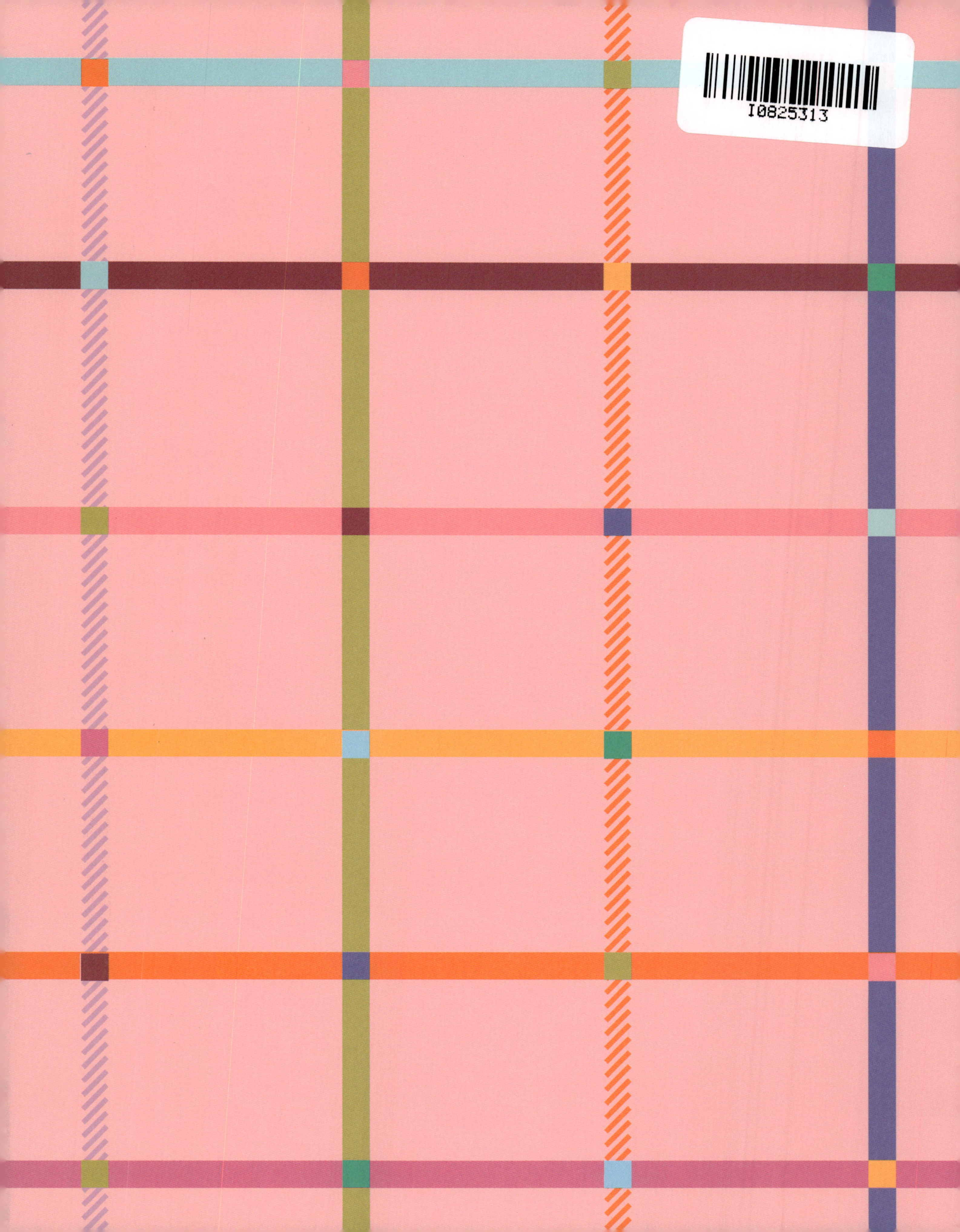
I0825313

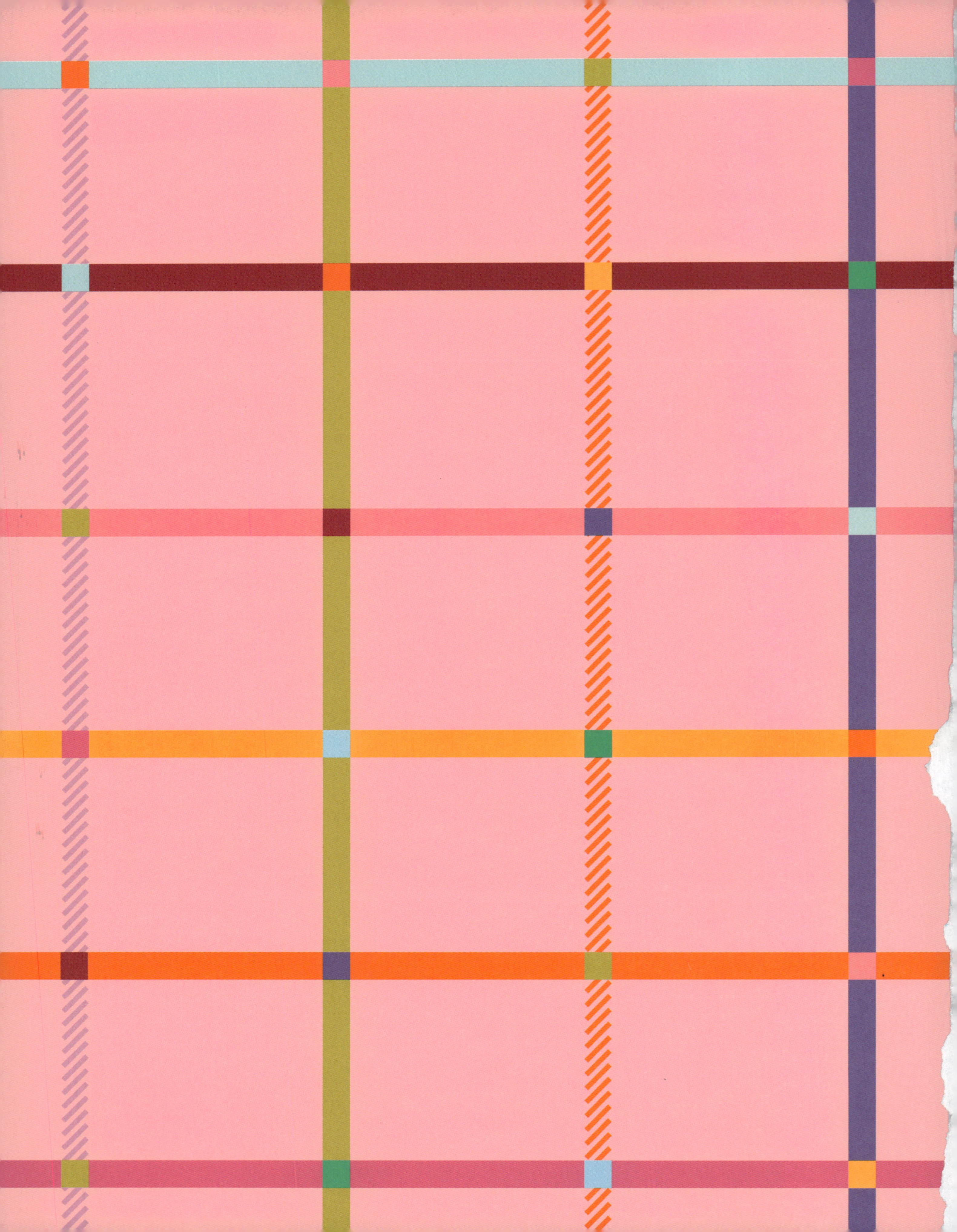

LOOP, HOOK, LOOM

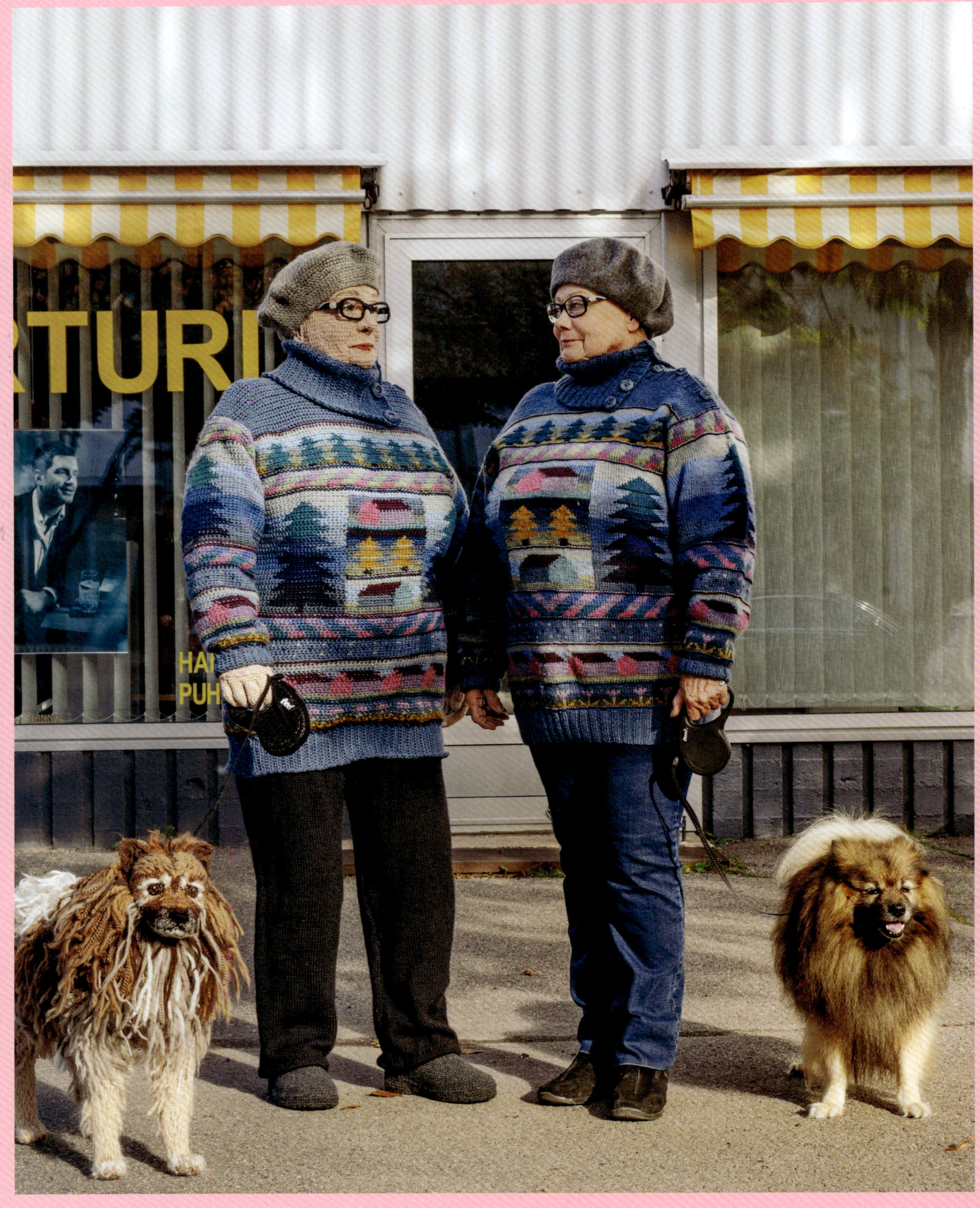

Artist Liisa Hietanen

A creative collection of textile art made with yarn and thread

LOOP, HOOK, LOOM

SOPHIA CAI 蔡晨昕

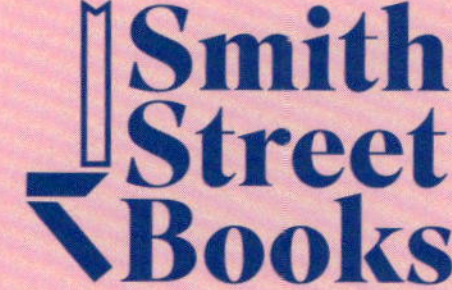

Contents

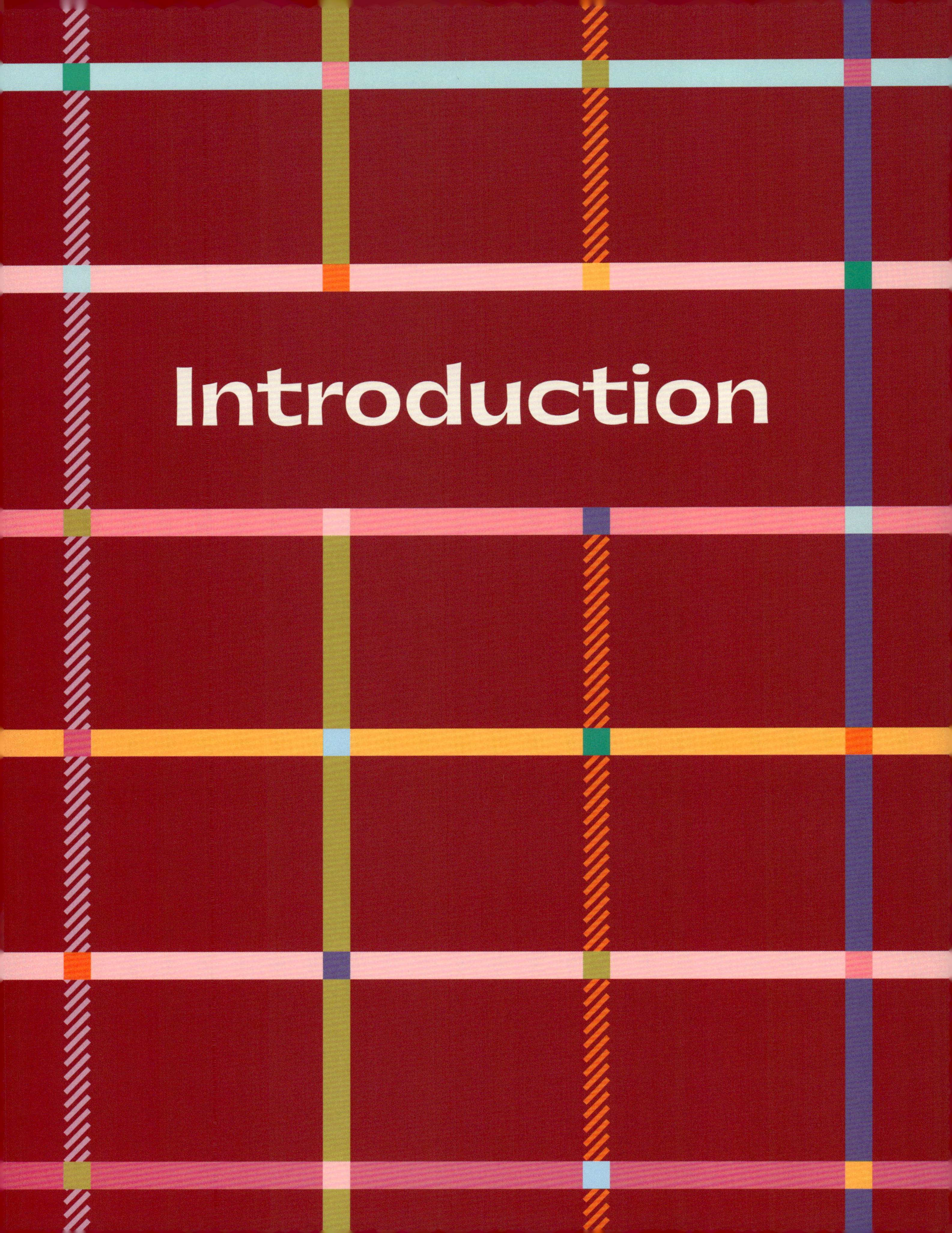

Introduction

I started working on this book of contemporary textile art in the summer of 2024, but my personal connection to the subject matter started in childhood.

Long before I ever picked up a knitting needle or crochet hook, I was raised by a mother who could do anything with textiles. When I was a young child in China, she would make us matching outfits cut from the same cloth; in photos from this period, I am her mini-me smiling at the camera, trying my best to match her pose. Whether by choice or by circumstance, making things by hand was something she was really good at. During my time as a teenager who wanted to keep up with the latest fads, my mother would always say no to my requests at the shopping centre: "I can make that for you at home." Although this almost never came to fruition, I knew that she was up to the task.

I bought craft books long before I could understand the instructions, inspired by the potential contained in their pages and dreaming of what I could make. My favourite books were vintage knitting titles from the 1980s, with their bold colours and patterns, as well as Japanese crochet books with instructions for making soft toys (or "amigurumi"). It wasn't, though, until a year spent living abroad as a postgraduate student that I finally taught myself how to knit by watching tutorials on YouTube.

I am now an avid knitter and crocheter, with a SABLE (aka a yarn "stash acquired beyond life expectancy"). The only artworks I have made are knitted: during pandemic lockdowns, I worked on a socially distanced sweater, *Safety Yellow Woman* (2020–21), that ended up in two exhibitions. During my time working at the Australian Tapestry Workshop in South Melbourne, I got to watch some of the most talented weavers in the world work on the loom every day – an experience that's impossible to come away from without being a fan of the process.

Loop, Hook, Loom is my love letter to textiles, shaped by a lifelong engagement with the topic and a drive to amplify underrepresented creative practices that we all can learn from. Stepping outside of my lived experience, my training as an art historian reminds me to think about art and artists in a bigger context: whether that be social, political, cultural or historical. When I apply this thinking to the breadth of textiles, I am struck by their endurance as artforms that have existed for millennia across global cultures and creative practices. Given the ubiquity of cloth and fabric in human civilisation, there are countless traditions to learn from, which makes for engrossing research. This also means that when we look at textiles, there is an almost limitless range of cultural viewpoints that can be brought into the conversation.

Perhaps because of this ubiquity, contemporary textile practices continue to contend with loaded historical and cultural connotations surrounding gender, class and race. This is not because textiles hold any less intrinsic value than other mediums. It speaks, instead, to what has historically been shown (or not shown) in museums and galleries. While art exists beyond these spaces, the conversations that happen within them uphold power. I am a stubborn person: the more that I am told something is or isn't art (the tired "but is it art or craft" debate), the more I want to put it centre stage. This is a view I share with many of the artists in the following pages.

Loop, Hook, Loom is a culmination of this thinking and research, which brings together the works of 38 contemporary artists from around the globe whose art reveals the creative possibilities of textiles. A deliberate choice was made to bring artists with long-established practices into dialogue with those who define themselves as early career. As with any project of this scope, I could not hope to encompass all that there is to textiles, and there are many perspectives I could not include (simply due to space). Instead, by highlighting three techniques that traditionally use thread or yarn – knitting, crochet and weaving – I wanted to provide some commonalities through which to examine textile artworks. As with any attempts at categorisations, these terms are tools to help us understand, rather than concrete boundaries: many artists in this book work across the three categories and beyond. While each artist sits within one chapter, profiles throughout the book also touch on their works created using other techniques.

My hope is that *Loop, Hook, Loom* does not just elevate and celebrate the artists it contains, but that it also inspires readers who might not think their own creativity can be deemed "art worthy". Life is too short for these categorisations and it is richer for the things that fill your time, your space and your surroundings with meaning. Long before any art museums and galleries came into existence, many artists experienced their first entry into creativity through textiles at home. I write this book for people like my mother, who would never call herself an artist, but was and is still my first creative inspiration.

Sophia Cai, August 2025

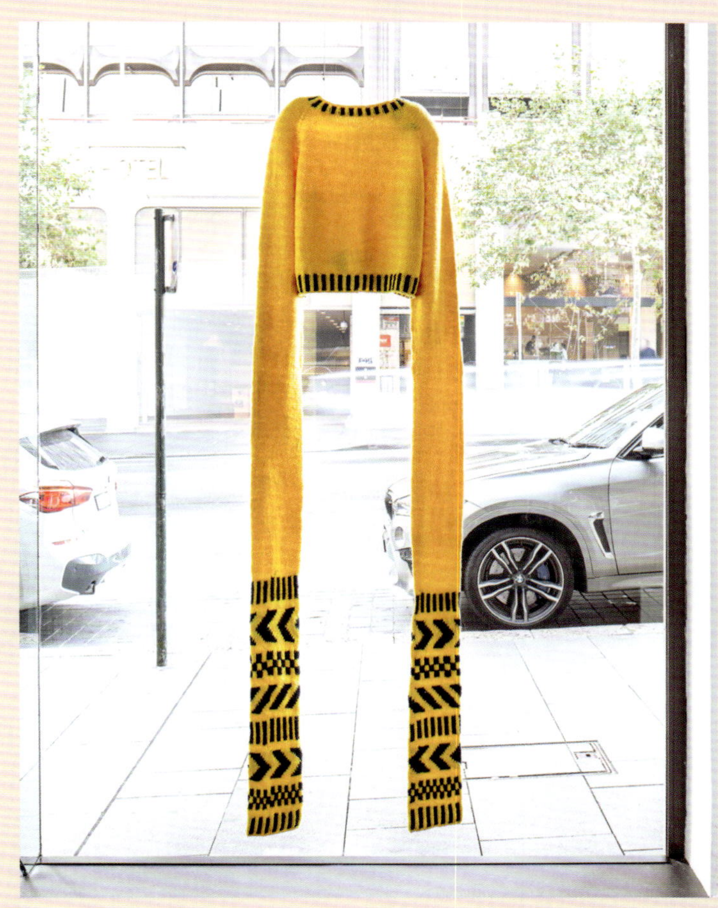

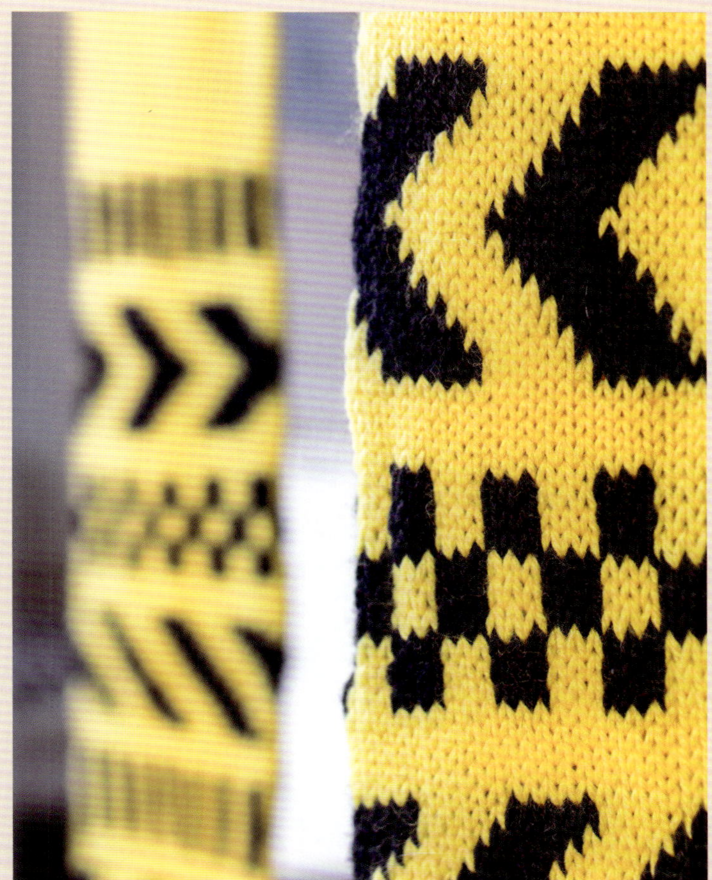

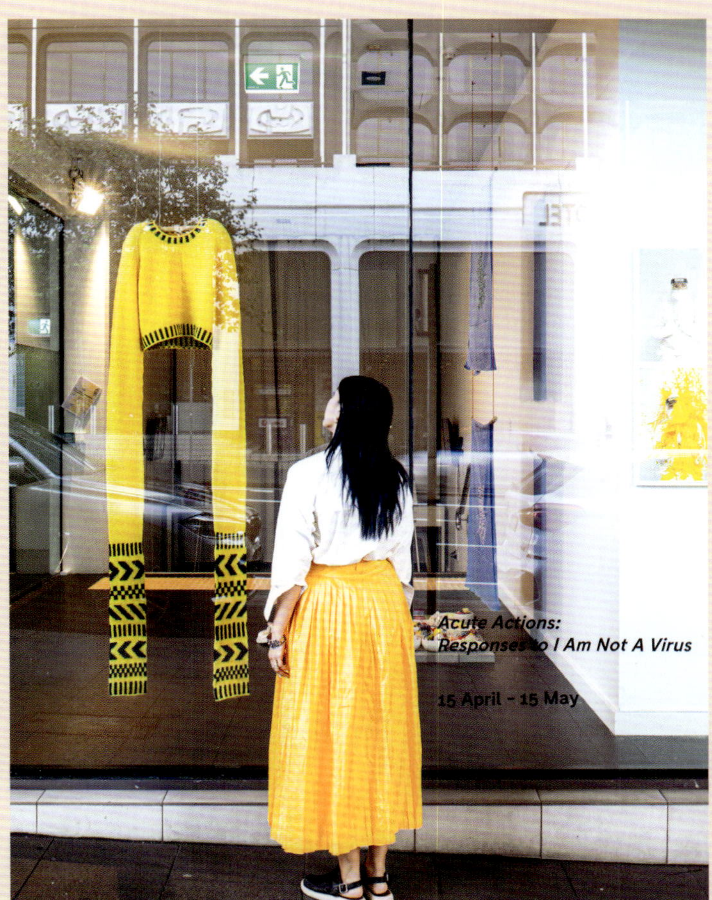

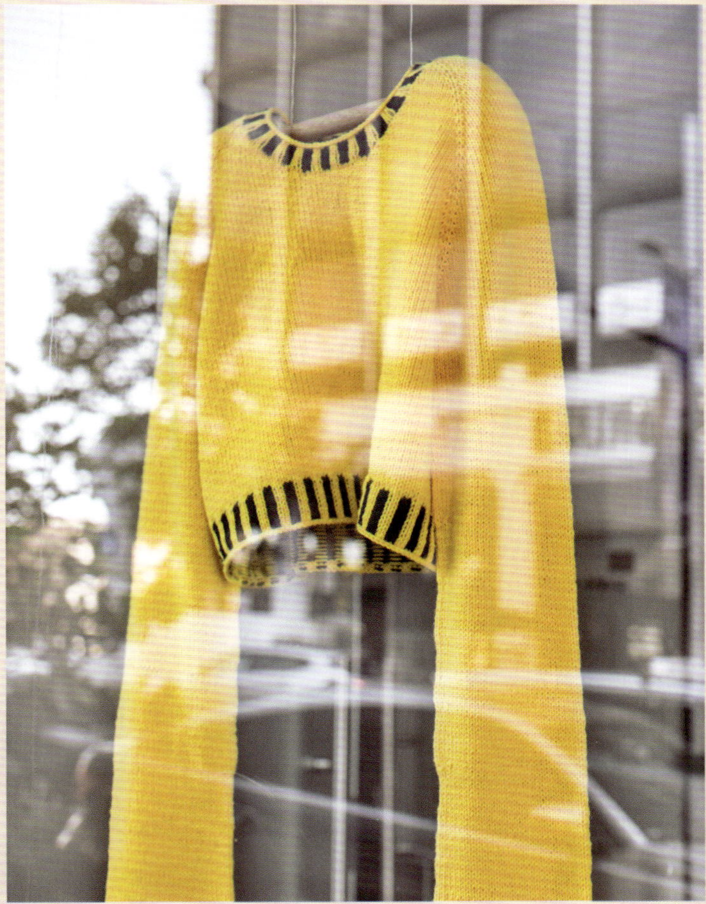

Safety Yellow Woman, 2020-21, Hand-knitting

Loop

Knitting is an artform that has been practised for centuries, if not millennia. While its exact date and place of origin is unknown, the oldest surviving example of knitting – a pair of socks from Egypt – has been dated between the 3rd and 5th centuries CE. Examples of double-knitting – using two colours to create patterns – have been dated to North Africa between the 12th and 14th centuries.

As a technique for creating fabric, knitting uses two or more needles (made of wood, bone, ivory or metal) to connect loops of yarn or thread together. There are two main ways to knit: flat (using two needles) or in the round (using three or more needles) to create tubes of fabric that can be turned into items, such as hats and socks. In contrast to crochet, which creates more rigid structures, knitting produces fabric with more drape. This makes it well suited to the creation of garments; for those looking to make clothes at home, the technique remains a popular choice.

A number of artists in this chapter carry on this lineage by knitting clothes as part of their creative practice. Sancia Ridgeway uses knitting to create unique pieces inspired by conversations with Aboriginal Australians, capturing stories centred on "Blak Joy". For Andrew Chan, knitting garments allows him to speak to issues of queer rights and HIV advocacy through an embodied lens. On the other hand, Lucas Morneau's works engage with the performance of gender through drag.

The works of Kendall Ross and Emma Buswell focus on topics related to labour. Ross creates wearable garments that read like personal diary entries by the artist. Through a combination of illustration and text, Ross examines topics related to the history of "women's work", challenging the so-called art vs craft distinction. Buswell, meanwhile, manually wields a knitting machine to situate her focus on labour within broader issues related to cultural production and class.

Themes of gender are also central in the works of Kate Just, Romina Chuls and Ben Cuevas, who each cite the influence of feminist theory and artists. In Just's work, this is seen in her ongoing series of knitted portraits that pay homage to her feminist art heroes. Cuevas takes inspiration from the 1970s feminist art canon to create textiles that challenge binary thinking around gender, while Chuls draws from Latin American feminism; this is visible in her use of cross-loop knitting – a technique that predates Spanish colonisation in Peru – connecting her modern work to ancestral knowledge.

Beyond the social and cultural meanings associated with knitting, this chapter's artists engage with the experimental possibilities the technique contains. Rather than work with conventional materials like yarn, Emma Roche creates long "threads" of paint that she knits into paintings to capture her experiences of motherhood and daily life. Emma Hasselblad, on the other hand, works six to eight strands of textured and varied yarns together to create large-scale sculptural works, based on the life cycle of flowers, as a comment on the transience of life.

Choice of materials is also central to the knitted works of Movana Chen and Shradha Kochhar. Chen shreds paper from books, passports and other sources to use as "threads", embedding her creations with stories and connections to others. In the works of Kochhar, kala cotton ties her works to the history of the crop, labour and colonisation in India. By processing the fibre from its seed and then hand-spinning it into yarn, Kochhar speaks to and with this past.

All 12 artists in this chapter use knitting in unconventional and creative ways to produce works. Ranging from garments to sculptural explorations, the artists use both flat and circular knitting methods to manipulate simple materials into expansive artworks.

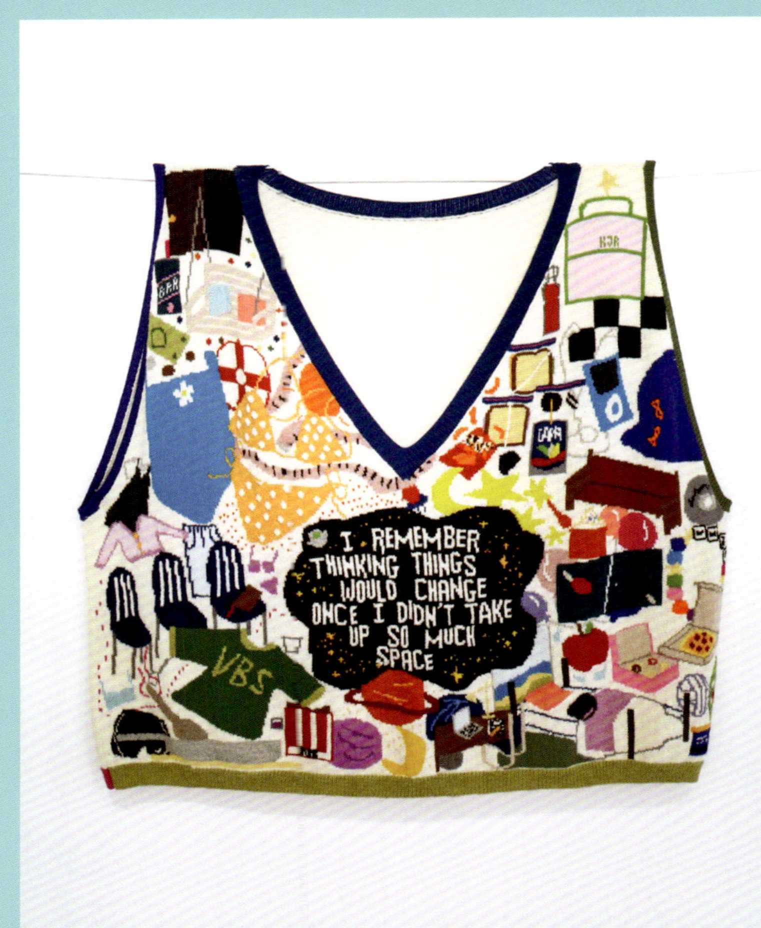
I REMEMBER THINKING THINGS WOULD CHANGE ONCE I DIDN'T TAKE UP SO MUCH SPACE
VBS

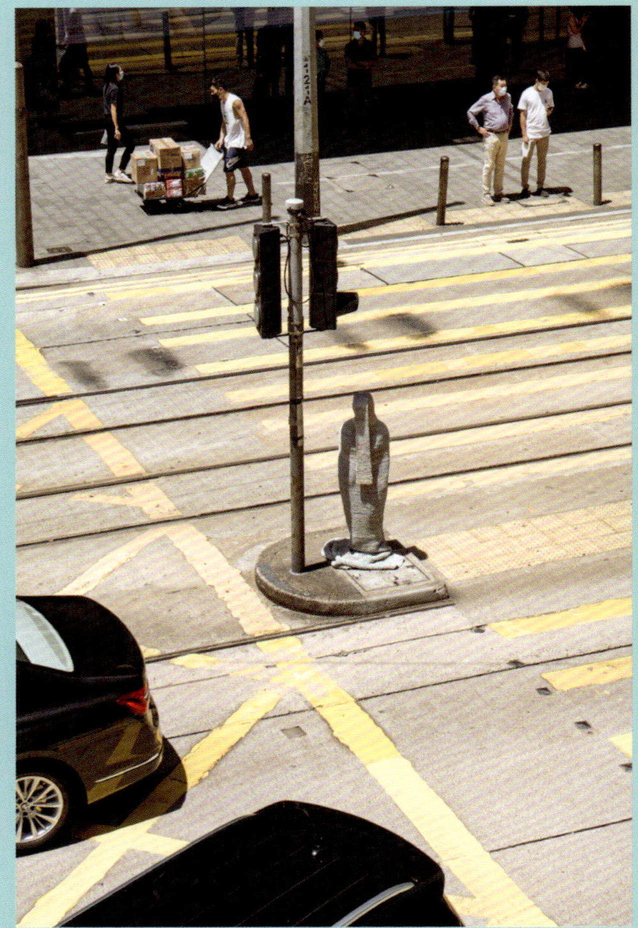

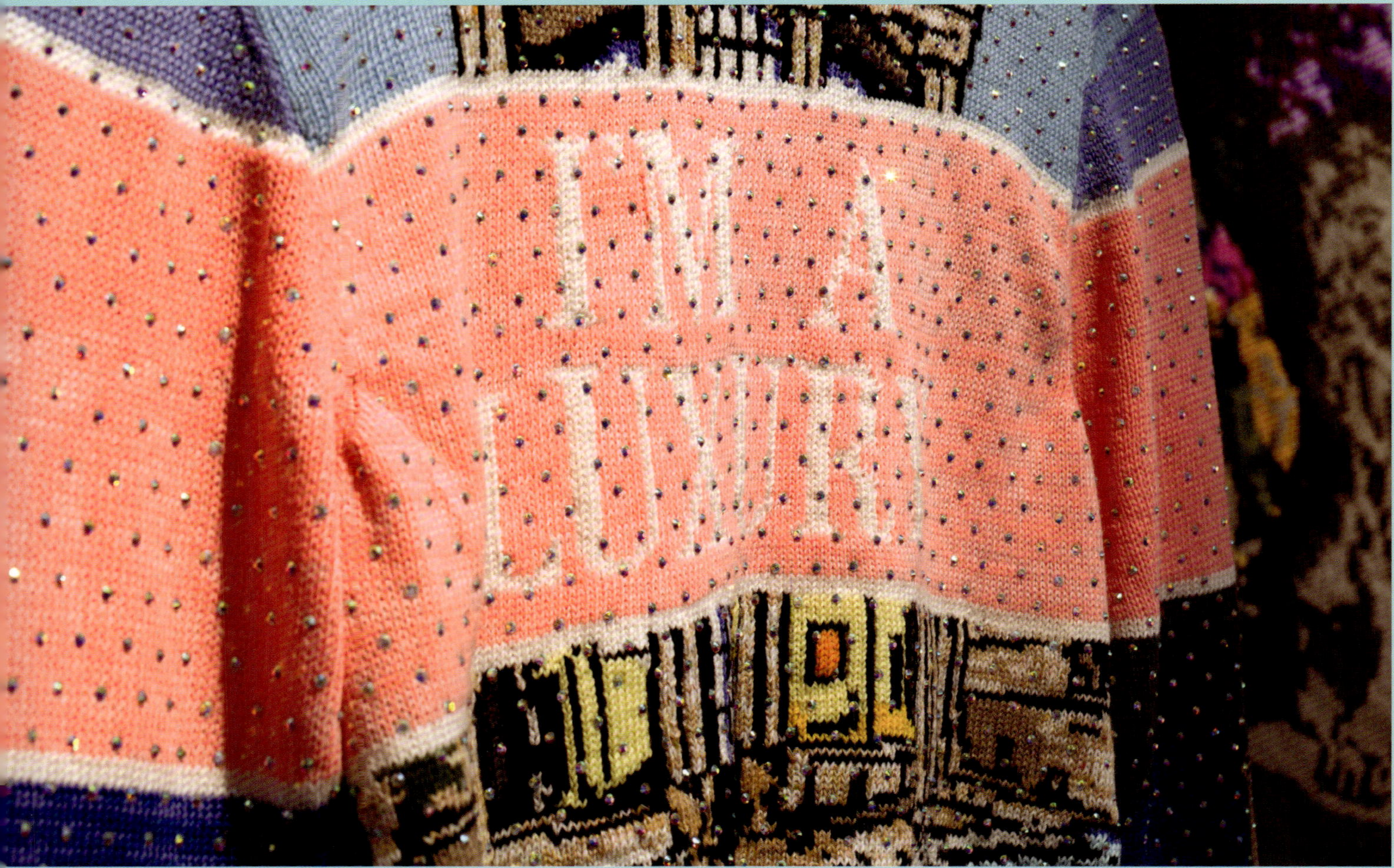

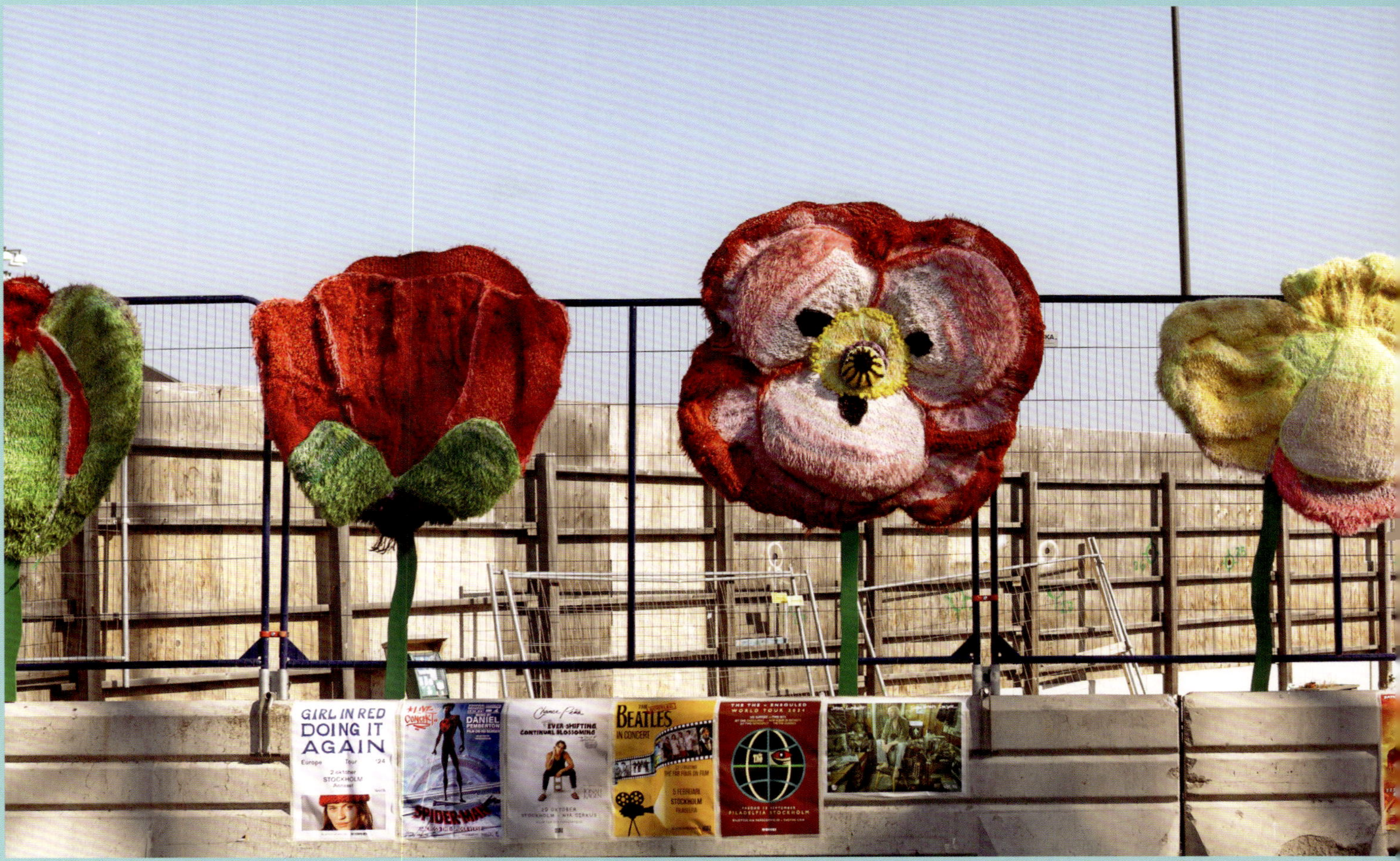

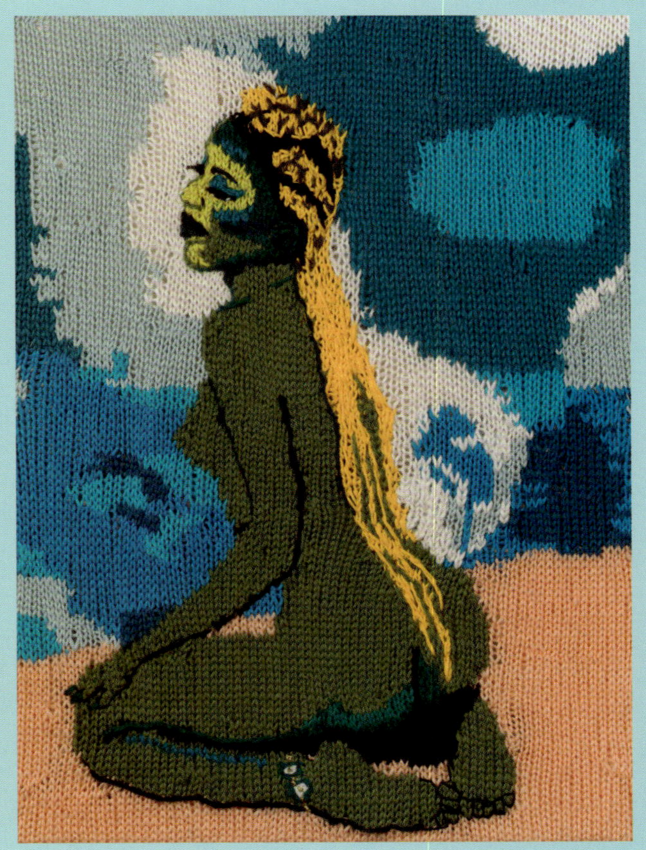

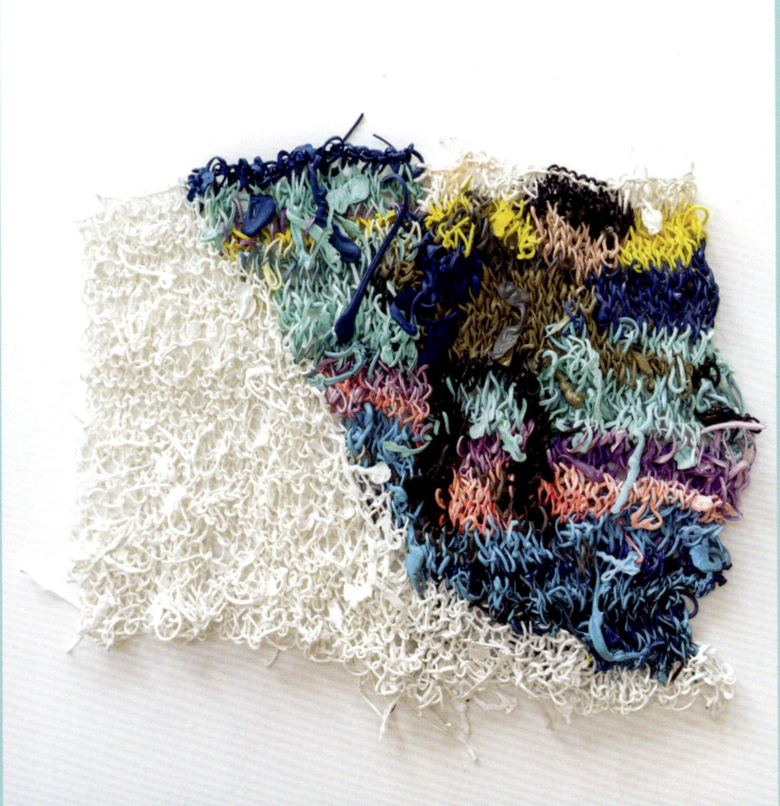

Artists clockwise from top left: Kendall Ross, Movana Chen, Emma Hasselblad, Emma Roche, Kate Just, Emma Buswell

Andrew Chan 編織的貓

NAARM/
MELBOURNE

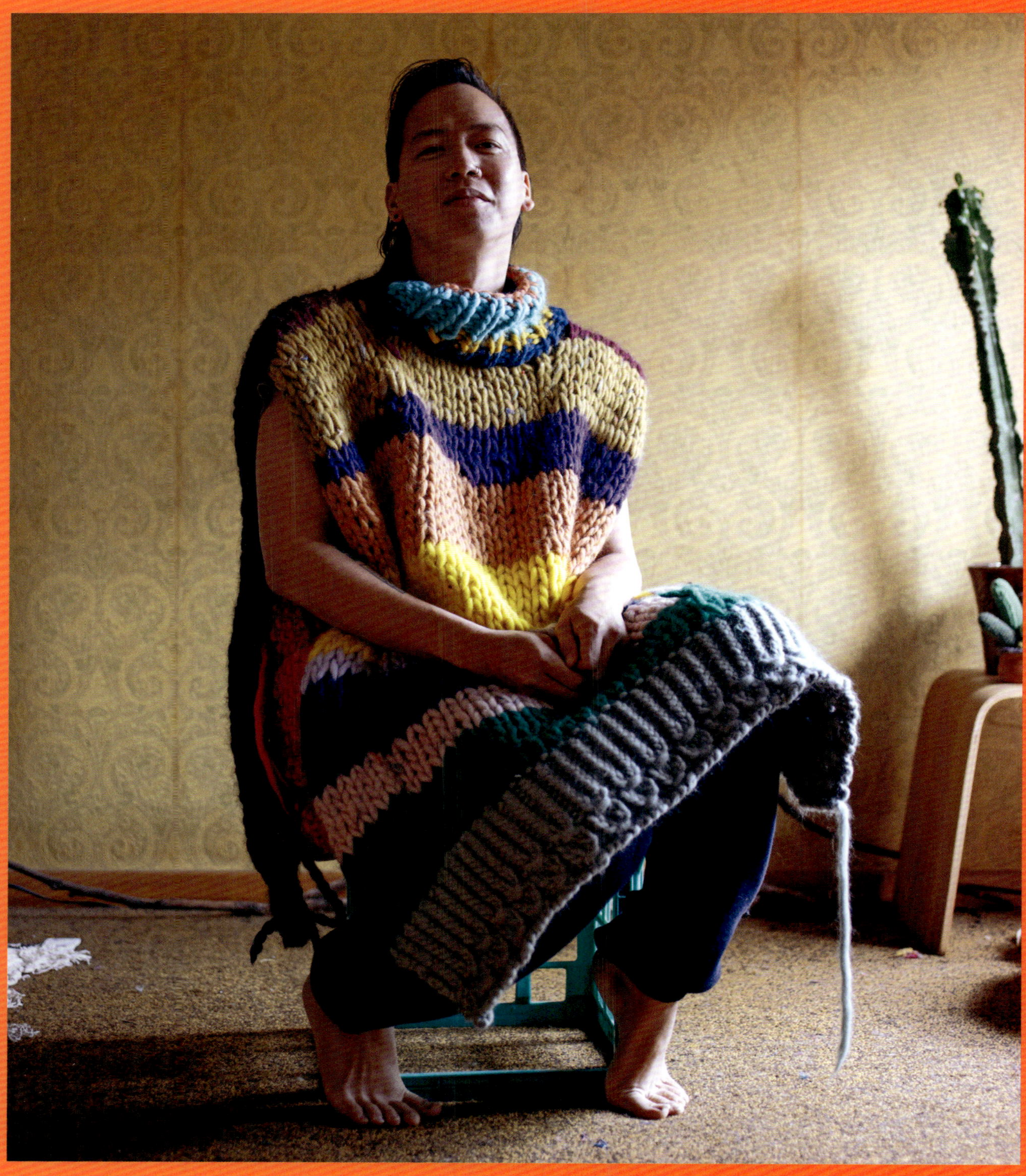

After working for 16 years as a graphic designer, Andrew Chan sought to return to creating with his "hands again rather than through a mouse" by learning to knit from a YouTube tutorial in 2019. While Chan, who now works under the name thecatwhoknits, grew up watching his grandmother make textiles for the home, he didn't fully appreciate the effort required until he started knitting himself. He was immediately struck by the malleability of the knitted fabric, "formed by making knots on knots", and the ability to "transform something so soft into something comforting and wearable".

After Chan learnt the basic knitting techniques of casting on, knit stitch, purl stitch and casting off, Melbourne's subsequent city-wide pandemic lockdowns during 2020 and 2021 afforded him a chance to hone his creative process and develop his particular artistic voice. During his free time from his job as a graphic designer, Chan worked in his home studio knitting one-off garments for clients based on their favourite colours and their references. Chan used wool as the main material, adopting the use of different stitches and jarring colour combinations to create patterns and designs.

It was this early foray into custom garments that led Chan to his first opportunity as an exhibiting artist in 2021 for Melbourne Fashion Week's Capsule Exhibition. Chan created a knitted work inspired by the iconic fashion of the late artist and designer Leigh Bowery, which also paid homage to the legacy of the AIDS Memorial Quilt. Chan's voluptuous head-to-toe red ensemble, consisting of a headpiece, a top and a skirt, is a "tribute to those who lost their lives to the HIV epidemic". The top is covered in the gold characters "U" and "=", a visual reference to Undetectable = Untransmittable (U=U): a campaign aimed at communicating the fact that a person living with an undetectable viral load cannot transmit the virus to their sexual partner. As Chan reflects, this set serves as a reminder "that there is still a lot of work to be done" in challenging biases and stigma.

Behind this work, and Chan's others, is an understanding that, "As a queer person, you carry the legacy of those who fought for your rights before you." Today, the same themes of HIV advocacy and queerness (particularly QTBIPOC experiences), remain central to Chan's art. In his first solo exhibition, Rebuilding Queerness (2022), he knitted five unique garments for five QTPOC artists based in Melbourne; the garments each tell a story tied to the artists' individual experiences. *Caught Between States* (2023) is a subsequent work created for the exhibition HIV Science as Art (2023), which paired an HIV scientist with an HIV-positive artist; inspired by the scientific work of Ryan Whitacre on the forced

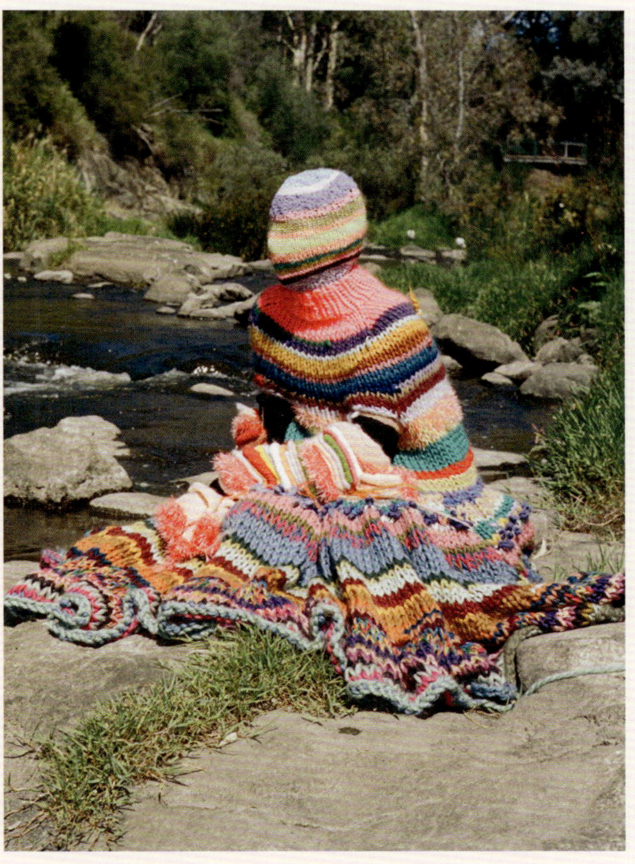

Still Knitting by the Merri Creek, 2024, Hand-knitting

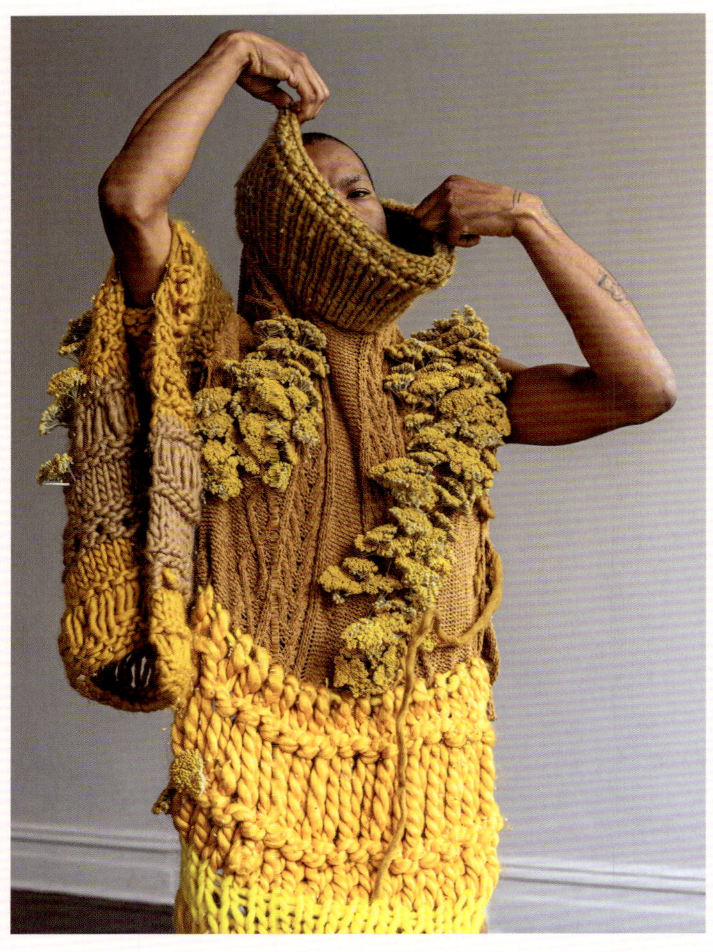

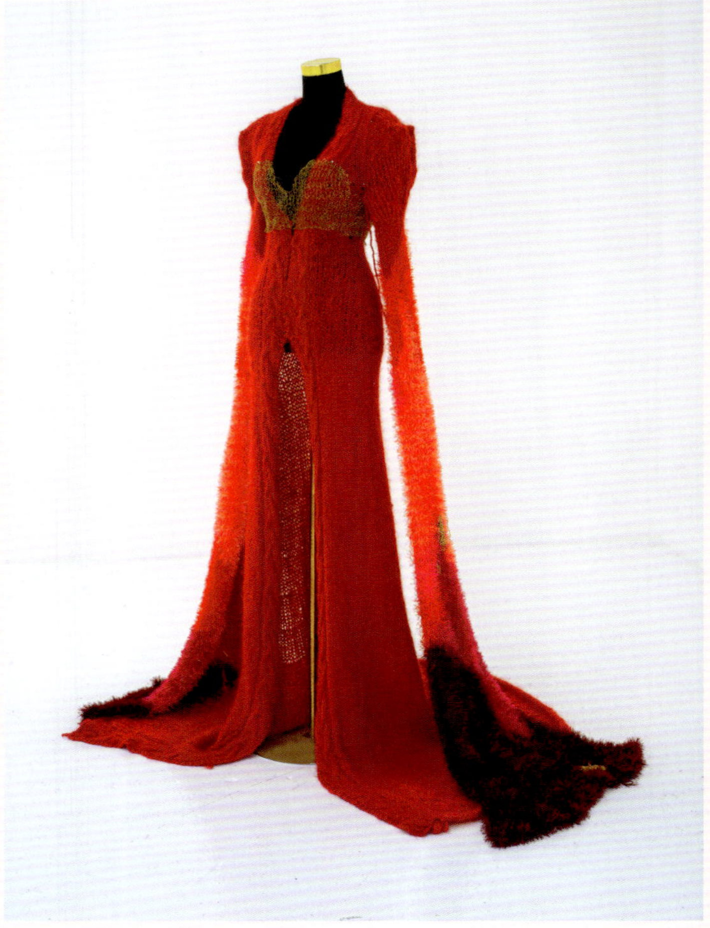

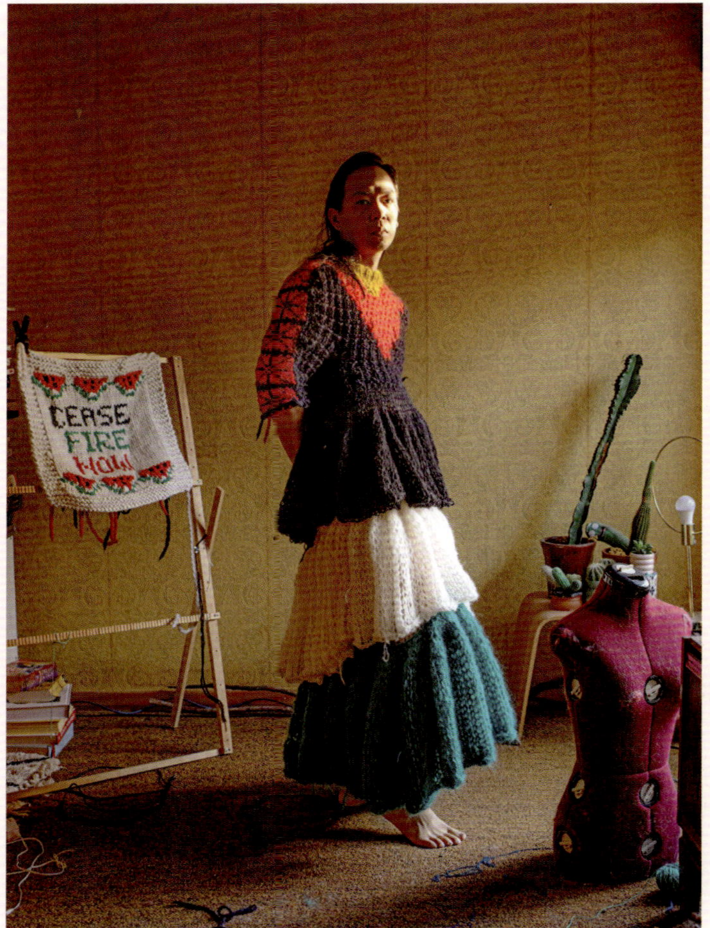

displacement of queer migrants, Chan's piece explores the ongoing impacts of homophobic policies on individuals. It speaks to the double marginalisation that occurs as a migrant and as a queer person, with the fist in the middle representing the "bureaucratic entanglements" that affect a person's safety and life.

Accessibility is a central focus in Chan's works, as he wants his pieces to speak to people of all ages and backgrounds; this is one of the reasons he mostly knits garments, worn either by himself or others. This close relationship to the body allows Chan to speak to audiences on a personal and direct level. While his works are "aimed at my community", he recognises the importance of sharing the messages and themes of his works with people who may not share the same lived experiences. Chan sees his artworks as a way to share stories, whether his own or someone else's, to challenge assumptions and foster greater empathy through a connection to others. ■

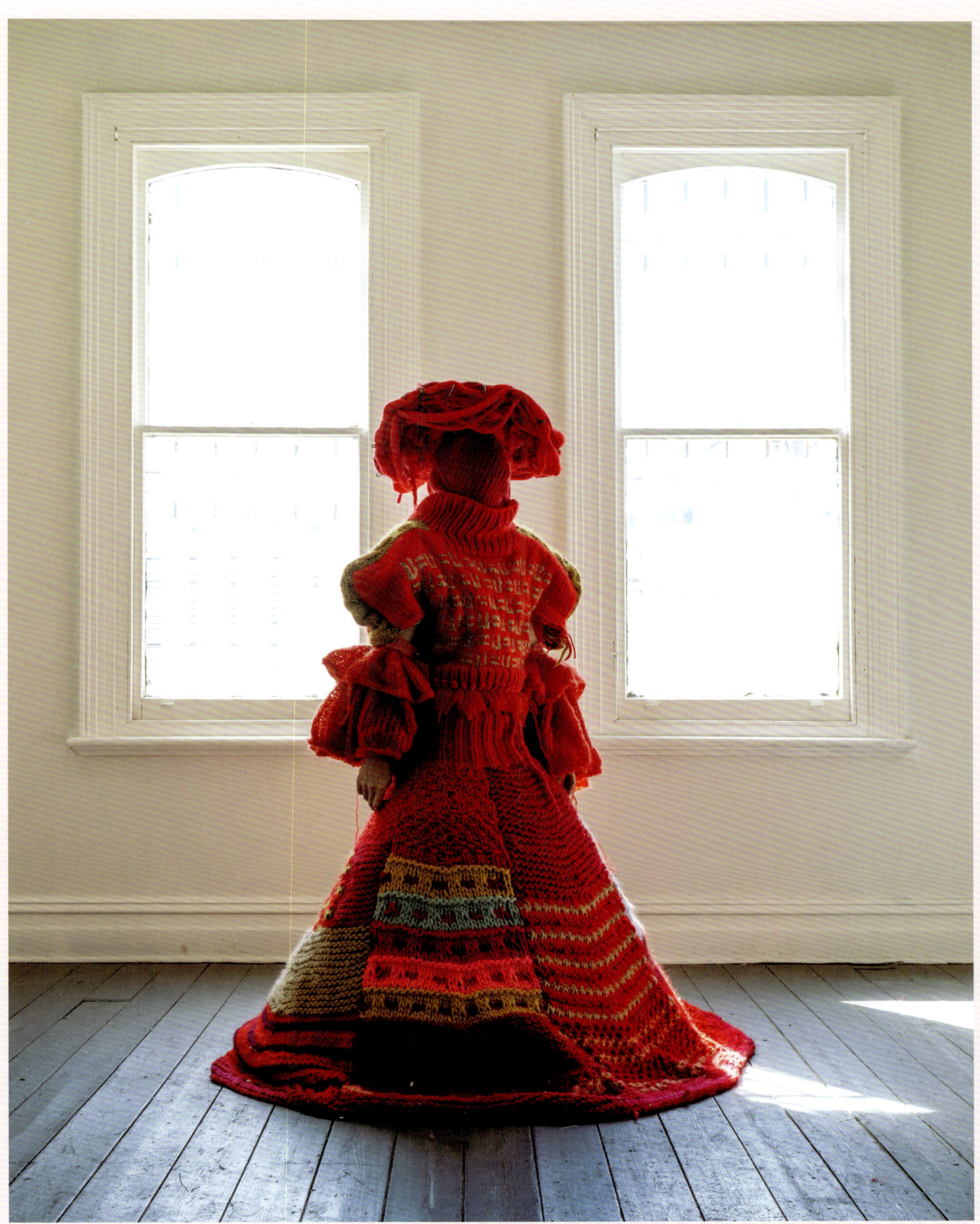

Opposite Clockwise from top left: *Achillea worn by Blu Jay*, 2021, Hand-knitting and upcycled jumper, floristry by Graham Ho; *It's You, Miss Hua*, 2023, Hand-knitting; *Solidarity Dress*, 2024, Hand-knitting **This page** *to u=u*, 2021, Hand-knitting

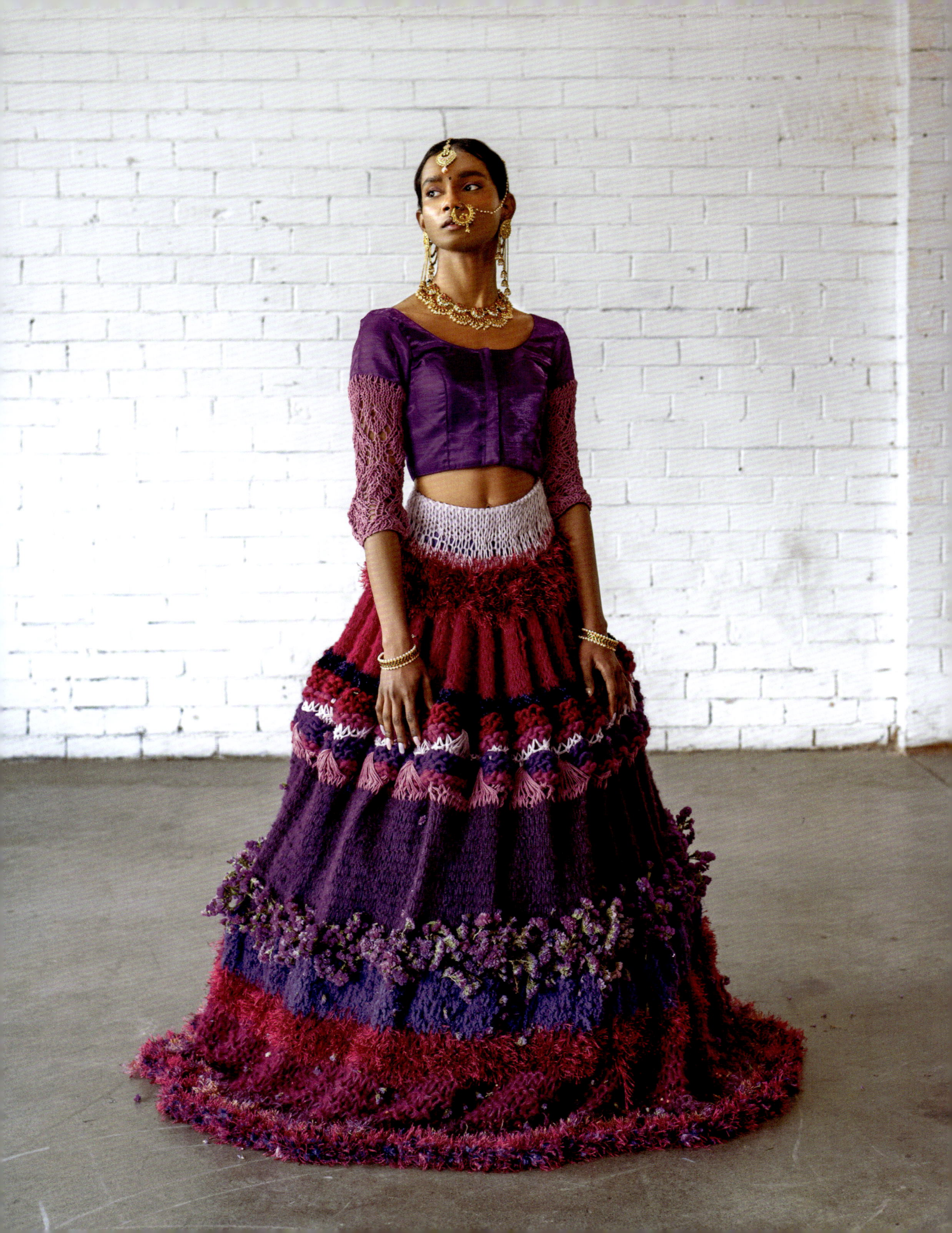

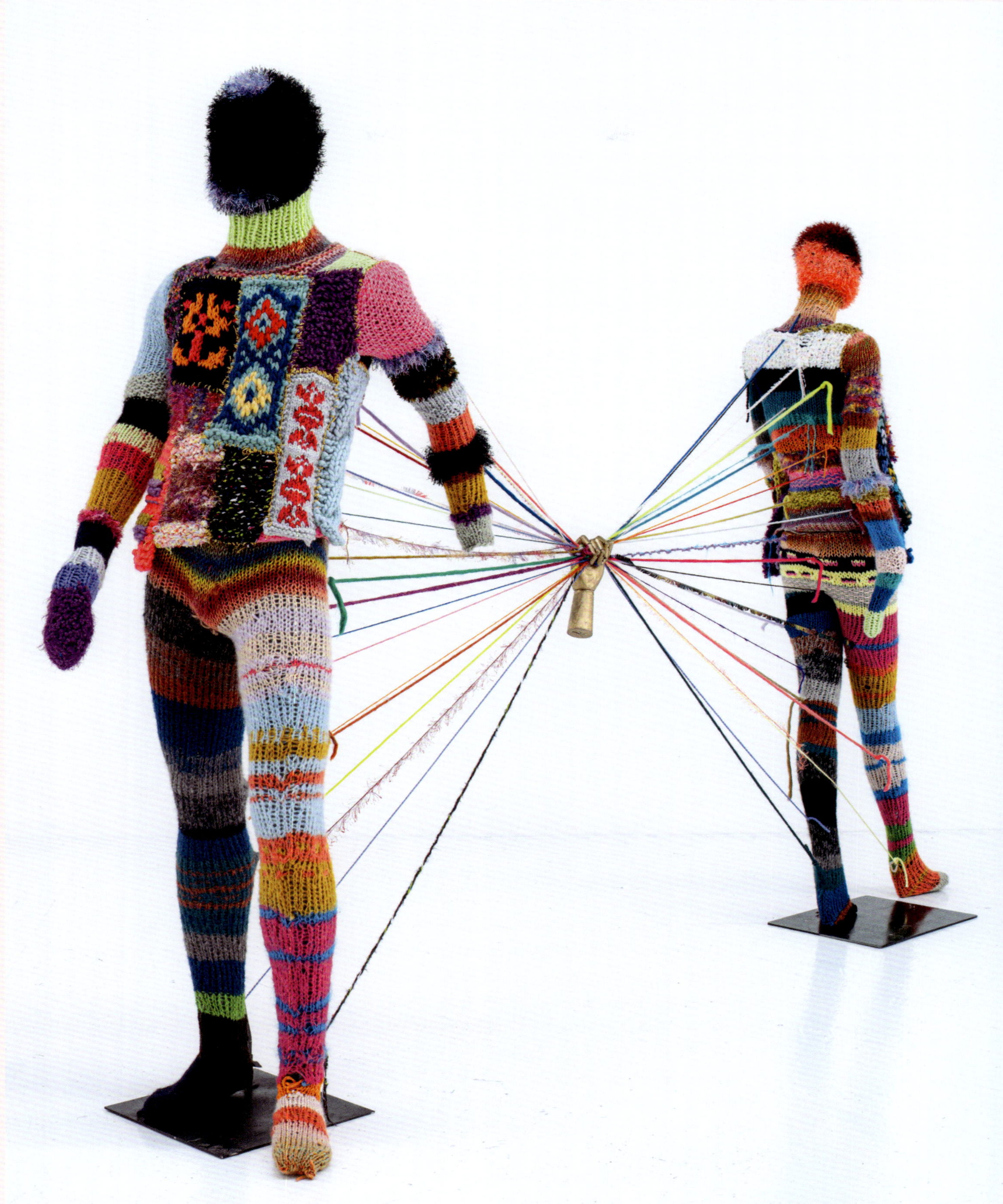

Opposite *Statice worn by Nupurasa*, 2022, Hand-knitting and upcycled sari blouse
This page *Caught Between States*, 2023, Hand-knitting

Ben Cuevas

LOS ANGELES

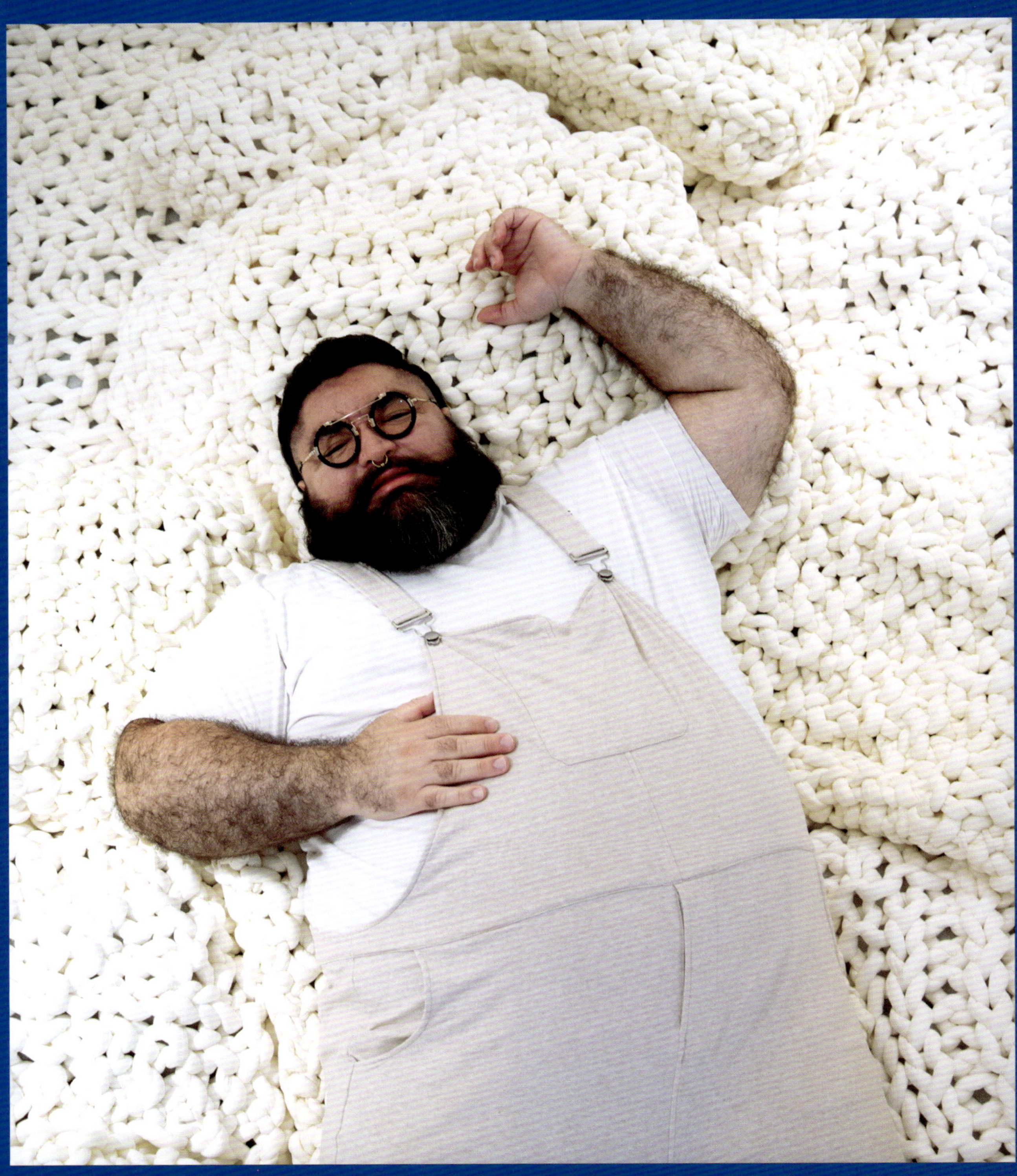

Ben Cuevas works as a multidisciplinary artist across installation, sculpture and photography, but knitting remains a constant feature in their art. After learning the technique from a friend as a young adult, Cuevas quickly began applying it to create objects for their sculpture classes at university.

For Cuevas, knitting affords a great freedom as it can be employed to create any form: a limitlessness that "opens up a lot of possibilities for creation". Cuevas, who works intuitively and without patterns, describes their process as "sculpting with yarn through trial and error". This process is "project orientated", and starts with imagining the piece "fully formed", the artist then working "backwards to figure out how to create it". Experimentation is a central part of their process, which includes the use of special knitting techniques including increases and decreases, cabling, fair isle, as well as unexpected materials such as macrame cord and jumbo acrylic yarn.

Cuevas cites the formative influence of seminal feminist artists from the 1970s, including Faith Wilding, Judy Chicago, Faith Ringgold and Miriam Schapiro. Cuevas follows in their artistic legacies, adopting textiles as a medium through which to explore the relationship between art and gender: "It is my hope to carry on this tradition in the work that I produce." This hope is visible in the performance piece *Man's Body Women's Work* (2014), in which Cuevas challenged the "deeply engrained, binary, cultural assumptions of work and gender" by highlighting the time and labour involved in knitting. From the hours of 9 to 5 over a full working week, Cuevas sat in a public gallery space in the nude, knitting themselves a flesh-coloured body suit, which they eventually wore.

The human body remains a central theme in many of Cuevas's artworks. This reflects their ongoing interest in themes of intersectionality, and how identity can be expressed through embodiment – "questioning what does it mean to have a body, to be a body, to be in a body, incarnated and interacting with this world". Works such as *The Hospital Room* (2010) translate the anatomical models of natural science museums into a knitted form, laid out on a lucite tabletop as if presenting a specimen. A closer look at each individual knitted organ reveals some surprises: a third eye, attached to the ocular nerve, as well as a depiction of what the artist terms "genitosexual", a gender-expansive depiction.

By bringing our attention to these details, Cuevas provides a space to challenge binary thinking. Reflecting on the "gendered connotations of knitting", they share that they "feel like working in a medium that is coded as feminine queers my gender expression and lets me express both the

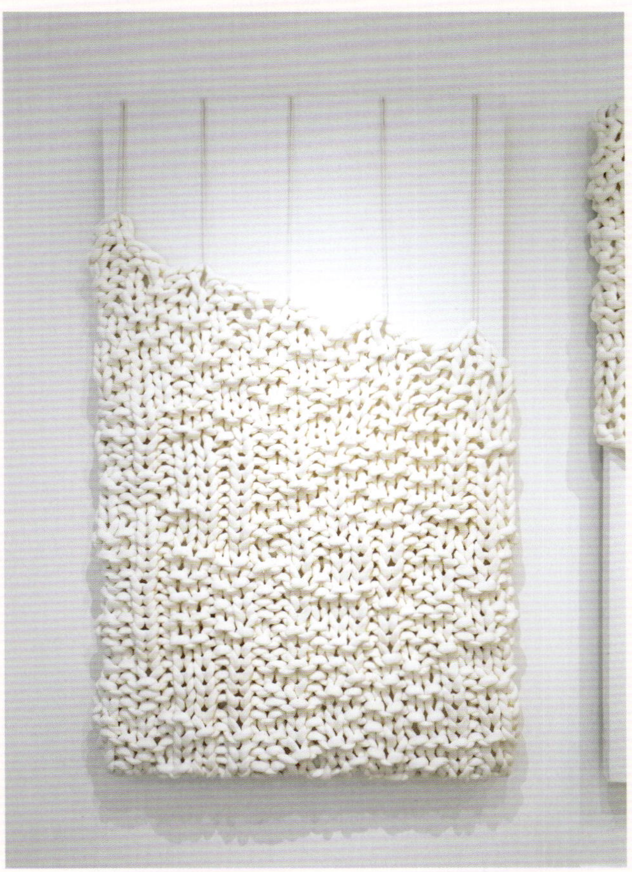

Pages 20–23 *Non-Binary Code*, 2023, Hand-knitting

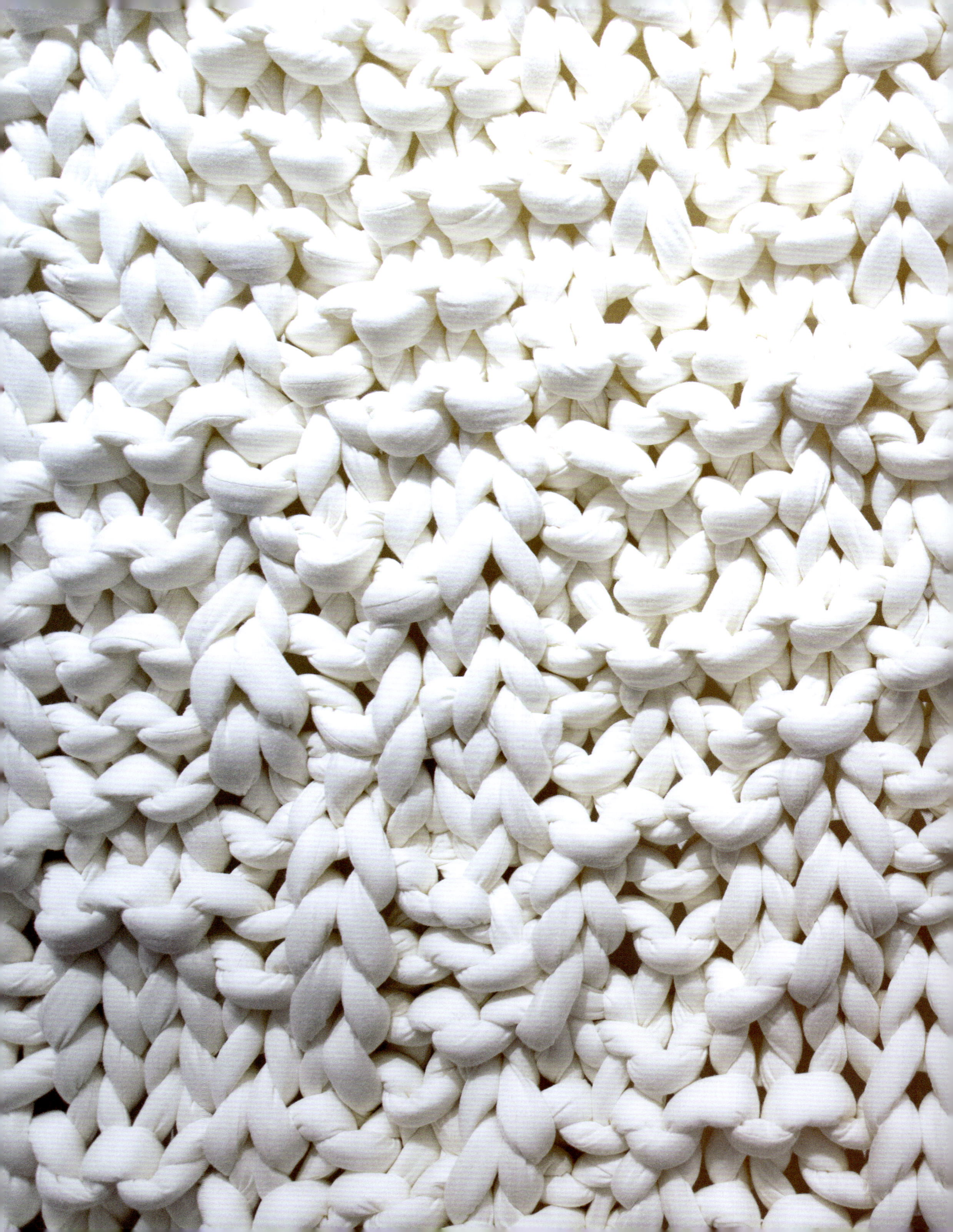

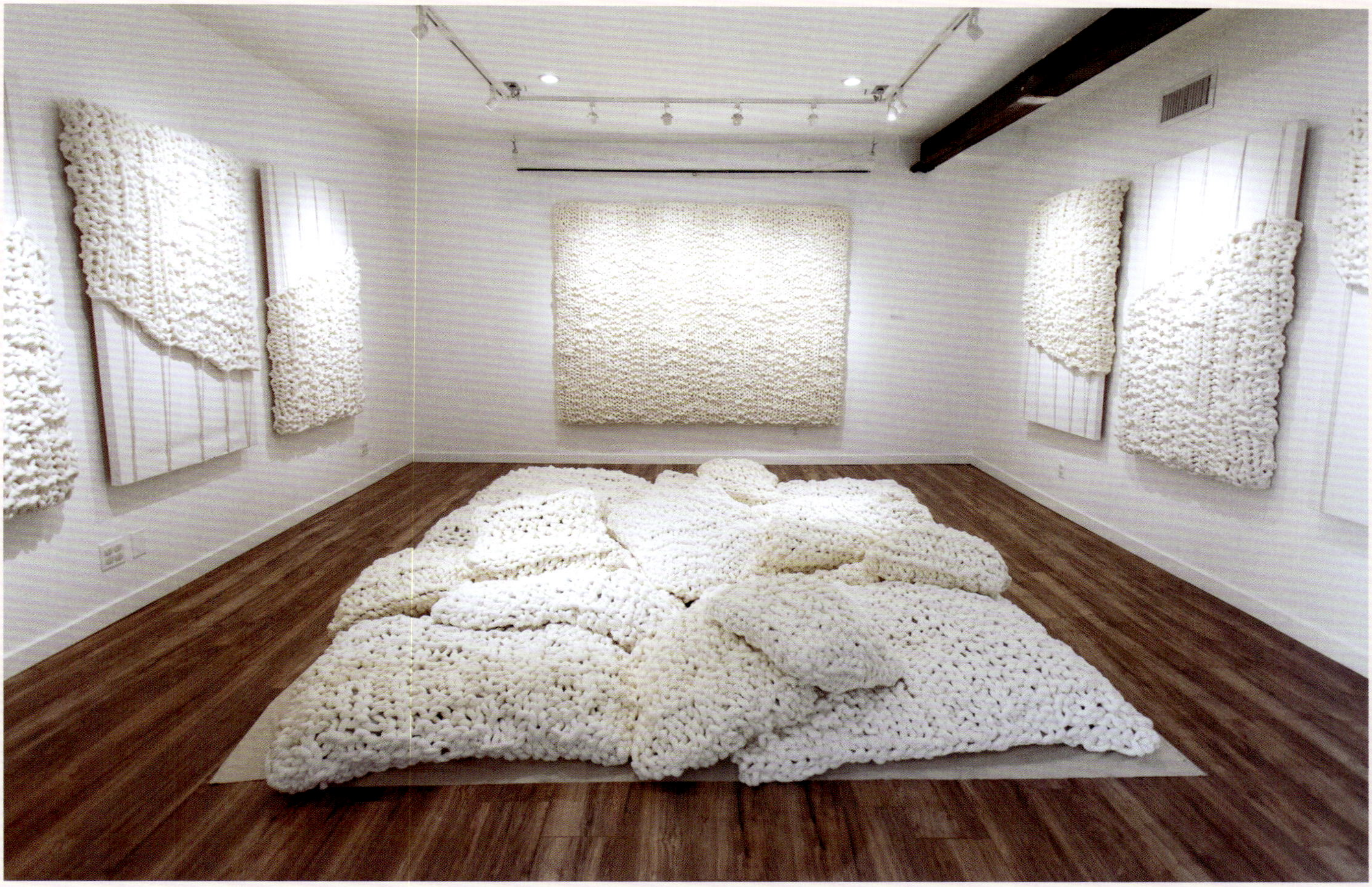

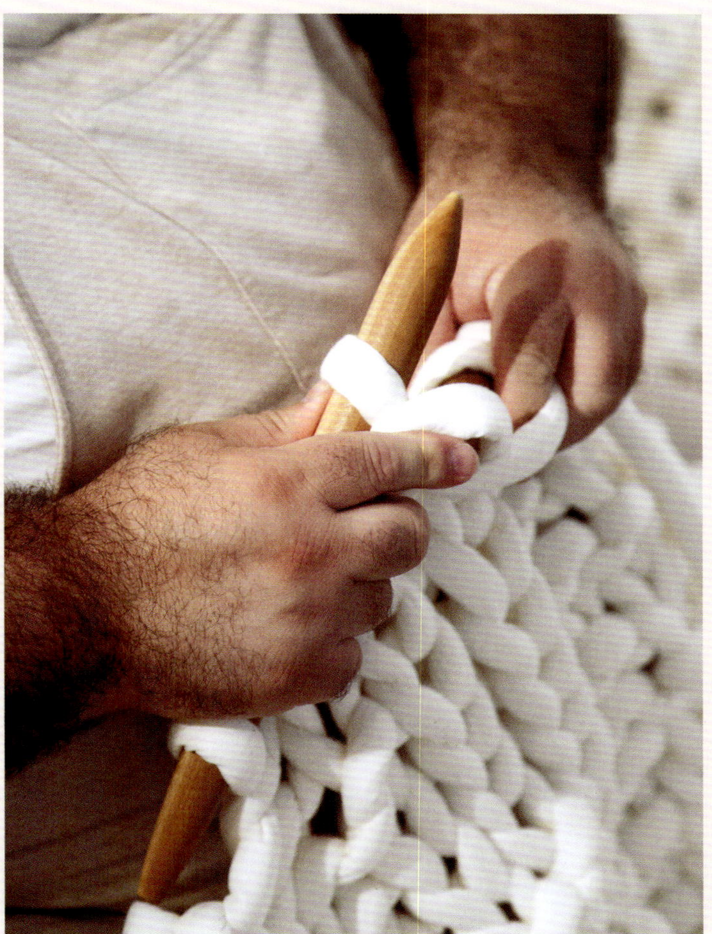

masculine and feminine sides of myself". This theme is continued in Cuevas's exhibition Non-Binary Code (2023), which uses the visual forms of the knit and purl stitch to translate the word "non-binary" into binary code (where the knit stitches are "1s" and the purl stitches are "0s"). By using only white yarn, Cuevas highlights the texture of the knitted surface to create a sensory interpretation grounded in softness and pensiveness.

While Cuevas makes their art for "anyone and everyone", they recognise that they "specifically make work for a queer audience". While their works might be resonant and can connect to anyone, they contain meaning that can only be understood through a queer reading: a gesture of solidarity that creates space for personal and intimate encounters. Cuevas identifies their favourite part of artmaking as "seeing moments of connection between the audience and the work. It's so fulfilling to see when someone feels something from the work I create." ■

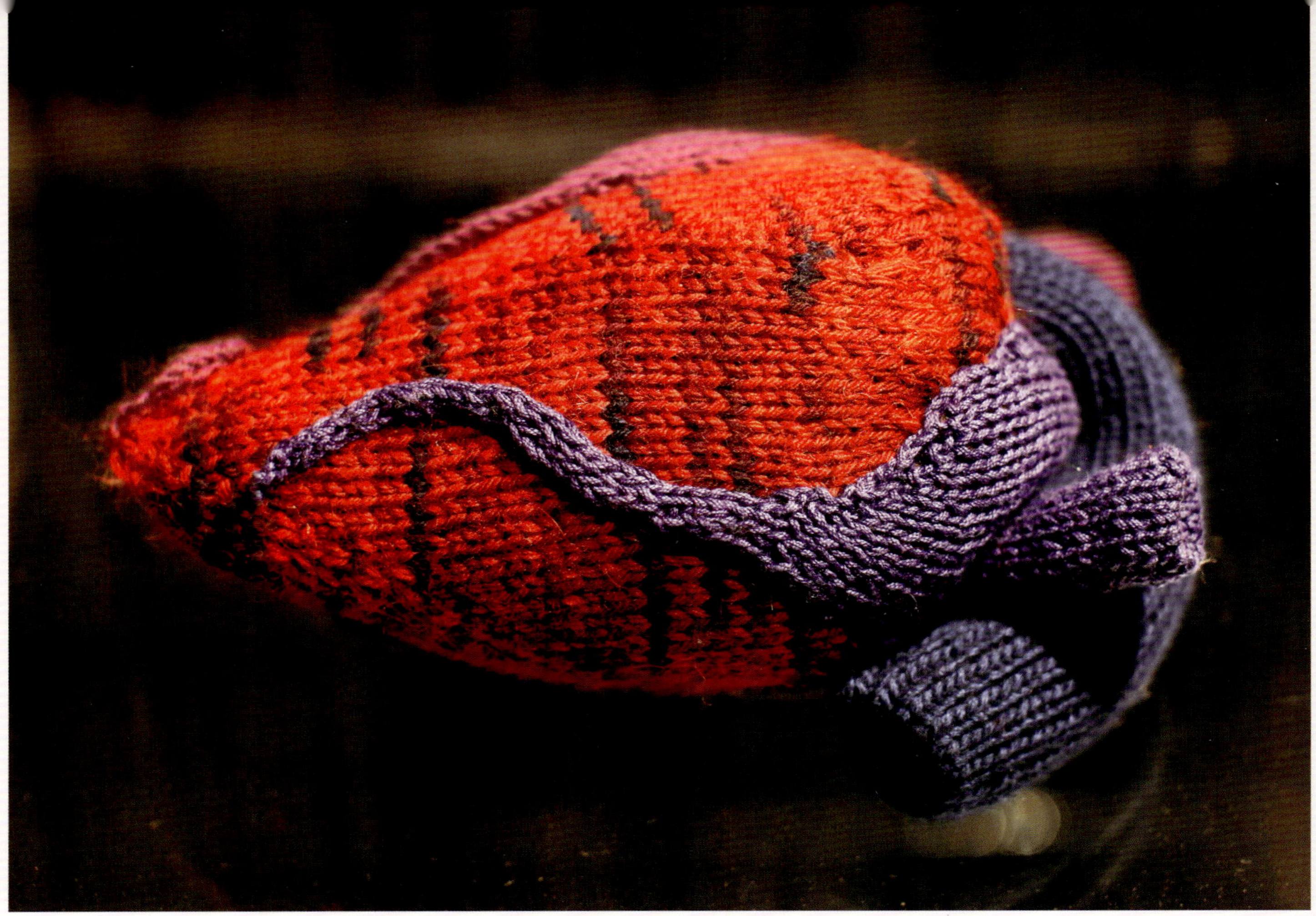

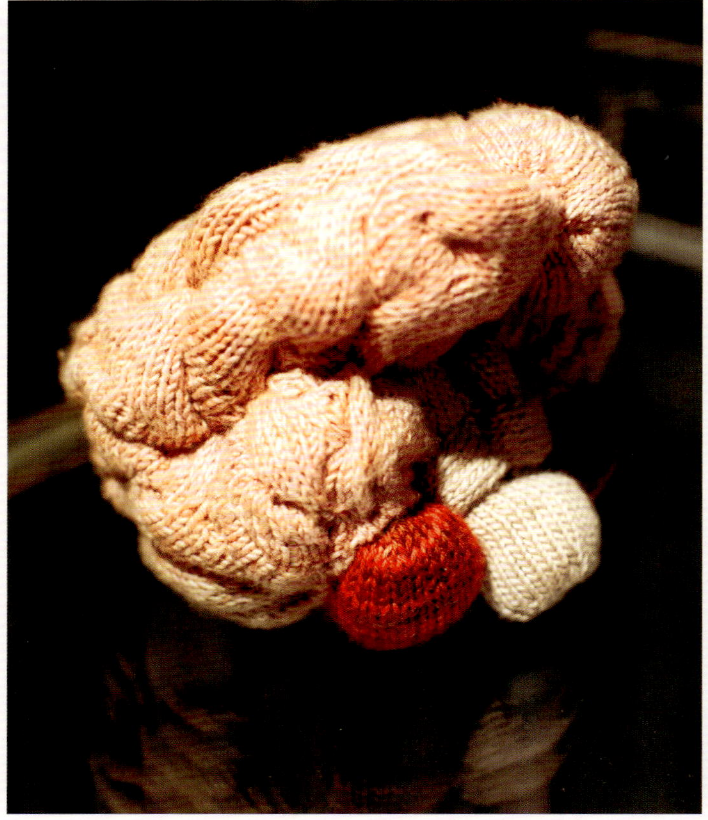

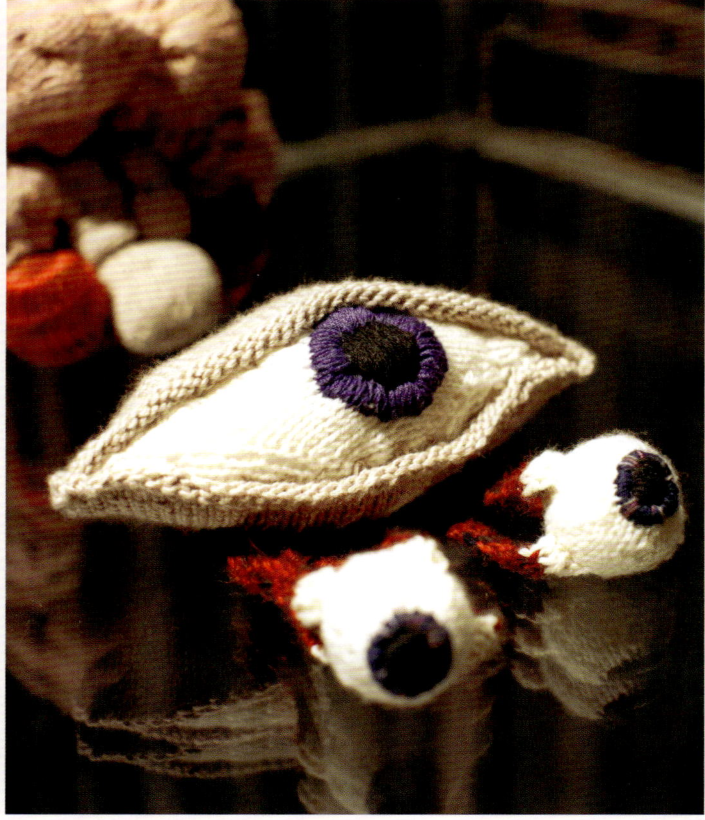

This page *The Hospital Room*, 2010, Hand-knitting
Opposite *Transcending the Material*, 2010, Hand-knitting

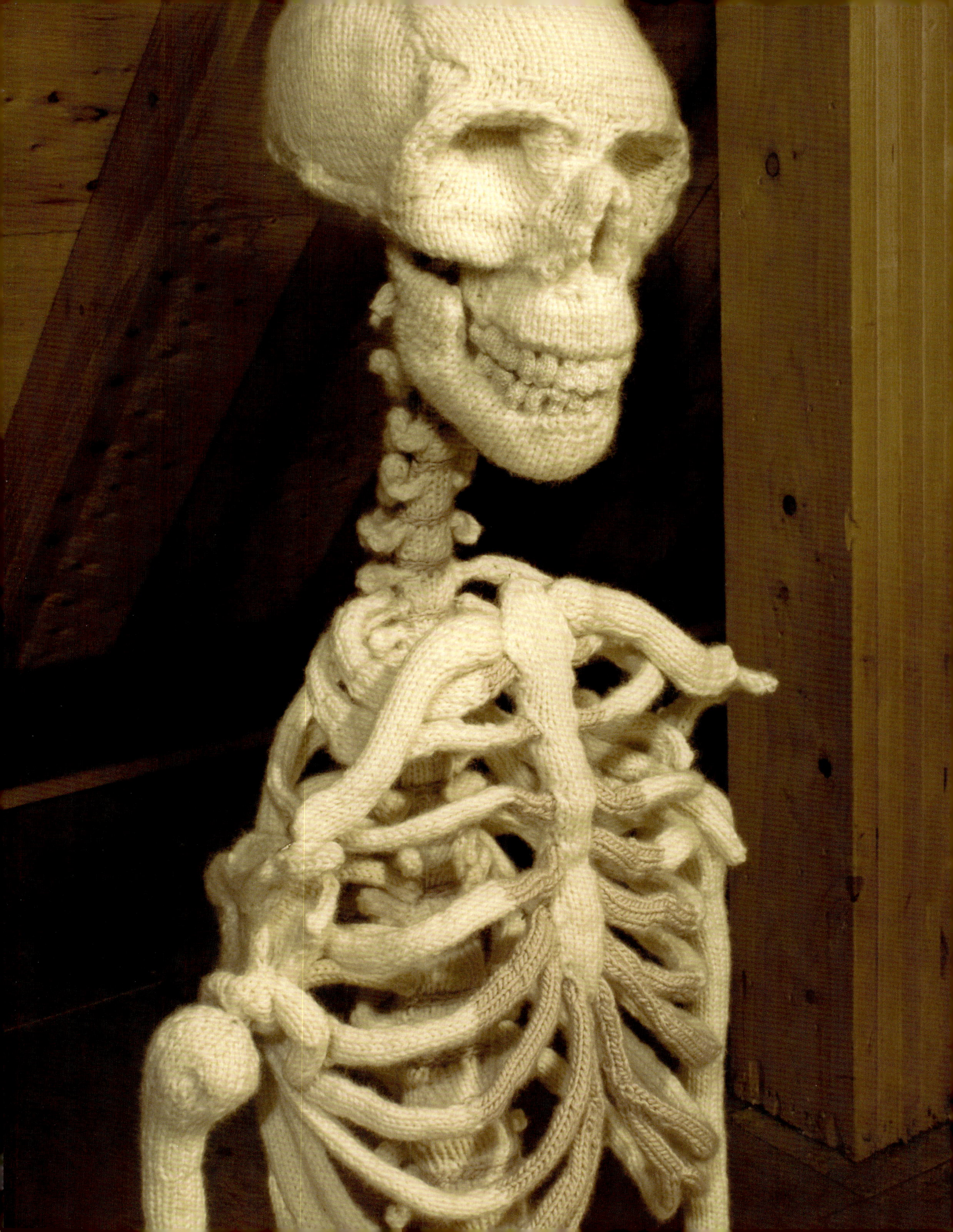

Emma Buswell

WALYALUP/EAST FREMANTLE

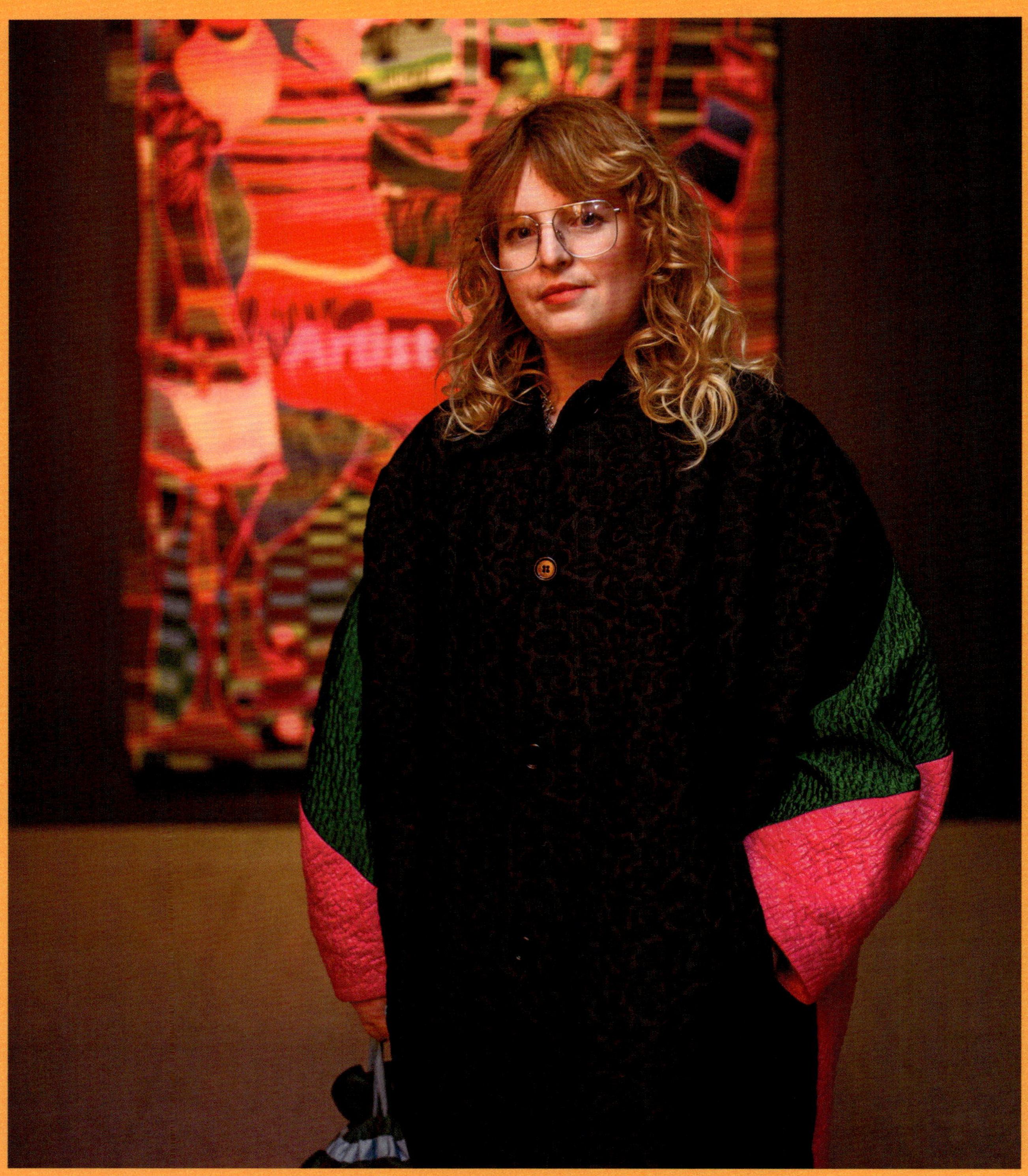

Emma Buswell uses textile materials and techniques to "[collapse] the space between kitsch and cultural expression". She works predominantly with knitting and beaded crochet to translate imagery and text into a fabric form. Her works are made to be shown in gallery contexts but also reside in the homes of friends and relatives – she has an "aversion to work which is made for an art audience exclusively".

Buswell came to textiles through a childhood spent making things, during which she learnt to knit from her mother and grandmother. She returned to knitting after art school, "[falling] back in love with the process, with stitch, and with the rhythms of making in that way" through the process of hand-knitting a jumper for an art prize. But while she enjoyed this mode of creating, she wanted to work more quickly, "in a way that could keep up with the pace of my ideas". After procuring a second-hand vintage knitting machine, Buswell used YouTube videos to teach herself how to "best translate my ideas from drawings and initial impulse into stitch". Since then, she has used the machine to create a range of works, from functional garments to large-scale installations.

One of the common themes that her works return to is storytelling, her textiles capturing "both local mythologies as well as grand narratives". Buswell brings together disparate visual and cultural references from art history, current day politics and personal narratives. Themes of Australian suburbia, humour and local touchpoints are ever present, from her first hand-knitted sweater that features her local landmark of Joondalup Shopping Centre, *So Glad You Were Here* (2017), to her ongoing series of "Chicken Bags": hand-beaded crochet interpretations of the sub-$10 roast chickens sold by big-chain supermarkets. Hand-beading a stitch at a time is a slow process, which imbues each "Chicken Bag" with a distinct identity and grandiose sense of purpose.

The everyday was also present in Buswell's exhibition Suburban Turrets (2022), which provided satirical commentary on aspirations of house ownership in Australia. Among the exhibition's knitted works was a sweater with the appearance of a construction worker's high-vis vest (albeit bearing the words "Hi Luxury"), as well as a contemporary interpretation of a 1980s sweater pattern that reads "I'm a luxury... few can afford". This play on ideas of "luxury" and the "Australian Dream" speaks to Buswell's interest in creating art that "communicate[s] ideas around working class and politics".

Buswell's more recent pieces have used knitting to replicate the grand scale and narratives of tapestry and Western history paintings, which often tell stories based in mythology and the classics. In *The Pool* (2024), Buswell references Greek mythology by depicting scenes drawn from Ovid's *Metamorphoses*. Buswell uses commercially hand-dyed sock yarns (favoured for creating self-striping socks) to create a variegated appearance that appears like "a broken code or glitch" on a large scale. Given the relationship between early computing and textile production (linked by the Jacquard loom), this disjointed appearance adds an additional layer of interpretation, bringing art historical sources into the present.

For Buswell, she is drawn to textiles because there is "something so purely human about them". She also recognises that they play a role in "how we communicate our identity, from gender to class, status, wealth, belief and so many other factors". The intricate labour required to make her work is also a deliberate choice that creates meaning, allowing Buswell to examine broader themes related to cultural production, the valuation (or undervaluation) of creative labour, and issues pertaining to class in both content and form. In her view, "labour and craft go hand in hand" as a "fundamental human expression that is deeply rooted in meditation, touch, skill and time". ■

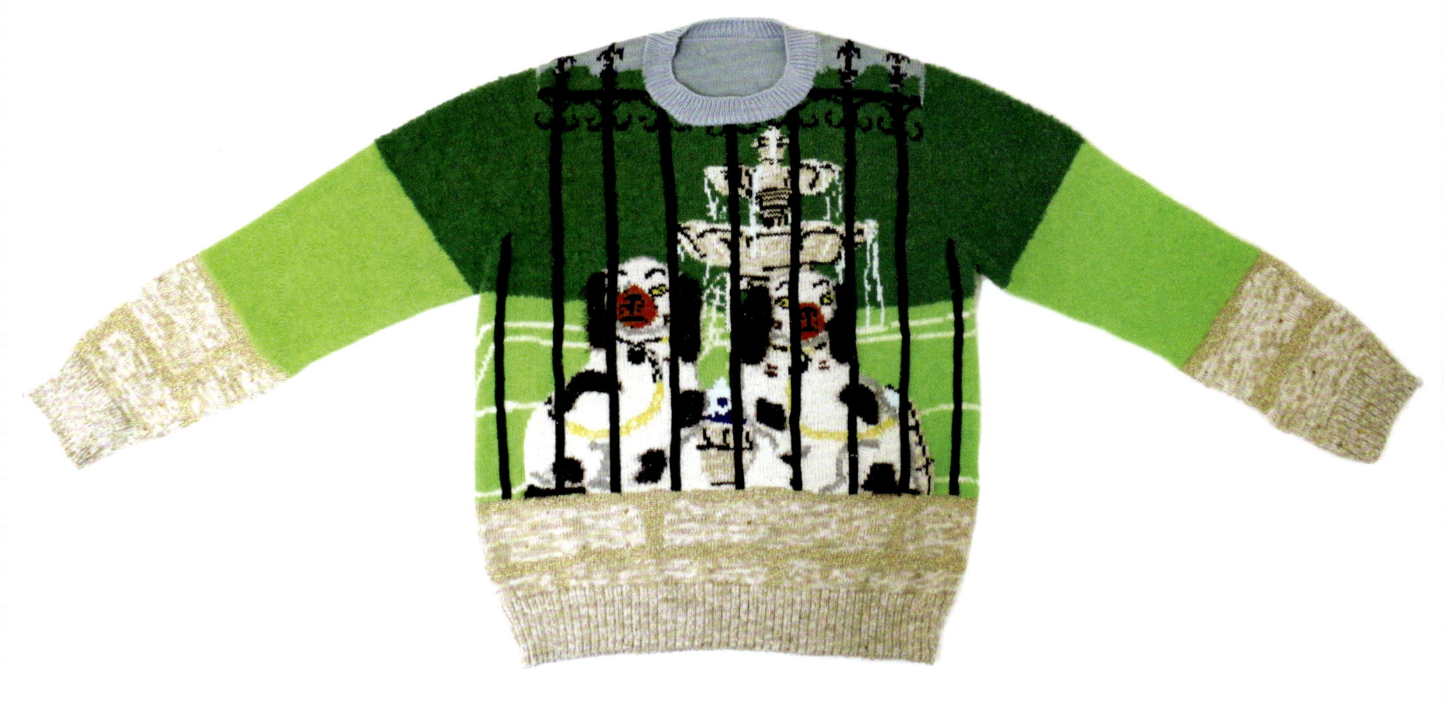

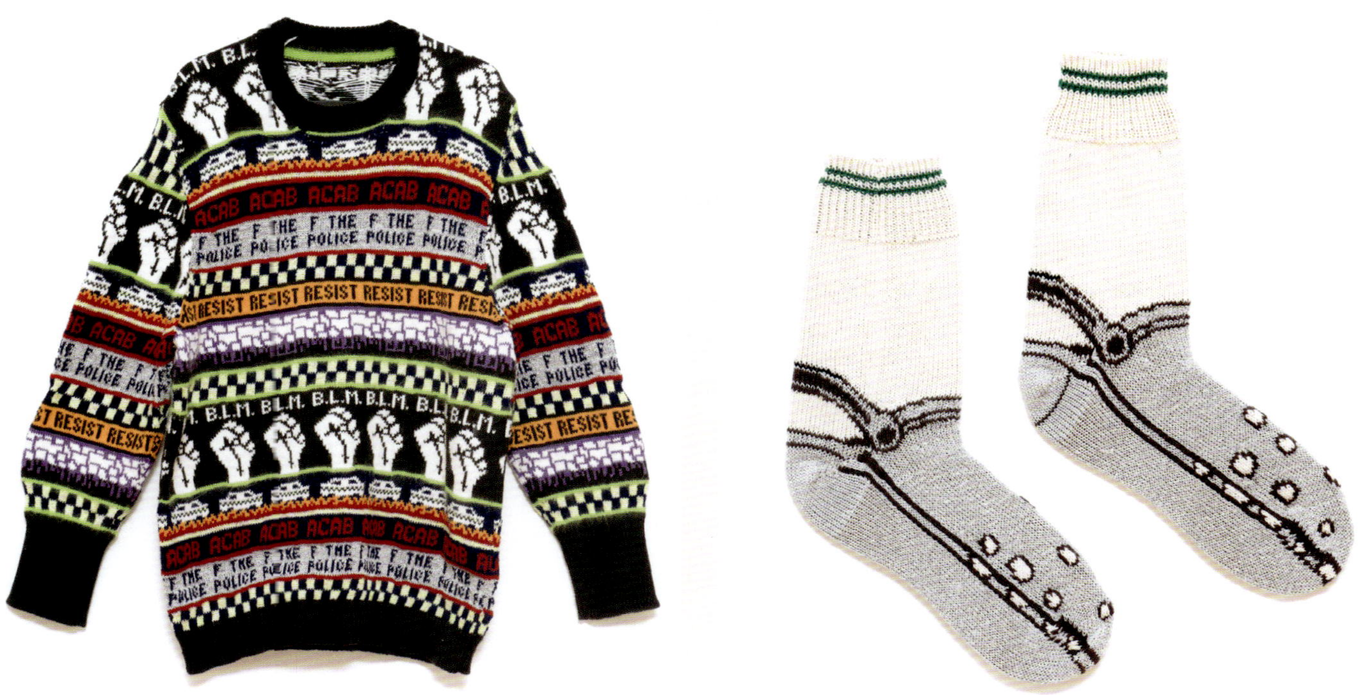

This page Clockwise from top: *A Dog's Life (Coco and Chanel)*, 2022, Manual machine knitting; *After Arachne, (October)*, 2021, Manual machine knitting; *After Arachne, (June)*, 2021, Manual machine knitting **Opposite** Top: *After Arachne, (September)*, 2021, Manual machine knitting; Bottom: *Chicken Bag the Third*, 2024, Crochet and beadwork

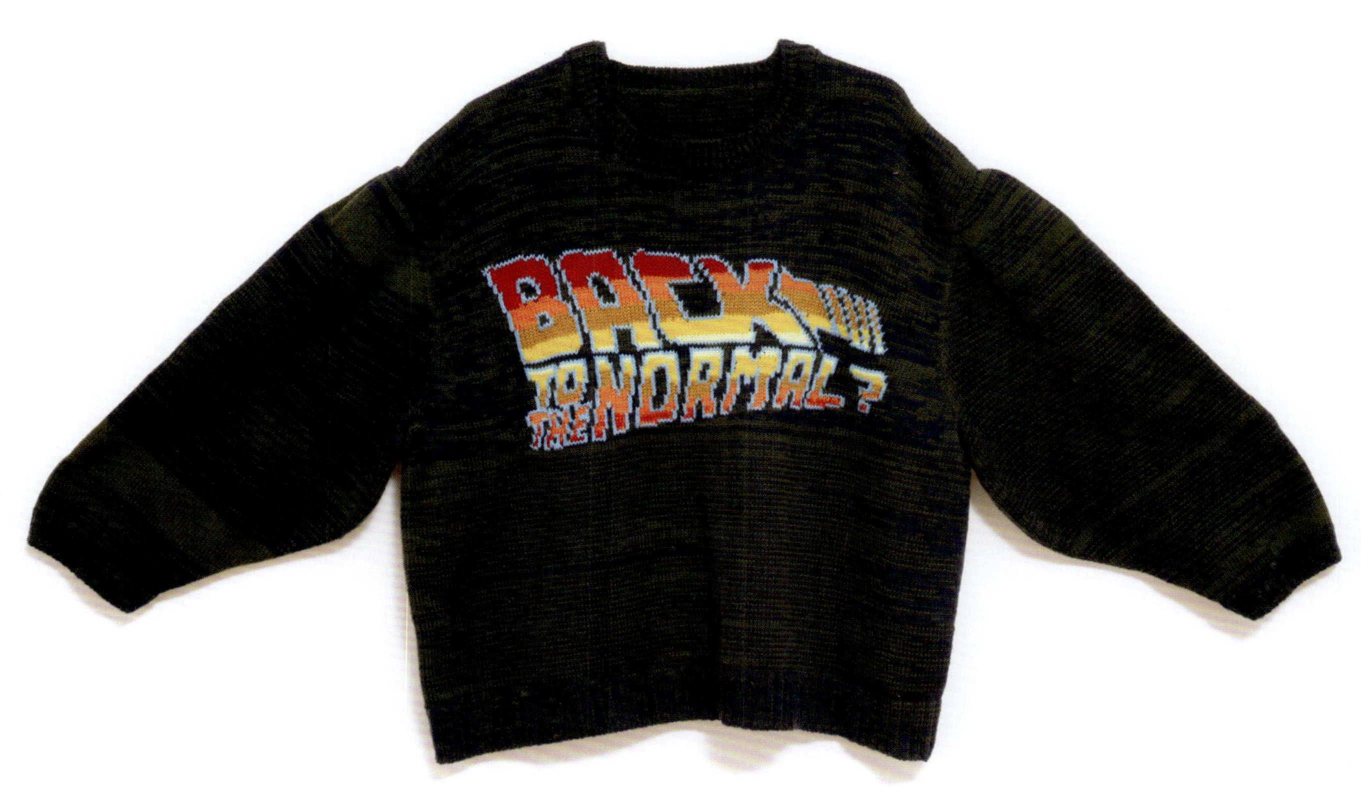
BACK
TO THE NORMAL ?

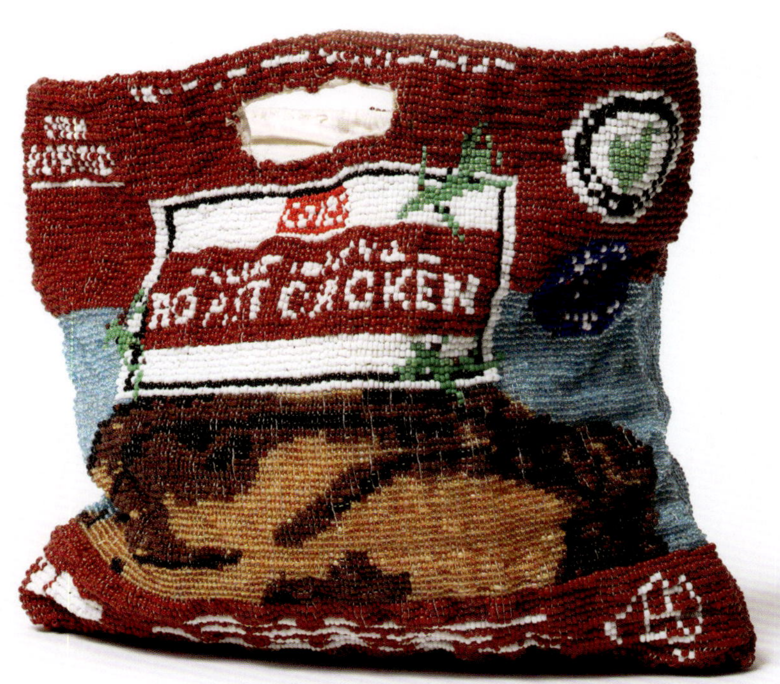

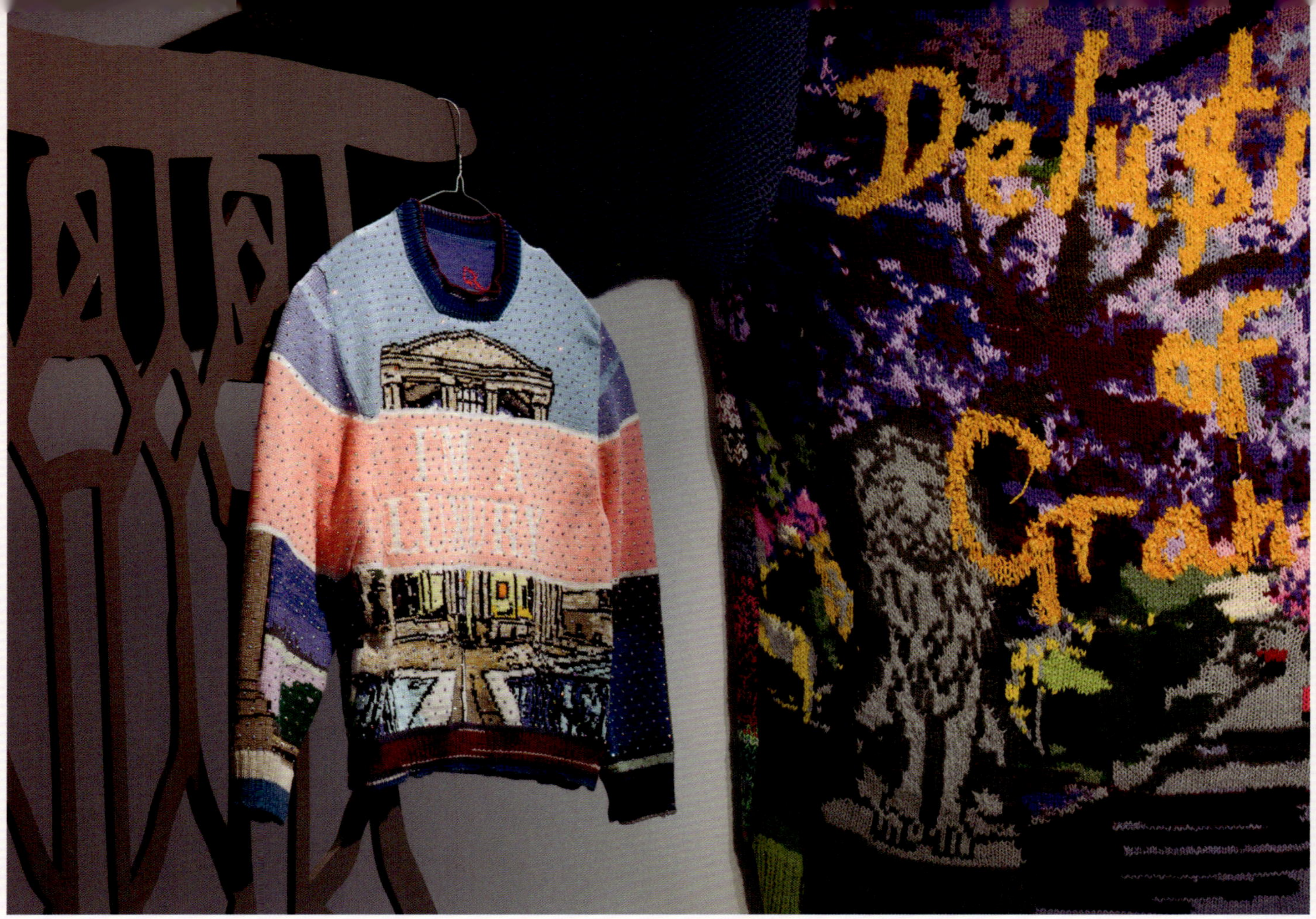

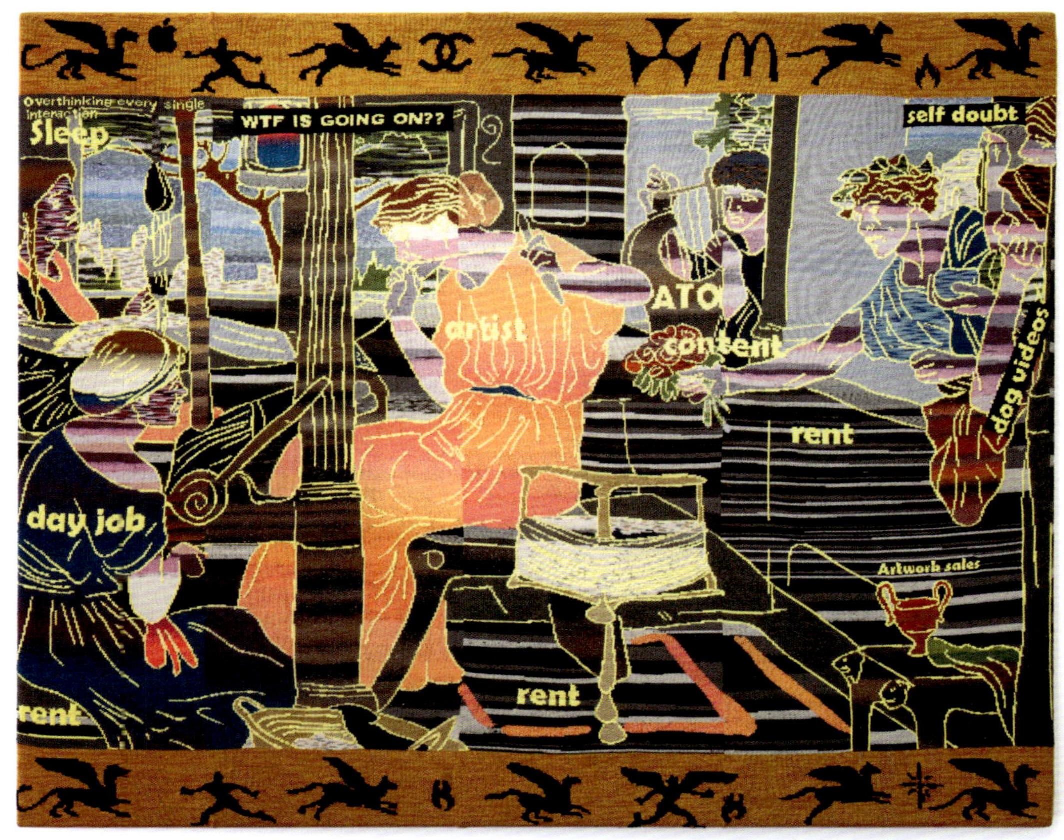
Overthinking every single interaction
Sleep
WTF IS GOING ON??
self doubt
ATO
artist
content
dog videos
rent
day job
Artwork sales
rent
rent

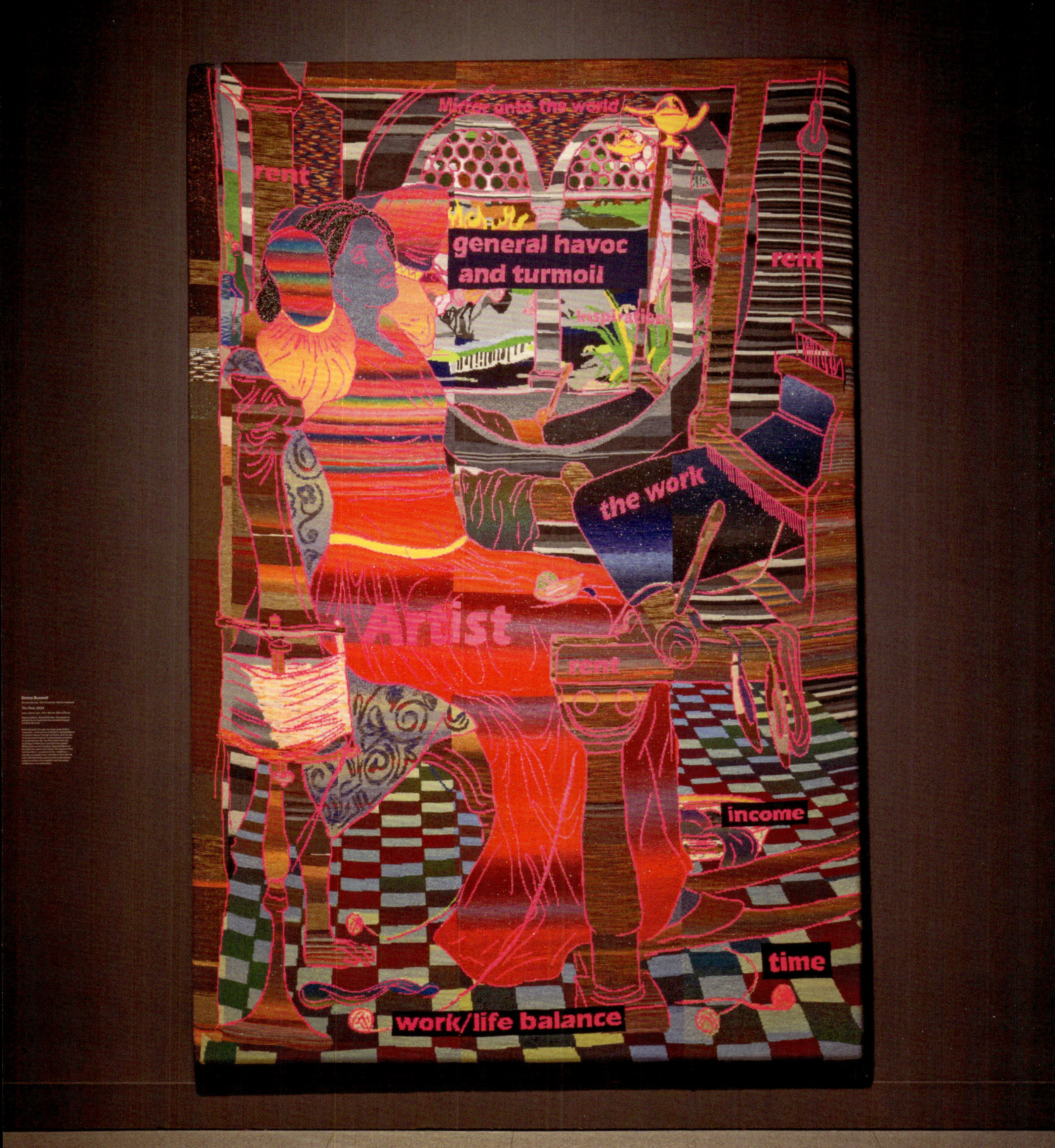

Opposite Top: *I'm a Luxury*, 2022, Manual machine knitting; Bottom: *Laertes and Lethargy*, 2023, Manual machine knitting **This page** *The Pool*, 2024, Manual machine knitting

Emma Hasselblad

STOCKHOLM

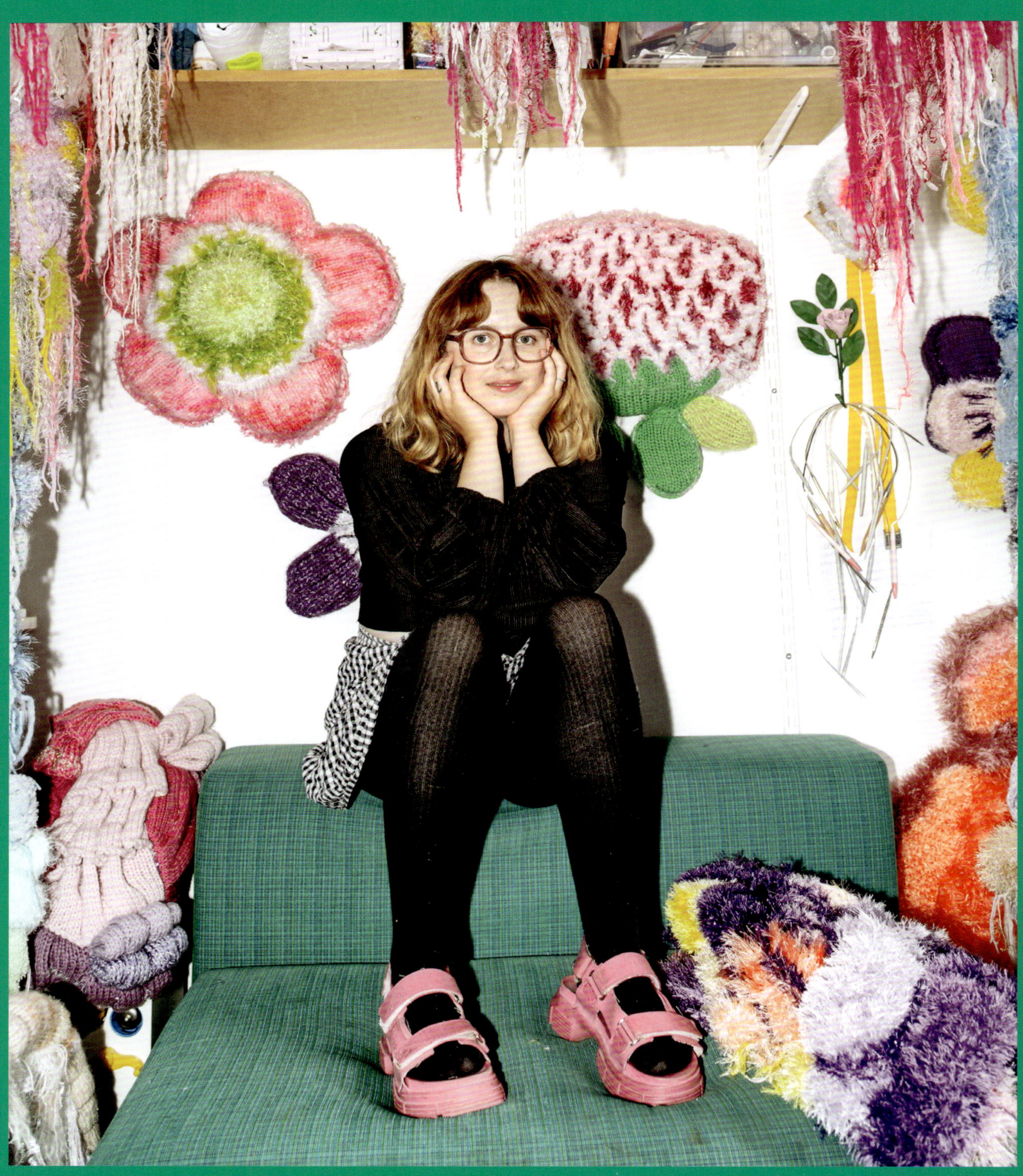

With a background in fashion design, Emma Hasselblad started knitting during her time at university. What started as a way to construct garments and an "interesting complement to my studies", though, soon became Hasselblad's "entire focus" and "the only thing I wanted to pursue". For her final collection at school, the artist knitted freeform sculptures, which were worn. These works set the foundation for Hasselblad's fascination with "the body and materials", which continues to the present day.

One of the central visual themes spanning Hasselblad's art is flowers – "whether as buds, in bloom, or wilting". This focus on living matter ("creating a kind of life cycle within the work itself") allows the artist to explore broader themes related to "fragility and beauty". In the same way that the vanitas tradition of still life paintings that came to prominence in Baroque-era Europe was used to represent life's transience, Hasselblad employs the motif of flowers at different stages to symbolise "the fleeting nature of existence". For the artist, "impermanence and time are deeply intertwined; they are inherent in us and perhaps the ultimate sign of life".

Much of Hasselblad's work employs scale to invite new perspectives and encounters. For her *Vallmo (Poppy)* (2024) series, she created five large-scale poppies measuring more than 1.8 metres tall, which each depict a distinct phase of the life cycle from bud to seed capsule. As with her other knitted flowers, this series pays attention to "structure and growth patterns", grounded in the artist's research into scientific depictions of flora. The pieces were exhibited as a public artwork, displayed outside in the city of Stockholm for five months. Over the seasons, the flowers were exposed to the outdoor elements of sun, rain and wind, transforming their colour and texture as time passed.

Hasselblad approaches her knitting with a deep love of colour, material and texture. In order to achieve the larger-than-life size of her sculptural forms, she often works with six to eight single threads of yarn made of wool, cotton and polyester, held together at once. She chooses threads that have different textures – including "fluffy, shiny and matte" – which creates a sense of three-dimensionality. This can be seen in Hasselblad's series of knitted *Pansy Flowers* (2020–ongoing), which adopt the use of novelty "eyelash" yarn, made of long threads that create the visual impression of a furry surface. Through these choices, Hasselblad is able to create interesting effects using simple knit and purl stitches, allowing the materials to shine.

While Hasselblad makes simple sketches, she relishes in the "openness and experimentation" that occurs during the hand-knitting process. Through working stitch by stitch, she can make "quick decisions" about how to "manipulate colours and materials directly", allowing her to turn her vision into tangible reality. For Hasselblad, this is a particular strength of knitting: a medium whose flexibility creates room for "intuitive, responsive and hands-on work".

Hasselblad approaches knitting not only as a "technical skill", but sees its use in her work as "an integral part of the expression itself". Reflecting on her love of the medium, Hasselblad shares that it "has always offered me a sense of freedom". For the artist, this arises not just from the fluidity of the process, but from knitting's versatility and portability, which allow her to take projects "back and forth between my studio and home". Her love also arises from place: Hasselblad grew up in Sweden, a country with an established knitting industry known for its colourwork designs. In her own contemporary artworks, Hasselblad draws inspiration from the country's "folk art and traditions". In this way, Hasselblad is continuing a cultural legacy of knitting as creative expression, pushing the medium to its dimensional limits. ■

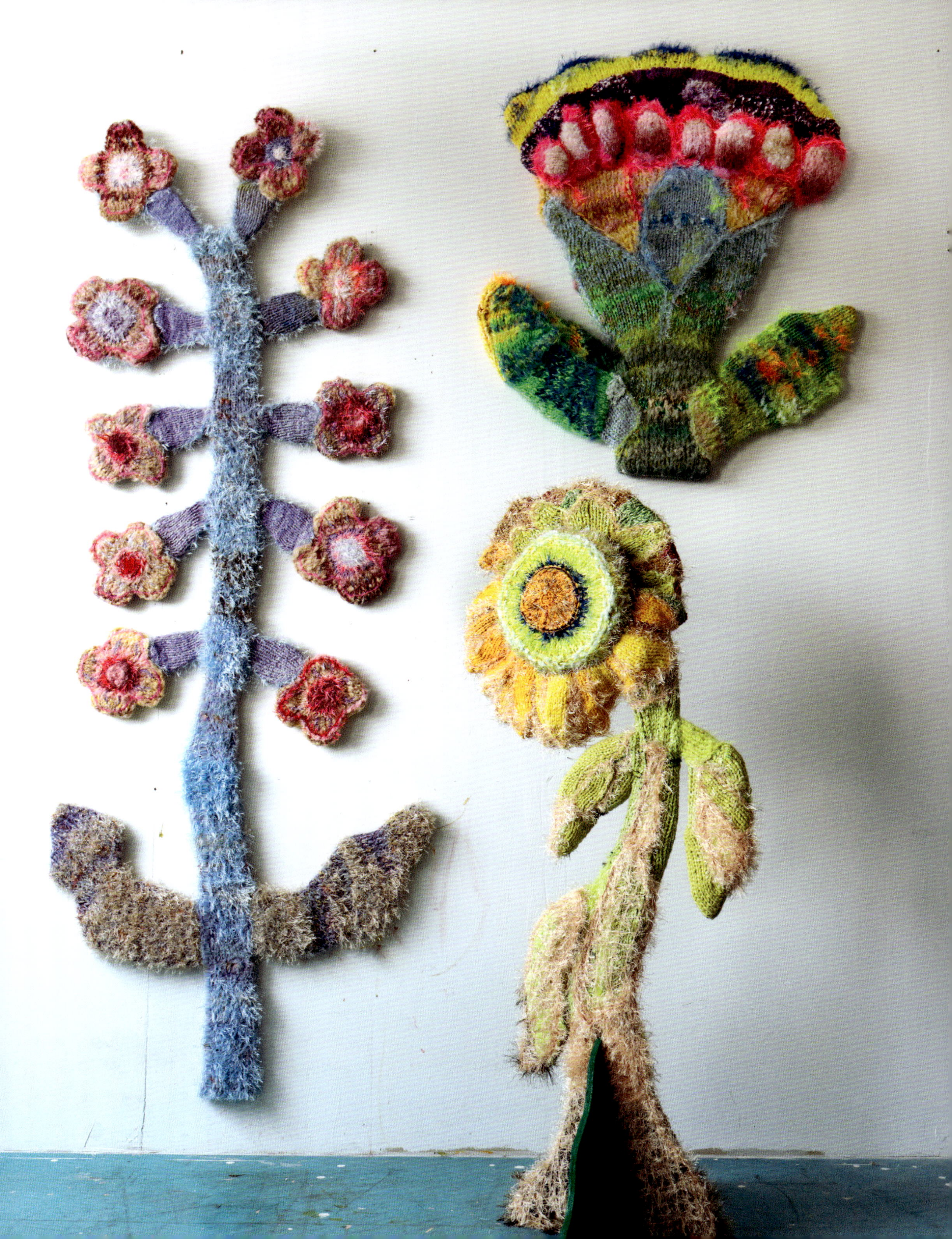

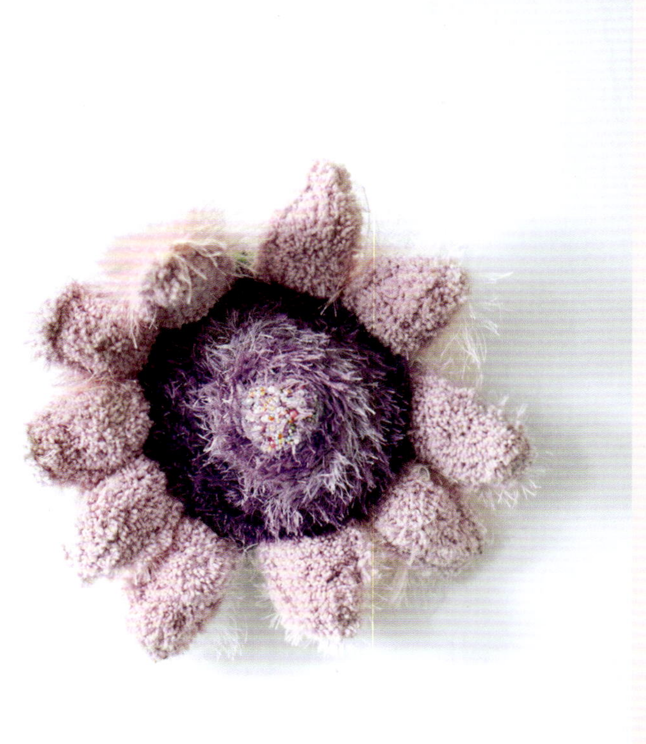

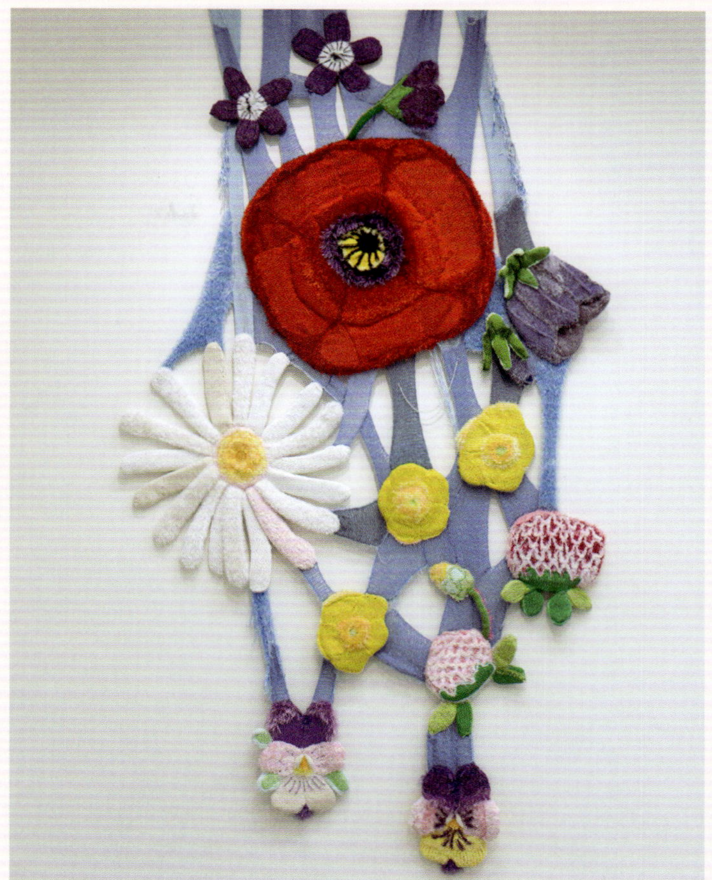

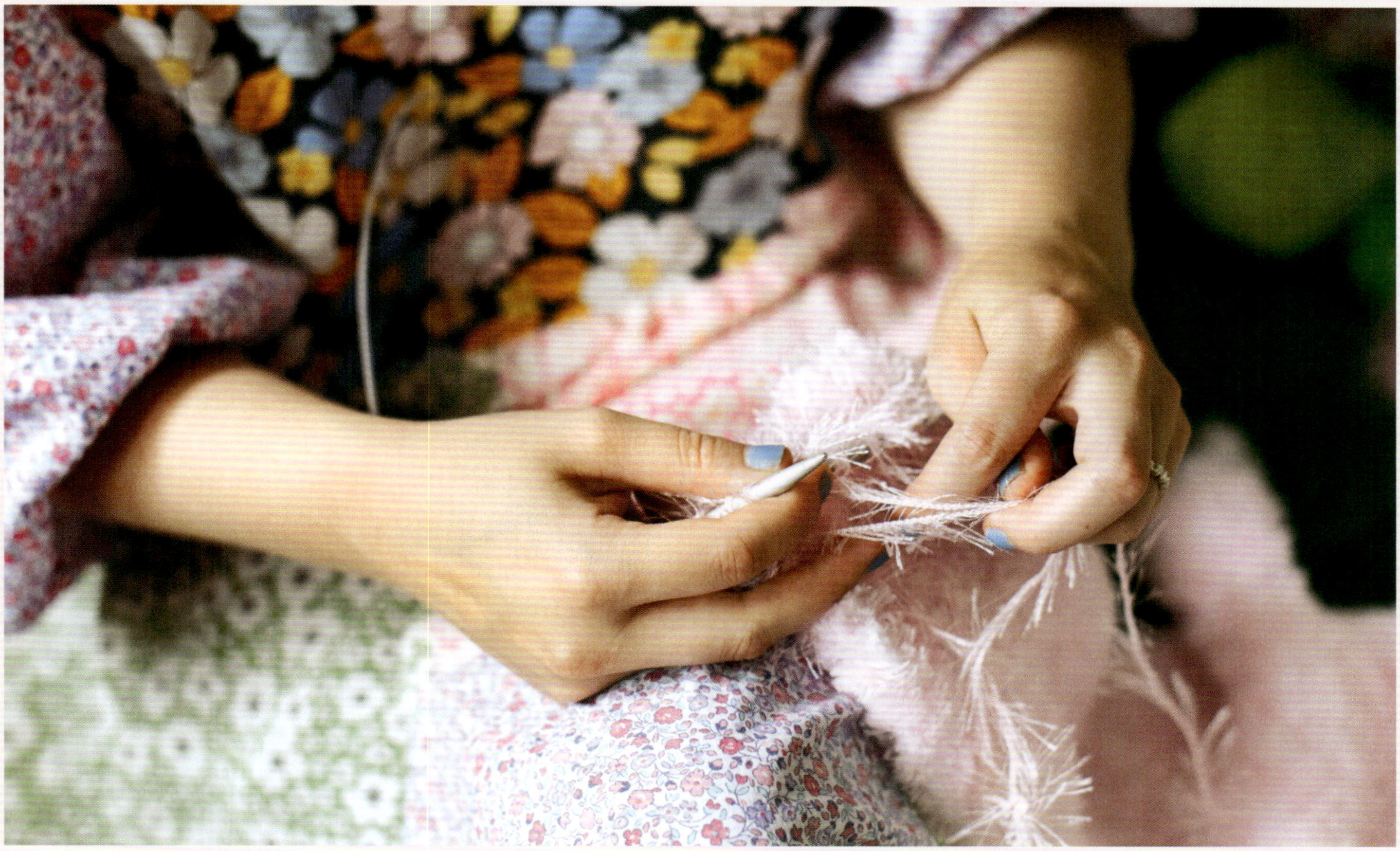

Opposite *Botanical Fantasia*, 2025, Hand-knitting **This page** Clockwise from top left: *Sunbleached Sunflower*, 2025, Hand-knitting; *Seven Flowers Under Your Pillow (Midsummer)*, 2022, Hand-knitting; Studio shot, 2022

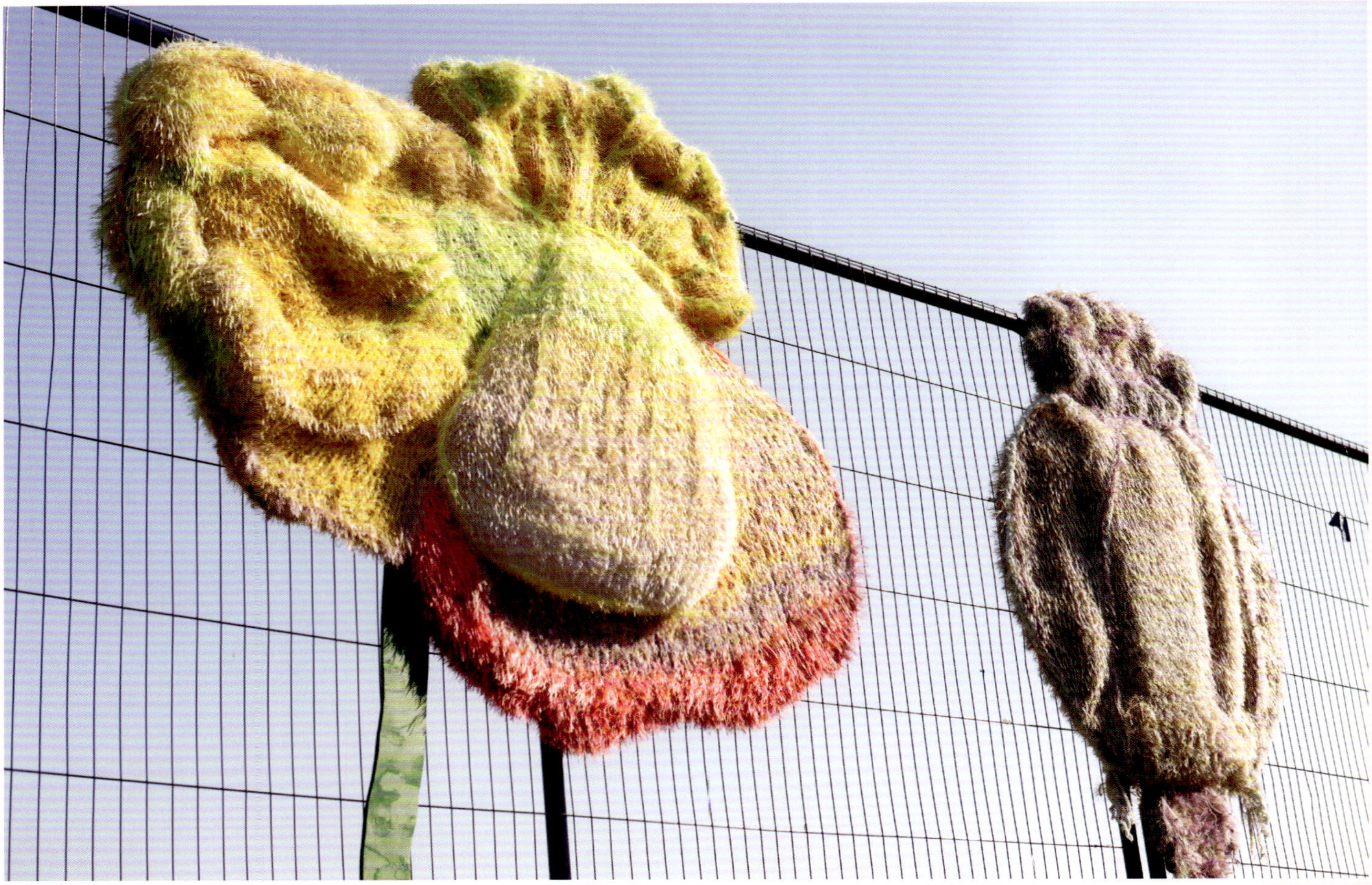

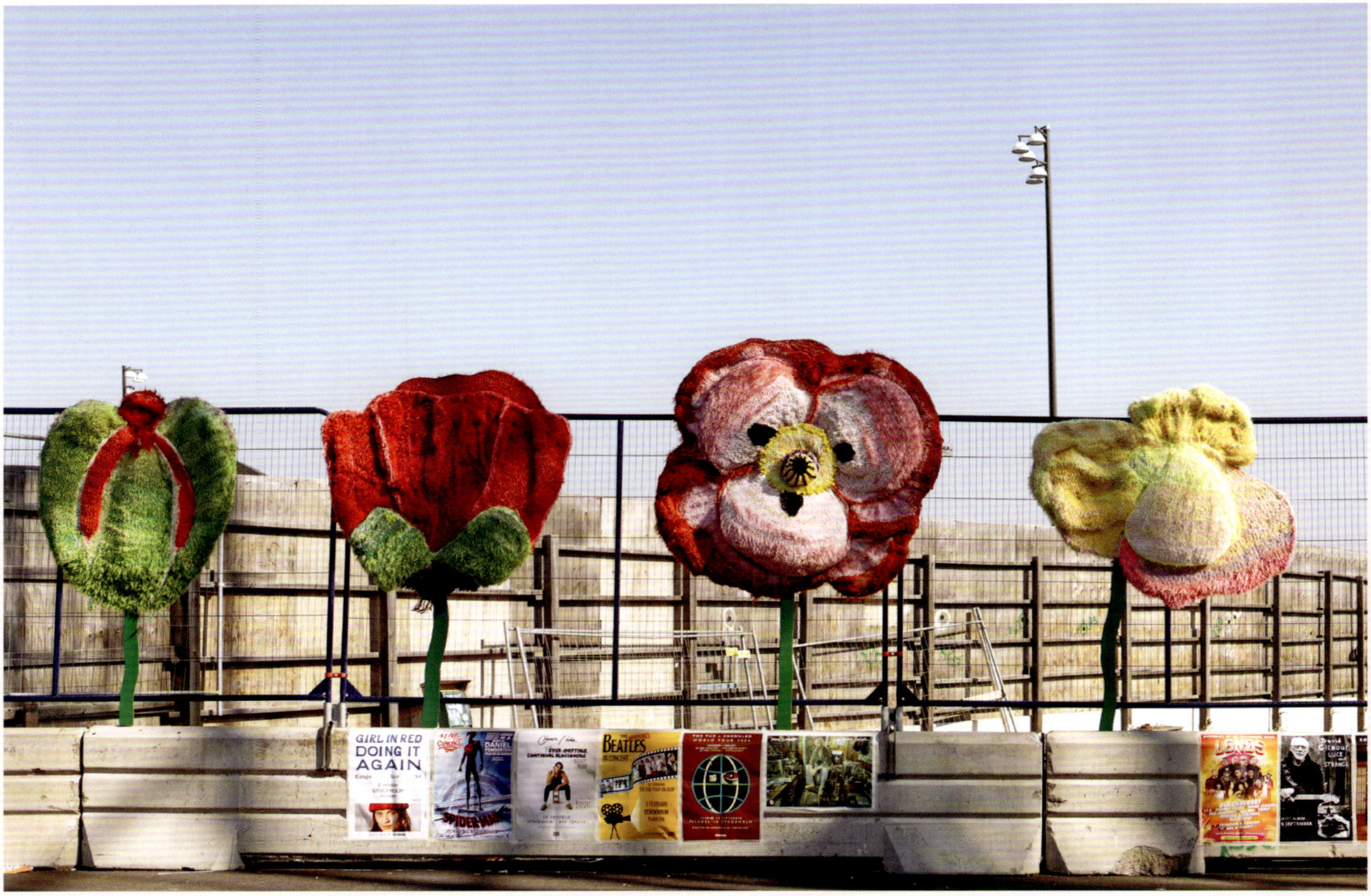

GIRL IN RED
DOING IT
AGAIN
BEATLES

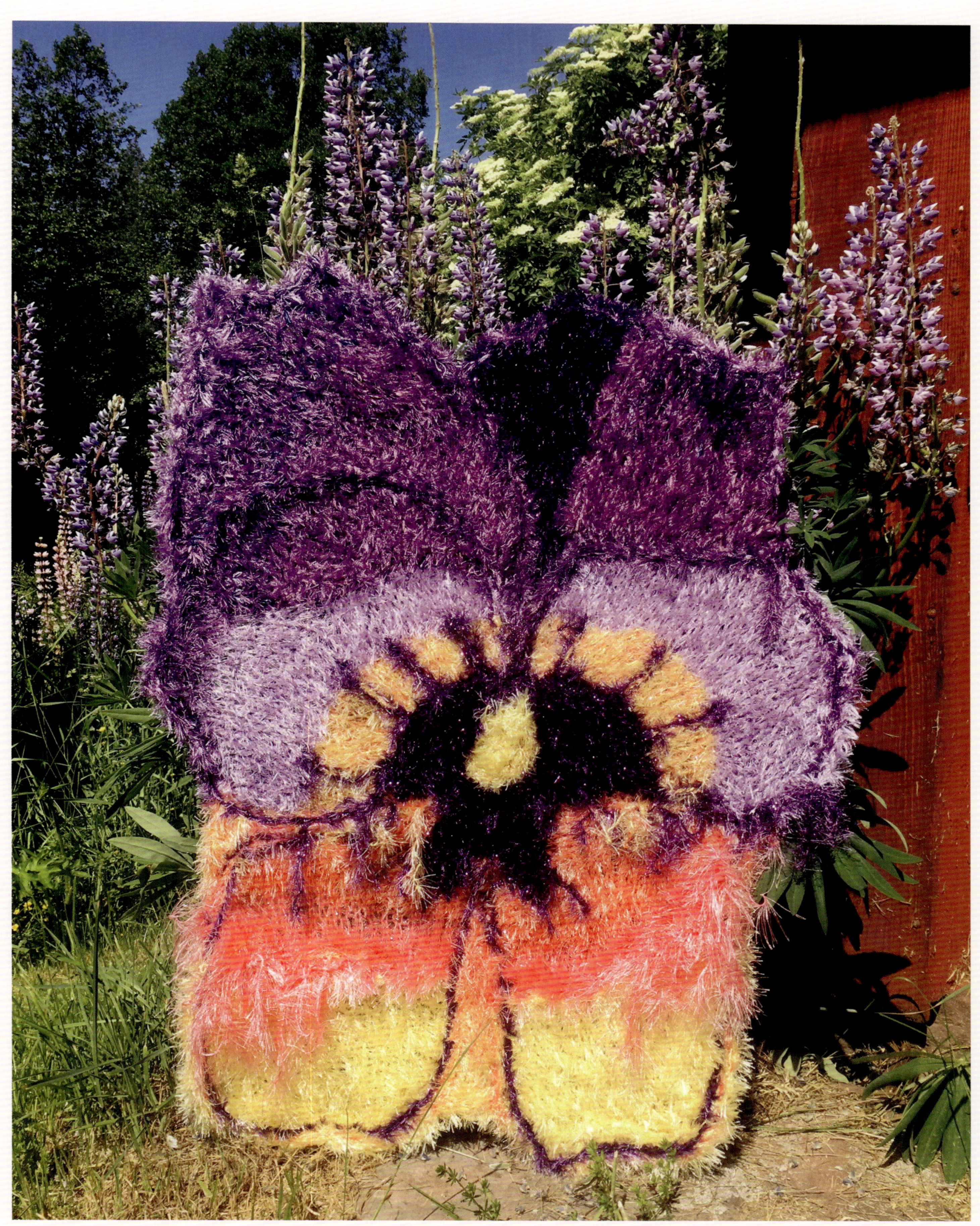

Opposite *Vallmo (Poppy)*, 2024, Hand-knitting
This page *Pansy Flower Purple and Peach*, 2020, Hand-knitting

Emma Roche

WEXFORD

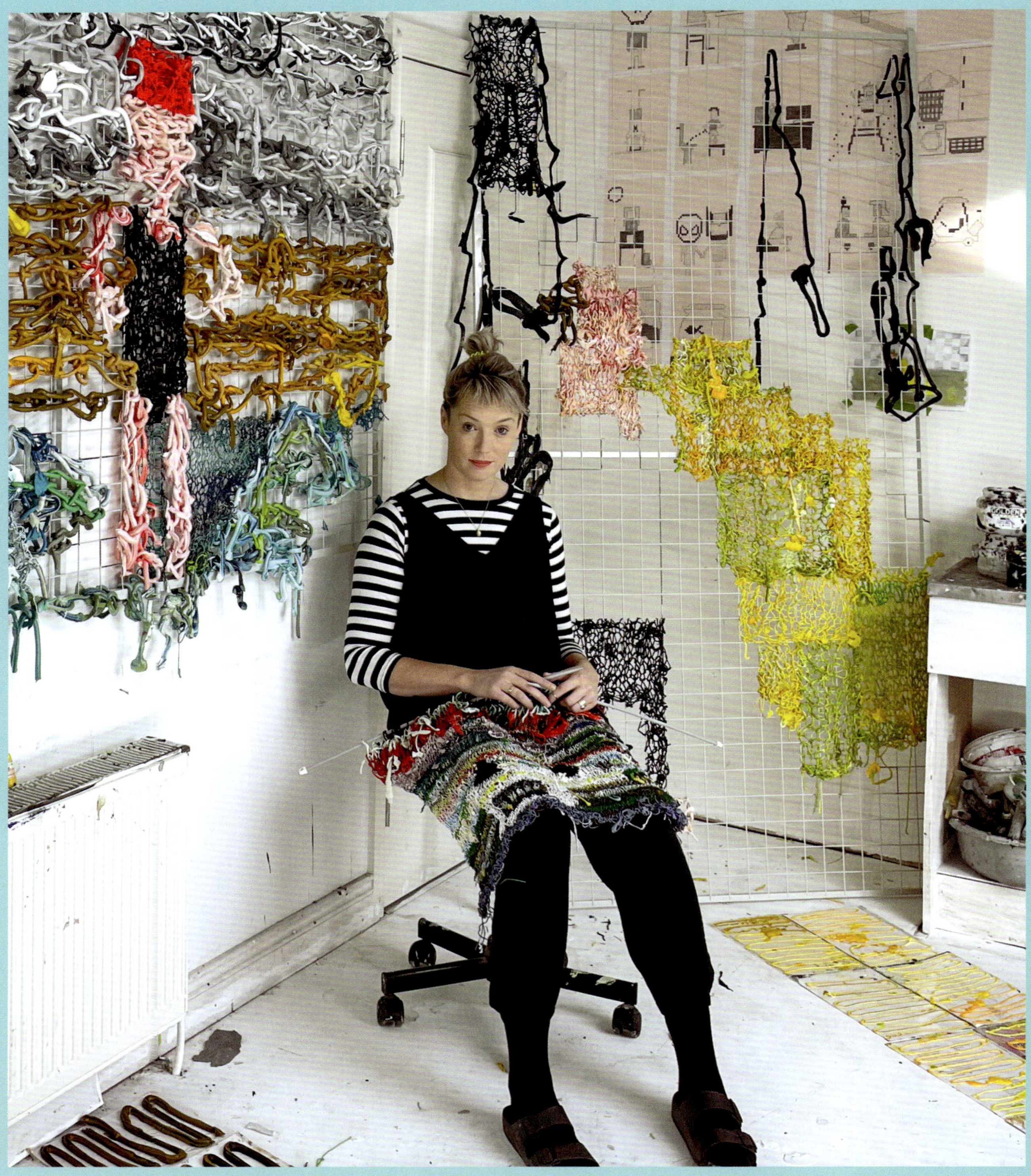

Emma Roche is a painter who employs textile techniques to push the limits of her materials. Her unique working method involves using syringes to make long lines of acrylic paint in different colours that are left out to dry. Roche then knits these dried "threads" as if they were yarn with knitting needles, adopting the use of intarsia knitting to create imagery from distinct blocks of colours like a jigsaw puzzle. Roche uses graph paper to map out the preliminary imagery and designs, each "grid" corresponding to one "stitch" on the final work. The completed flat pieces are then stretched over wooden laths like a canvas, which can be hung on walls.

Roche's paintings, with their three-dimensional surfaces, convey "a haptic approach to painting materials and processes" that challenges visual perceptions and assumptions. One may not think of paintings as "soft", but the appearance of knitted surfaces contradicts that physical expectation, even if it's an illusion created with dried paint. Roche further situates her work within the lineage of abstract painting and the freedom of painterly experimentation. As she shares, "knitting has allowed me to build an image and introduce figuration while still playing with abstraction in a tangible way". The resulting pieces test the boundaries of both textiles and painting, creating what Roche refers to as "anti-painting paintings with holes in them that droop or seem they might slip off the wall".

A central theme in Roche's art is a consideration of labour and work. Many of her pieces are influenced by scenes from daily life, including "unsolicited advice, day jobs, liquids, the body, screens, background noise, lists, interruptions, computer games, iconography, my kids and various everyday activities". Among this imagery, video game characters are another common theme, such as the Super Mario Brothers and Sonic the Hedgehog, whose translation from digital pixels to paint is particularly suited to the grid-like appearance of Roche's knitting. Other common visual motifs include bodily waste and functions, seen for example in the bright yellow vomit stream at the centre of the aptly titled *Hurl* (2023). This work playfully uses the messy, droopy lines of the paint to capture a vomiting child: a fitting commentary on the dualities of child-rearing and motherhood from Roche, who is a mother of three young children herself.

Roche lists a number of cultural and familial connections to knitting. In Ireland, where she was raised and still lives, the harsh climate and weather means knitting is a "significant and symbolic" part of culture. Within her own family, her grandmother taught Roche's mother, who taught Roche, in turn, to knit, and both her grandfathers were knitters in their own time. A small textile piece by her late grandfather Jim, who she never met, continues to hang in Roche's studio to the present day and is a visible connection to this lineage. While she works within a long knitting tradition, though, Roche also breaks with it, refusing for her pieces to be read strictly in terms of craft or art, demanding instead for her paintings "to be both".

For Roche, her marriage of knitting and painting invites discussions of gendered biases and value. Painting, particularly in Western art history, has historically privileged white male voices; even today, there remains a gender disparity in art sale prices and auctions. Roche's choice of mediums is an attempt to "challenge established assumptions", and the "systemic intersectional misogyny and gate-keeping within the art market". Within her practice, Roche recognises that there is a "refusal and joy in tying 'straight-male-dominated-materials' into knots". Her imaginative blend of painting and knitting indicates new possibilities and ways of creating that exist beyond binary distinctions of form and function. ■

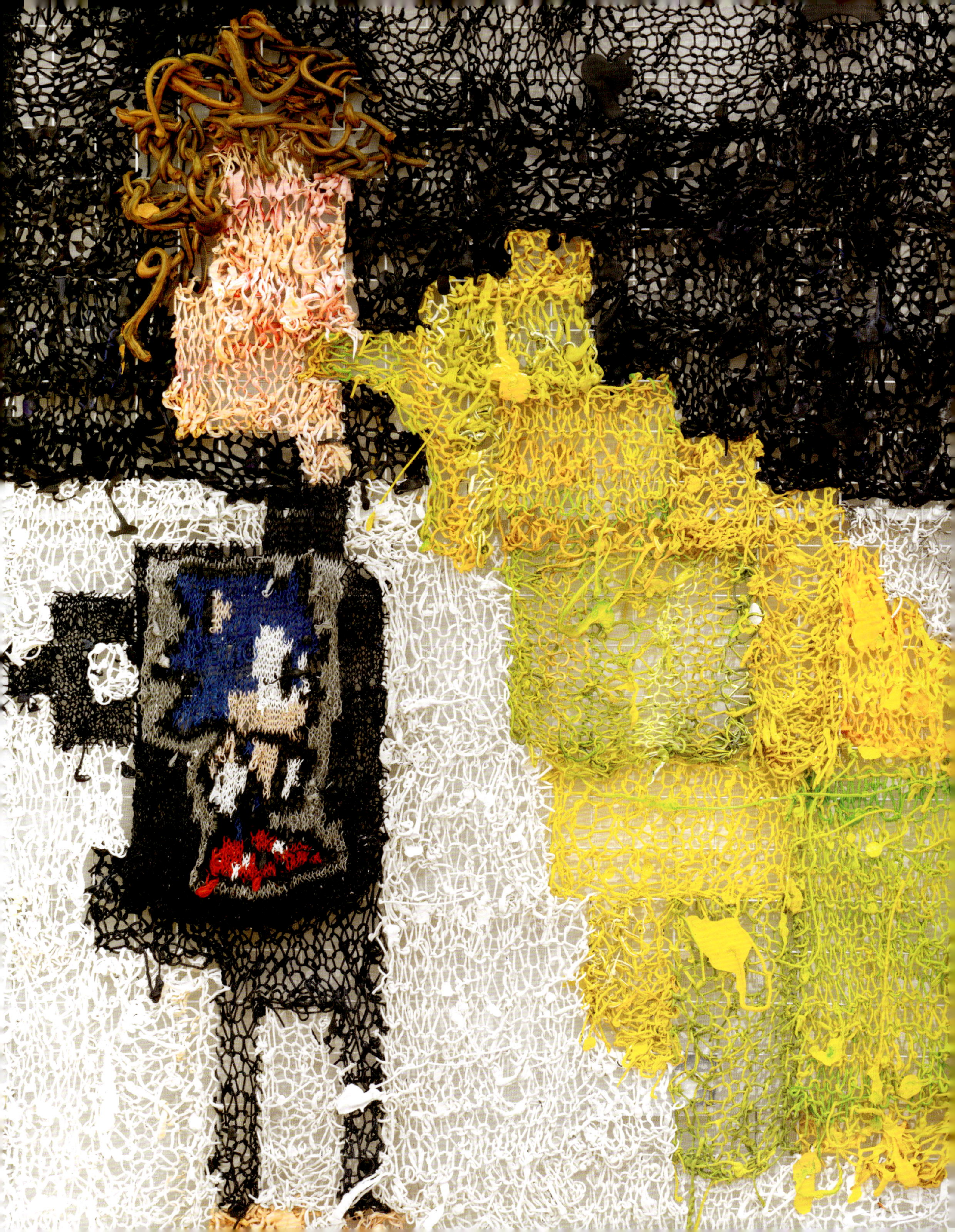

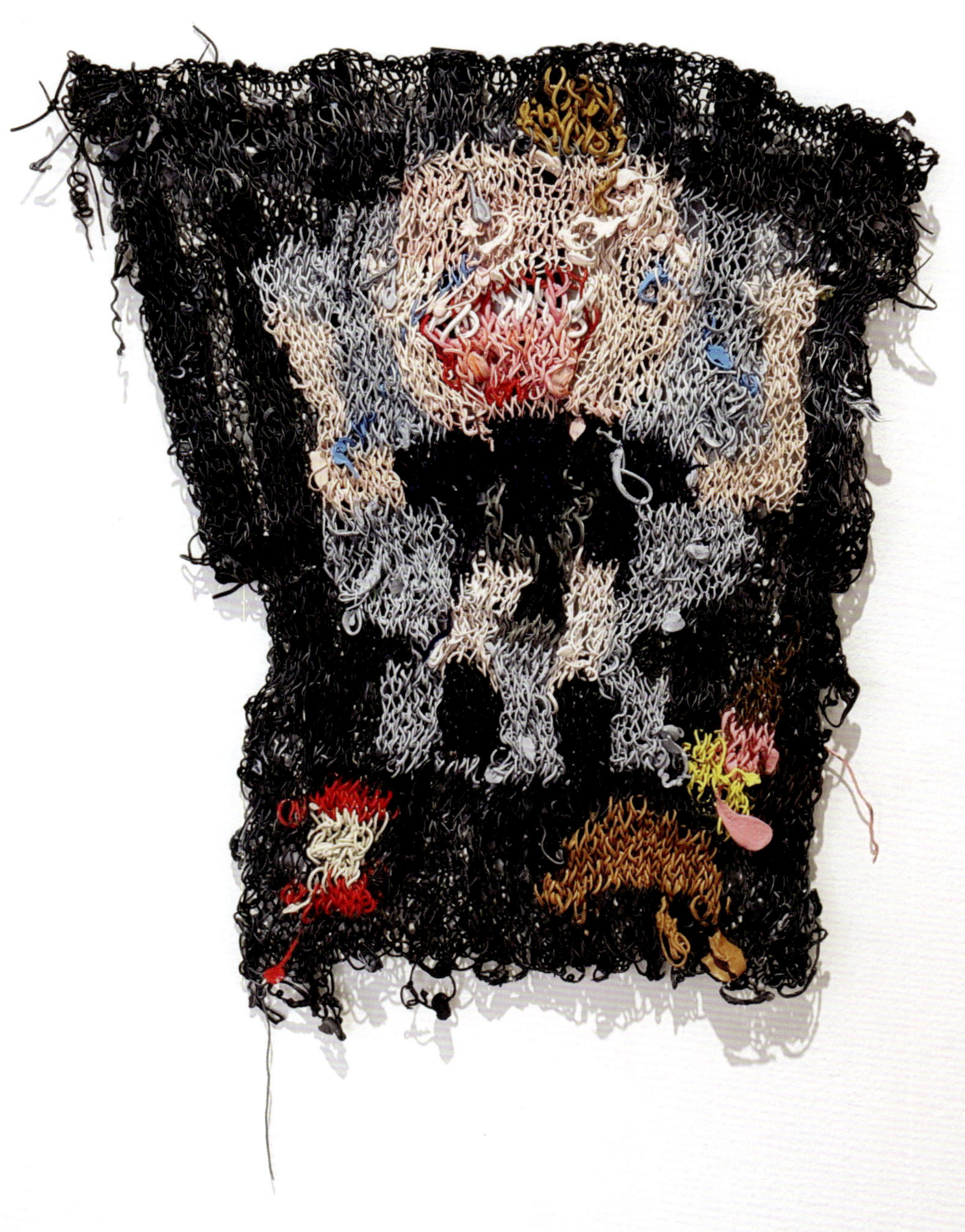

Opposite *Hurl*, 2023, Hand-knitted acrylic paint
This page *Back Seat*, 2023, Hand-knitted acrylic paint

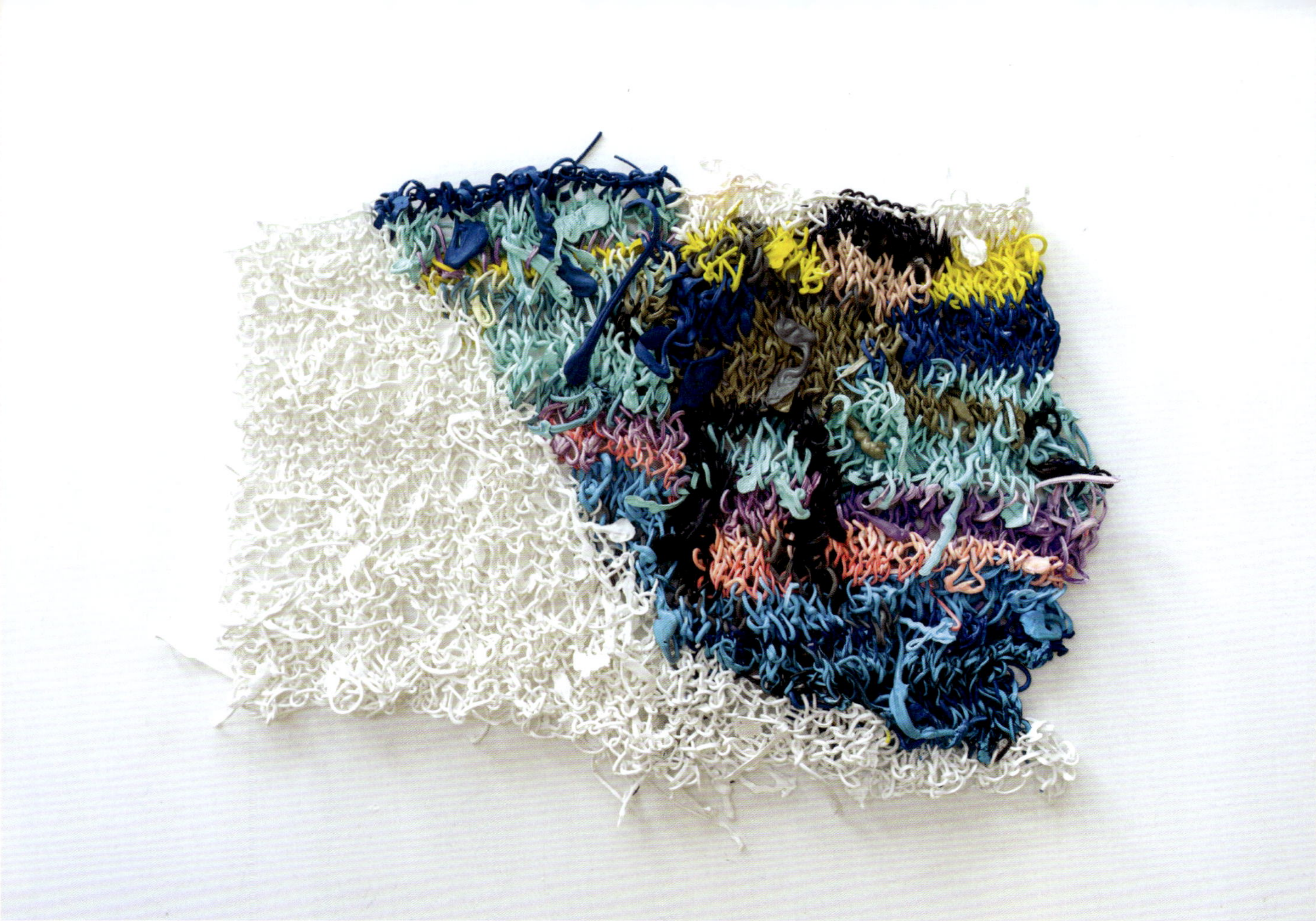

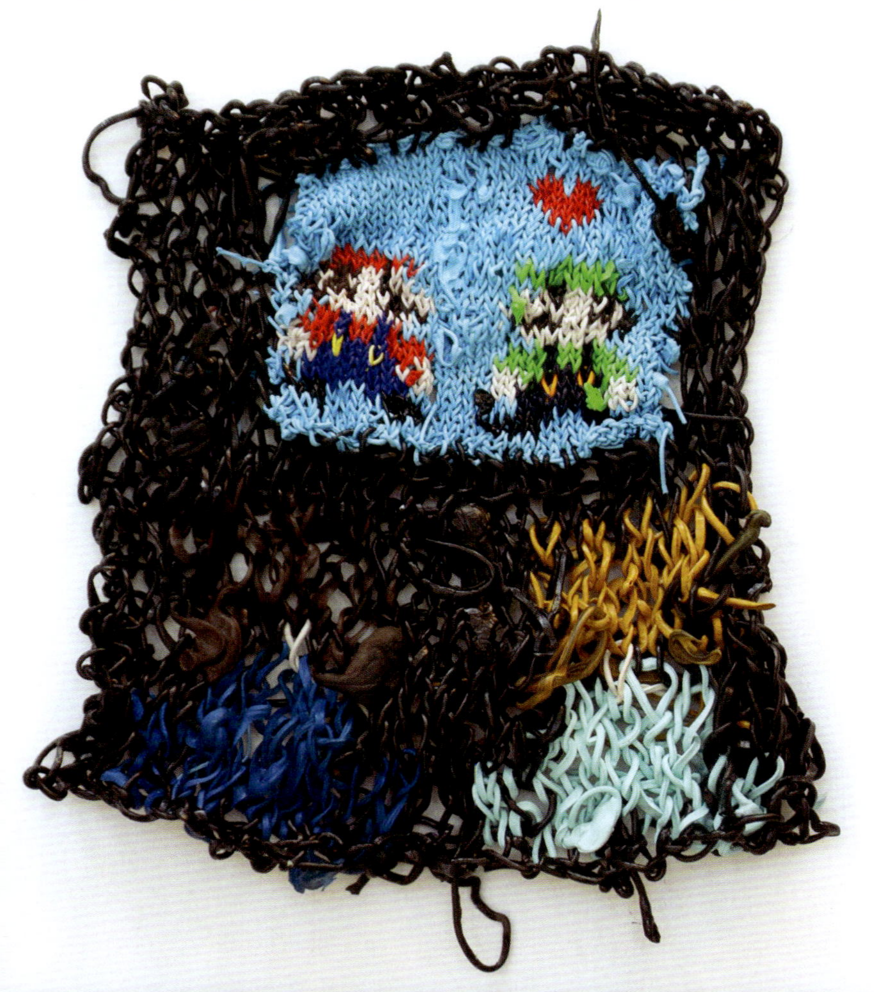

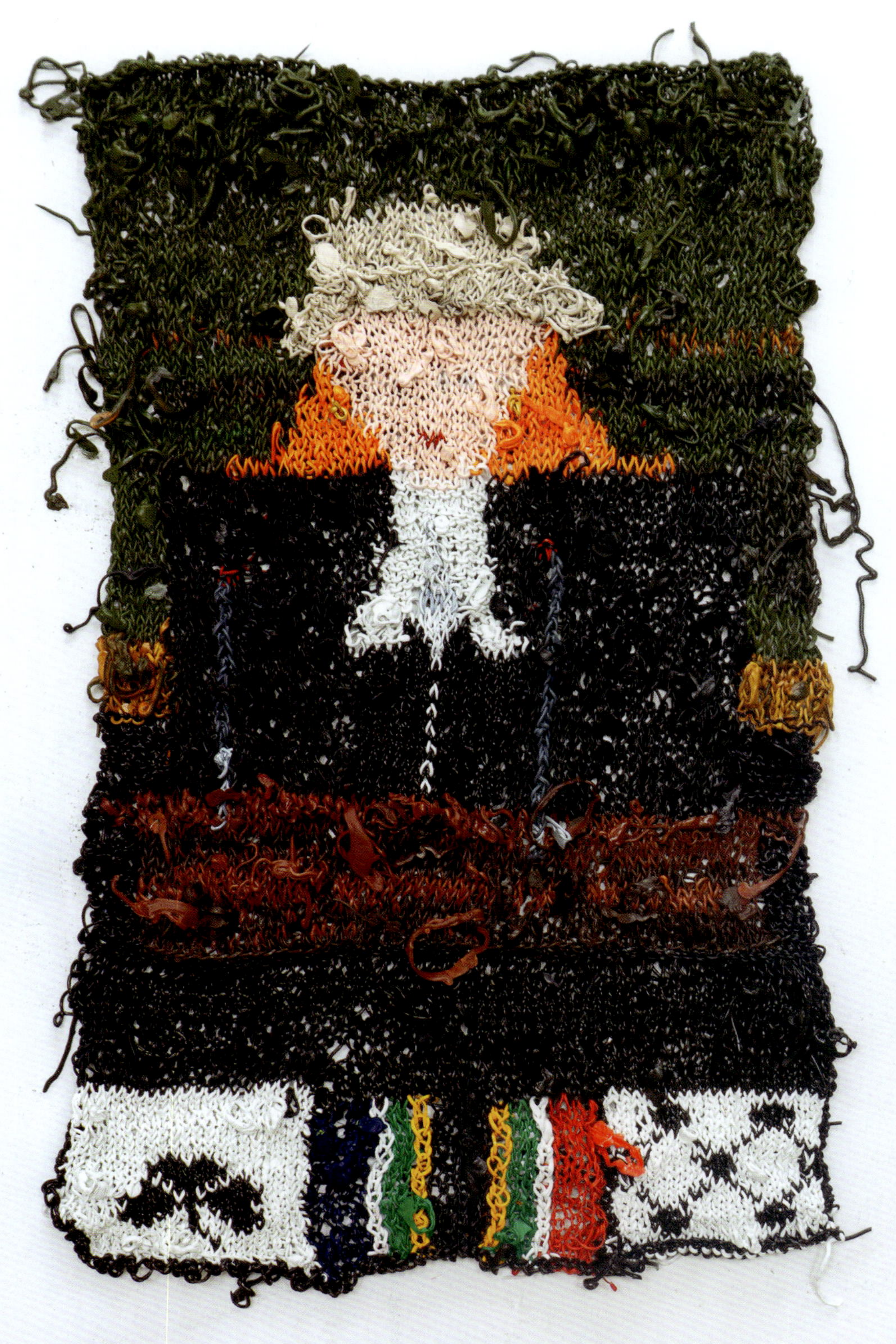

Opposite Top: *Off-piste Jacques*, 2025, Hand-knitted acrylic paint; Bottom: *Two-player*, 2025, Hand-knitted acrylic paint
This page *Blinne*, 2025, Hand-knitted acrylic paint and gold leaf

Kate Just

DJANDAK/CASTLEMAINE

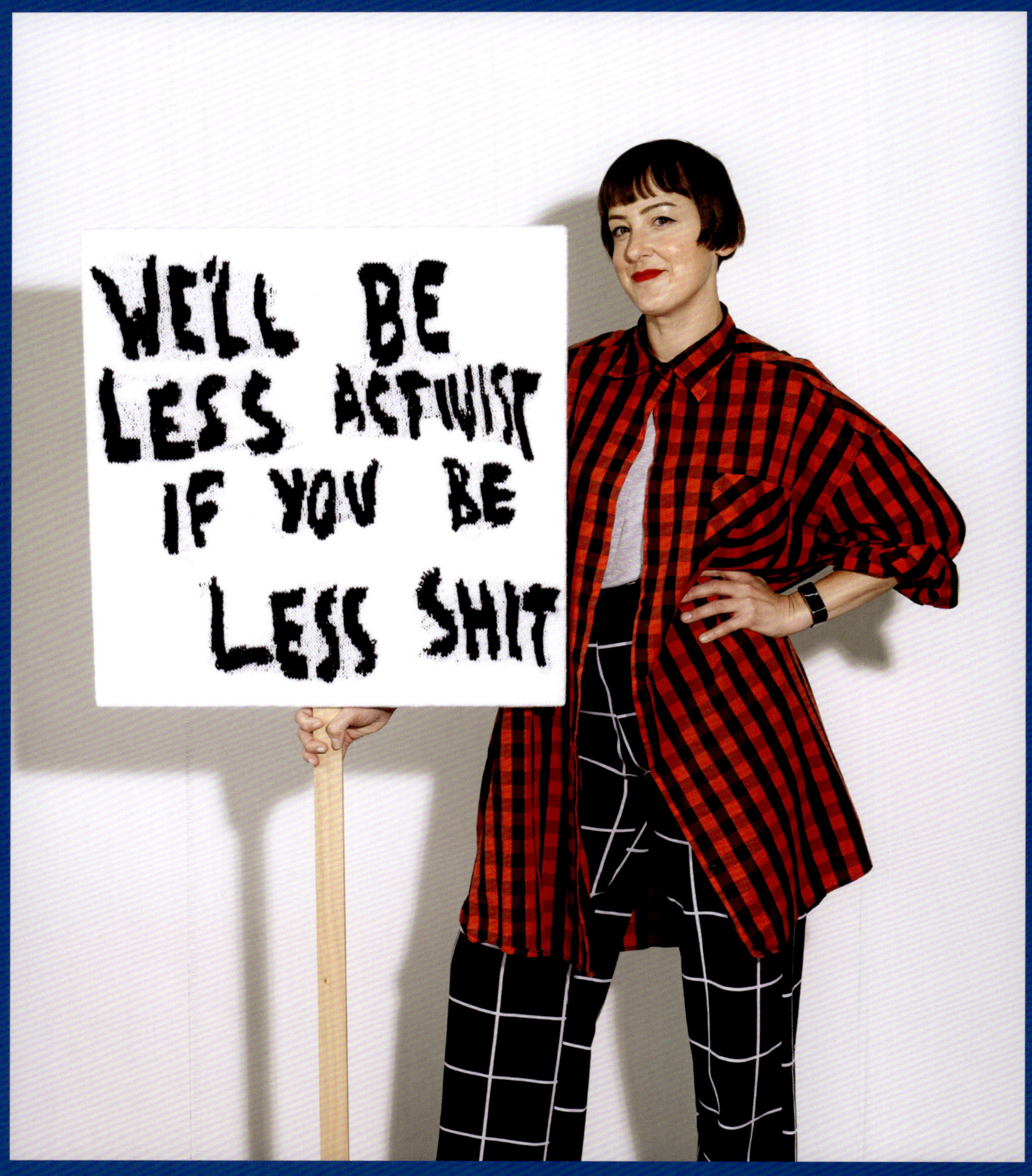

Kate Just is an artist whose works highlight the political and radical possibilities of textiles. Her approach to knitting is informed by her life and draws on feminist and queer histories of protest and solidarity. This challenge to historical, Eurocentric dismissals of craft as simply "women's work" "reinvent[s] knitting's potential as an embodied material language, a way of speaking one's truth, sharing stories, or agitating for change". Just's creative, defiant approach centres "feminist issues and ideas: of love, care, repair, gender-based violence, protest, and the reclamation of our bodies, lives and artwork for ourselves".

Just's art has always been autobiographical. She first learnt to knit from her mother in a moment of grief after the tragic loss of her younger brother. It was this experience of being physically present with another that led her to recognise that knitting can "be a powerful personal tool for narrating stories and creating new bonds". This connection to others is present in Just's public knitting circles and her participatory artworks that invite others to contribute; two examples of the latter are *HOPE* (2013) and *SAFE* (2014), both made in response to violence against women. Just invited people from Edinburgh and Melbourne to join her in knitting squares in night-reflective fluorescent yellow (*HOPE*) and black (*SAFE*) yarns, which she then joined together to create large, knitted banners that were carried during late-night walks led by the artist.

Just's work is marked by an ongoing use of text, inspired in part by graffiti and protest signs. For Just, text's incorporation in knitted works "explore[s] the erasure of women from the canon of art and society more broadly, the significance of protest movements, the importance of self-care to activist and artistic practices, and the ways artists use text as messages to others in public space to inspire change". *PROTEST SIGNS* (2022) translates actual protest signs into knitted versions, stretched on canvas and then attached to wooden pickets. Real-world protest signs may be discarded after one use, but in this series, Just archives the originals' messages through knitting in "an act of love and preservation".

Even when she knits alone, Just's works are still grounded in community and shared values. Her ongoing *Feminist Fan* series are Just's tribute to the feminist and queer artists who have shaped and influenced her work and thinking; among them are depictions of art historical names such as Louise Bourgeois and Frida Kahlo, alongside contemporary inclusions such as Juliana Huxtable and Mithu Sen.

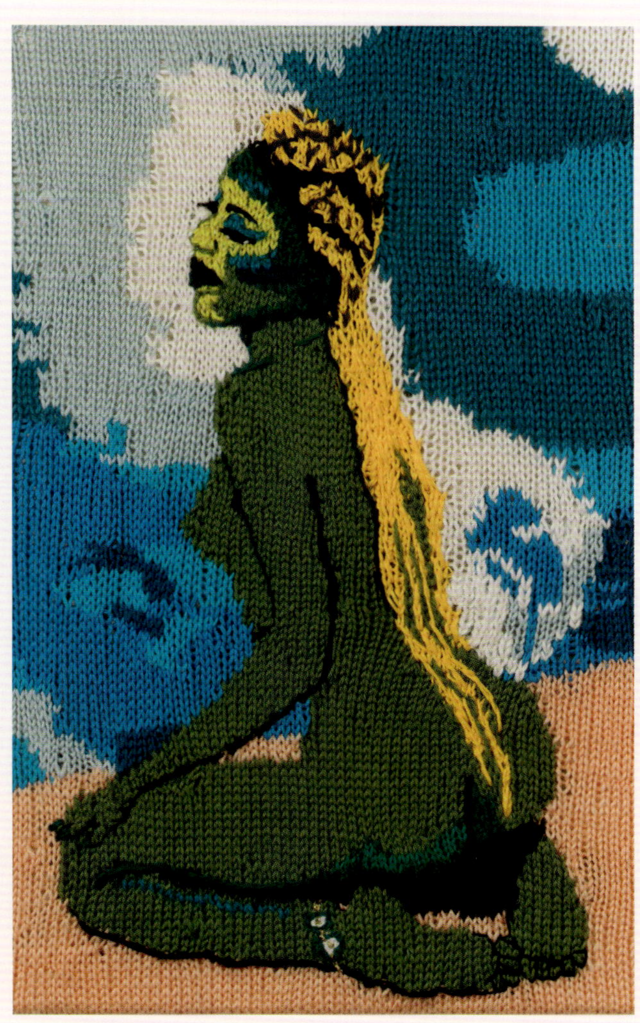

Opposite *We'll be less activist if you be less shit*, 2022, Hand-knitting stretched around plywood with timber handle

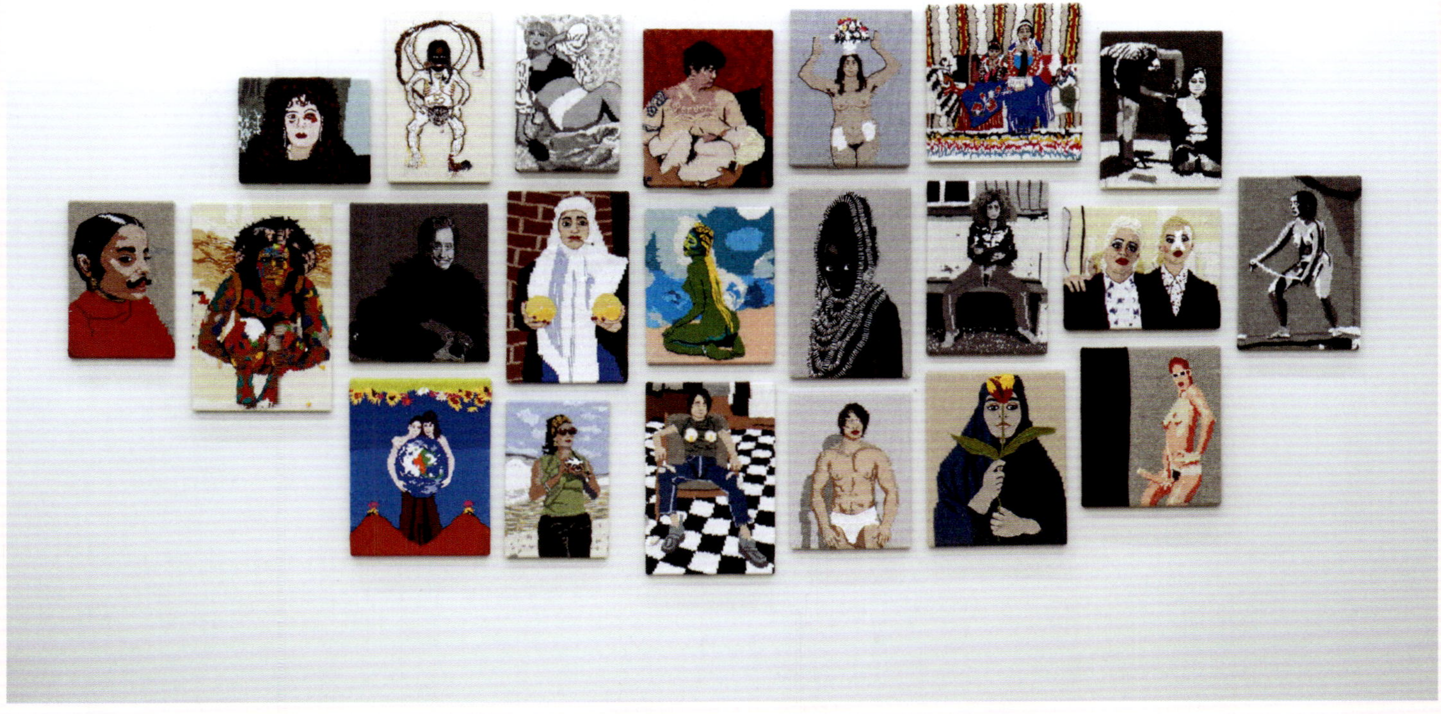

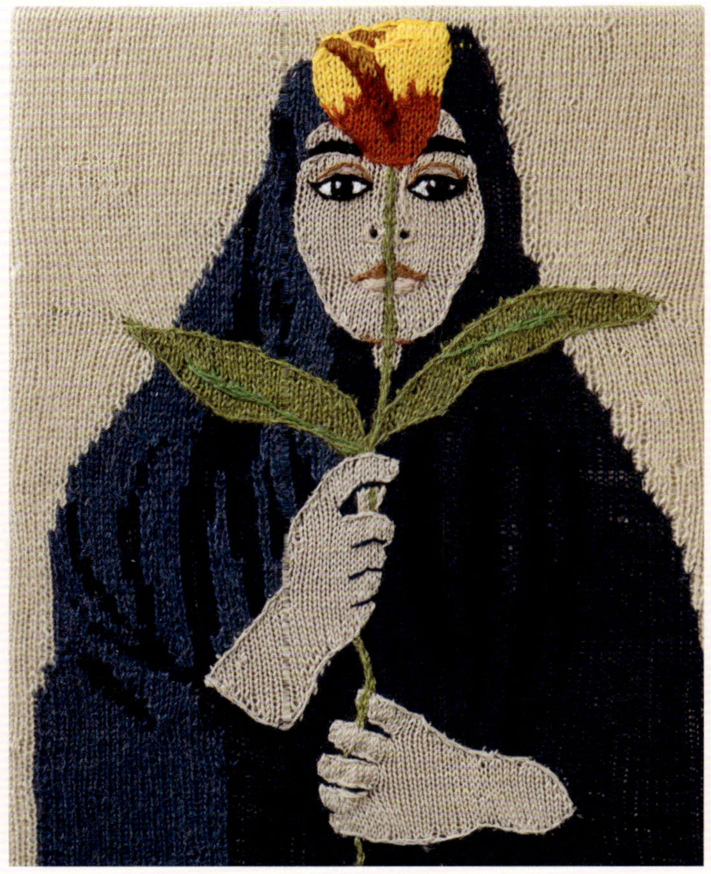

As an ongoing collection, *Feminist Fan* can be considered as an expanded "family portrait" of artists that captures lineages and connections across the globe and time. Just spends more than 80 hours on each portrait, which she says "constitutes a time-intensive act of devotion". Part of this process includes translating photos of the subjects into a gridded image, determining which details to capture and which to simplify. Knitting's soft materials further imbue each portrait with associations of "love, care and comfort".

Reflecting on her 25 years of knitting, Just shares that part of the medium's appeal is that "it exists in the real world as a comforting, accessible material that almost everyone has some relationship with or association to". Just uses knitting as a creative and political tool through which to understand the world around her, and in the process, proposes a future rooted in softness and solidarity. Her works remind us that we too can, "with our own two hands", create or make something new. ■

Page 45 *Feminist Fan #19 (Juliana Huxtable, Untitled in the Rage, Nibiru Cataclysm)*, 2017, Hand-knitting stretched around canvas and timber **This page** Top: *Feminist Fan (selection)*, 2017, Hand-knitting stretched around canvas and timber; Bottom: *Feminist Fan #33 (Shirin Neshat, Untitled, 1995)*, 2017, Hand-knitting stretched around canvas and timber

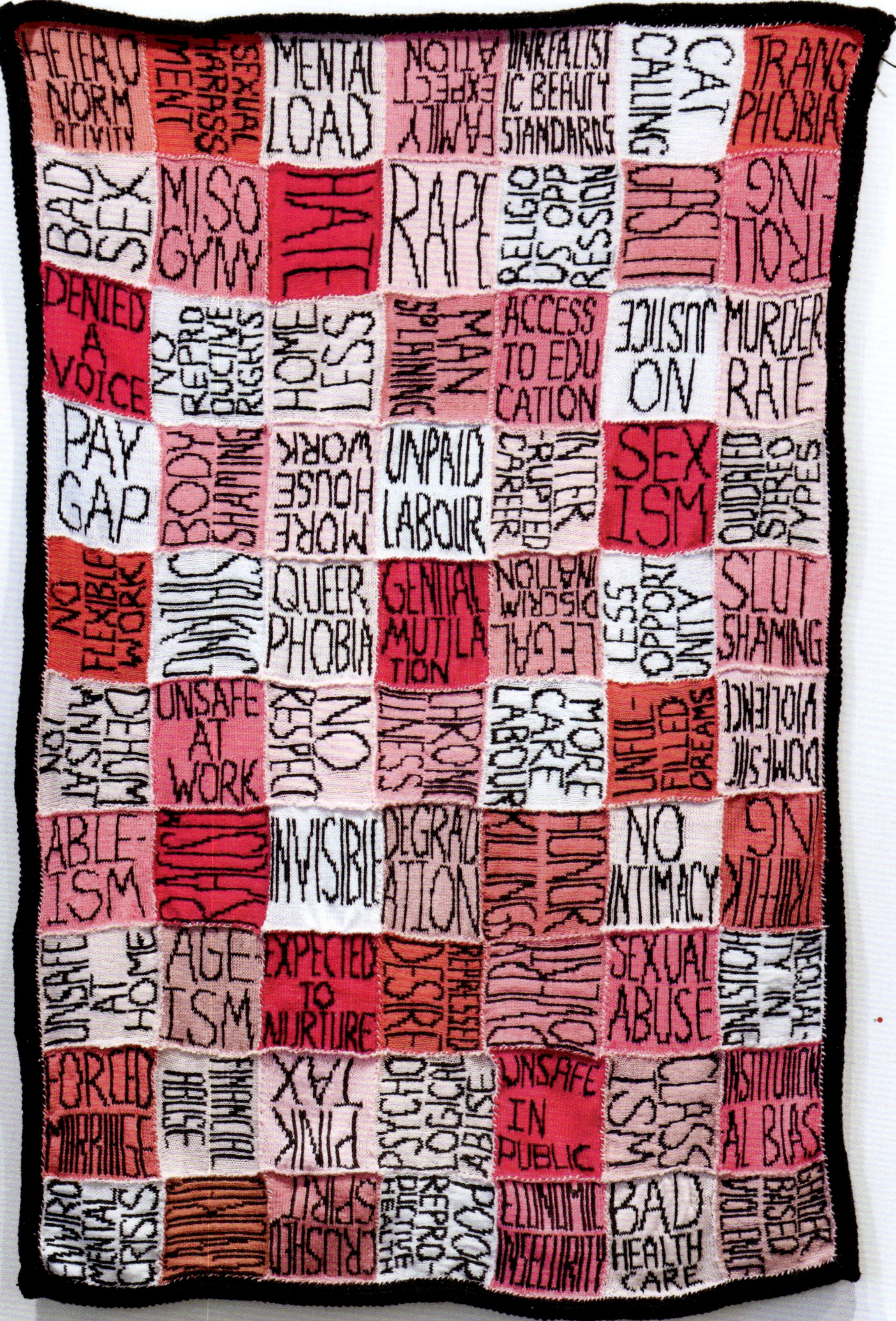

HETERO NORM ATIVITY
SEXUAL HARASS MENT
MENTAL LOAD
FAMILY EXPECT ATION
UNREALIST IC BEAUTY STANDARDS
CAT CALLING
TRANS PHOBIA
BAD SEX
MISO GYNY
HATE
RAPE
RELIGIOUS OPP RESSION
TROLL ING
DENIED A VOICE
NO REPRO DUCTIVE RIGHTS
HOME LESS
MAN SPLAINING
ACCESS TO EDU CATION
JUSTICE ON
MURDER-RATE
PAY GAP
BODY SHAMING
MORE HOUSE WORK
UNPAID LABOUR
INTER -RUPTED CAREER
SEX ISM
NO FLEXIBLE WORK
QUEER PHOBIA
GENITAL MUTILA TION
LEGAL DISCRIM INATION
LESS OPPOR TUNITY
SLUT SHAMING
UNSAFE AT WORK
NO RESPECT
MORE CARE LABOUR
UNFUL-FILLED DREAMS
DOMESTIC VIOLENCE
ABLE-ISM
INVISIBLE
DEGRADATION
NO INTIMACY
UNSAFE AT HOME
AGE ISM
EXPECTED TO NURTURE
REPRESSED DESIRE
SEXUAL ABUSE
FORCED MARRIAGE
FINANCIAL ABUSE
PINK TAX
UNSAFE IN PUBLIC
CLASS ISM
INSTITUTION AL BIAS
CRUSHED SPIRIT
ECONOMIC INSECURITY
BAD HEALTH CARE
GENDER BASED VIOLENCE

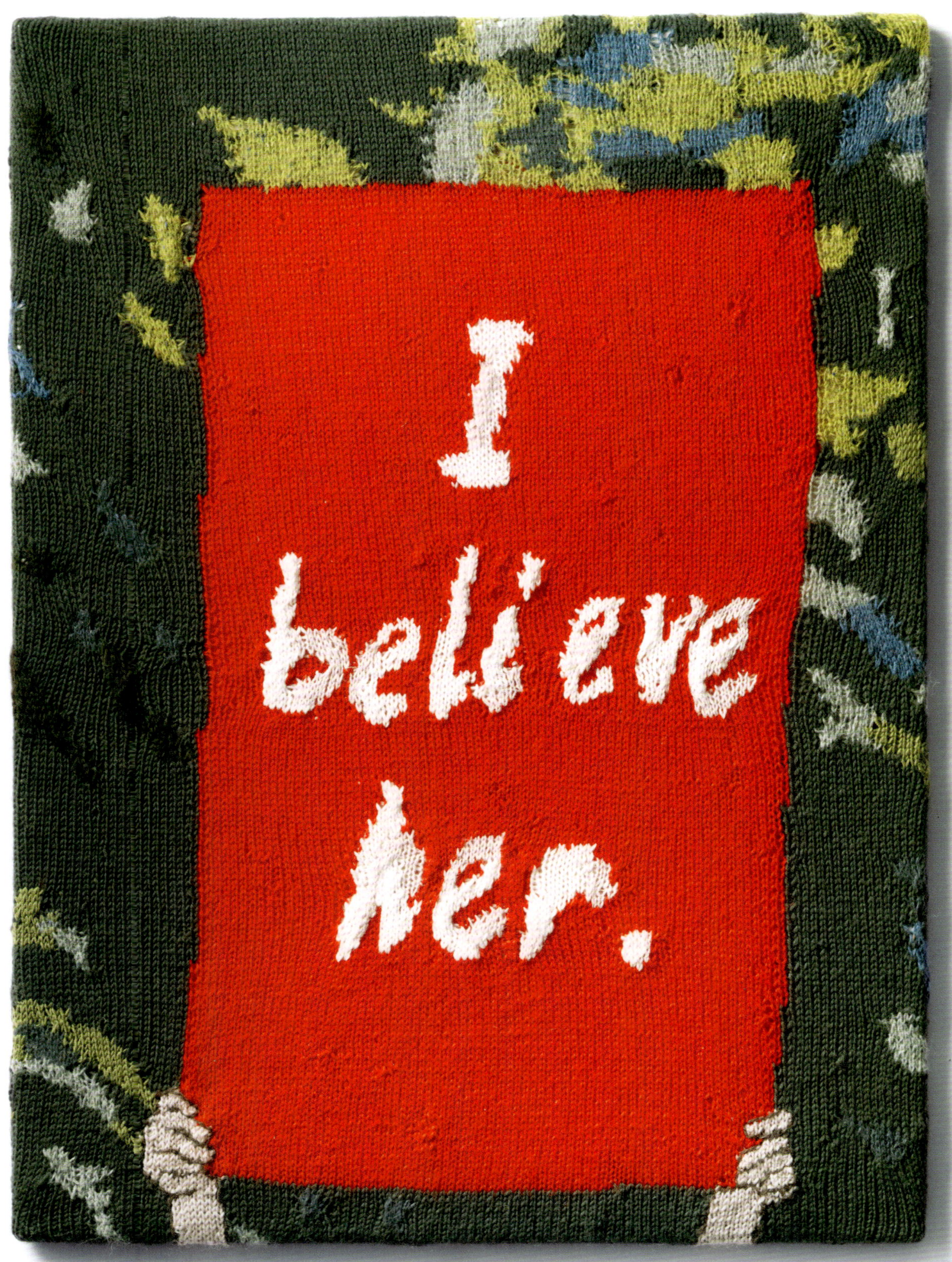
I
believe
her.

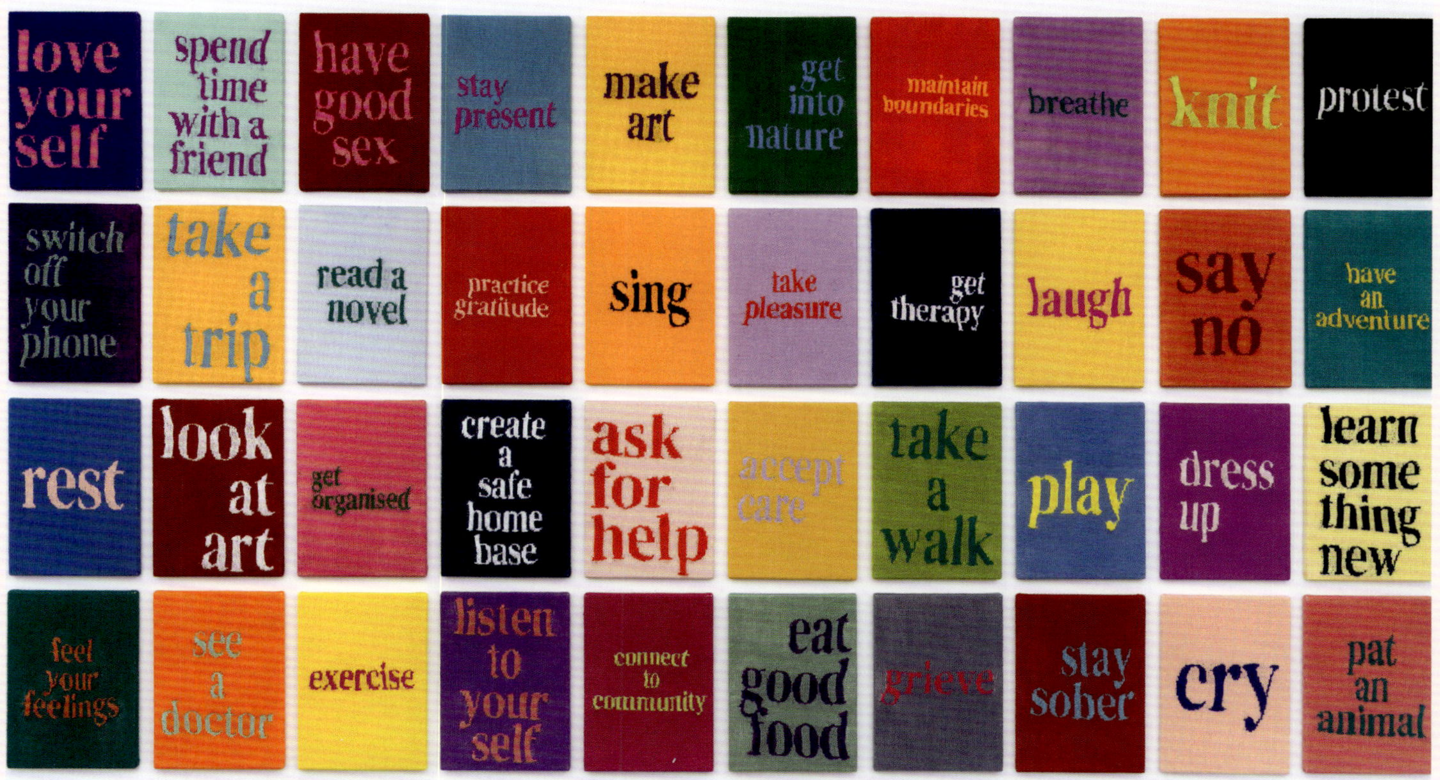

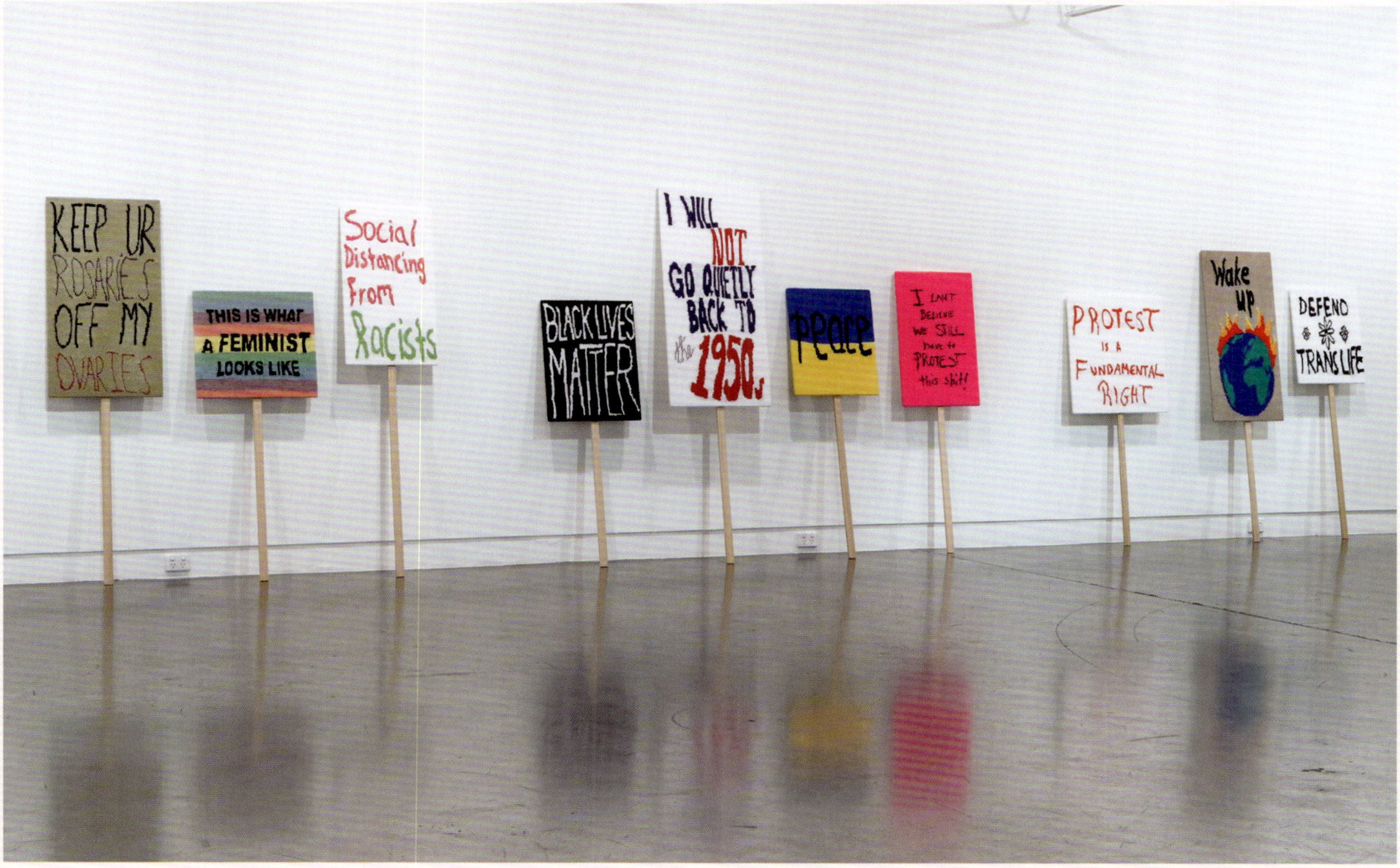

Page 47 *Tickled Pink to Be a Woman*, 2023, Crochet border and hand-knitted squares **Opposite** *I Believe Her*, 2022, Hand-knitting stretched around canvas and timber **This page** Top: *Self Care Action Series*, 2022, Hand-knitting stretched around canvas and timber; Bottom: *PROTEST SIGNS*, 2022, Hand-knitting stretched around plywood with timber handles

Kendall Ross

OKLAHOMA CITY

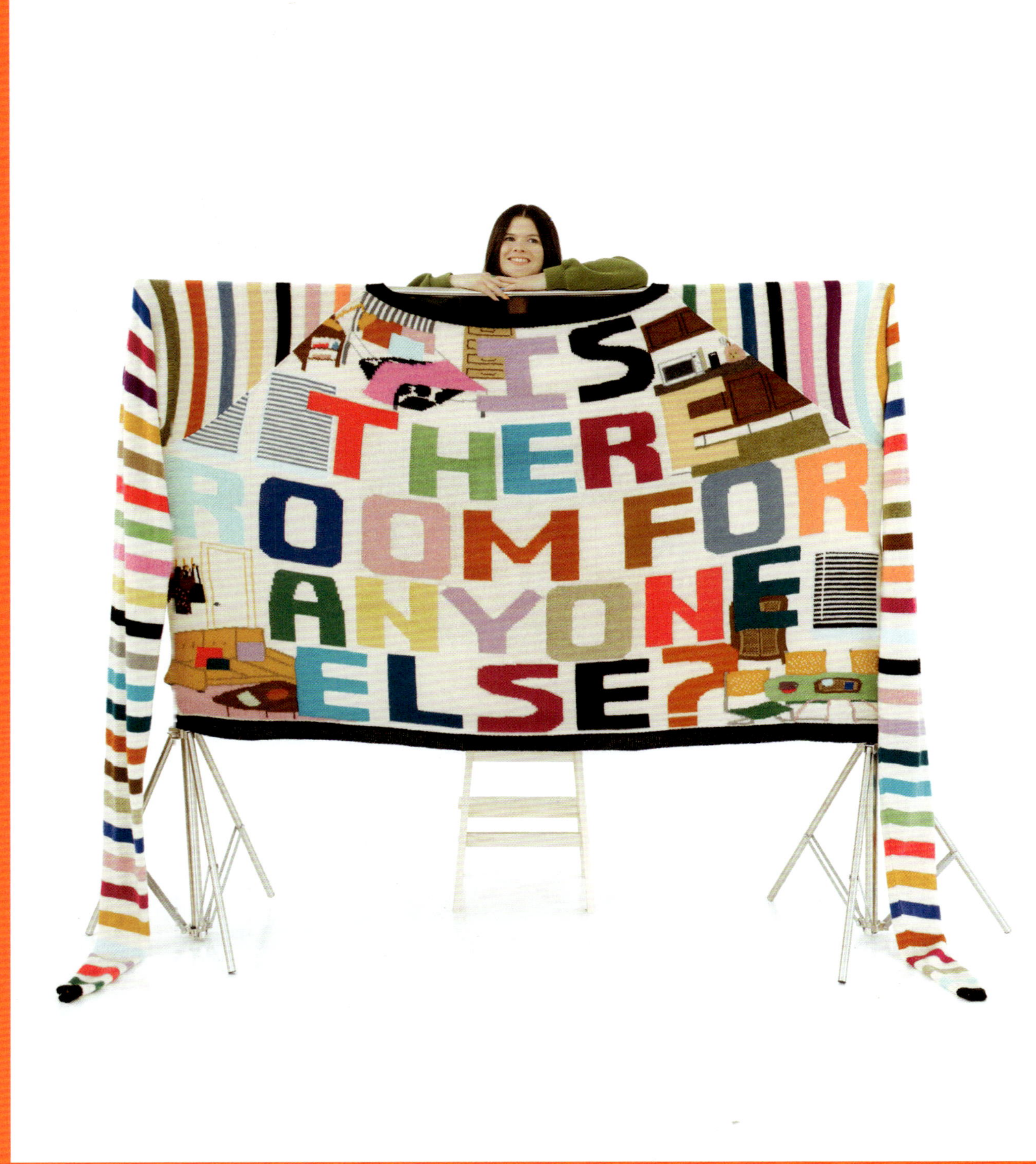

Kendall Ross is known for her brightly coloured, wearable sweaters that incorporate original text alongside illustrations. Ross's works are deeply personal: a way for the artist to process her "emotions, experiences and memories" through knitting as "journalling". Her works are made by hand using between 10 and 25 different balls of yarn at once. In order to convey the details of her illustrations, as well as make the text legible, Ross uses a combination of both stranded and intarsia knitting techniques, swapping between working with multiple threads to working a single thread at a time. All of her pieces are knitted as "flat" portions, which are then stitched or joined together to create garment shapes; for her large-scale works, this includes using lengthy custom circular knitting needles measuring over 1.5 metres to capture the full length of the stitches required.

Ross enjoys every part of the process of hand-knitting garments, which includes weaving in ends and blocking (the process by which finished pieces are shaped through moisture). As she is in total control of every step, this work offers "a rare space where I'm able to express myself fully" from start to finish. Ross knits everywhere, taking simpler projects with less colours on the go, while completing the more complicated colourwork pieces at her home studio ("aka my dining room table"). This consistency helps Ross maintain her routine.

While Ross's works are deeply personal, they are also shaped by broader historical considerations of women and "women's work". Growing up, the relationships she built with the women in her family through knitting and crochet led her to study women's history at university. She cites this tertiary background as a historian as a central inspiration for both the "content and purpose" behind her work as an artist. Namely, she is interested in "using this historically female-dominated skill to tell unapologetically emotional and vulnerable stories from my perspective as a young woman". She further reflects that she "love[s] what knitting means within my family and within women's history", sharing that her mother, who is constantly "expressing herself through textiles", was her "first favourite artist" – a title she still holds.

In more recent years, Ross has been making large-scale works that aren't necessarily wearable ("Is it still a garment if you can't wear it?") to further explore what it means to "unapologetically take up physical space as a woman". Growing up in the Bible Belt, in "one of the most conservative states in America", Ross felt like "only men could speak and were listened to". Her works today, such as *I Remember Thinking Things Would Change Once I Didn't Take Up So Much Space* (2024), are defiant. In this work, the central words are situated against a knitted backdrop of personal objects and artefacts. Among these are

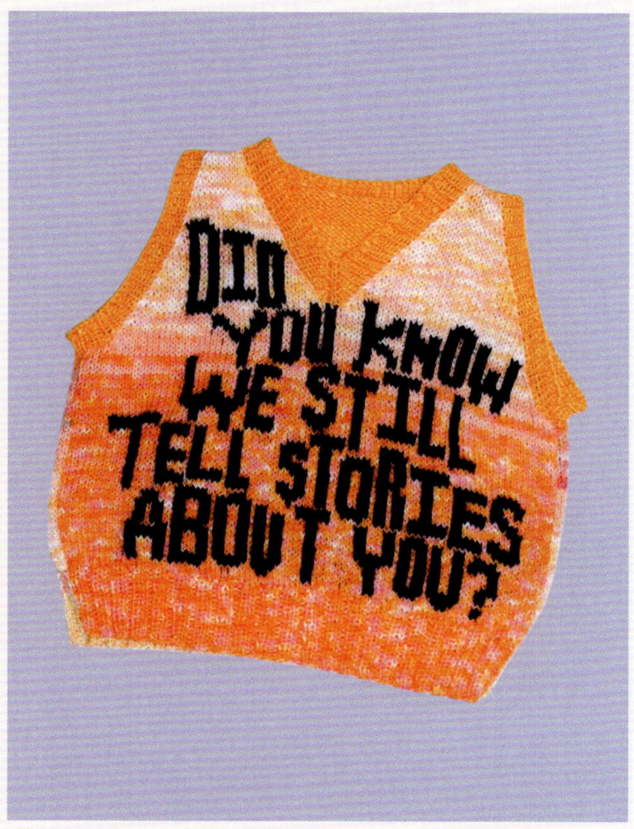

Opposite *Is There Room For Anyone Else?*, 2025, Hand-knitting **This page** *Storyteller*, 2022, Hand-knitting

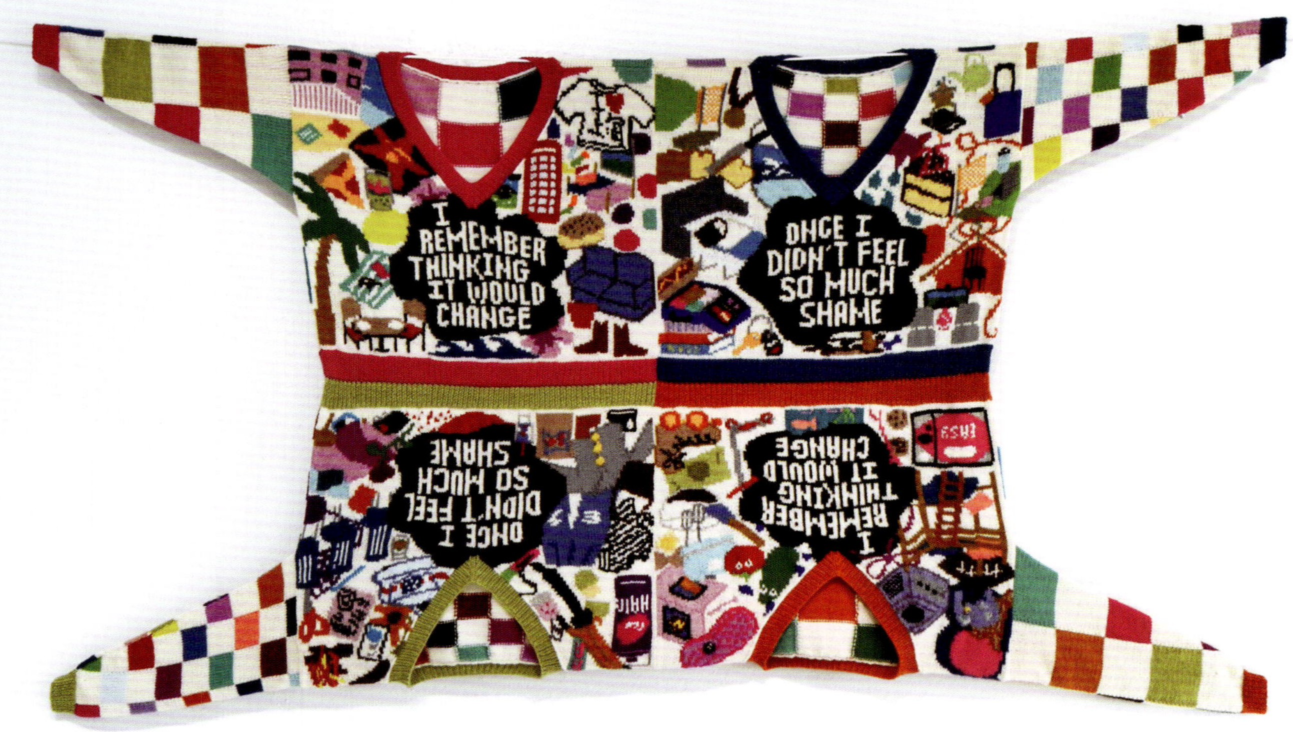

clear indicators of a millennial girlhood: clothes, iPods, friendship bracelets and more. The scale of the piece commands a viewer's attention, making each individual object larger than life.

Another central theme in Ross's works is the assertion of knitting's value as an artform. Works such as *Crafty* (2022) tackle the gendered double standard applied to textile mediums through humour, using a combination of shocking pink and bright blue to further challenge gender binaries. Ross shares that she hopes her work empowers other fibre artists in their own practices. One of her ongoing goals is to shift the perception of knitting "both in institutions and in individuals", and to validate the importance of this work. She's drawn to knitting because she "love[s] and respects the work and patience" that it requires, and she wants to honour the high level of dedication and commitment behind every finished piece. In this way, Ross seeks to not only value her own work, but the work of generations past, present and future. ■

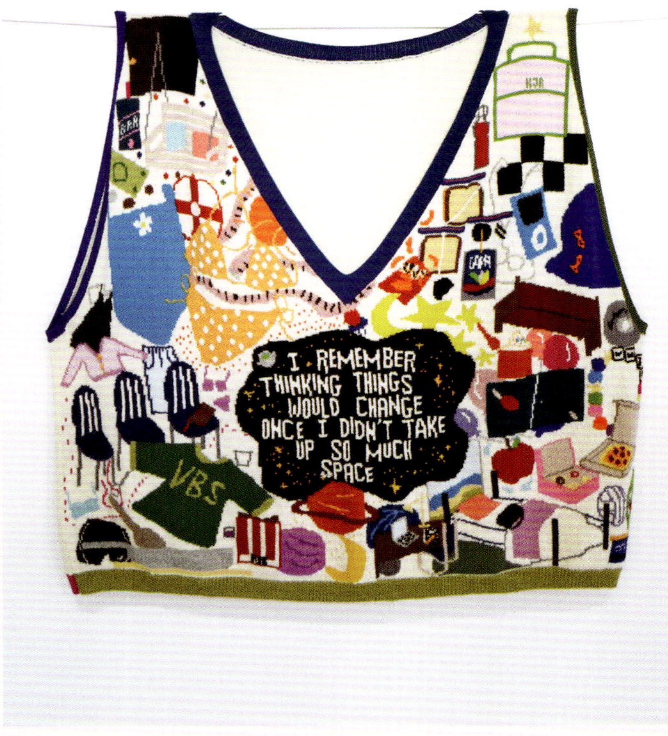

Top: *I Remember Thinking It Would Change*, 2024, Hand-knitting; Bottom: *I Remember Thinking Things Would Change Once I Didn't Take Up So Much Space*, 2024, Hand-knitting

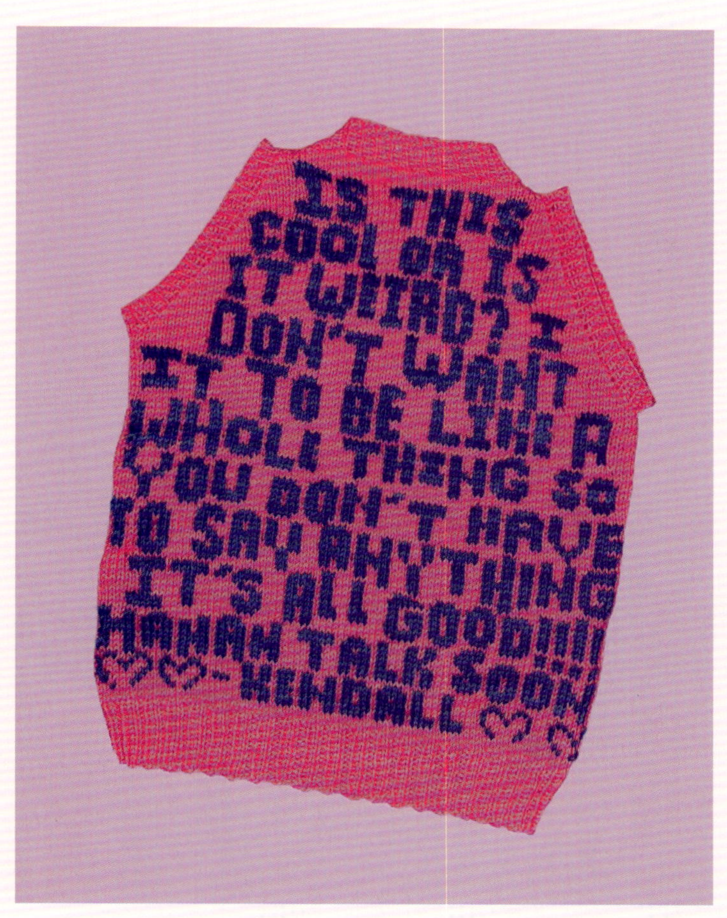

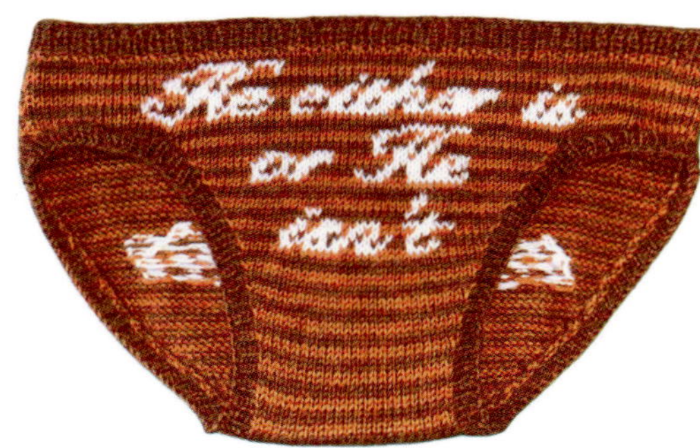

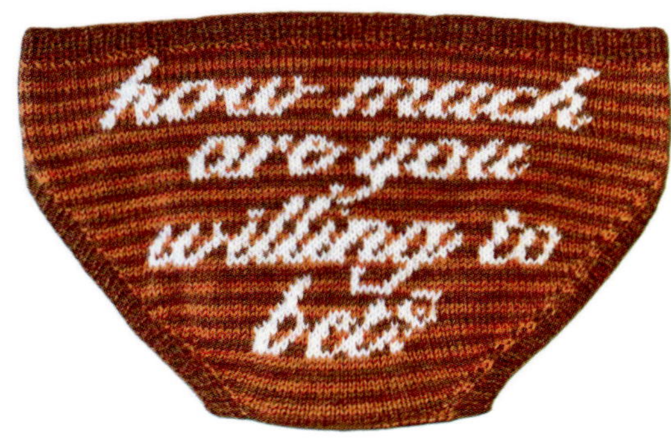

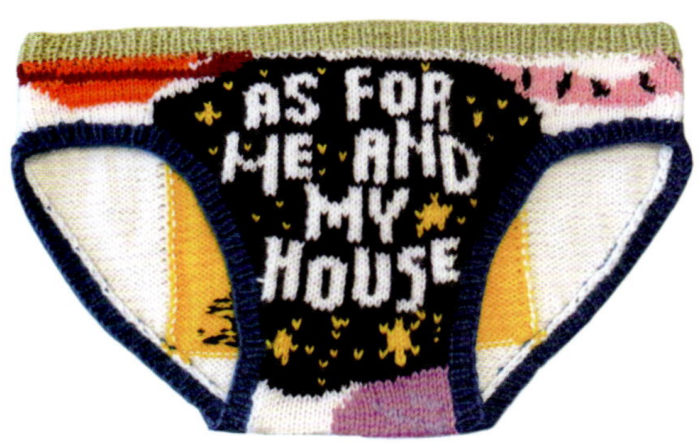

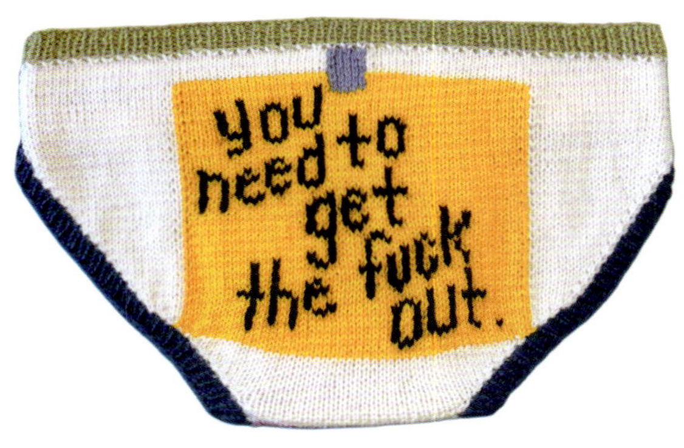

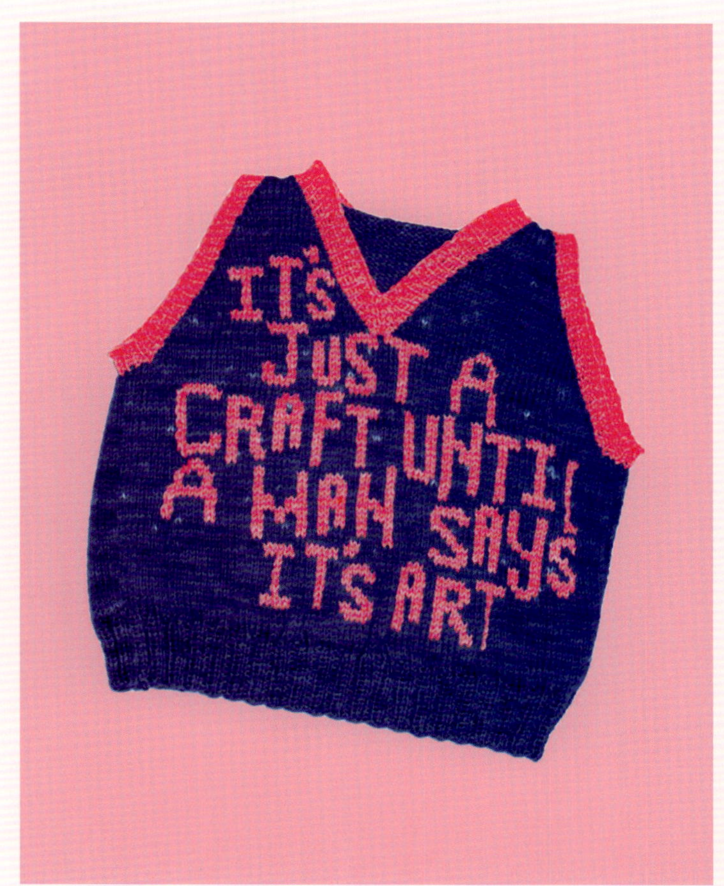

Clockwise from top left: *I Made This For You I Hope It Fits*, 2022, Hand-knitting; *How Much Are You Willing to Bet?*, 2025, Hand-knitting; *Crafty*, 2022, Hand-knitting; *As For Me and My House*, 2025, Hand-knitting

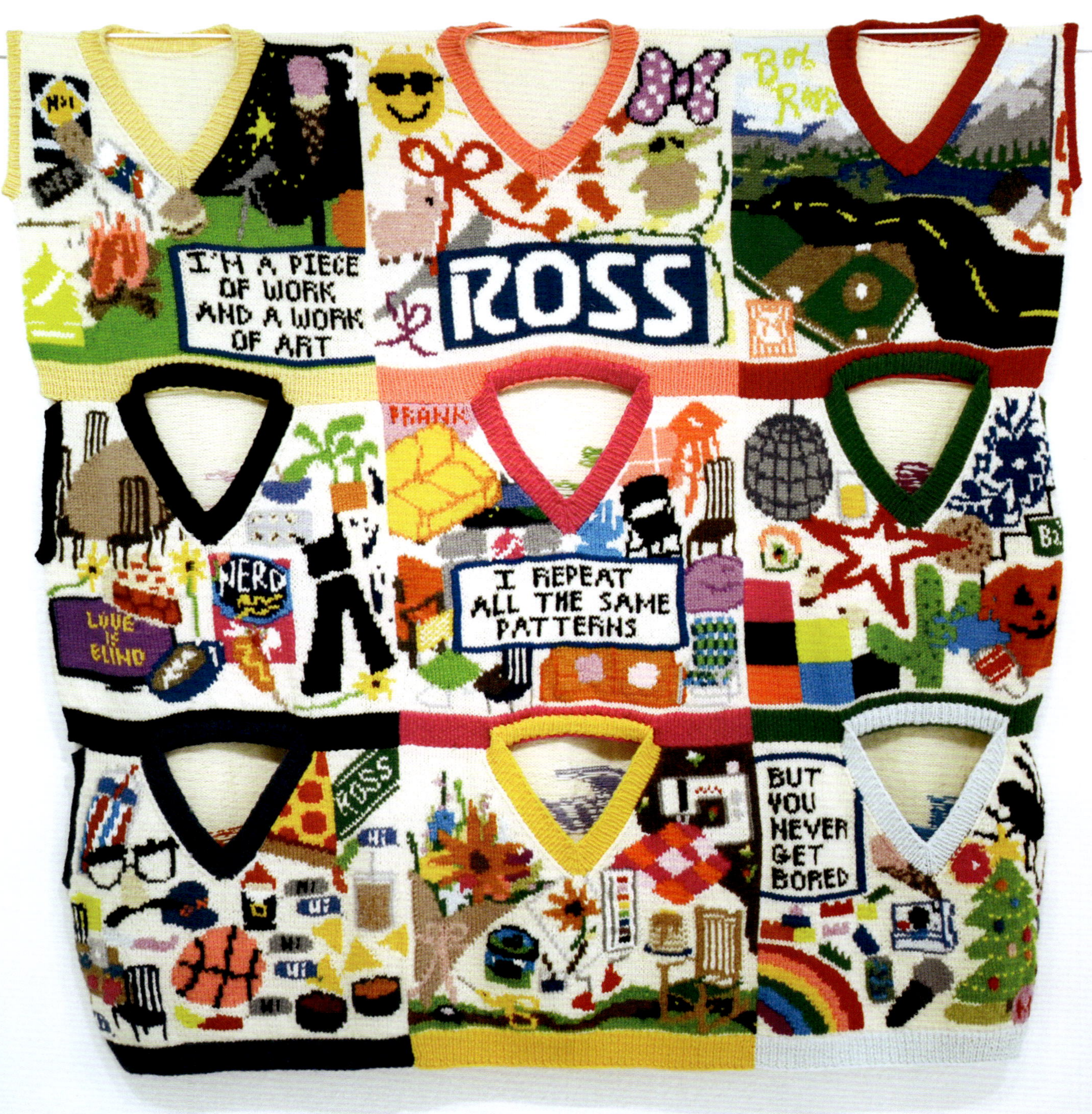
I'M A PIECE OF WORK AND A WORK OF ART
ROSS
I REPEAT ALL THE SAME PATTERNS
LOVE IS BLIND
NERD
FRANK
BUT YOU NEVER GET BORED

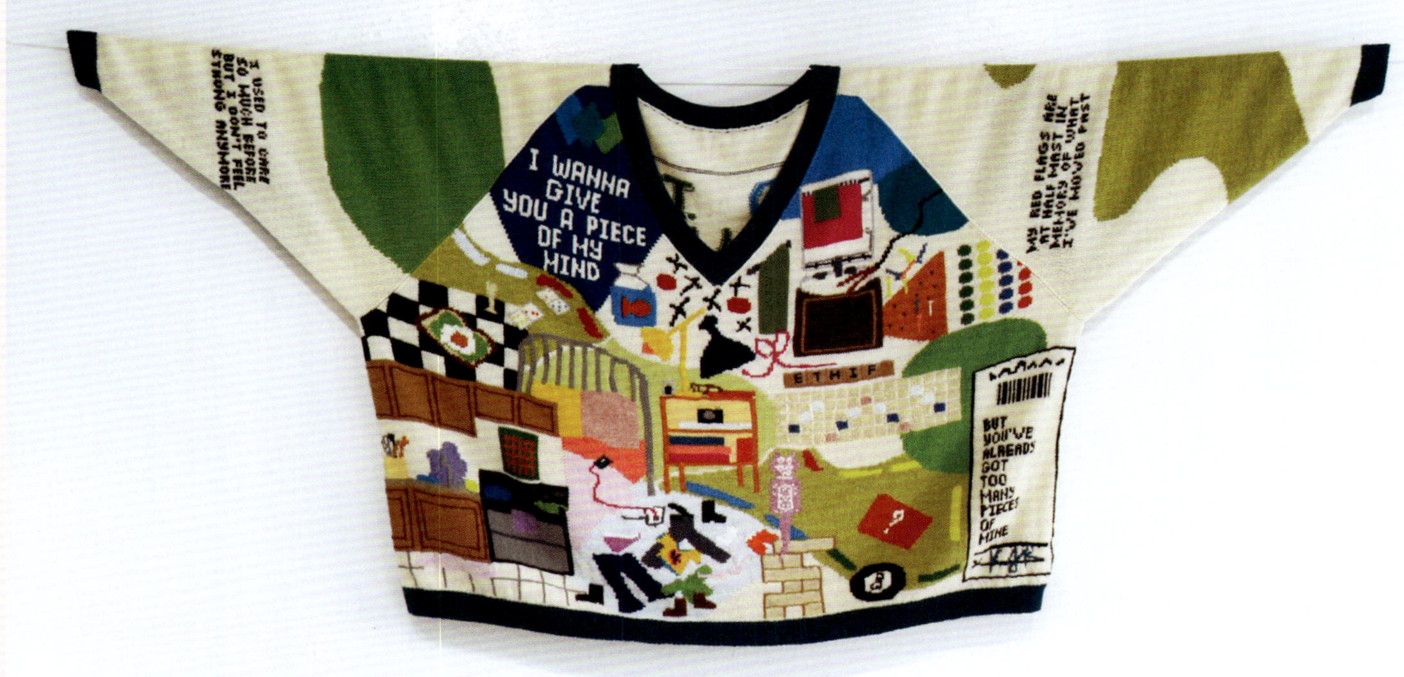

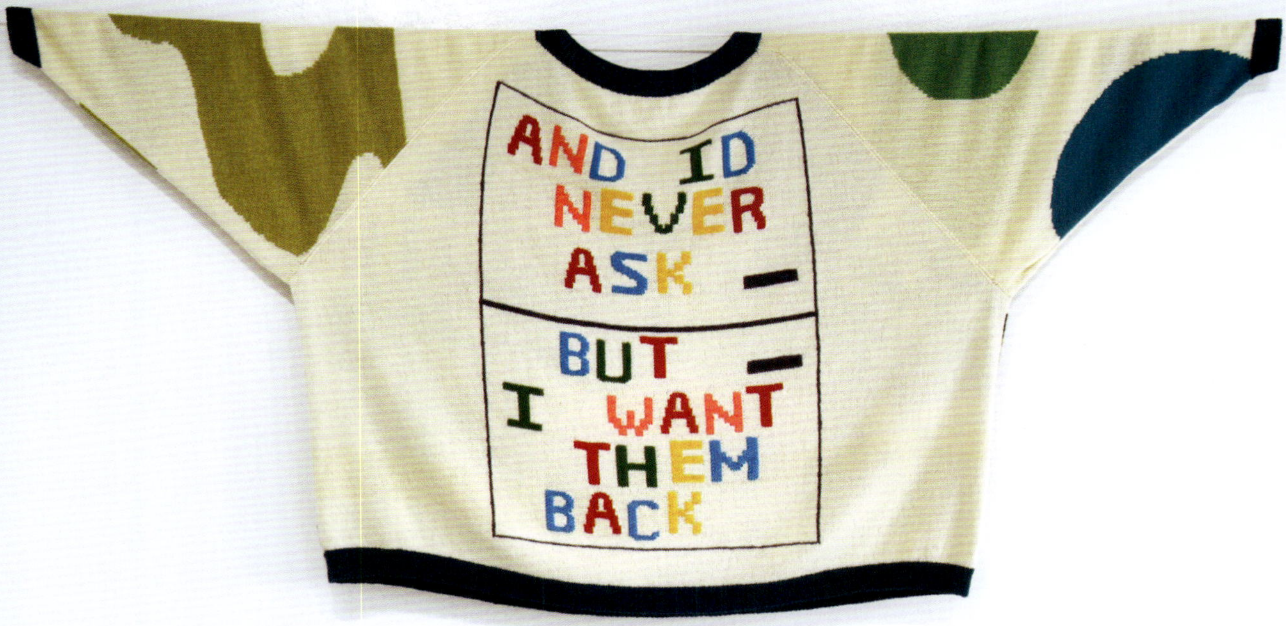

Opposite *Dress For Less*, 2024, Hand-knitting
This page *SET Piece*, 2024, Hand-knitting

Lucas Morneau

SACKVILLE

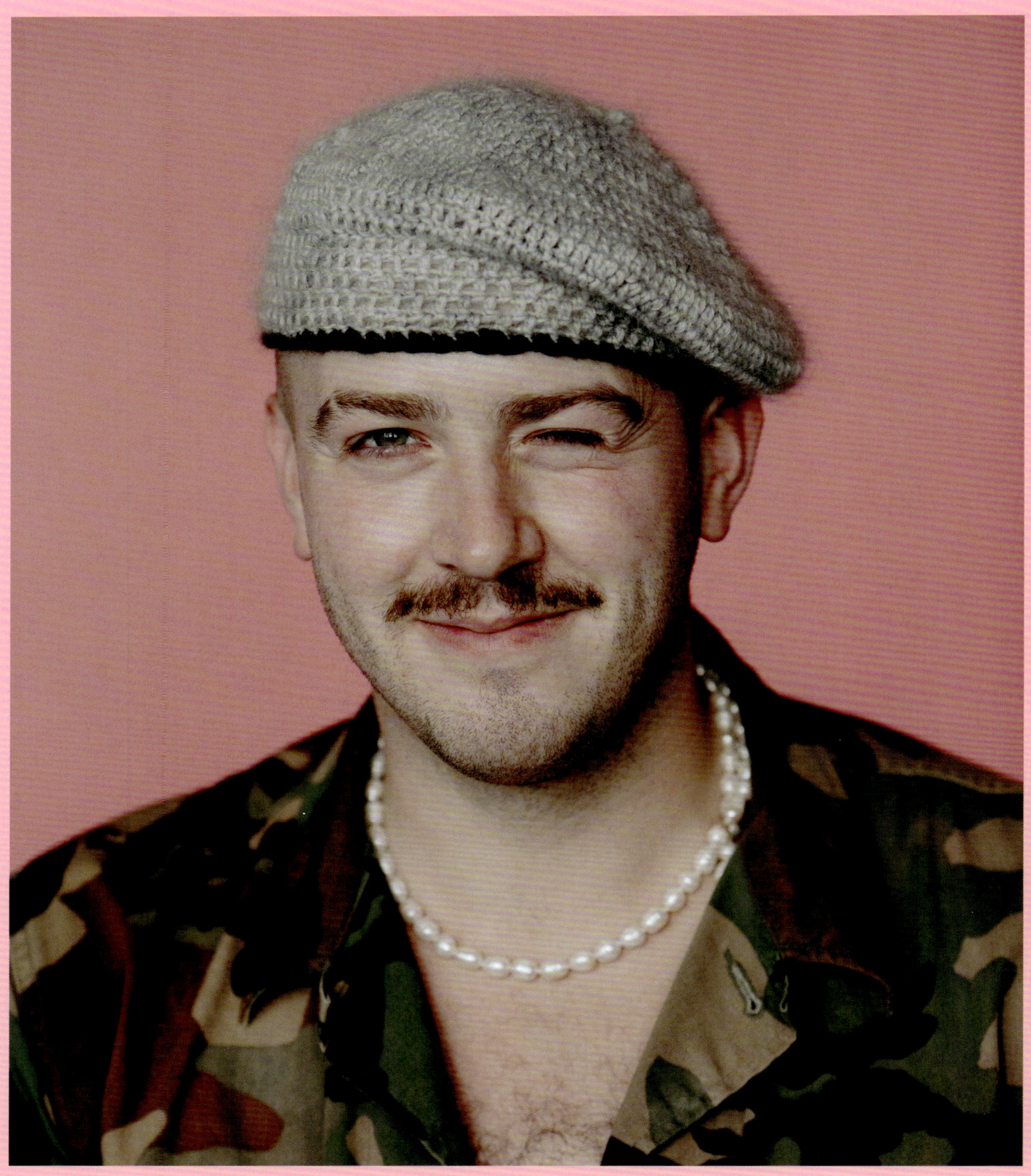

Spanning knitting, crochet, photography, video, sculpture and performance, Lucas Morneau's artistic practice "is an ongoing exploration of identity, culture and the subversive potential of tradition". As someone born and raised on the island of Ktaqmkuk/Newfoundland, Canada, which is widely known for its rich history of textile crafts, Morneau seeks to question the "heteronormative and patriarchal systems" that have shaped the region's cultural practices.

In Newfoundland, where knitting is taught to both women and men, Morneau grew up surrounded by textiles; his mother was part of local quilting clubs, while his grandmother taught Morneau and his brother and cousins how to knit. He didn't pursue this practice further, though, until his undergraduate studies under Canadian textile artist Barb Hunt, who taught Morneau how to knit again in a new context. He reflects that he "loved learning new textile processes from Barb", and that she both "introduced and legitimised fibre art" to him. Today, from his home in New Brunswick, he is interested in "playing with multiple mediums" to blur and deliberately muddle the distinctions between art and craft; for Morneau "these binaries tend to not truly exist", and have historically been used to divide along class, gender and racial lines.

One of the key themes in Morneau's work is the "performative aspects of culture, particularly gender performance", and the role of drag in usurping norms. Morneau started performing in drag at local gay bars after moving away from Newfoundland, and has since incorporated the practice into his broader art.

The Queer Mummer (2018) is a work that combines contemporary expressions of drag with mummering, a Christmas-time tradition practised in Newfoundland in which people wear costumes to visit their neighbours' houses. In Morneau's interpretation, mummering "becomes a site for queer intervention". Dressed in hand-made crochet garments that celebrate drag aesthetics, Morneau adopts the Queer Mummer as an artistic alter ego, openly embodying queerness through performance.

Morneau sees himself as a "lifelong learner" who "tends to work with a new medium for each project". He taught himself to hand-crochet for *Queer Mummer*, and has more recently learnt how to use a knitting machine for the project *Heels and Faces* (2023–ongoing). This adoption of knitting follows Morneau's struggles with chronic pain from the repetitive motions of crochet, and has allowed him to keep making textiles without the same physical strain.

Heels and Faces continues Morneau's interest in gender performance through the lens of professional wrestling. "Wrestling, much like drag, is a spectacle where characters perform exaggerated versions of gender and identity, playing with the same tropes that drag performers manipulate on stage." Morneau uses embellishments common to drag to complete each knitted piece, including sequins, rhinestones and furs. The result is vibrant, joyous works, such as *Paradise Poof* (2024) and *Star Fvck* (2024), that offer "radical reimaginings of identity" to challenge toxic heteronormative masculinity.

Reflecting on the use of textiles in his artistic practice, Morneau shares that working in this way "[brings] more fun into my practice". Crochet and knitting allowed him avenues to "explore areas of my imagination that I had been wanting to explore" by offering a way to work "character and gender play" into his art. By using humour and performance to speak to difficult topics, Morneau seeks to bring forth greater understanding and empathy. Reflecting on his own experience and strong connection to Newfoundland, Morneau wants to make his art "for [other] queer Newfoundlanders who've had to deal with growing up on an isolated island". In this way, Morneau's works can be viewed as a way for the artist to connect with his past, but also a generous invitation to a positive path towards the future. ■

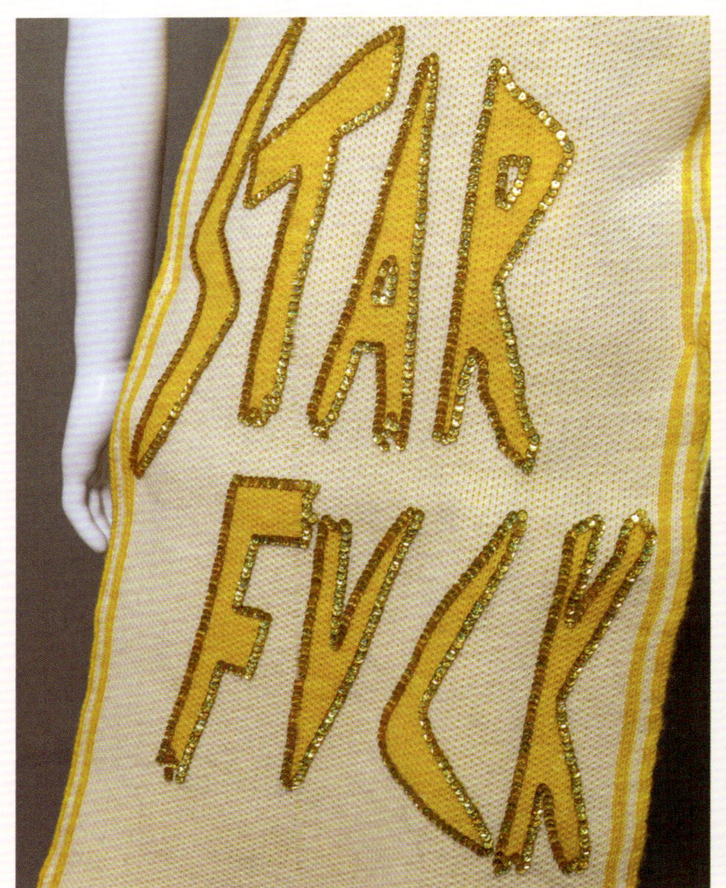

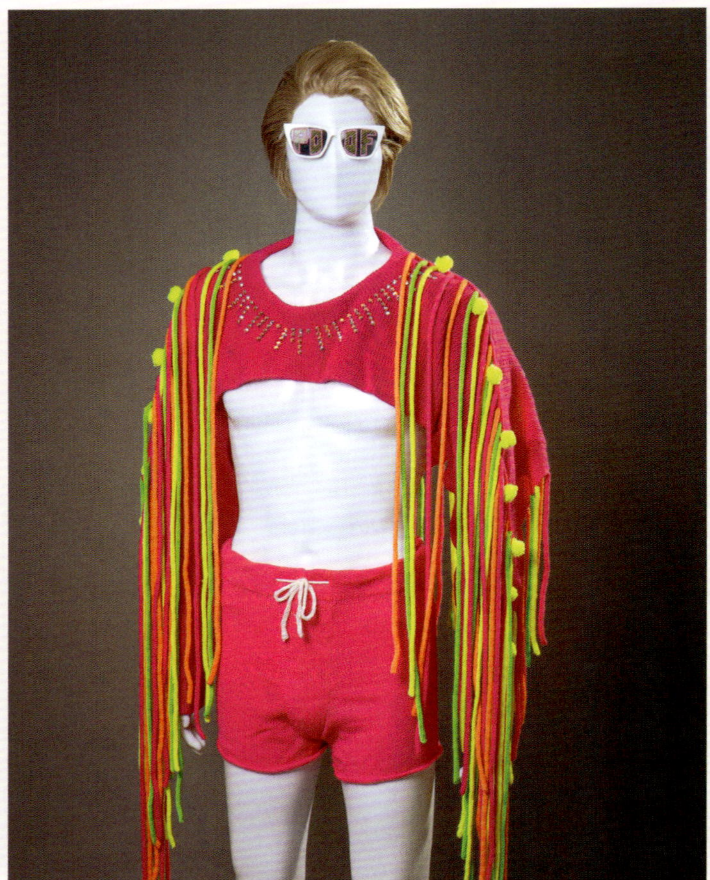

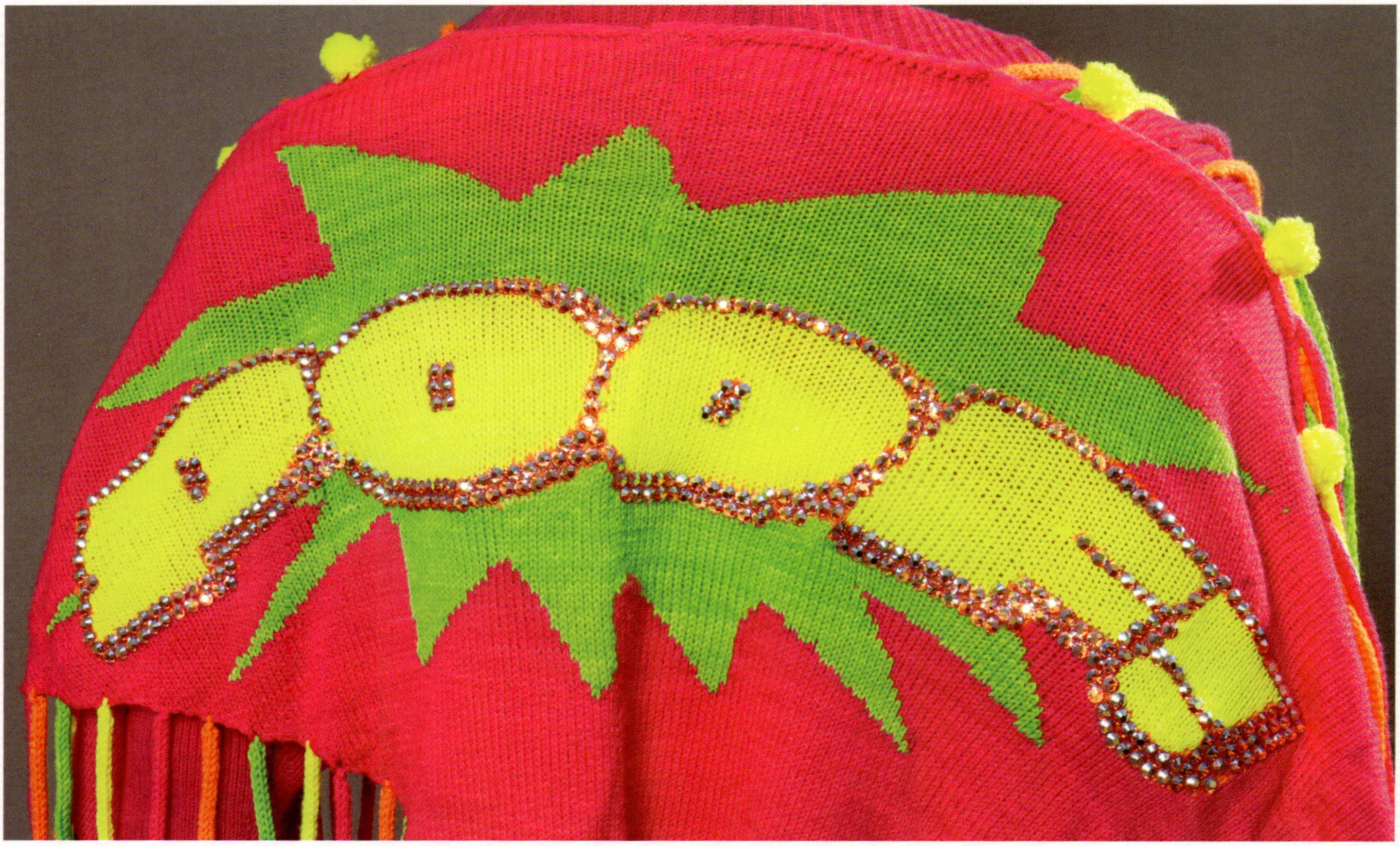

This page Top left: *Star Fvck*, 2024, Manual machine knitting; Top right and bottom: *Paradise Poof*, 2024, Manual machine knitting **Opposite** *Bae Fae*, 2024, Crochet

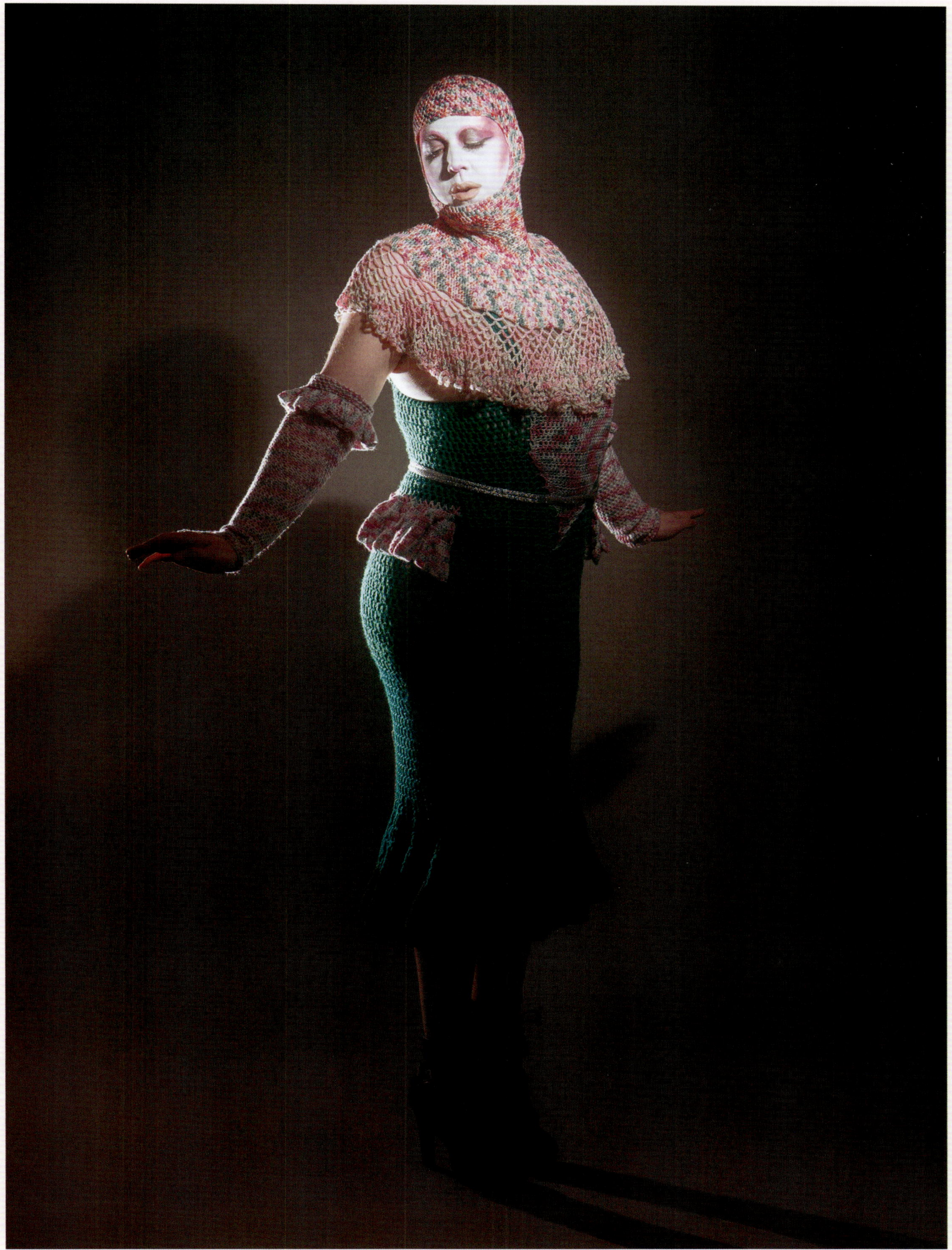

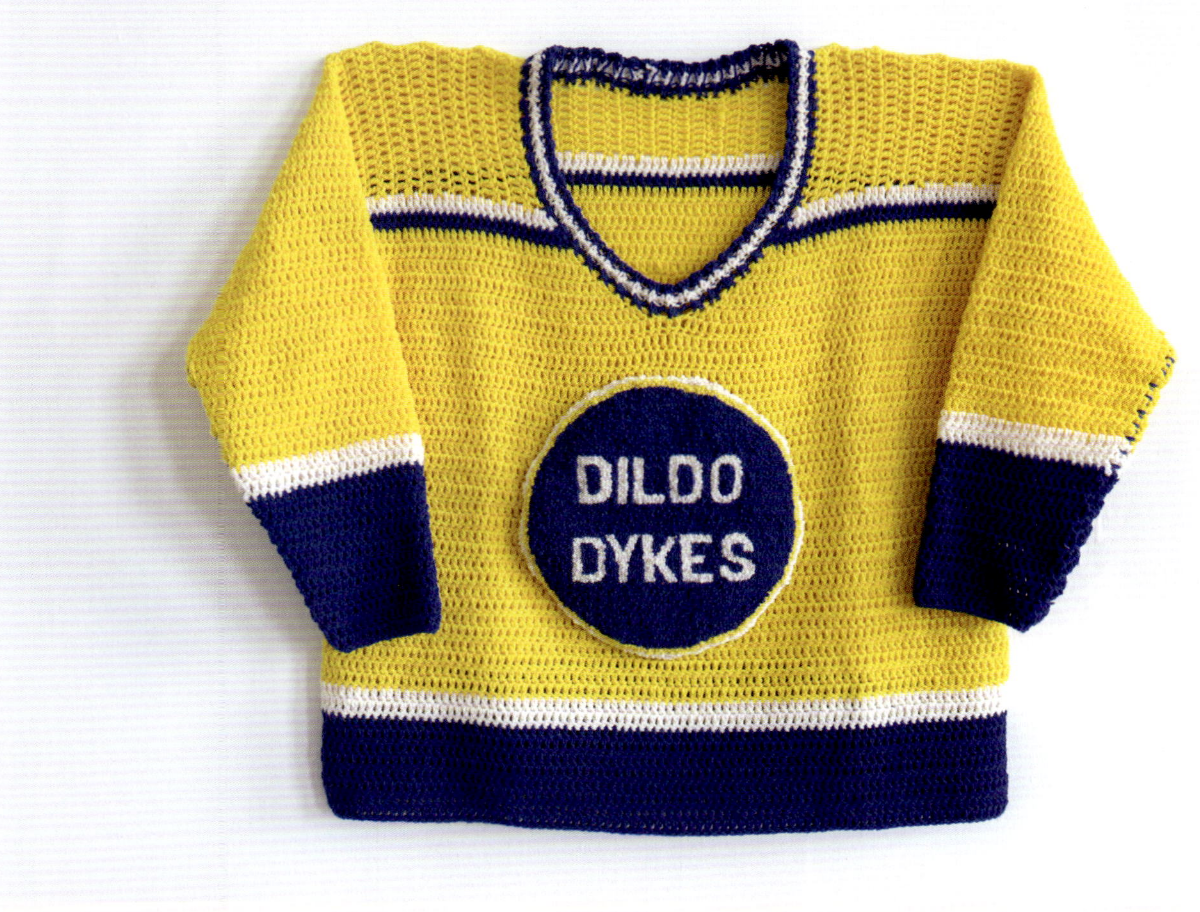

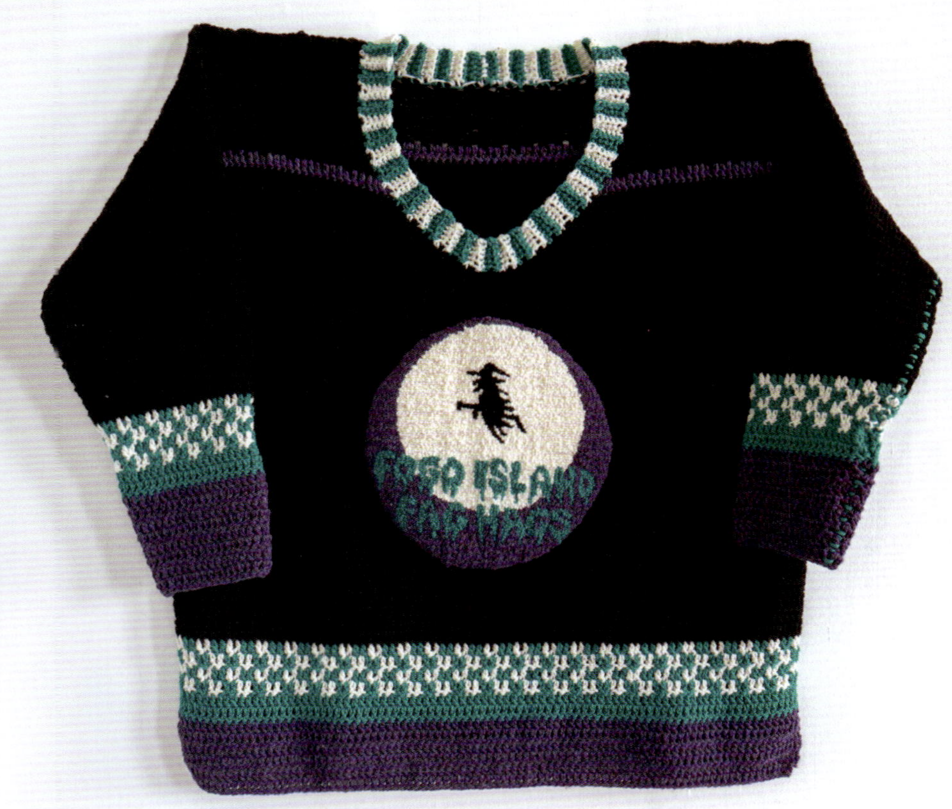

This page Top: *Dildo Dykes*, 2020, Crochet and rug hooking; Bottom: *Fogo Island Fag Hags*, 2020, Crochet and rug hooking
Opposite *Big Poppa Bear*, 2025, Manual machine knitting

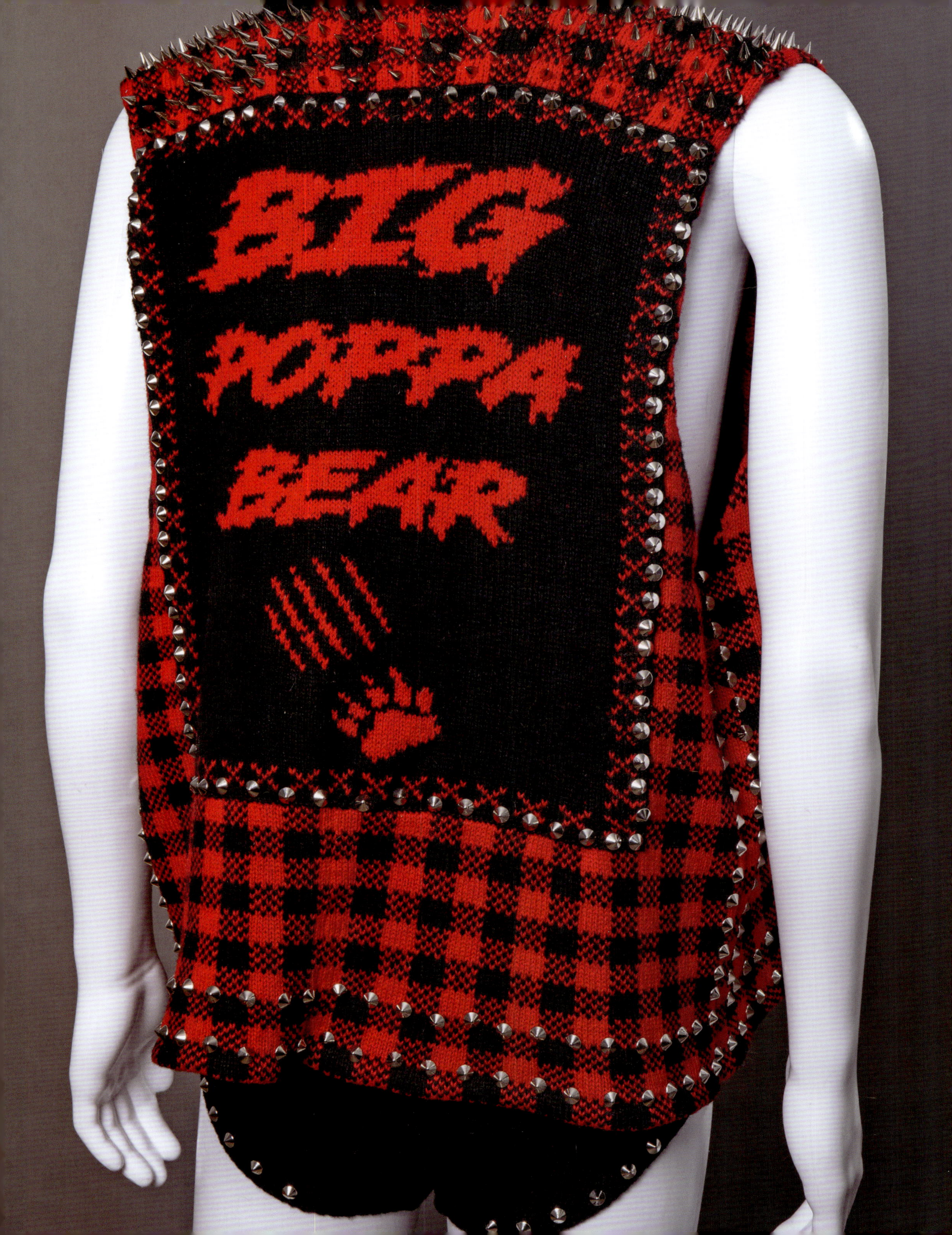
BIG
POPPA
BEAR

Movana Chen 陳麗雲 LISBON AND HONG KONG

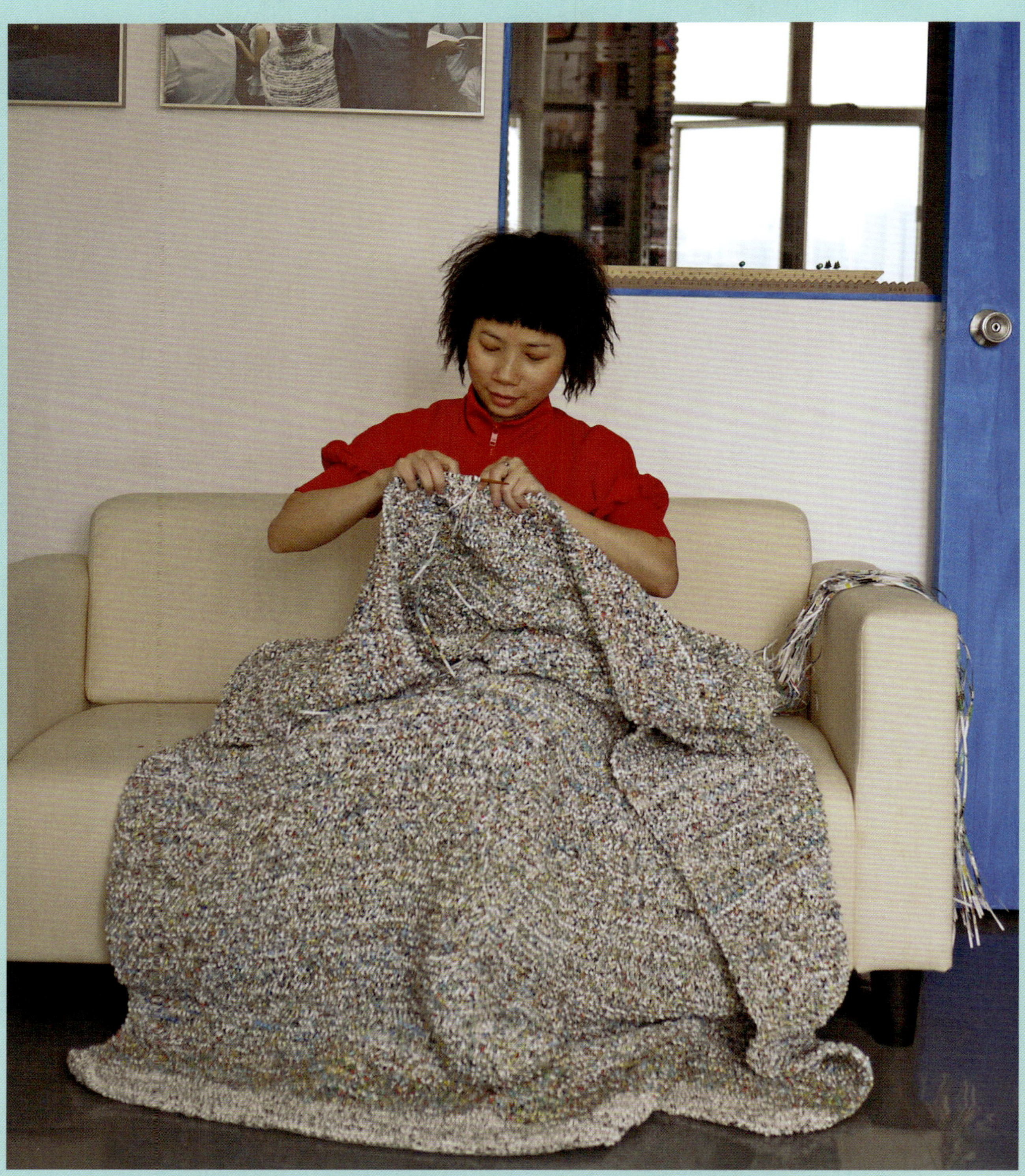

Movana Chen learnt to knit from her grandmother at the age of 10. Today, she is known for her thoughtful and empathetic artworks that she makes using shredded magazines, books, maps and documents to explore themes of human connection and belonging. She first began experimenting with paper as a knitting material after working in her father's office in Hong Kong, where one of her administrative tasks was the shredding of confidential documents. Chen was inspired by the creative possibilities of the long, thin paper strips that emerged from the shredder, akin to pieces of thread or yarn. Inspired, Chen created her first paper artwork, *i-D magazine dress* (2004): a life-size knitted dress made with a cut-up copy of the publication.

Since this initial spark of inspiration, Chen has continued to experiment with different sources of paper to create knitted sculptures and installations. Among this range of source materials are old books and expired passports: deliberate choices that add layers of interpretation and meaning to the works they create. Many of these paper documents and items are donated by the artist's friends or by people she encounters in her extensive travels, which deepens the connections these works hold to others.

These connections are a central driving force in Chen's artistic output. She describes her work as being "about hope, about meeting, about collaboration, bringing people together in a very simple way: sitting, knitting, sharing and weaving the world we want to live in". Her series *Questioning the line* (2023–ongoing) visually represents these themes through activating two-person sculptures. Together with a dancer, the artist "performs a dialogue of movement and stillness – investigating the space between and the seams that connect them". These performances are an extension of her *Body Containers* (2012–ongoing) series; during the pandemic, Chen modified these works by knitting them in pairs, connected by 2-metre tubes – a visual representation of the period's shared experience of social distancing.

Travelling into your bookshelf (2009–ongoing) is another series defined by the interpersonal. For these works, Chen invites people she encounters on her travels to donate their favourite book, which she then shreds and knits. Chen reflects on this series' ongoing nature: "It is always a moment of joy at being together, being connected, and especially knitting new relationships." In each of these works, the shredded and knitted words may no longer be legible, but their weight is still present,

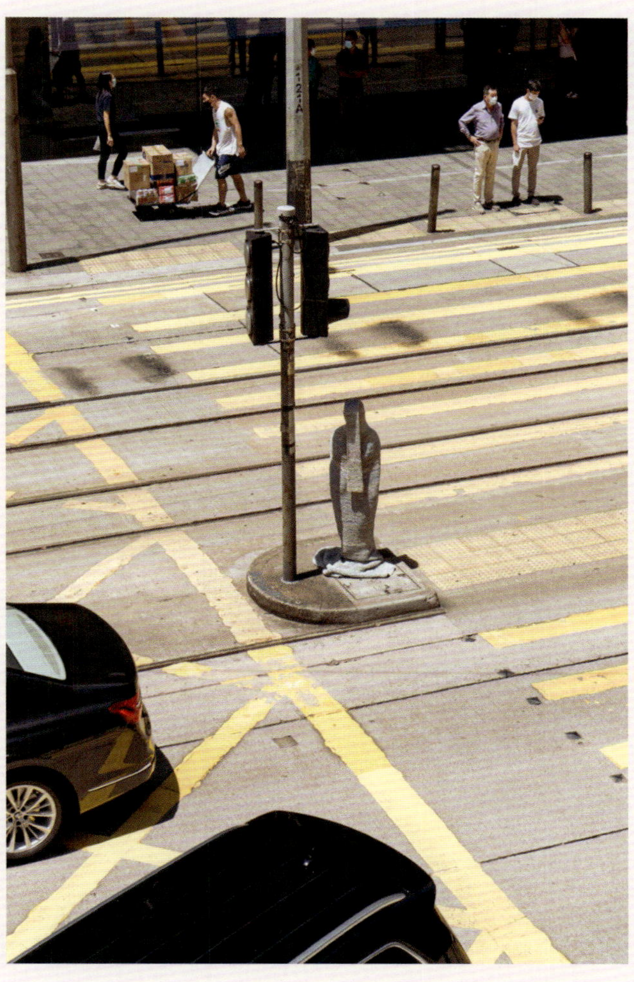

Body Container comes to life in Hong Kong, 2023, Hand-knitted shredded maps, Performance by Movana Chen

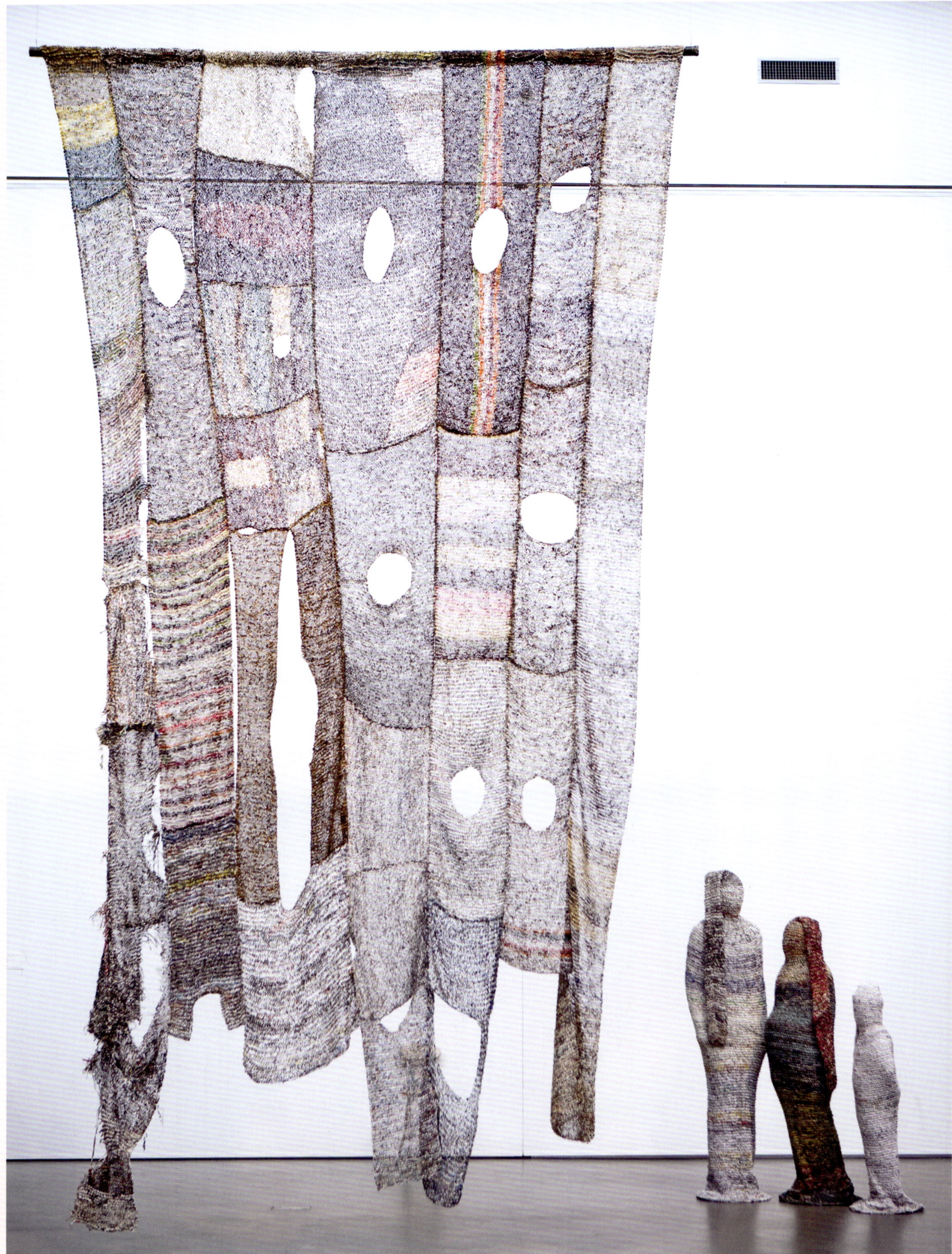

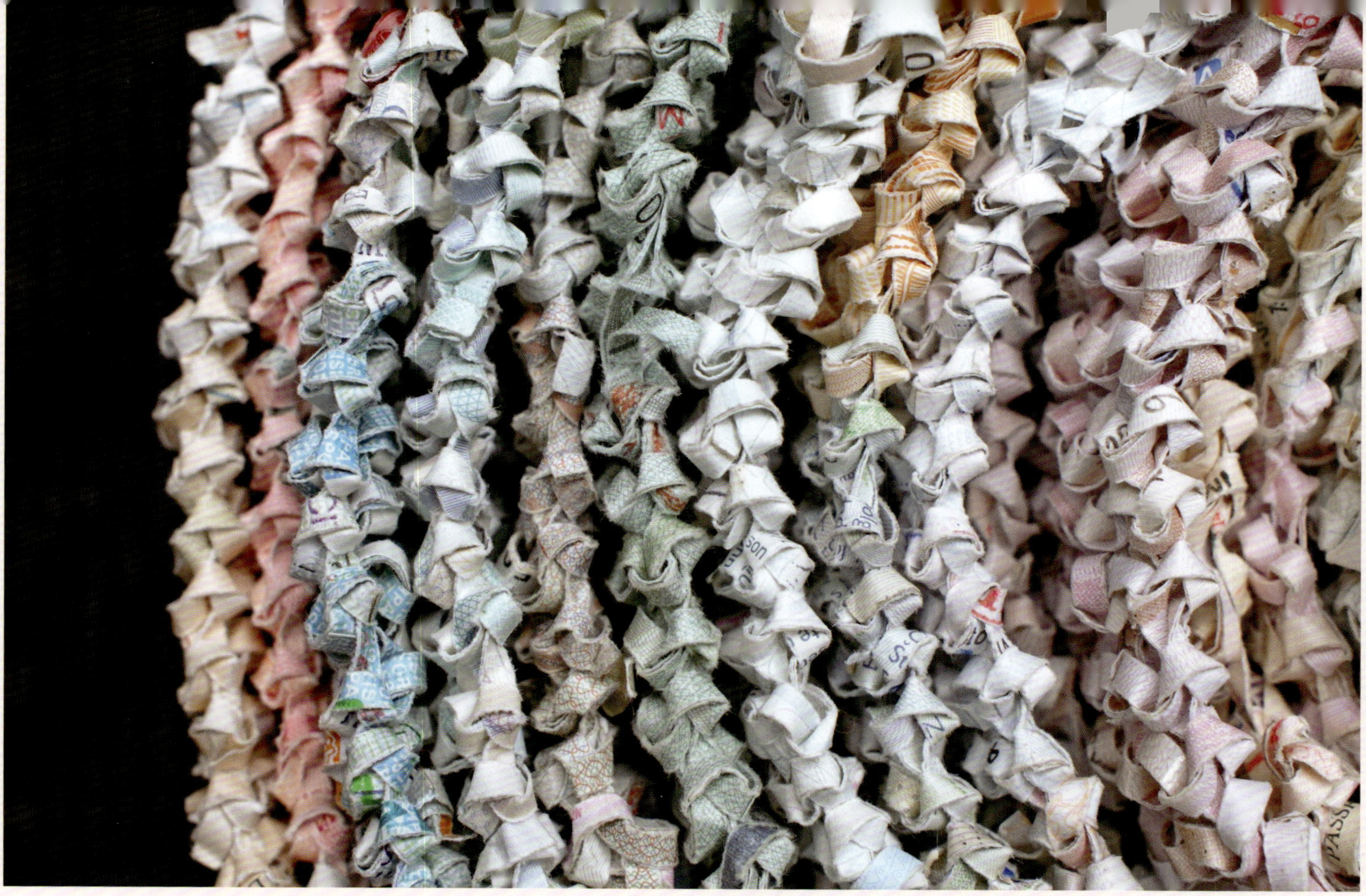

and with them, the person who picked the book, embedding Chen's final creations with others' experiences and perspectives.

The choice of using paper – especially printed paper – carries additional connotations of language, place and culture. In *Beyond the Surface* (2024–ongoing), Chen works with shredded passports to create one piece from hundreds, if not thousands, of expired passports from around the world. The work's title alludes to the artist's interest in literally and metaphorically "shredding an individual passport, symbol of identity and nationality", to ask, "Can we look together, beyond the surface?" This focus on shared humanity, and on recognising people's existence beyond their documentation, reflects Chen's desire to search for what's "underneath the blinding concept of nationality: another human being looking for happiness". By knitting these documents into a single artwork, Chen invites us to discover the commonalities that bind us together. ■

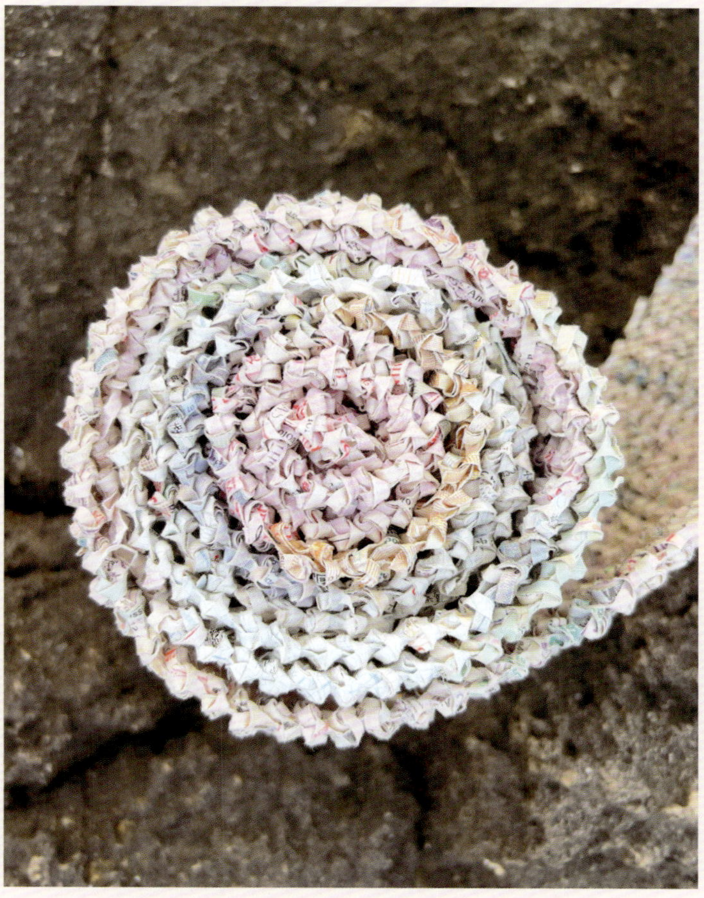

Opposite *Dreconstructing*, 2009, Hand-knitted shredded magazines **This page** *Beyond the Surface*, 2024–ongoing, Hand-knitted shredded passports

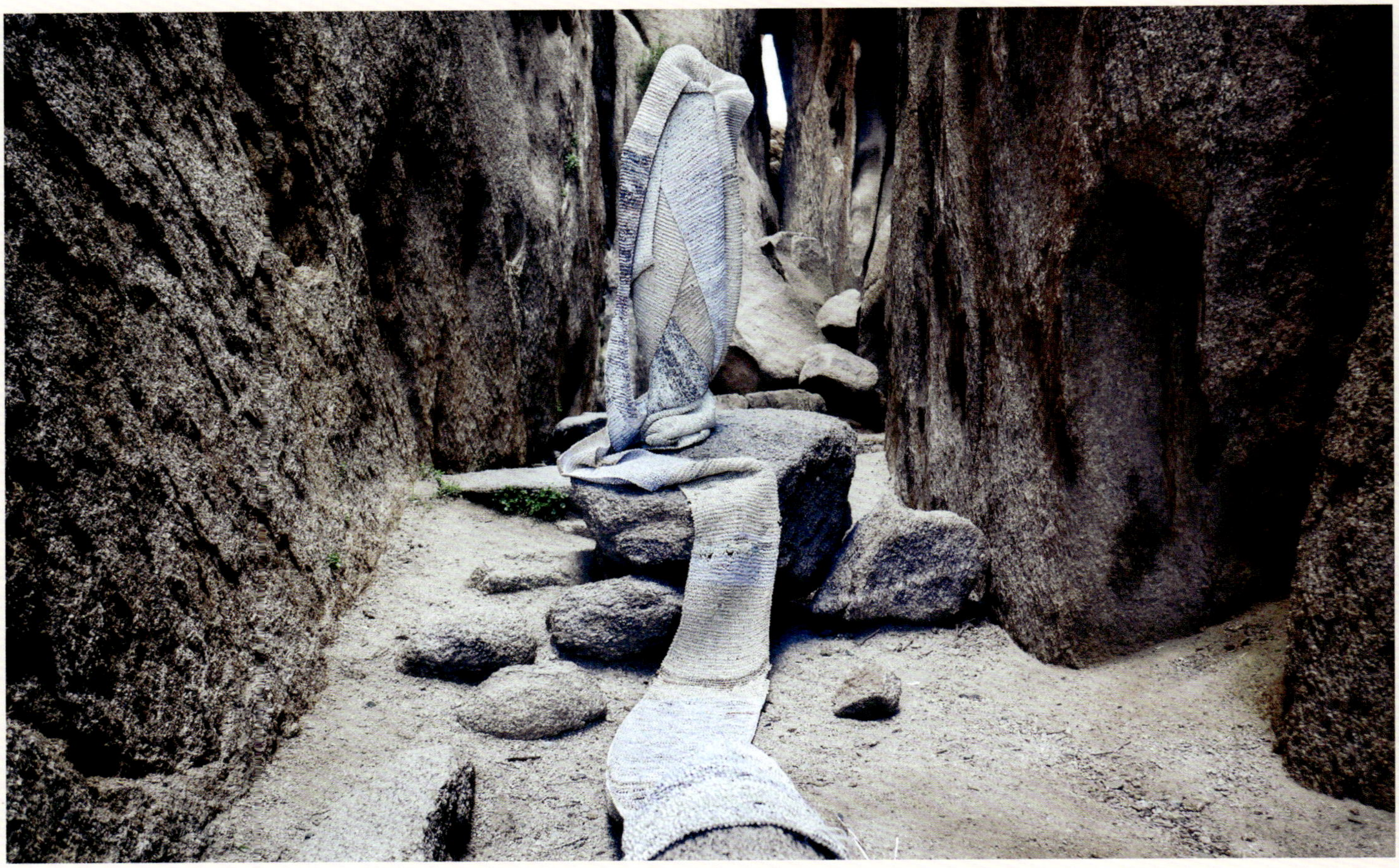

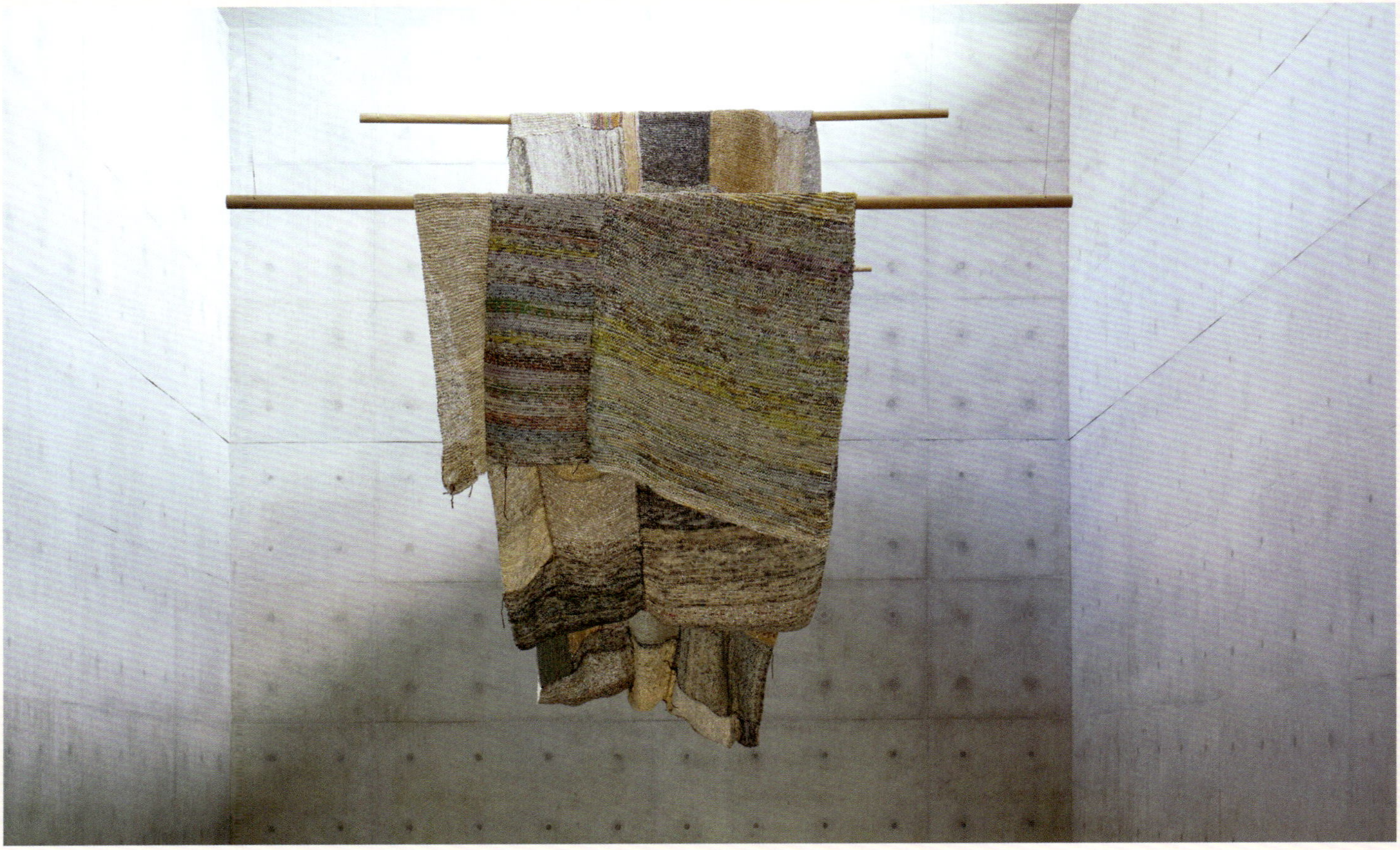

This page Top: *Travelling into your bookshelf - Joshua Tree*, 2017, Hand-knitted shredded books, Performance by Movana Chen; Bottom: *Knitting Conversations*, 2024, Hand-knitted shredded books **Opposite** *Questioning the line*, 2023, Hand-knitted shredded maps, Performance by Movana Chen and Francisco Borges

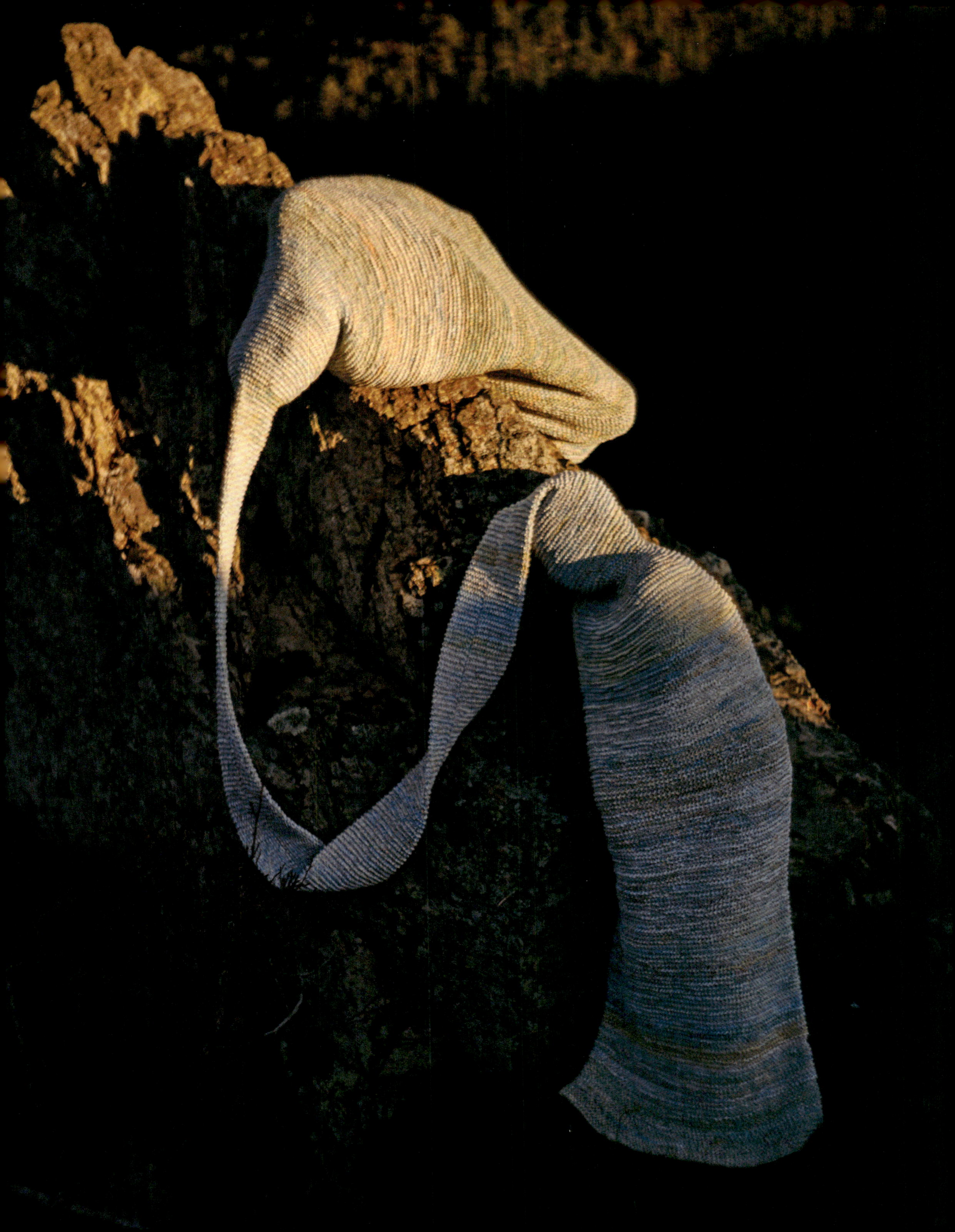

Romina Chuls

NEW YORK CITY

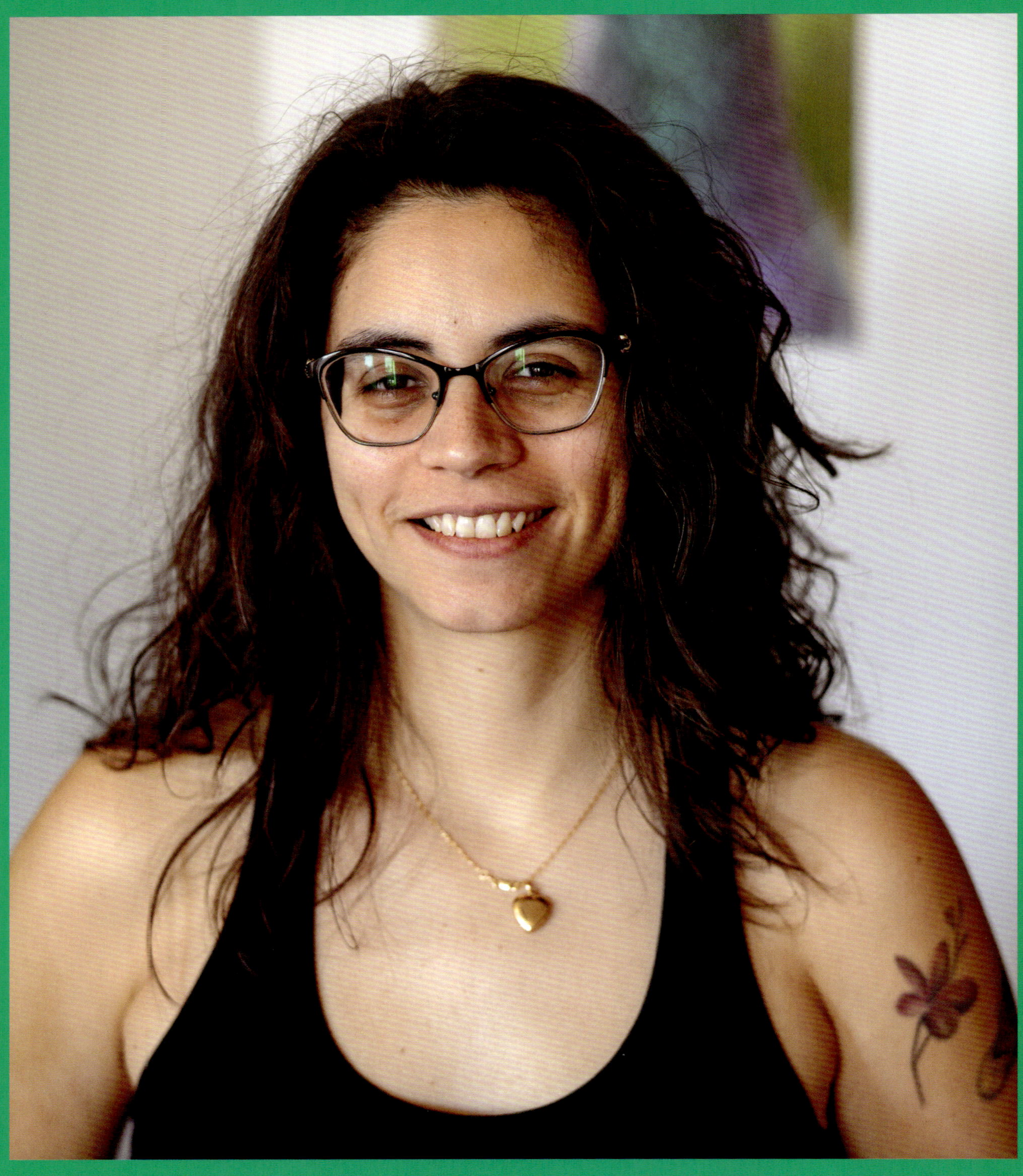

Romina Chuls started using textiles in her art after the passing of her grandmother, who she describes as a "master knitter". This period coincided with Chuls' exposure to Latin American feminism as an art student in Peru, which deepened her understanding of cultural constructions of gender and the way that systems of control are imposed on women's bodies. Soon after, Chuls turned to knitting to tackle societal issues related to gendered violence, sexuality and reproduction rights.

Chuls' works are shaped by her ongoing interest in the "relationship between textiles and gender, both within and outside Western culture". She largely uses two knitting techniques: machine knitting and cross-knit looping, which she pairs frequently with drawings and ceramics. Cross-knit looping dates to pre-Hispanic Paracas and Nasca cultures in Peru, which existed around 800 BCE–650 CE; the technique creates knits with a braided structure, like domestic knitting machines. For Chuls, it connects her contemporary art with practices predating Spanish colonialism, highlighting the ongoing centrality of textiles to Andean cultures. It's also a way for her to centre the "rich and diverse history of textiles" in Peru, where she grew up in proximity to a diversity of craft traditions.

Chuls' art aims to express "stories that remain untold, buried in the global South". Her early works focus on themes of "memory and the male gaze", combining cross-knit looping, worked flat as embroidery, with charcoal drawings. Art from this period includes the *Con P de Patria* series (2018), in which Chuls mirrors "systems of violence" with environmental exploitation enacted for economic development. She represents these connections by placing knitting atop drawings of women's bodies. These knitted sections take the shape of regions in Peru with high rates of systemic sexual assault committed by the military during the 1980s, as well as forced sterilisation in the '90s. The works offer a critical view of a "heteropatriarchal extractive system", in which women's bodies become "spaces to master" like the territories they live on.

Chuls' more recent works "[revolve] around reproduction practices" and the need to "release the body from surveillance and control". The series *Parir los Pétalos* (2023), which translates to "Give Birth to the Petals", responds to discussions around abortion. In the artist's view, abortion rights are "defined by neoliberalism", which confines them to "the notion of self-determination". Instead, Chuls looks past the individual to explore the issue "from the perspective of our interdependencies". In *Parir los Pétalos*, Chuls uses cross-knit looping in both flat and three-dimensional ways, wrapping the textiles around ceramics and metal. These pieces integrate interpretations of fertility symbols, based on Chuls'

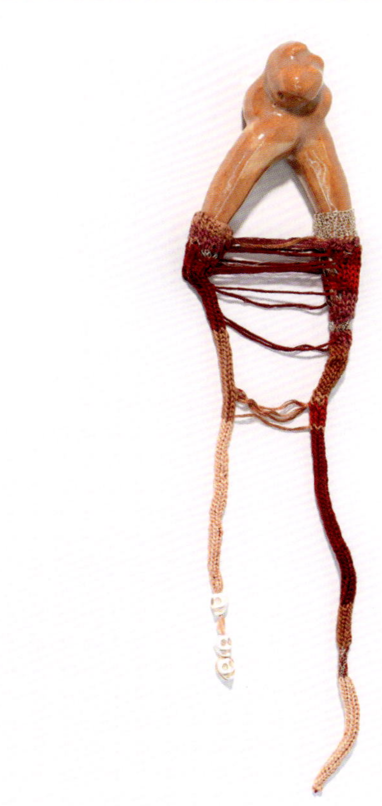

Acaríciame hasta el aborto, 2023, Cross-knit looping and ceramics

research into customary Nasca practices, including both harvesting and funerary traditions. Through these connections to the past, the artist seeks to "challenge our understanding of history" and reproductive knowledge, which has been shaped by "colonial and patriarchal narratives".

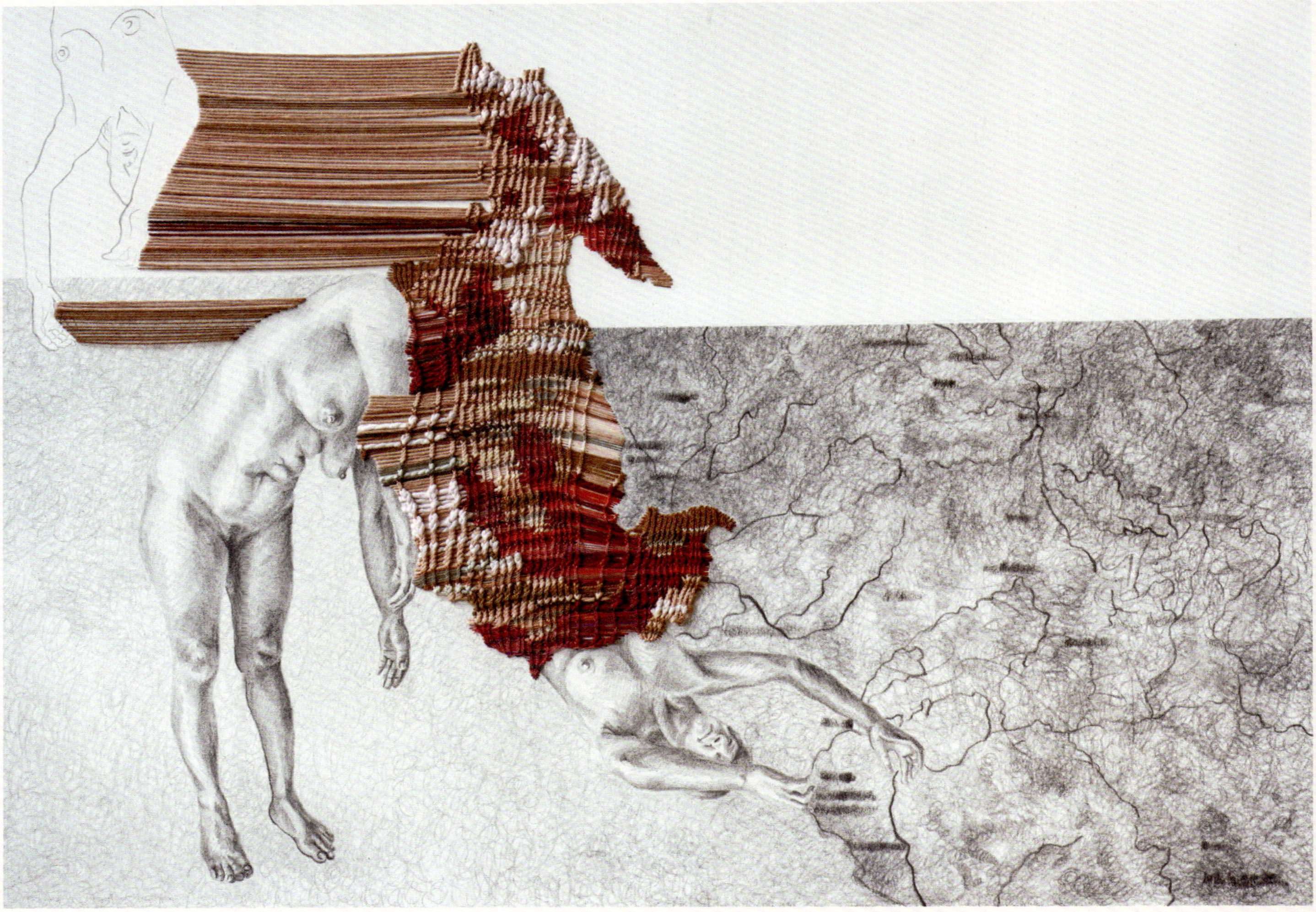

For Chuls, textiles are deeply personal. As she reflects, this "whole love affair…started with the death of my grandmother, and maybe all of this is to learn how to grieve". But beyond the familial, Chuls recognises the ability textiles contain to "create some disruption, some magic". This is because "there is power in the looping of each thread, as if by doing that I was making something imperceptible in the world happen, affecting something far away". A part of this magic arises, as Chuls describes, from how textiles centre touch, not just sight, allowing for intimate encounters with audiences who can recall how fabrics "feel on our skins…without touching them". ■

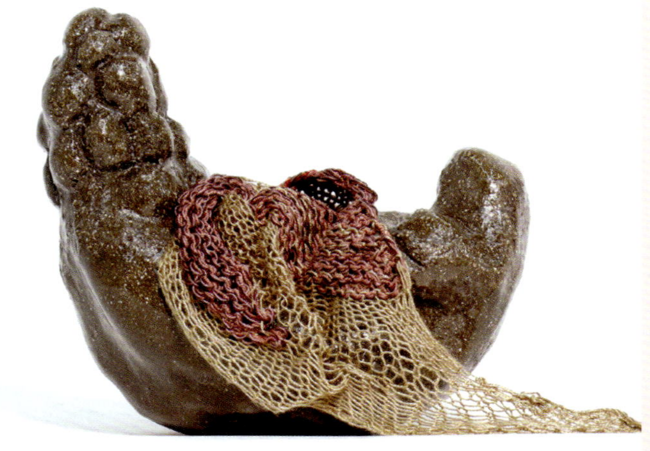

This page Top: *La montaña en sus venas*, 2018, Cross-knit looping and charcoal drawing; Bottom: *Germinada I*, 2023, Manual machine knitting and ceramics **Opposite** *Sembrando mis tierras*, 2018, Cross-knit looping and charcoal drawing

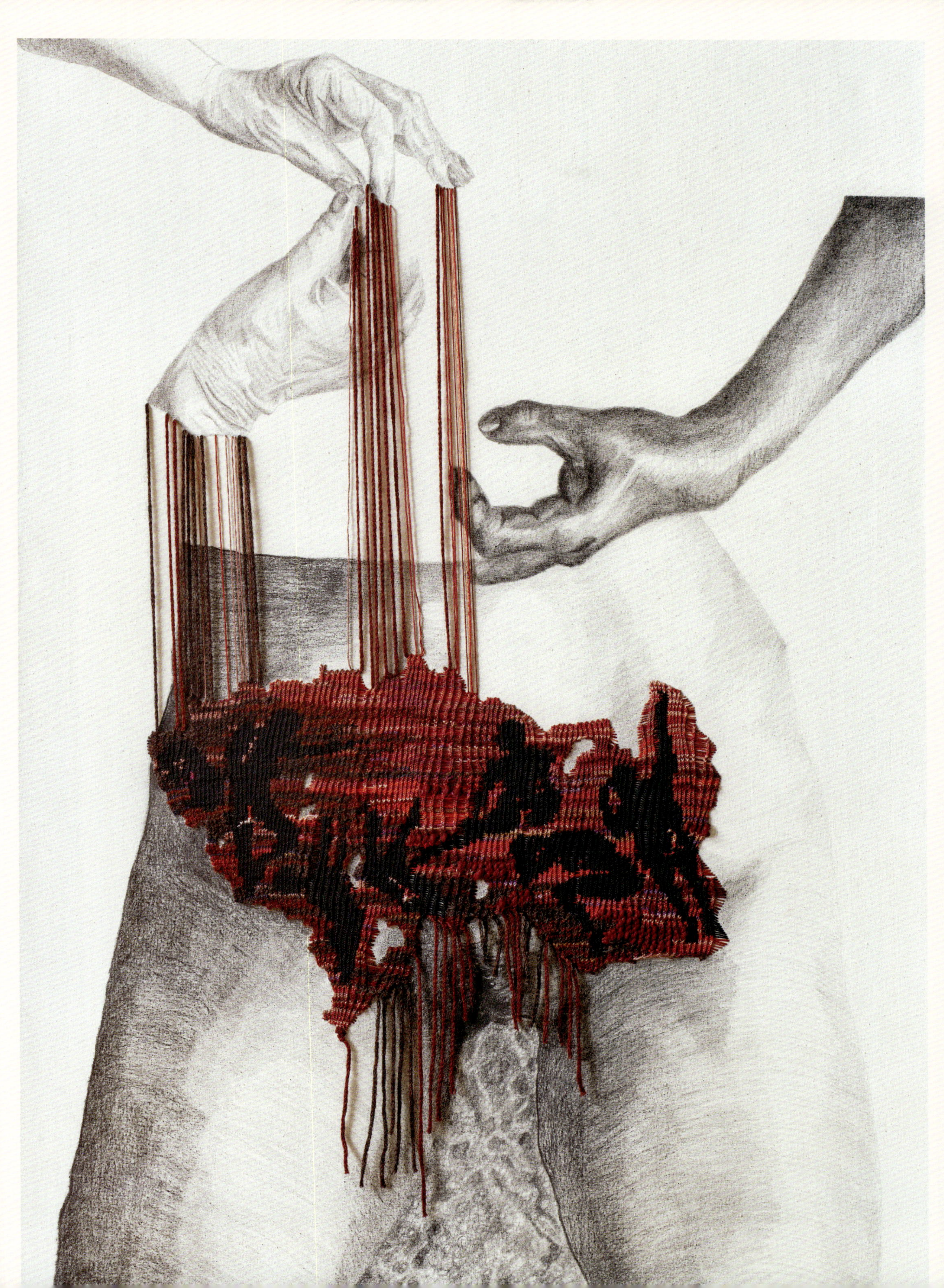

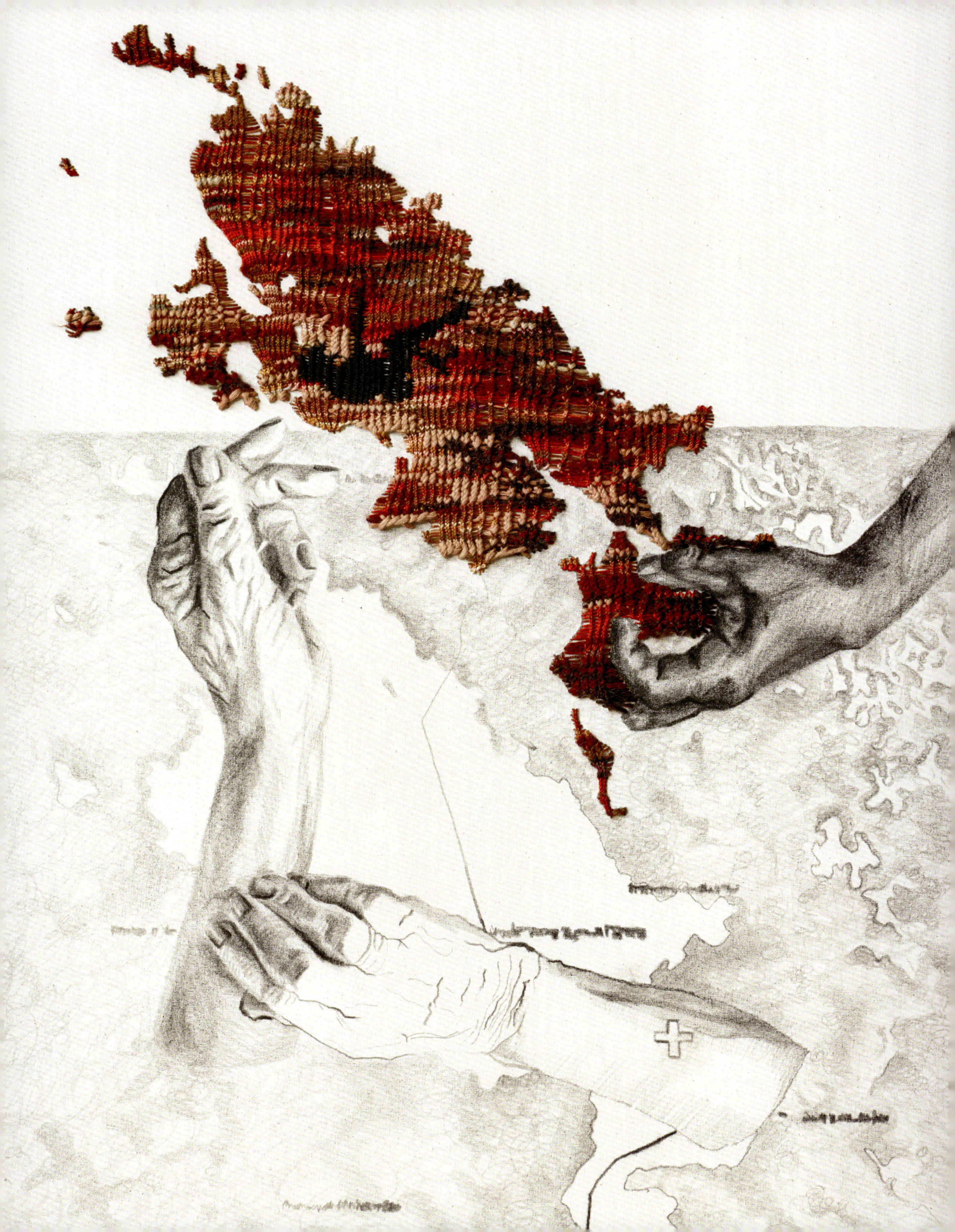

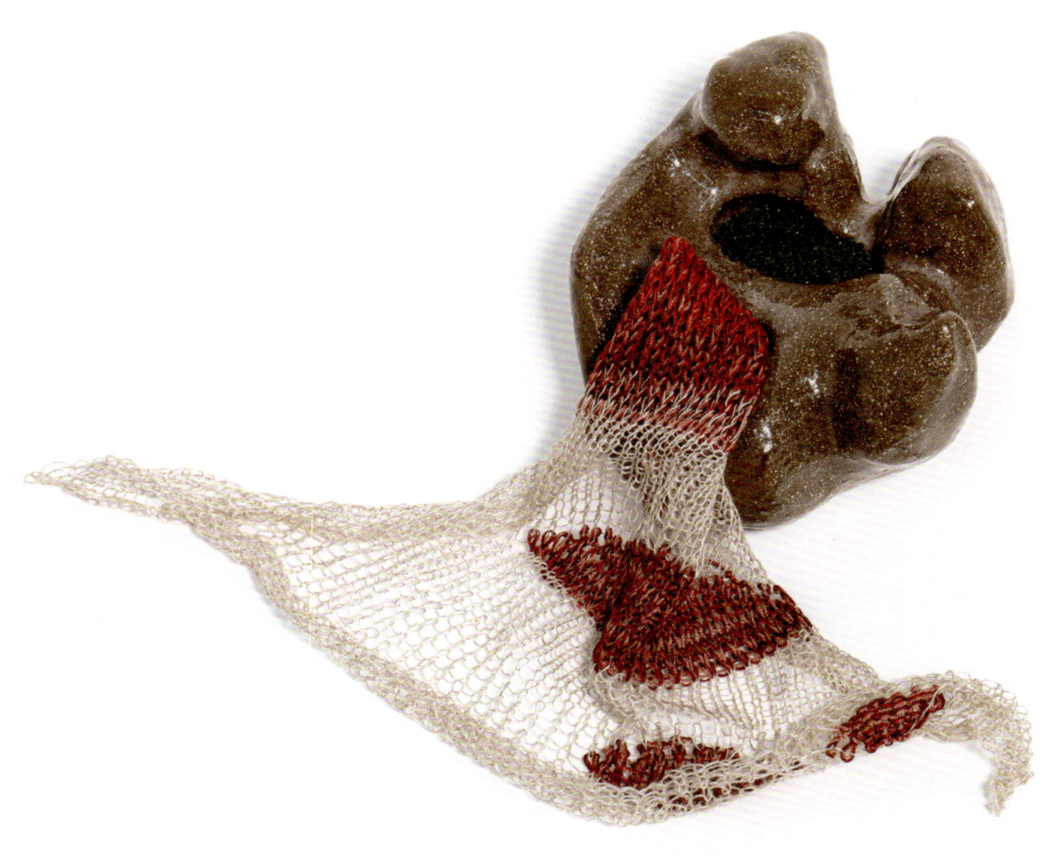

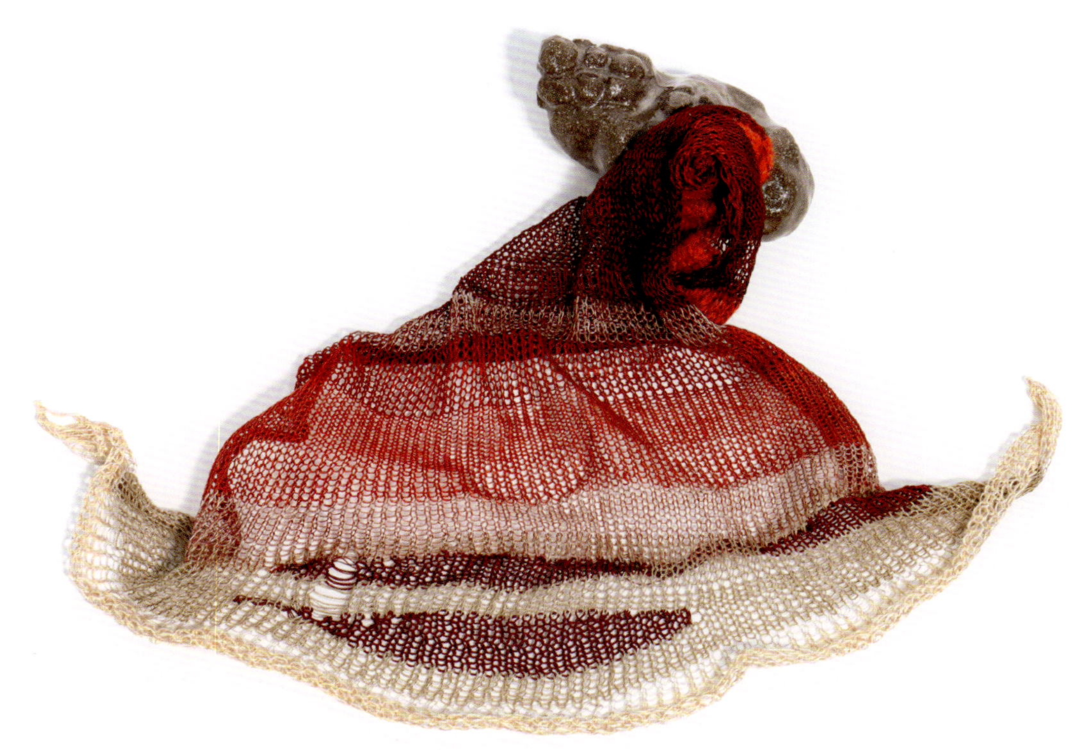

Opposite *Cosechando mis mares*, 2018, Cross-knit looping and charcoal drawing **This page** Top: *Germinada II*, 2023, Manual machine knitting and ceramics; Bottom: *Germinada III*, 2023, Manual machine knitting and ceramics

Sancia Ridgeway

GADIGAL COUNTRY/
SYDNEY

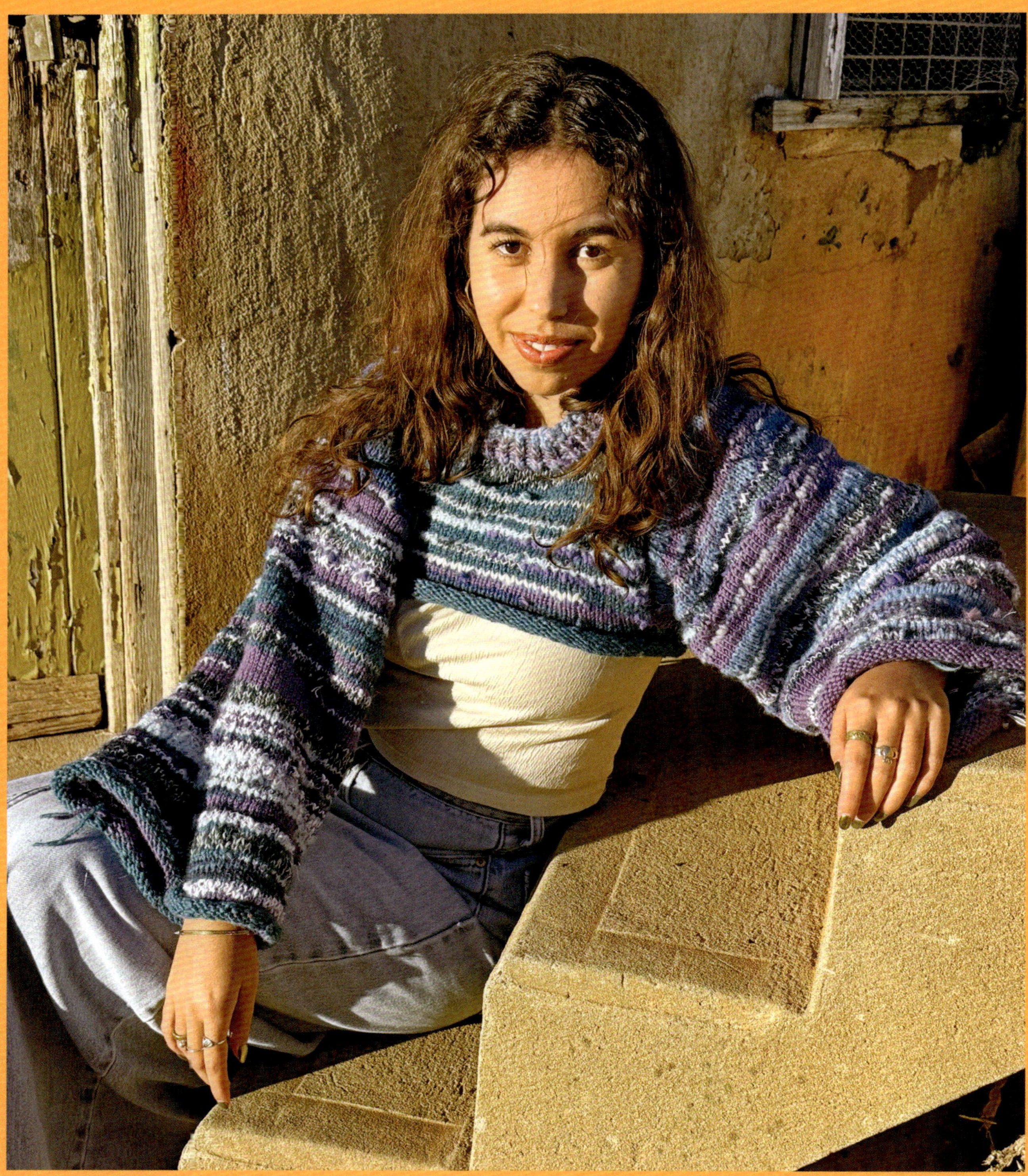

Sancia Ridgeway first learnt to knit by watching YouTube tutorials. She was in her final year of her undergraduate degree in graphic design, and "immediately became obsessed" with this new hobby. Soon after, Ridgeway decided to apply for an additional year of study, determined to include knitting as part of her degree's final project. The result, *Yarns About Blak Joy* (2024), was a publication that features conversations with six Aboriginal Australians alongside photographs of each participant wearing hand-knitted pieces inspired by their individual experiences. This project combines Ridgeway's background in graphic design with her love of hand-knitting to tell stories that centre not only her own "Blak Joy" – the practice of knitting – but also the joy of each individual interviewee.

The term "Blak Joy", as used by Ridgeway, is an adaptation of the term "Black Joy" coined in 2015 by writer Kleaver Cruz in response to police brutality and oppression against Black Americans. As Ridgeway explains, Cruz created the term to "acknowledge the collective struggles of Black people whilst holding space for joy as a vessel for a better future". Ridgeway wanted to "reimagine Cruz's concept into an Australian context" by adopting the spelling of "Blak" (first used by Aboriginal artist Destiny Deacon) to represent Aboriginal and Torres Strait Islander people in her own project. This choice recognises the similar experiences that face Black and First Nations people, while also recognising local context and history.

Ridgeway's ongoing cultural connection to Gumbaynggirr Country is maintained in both the environmental themes of her work, as well as her choice of materials. She prefers to work with donated materials or scrap yarns ("leftover yarn from other projects and odd random balls from op-shops"), combining small amounts of yarn in different fibres, textures and colours to create colour-shifting fabrics. Ridgeway continues to draw inspiration from her local environment, including both "cultural and family artefacts" as elements. For instance, one of her pieces is a knitted dress made with shells, which she views as a "visual metaphor for the power of Songlines", while other pieces in her *Blak Joy* series suggest fishing nets with their open design. For her Aunty Bea, Ridgeway knitted a cloak to represent her seniority as an Elder, a position in which one might traditionally wear a possum-skin cloak.

Ridgeway cites environmental sustainability as a key concern, sharing that "knitting has given me the ability to feel a sense of control of my waste output and my climate footprint – even if it is only in this one small area of my life". Part of Ridgeway's commitment to sustainable practice is reflected in her approach to maintaining net-zero or waste-free output: for yarn scraps that are too short to knit with, Ridgeway combines them with other remnants to create rolags (rolls of fibre) that are then hand-spun into recycled yarns using a spindle. When buying new yarn, she always tries to opt for natural fibres, only working with acrylic yarns if they are second-hand or donated.

Ridgeway's knitting has paved the way for her to form stronger connections with her family, as well as uplift the stories of other First Nations people in her broader community. For Ridgeway, knitting is an active form of activism and self-determination; as an embodied form of artmaking, her work directly correlates with the manual effort required, while her freehand approach allows her to adapt as she goes, accepting mistakes or individual quirks that might arise. Ridgeway relishes the freedom that comes with turning "creativity into something real… with your own bare hands". This immediacy, she reflects, is different to creating something via digital screens, which maintains "a level of disconnect". Ridgeway's knitting practice recognises the small power and impact that making by hand can effect: not just on the individual, but perhaps the world around her. ■

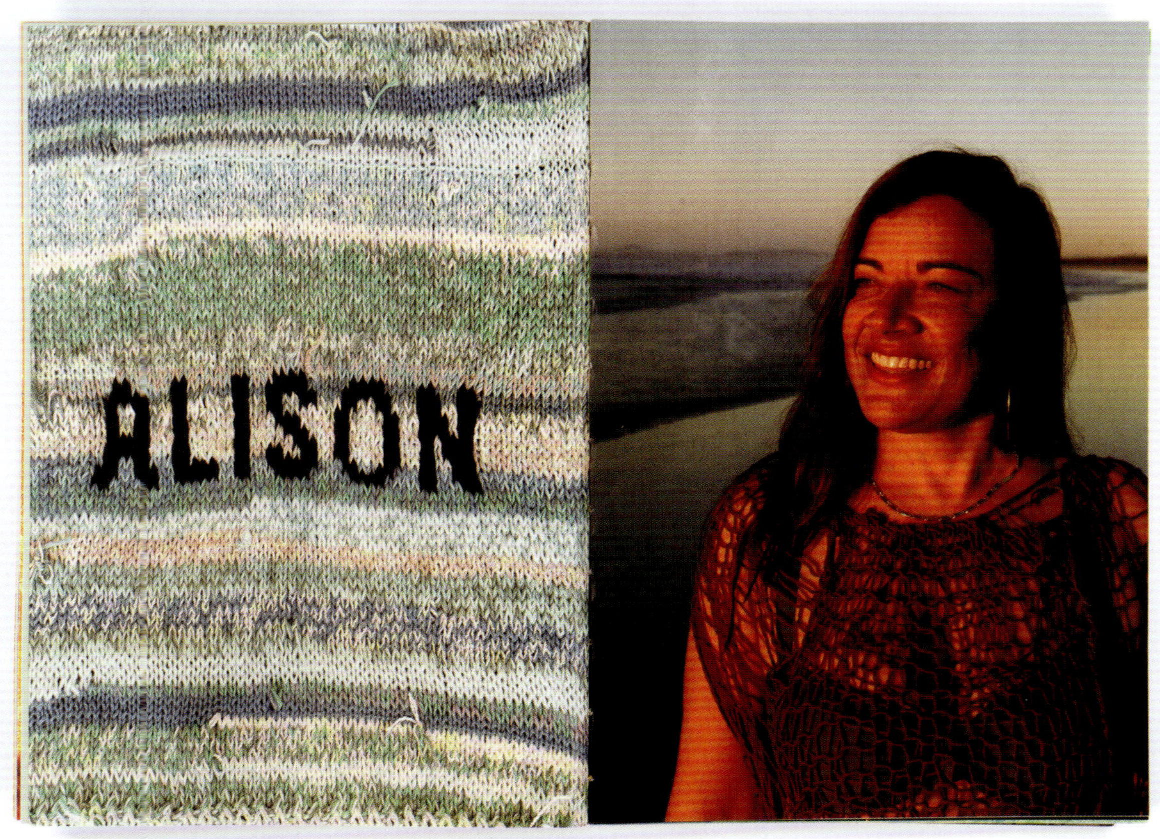

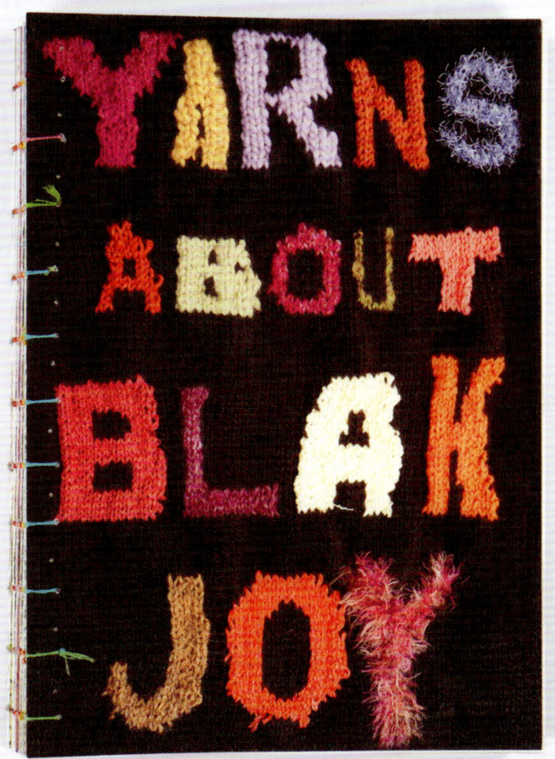

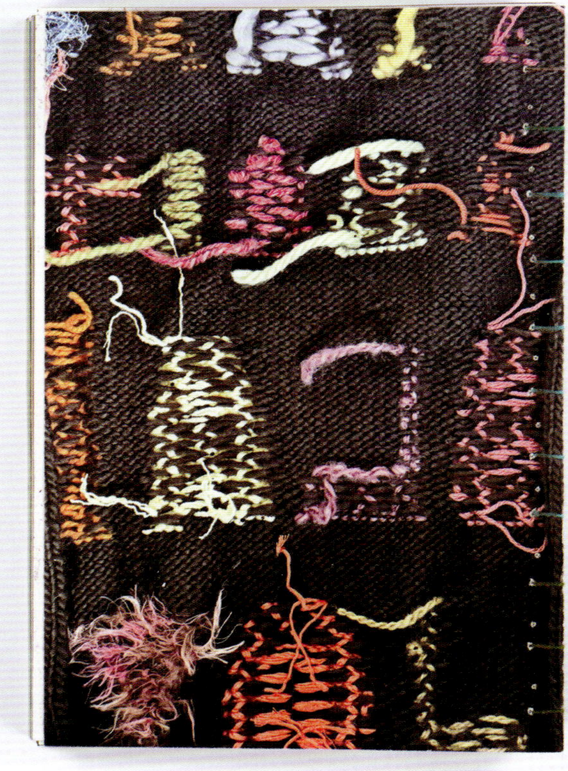

This page *'Yarns About Blak Joy' publication project for Sancia's honours year at university*, 2024, Hand-knitting
Opposite *Sancia wearing a knitted cloak*, 2024, Hand-knitting

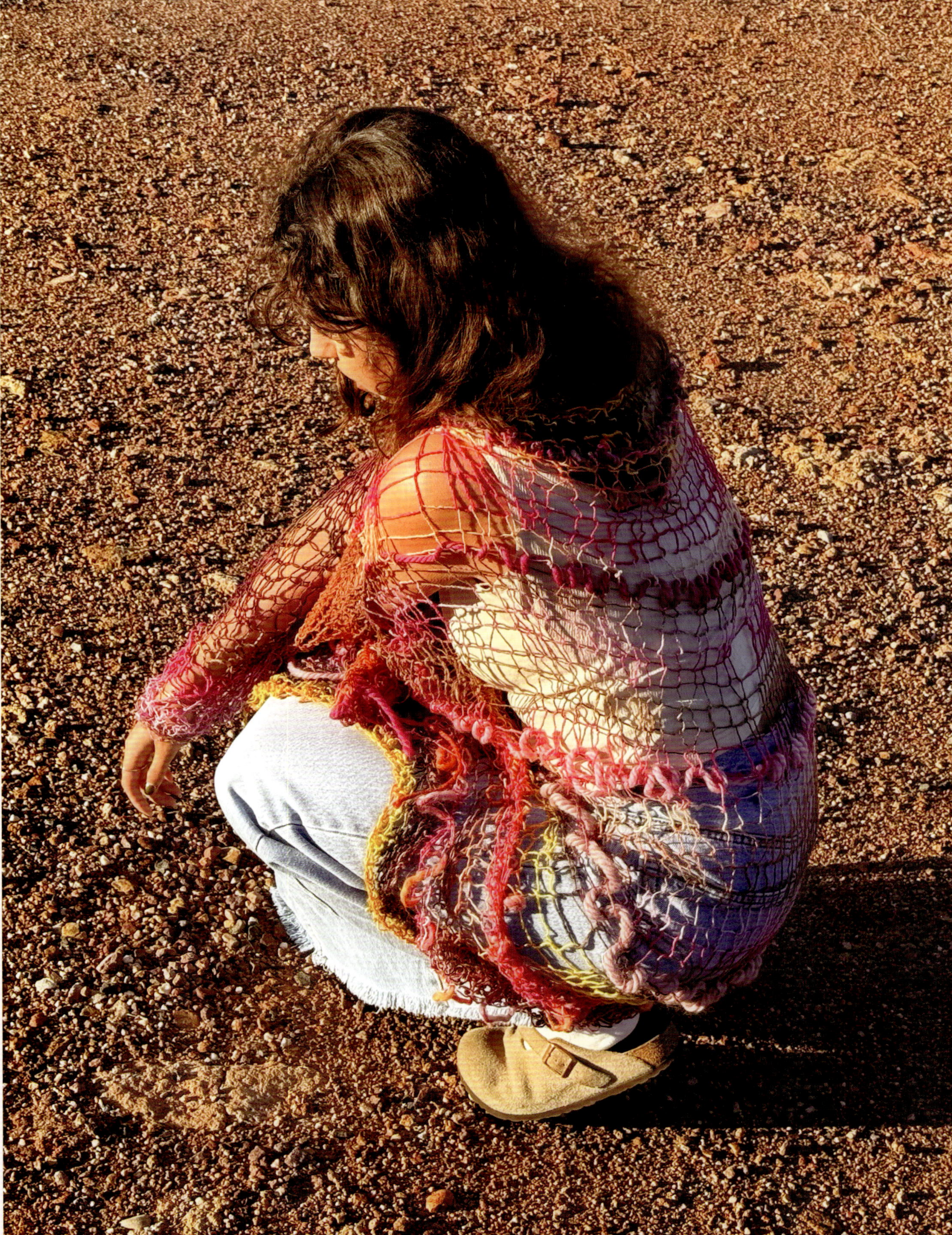

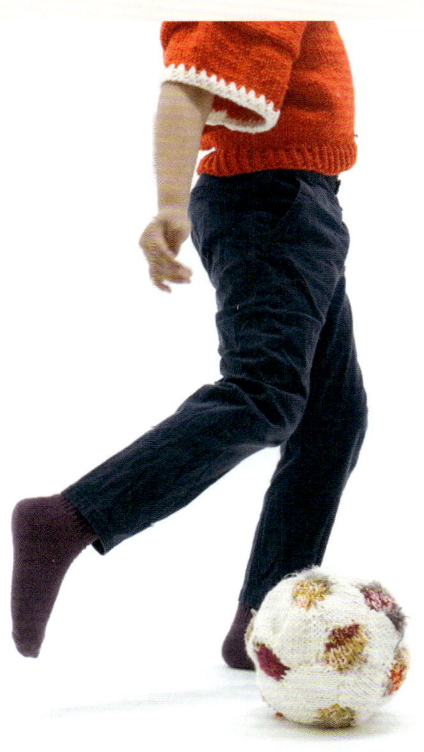

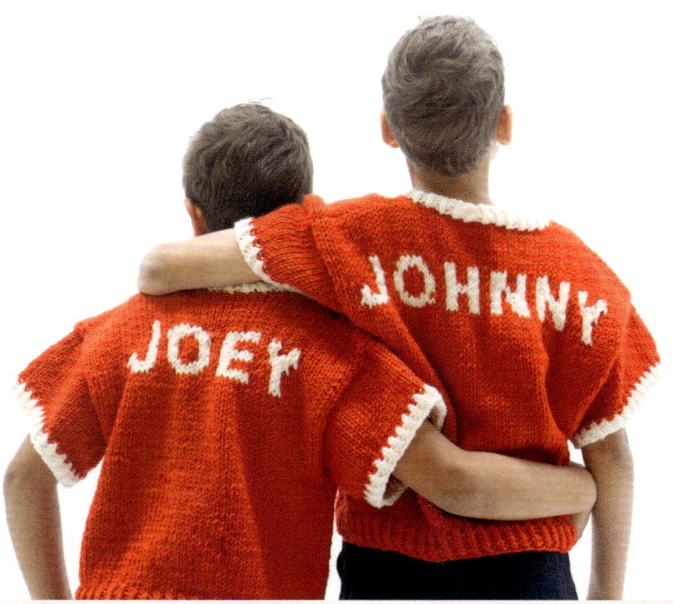
JOEY
JOHNNY

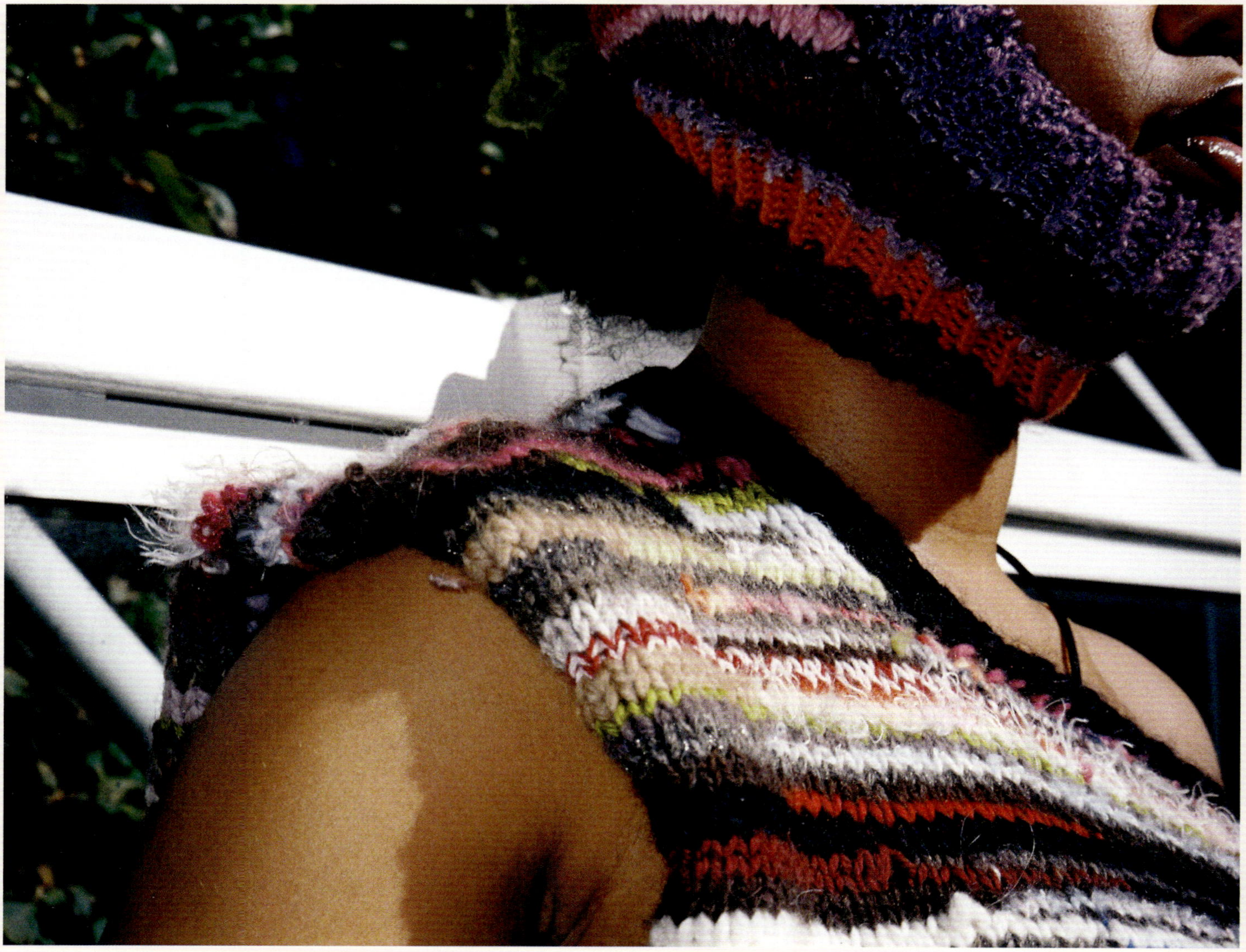

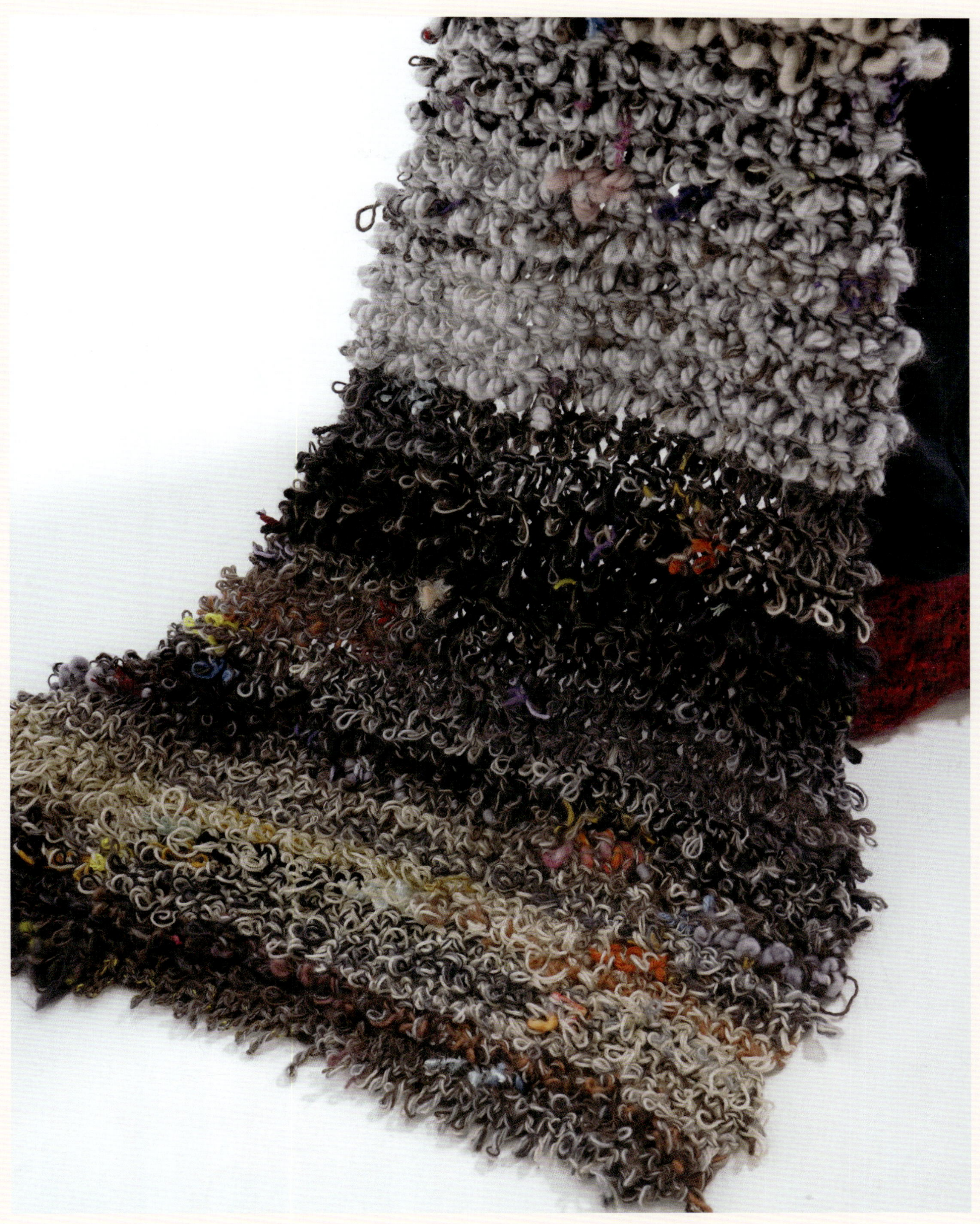

Opposite Clockwise from top left: *Joey booting the knitted soccer ball,* 2024, Hand-knitting; *Johnny and Joey in their knitted sports jerseys,* 2024, Hand-knitting; Bottom: *Majeda wearing some of Sancia's garments*, 2024, Hand-knitting
This page *Aden (Sancia's Dad) in his scrap yarn knitted 'possum' cloak*, 2024, Hand-knitting

Shradha Kochhar

NEW YORK CITY

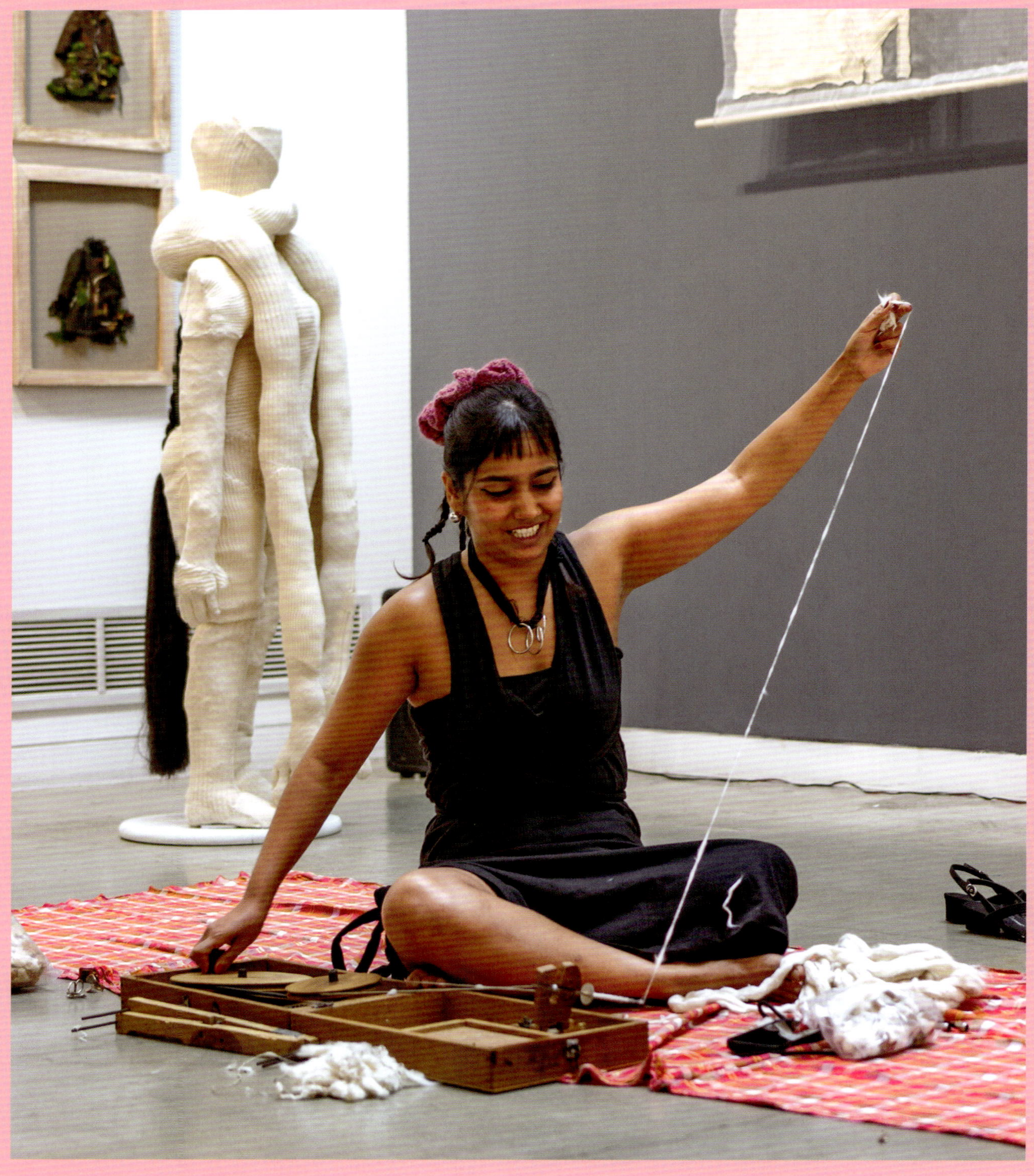

Shradha Kochhar's art is inspired by the history of cotton, women's labour and colonisation, through both a personal and collective South Asian lens. The artist grew up in "a family deeply embedded in textiles", in which fabric was not just a practical part of daily life, but also an essential part of "our survival", self-sustenance and livelihood.

Kochhar's works are shaped by these early experiences, and result from her "desire to understand cloth, cotton specifically, at a deeper level". For the artist, this includes understanding not only the processes that create cotton (from seed to fibre to thread to textile), but also its histories of production and distribution. Kochhar views the fabric as a "living archive" through which she can map "personal and collective histories" between India, the country where she was born, and the United States, where she now lives.

Kochhar's recent works are made primarily from kala cotton, a strain which is indigenous to India. Her creative process begins with ginning, or separating the raw cotton fibre from its seed, which she then hand-spins into yarn. She uses a peti charkha: a special modular spinning wheel that became a "pivotal part of the civil disobedience movement in India" in the early 20th century through its use by incarcerated protesters who spun cotton behind bars to boycott foreign-made material. Once her yarn is spun, Kochhar hand-knits it into pieces of cloth that are then either appliqued or sewn onto sculptural forms or used to create flat pictures that she terms "knitted essays". In Kochhar's words, "every gesture, every pull, every twist, every loop, becomes a ritual of creation and remembrance" through which she can look to the past, while also "actively reshaping the present".

Some of the common themes Kochhar explores in her "knitted essays" include interpersonal relationships, and how stories (both personal and cultural) can be transmitted through textile practices. A visual motif that she returns to frequently is the familial dining table, as seen in *Last Meal Together* (2023) and *7 Ways to Sit Around A Table* (2023). The focus on the table in each of these knitted compositions speaks to its role as central to family dynamics: a place where lifelong connections can be formed or ruptured over shared meals.

In other pieces made from kala cotton, Kochhar creates life-size sculptures that stretch hand-knit fabric around "delicately carved bamboo vessels". Works such as *I'm Cocooning* (2021) are made at a scale that is able to hold a human body, offering a soft protective layering between the wearer and the outside world. As a stand-alone object in the absence of a wearer, though, the piece can still be interpreted via embodiment – the cloth not only covers the human body, but is also a being with its own histories and identities.

This relationship between cloth and body is further explored by Kochhar in *Family Portrait* (2019), which depicts an entanglement of human forms made from stitched fabric dyed with tea leaves. Whether in an embrace or caught in strife, the figures in this sculpture capture "the imperfect choreography of belonging, where affection and friction coexist". As with her "knitted essays", the figures have no identifying features, intentionally devoid of colour. Instead, the "blank" slate allows viewers to "reflect, and imprint their own narratives onto the work".

For Kochhar, her artmaking is an "active place of healing and survival". By connecting with the histories of cotton production in India, and the myriad of ways that textiles are present in our lives today, Kochhar prompts audiences to "recognise the stories embedded in the things we often take for granted". In doing so, she seeks to uplift the often invisible labour behind textiles while drawing attention to the possibilities found through the physical act of crafting. ■

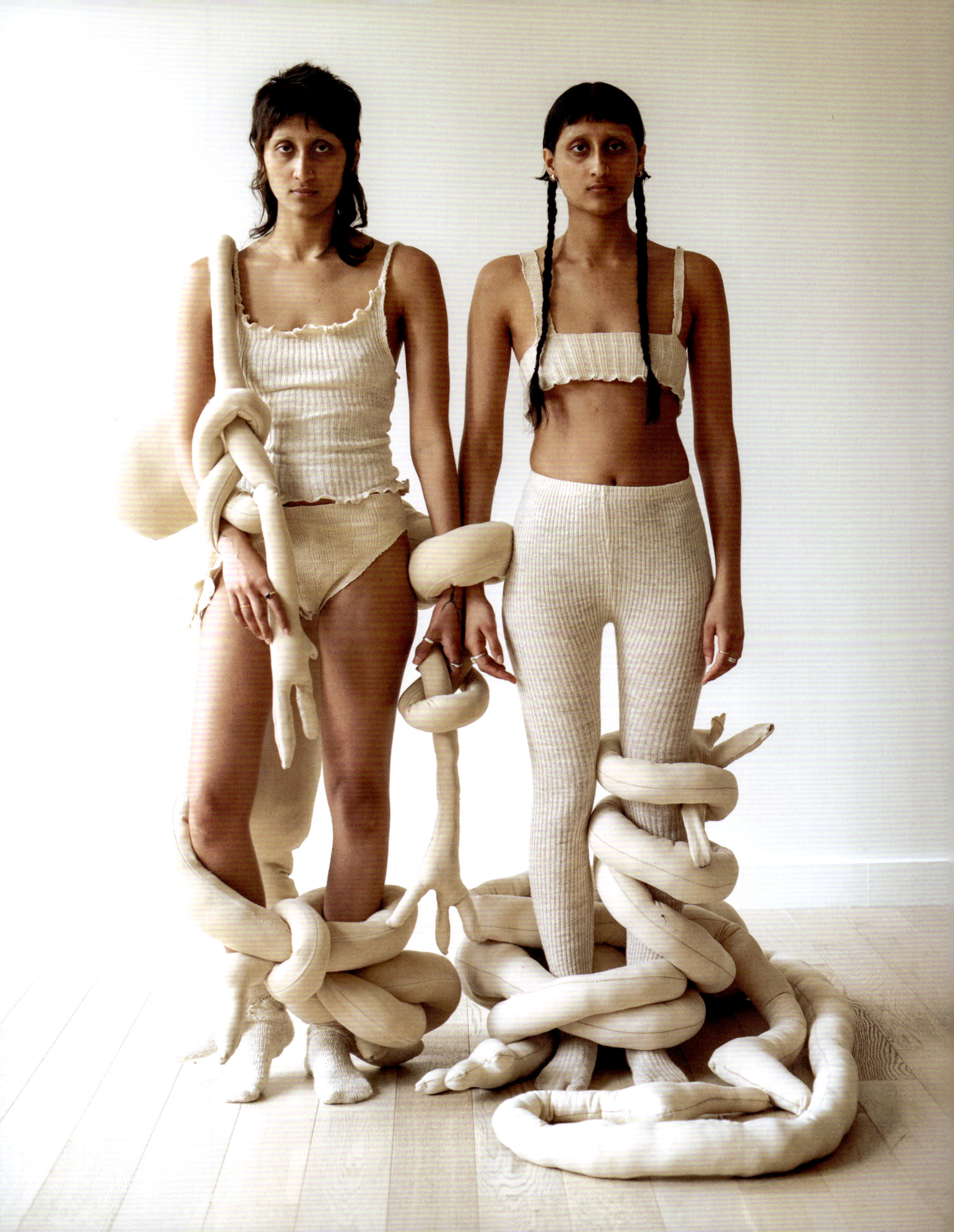

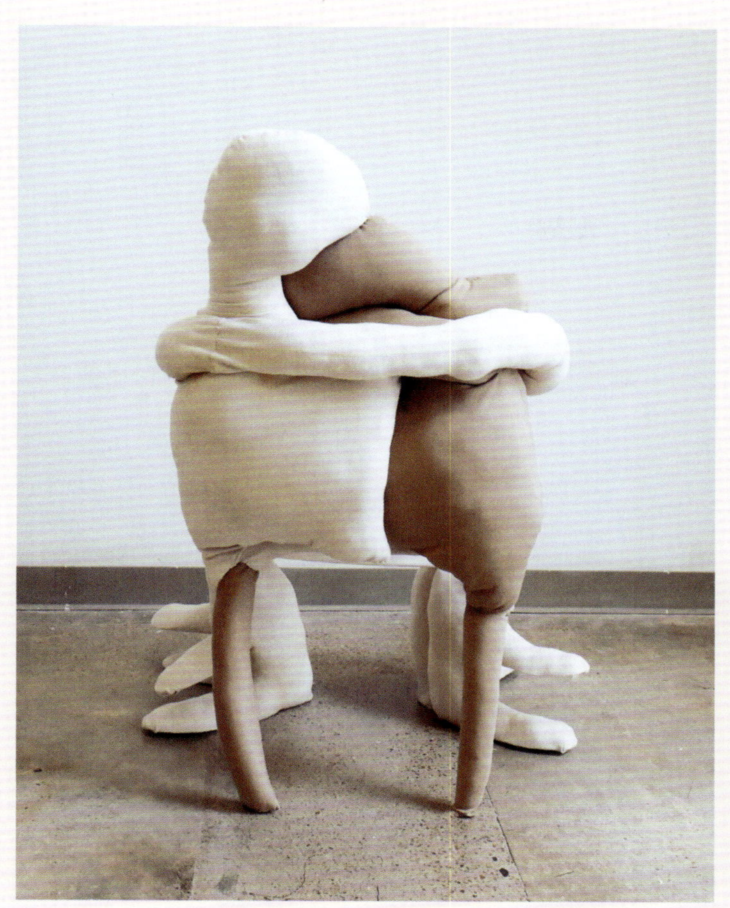

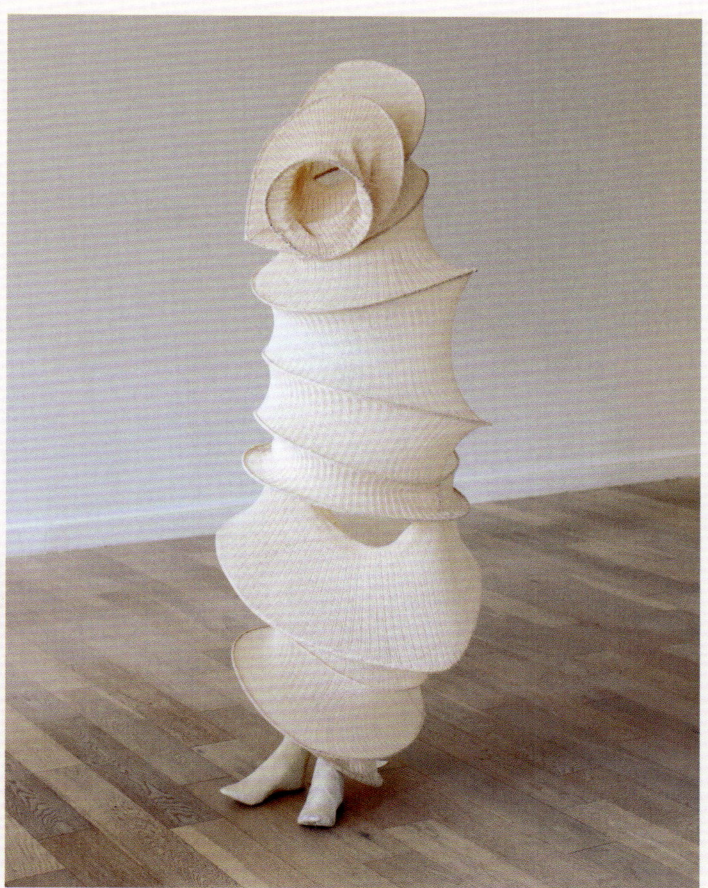

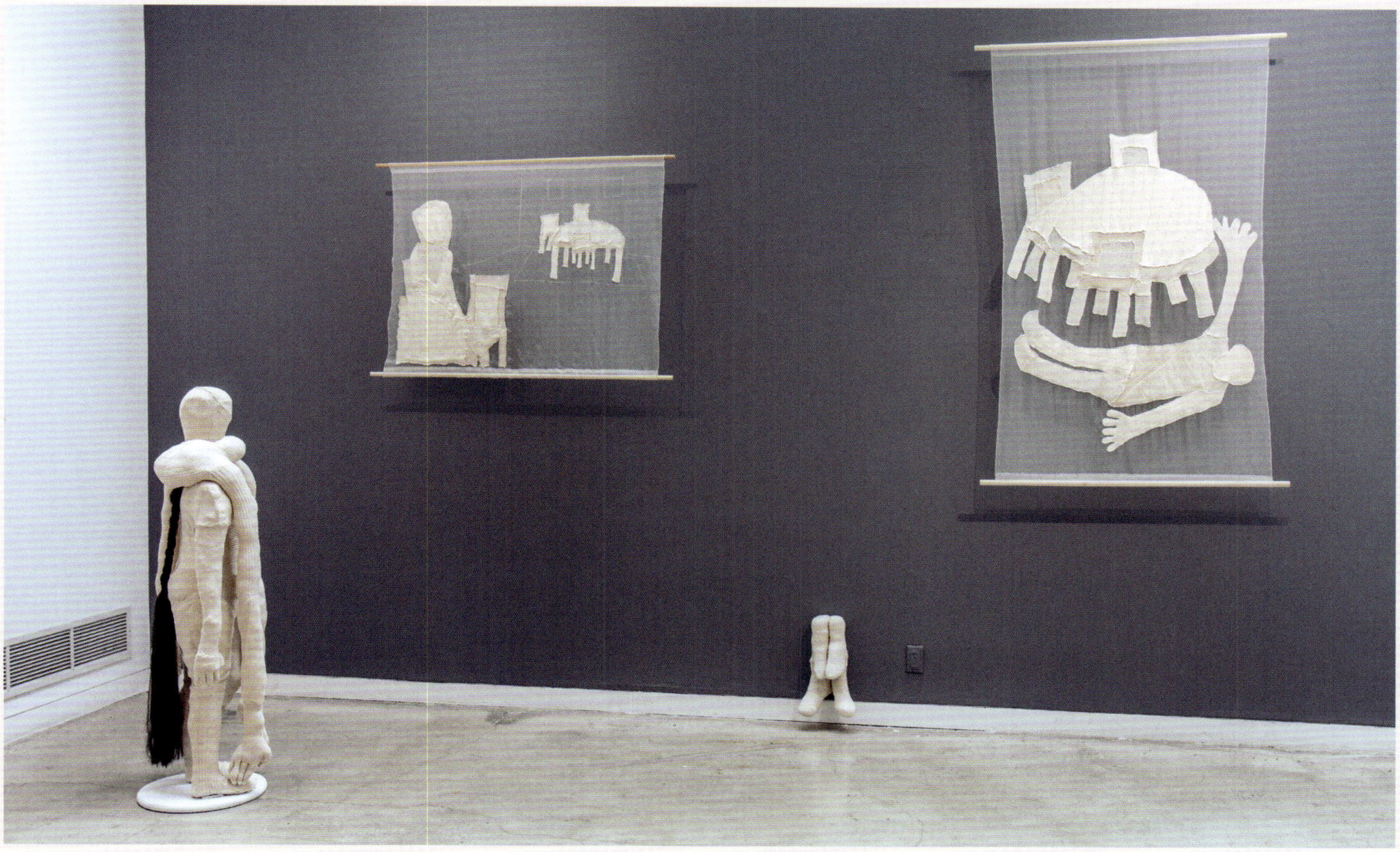

Opposite *Closer not far - Family Portrait,* 2019, Sewing, featuring Mannat and Sirat
This page Clockwise from top left: *Gaping Silence,* 2024, Sewing; *I'm Cocooning,* 2021, Hand-spinning and hand-knitting; Installation view, 2024

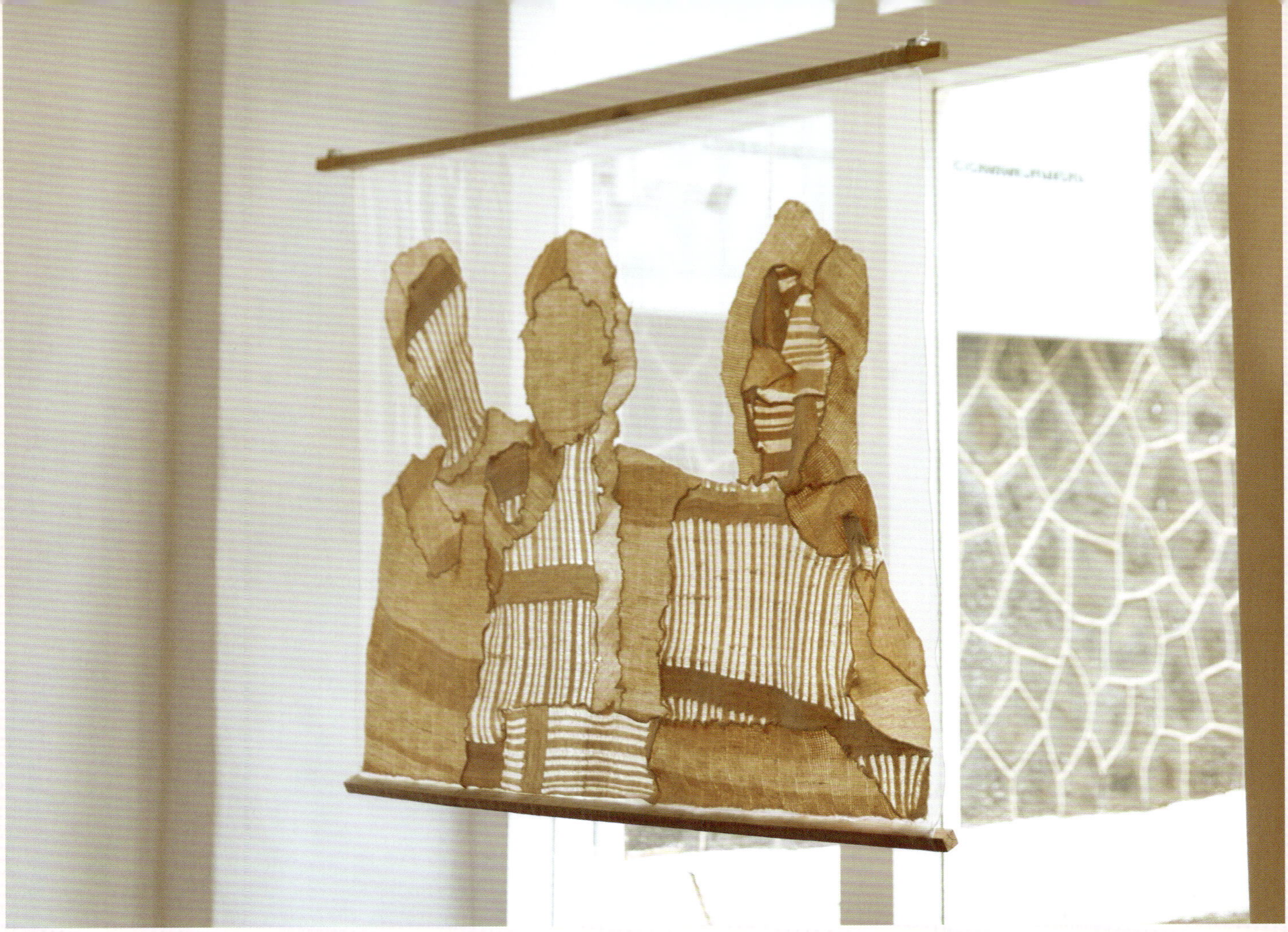

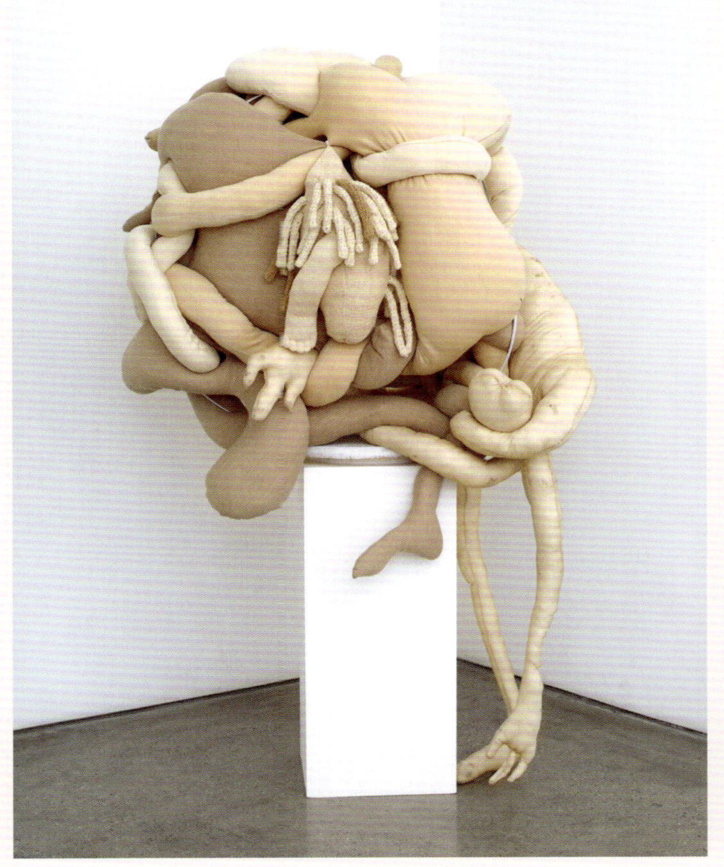

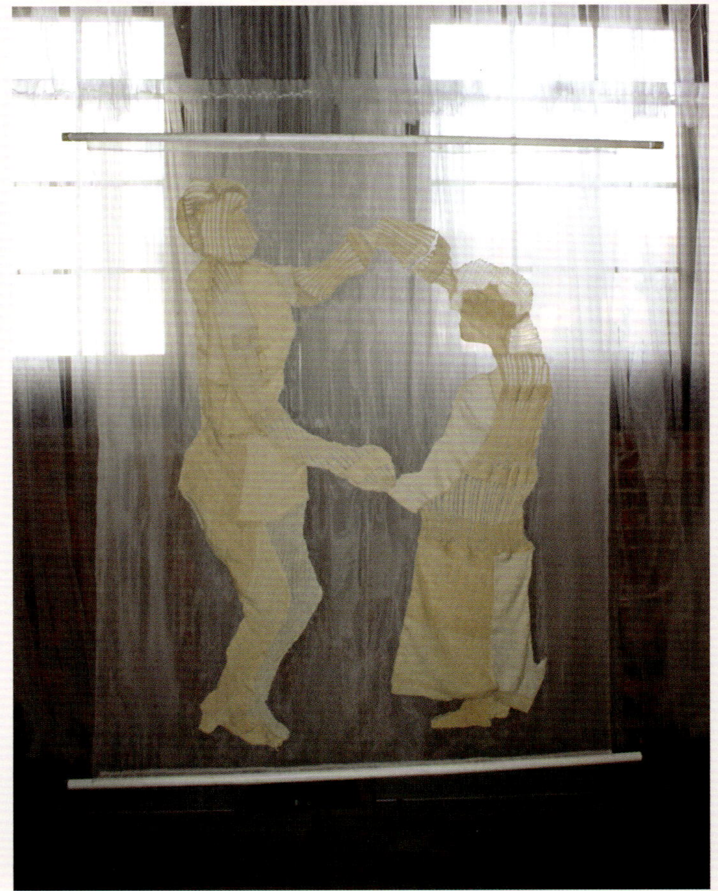

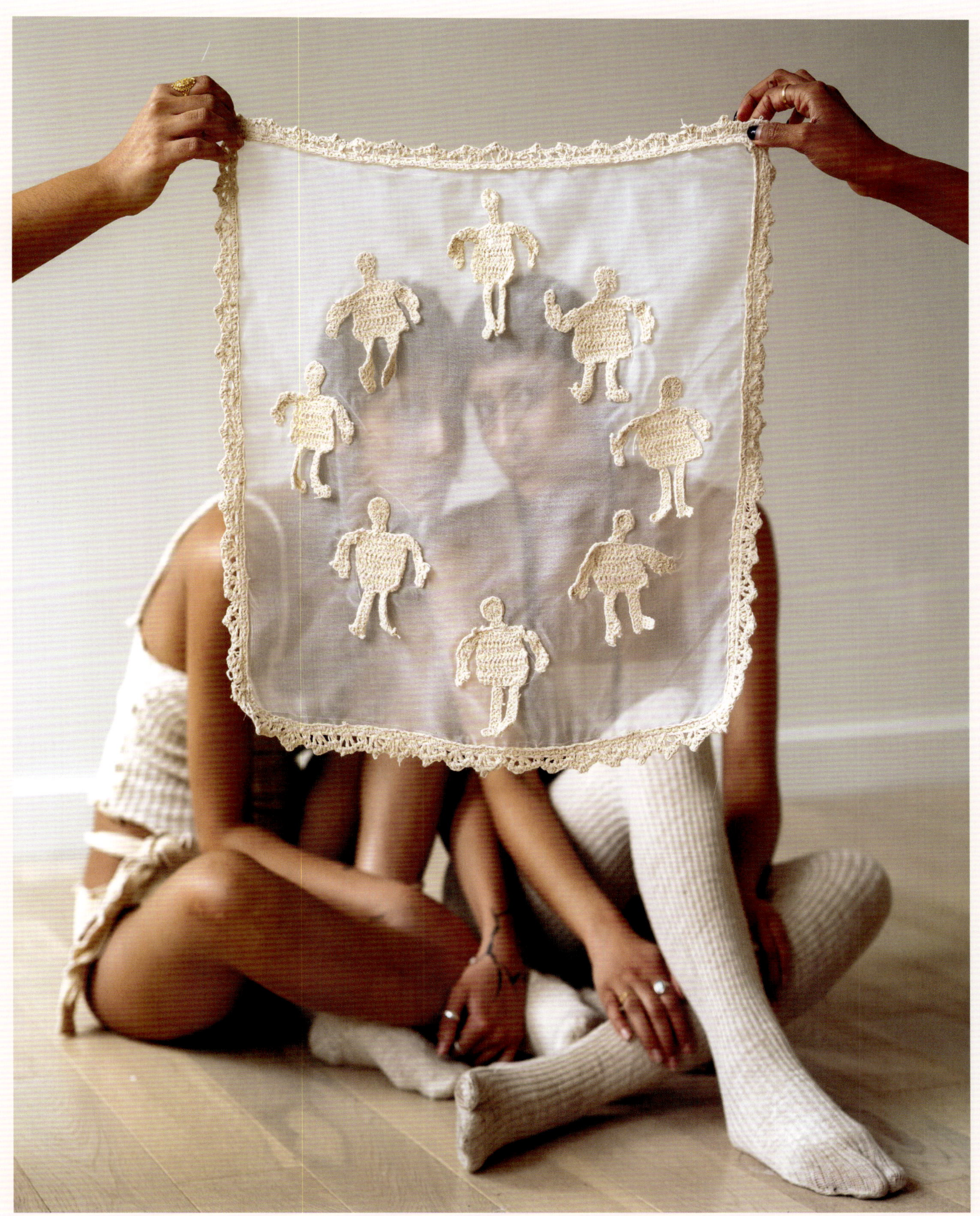

Opposite Clockwise from top: *Just Us Now,* 2021, Hand-spinning, hand-knitting and applique; *Untitled,* 2022, Hand-spinning, hand-knitting and applique; *Family Portrait,* 2019, Hand-spinning and sewing **This page** *Closer, not far - For those who came before and after,* 2021, Hand-spinning, hand-knitting and crochet, featuring Mannat and Sirat

Hook

Of the three textile techniques covered in this book, crochet can be considered the "youngest" sibling. While there are examples of cultures using looped or chained threads as a foundational stitch across Asia, South America and Africa, crochet as we know it today became popularised in early 19th-century Europe.

As a technique, crochet uses a hook, which can be made from a range of materials including wood, plastic and metal. Loops of yarn (or other materials like thread) are pulled through other loops to create stitches, producing interlocked structures and patterns. In contrast to knitting, where an entire line of stitches is worked at once, each crochet stitch is completed before a new one is started.

This difference means that crochet is a forgiving medium for mistakes, and that it lends itself to creating more structural shapes, which makes it well suited to three-dimensional forms. This is seen in the works of the artists Kat Leonardo, Liisa Hietanen and Philippa Rice, who each use basic crochet stitches to create sculptural works out of wool. For Leonardo, this includes imaginative wearable pieces, which bring a sense of whimsy to the everyday. Hietanen makes crochet portraits based on her interactions with her local community, which are then presented in public settings. Rice crochets toys that have a unique personality of their own; with the use of stop-motion animation, she brings each character to life.

Paula do Prado and Baylee Schmitt harness the freeform possibilities of crochet to create distinct and imaginative works based on intuition and memory. For do Prado, this involves the use of a simple crochet slip stitch, in combination with a range of materials, to create large-scale works that are guided by experimentation and playfulness inspired by her cultural ancestry. Schmitt, on the other hand, works from memory. She uses crochet as an "engineering" process to recreate her childhood home from scratch.

The artists Lissy and Rudi Robinson-Cole and Mulyana further demonstrate crochet's sculptural possibilities by creating immersive installations. In Lissy and Rudi's works, crochet is used to connect to their whakapapa (ancestral ties) by interpreting Māori history and culture through bright yarns. For Mulyana, the ability to use individual parts to create large-scale forms reflects the ways in which nature is shaped through evolution, but also by human actions.

A number of artists in this book use crochet in a tapestry form, wielding multiple colours together to create interpretations of existing imagery. In the works of Nicole Nikolich, this includes crochet recreations of digital culture and the internet, each pixel of the screen transcribed into crochet stitches. Wells Chandler's works reference images from art history, as well as his own ensemble of characters to celebrate queerness and joy. For Chandler, his use of crochet is intimately connected to the history of painting.

While most of the artists in this chapter use materials like yarn and thread, the works of Omar Badrin and Kelly Jin Mei use unconventional materials to create meaning. Badrin creates masks from materials that are closely connected to Newfoundland, where he grew up, in part to reflect on the region's maritime industries. Jin Mei, on the other hand, deliberately uses nylon thread so she can burn her crochet vases without turning them to ash.

Crochet is a versatile medium, and the many possibilities of its application is seen in the works of Blake Ballard and Beth Williams. In addition to his works using filet crochet (a technique that mimics lace work), Ballard explores the meanings of crochet symbols as a cultural artefact by highlighting the patterns themselves. His works reveal how artists use crochet not just as a technique, but also as a subject. Williams, on the other hand, focuses on the creation of the fibre itself. They make "living textiles" that grow and change over time, returning to the earth at the end of their natural lifespan.

The 14 artists in this chapter demonstrate a wide range of creative approaches to contemporary crochet. Their works show us how through single stitches, built up one on top of another, profound and creative storytelling is possible.

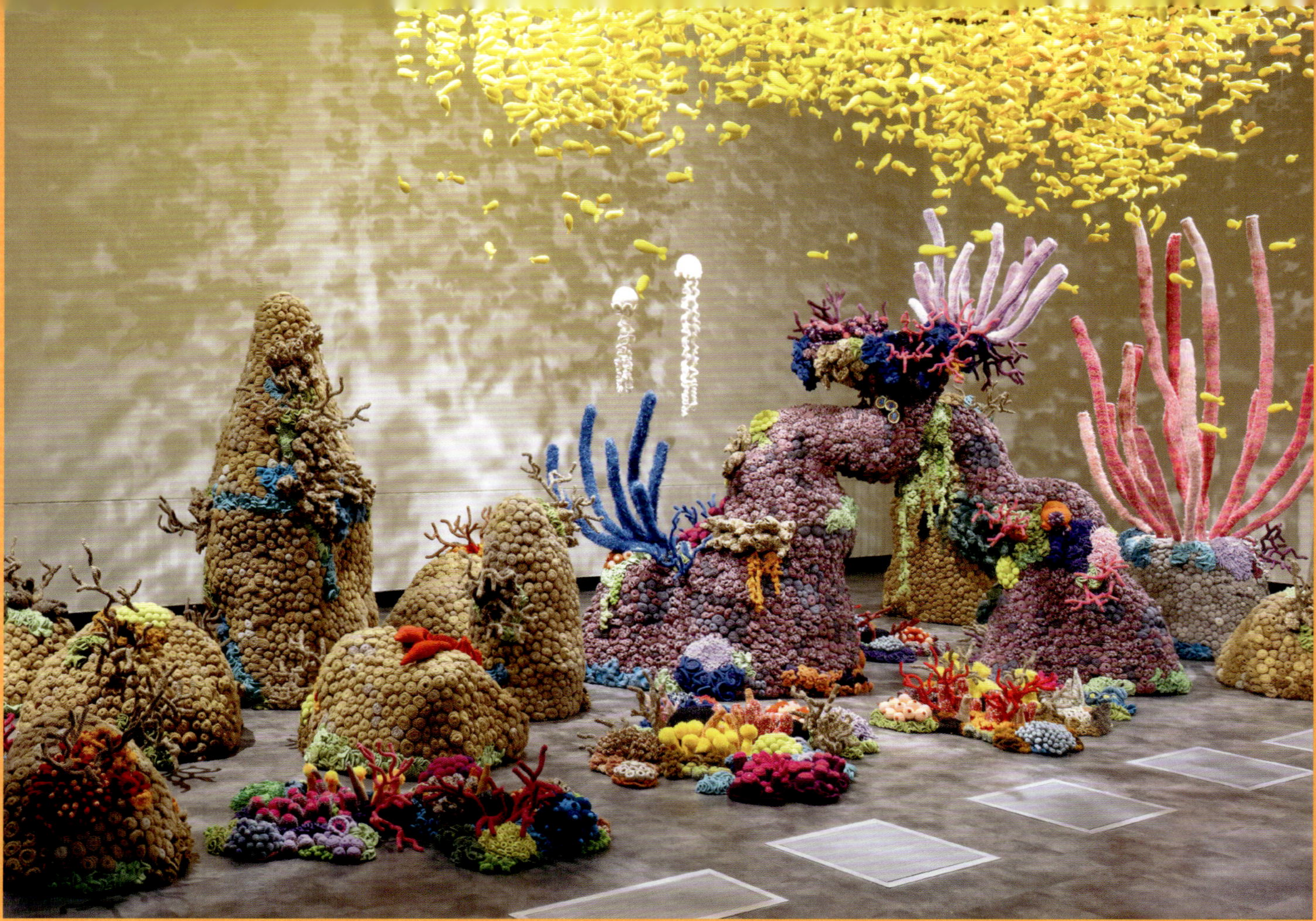

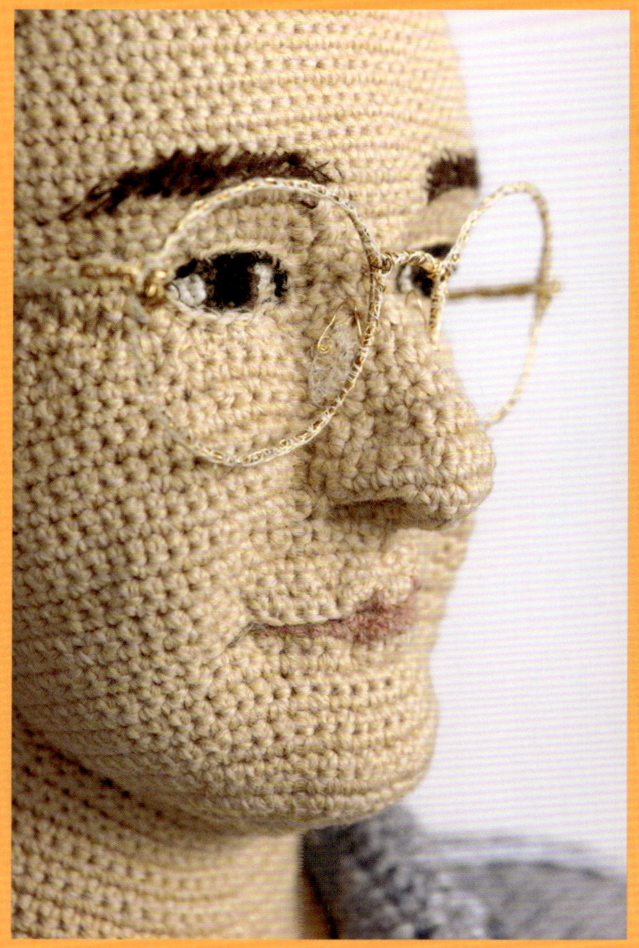

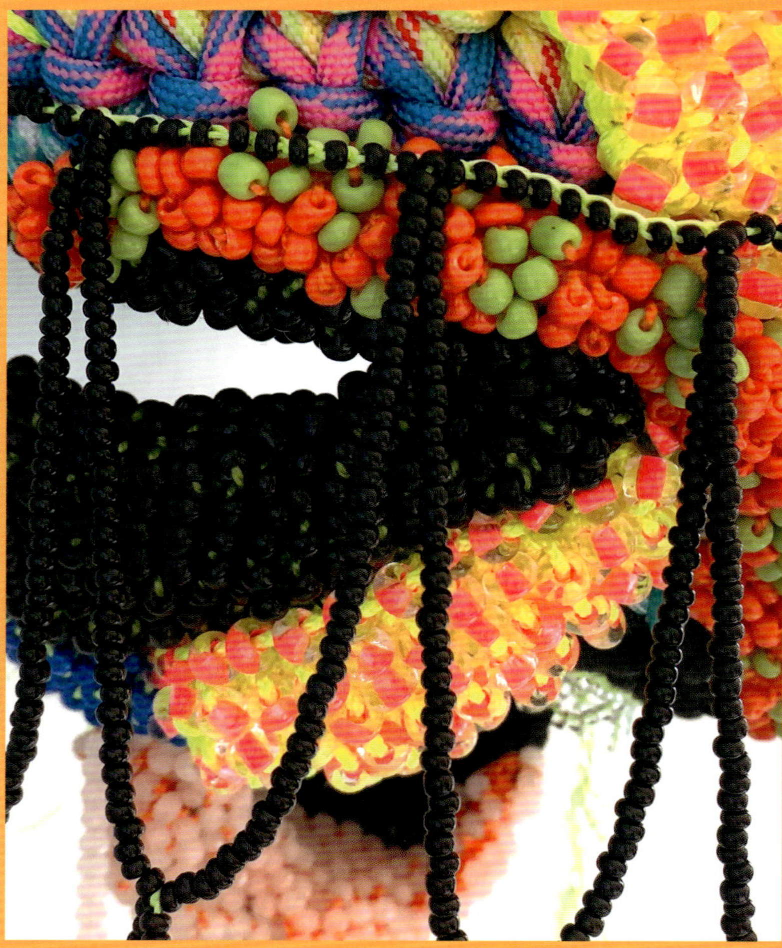

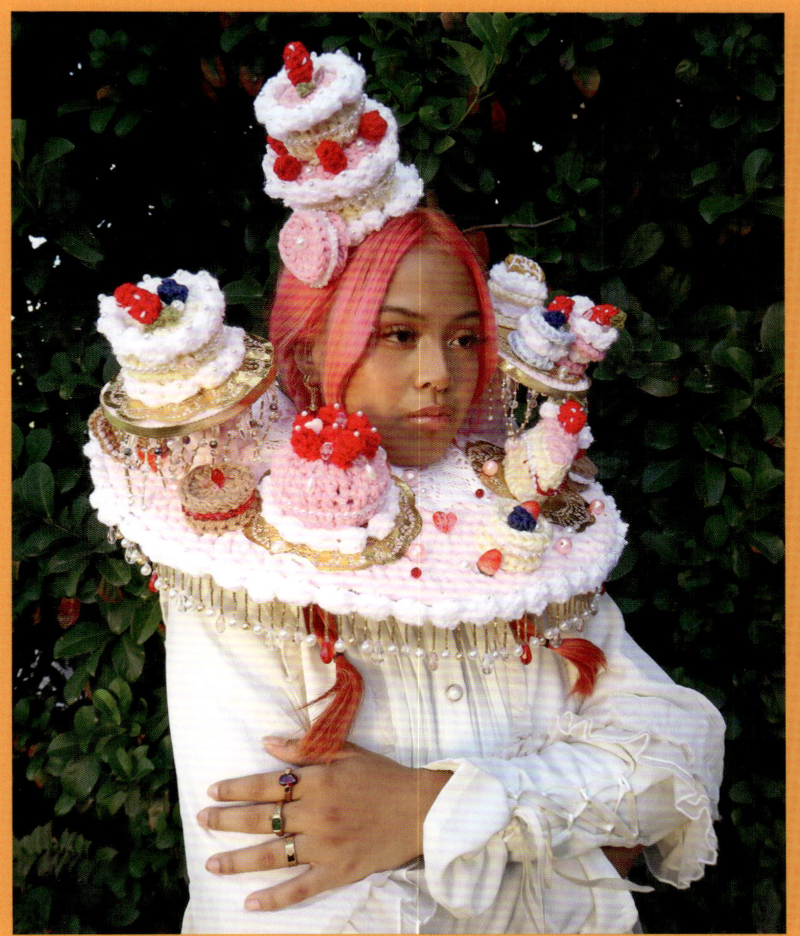

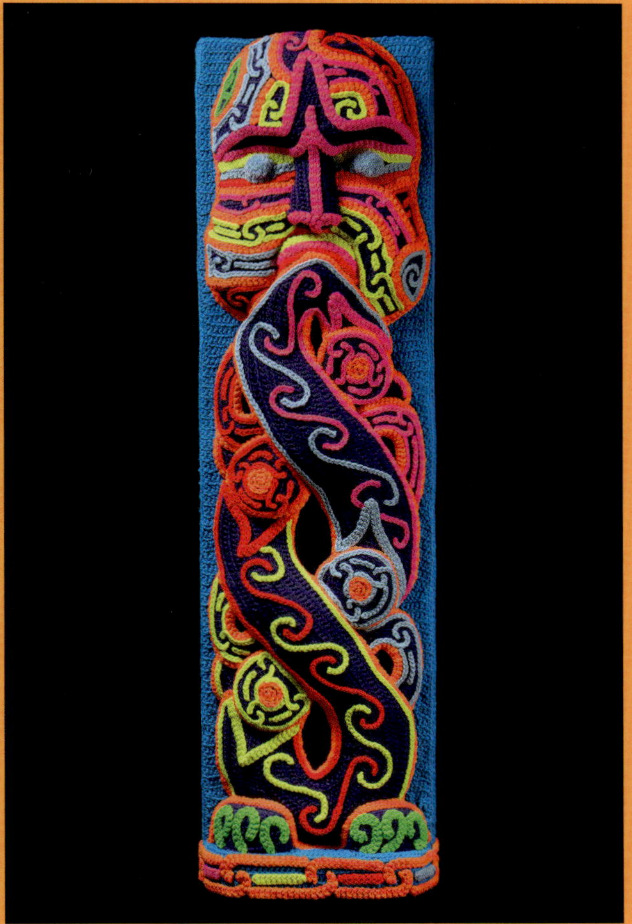

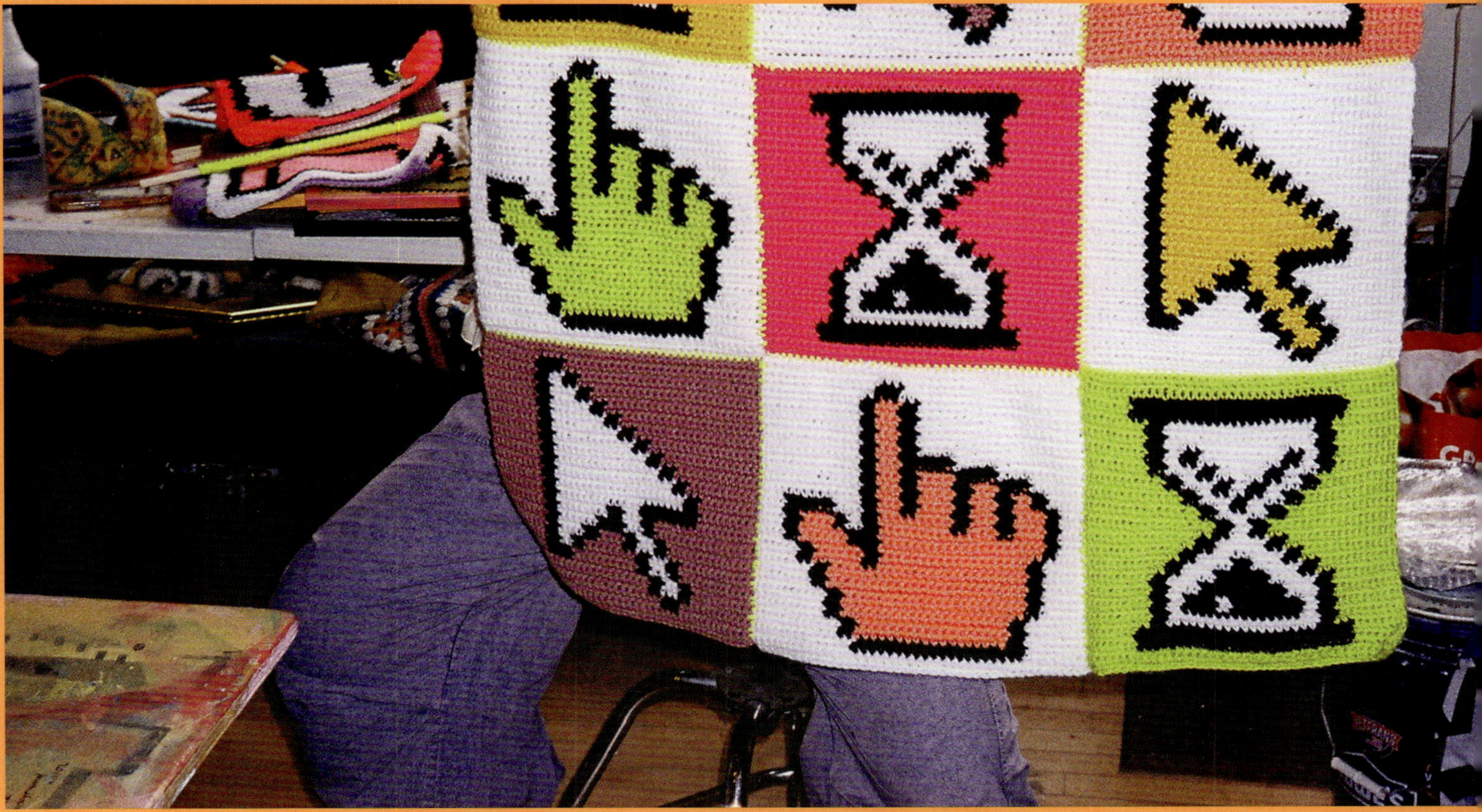

Artists clockwise from top left: Mulyana, Kat Leonardo, Lissy and Rudi Robinson-Cole, Nicole Nikolich, Omar Badrin, Liisa Hietanen

Baylee Schmitt

CINCINNATI

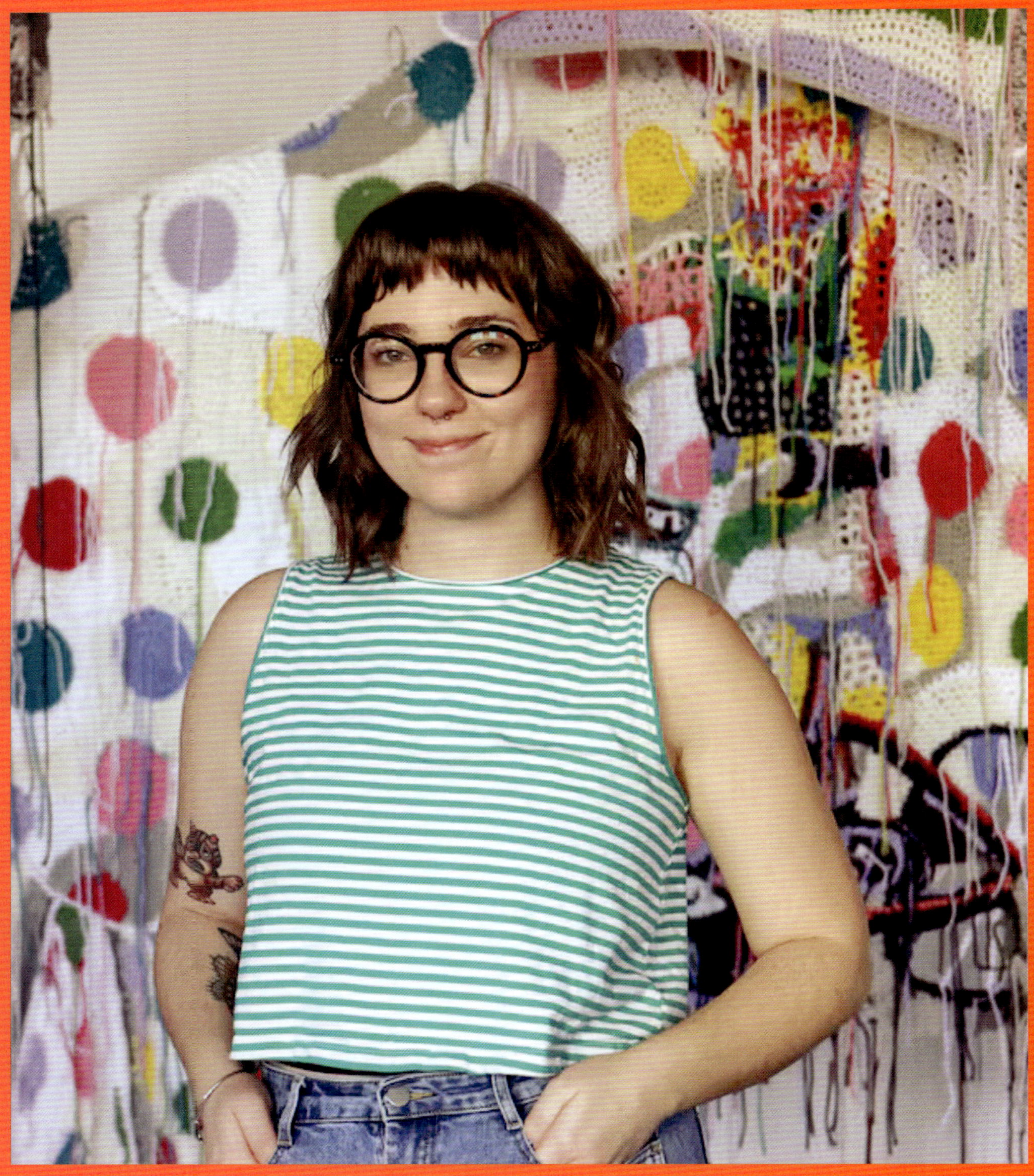

Baylee Schmitt grew up in a close-knit family in a small town in Ohio, USA – a place with "one stoplight, two gas stations, and a Subway". She is the only member of her family who has moved away, although her connection to home remains central to her creative process and art, which takes the form of crochet interpretations of her childhood memories. Schmitt reflects that "perhaps it comes down to taking the girl out of the small town but not the small town out of the girl. Perhaps it's harder to let go than I thought."

306 West Church St. (2022–23) is a life-sized interpretation of Schmitt's entire childhood home in yarn: an alternate soft world that acknowledges the minutiae that make up a life. While each crochet work is suspended from the ceiling as a flat piece, Schmitt creates the illusion of depth through layering – a process that further highlights the artifice of the scene. The goal here is not truthful replication, but instead an interpretation that acknowledges the murky lines between fantasy and memory, exacerbated by a distance from childhood. Schmitt explains that she used to work from family photos, but found this process too much of a "one-to-one copy". Nowadays when she makes her pieces, Schmitt deliberately does not look at old images or other source materials, choosing instead to rely entirely on her memories.

Crochet is an ideal medium for Schmitt to undertake this process of recollection through reconstruction; she initially began working with yarn and textiles after "becoming frustrated with photorealistic painting" and how it was beholden to the source material. By contrast, crochet's freeform capacity allows Schmitt to create an image from scratch, while also offering a "compelling way to complicate the act of making something". She describes the technique as akin to "engineering", her work forming from "a series of units that stack on top of each other". Crochet, considered in this way, is a form of worldbuilding that reflects Schmitt's own thoughts around "the way memories, relationships, and experiences seem to make up a person" when stitched together. This lateral thinking is reflected in Schmitt's finished works, which are built in the same way one might assemble flatpack furniture: piece by piece to create a whole.

Schmitt's crochet elevates the emotional memories contained within everyday objects through a process of personal identification and storytelling. In her subsequent series, *we settle into corners with the dust and mites* (2025), Schmitt turns her focus to the bedroom she shared with her twin sister. This intimate work encapsulates the artist's "practice of understanding myself in relation to my sister and our twinness". The focus here is on differences, as well as similarities, as shown through shared items and individual markers (such as an alphabet pillow for each sister). Within these crochet artefacts, a shared experience of childhood can also be viewed more broadly through references to pop culture, including a portrait of Jacob from *Twilight*. These cultural touchstones expand Schmitt's work beyond purely personal memories, to the social memories of a generation.

The poetic pathos of Schmitt's translation of the past into yarn is deepened through her choice of a labour-intensive process. This acknowledgement of labour is important for Schmitt, as she finds "immense satisfaction in the pure work of it": work that "requires intense involvement from beginning to end". By instilling this labour into her recreations – building up an image from a single stitch that clearly contains her hand – Schmitt instils each object with devotional love and care. This is a love and care that is, by extension, granted to her family and close ones. Considered in this way, Schmitt's work can be regarded not only as a self-portrait as told through the past, but as a love letter to her childhood years. ■

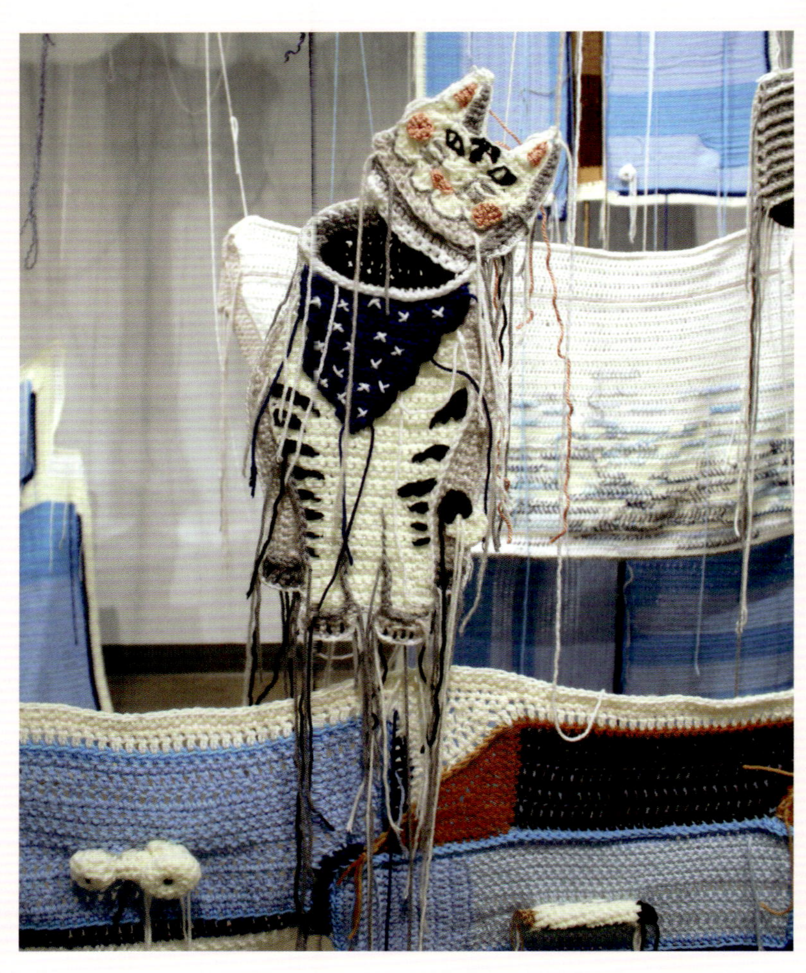

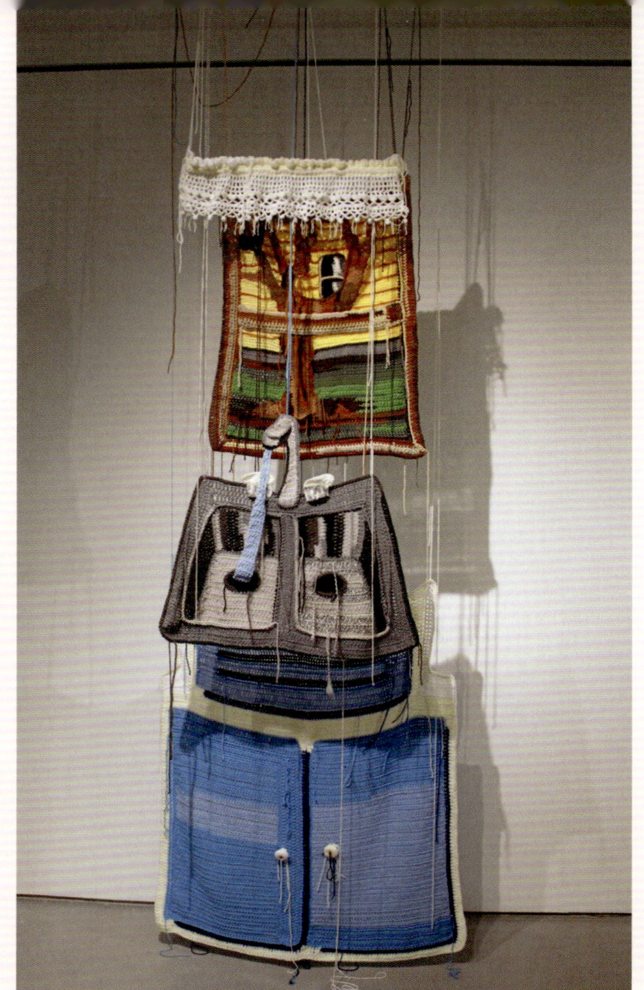

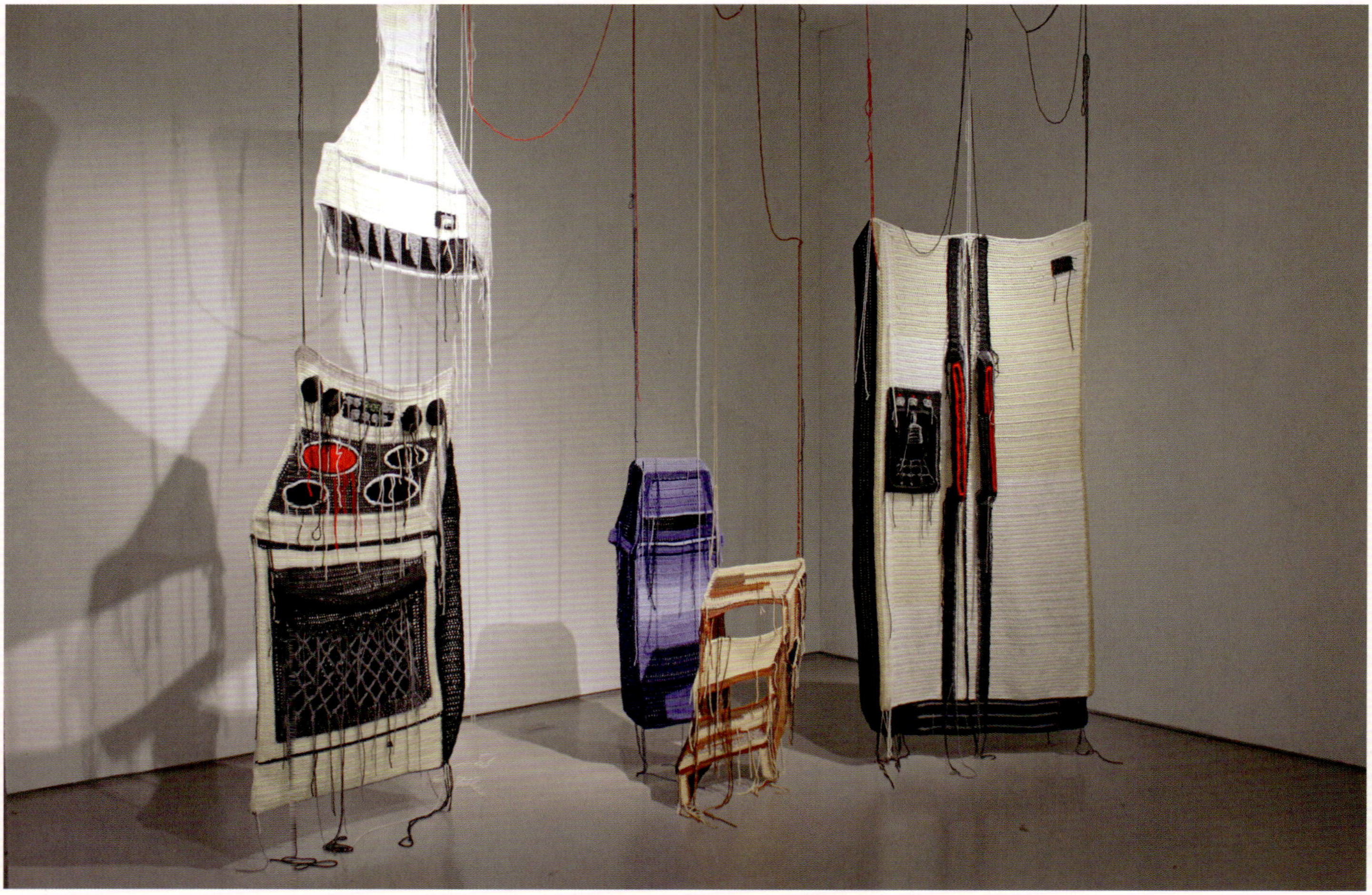

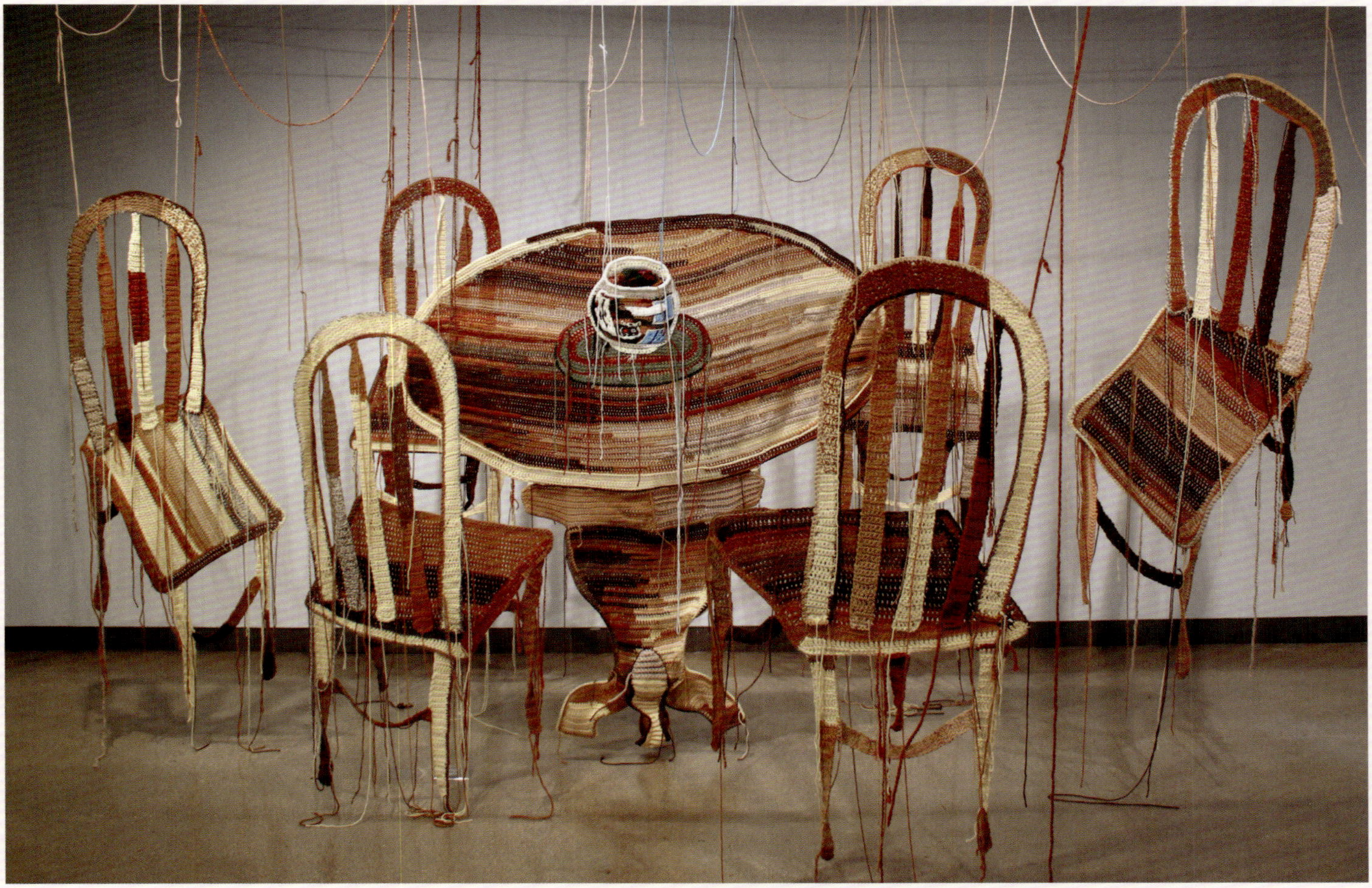

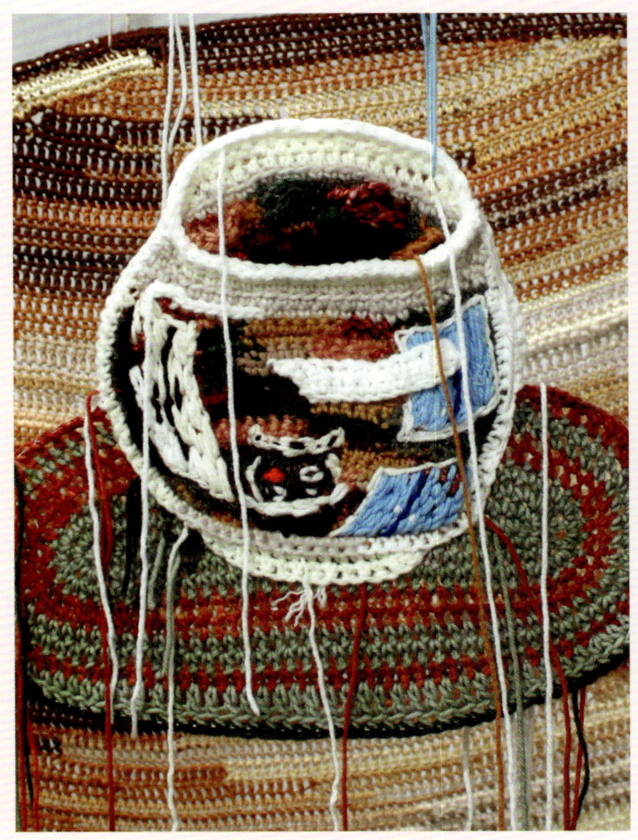

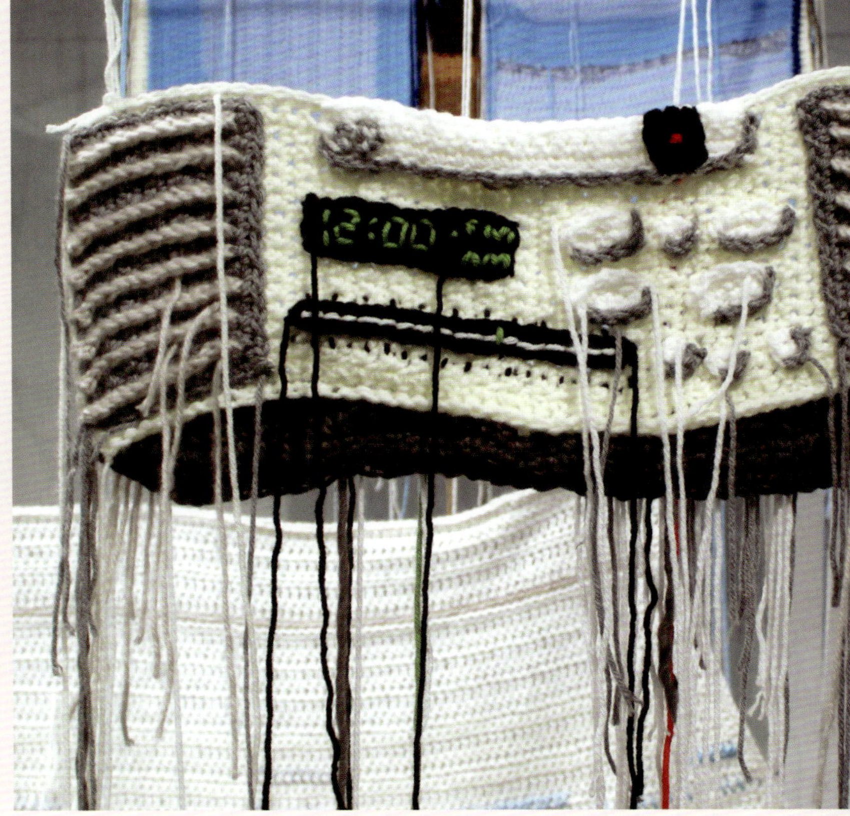

Opposite Clockwise from top left: *Cat Cookie Jar*, 2023, Crochet; *Perfect for sitting, but too tall to climb*, 2023, Crochet; *Supper Soon*, 2023, Crochet **This page** Clockwise from top left: *Oak Table and Chairs*, 2023, Crochet; *Radio*, 2023, Crochet; *Oak Table and Chairs* (detail)

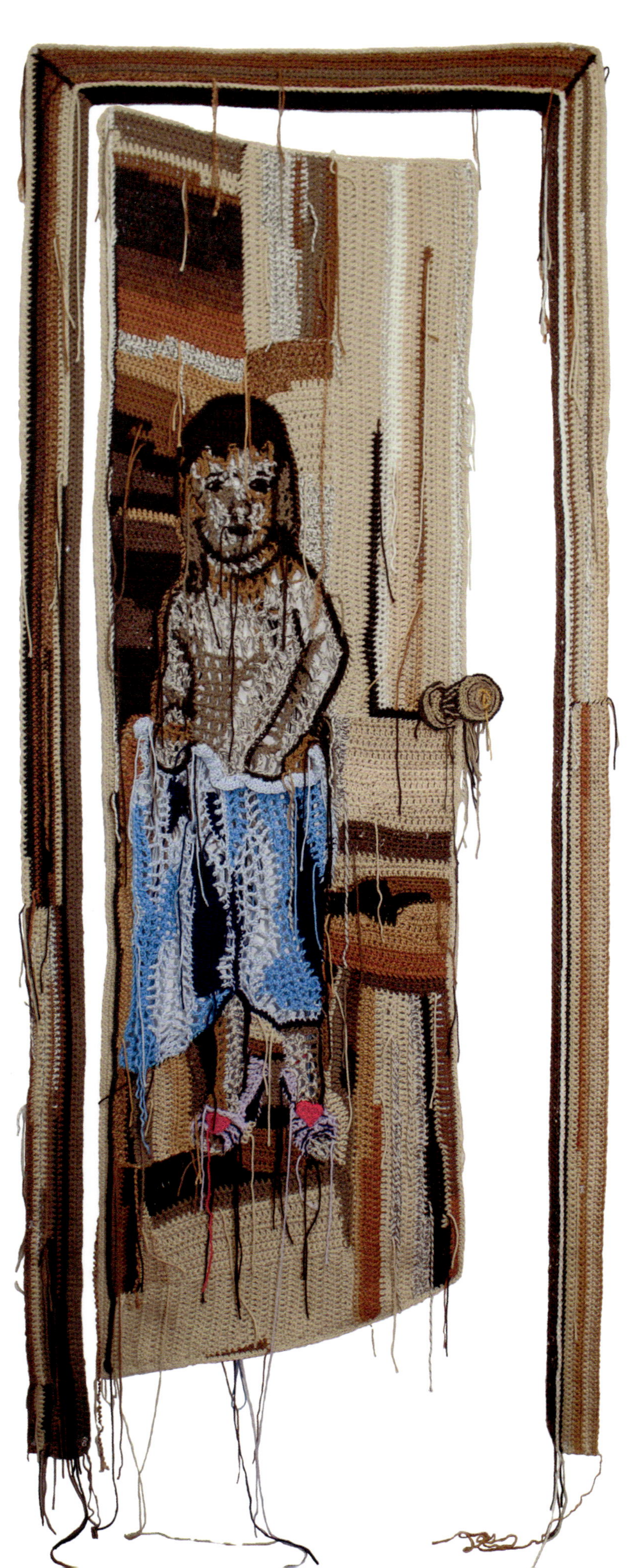

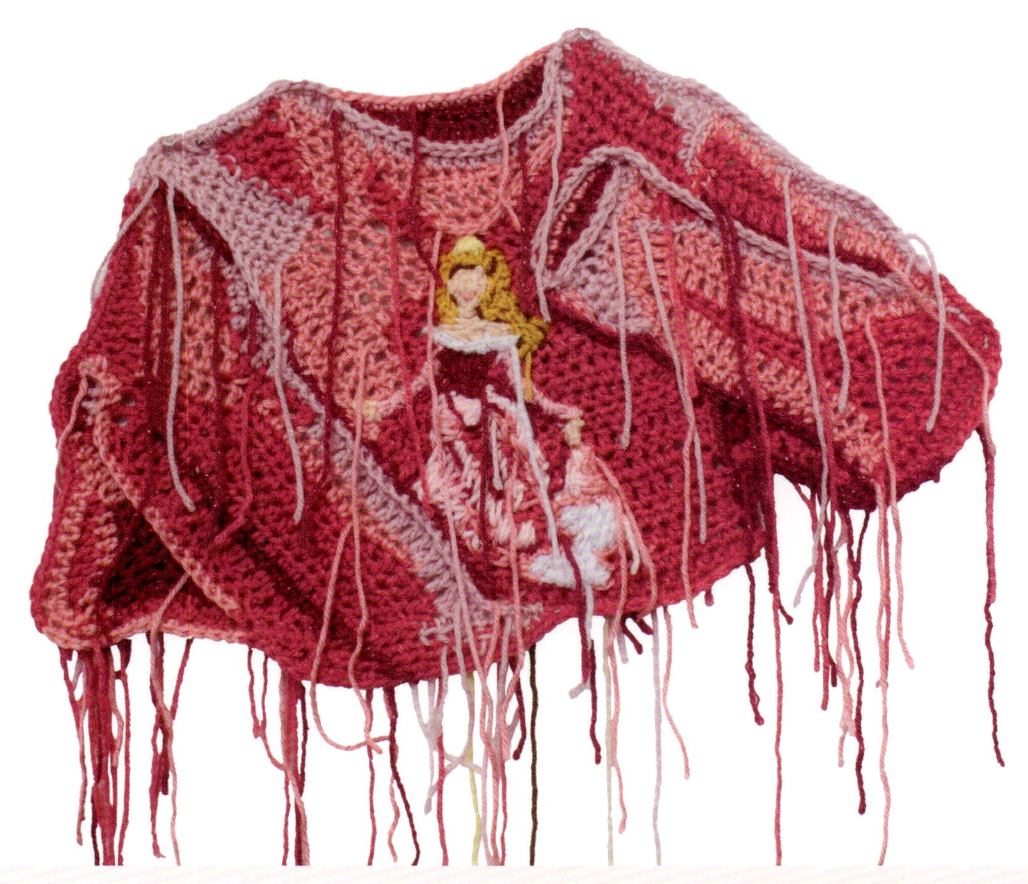

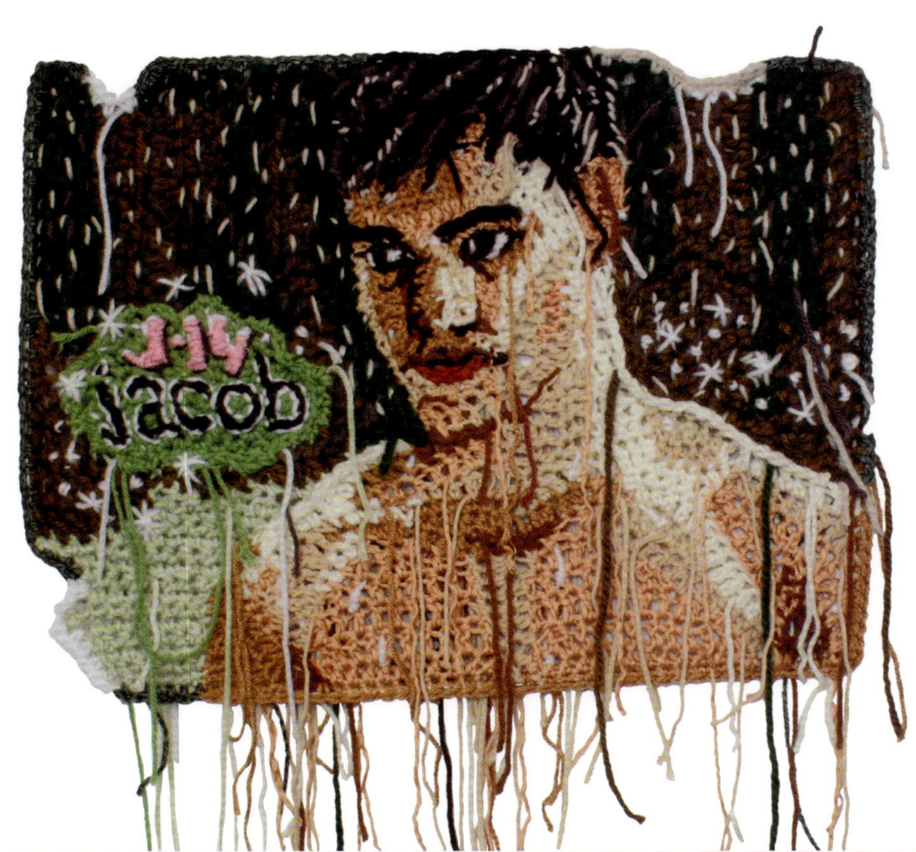

Opposite *Door B*, 2025, Crochet

This page Top: *Sleeping Beauty Sweater*, 2025, Crochet; Bottom: *We can't be friends anymore, Bella…*, 2025, Crochet

Beth Williams

LONDON

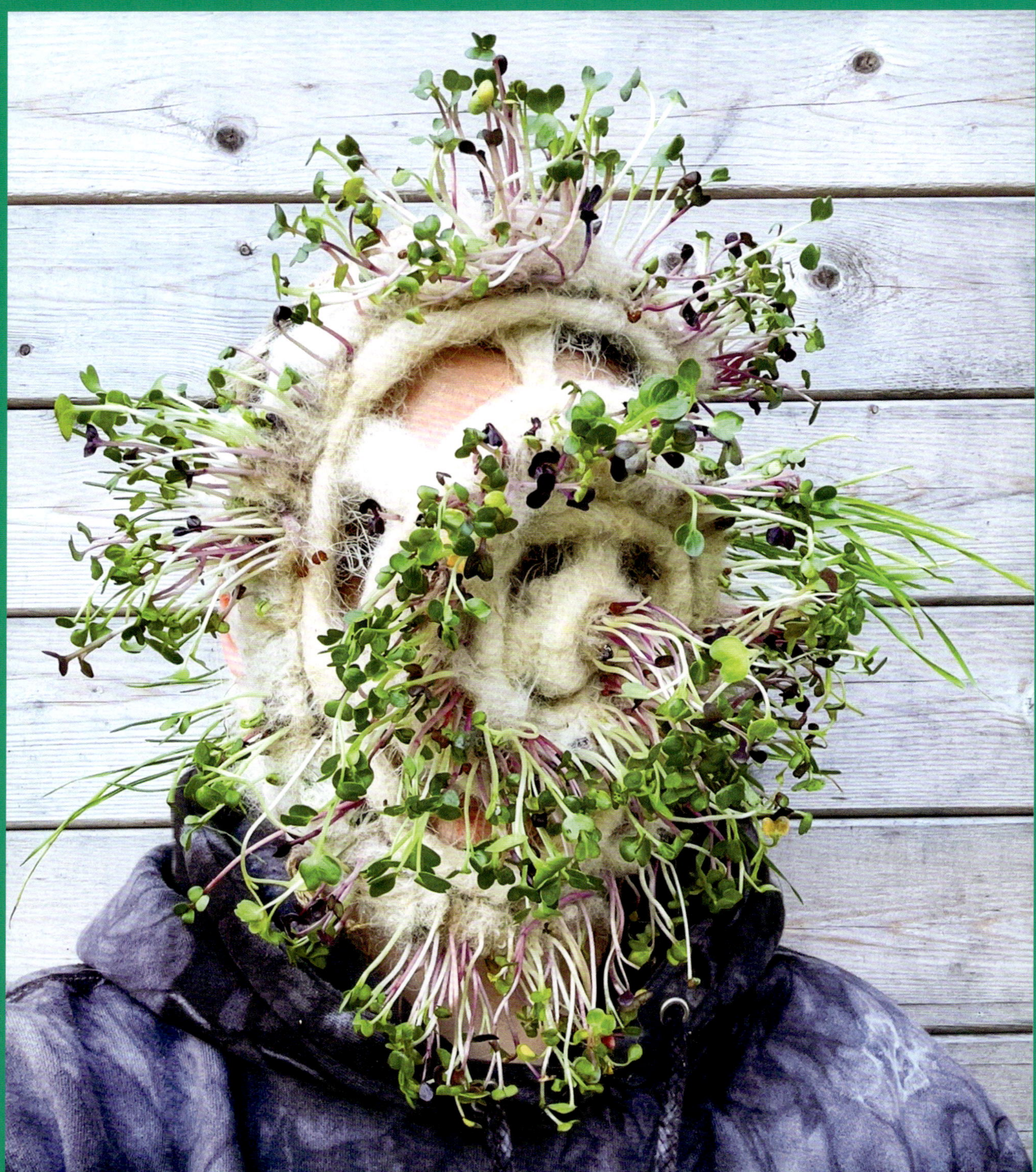

Beth Williams is an artist who works "in collaboration with nature" to make what they call "living textiles" that grow and change over time, with the help of living bio matter. Williams' shift to a sustainability-minded approach was driven by their growing frustrations at the excess, exclusivity and wastefulness of the fashion industry, as well as their experience of "living in an inaccessible world" as a disabled person. By creating textiles that naturally decompose, mitigating their environmental impact, Williams seeks to produce works that "make humans rethink their relationship with nature and create a sense of awe".

Williams was initially drawn to fashion because it's a "language everyone understands and can relate to". The use of textiles across "many histories, cultures, and politics" means these materials have an ongoing relatability and power to communicate to different audiences. However, Williams describes their time studying fashion at university as disillusioning, in large part because of the industry's inaccessibility for disabled people. But while they were studying, Williams encountered the historical use of wool in 19th-century England "as both mulch and compost" in agriculture. This discovery led the artist to consider the relationship between yarn and compost, and how to create a "growable yarn" that is then crocheted or knitted into living artworks. The resulting pieces grow alongside the artist, changing appearance and form: a process that Williams calls both "enlightening and terrifying".

The production of living textiles involves the careful combination of a fibre, a seed and different propagation techniques. Williams arrived at their process following extensive trial and error while testing methods and materials: "Usually it takes a lot of sampling to find the right combo, but I really enjoy the experimentation." To get started, the artist had to grow their own dye and fibre plants, including Japanese indigo, Hopi sunflowers, dyer's coreopsis, calendula, marigolds and scabiosa black knight, as well as learn how to process raw materials and spin different yarns. This was followed by trialling seed propagation using different natural fibres (among them, silk, plant fibre and wool) to see what sprouts and grows over time, creating the artist's own ecosystem of textile fibres. This process of testing and experimentation is ongoing, which means Williams' pieces continue to evolve, each unique but with a finite usable period ranging from a few weeks to a few years.

Each piece by Williams explores different ways to construct growing, changeable garments, capturing the circular design process of soil-to-soil textiles that connects the pieces to the earth that they came from. *In Compost Vest* (2023), Williams knitted a top with pockets that they filled with growable paper, which sprouted over time, turning the piece into a field of green. *Life is Like Compost* (2023) is a freeform garment created from hand-spun and hand-dyed

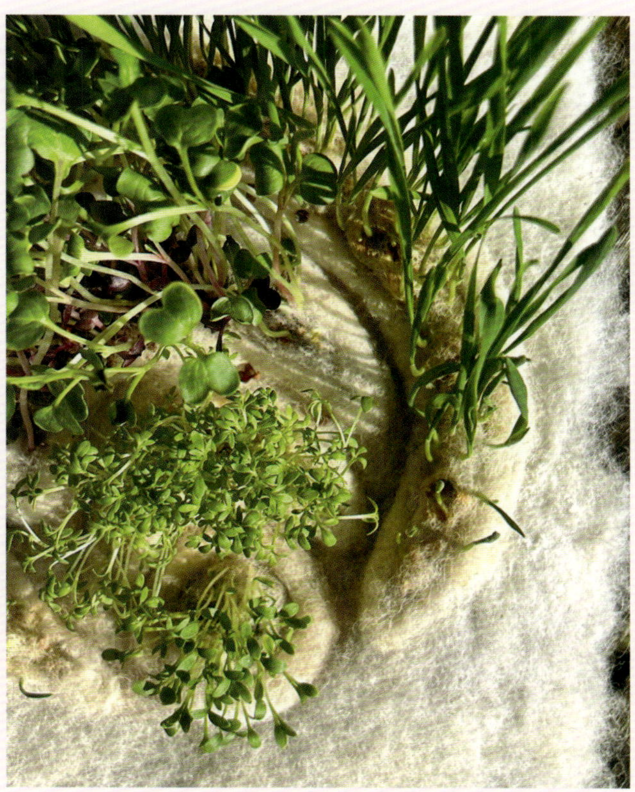

Opposite *Uzumaki's Mask*, 2023, Crochet and plant propagation **This page** *Survivor's Offering*, 2023, Needle felting and plant propagation

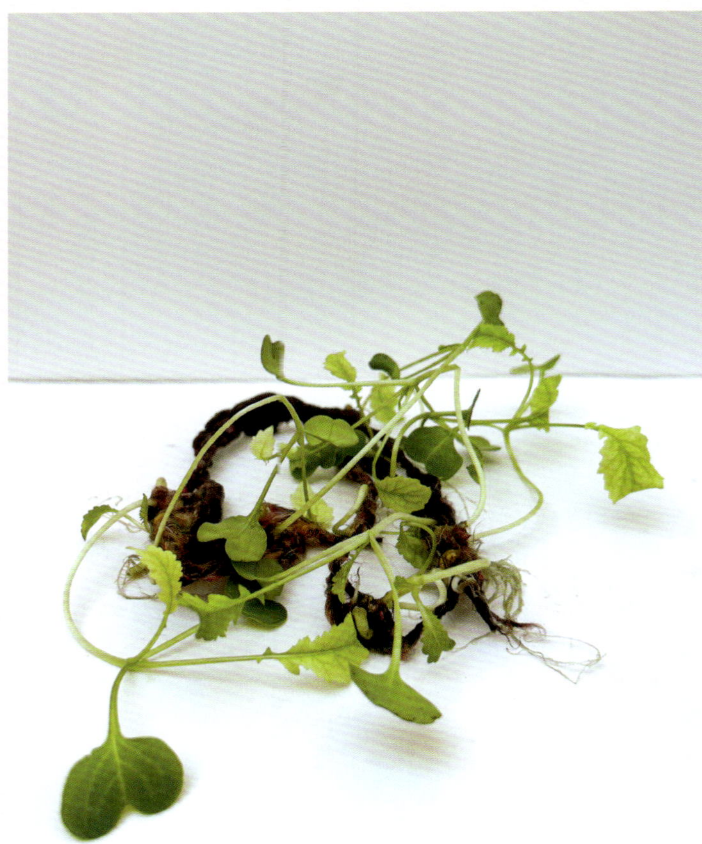

lotus fibre. The letters that form the piece (which spell out *Life is Like Compost*) provide a home for pink oyster mushrooms to grow, transforming the work into an embodiment of its title. *Uzumaki's World* (2023), meanwhile, is a series inspired by the horror manga by Junji Ito; these pieces feature plants propagated on spiral-shaped substrates. Whereas Ito's spirals are a symbol of horror, Williams' reference the cyclical nature of the environment.

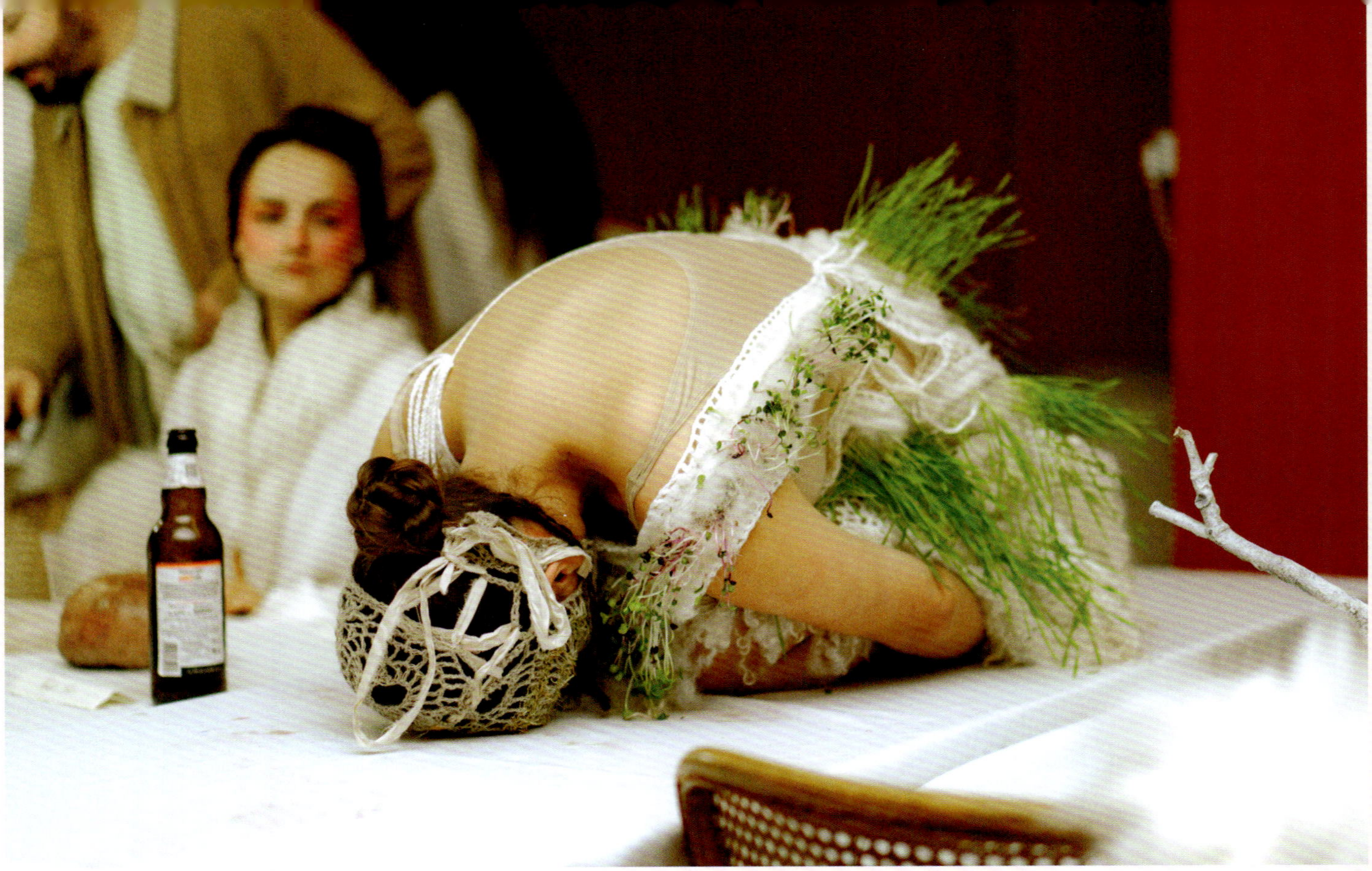

Williams' work raises pertinent questions about accessibility and sustainability in fashion – instead of privileging only the human experience, their garments "provide an environment for non-human life to thrive". Because of their nature, these pieces are short-lived, which Williams recognises creates a contradiction position: "Is the most accessible piece of clothing… entirely inaccessible to all?" Williams seeks, through their work, to make "people feel seen, especially other disabled artists or anyone else who has faced barriers within the industry". There is hope embedded in Williams' art, which draws attention to both the fragility and beauty of nature, and which challenges capitalist ideas of value and output. ■

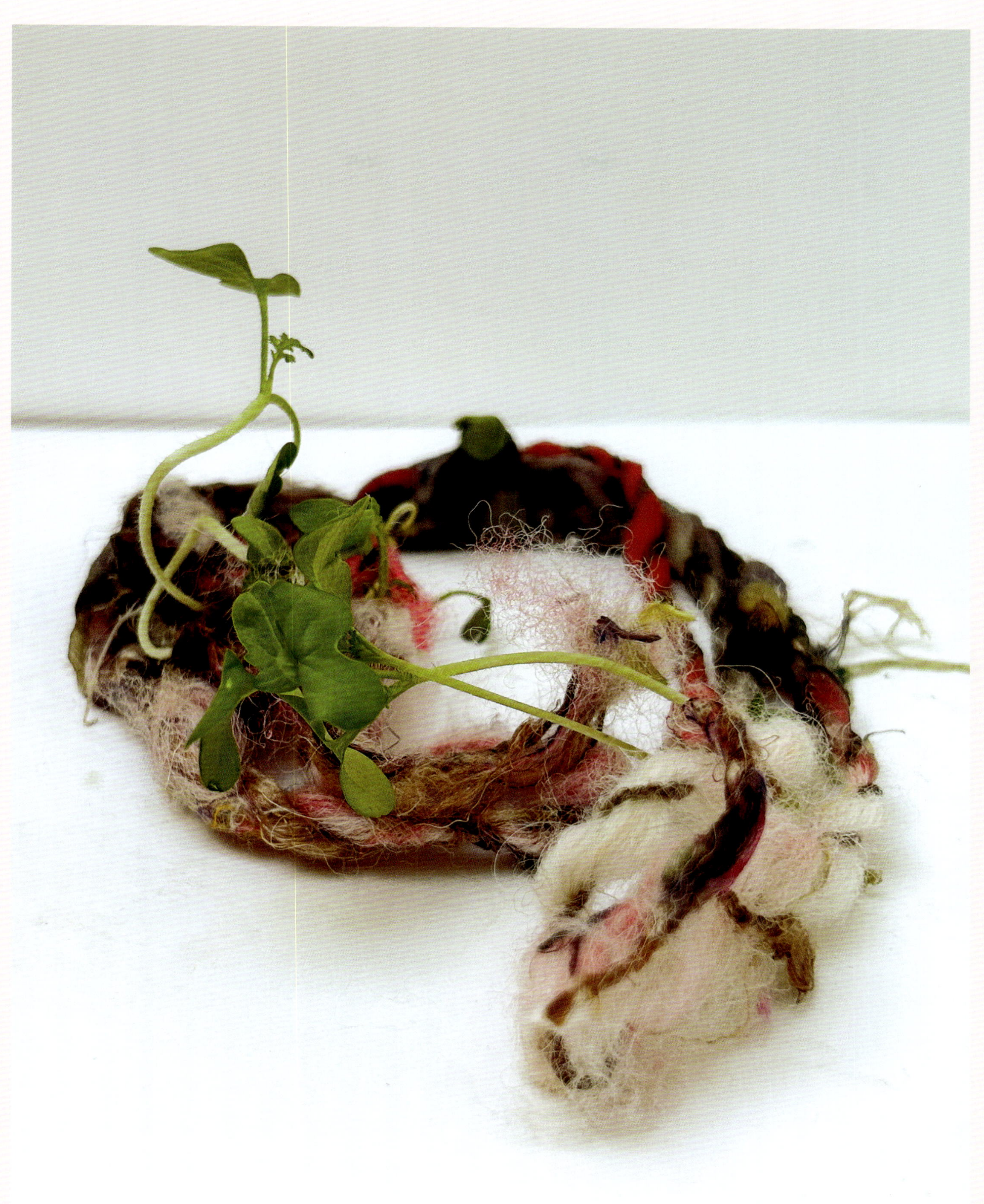

Opposite Top: *Twin Two*, 2023, Crochet and plant propagation; Bottom: *Handspun silk yarn with mustard seed*, 2022, Plant propagation **This page** *Handspun wool yarn with radish seed*, 2022, Plant propagation

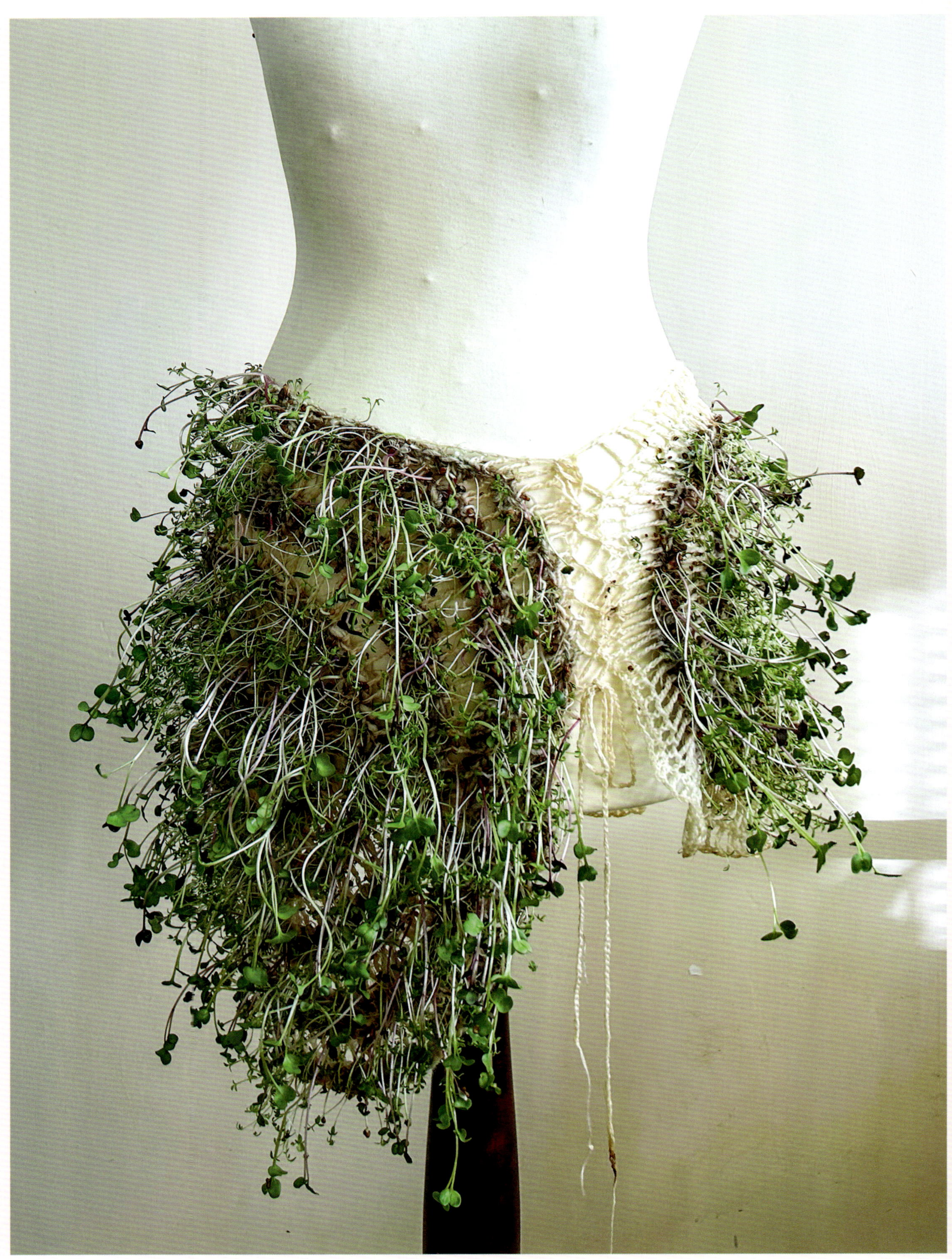

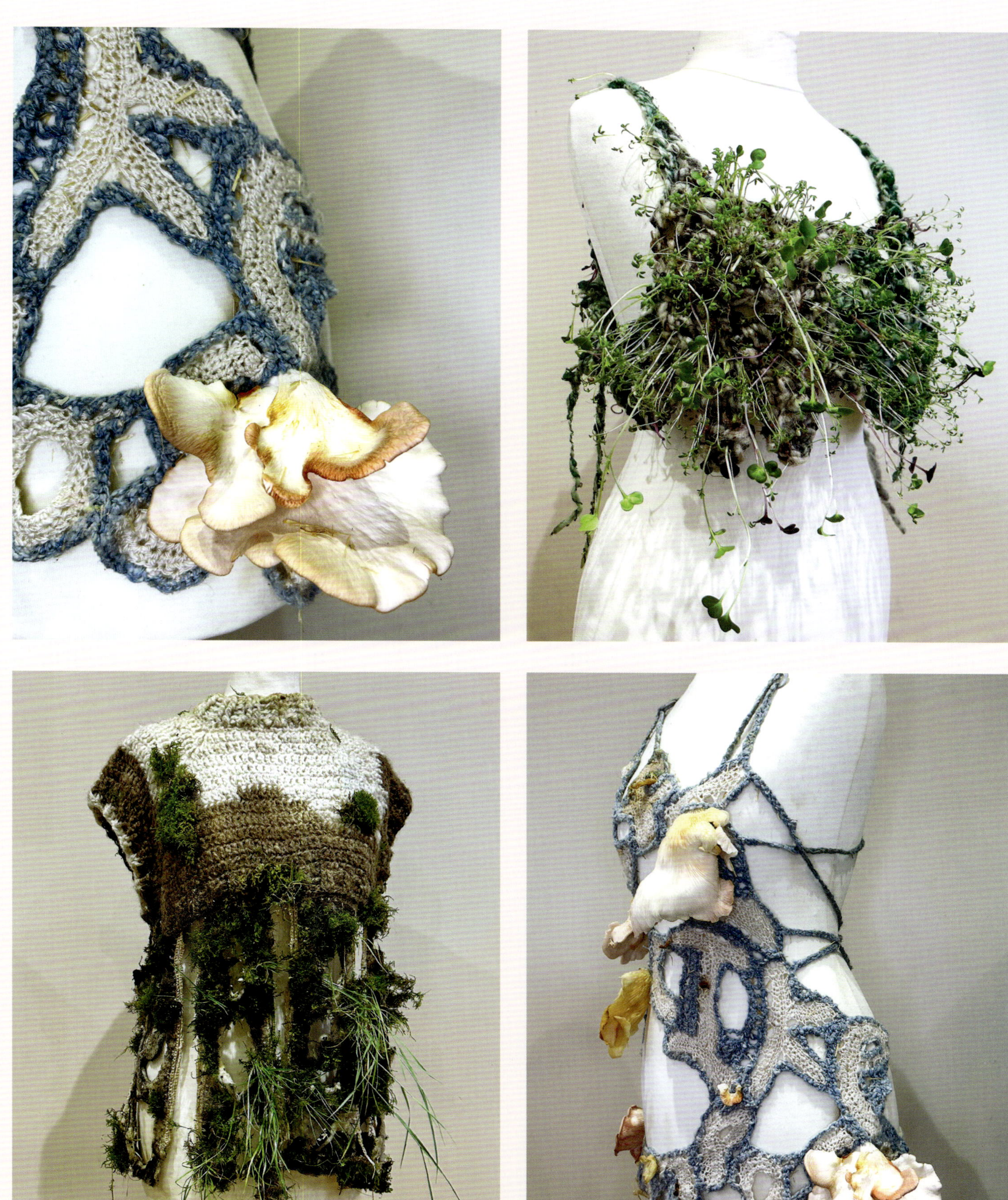

Opposite *Uzumaki's Skirt*, 2023, Crochet and and plant propagation **This page** Clockwise from top left: *Life is Like Compost* (detail), 2023, Crochet and plant propagation; *Hands Top*, 2022, Crochet and plant propagation; *Life is Like Compost*; *Nature Breaks the Code*, 2024, Crochet, felting and plant propagation

Blake Ballard

DENVER

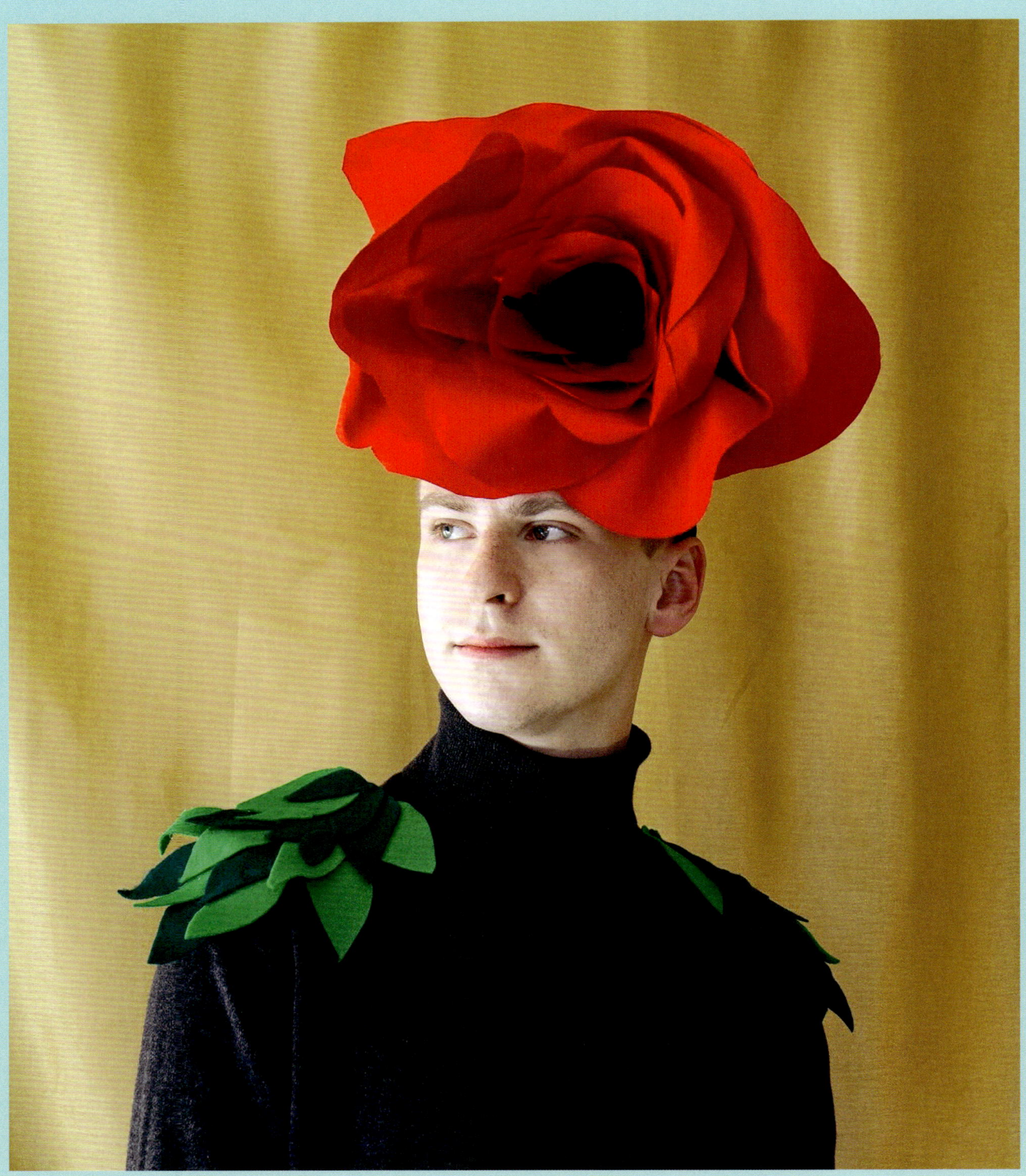

Blake Ballard continues a matrilineal tradition of crochet in his family. He first learnt the technique as a child from his mother, who learnt from her grandmother. Growing up in rural America, his home brimmed with crochet objects crafted by family members bearing religious or cultural significance, including prayer doilies and angel Christmas tree toppers made of starched yarn. Central among these was a crochet filet doily made by his mother bearing the family surname that has hung on the living room wall for decades, where it still features today.

While Ballard recognises that family history has influenced his thinking, he is also interested in the "complex narratives that craft can bring to any art practice". In particular, he is interested in using craft methods and techniques to "investigate the innocuous connections textiles have to colonialism, white supremacy, and Christian conservatism", recognising that politics is an inherent part of crochet's past and present. For Ballard, this means first engaging critically with crochet's usage, and then transforming the medium as a tool to convey "inclusivity, hope, and equity".

Underneath the Antimacassar (2024) is one work in which Ballard grapples with the relationship between textiles and politics. It was inspired by his interest and research into the antimacassar, a crochet doily originating in Victorian-era England, typically placed on upholstered furniture to protect the fabric from men's hair oil. While this doily appears innocuous, during his research, Ballard learnt of the historical connection between the Macassar oil used in men's hair in 18th- and 19th-century Europe and the Dutch's colonisation of Indonesia; access to ingredients from Makassar led to Europeans producing the hair oil. This, in turn, led to the invention of the doily. Ballard's work casts a critical look at this history, complete with hand-embroidered text that poetically responds to the colonial legacy.

Beyond this piece, text appears as a crucial component across many of Ballard's works, with a number created through filet crochet. This centuries-old technique uses a grid-like structure, consisting of "open" and "solid" squares, to form a design; while these designs were traditionally mapped out on graph paper by hand, online graphing tools like the one used by Ballard are available today to fulfil this task.

No Place Like Home (2021) is among the first large-scale text pieces Ballard created with this technique. A queer ode to the *Wizard of Oz*, the work was created by the artist during a time of personal change and upheaval, when he sought a sense of belonging "no matter the location or circumstance". The work pays homage to the actress Judy Garland as a gay icon, and the queer subtext of Dorothy's escape from small-town Kansas to the technicolour Oz. The phrase "friends of Dorothy" was used colloquially in the United States in the mid-20th century by gay men to covertly identify each other. Many decades later, Ballard's large doily bearing the words "No Place Like Home" links the artist's personal experiences to this queer legacy, emphasising the importance of forming communities and belonging.

While invested in the histories of craft, Ballard does not just work with the traditional materials. His project *Who Sets the Ground Rules?* (2023–ongoing) translates vintage crochet patterns, found in his family's pattern library, into large-scale floor chalk drawings akin to hopscotch patterns. These crochet patterns are a set of pre-established rules, which produce repeated results from the past if followed. By placing the crochet instructions on the floor, and inviting viewers to smear and smudge these chalk lines, "the ground becomes a contested location where walkers are negotiating their role". In this way, Ballard's works ask viewers to "engage with their present role in society", and to consider the ways we all uphold "systems and structures that guide our life".

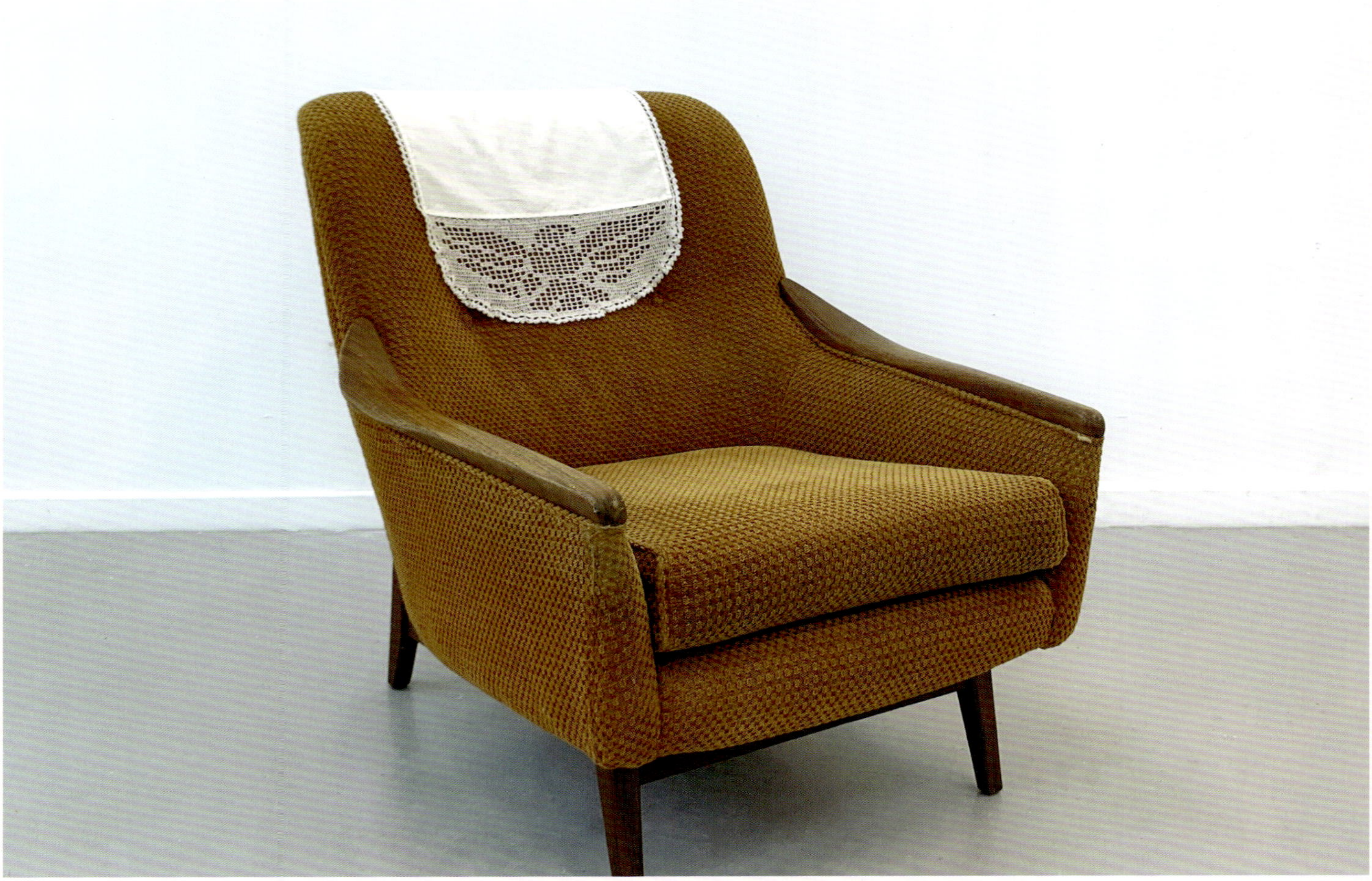

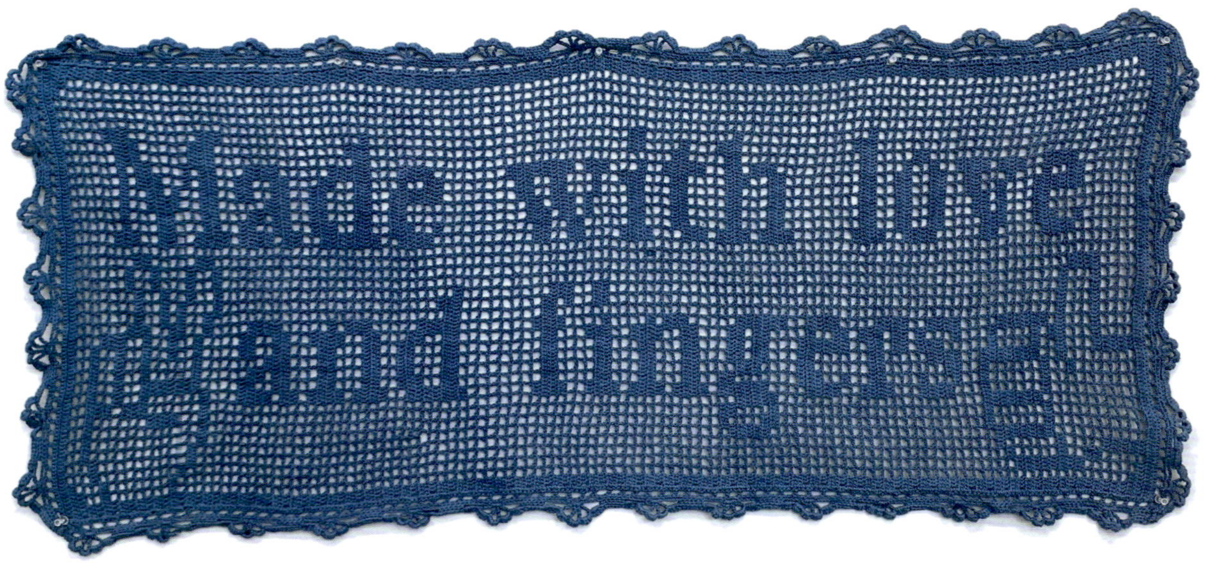
Made with love
and fingers

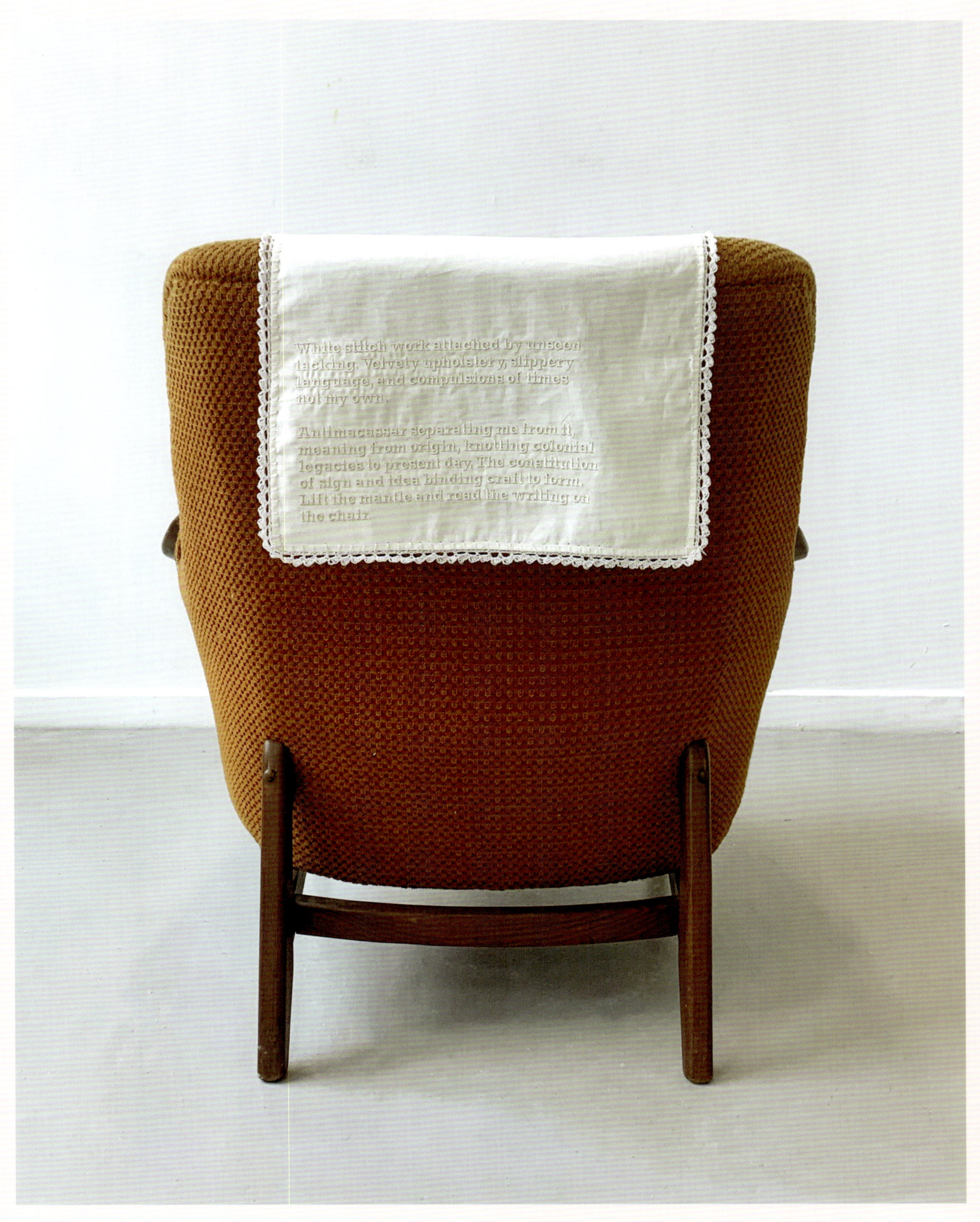

Opposite Top: *Underneath the Antimacassar*, 2024, Crochet and embroidery; Bottom: *Made with Love and Fingers*, 2023, Filet crochet **This page** *Underneath the Antimacassar*

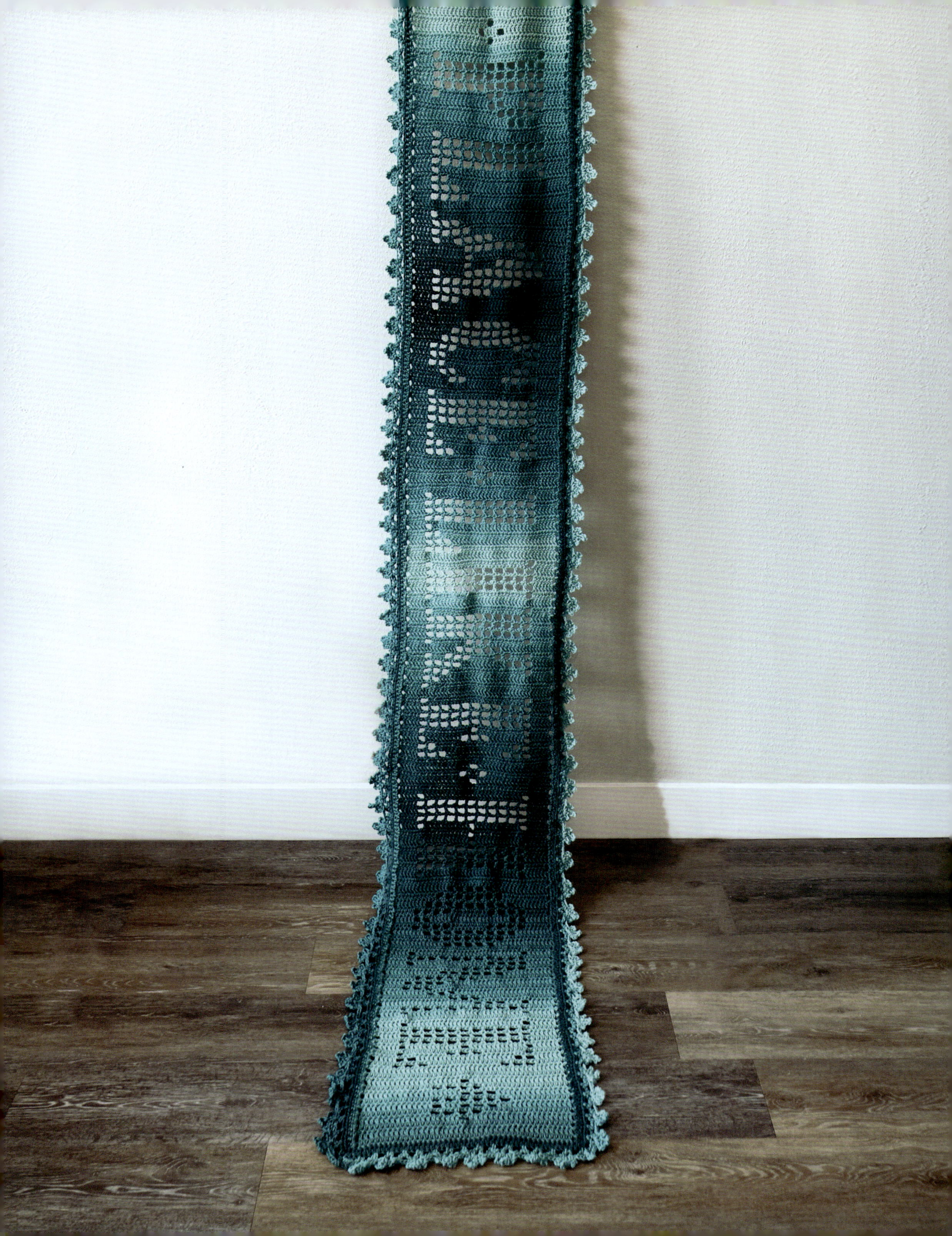

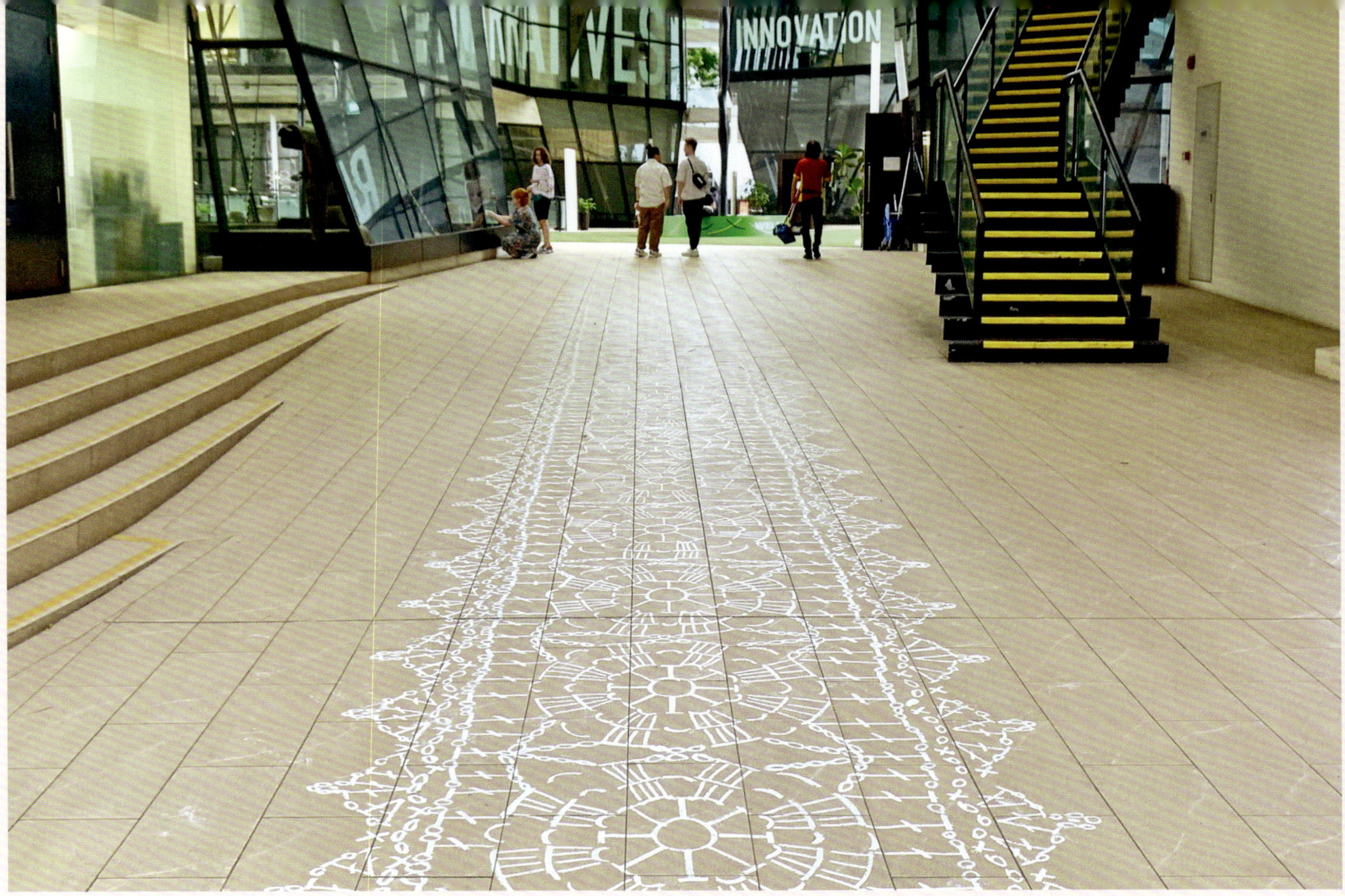

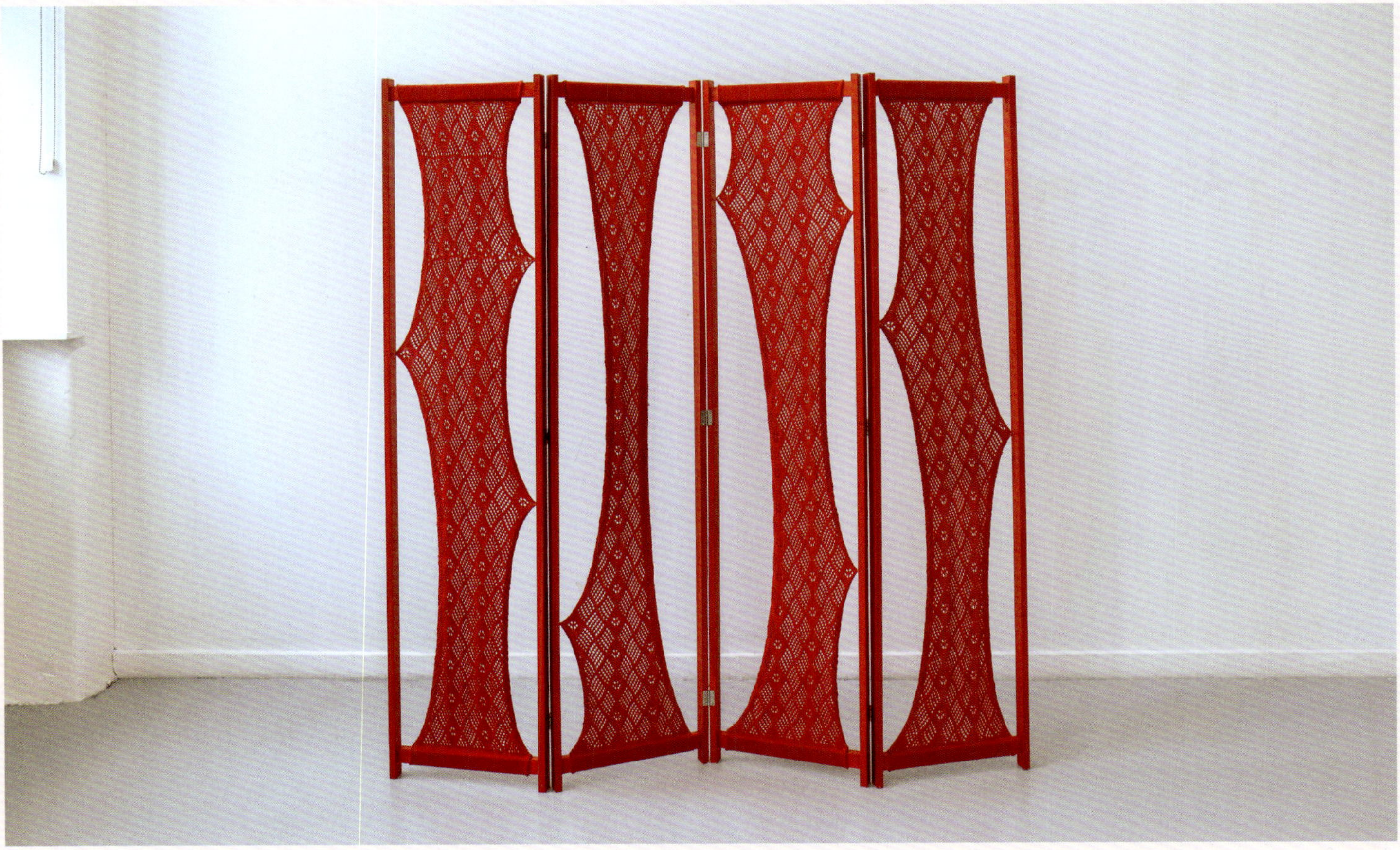

Opposite *No Place Like Home*, 2021, Filet crochet
This page Top: *Who Sets the Ground Rules?*, 2023, Chalk drawing; Bottom: *See-through*, 2023, Hand-knitting

Kat Leonardo

GADIGAL COUNTRY/SYDNEY

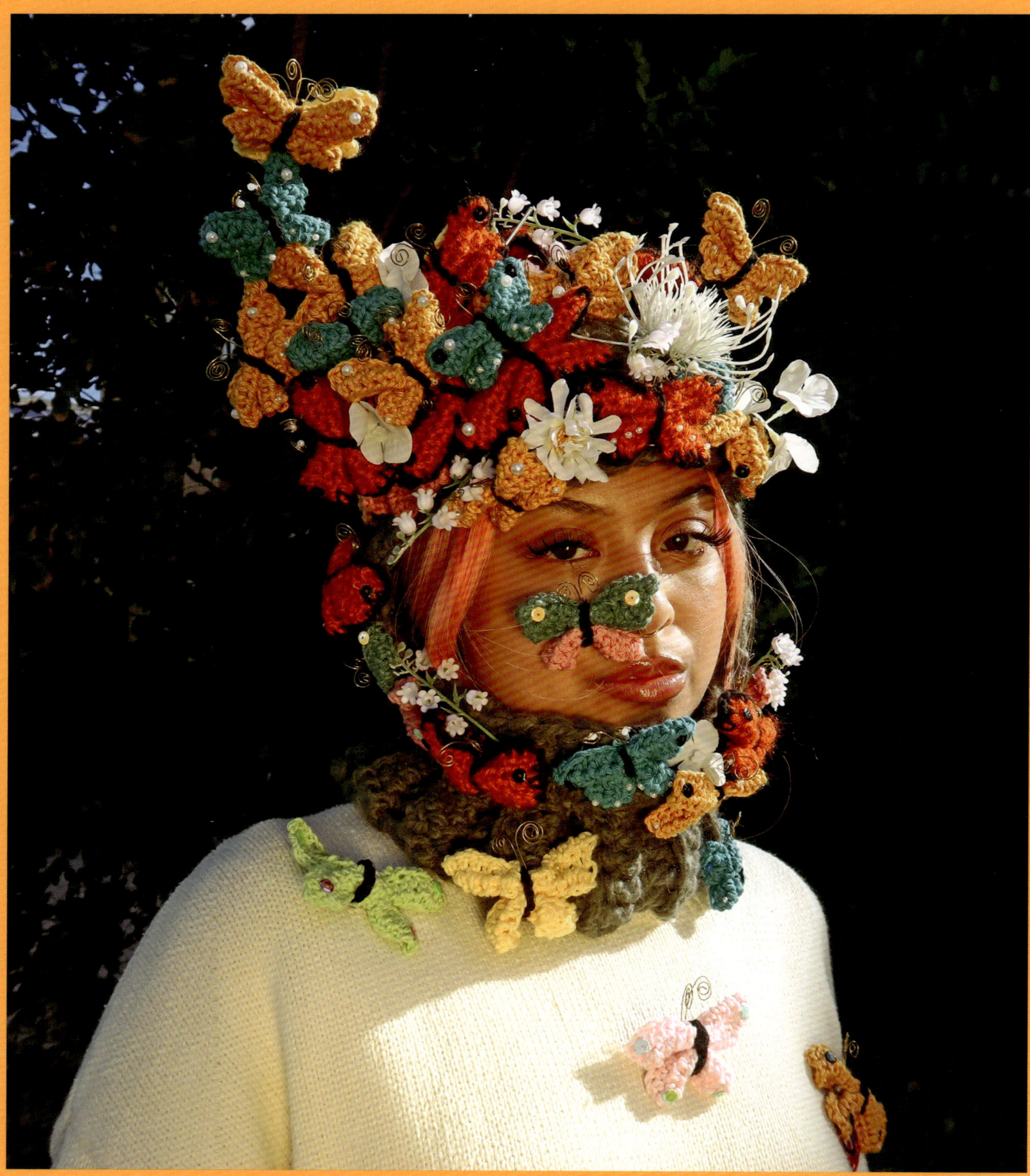

Kat Leonardo, who works under the artist name tataykatelyn, is known for her wearable crochet pieces that combine functionality with extravagant and fantastical design elements. This includes crochet covers for headphones, sculptural headpieces, balaclavas and parasol covers, as well as head-to-toe ensembles. She seeks to "make obscure, inconvenient objects" that have the "sole purpose of being beautiful". The goal is not for these objects to be practical: she hopes, instead, for her works to get "a second glance" from viewers.

Like many other people looking for ways to keep their mind and hands busy during the height of pandemic lockdowns, Leonardo started to crochet. Her quick adoption of this medium follows a creative upbringing and prior forays into a variety of different creative pursuits including "painting, drawing, rug tufting, knitting, candle making, and more". Crochet, however, was the medium that stuck around. Leonardo cites the ongoing influence of her two grandmothers as women who are both "quite versed when it comes to textiles, in terms of sewing, knitting and crocheting. Both were from the Philippines; one was a seamstress working in a factory, and the other was always seen knitting when I was younger."

Today, these familial influences shape Leonardo's crochet, one of her grandmothers continuing to teach her stitches she's "never heard of". Leonardo uses a number of basic crochet stitches – half-double crochet, double crochet and triple crochet – finding they form a "great foundation" that can be adopted for a variety of needs. Depending on the individual complexity of a piece, it may go through a prototype process; this might involve creating a solid, supportive structure using wire, or testing functional structure and form.

One of the most striking aspects about Leonardo's crochet is its ability to challenge the limits of our perception and the possibilities of the medium. In *Ferris Wheel* (2025), she has incorporated motorised elements as well as fairy lights to replicate the movements of a ferris wheel, which gives the resulting work a whimsy and life-like appearance. *Knight Armour* (2024) uses the soft fibres of acrylic yarn to create a piece of armour – complete with a helmet. While armour's functionality relies on its tough materials to protect the wearer, Leonardo's soft interpretation draws attention to the decorative surfaces and how they follow the shapes of the body.

Leonardo is drawn to the "unlimited amount of ideas and potential" of crocheting. She regards her working process, in which she experiments with yarn and shape to create a sculpture, as akin to "figuring out a puzzle", and shares that it's highly rewarding to see an "idea in your head come to fruition with your hands", sometimes exceeding her initial ideas or concepts. On the expansiveness of her creative vision, Leonardo cites the influence of drag queens, naming Violet Chachki, Raja Gemini and Plastique Tiara as her favourite artists. She finds inspiration in drag's pioneering elements, sharing that it "is such a beautiful art form that it is so limitless in its expression". The detail and thought that is embedded in drag has motivated Leonardo to keep pushing herself in crochet.

Although Leonardo has only been working with the technique for a short time, she comes from a new generation of artists who have found a community of like-minded peers online. She shares that in addition to the excitement of seeing her ideas realised, she is also moved when women, both younger and older, are inspired by her work to crochet themselves. She says: "I'd like to encourage everyone to try crochet at least once. It is such a great stress reliever, and you do learn so many things." ■

Opposite *Butterfly Balaclava*, 2025, Crochet

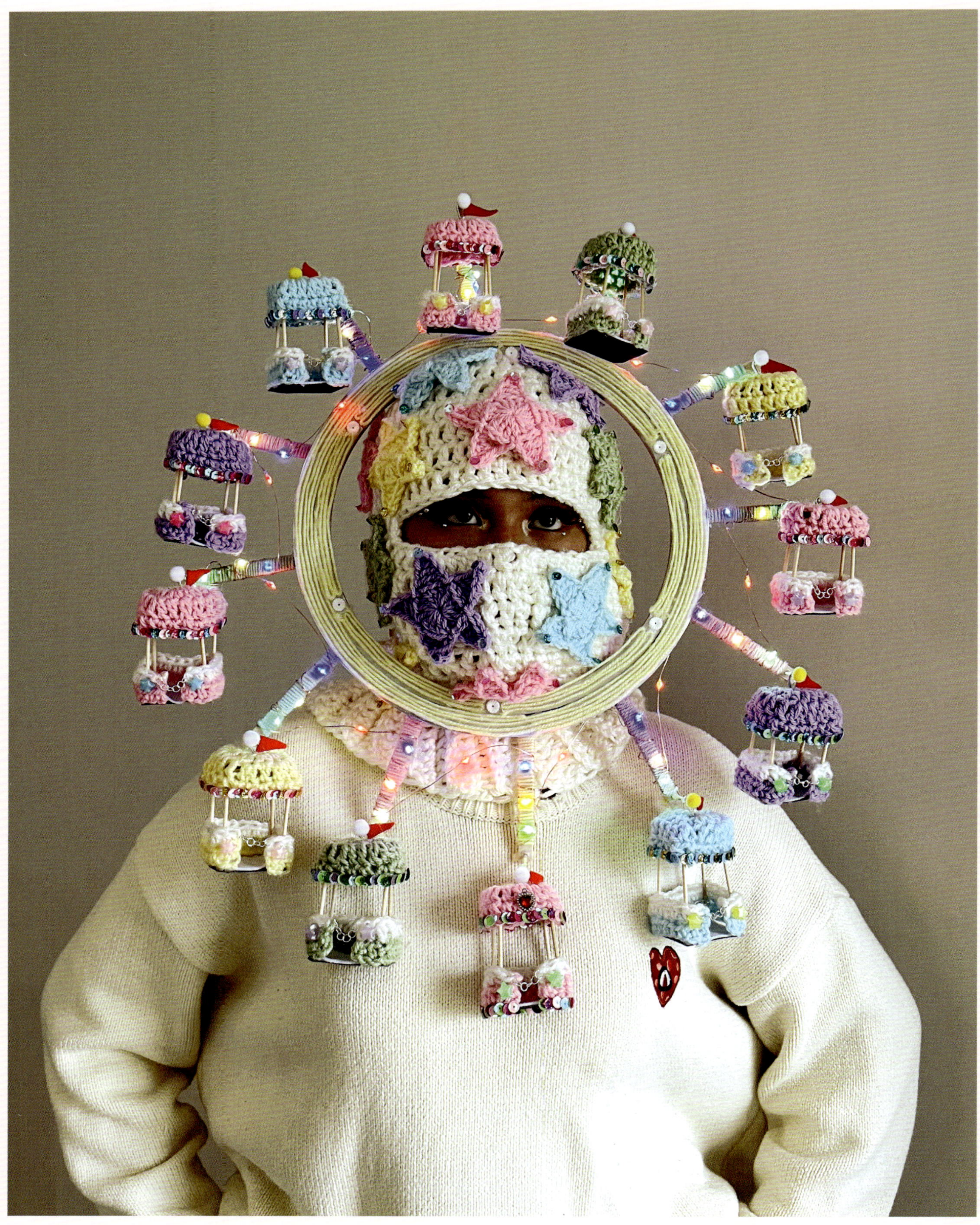

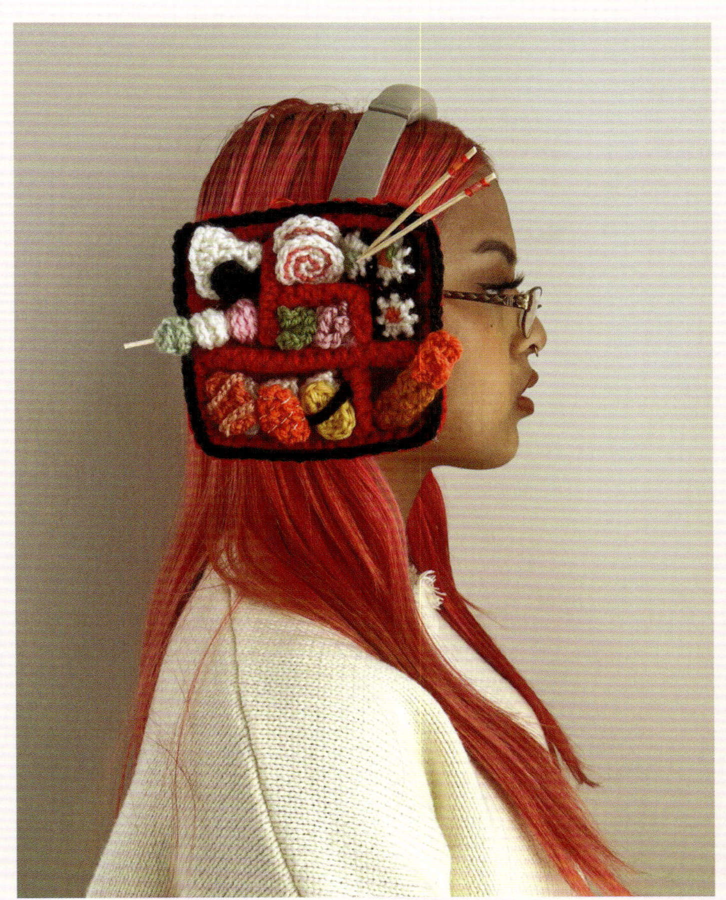

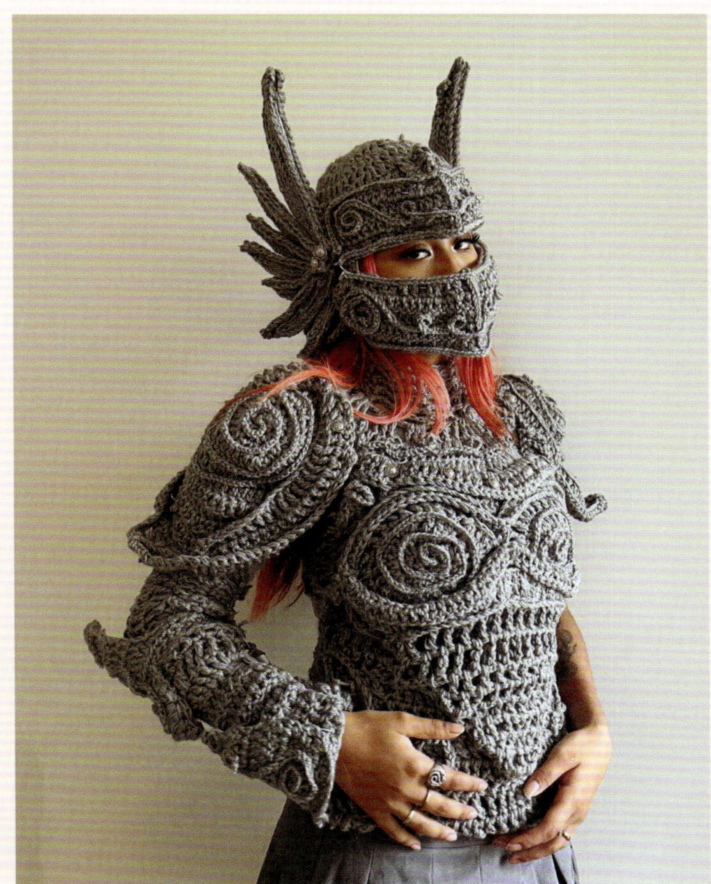

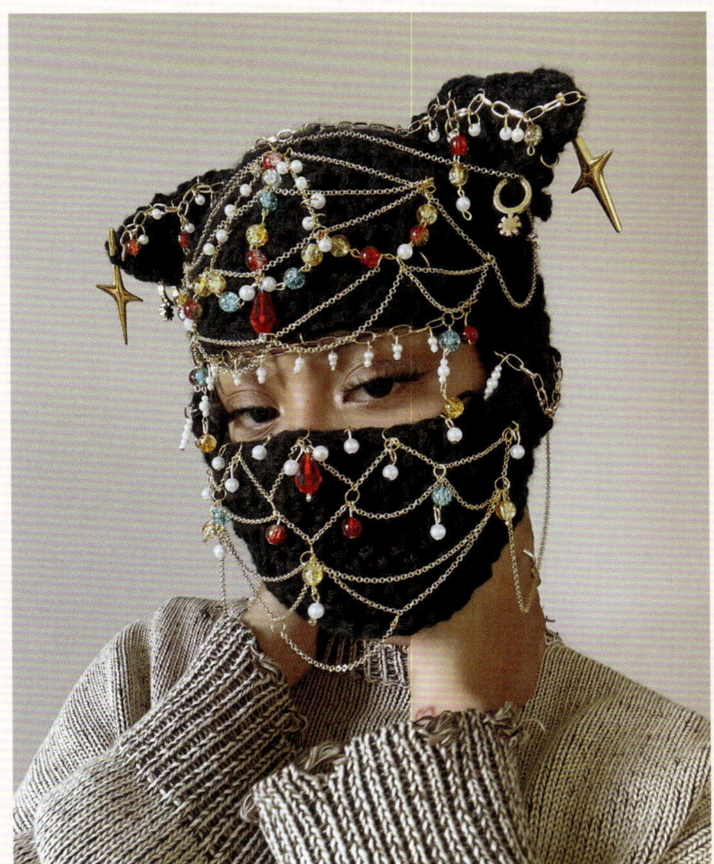

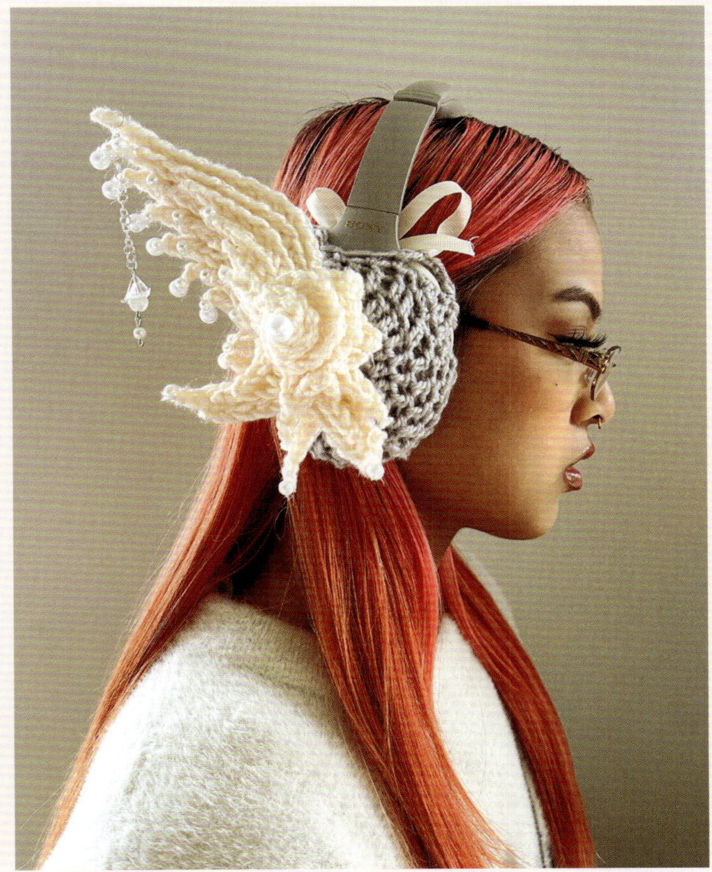

Opposite *Ferris Wheel*, 2025, Crochet **This page** Clockwise from top left: *Bento Covers*, 2024, Crochet; *Knight Armour*, 2024, Crochet; *Angel Covers*, 2024, Crochet; *Gold Cat Balaclava*, 2025, Crochet and beadwork

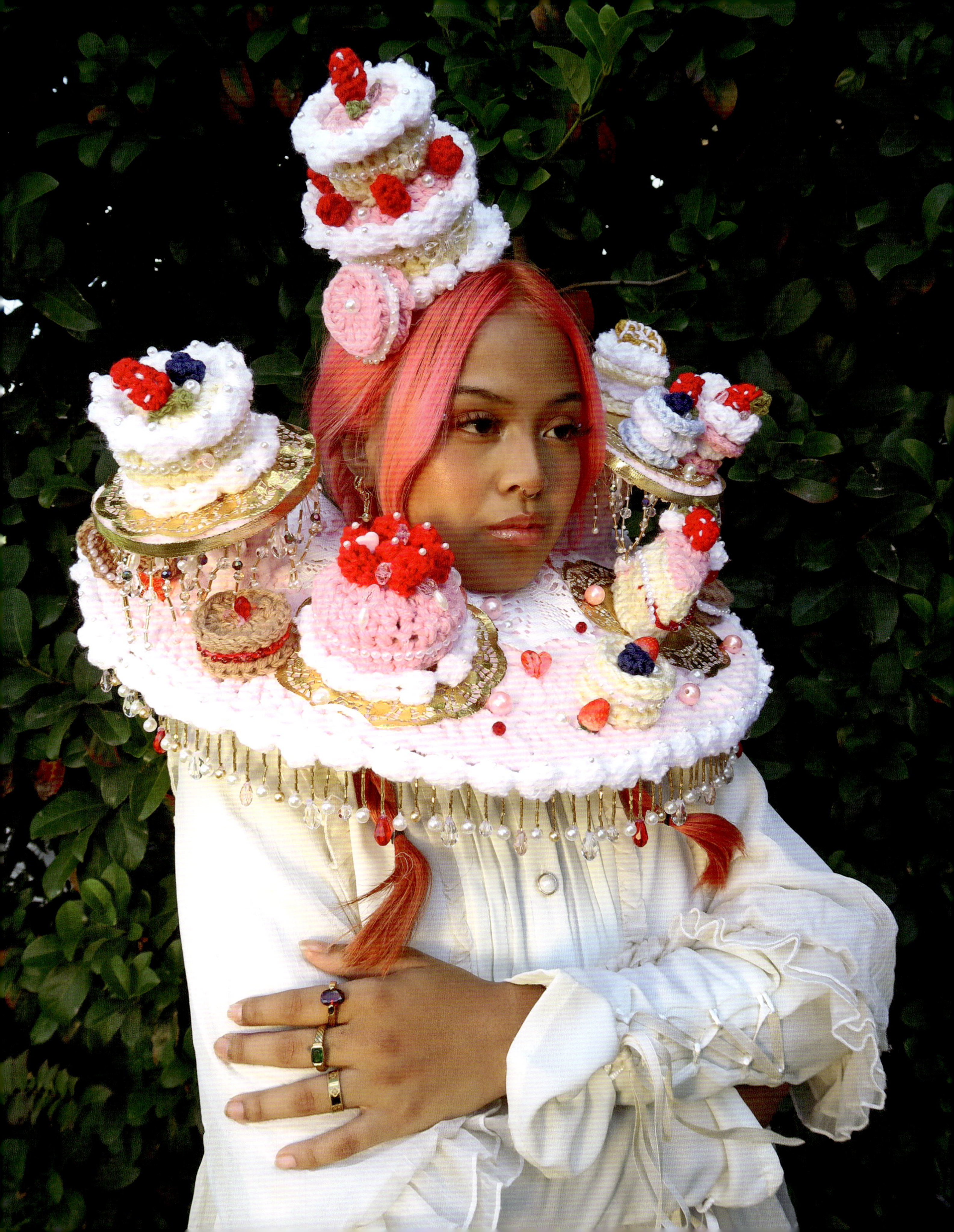

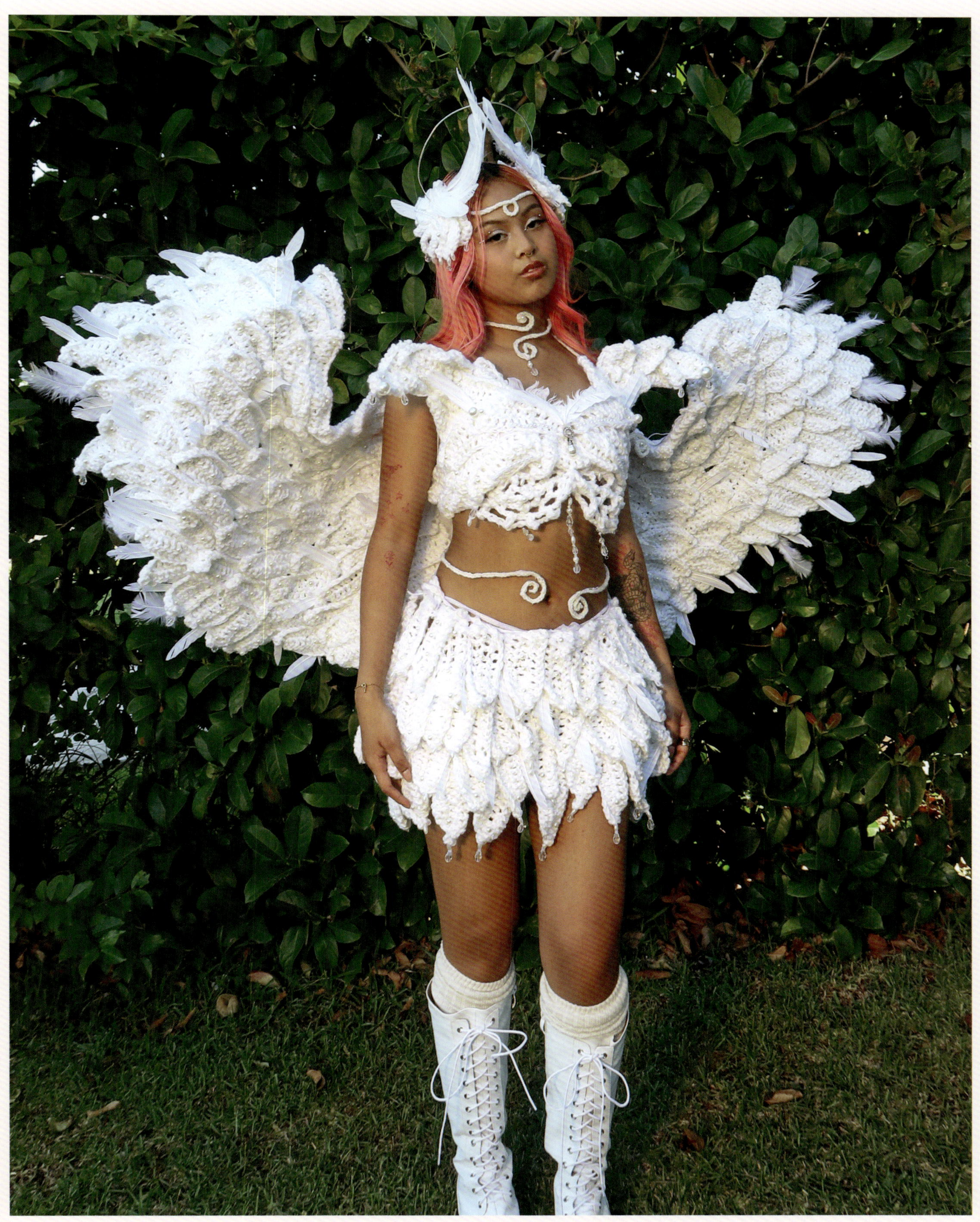

Opposite *Dessert Platter*, 2025, Crochet and beadwork
This page *Angel*, 2024, Crochet

Kelly Jin Mei

SINGAPORE

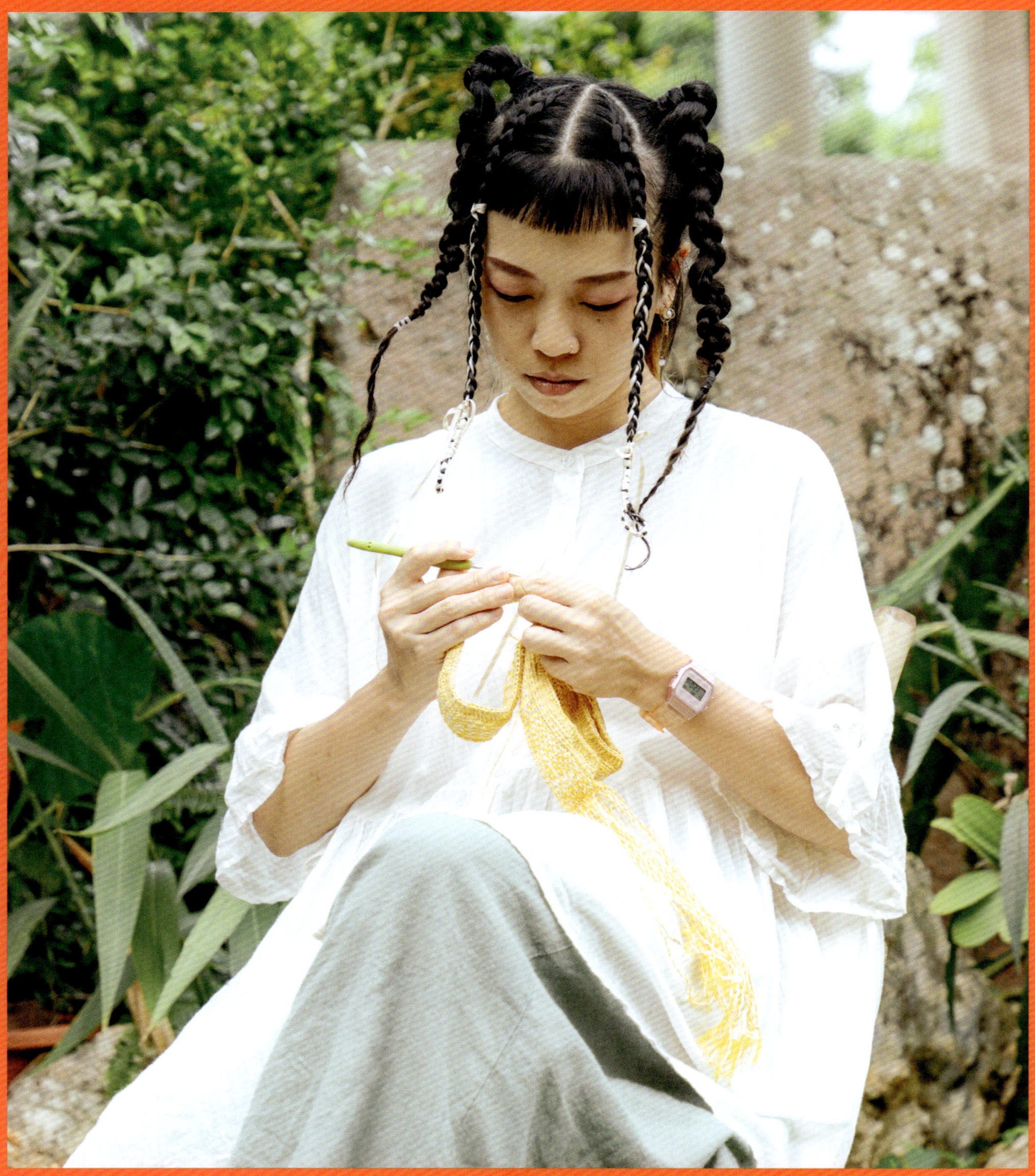

Kelly Jin Mei is an artist with a lifelong affinity for making textiles. She has crocheted since she was seven and describes her early discovery of the technique as a "magical way of turning a piece of yarn into a 3D object". As a teenager she made toys and pouches for friends. After high school, she went on to study fashion design, after which she lived in Japan. During her years there, her perspective on art and its relationship to her life transformed. In particular, Jin Mei was inspired by her experience volunteering at the Setouchi Triennale, where she saw first-hand how public art projects can bring diverse audiences together beyond gallery walls. Her time there inspired Jin Mei to seek ways to bring art to people outside of pre-established art circuits, which inspired one of her first large-scale crochet installations, *Portal of Patterns* (2018), made with 63 volunteers.

Today, Jin Mei works as an artist across many forms including sculpture, installation and multimedia. She continues to crochet unique one-off characters as part of her *Creatures* series (2012–ongoing), but perhaps she is now best known for her burnt crochet vases and vessels, which translate historical forms into contemporary expressions.

For *Qiān Jīn (千金)* (2024), Jin Mei created four works based on the shapes and colours of the "willow leaf vase", which originated in China during the Qing dynasty. The "peach bloom" glaze typical of these vases has been reinterpreted by Jin Mei through yarns in shades of reds, pinks and oranges. Historically, the slender shape of the willow leaf vase meant it often required an additional support structure at its small base. This precarity of form is maintained in Jin Mei's interpretation through her use of hair to suspend the vases. Hung at a low angle, on the edge of the display shelf, this work can be read as a feminist critique on the parallels between historical practices of foot-binding in China, and the way that women's freedoms are controlled today. As Jin Mei says, "This hair saves these vases from falling, yet simultaneously chokes them like a noose."

Whereas stereotypical images of crochet might conjure images of "cosy" granny square blankets or softness, Jin Mei presents crochet as something hard, stiffened and even violent through its destruction. For the artist, burning her works explores "destruction as a secondary technique", inviting interpretations that go beyond the appearance of "perfectly" crafted objects. The act of destruction invites intimacy with a viewer, as it "makes us develop empathy for an inanimate object, because it shows the passing of time, which is life itself". For the pieces she burns, Jin Mei uses nylon thread instead of organic yarn, which would turn to ashes. Through exposure to flames via a heat gun or an open flame torch, the nylon threads harden, turning into brittle plastic that takes a shape of its own.

For Jin Mei, crochet affords many freedoms and liberties for experimentation. It is both "portable, and forgiving", allowing her to unravel and rework the threads as many times as she needs. This malleability forms a core part of *100* (2023), a stop-motion video work that documents Jin Mei crocheting 100 objects one after another from the same ball of yarn. Over time, the yarn becomes discoloured and frayed from use, encapsulating what the artist calls the "accumulated experience" of time.

While Jin Mei has worked with textiles for most of her life, she has only adopted the label of "artist" more recently. Feeling frustrated with a lack of opportunities offered to her in traditional gallery spaces, Jin Mei burnt her first vases in 2021. Ironically, it was this initial act of destruction that led to artistic opportunities and a shift in her own thinking. She reflects, "I found it funny that the destroyed vessel which has lost its function, has more value as an art piece than what it was before." Leaning into this paradox, Jin Mei creates works that prompt a consideration of duality and contradiction, with the hope they spark interest and dialogue, no matter the viewer's background or knowledge of art. ■

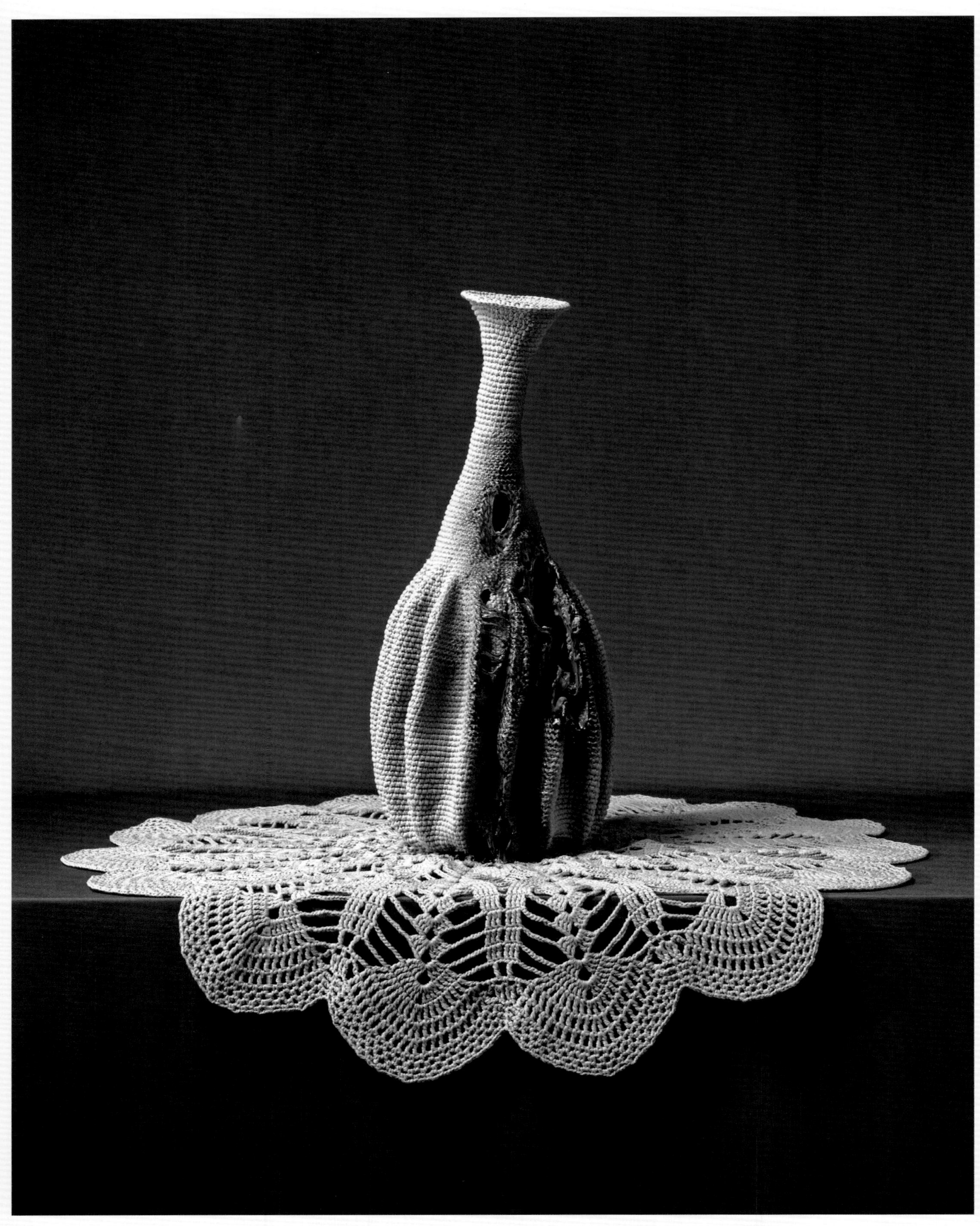

This page *Carefree*, 2022, Melted crochet
Opposite *100*, 2023, Crochet

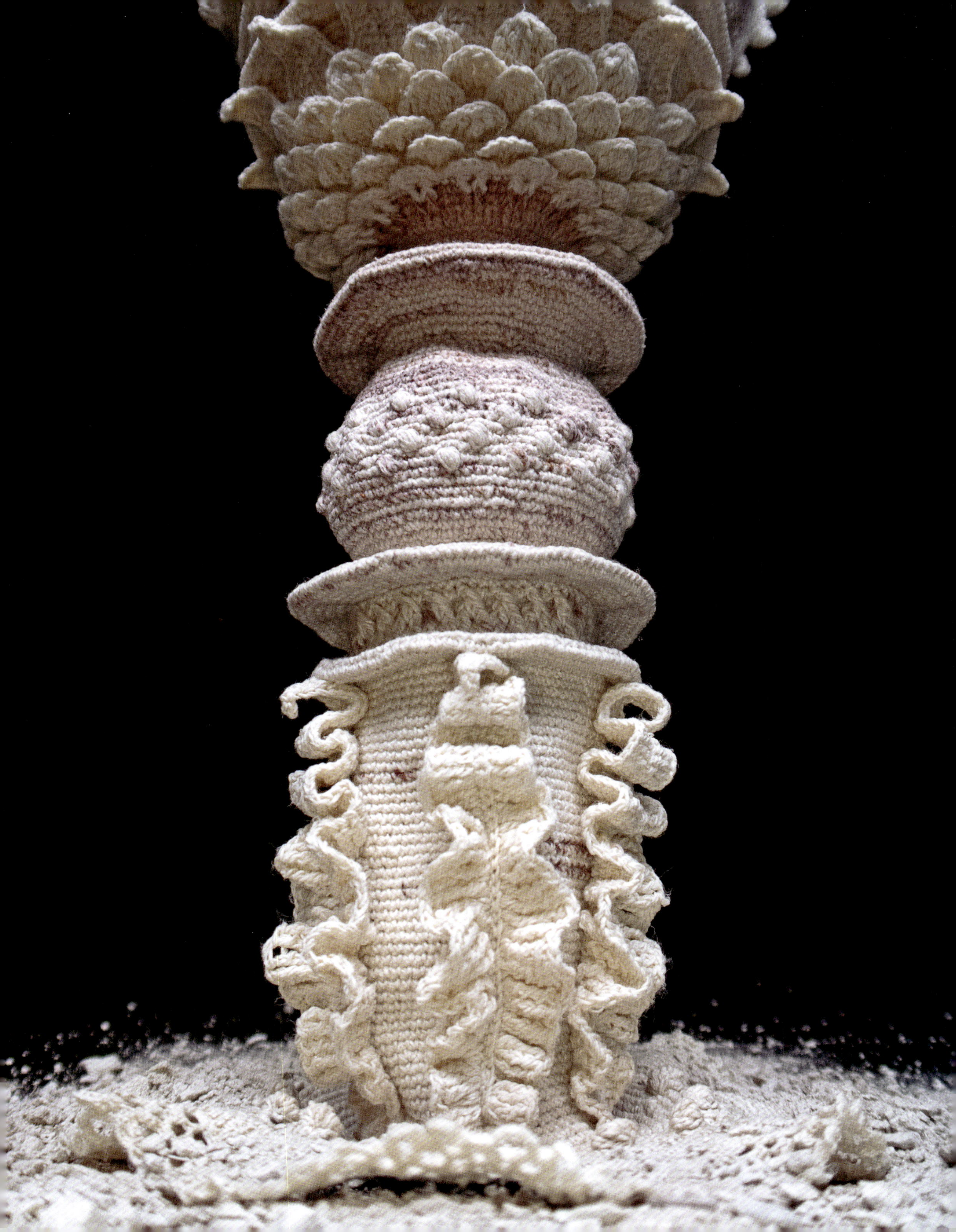

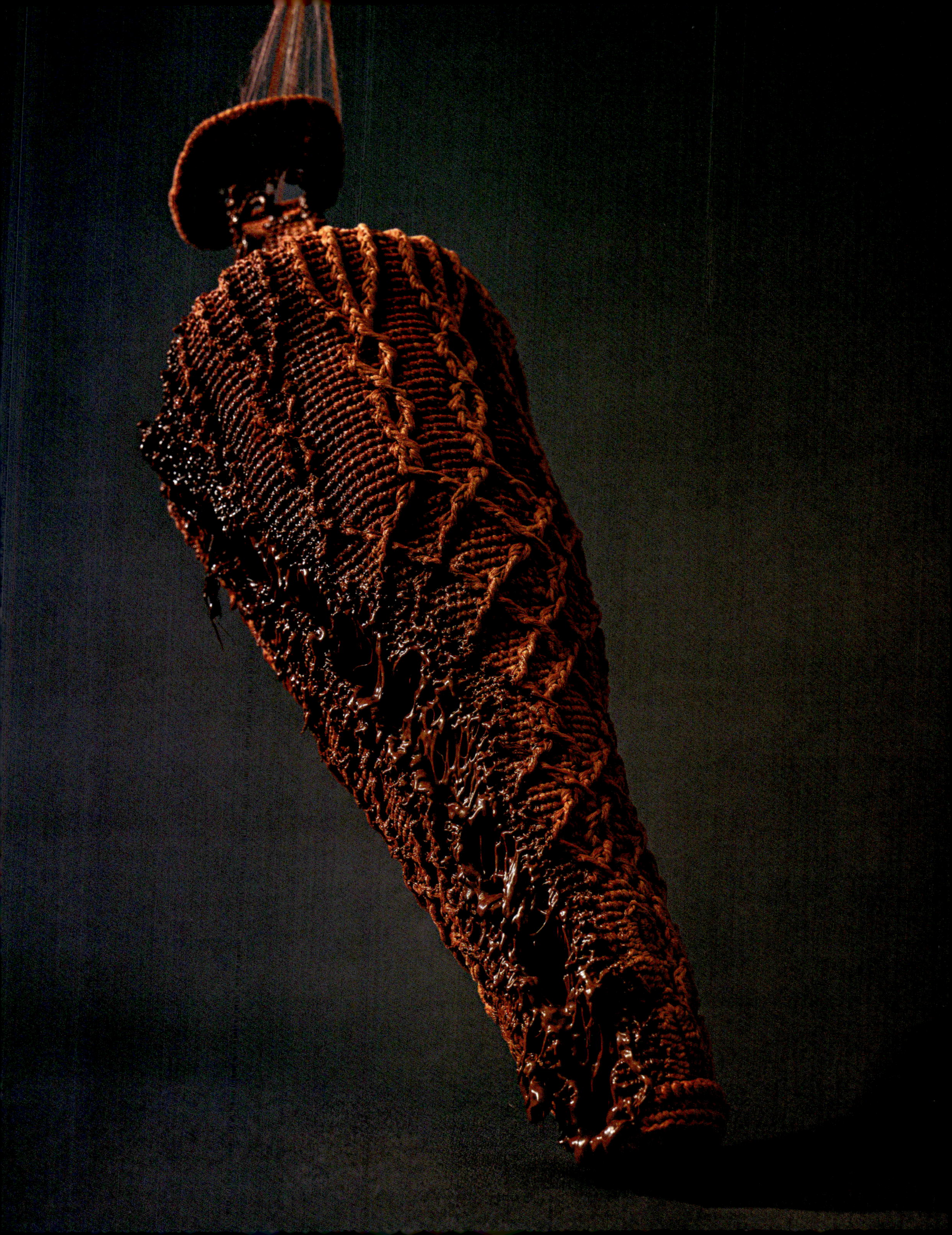

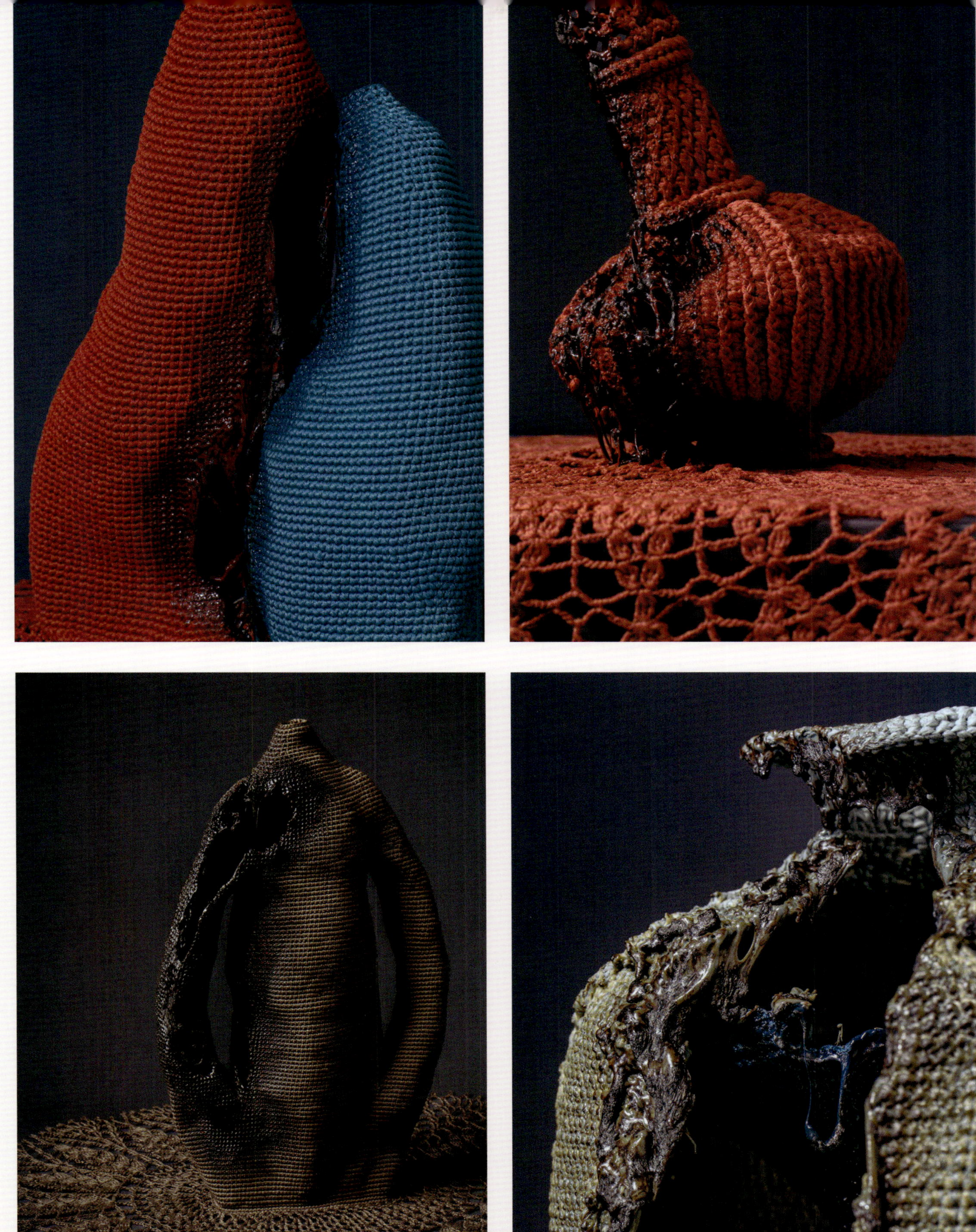

Opposite *Qiān Jīn (千金)*: *Dīng 丁*, 2024, Melted crochet **This page** Clockwise from top left: *Committed*, 2022, Melted crochet; *Demure*, 2022, Melted crochet; *Dignified*, 2022, Melted crochet; *Steadfast*, 2022, Melted crochet

Liisa Hietanen

HÄMEENKYRÖ

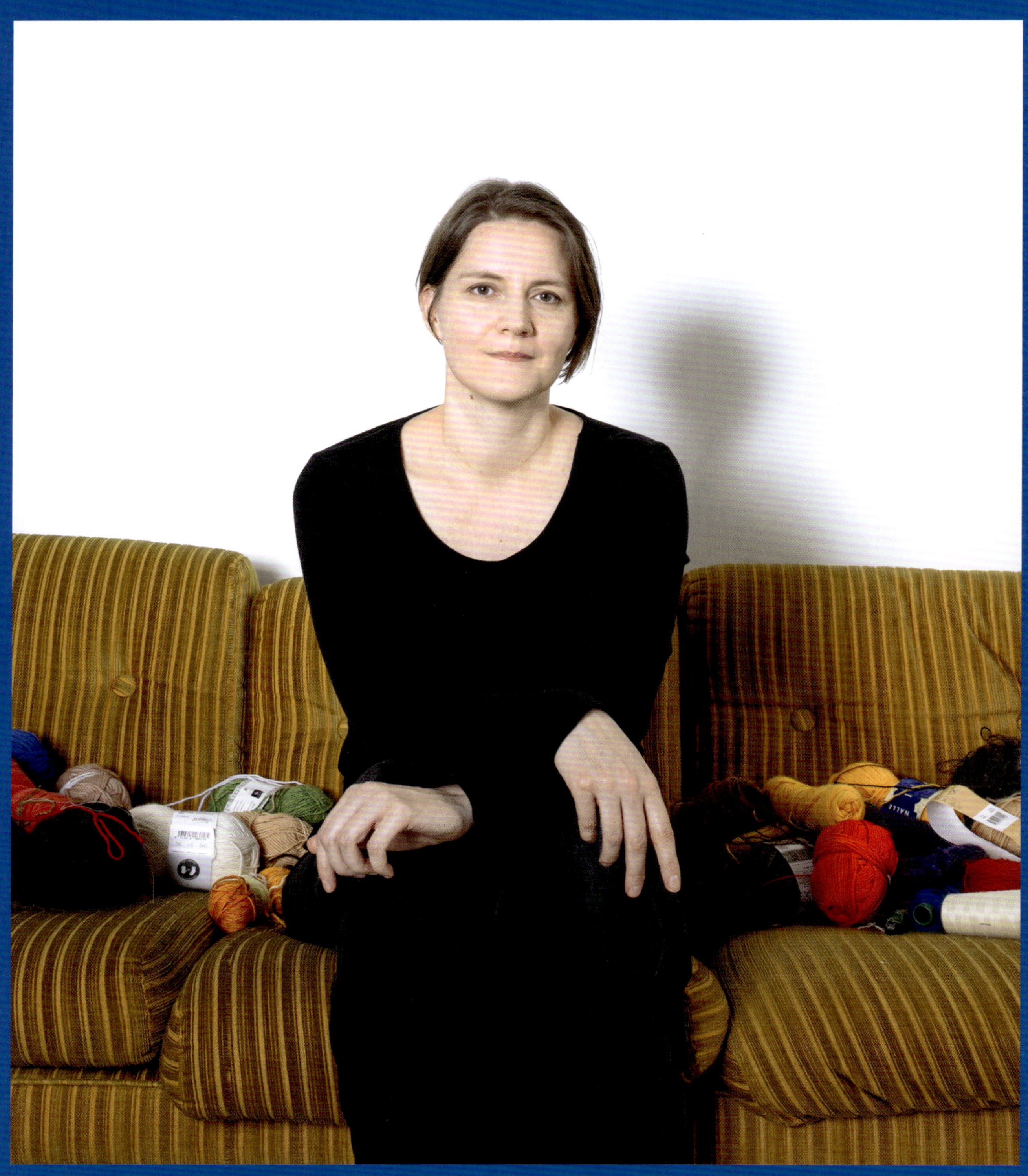

In 2012, Liisa Hietanen moved back to her childhood home of Hämeenkyrö, Finland, a town that currently has a population of approximately 10,300. Returning to her home as an adult, Hietanen sought to reconnect with her local community as an artist by creating crochet and knit versions of the town's residents. The resulting *Villagers* series (2012–ongoing) takes the form of life-size textile portraits of townspeople in everyday settings, from breastfeeding mothers to people walking their dogs. Hietanen is an observer of life and chooses her subjects through an intuitive process guided by daily encounters: "The person depicted might be someone I meet in the library, in the locker room of the gym or walking their dog on the way home."

What is immediately apparent from viewing the meticulousness of Hietanen's portraits is the translation of curiosity about and care for her subjects. The choice of yarns, both in texture and colour, and the application of crochet and knitting techniques captures the individuality of each subject. Given the length of time it takes to finish a *Villager*, Hietanen works from photographs taken from all angles, accompanied by in-person meetings. While most of Hietanen's subjects start as strangers, over the four to five months it takes to finish their yarn counterpart, she gets to know them as individuals.

The sculptures are created around a steel frame and shaped through soft materials like wadding and foam. The surface, mostly made of crochet pieces, is sewn together on top. Hietanen still uses the same crochet techniques she learnt in elementary school, but she now applies a sculptural mindset to her approach. Hietanen describes her working method as "an intuitive process where using hands and thinking are inseparable, and the work consists of constant immediate or unconscious decisions with each loop". Reflecting on her use of crochet, the artist shares that it "is a very natural and organic way to make forms", although it requires a certain level of immediate precision. In more recent works, Hietanen has adopted the use of knitting and surface embroidery to complete the pieces, adding details to the items of clothing and accessories adorning each subject.

In photographs from the series that place the sculpture alongside the real-life subject, an uncanny effect is conjured: a twin in another form. But while each *Villager* is based on a unique person, Hietanen is interested in exploring "familiarity and shared experiences". Audiences may see themselves in "the subjects or materials that are common to many people", whether that identification is based in "everyday life", or in personal experience making handcrafts. We may not know *Anna and Edith* (2016) personally, but in their depiction, we can recognise common experiences of motherhood. In this way,

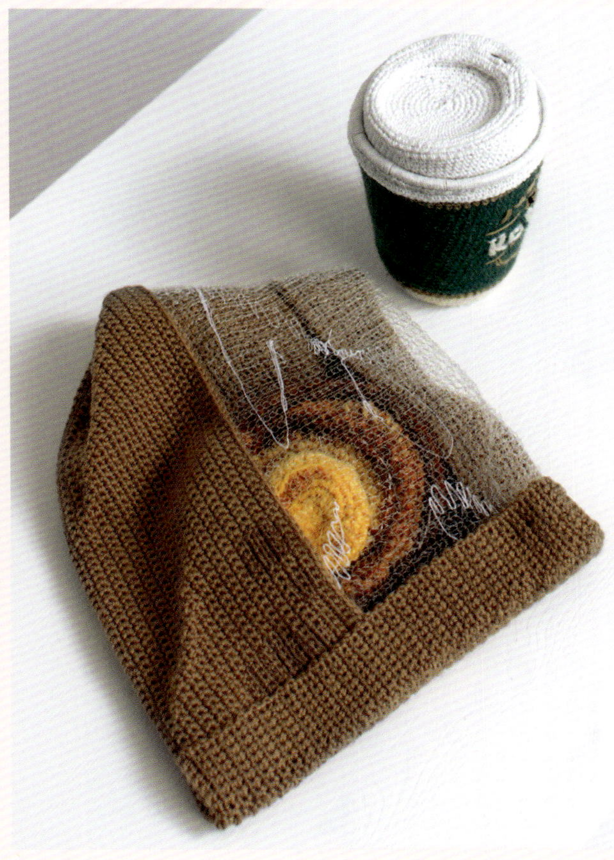

Dallas, 2019, Crochet

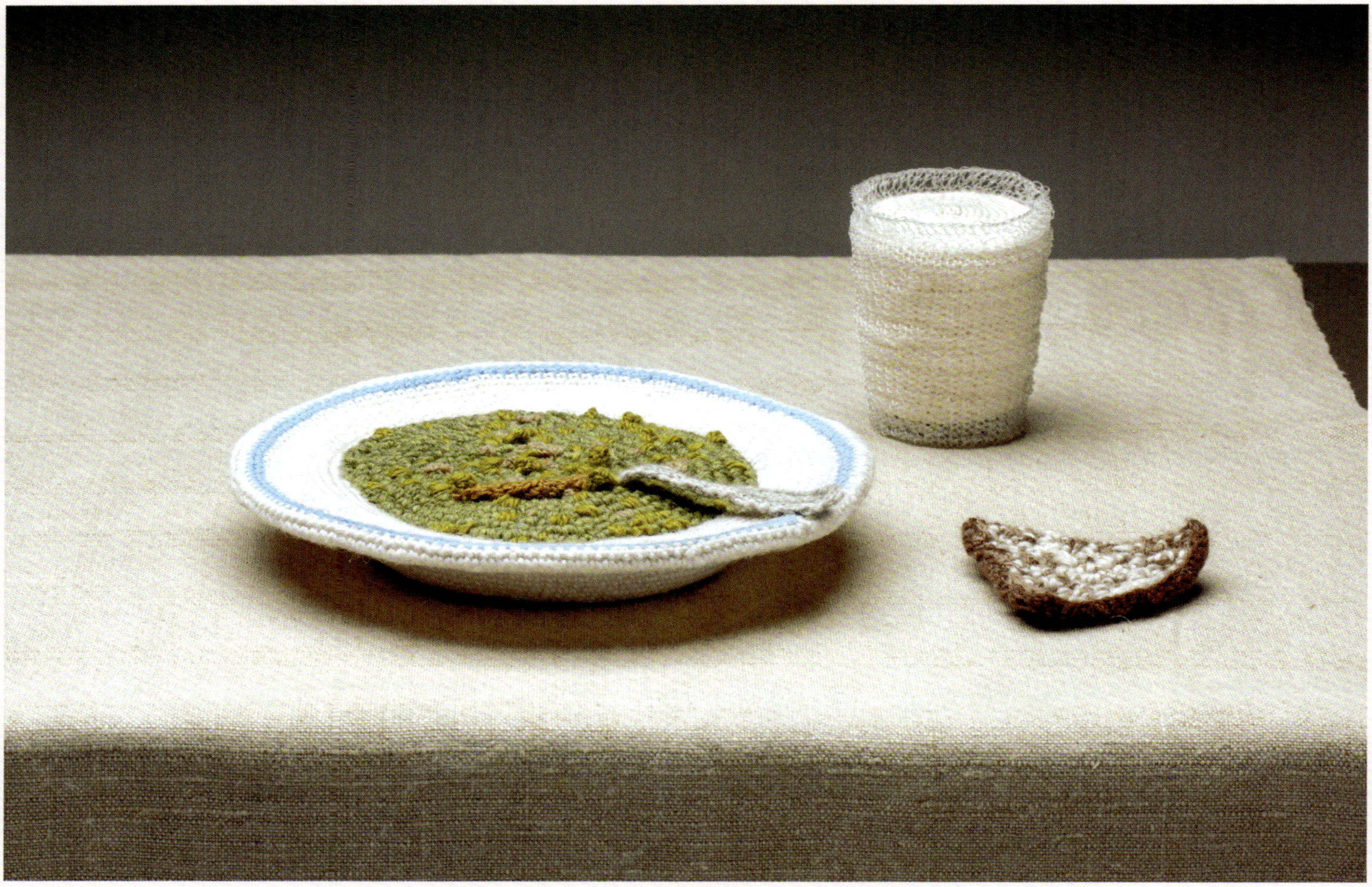

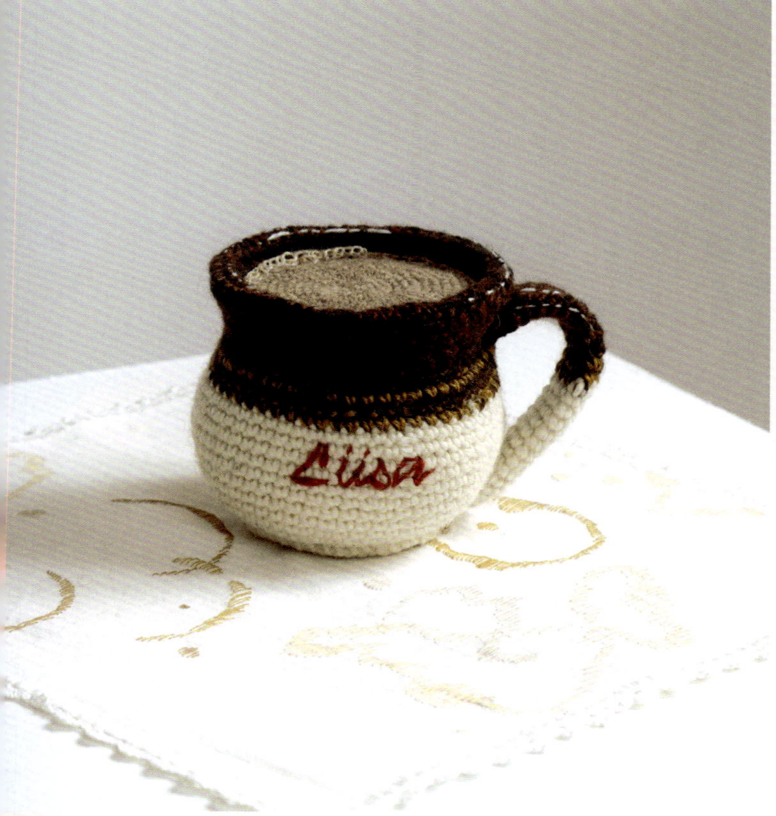

while each work is based on an individual, they also represent shared moments, both cultural and personal, which creates an intimate engagement with viewers.

A significant component of the *Villagers* series is the public display of each sculpture. Once they are complete, Hietanen places her works in public spaces, allowing passers-by to encounter them in a setting outside of typical art galleries or museums: places that have hosted the portraits include a flower shop, a cafe and a public library. For the artist, this choice of location is essential to the series' meaning, as she strives to create "a dialogue with the people directly in my surroundings". It's this attempt to create conversations and relationships that marks Hietanen's skill as an artist, which resides not only in her masterful use of thread and yarn, but in her recognition that it is human connection that gives meaning to her work. ■

This page Top: *Thursday*, 2017, Crochet; Bottom: *Liisa*, 2020, Crochet
Opposite *Raija*, 2018, Crochet, hand-knitting and embroidery

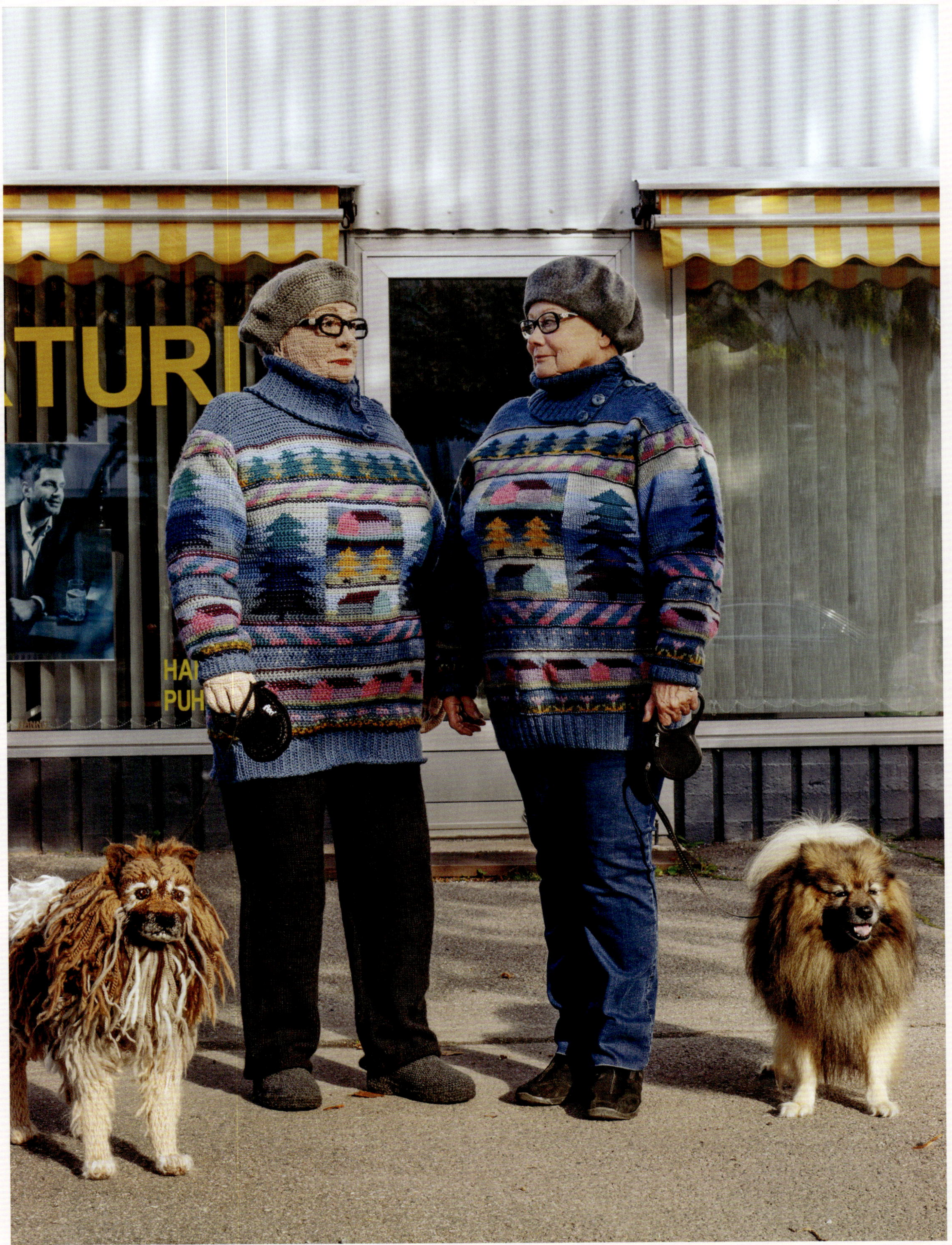
TURI

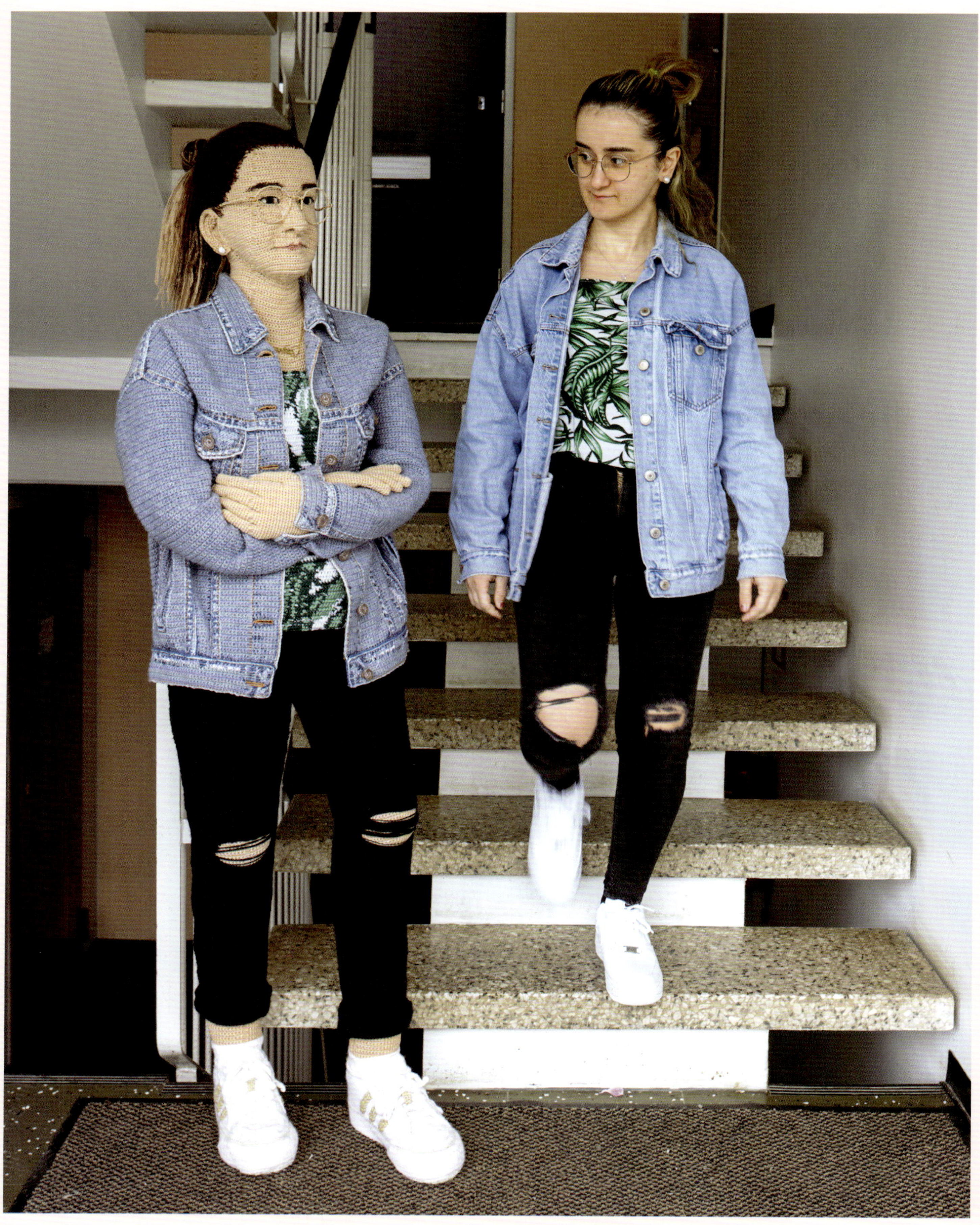

This page *Dilara*, 2023, Crochet, hand-knitting and embroidery **Opposite** Clockwise from top left: *Suvi*, 2022, Crochet, hand-knitting and embroidery; *Aulis*, 2020, Crochet, hand-knitting and embroidery; *Anna and Edith*, 2016, Crochet, hand-knitting and embroidery

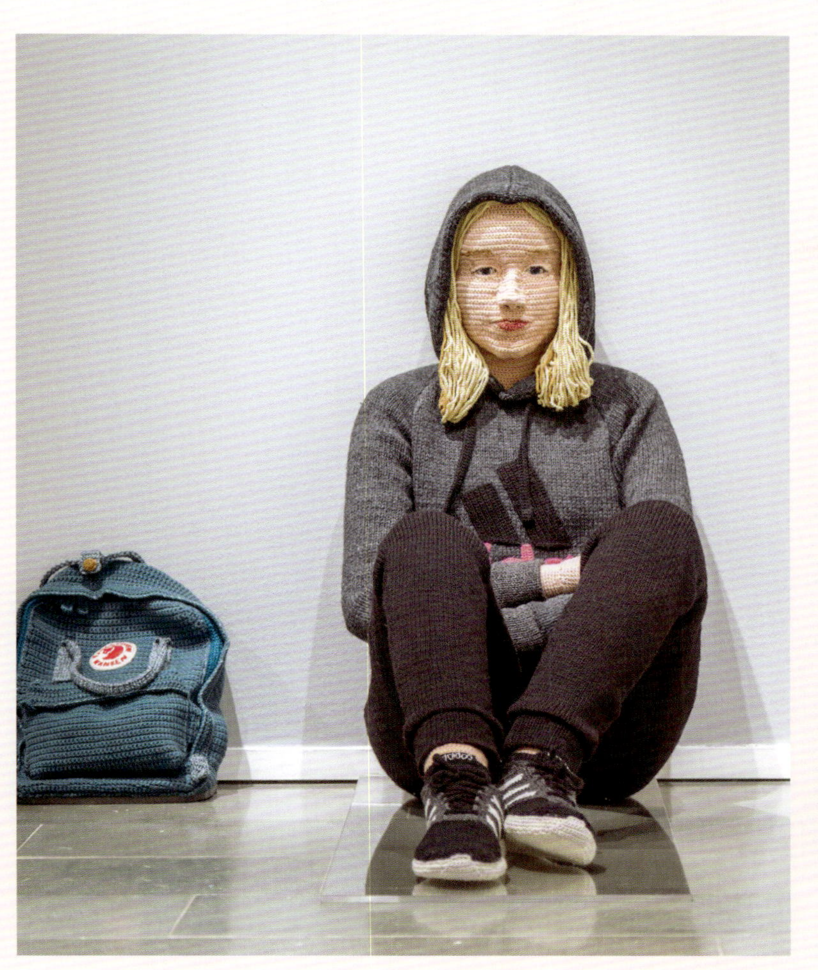

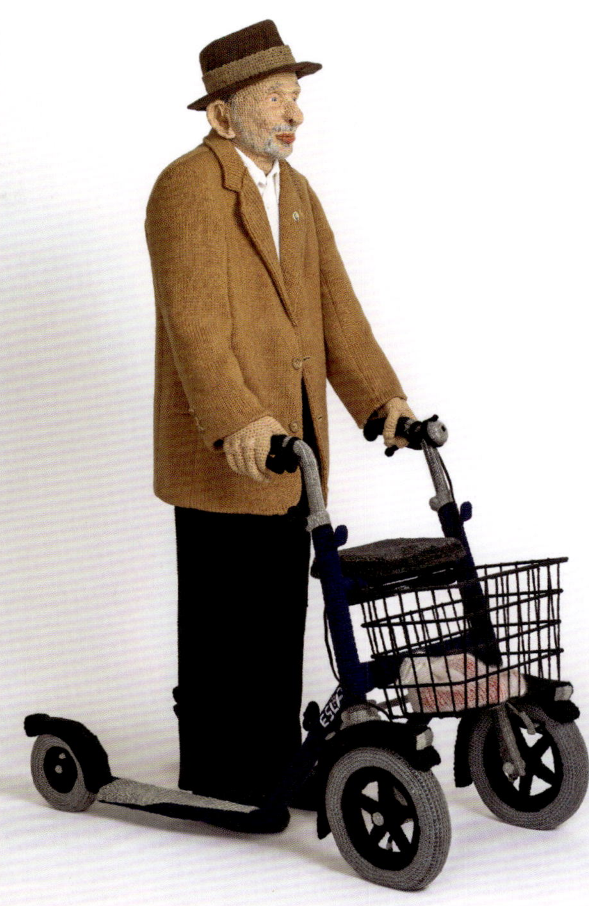

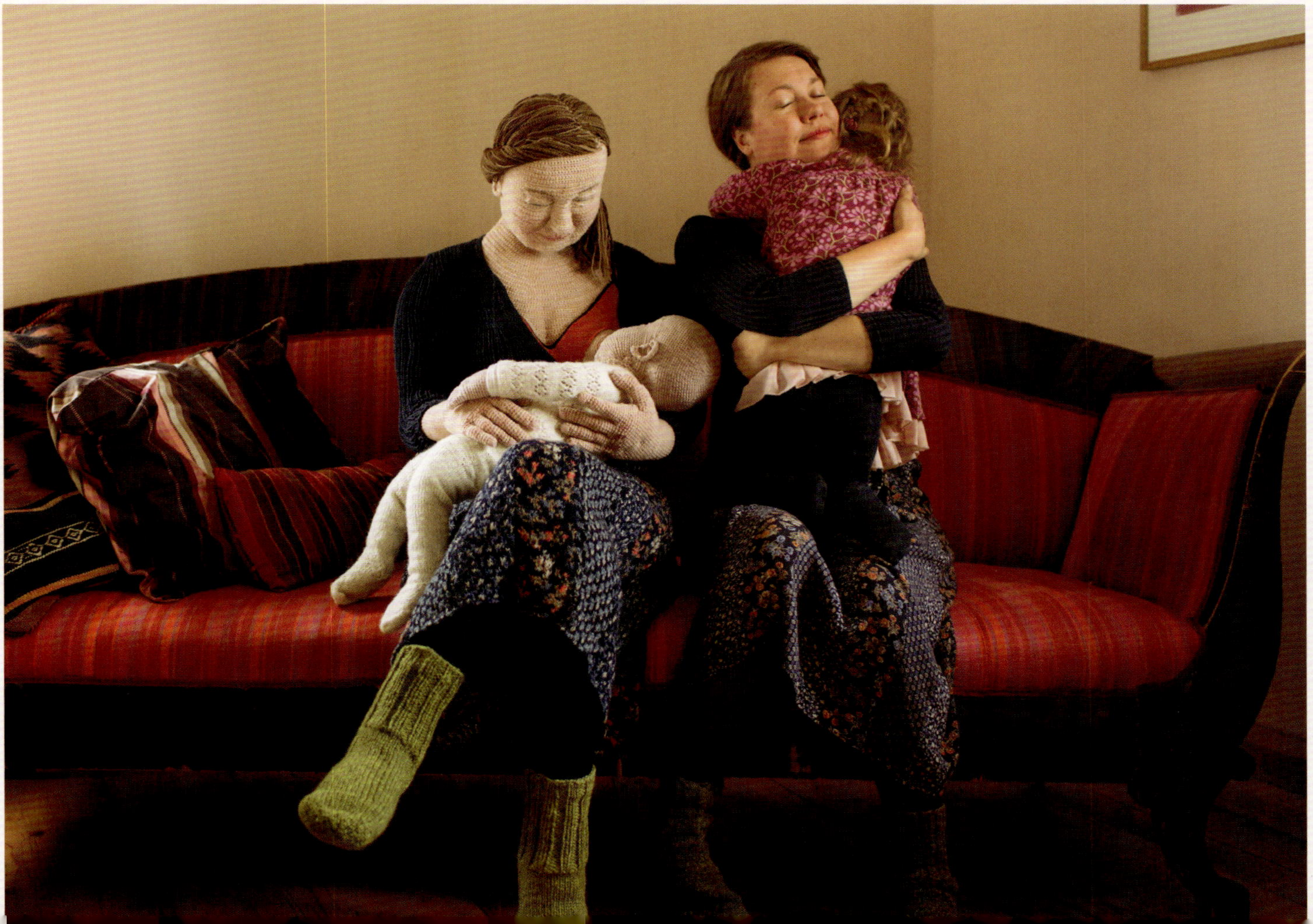

Lissy & Rudi Robinson-Cole

TĀMAKI MAKAURAU /AUCKLAND

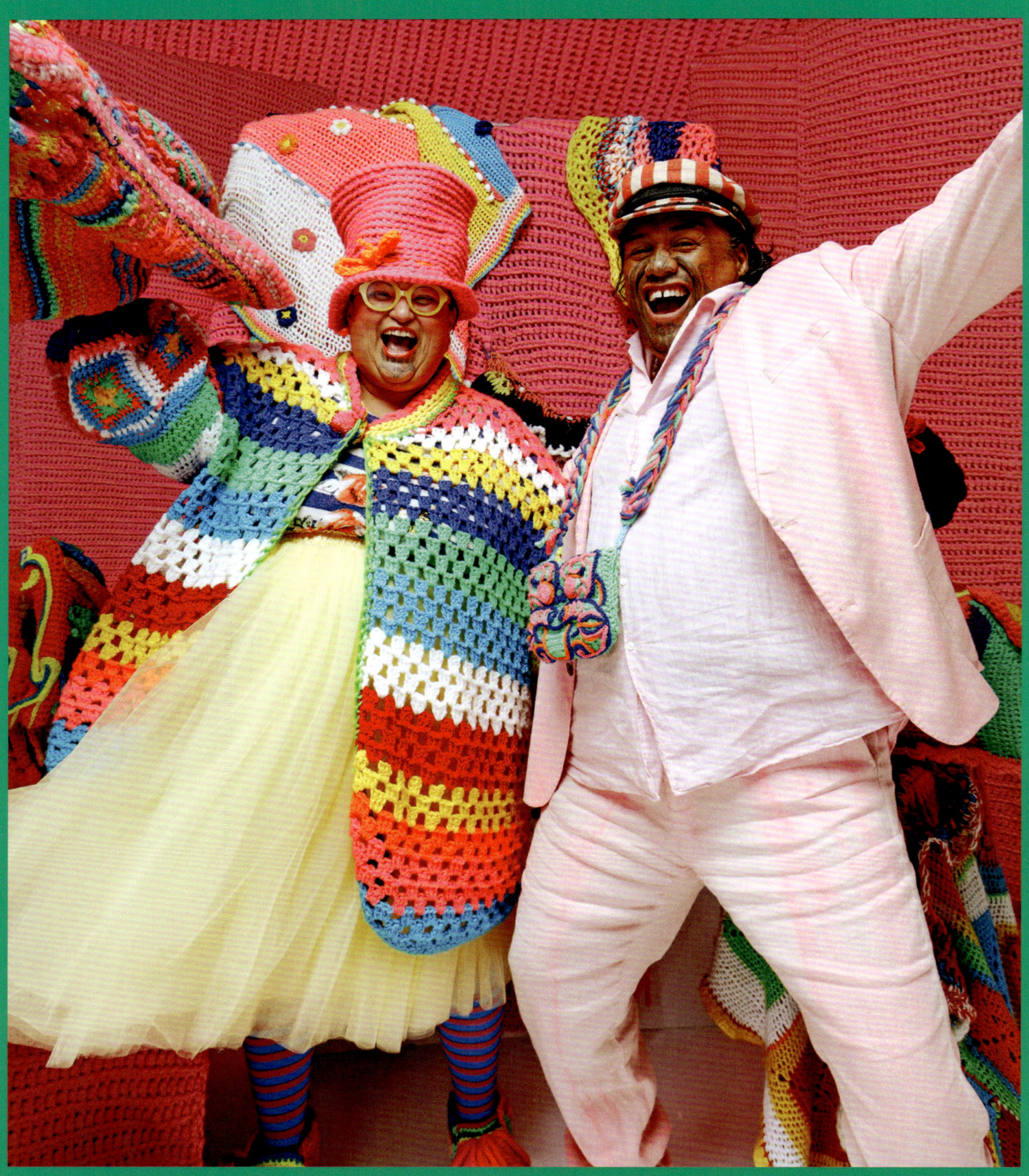

Lissy and Rudi Robinson-Cole believe crochet found them. The Māori husband and wife duo from Aotearoa/New Zealand first met 10 years ago and now work together to create colourful and bold crochet installations and sculptures that celebrate Indigenous joy, informed by their whakapapa (ancestral ties): "We are on a journey led and inspired by our Tūpuna (ancestors) and our uri (descendants). Everything we create is in celebration of them, for them, because of them."

Lissy and Rudi's earliest crochet projects took the form of yarn bombing – using the materials and techniques of textile crafts in a street art context. Their first collaborative work was a display of crochet poppies, both large and small, on the Ōtāhuhu motorway for ANZAC Day. Quickly, the artists came to recognise the positive, immediate ways that crochet speaks to different audiences. As Lissy and Rudi reflect, "As soon as we began our journey with crochet, we were able to see that this material gave us the ability to express our deepest connection to the wairua (spirit) realm in a visual and tangible way." This is because, in the artists' experiences, the materiality of crochet and the memories that are lovingly embedded in objects made by family members translate into a moment of connection with "people from all cultures, ages, genders, abilities". For Lissy, this personal connection to textiles was also instilled from a young age by her father Colin Cole, a renowned fashion designer.

Lissy and Rudi's works take visual cues and inspiration from Māori history and culture, which is interpreted through striking fluorescent yarn choices. The artists combine bold colours, including bright pinks, neon yellows and acid greens. The colours are assigned meanings by the artists – for instance *Harikoa* (pink, joyful), *Paki* (blue, a clear vision) and *Taumata* (red, passion). These meanings are then embedded in the material outcome of the work. But the artists' colour choices go deeper than an ability to command a joyous presence: "The use and love of fluorescence lies deep within our whakapapa." The artists share that "there is some thought that our Tūpuna used phosphorescence as a navigation tool" on the base of their canoes when travelling great distances by water; for Lissy and Rudi, fluorescence serves as "a tool to navigate" to their roots.

The pair's collaborative method is centred on clearly "definite roles within our practice, both spiritually and physically". Lissy describes herself as the "kite flying high in the sky", while Rudi acts as the anchor, "holding on to the string". In terms of their process, Rudi designs and creates the structural forms from polystyrene, which hold the works together, while Lissy freestyle crochets pieces to cover the surfaces in colours the artists collaborate to pick. Lissy works with a single crochet stitch, preferring the straightforwardness and simplicity of using the same stitch over and over. Neither work from a pattern, instead creating in a more intuitive manner through trial and error.

One of their most ambitious and large-scale projects to date is *Wharenui Harikoa* (2023), translated as "House of Joy". This full-size crochet structure takes the form of a *whare whakairo*, or carved meeting house, which is a significant communal space in Māori culture where rituals and meetings take place. Created in collaboration with an international network of Indigenous communities and artistic collaborators, Lissy and Rudi describe *Wharenui Harikoa* as "manifesting intergenerational healing and joy for our people, past, present and future". For the artists, "This is the space where we are our truest selves as beings exist, where we are with our Tūpuna and with each other in the space of love. The place of our dreams and all the magnificence we are in this universe." Reflecting on the intended audiences for their artworks, Lissy and Rudi share that they are "a love letter… for our children and grandchildren, our ancestors and the rest of the world". ■

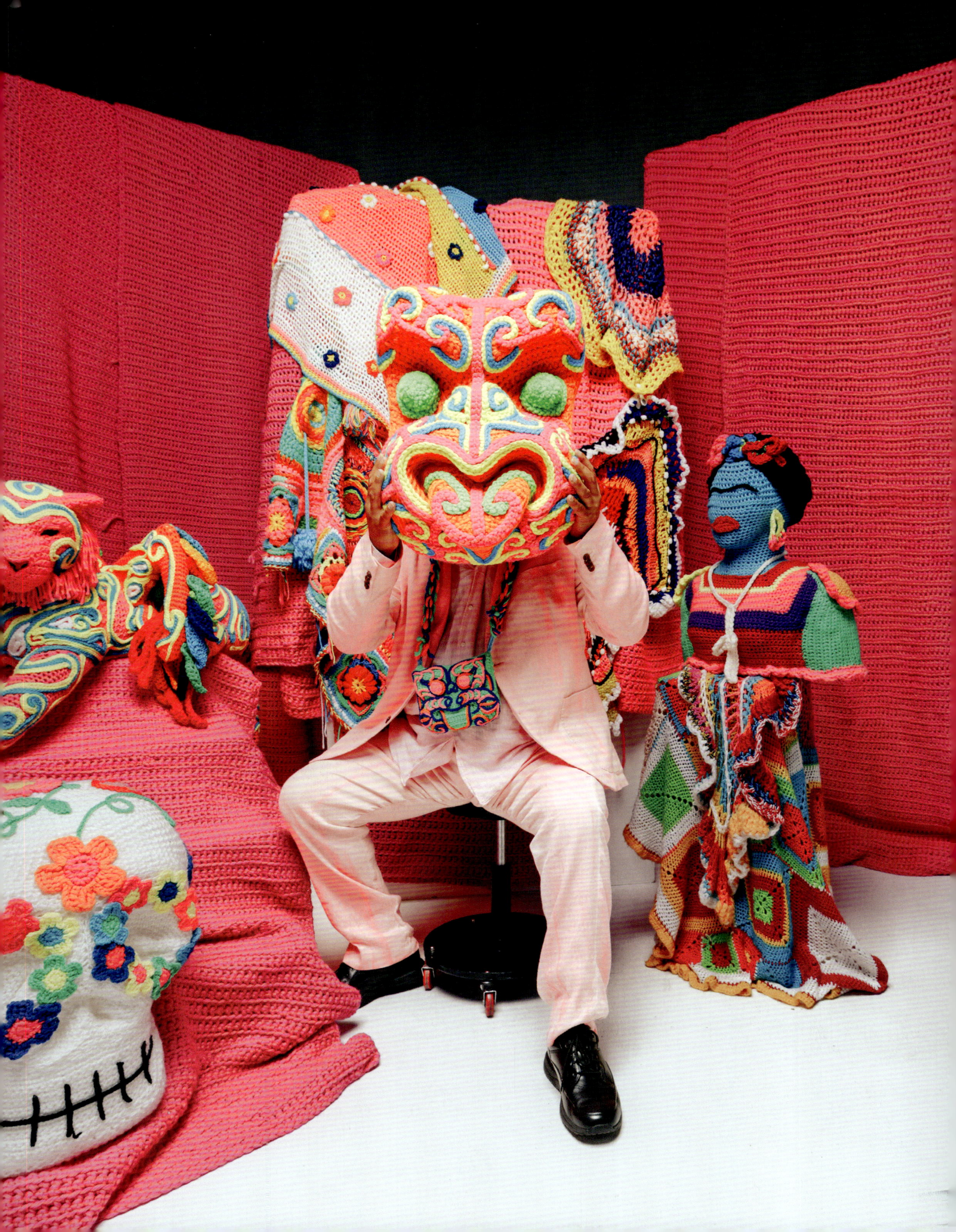

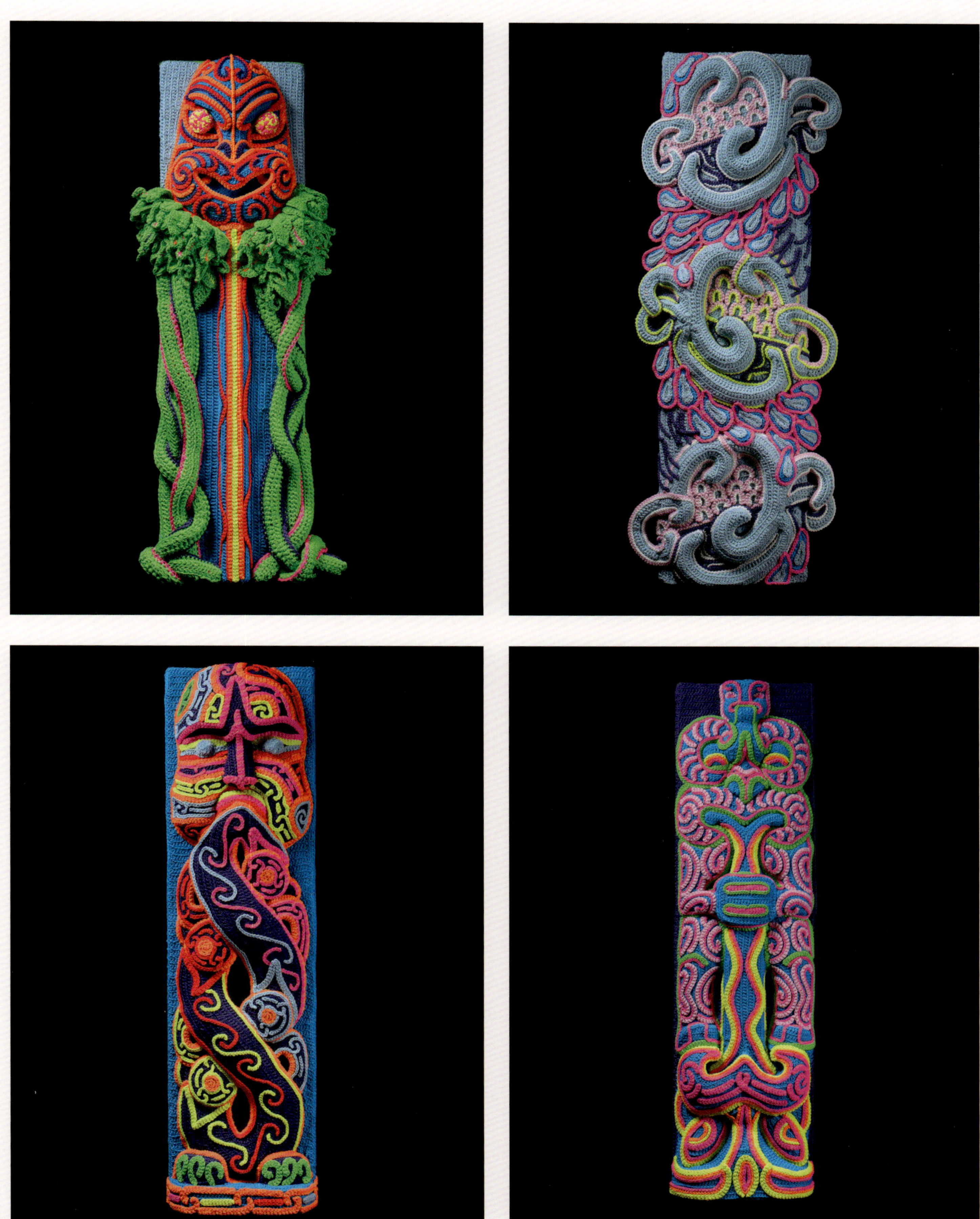

Opposite *Harikoa*, 2023, Crochet **This page** Clockwise from top left: *Tupuārangi*, 2023, Crochet; *Waipunarangi*, 2023, Crochet; *Waitā*, 2023, Crochet; *Ururangi*, 2023, Crochet

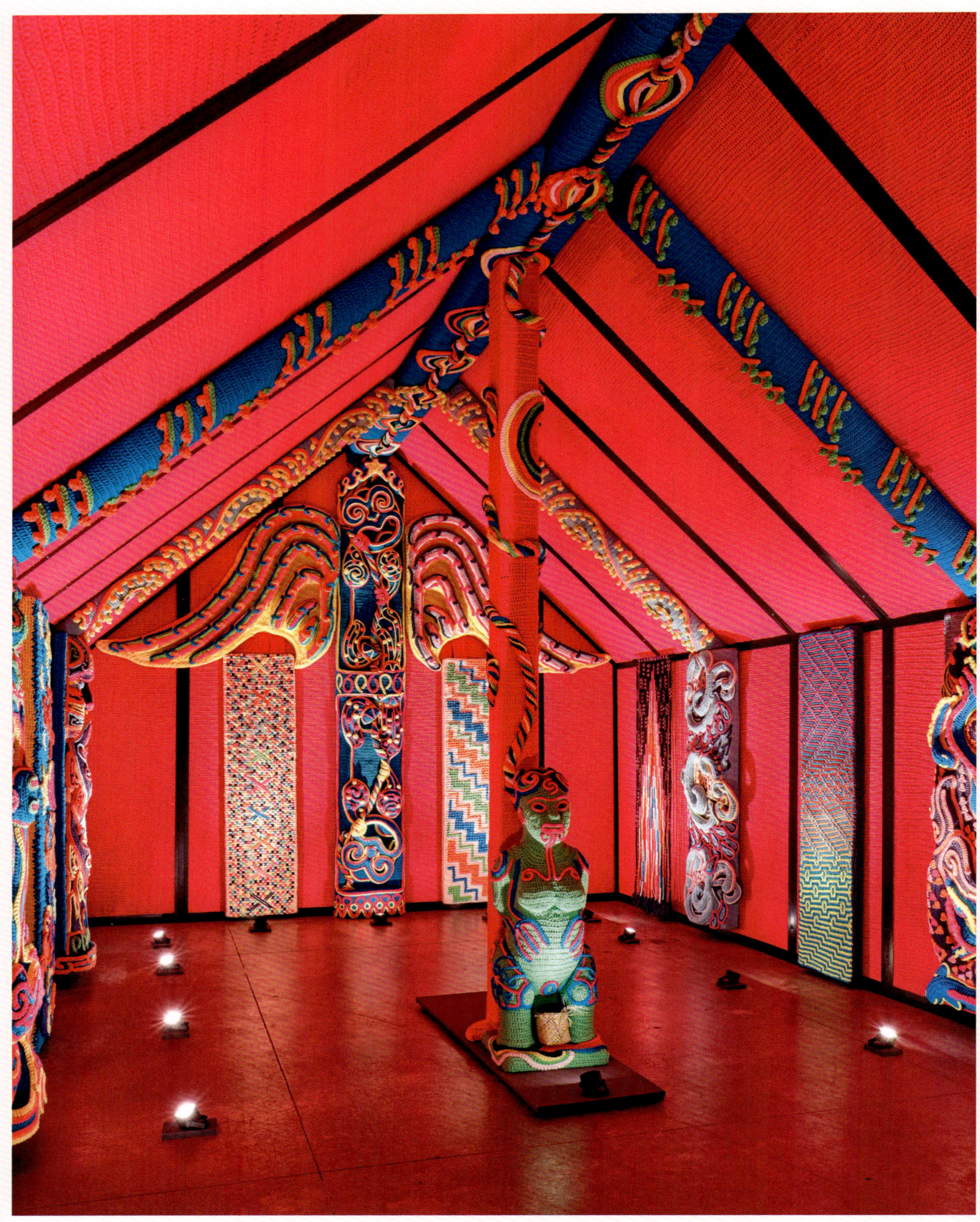

This page and opposite *Wharenui Harikoa*, 2023, Crochet

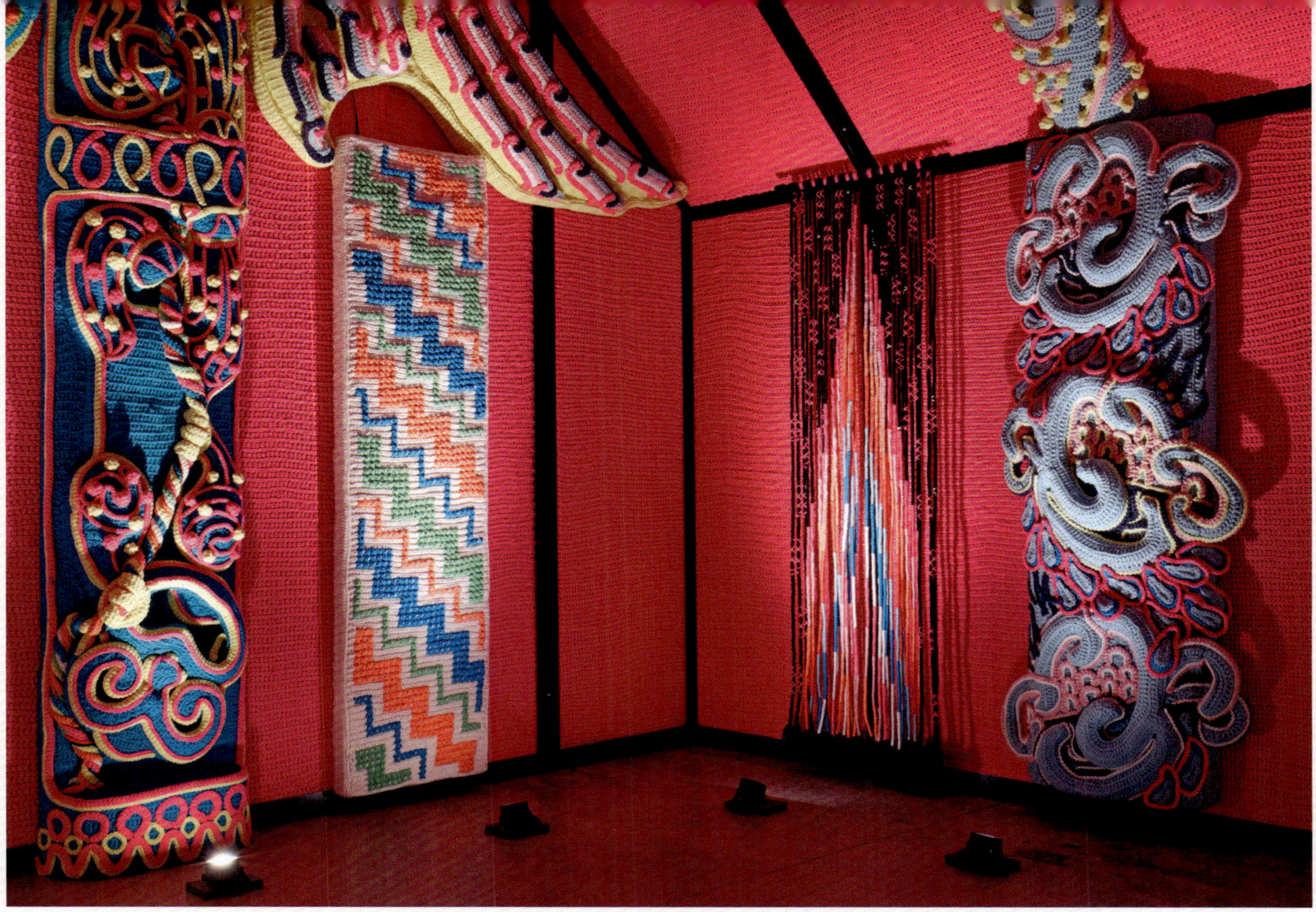

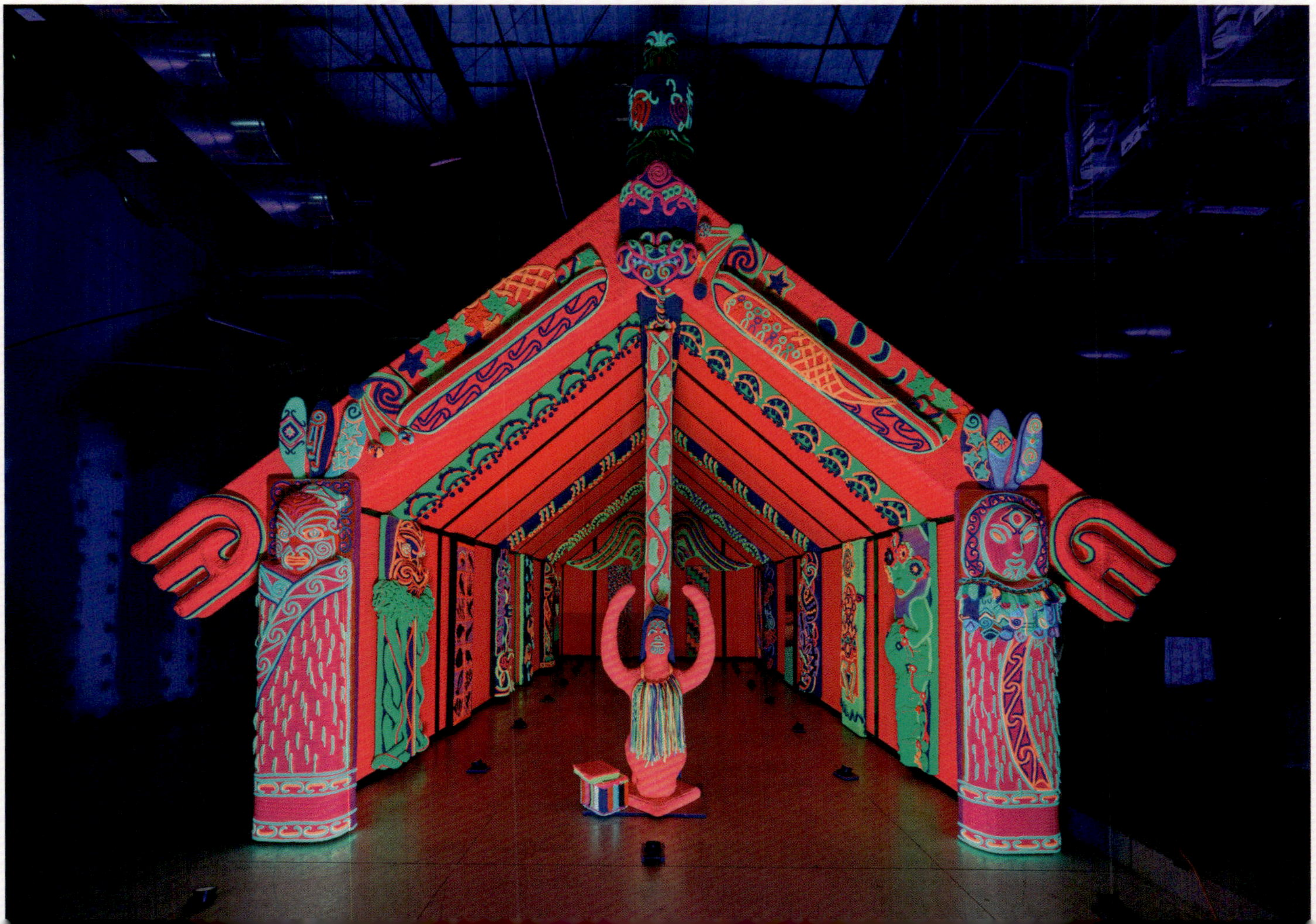

Mulyana

YOGYAKARTA

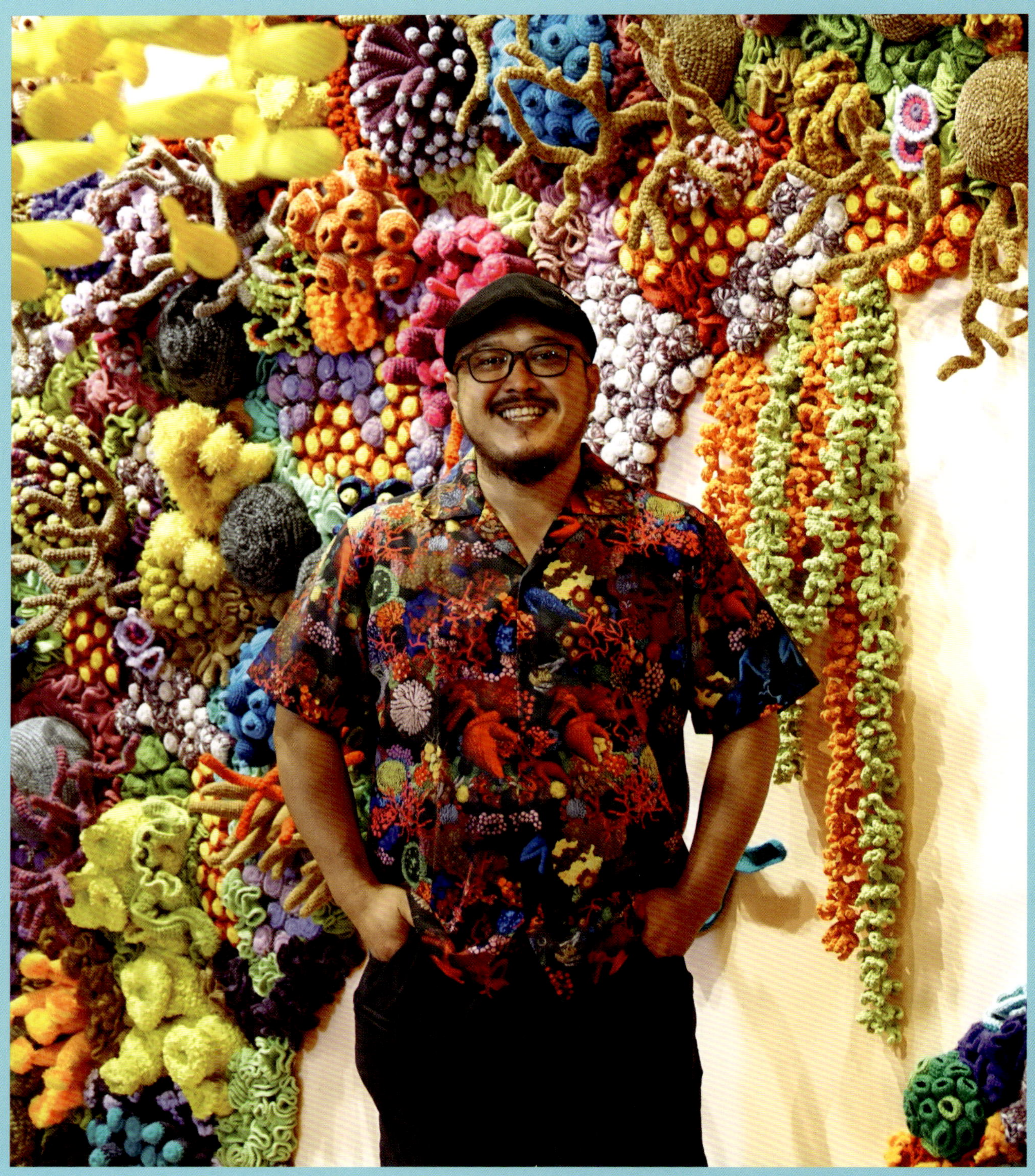

Mulyana is known for his immersive crochet installations encompassing fantastical "monster ecosystems" and life forms. At the heart of many of his works is Mogus, a character whose name is derived from a combination of Mulyana's family name and the Indonesian word for "octopus". Mogus, who acts as a creative alter ego for the artist, is partly inspired by the rich cultural traditions of puppetry and Indonesian theatre dating back thousands of years. The character first appeared in 2008 in crochet form and has continued to feature as one of the central motifs in Mulyana's works since.

Over the last decade, as his projects grew more ambitious in scale and theme, Mulyana says he became increasingly "fascinated with modularity and transformation", leading him "to develop an artistic practice that revolves around interactive and evolving artworks". Mulyana's installations invite audiences to engage directly through "touch, movement, or participation", "challeng[ing] the notion of passive spectatorship" typically expected in a gallery setting. For those viewing or interacting with Mulyana's artworks, their handcrafted nature fosters an immediate "sense of warmth and familiarity", which contributes to their meaning. Reflecting on his affinity for crochet, Mulyana describes the technique as a "deeply personal and meditative process that connects my physical movements directly to the creation of each piece".

Encountering one of Mulyana's installations is to enter a wondrous landscape that recreates familiar visual cues from our world with a playful spin. Each installation is the sum of its parts: small crochet elements are combined to create a larger whole. The modularity of Mulyana's art means that his works are "constantly chang[ing], much like identity and nature, which are always evolving". Crochet, made up of individual stitches that can be "joined, altered, or rearranged", affords the artist a degree of freedom in building large-scale forms that maintain a hand-made quality with structural flexibility and cohesion. This ability to construct, deconstruct and reassemble allows Mulyana to mirror the ways in which evolution and change shape the natural world.

Nature, and in particular ocean life, is a central visual theme for Mulyana. This motif is inspired by his experience snorkelling off the coast of Indonesia, and what he encounters in those waters. Works such as *Ocean Wonderland* (2019) is a joyous experience that captures the multitudes of oceanic life forms. The bright colours of yarn are an ideal medium for the crochet depictions of corals, above which a school of felt yellow and orange fish is suspended. By contrast, Mulyana adopts a black and white colour palette in another ocean-inspired installation, *Kosong (Zero)* (2018), which is marked by a suspended ring of black octopus. Whereas the colours in *Ocean Wonderland* can be interpreted as a celebration of the diversity of life, *Kosong*'s monotone scheme serves as a stark reminder of the realities of climate change and coral bleaching, which are adversely impacting our

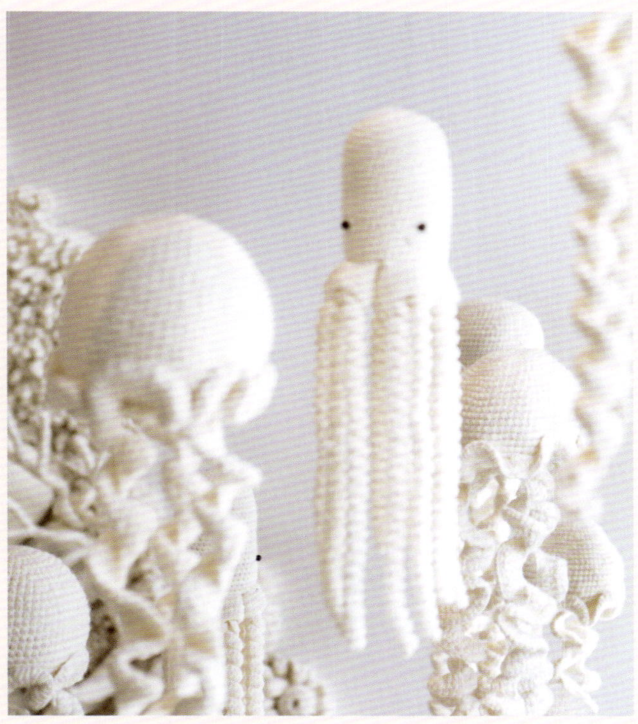

Opposite *Imagery of Eastern Nusantara Sea* (detail), 2024, Crochet **This page** *Satu (One)* (detail), 2018, Crochet

oceans' present and future. While Mulyana's works highlight the beauty found in our natural world, they also speak to the toll of human expansion and industry.

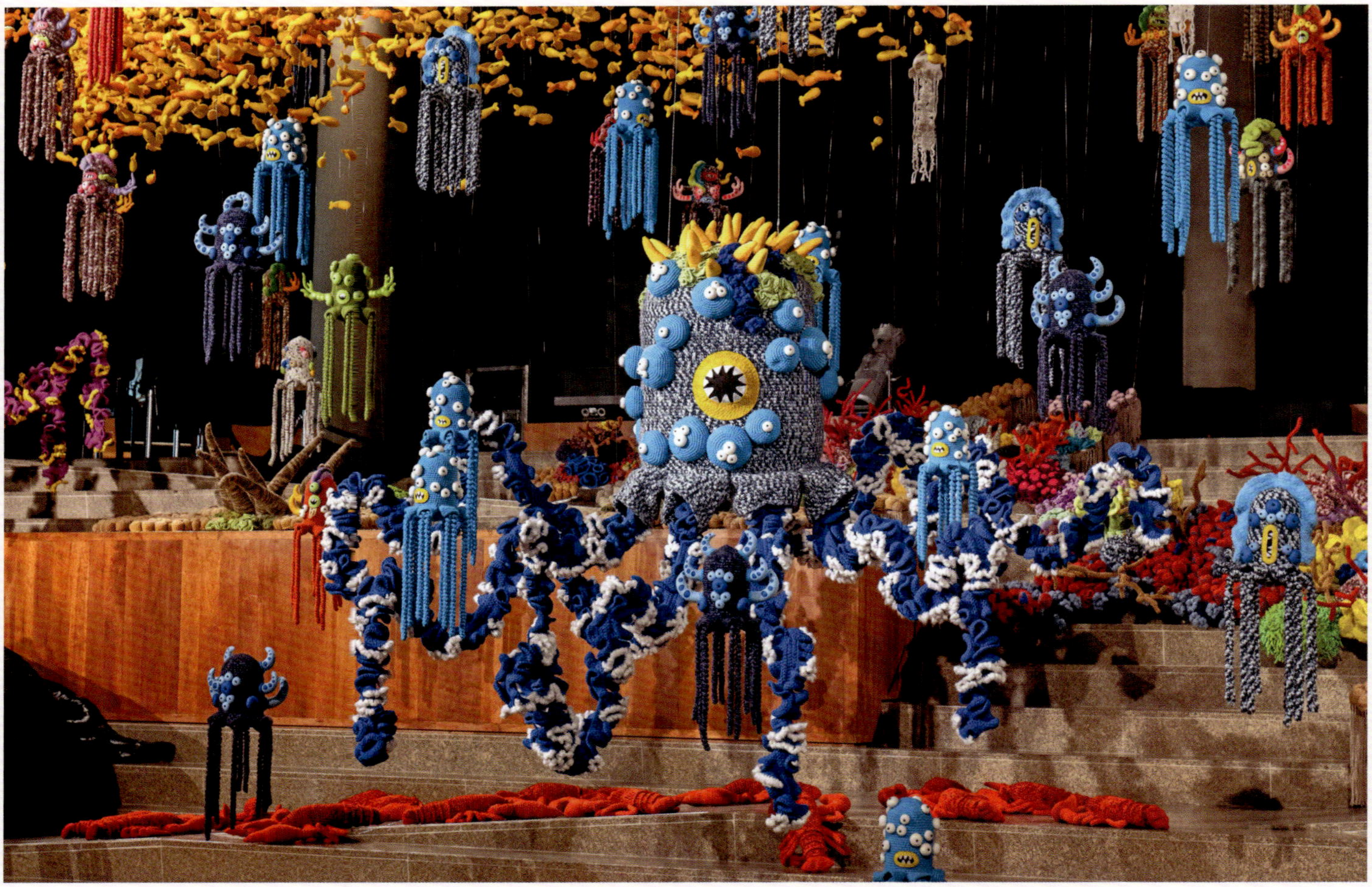

Despite these pressing themes, Mulyana's works continue to bring hope to audiences by instilling a sense of agency and a shared responsibility for collective action. This focus on togetherness is also encapsulated in Mulyana's working process. Now based in Yogyakarta, Mulyana's studio employs a number of collaborators who help him fabricate his works. Making crochet installations at his scale, consisting of between hundreds to tens of thousands of individual pieces, is a labour-intensive process. By bringing in other artists, Mulyana is able to make the "process communal and dynamic". This focus on community is also maintained through the range of workshops that he hosts as an extension of his artistic output, sharing the craft of crochet with audiences of different ages. In these workshops, like in his artworks, Mulyana fosters an inclusive outlook that widens not only how his installations and their themes are viewed, but who is invited to be part of the crochet process. ■

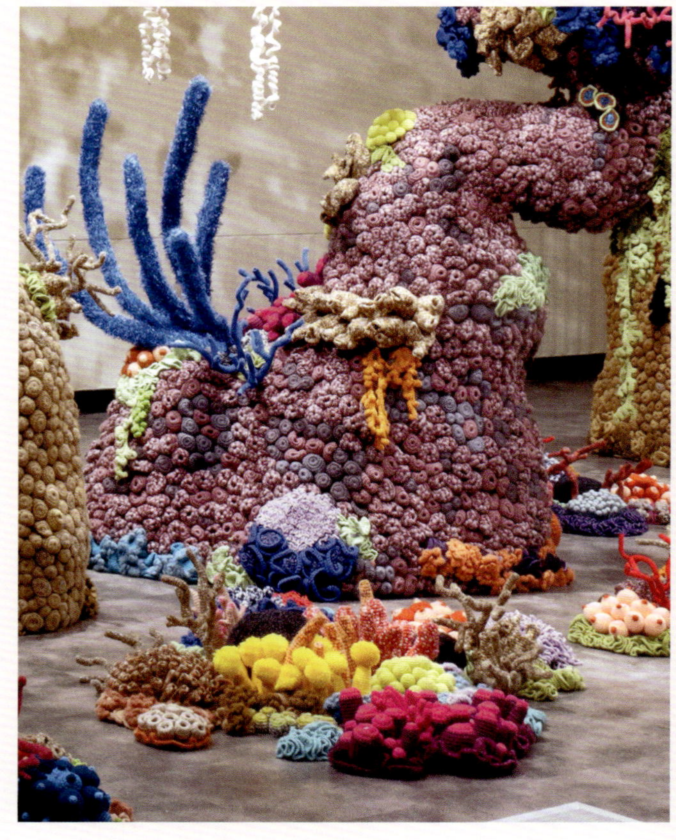

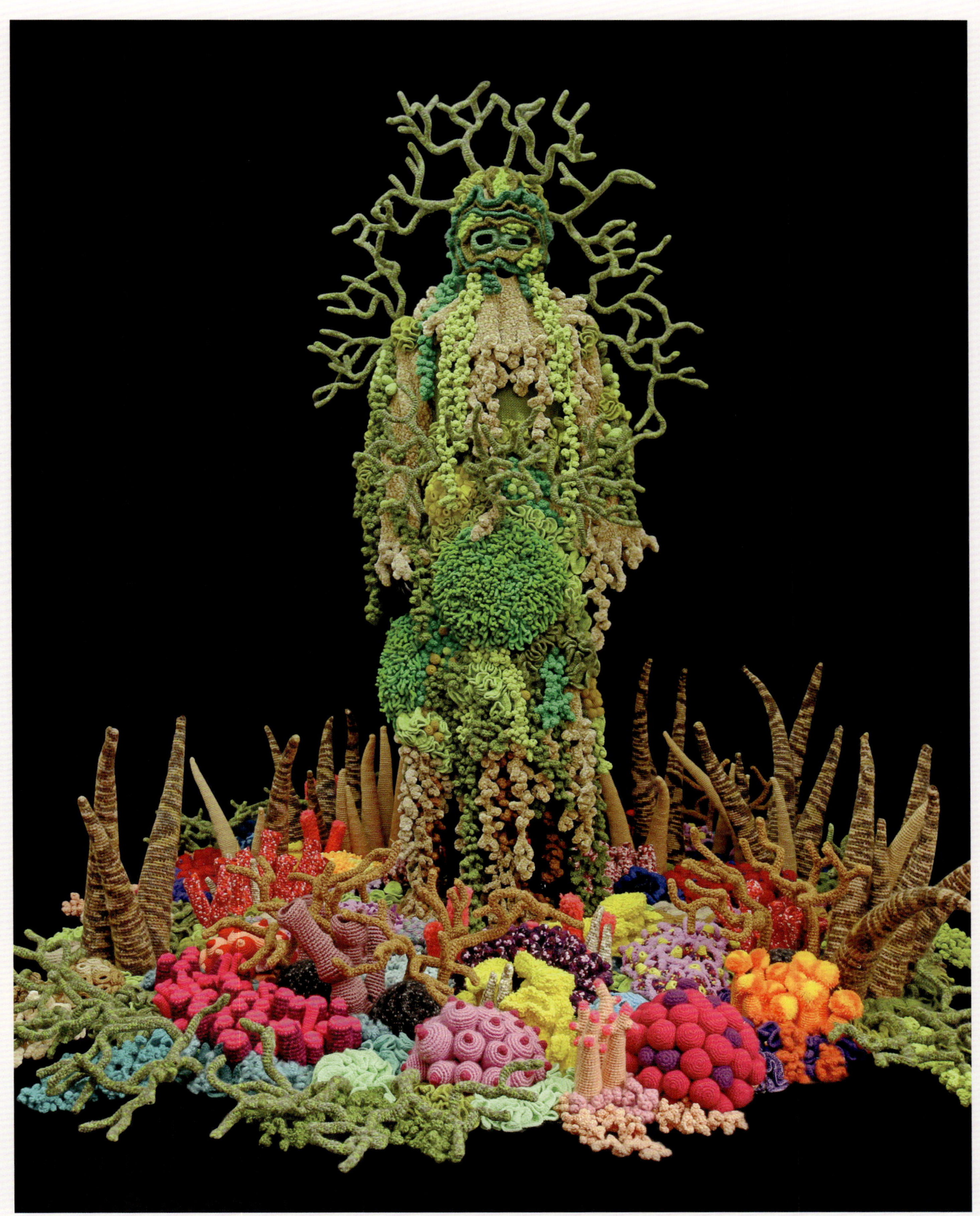

Opposite Top: *Diver(sea)ty*, 2020, Crochet; Bottom: *Ocean Wonderland* (detail), 2020, Crochet **This page** *Adikara*, 2020, Crochet **Overleaf** *Ocean Wonderland* (detail); **Page 137** Top: *Ocean Wonderland*; Bottom: *Satu*, 2018, Crochet

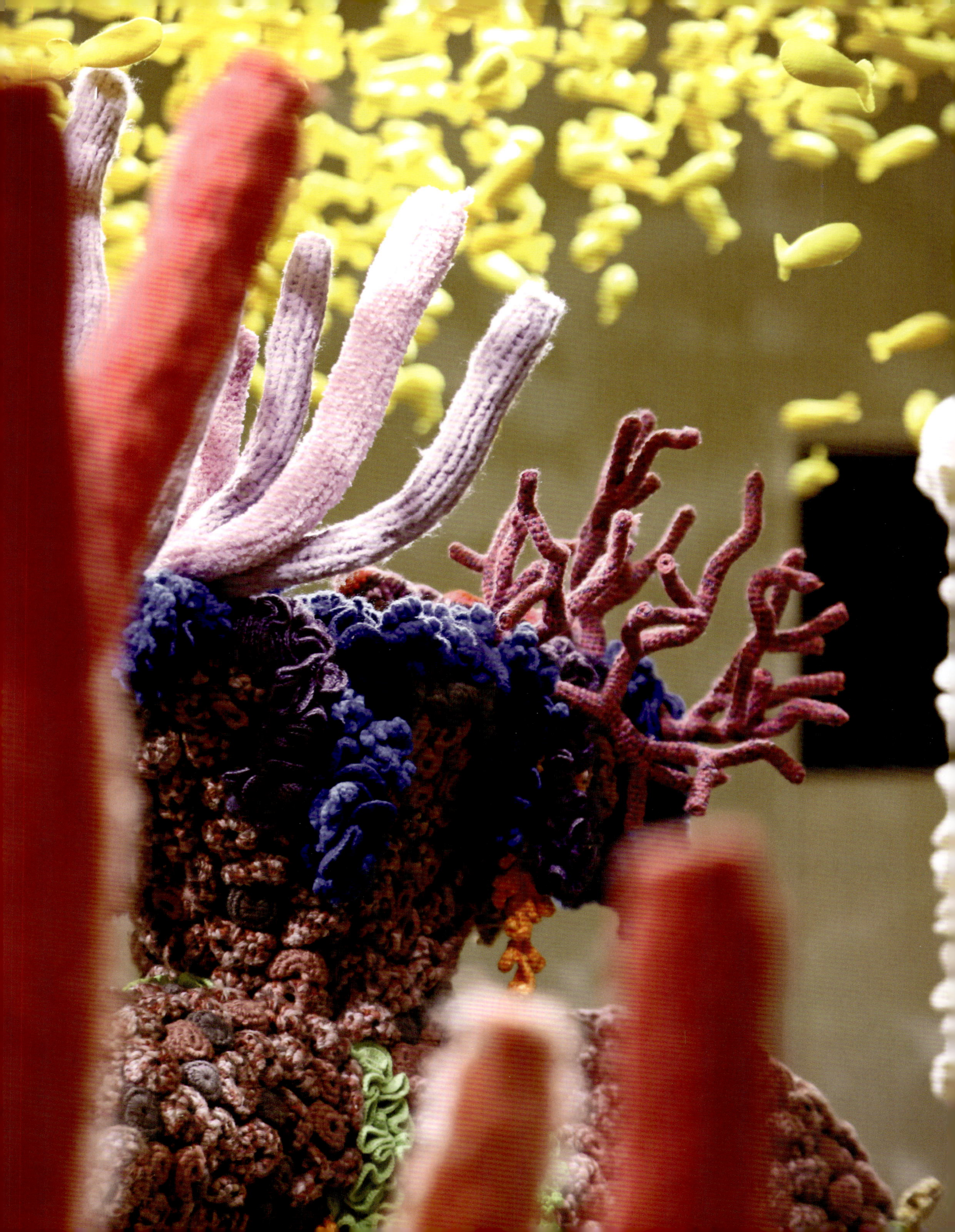

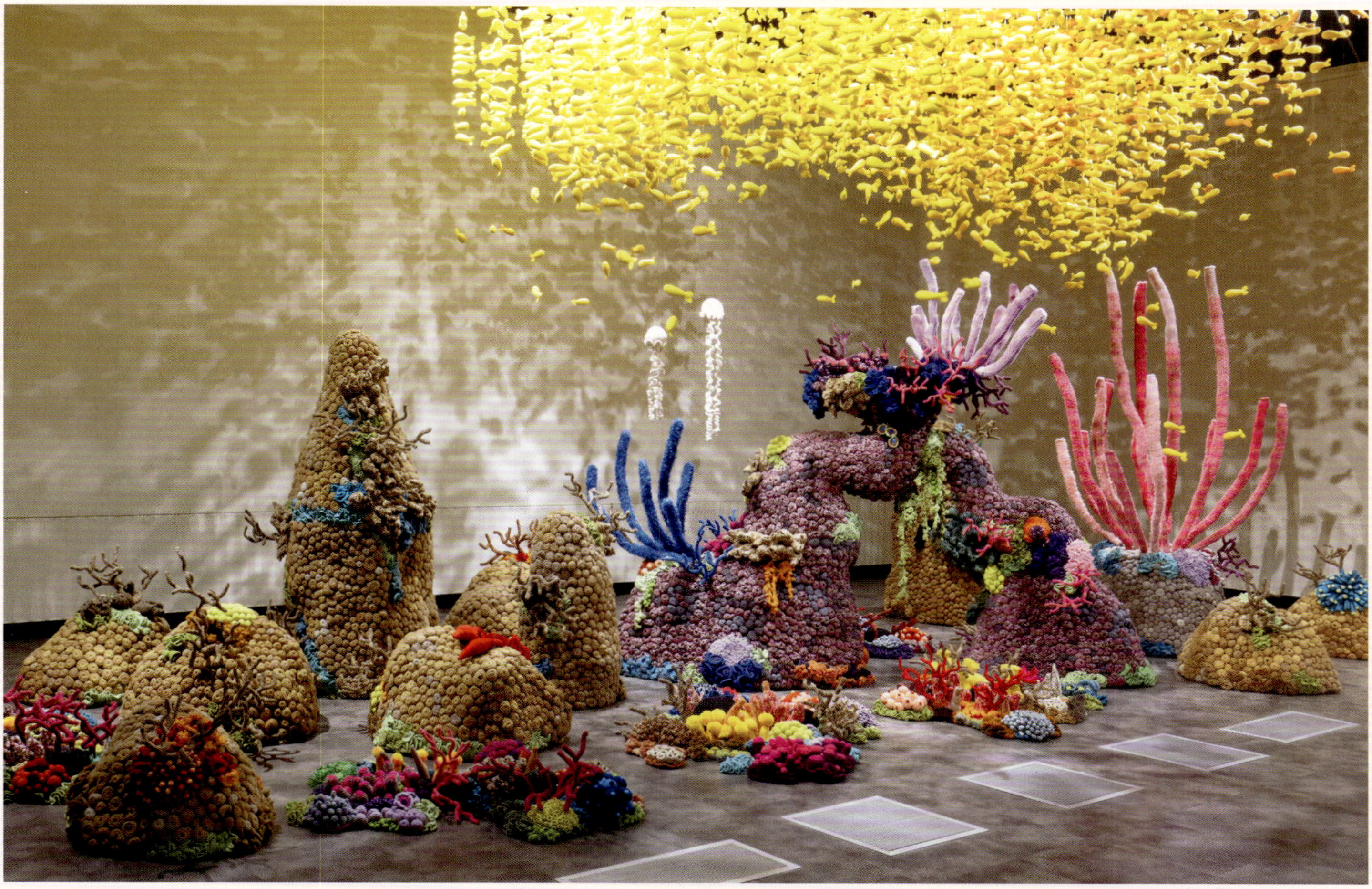

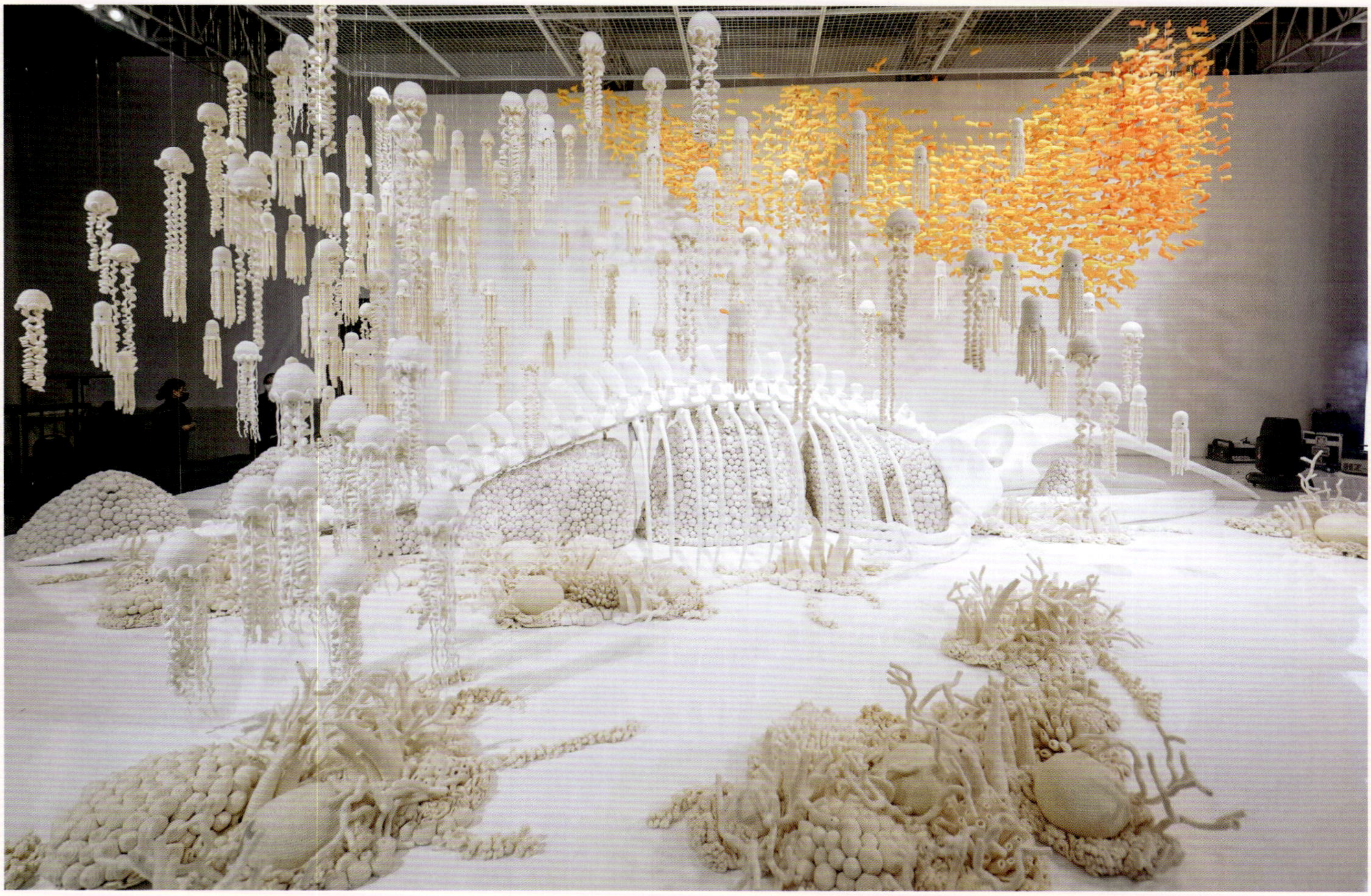

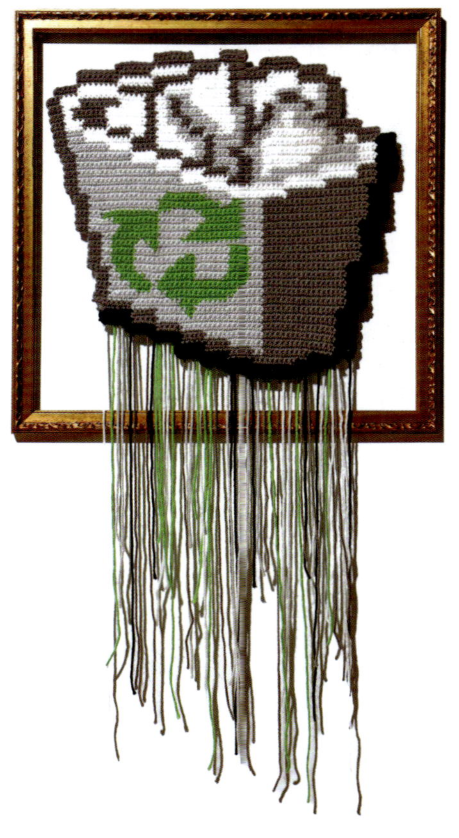

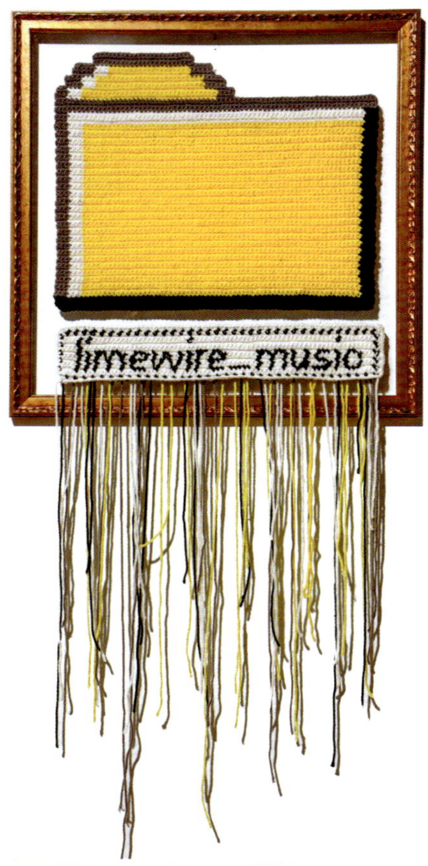

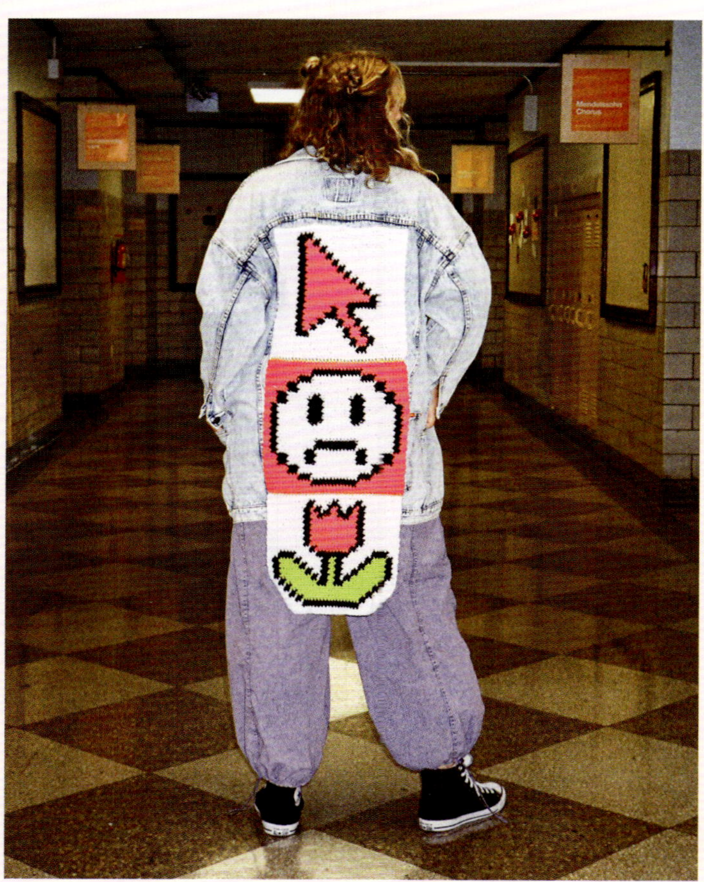

This page Clockwise from top left: *Recycling Bin*, 2023, Crochet; *Music Folder*, 2023, Crochet; *Untitled*, 2023, Crochet
Opposite *Untitled*, 2023, Crochet

crochet pieces, which each represent different computer "windows", are physically connected to a desktop computer in the centre of the room through loose yarn ends. In the windows, larger-than-screen depictions of *Neopets*, *The Sims*, *Minesweeper* and *Solitaire* are meticulously translated into yarn forms. The techniques of tapestry crochet, in which multiple colours of thread are carried through each individual stitch, allows for limitless colour changes. This expansive palette helps Nikolich to more accurately recreate pixel-for-pixel the digital screenshot on a larger scale.

When asked about who she makes her work for, Nikolich shares that a lot of her art is for "little Nicole". Reflecting on her childhood and her struggles with mental health, Nikolich says, "I spent a lot of time on the internet as a kid. I used the internet as an escape, as a playground, a hiding spot." Today, making art that references this time is "healing". By translating these memories into large-scale, awe-inspiring crochet installations and murals, Nikolich is hoping to speak to audiences who may recognise these shared nostalgic experiences.

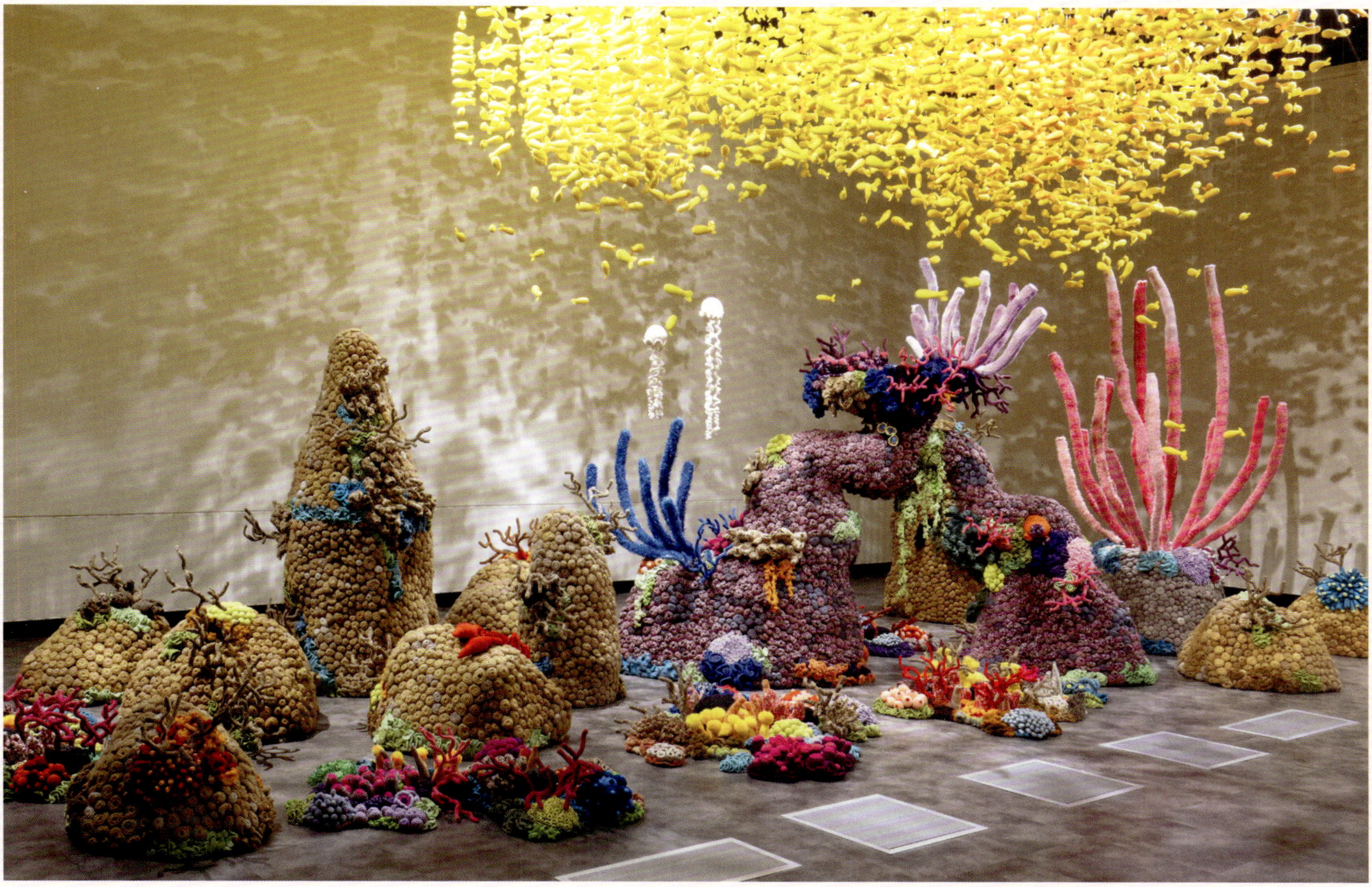

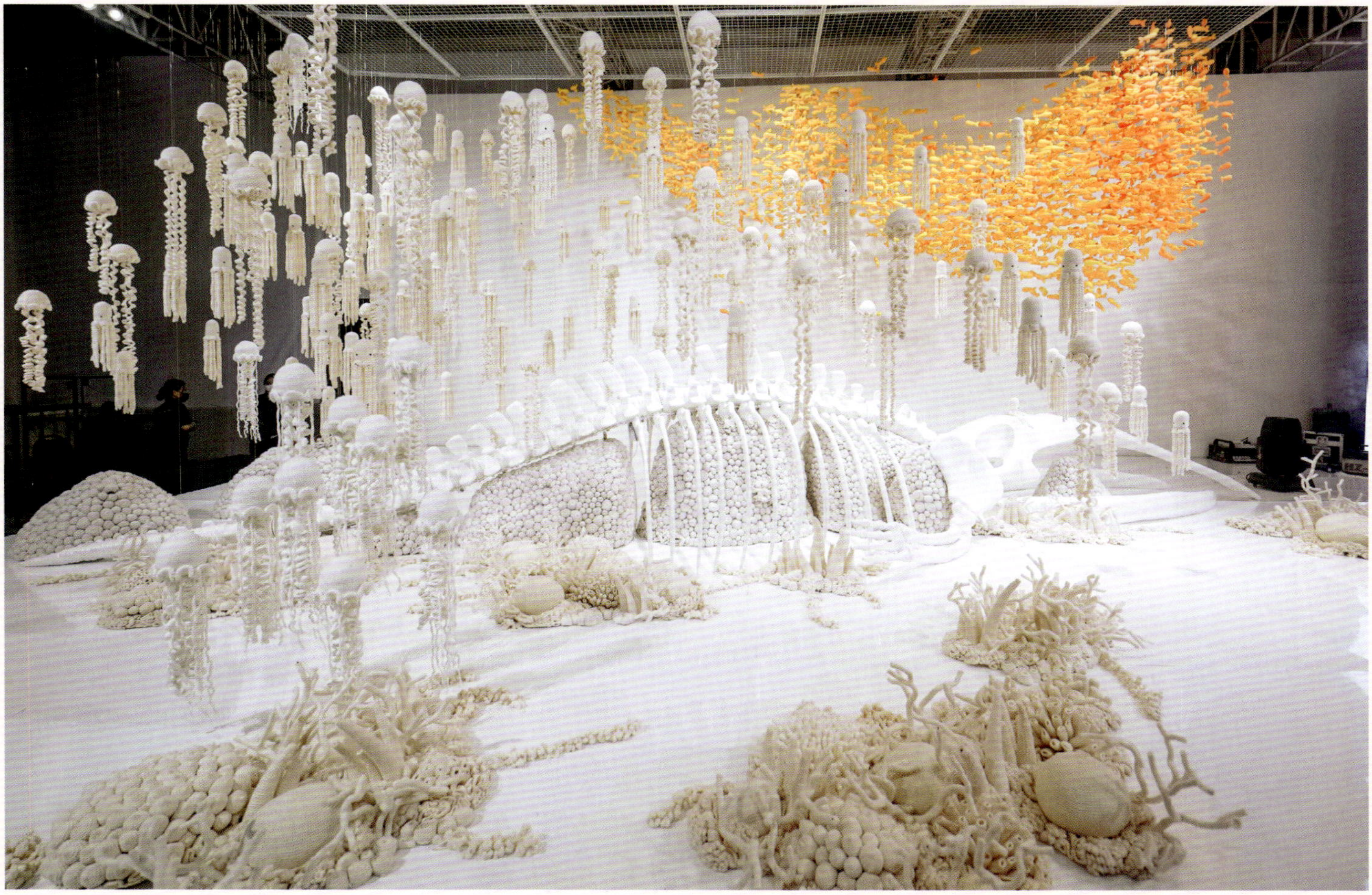

Nicole Nikolich

PHILADELPHIA

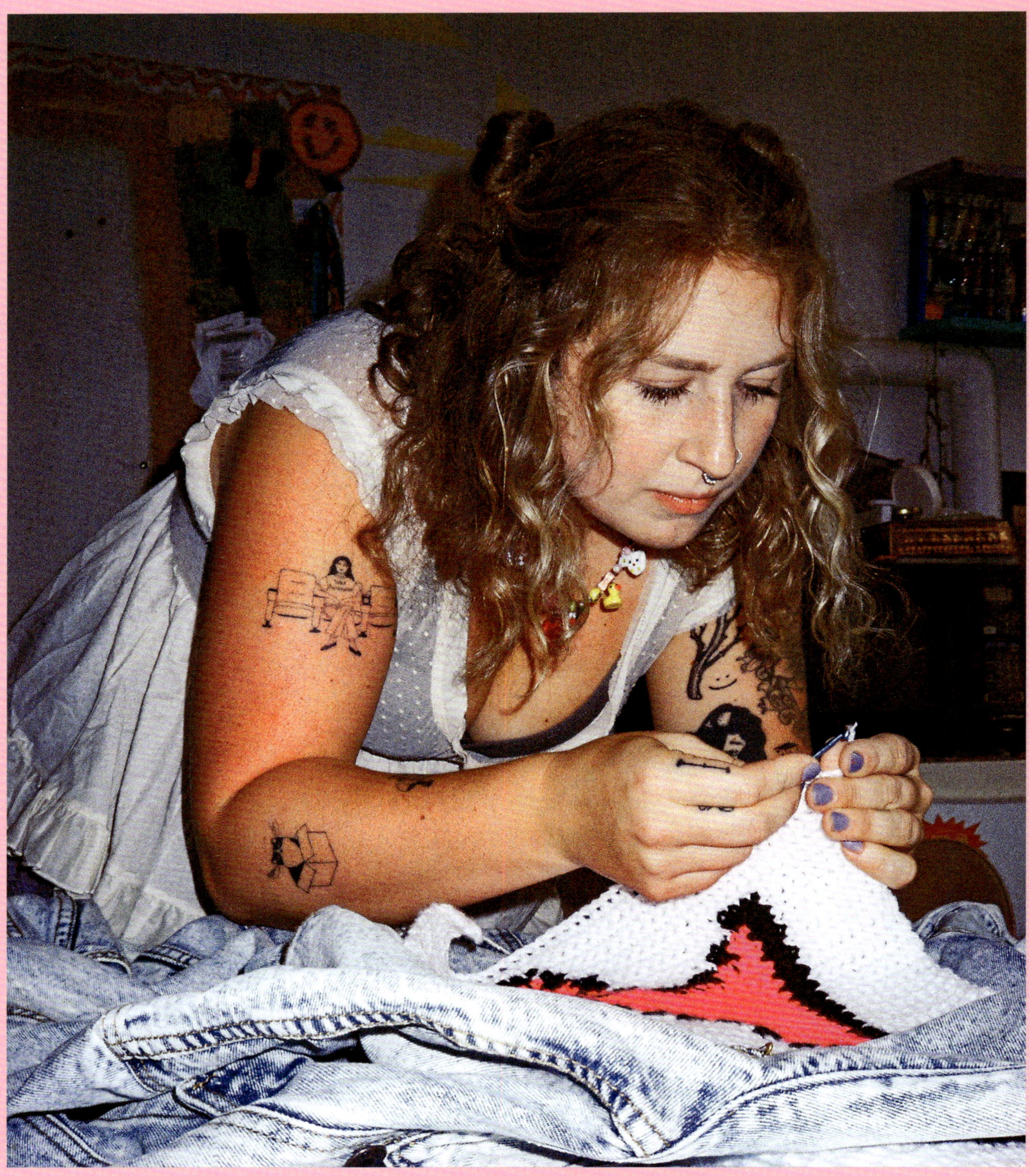

Nicole Nikolich, known as Lace in the Moon, is a full-time crochet artist working across exhibitions and public art. She first learnt to crochet from YouTube in 2017, after her doctor recommended the craft to help her cope with anxiety and depression. Of this first encounter with the technique, Nikolich says, "When the yarn hook met my hands, that was it." She'd grown up as someone who loved art but never felt like she found the right medium; crochet and its colours and textures afforded Nikolich a peaceful and meditative way of working that suited her well. "It's really peaceful and fun and it just clicked for me."

Now based in Philadelphia, a city with a vibrant street art culture ("We have the most murals per capita of any city in the world"), Nikolich got her start as an artist through yarn bombing, or the act of decorating public spaces with crochet or knitted fabrics. She installed these early artworks, which often paired floral shapes with text, around her neighbourhood – tied up to fences, wrapped around poles or hung from walls. These roots are still present in Nikolich's public artwork commissions today, which take the form of ambitious installations and immersive experiences that engage creatively with space.

Nikolich's works explore themes that include mental health, healing, LGBTQI+ issues and pop culture (she met Taylor Swift as a result of crocheting her lyrics). Flowers are a common motif, from the simple blooms of her early days to more recent installations such as *From The City Cracks* (2022), a series of free-standing flower sculptures measuring between 3 and 5 metres tall that were installed at a park for the Philadelphia Flower Show.

Some of Nikolich's more recent works are inspired by personal experiences of growing up on the internet in the late 1990s/early 2000s and a nostalgic recollection of technologies and platforms during the early transformations of the World Wide Web. For Nikolich, the grid-like form of crochet is well suited to exploring these themes, as "individual stitches [represent] 8-bit pixels" and yarn strings the "wires or the insides of old monitors". Beyond physical correlations, crochet and computers also share a thematic commonality: "I love how crocheting is often a solo activity, and the early days of the internet were often spent alone in a computer room, as you could usually only access the internet from a small box in a small room." Nikolich's works inspired by this period include yarn representations of old Microsoft Windows icons, as well as glitchy portraits of "MySpace Tom" – the latter a visual nod to MySpace's "Top 8 friends" and a visual representation of how our memories and recollections change over time.

Nikolich's recent installation *Can I Please Eat In The Computer Room Tonight?* (2024–25) brings this personal experience of growing up online into a public space. In this work, four large-scale tapestry

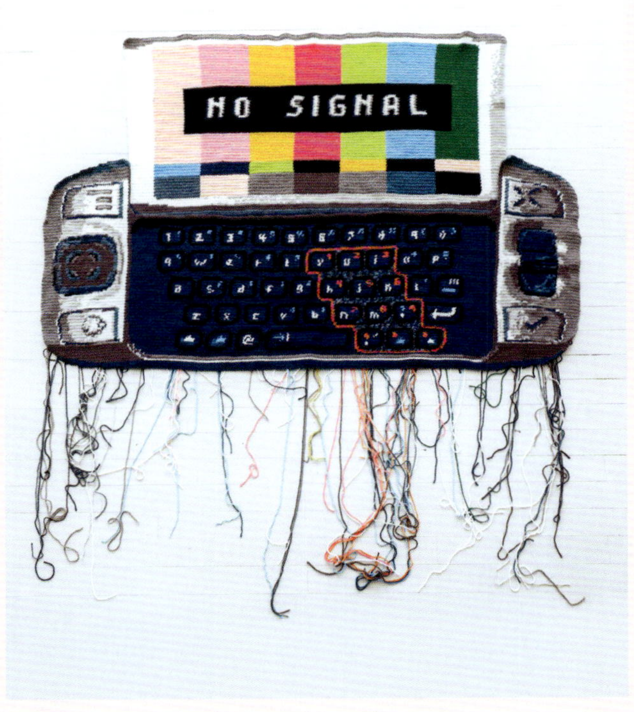

T-Mobile Sidekick II, 2023, Crochet

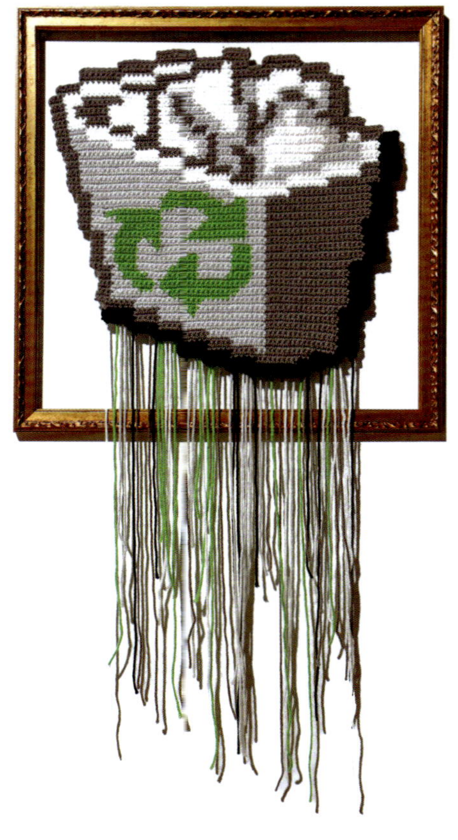

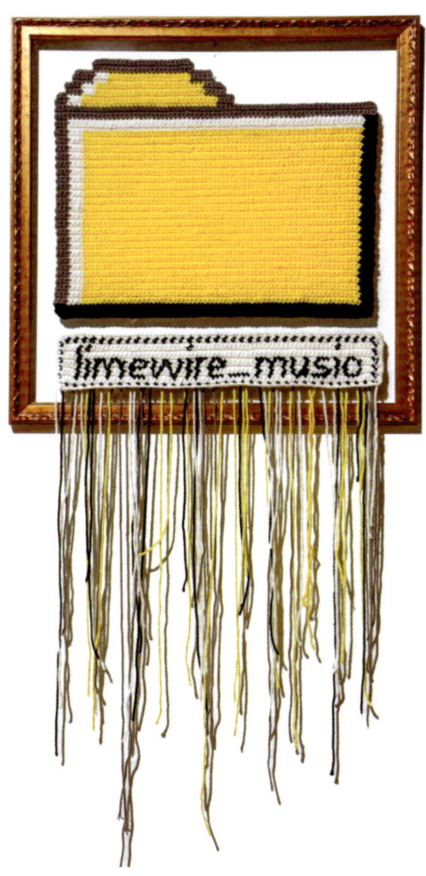

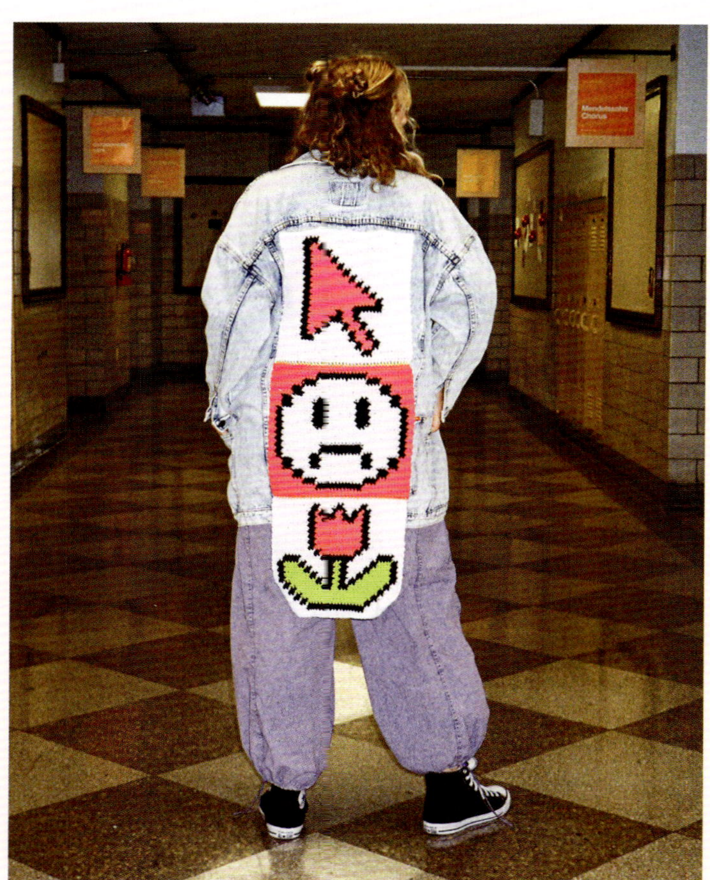

This page Clockwise from top left: *Recycling Bin*, 2023, Crochet; *Music Folder*, 2023, Crochet; *Untitled*, 2023, Crochet
Opposite *Untitled*, 2023, Crochet

crochet pieces, which each represent different computer "windows", are physically connected to a desktop computer in the centre of the room through loose yarn ends. In the windows, larger-than-screen depictions of *Neopets*, *The Sims*, *Minesweeper* and *Solitaire* are meticulously translated into yarn forms. The techniques of tapestry crochet, in which multiple colours of thread are carried through each individual stitch, allows for limitless colour changes. This expansive palette helps Nikolich to more accurately recreate pixel-for-pixel the digital screenshot on a larger scale.

When asked about who she makes her work for, Nikolich shares that a lot of her art is for "little Nicole". Reflecting on her childhood and her struggles with mental health, Nikolich says, "I spent a lot of time on the internet as a kid. I used the internet as an escape, as a playground, a hiding spot." Today, making art that references this time is "healing". By translating these memories into large-scale, awe-inspiring crochet installations and murals, Nikolich is hoping to speak to audiences who may recognise these shared nostalgic experiences. ■

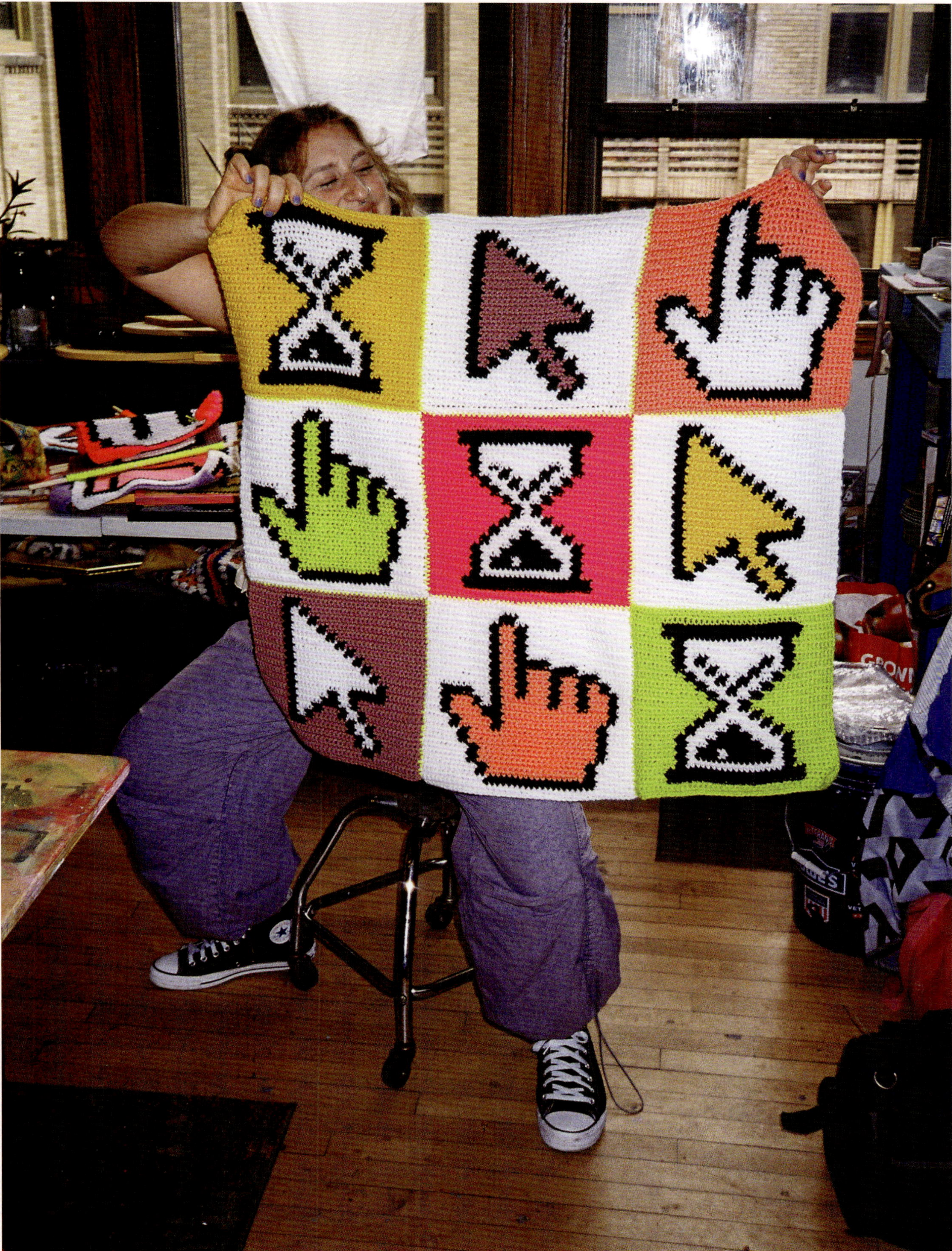

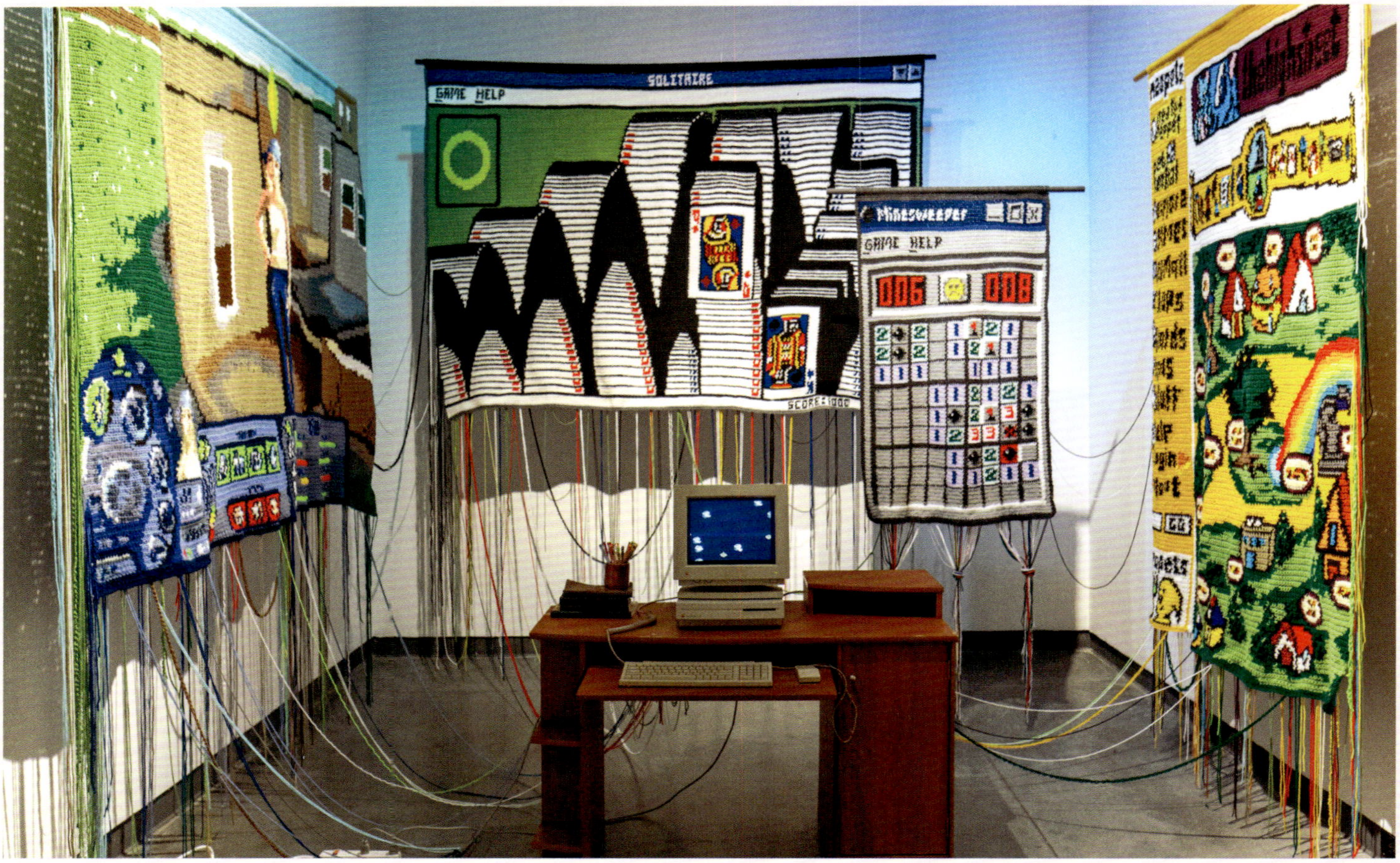

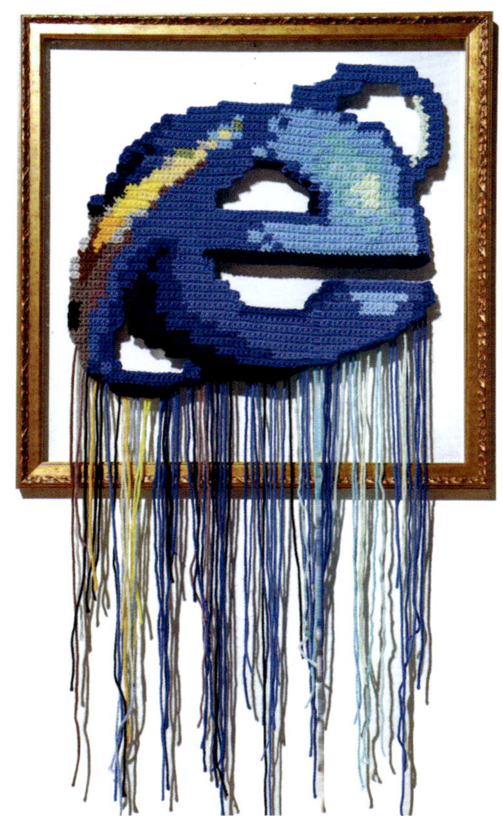

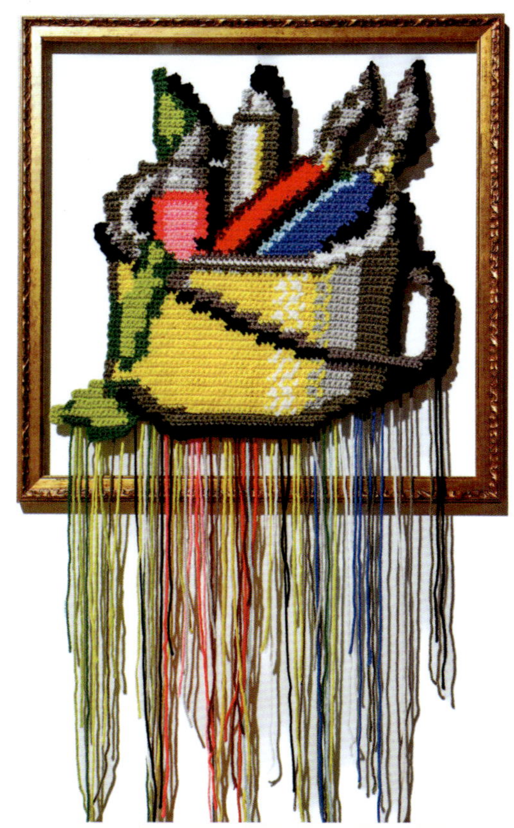

This page Clockwise from top: *Can I Please Eat In The Computer Room Tonight?*, 2024–25, Crochet; *MS Paint*, 2023, Crochet; *Internet Explorer*, 2023, Crochet **Opposite** Clockwise from top left: *MySpace Tom no. 1*, 2023, Crochet; *MySpace Tom no. 3*, 2023, Crochet; *Can I Please Eat In The Computer Room Tonight?* (detail)

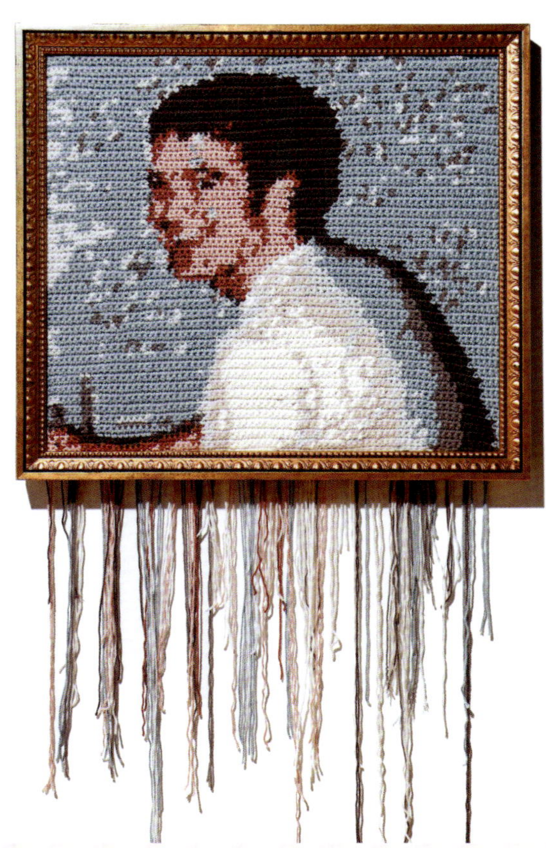

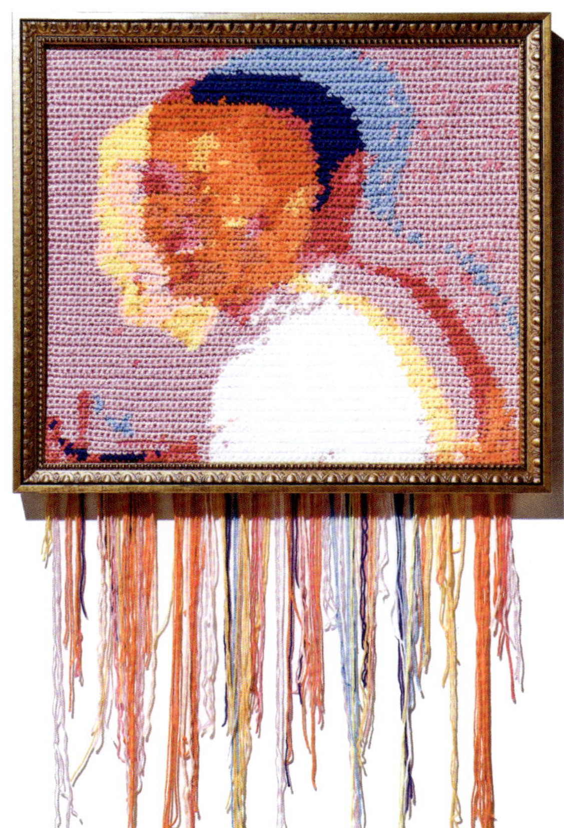

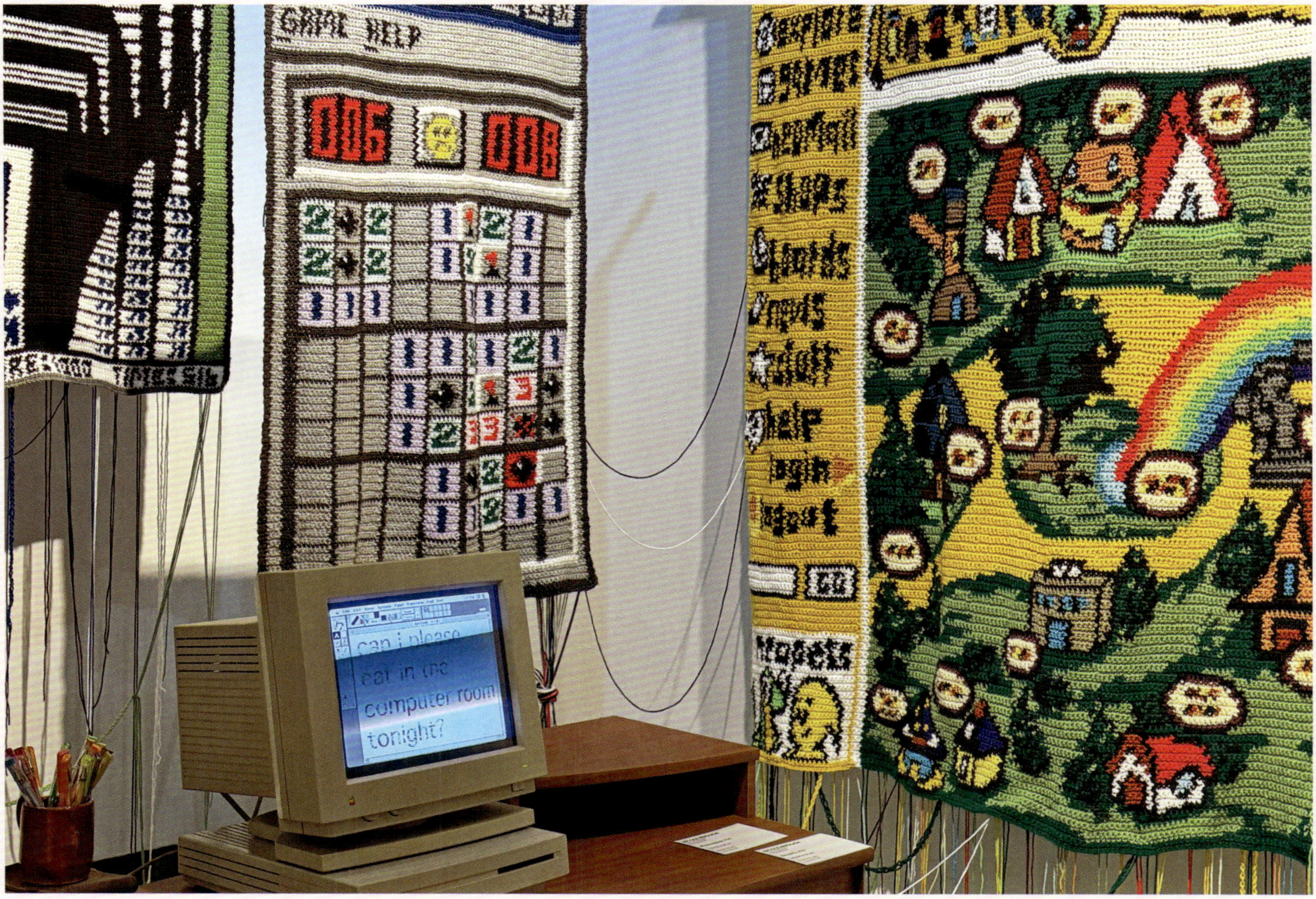

Omar Badrin

TORONTO

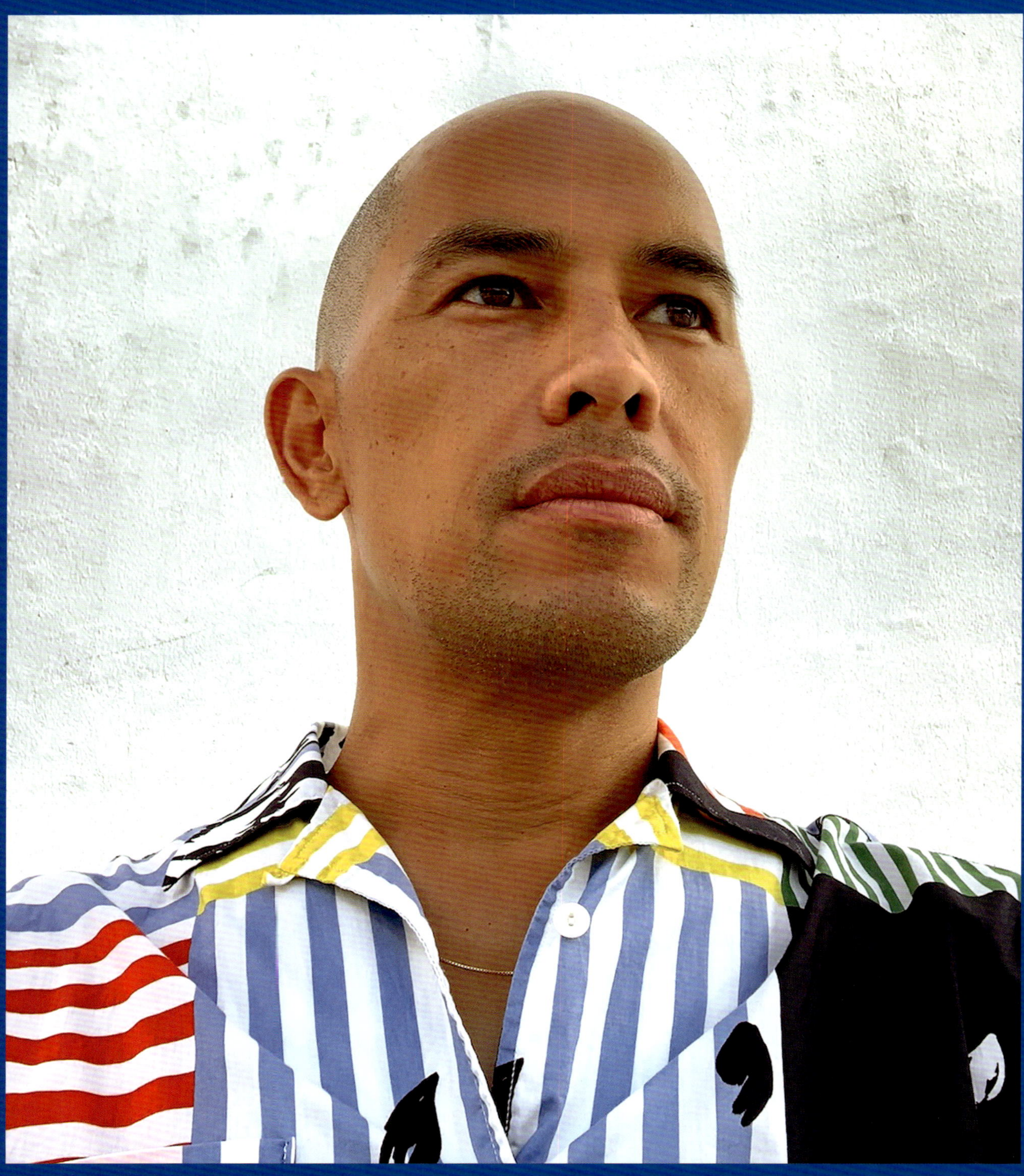

Born in Kuala Lumpur, Malaysia, Omar Badrin relocated to the province of Newfoundland, Canada, with his adopted family. As a person of colour raised in a predominantly white community, Badrin makes artworks that grapple with themes of belonging and otherness through a racial and cultural lens, informed by his own experience of transracial adoption. Today Badrin lives and works in Toronto, but his personal connections to Malaysia and Newfoundland continue to inspire his art.

Badrin's affinity for crochet started in his family home. The artist grew up surrounded by needlework, although he explains that he didn't fully come to appreciate the knitting and crochet skills of his mother and grandmother until later in life. In particular, the experience of watching his grandmother crochet during his childhood was formative. Badrin explains, "I was very close with her. I was inspired to crochet because I wanted to keep family traditions like this going." He goes further to reflect that "the medium to me is symbolic of adopted family traditions and history". Contextually within Newfoundland, where textiles and handcrafts are very popular, Badrin's adoption of crochet can also be regarded as a symbolic gesture of connection to this region.

One common feature across many of Badrin's works, which include sculptures, videos and animations, are masks. Masks, of course, can take many different meanings depending on context and utility: whether they conceal, protect or embellish. Badrin's masks straddle the grotesque and the visually enticing; they are bright and colourful, yet their forms (with open eyes and gaping mouths) can also suggest more complex interpretations regarding death and the body.

For Badrin, these masks "serve to reveal, rather than hide", reflecting in part the artist's own journey of self-acceptance as he embraces lifelong feelings of "otherness". The use of bold nylon colours immediately attracts the attention of viewers, yet the masks also fail in their functional task to shield as Badrin creates them at a loose gauge: they can't hide or protect wearers. Beyond the physical forms, there is also a metaphorical association with "masking", or the act of concealing parts of yourself to fit in. Badrin's crochet masks suggest a sense of alienation or an emotional distance, but there's also whimsy and fun within their bold appearance. He's not concerned with being highly proficient at crochet", but instead is interested in how the medium can be used "in a basic way to translate ideas".

Badrin's crochet masks creatively use a range of unexpected materials. Instead of conventional yarn and fibres, the artist crochets with materials including nylon thread, paracord and flagging tape as well as nylon fishing twine. While some of these materials connect to Badrin's experience working on construction sites, they are also visual cues of Newfoundland, with its history of maritime industries. The open structure on some of his works, such as the mask *See Me* (2017), evokes a net-like quality, strikingly similar to those used for fishing. In fact, before Badrin started crocheting, he explored the regional art of making fishing nets. It was ultimately, however, the connection to his family that led to crochet as his ongoing choice.

As each of Badrin's works are made spontaneously, without pre-planned sketches or plans, they are all unique. In this way, they can be viewed as a rejection of homogeneity, and an embrace of what makes people individual. Badrin's works are created from the particular regional histories and lived experiences of the artist, but they also speak to our broader shared desires for belonging and acceptance. He leaves the interpretation open to the viewer. ■

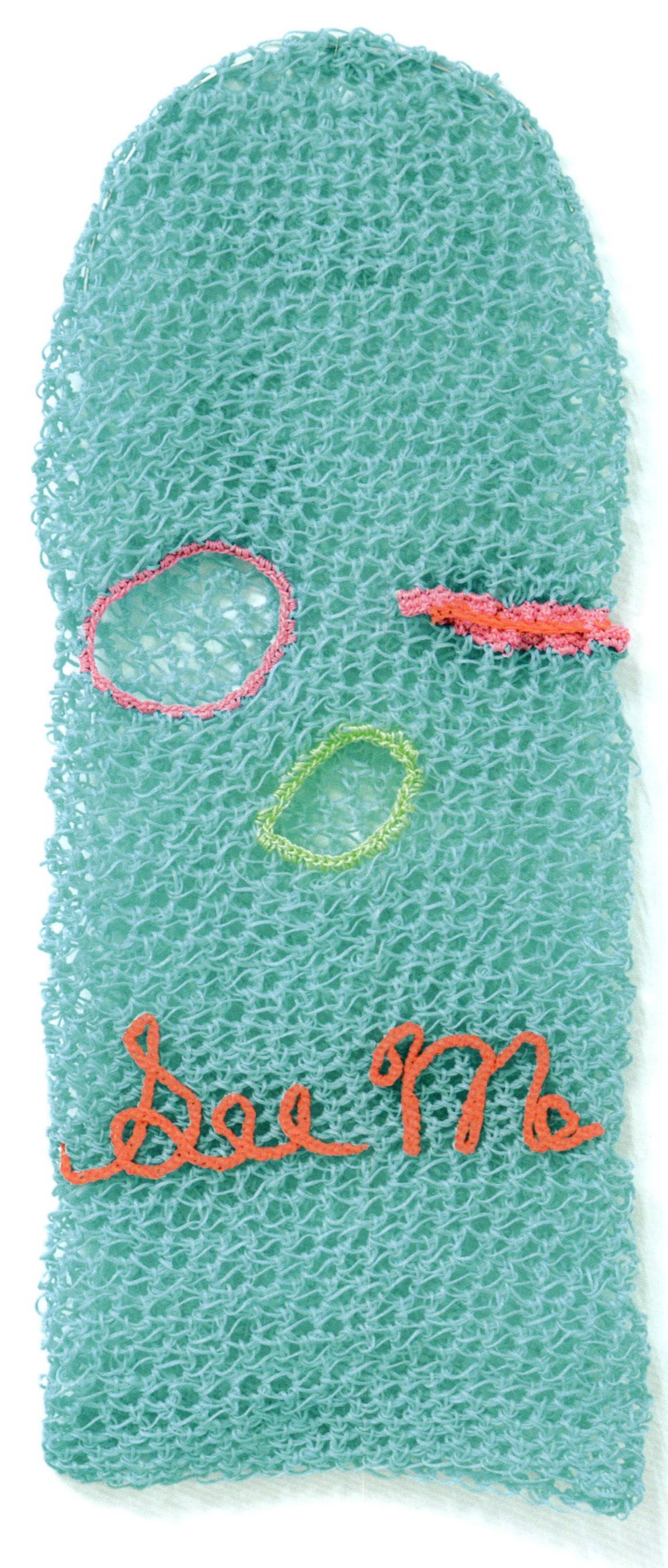
See Me

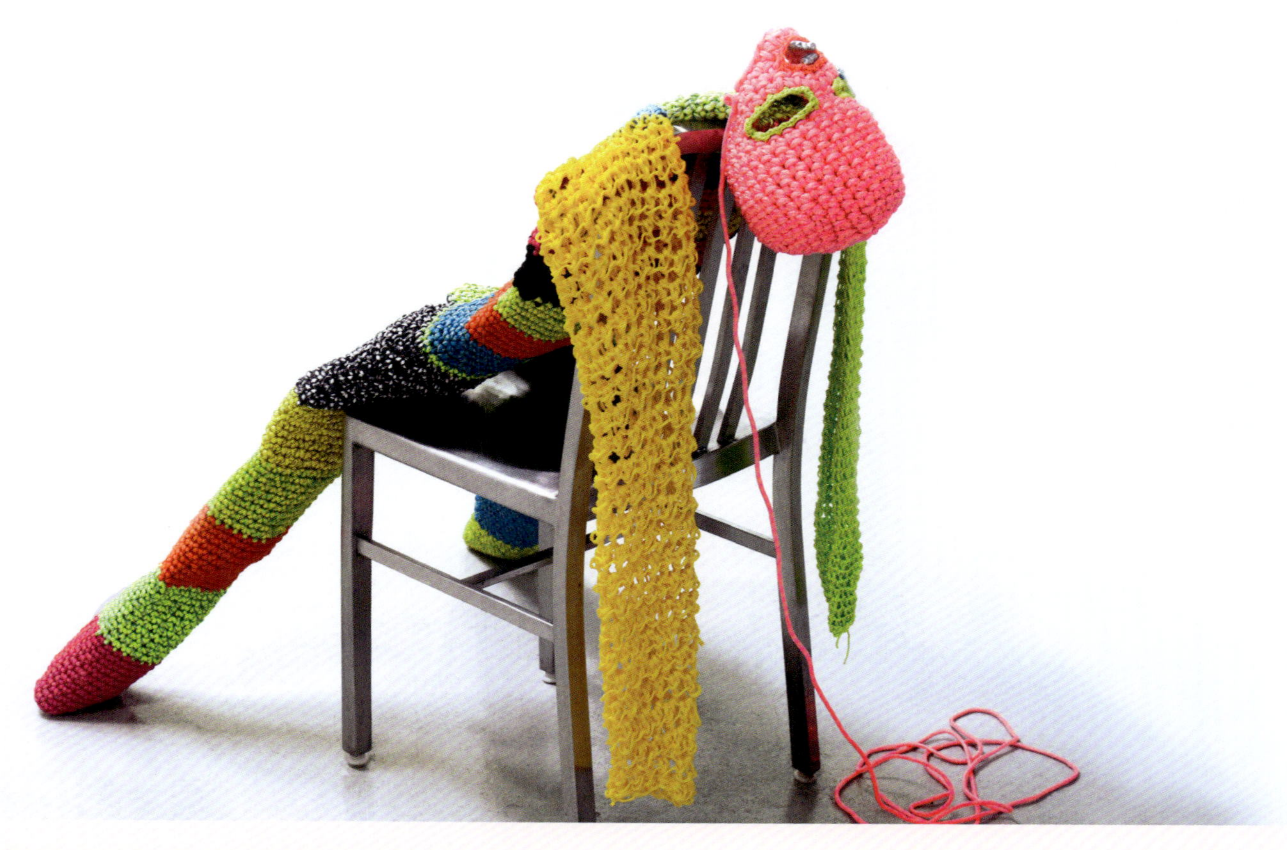

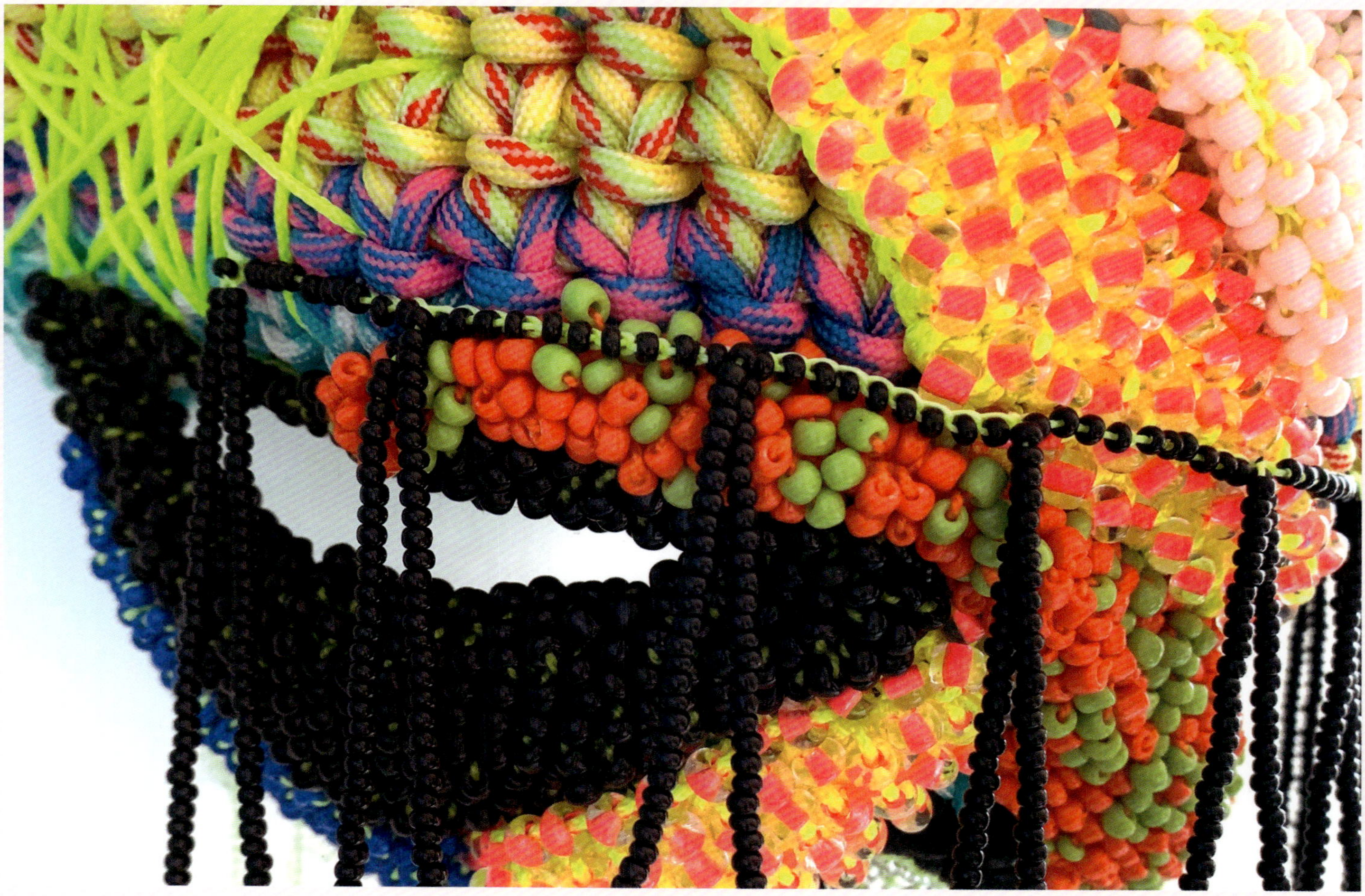

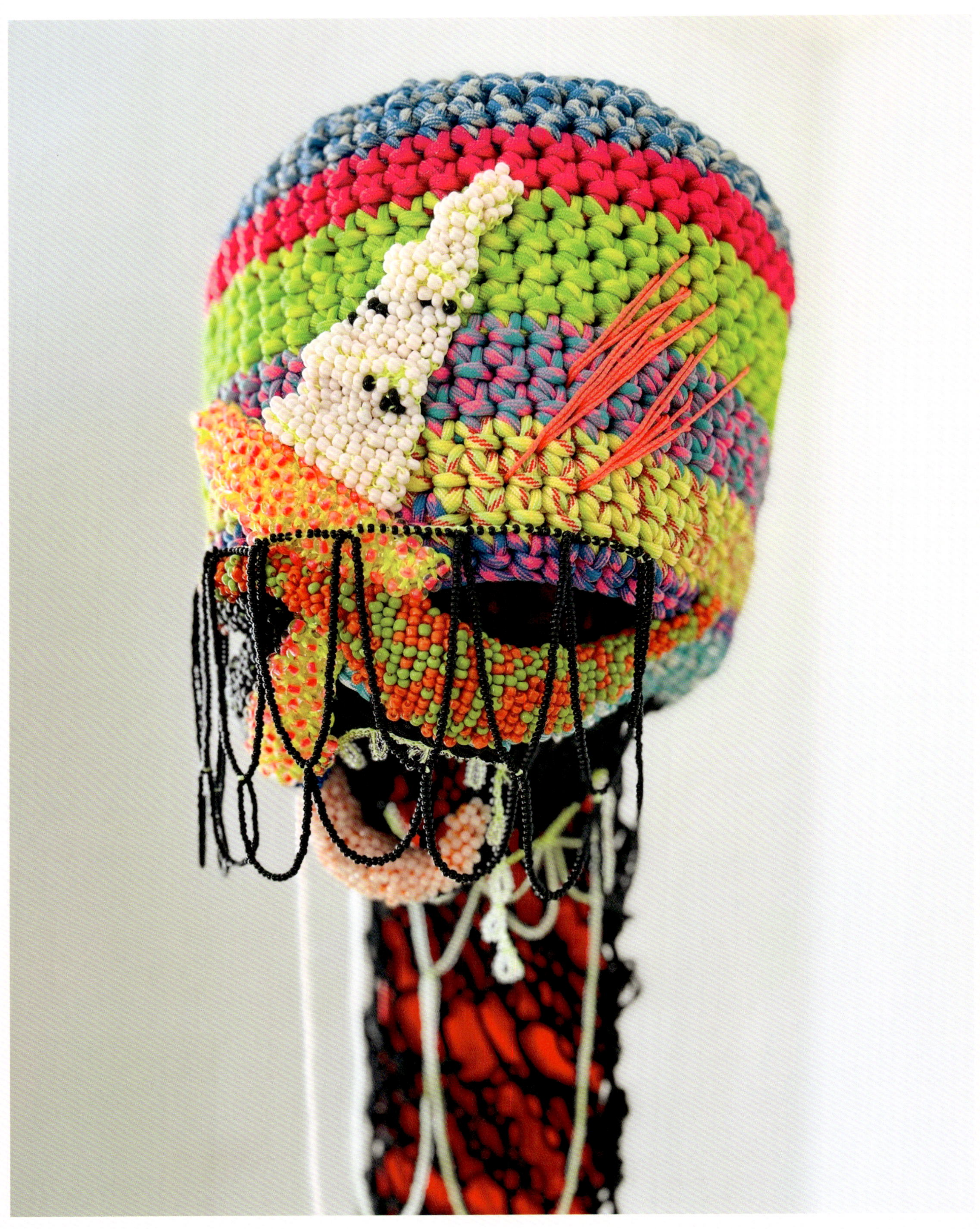

Page 146 *See Me*, 2017, Crochet **Page 147** Top: *Lacuna*, 2018, Crochet; Bottom: *Adornment I* (detail), 2023, Crochet and beadwork **This page** *Adornment I*, 2023, Crochet and beadwork **Opposite** *I Still Think About You Often*, 2024, Crochet and beadwork

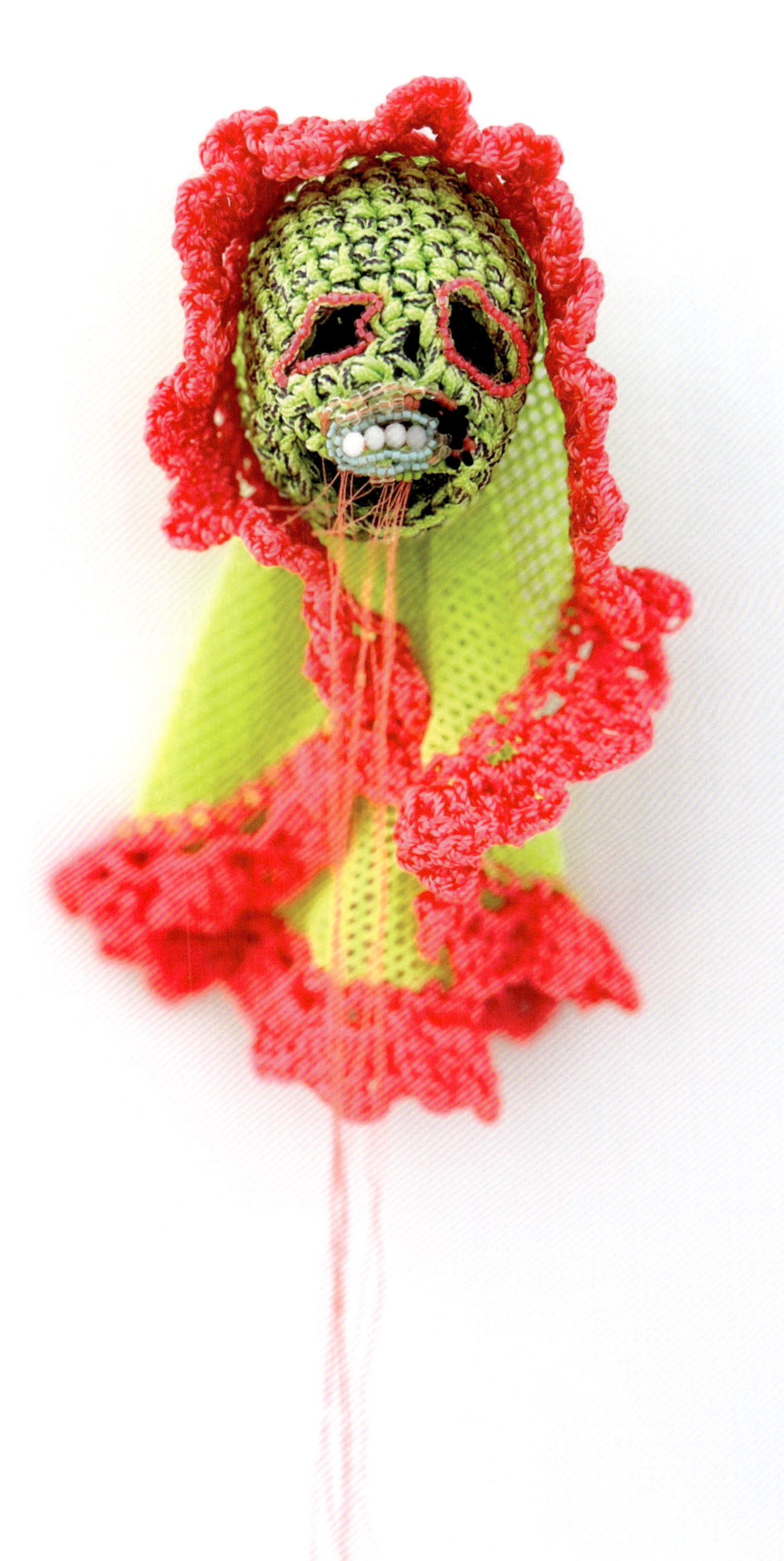

Paula do Prado

GADICAL COUNTRY/
SYDNEY

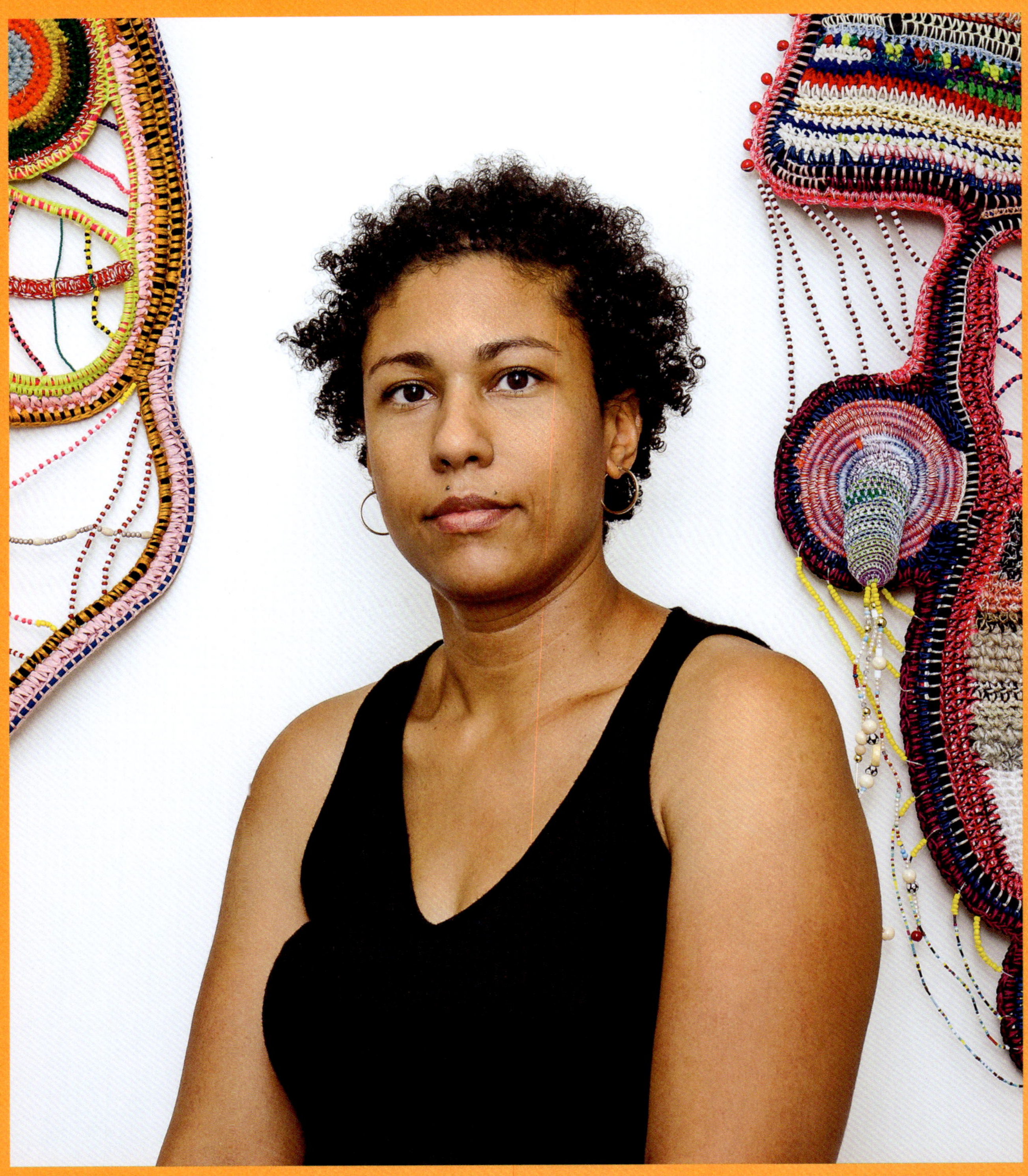

Born in Uruguay and migrating to Australia as a child, Paula do Prado is a contemporary artist who engages with textile and fibre art to explore the intersections of her African Bantu-Kongo, Iberian and Charrúa (Indigenous Uruguayan) ancestral heritage. Do Prado recognises that her artistic output is intimately connected to her family, cultural storytelling and spiritual practices: "For me there is no sense of, need or desire to create a separation between creating art and all of the other roles I fulfil as a mother, a daughter, a friend and human in the world. My art practice is indivisible from the ancestral and community relationships, both human and more than human (wetlands, rivers, salt and sweet water) that I cultivate and tend to."

What is immediately striking about do Prado's works are her highly attuned senses of colour, texture and form, which are brought together in her art to create unique sculptural forms and installations that employ techniques including crochet, coiling and embroidery. Do Prado uses a range of materials, from textured and fluffy yarns to beads, felt rope and cooking twine, which are combined to form large-scale expressive works. She still uses the same crochet slip stitch she first learnt 20 years ago, based around a simple "looping" technique: a foundational stitch common to many cultures and textile traditions. Relishing in the creative freedom of crochet as a freeform medium, do Prado doesn't "sketch, pre-plan work or use any sort of patterns or templates, or count stitches". Rather, she is led by experimentation and "surrendering to the materials and process", allowing curiosity and playfulness to guide her. While there may be recognisable motifs, such as animal forms or shapes that suggest land and waterways, her visual language is wholly unique and left open-ended for audience interpretation.

This fluidity translates to do Prado's working process, and the collapse between studio life and home life. Motherhood has shifted her relationship to artmaking; as do Prado reflects, it has "perhaps been a main factor in the development of my working process, because I had to be flexible and make time for my practice as well as all my care responsibilities". These care responsibilities have also meant do Prado chooses materials and processes that are safer around children.

While do Prado's working techniques and materials have adapted over her years as an artist, one thing that's remained constant are her themes, which she describes as encompassing "ancestral connections, diaspora, the cosmos, nature spirits, relationships to place, complicity and my position as a settler-migrant inextricably implicated in the ongoing colonial project that is so-called Australia". Do Prado is particularly interested in how artmaking can offer more "textural or haptic" ways to explore questions and themes that are difficult to approach through more rational or linear means: an approach afforded by do Prado's intuitive and fluid style.

Crochet acts as a way for do Prado to "process and work through whatever is happening in my own personal and family life, as well as what's happening in the world more broadly". The bold colours and exuberance of her works gives the artist space to contest with the difficulties of the world around her, offering a creative outlet to challenge "a lot of the rage and anger I feel at injustices and the frustrations, feelings of smallness and impotence". She shares, "My [textile] practice has also been fundamental for me in processing and remaining open-eyed and soft-hearted to bear witness to so many atrocities occurring concurrently – Gaza, Congo, Sudan – whilst also recognising the ongoing violence First Nations people face on a daily basis." In this way, it is not just the material output, but also the *process* of creating work that instils meaning in do Prado's works. To encounter them is to be reminded of the multiplicity of ways that artmaking can positively shape culture and heal the self. ■

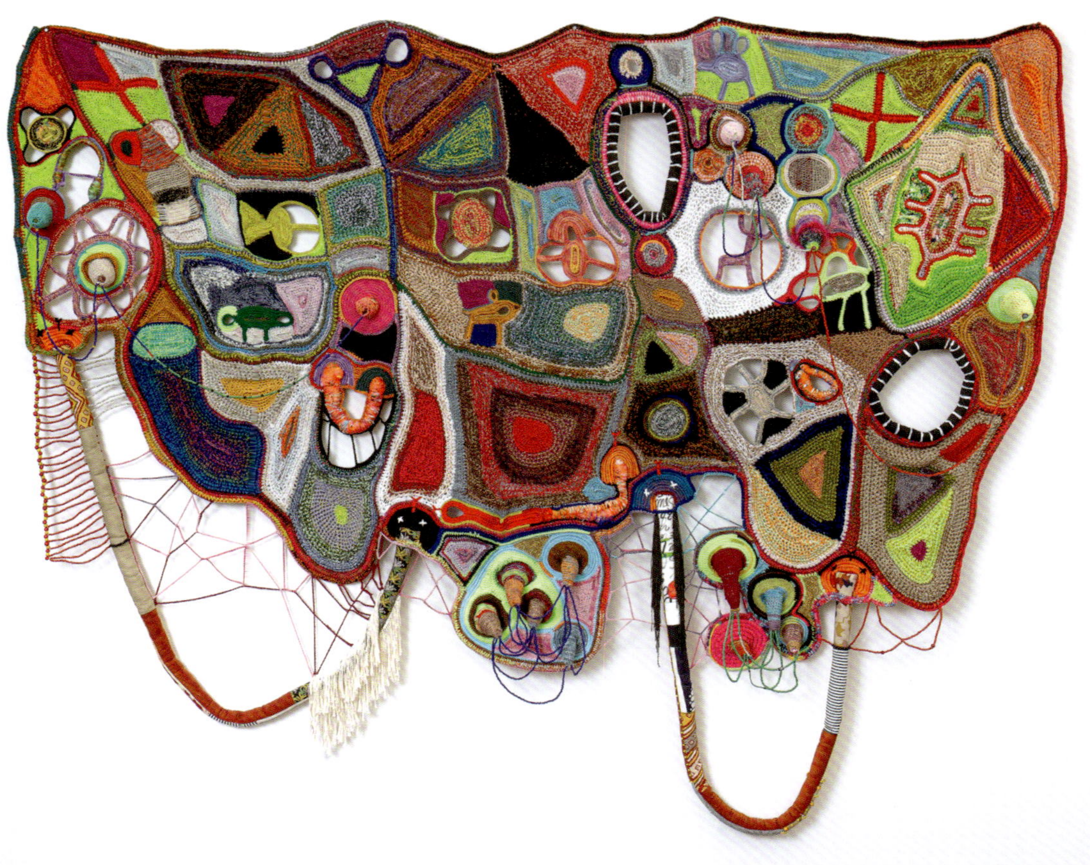

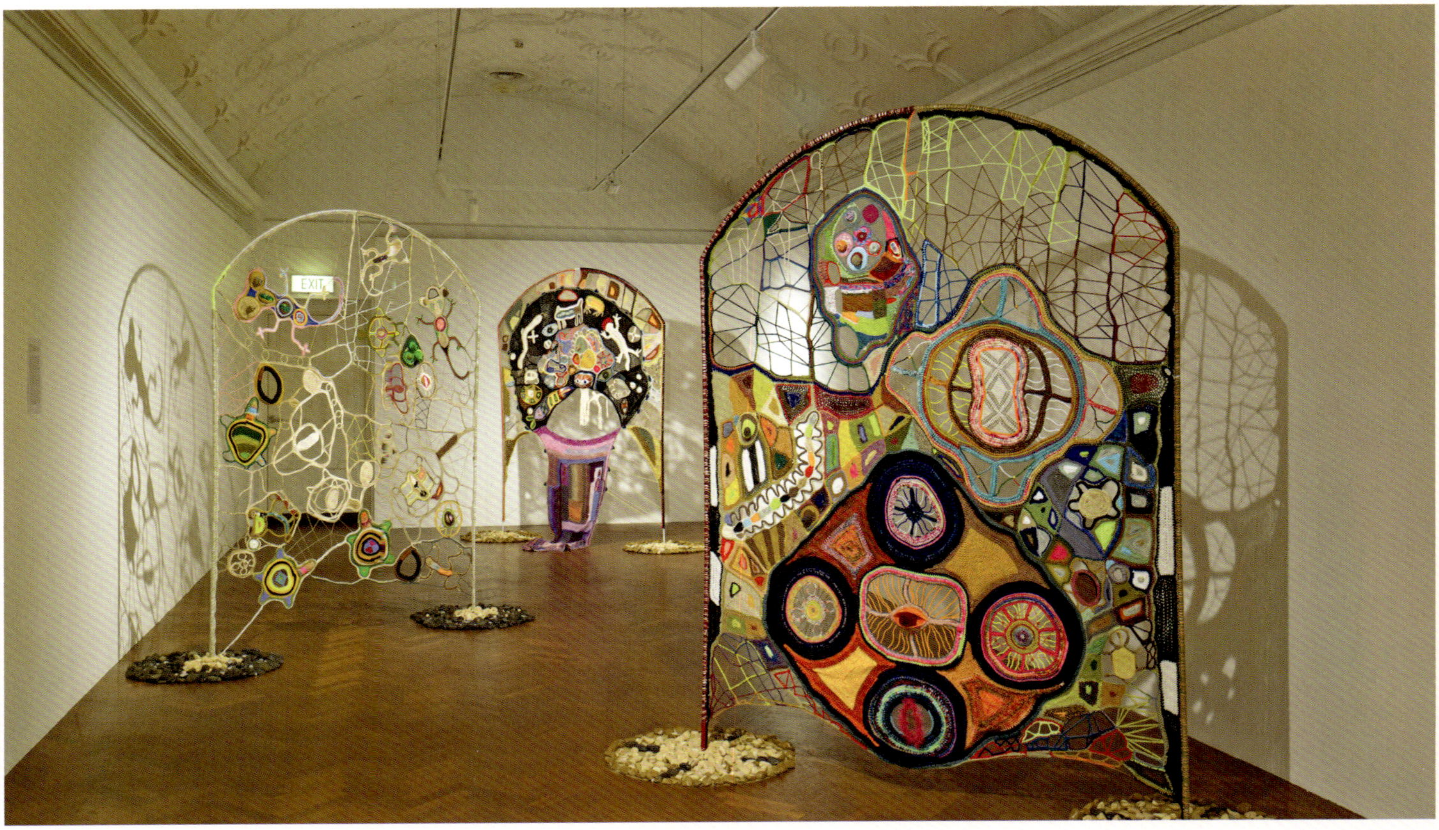

This page Top: *Abya Yala*, 2022, Crochet, hand-stitching, wrapping, coiling and beading; Bottom: *Remembering my Charrúa roots*, 2024, Crochet, hand-stitching, wrapping, coiling and beading **Opposite** *Abya Yala* (detail)

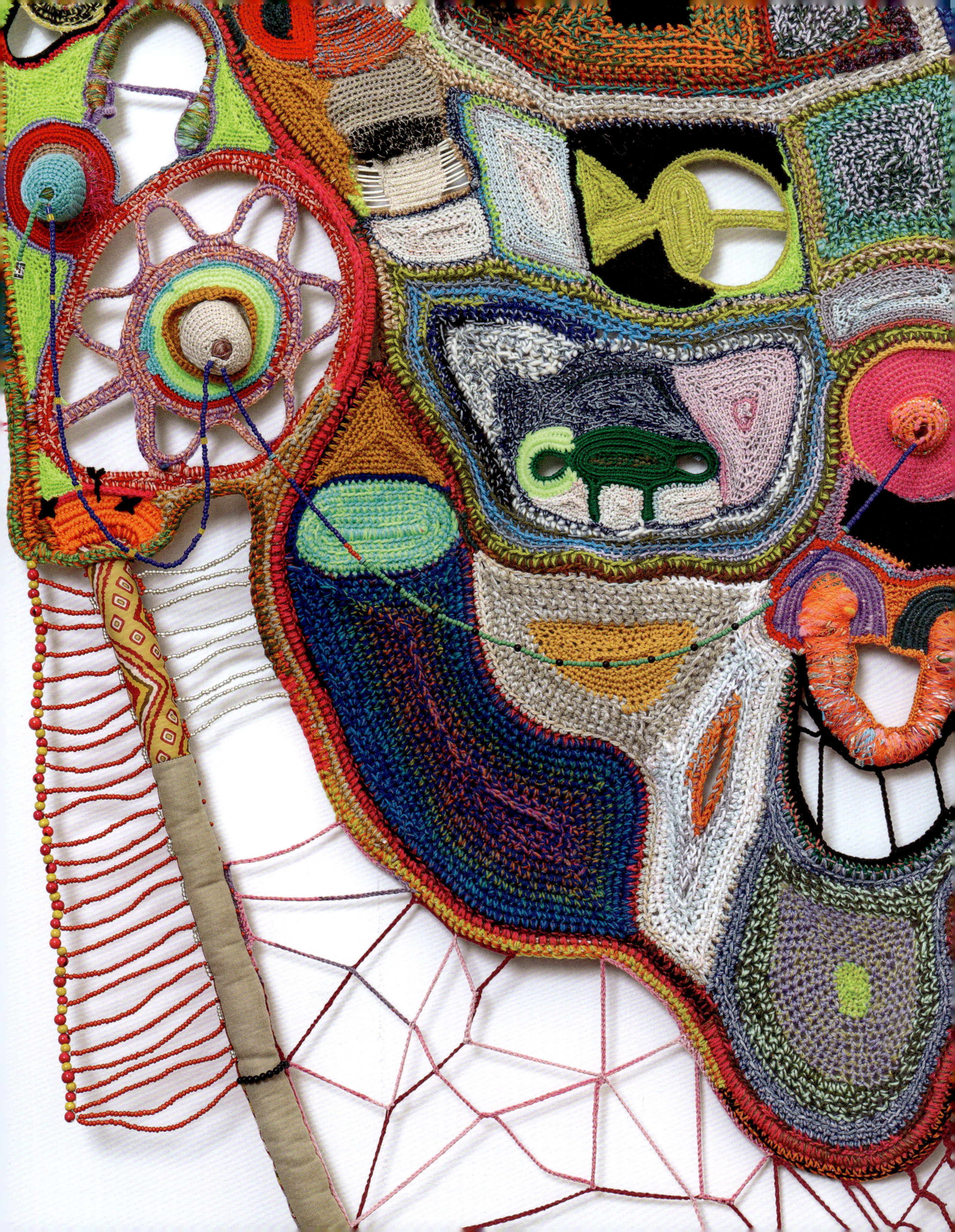

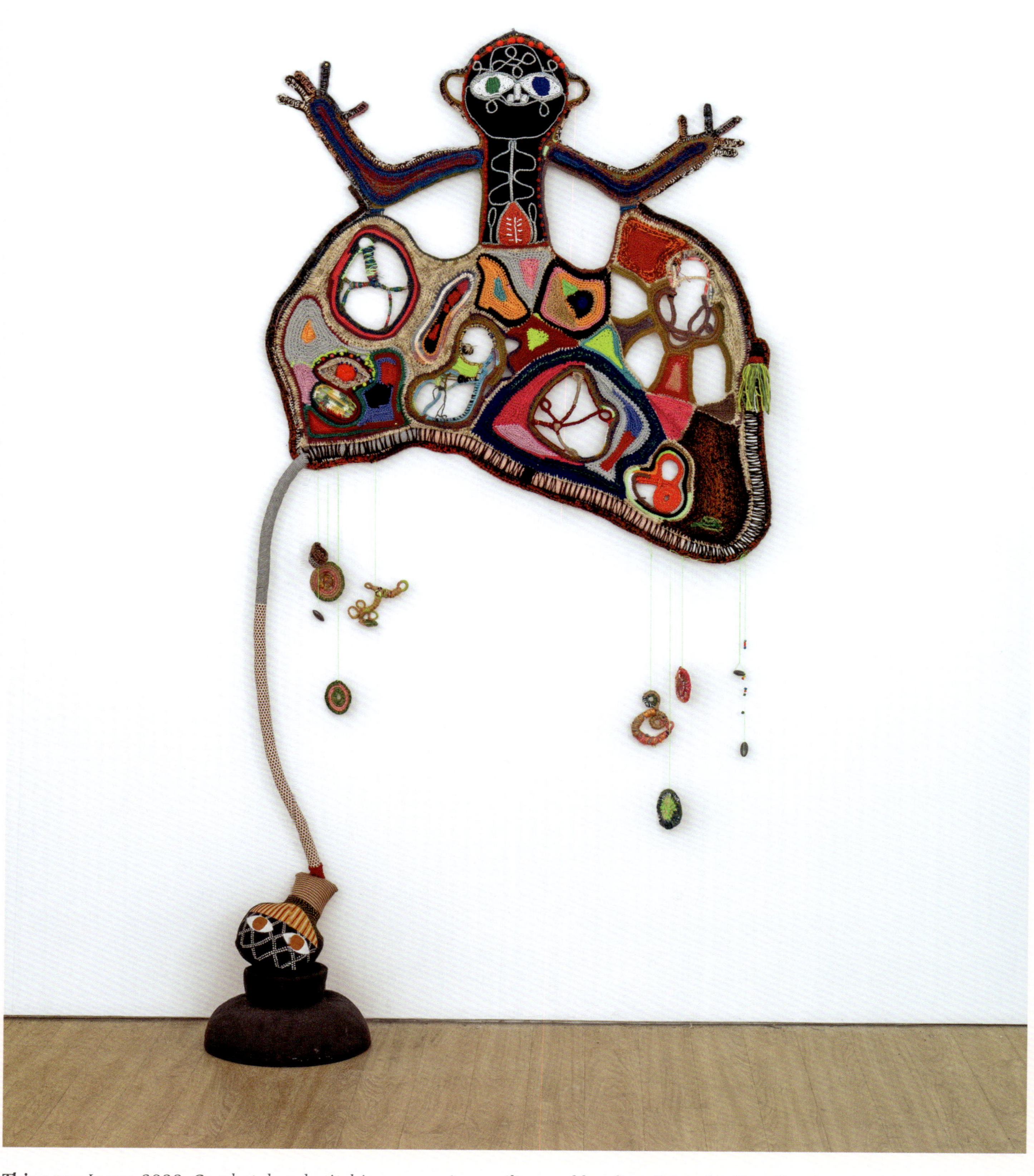

This page *Lenge*, 2023, Crochet, hand-stitching, wrapping, coiling and beading **Opposite** Top: *Barriga Negra/Coral Negro* (detail), 2024, Crochet, hand-stitching, wrapping, coiling and beading; Bottom: Studio shot, 2020

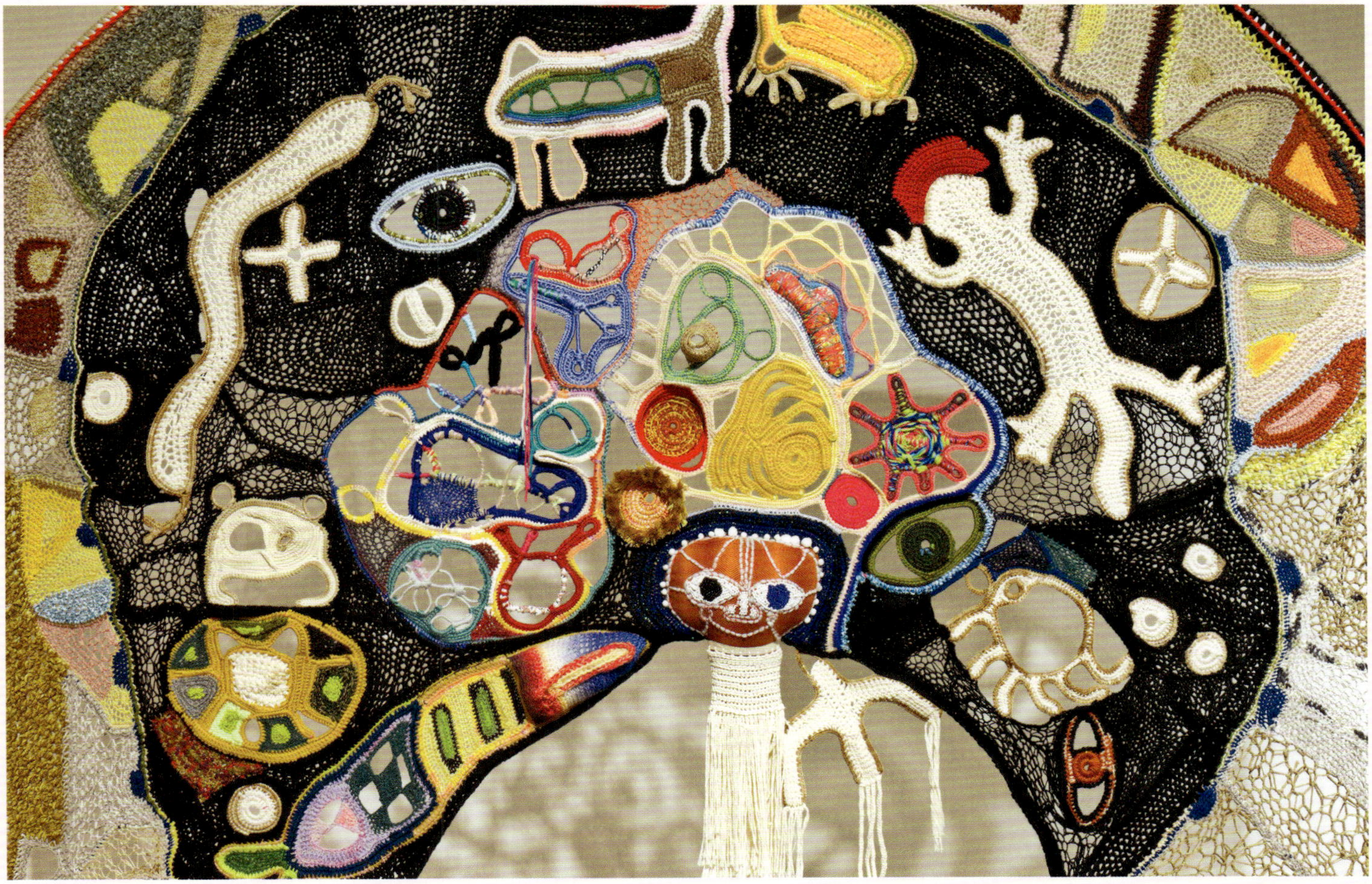

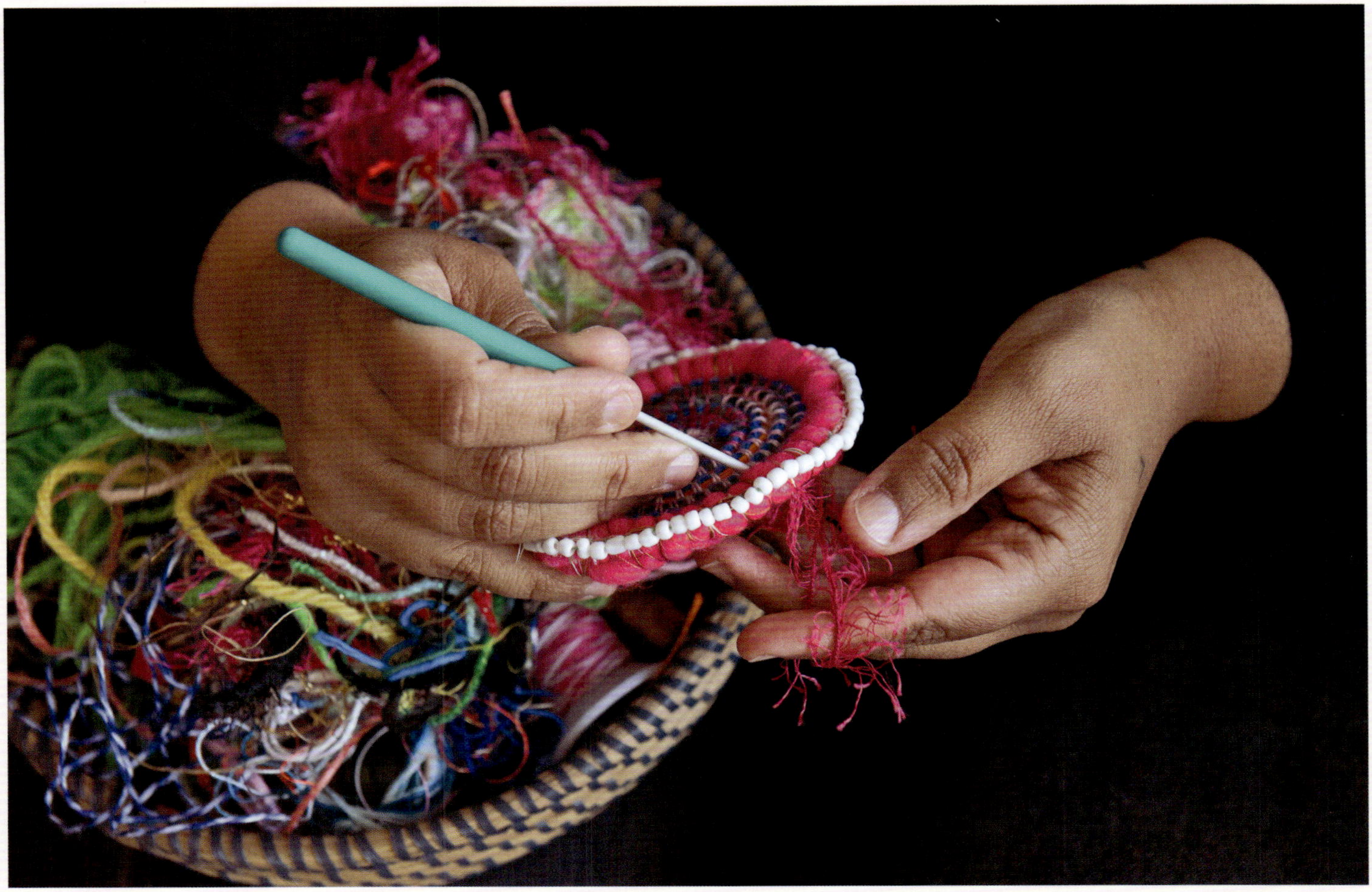

Philippa Rice

NOTTINGHAM

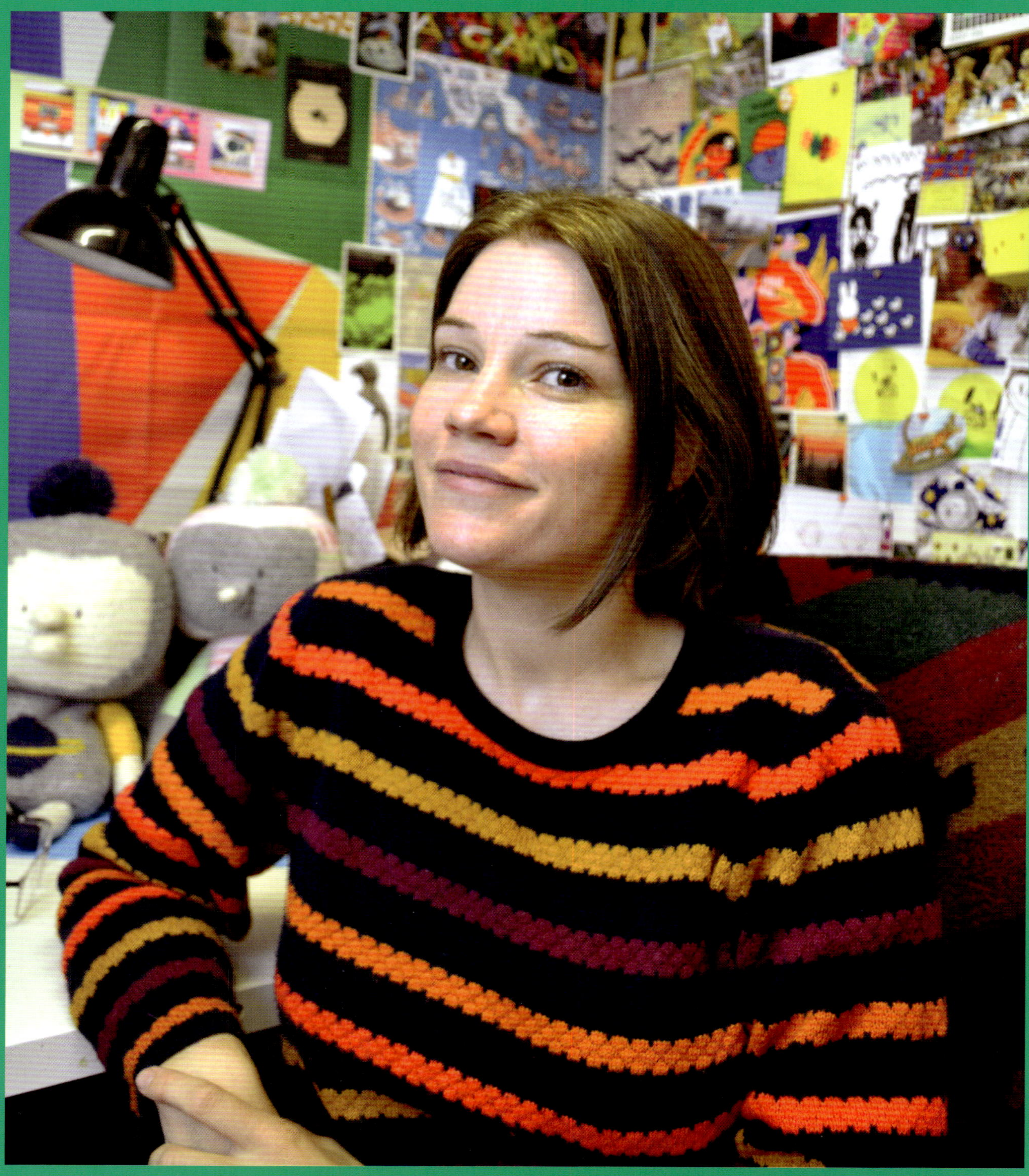

Philippa Rice is an artist and author who makes works inspired by both her personal life and fantasy. With a tertiary background in animation, she works across multiple artforms including illustration, stop-motion, model-making and sculptures, and has published a number of best-selling comic books. Among her varied output, crochet is something she "always comes back to". For Rice, she enjoys the medium because, in contrast to other textile practices like sewing or quilting, crochet can be very forgiving: "There aren't too many stages, just one stitch at a time 'til it's finished and everything comes out looking neat and tidy all by itself."

Rice's crochet creatures are an extension of her creative visual world and "come from a narrative place". They range from animals like cats and pigs dressed in stylish outfits to more alien or imaginative forms. Each is individual: a character whose personality and attitudes are expressed through "colour combinations, shape and scale" to tell stories and build connection to audiences. Rice shares, "When I make a crochet character, I think I'm always trying to make something that people empathise with. If I can make an inanimate object seem friendly or feel like it has a real personality, then I've succeeded." Part of this empathy is achieved through the personality Rice imbues each character with through attire and details, like patterns and texture, as well as through giving each creature a unique name. When placed together, Rice's creations invoke a welcoming scene.

While Rice works from rough ideas, her crochet creatures aren't pre-planned: "I tend to keep it vague and make it up as I go along." Stylistically, Rice's creatures share similarities with amigurumi (crochet stuffed toys popularised in Japan, often made with single crochet stitches in the round); however, Rice's choice of crochet techniques offers a distinct point of difference. One of the most distinctive features of her works is that she crochets on the "wrong" side, preferring the more textured fabric that is created when crocheting from the inside out. In other words, what might usually be hidden is utilised by Rice as a distinct design feature.

Rice uses a combination of double (looped twice) and single (looped once) crochet stitches, building each character up from the bottom. Design choices such as popcorn stitches (where multiple stitches are made into the same loop) for texture or colour-changing patterns are also used to provide unique design features. *Ryan* (2016) for instance, cleverly uses so-called "eyelash" yarn on the legs to create the appearance of fringed trousers – a bold, fashion-forward statement. Rice works with a range of gifted, thrifted and store-bought yarns. She shares that many people give her unwanted yarn, which allows her to

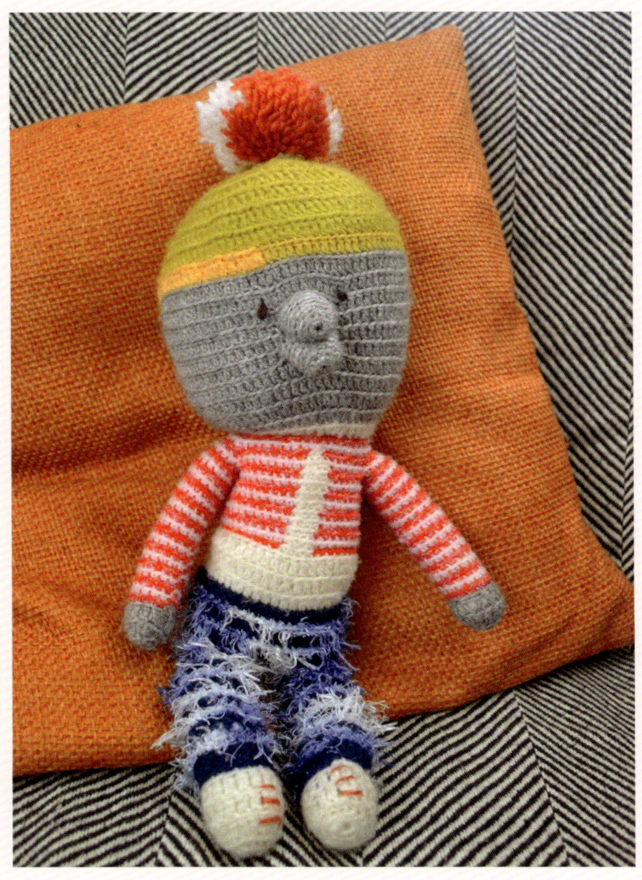

Ryan, 2016, Crochet

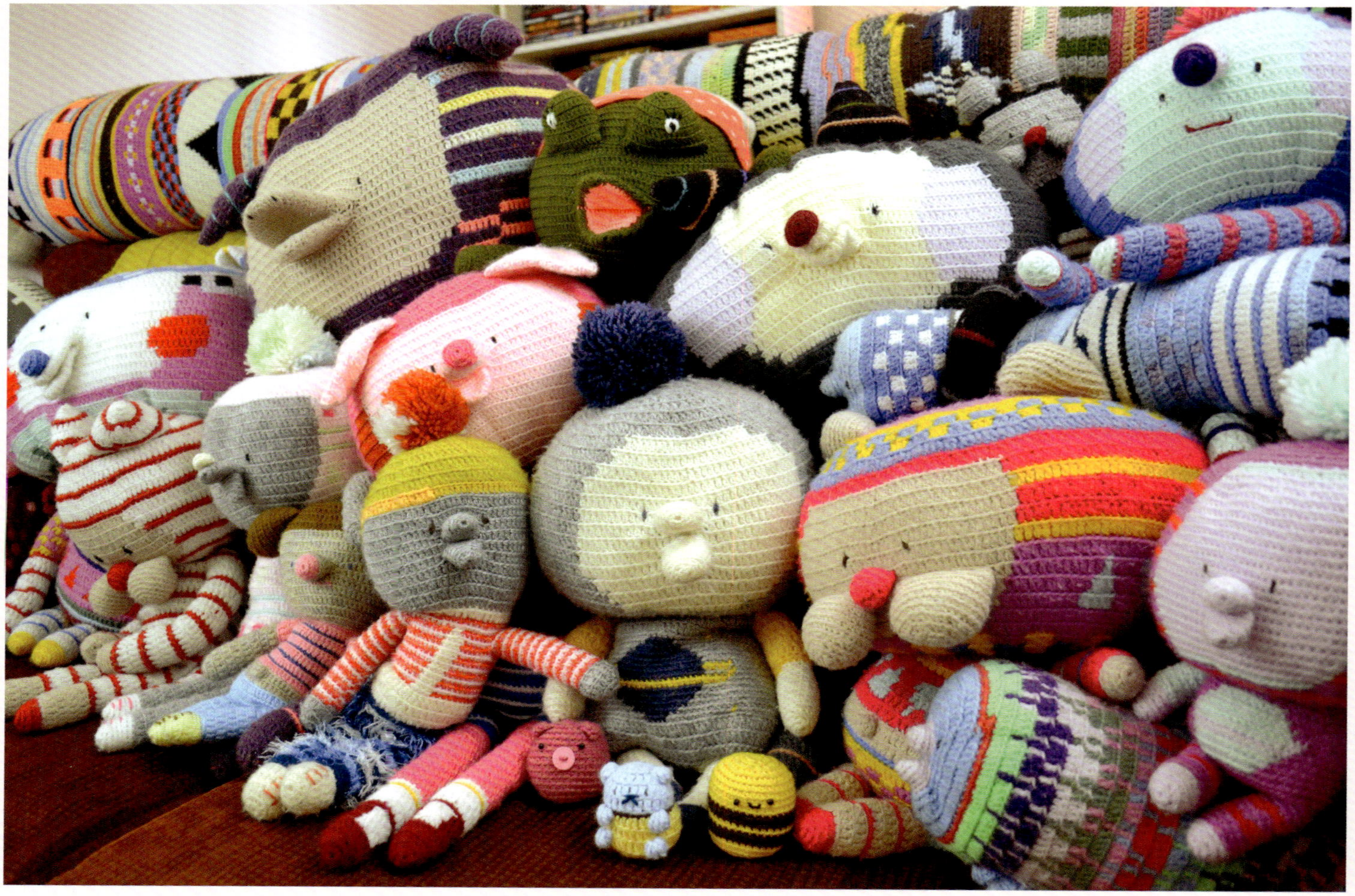

embed different personal stories and histories into each finished object. This thrifty approach is visually represented in the design for each creature, and in the coupling of colour combinations.

For Rice, crochet is an activity that allows for multitasking: not only can she do it while watching television or movies, but as a mother of three, the medium's flexibility makes it easy to work with, even after a full day attending to other tasks and working on projects. She shares that while her brain can't work on writing or admin after six o'clock, she "can crochet any time" and that "working on a crochet project [is] almost like a break between other things". Her favourite part of crochet is completing a project, as she "can look the finished character in the face and it looks back". When further coupled with her skills in stop-motion, which she uses to animate her creatures, Rice's mastery of crochet resides in her ability to bring personality and life to these otherwise inanimate handmade objects. ■

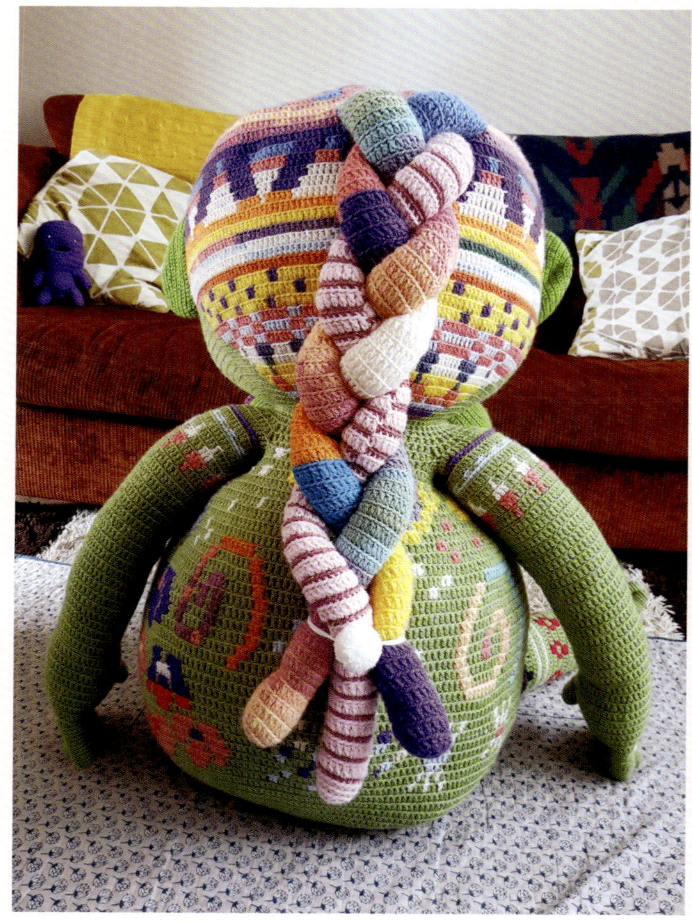

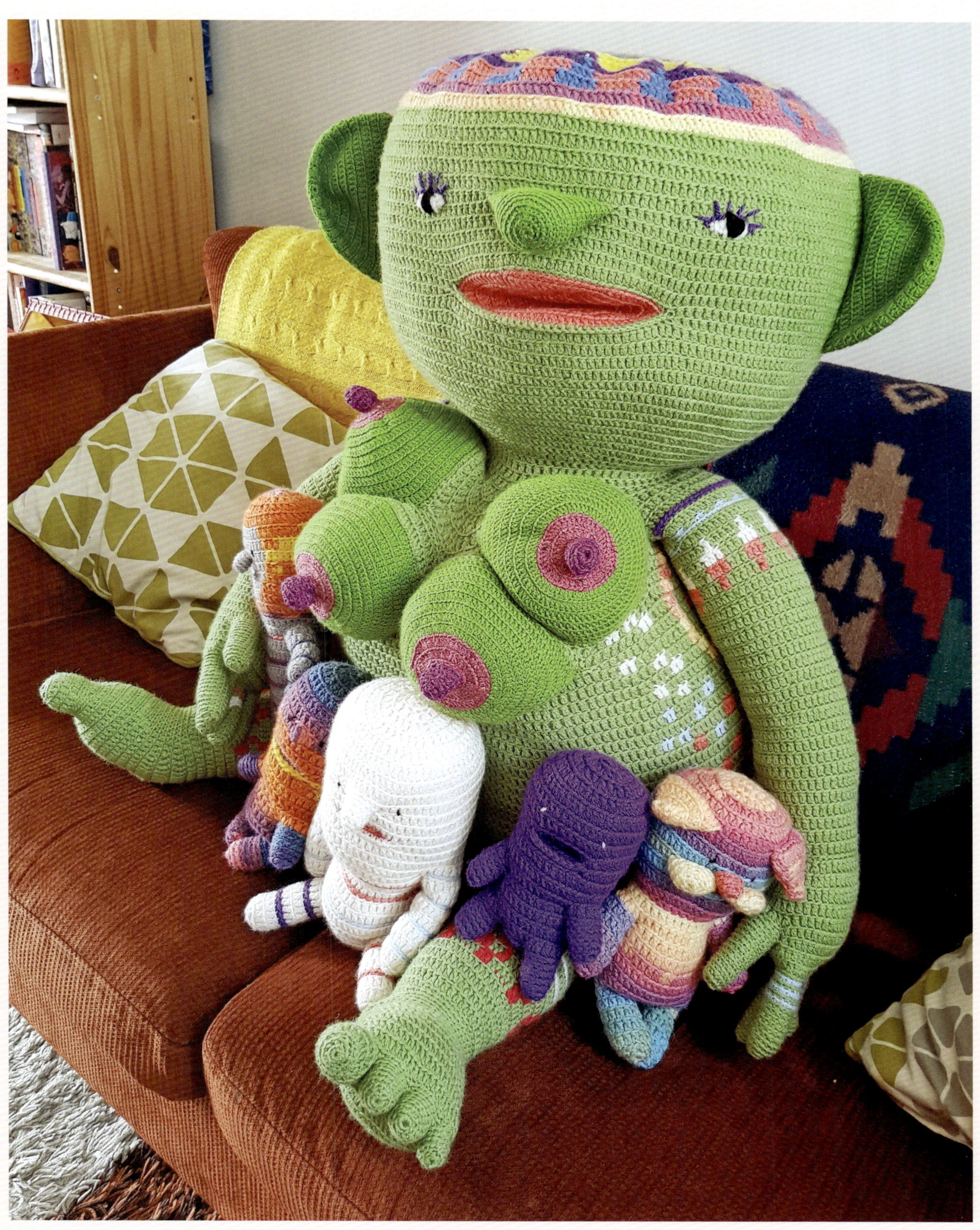

Opposite Top: *Group of crochet characters*, 2015, Crochet; Bottom: *Mother Earth*, 2019, Crochet
This page *Mother Earth* **Overleaf** *George*, 2015, Crochet **Page 161** *Anika*, 2018, Crochet

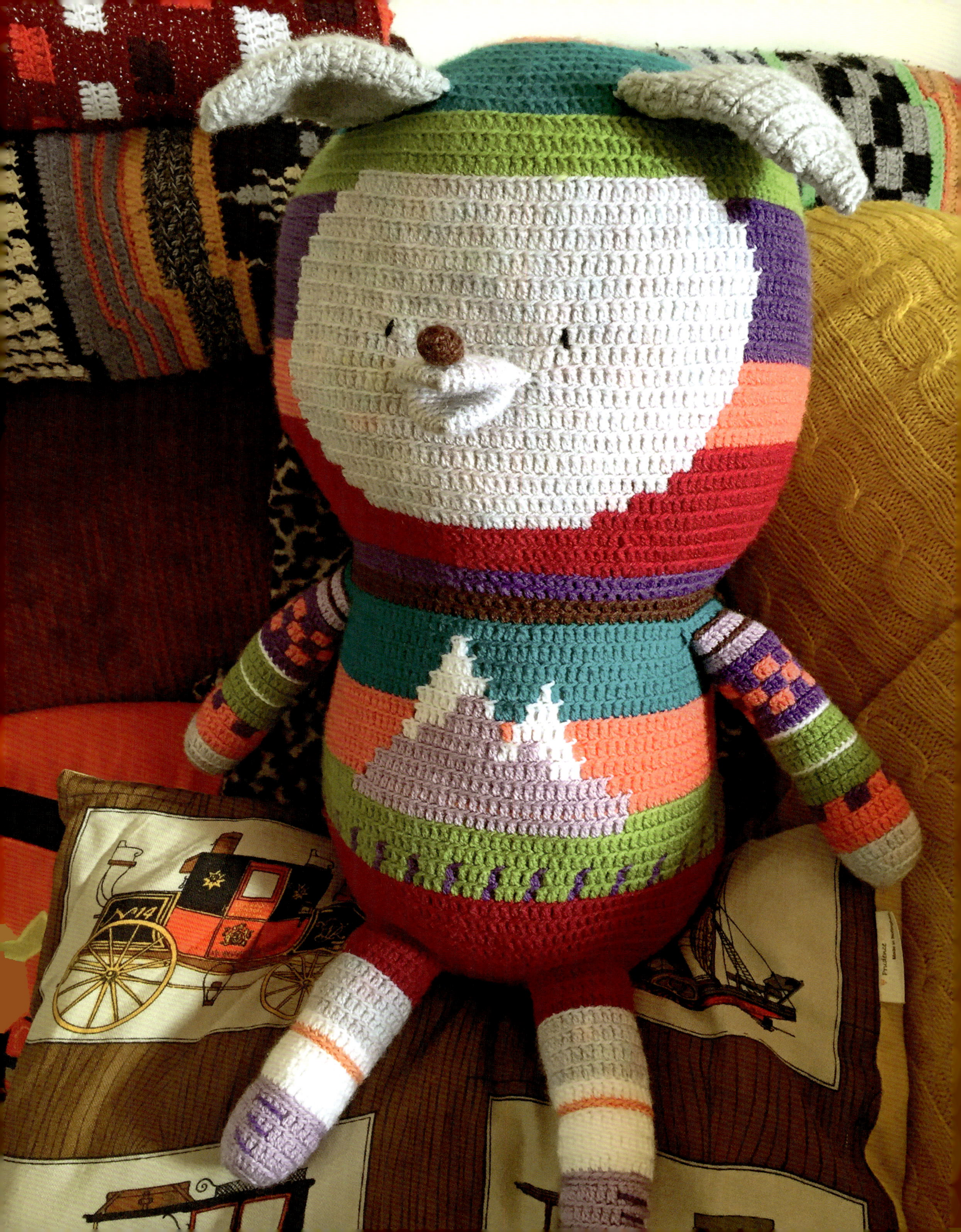
№14

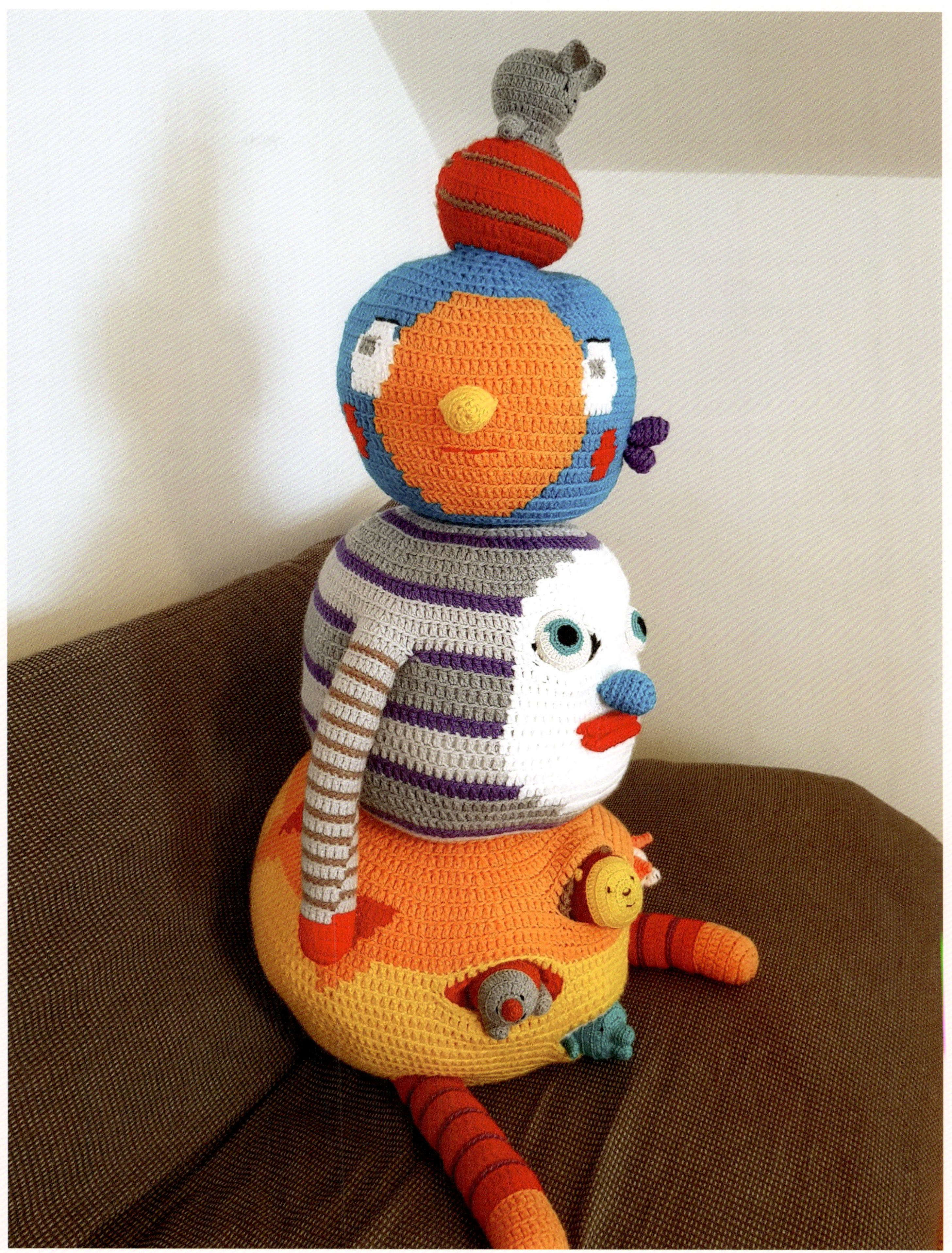

Wells Chandler

NEW YORK CITY

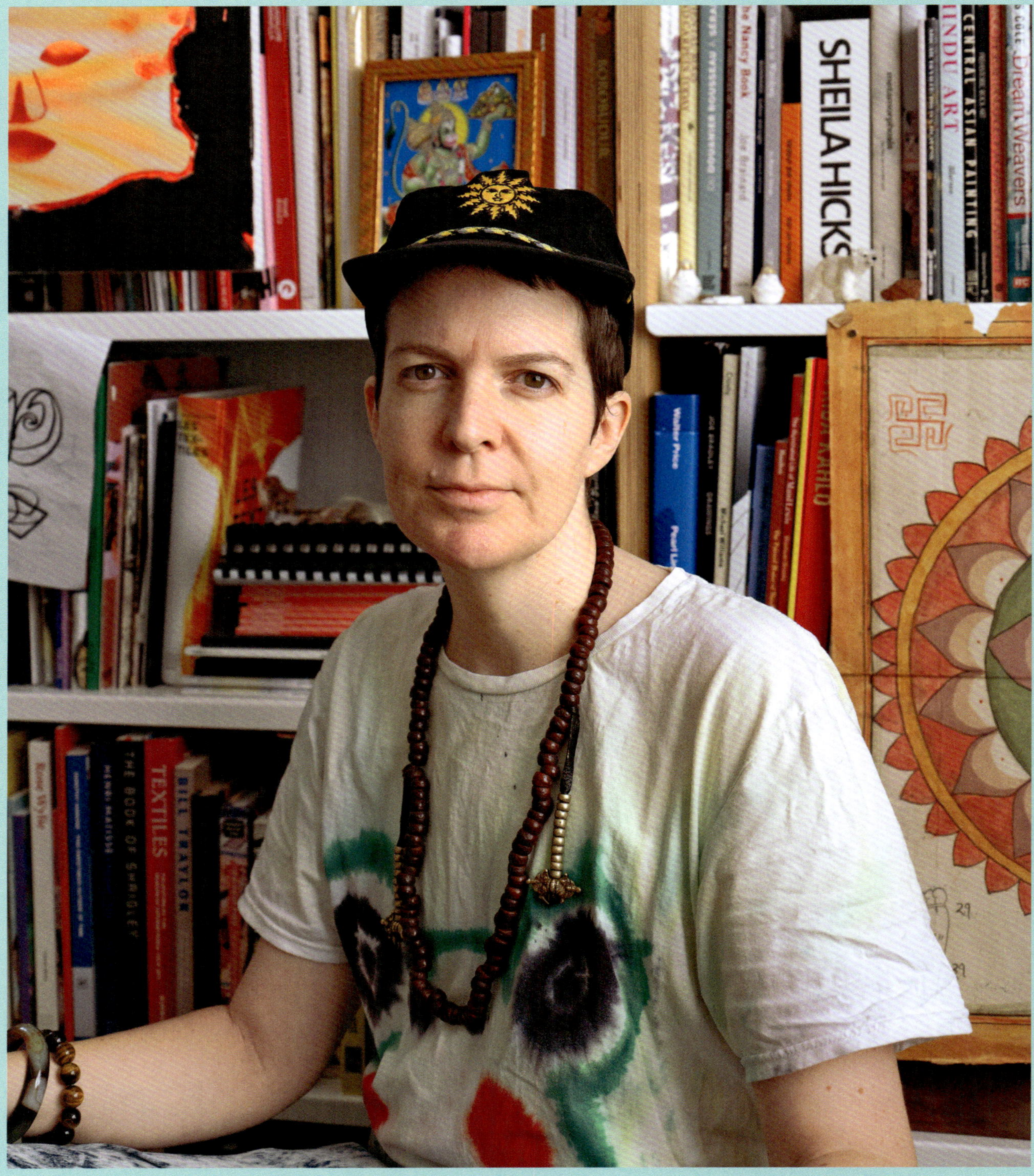

Wells Chandler creates joyous, vibrant artworks that "affirm queerness as foundational to reality". His crochet works take the form of a cast of gender queer characters, whose smiling expressions and lively poses centre joy as a radical proposition. Among this cast are cowboys, cape-donning superheroes, athletes, the Village People and bathers. One of his most frequently depicted forms are "Orgins" (a combination of the words "origin" and "organ"), which are figures floating in the air, a vibrant rainbow radiating from between their split legs. Many of Chandler's figures bear double mastectomy (top surgery) scars.

Chandler's works are shaped by a number of diverse and esoteric influences that look beyond traditional culture and knowledge. While his formal education means he is always "thinking about the history of painting", he also recognises his personal affinity for so-called "Outsider" artists (a term problematically applied to those who aren't trained or who don't work within the established art world circuit). In his own work, Chandler first started experimenting with crochet after learning the technique from an undergraduate professor, and he considers his art today to sit within "the category of expanded field painting", in the legacy of devotional art.

Crochet fulfils what Chandler regards as an etymological link in his practice. Here, he is drawing on one linguistic theory that the English word "queer" links to the Indo-European root "terkw-", and the Latin word "torquere", both meaning "to twist". Fittingly, crocheting involves twisting yarn with a hook, linking Chandler's chosen technique to the topics he uses it to explore.

Art historical references are rife in Chandler's oeuvre. *Lesbian Lovers, Mothers, Brothers and Sisters Past, Present, and Future* (2023) is a crochet interpretation of Henri Matisse's *Dance* (1909–10) that translates the original's dynamism into a contemporary expression of transgender and lesbian joy. *Big Red (The Bather)* (2016) adopts the same pose as Cezanne's *The Bather* (1885), but with a confidence amiss in the original. Chandler queers Cezanne's study of the male form through the use of gaudy colours, coupled with visible mastectomy scars and a straight red line through the crotch region. Like other figures that share the same outward traits in Chandler's works, these expressions are freeing.

Reflecting on his art, Chandler shares that he "want[s] the work to feel hopeful and silly but also profound. I hope it fosters connecting, tapping in, lightening up and embracing the weirdness of being alive and in a body." These sensibilities are present in pieces such as *Centaur* (2019), which was made in response to remarks the artist heard in Texas claiming that legalising gay marriage meant people would marry horses; *Centaur* is Chandler's humorous answer to this homophobia – a love child of forbidden desire.

Chandler doesn't read crochet patterns, instead working from drawings made with black ink markers on computer graph paper. He crochets everything himself without assistants, using skeins of mixed acrylic and wool yarns in bright colours and tones sourced from specialist yarn stores, as well as everyday craft stores like Michaels Arts and Crafts. These freeform crochet works are then directly stapled onto walls. All of Chandler's crochet pieces are made specifically for exhibitions and are planned with the gallery's size and specifications in mind, the entire space considered as the canvas. In pieces such as *Freestyln* (2016) for example, the dynamic pose of each figure is coupled with the use of negative space to suggest movement. Chandler cites the Italian painter and architect Giotto as an influence on how he wants viewers to engage with his work – that they are both inside and part of it. Chandler's art invites deep care and introspection, radiating more joyous possibilities for all.

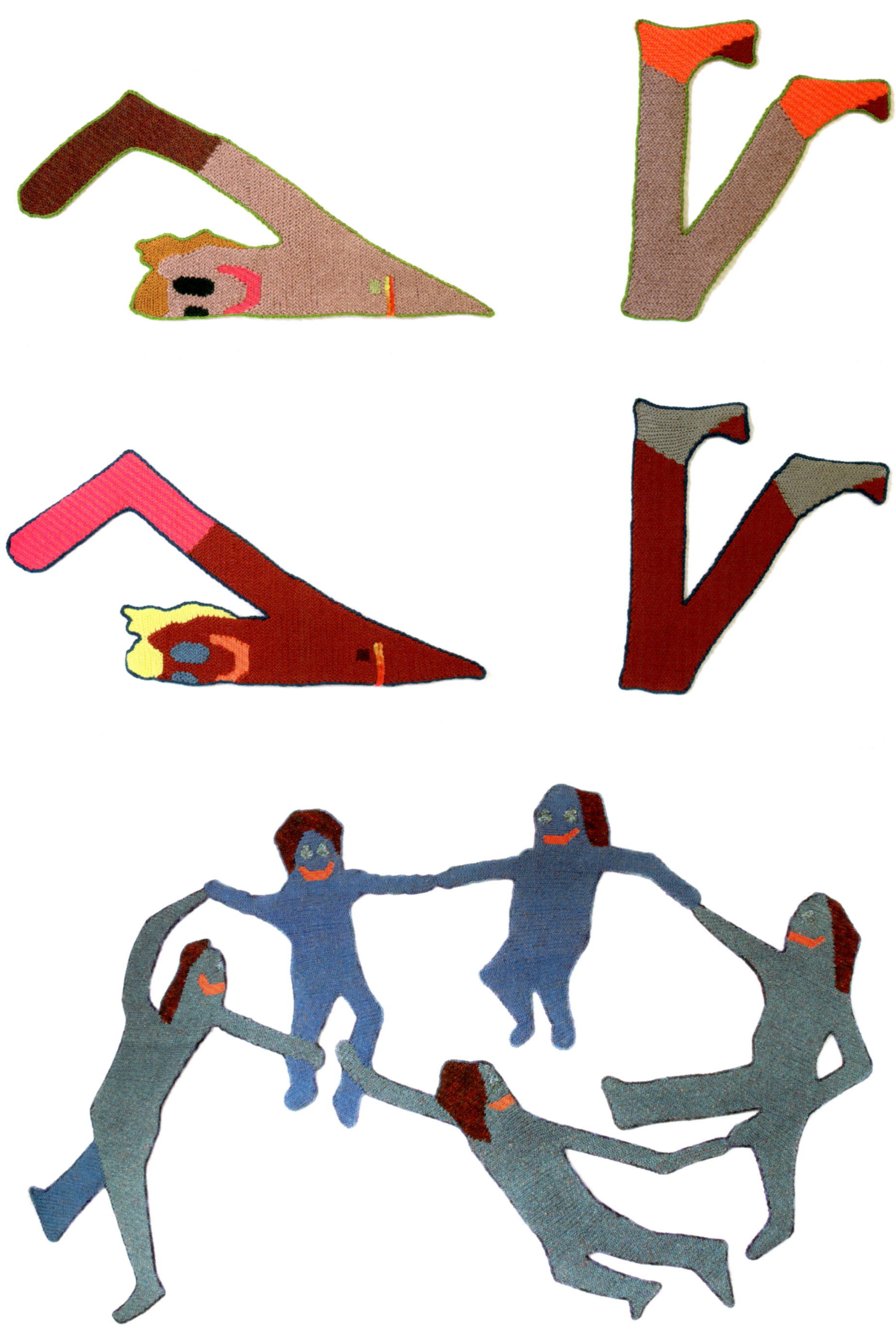

This page Top to bottom: *Freestyln (light mauve)*, 2016, Crochet; *Freestyln (shiny red)*, 2016, Crochet; *Lesbian, Lovers, Mothers, Brothers and Sisters Past,Present and Future*, 2023, Crochet **Opposite** *Cruising Utopia*, 2023, Crochet, quilting and sewing **Overleaf** *Big Red (The Bather)*, 2016, Crochet **Page 167** *Feminist Bird Club Presents Luncheon on My Ass*, 2023, Crochet

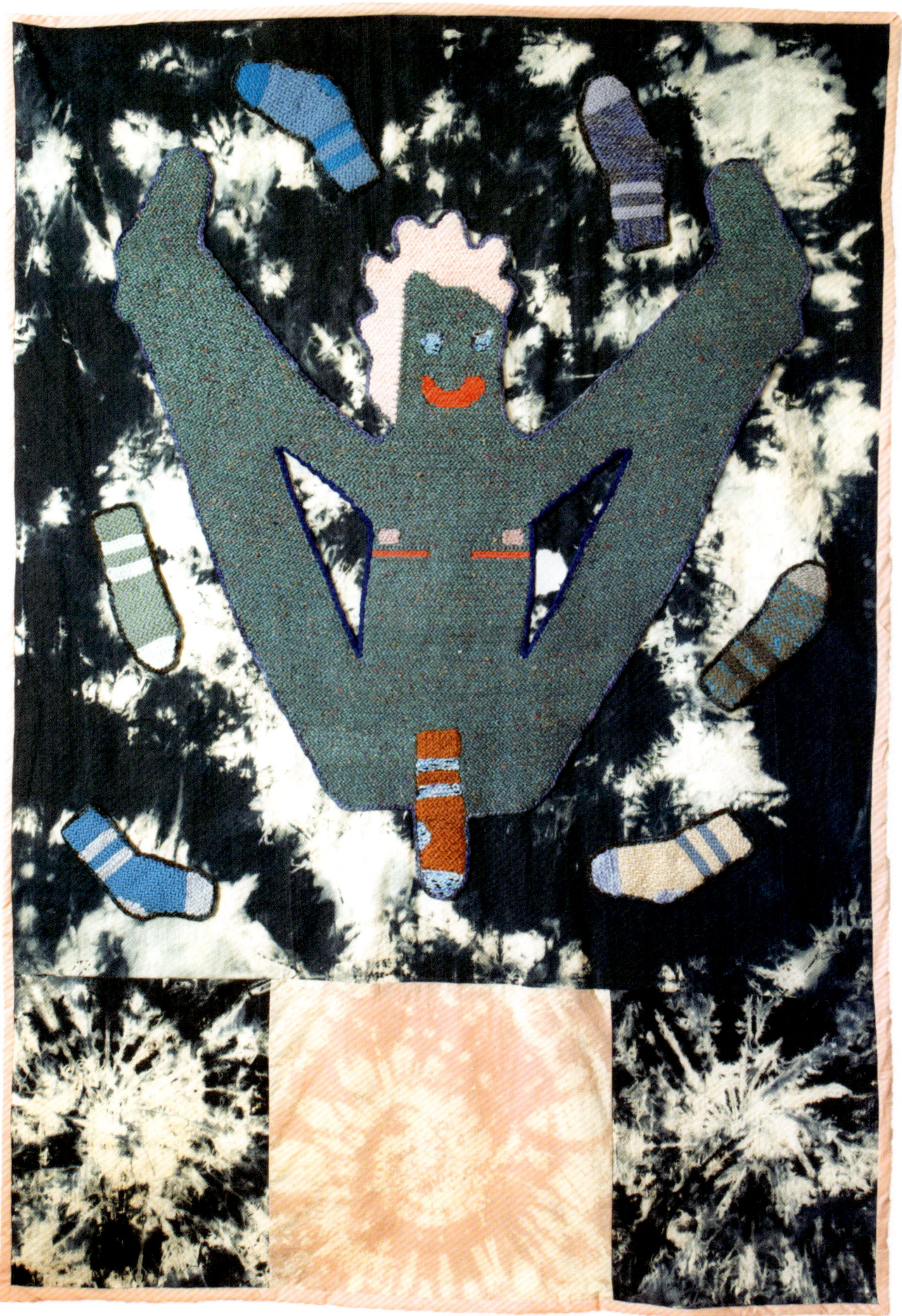

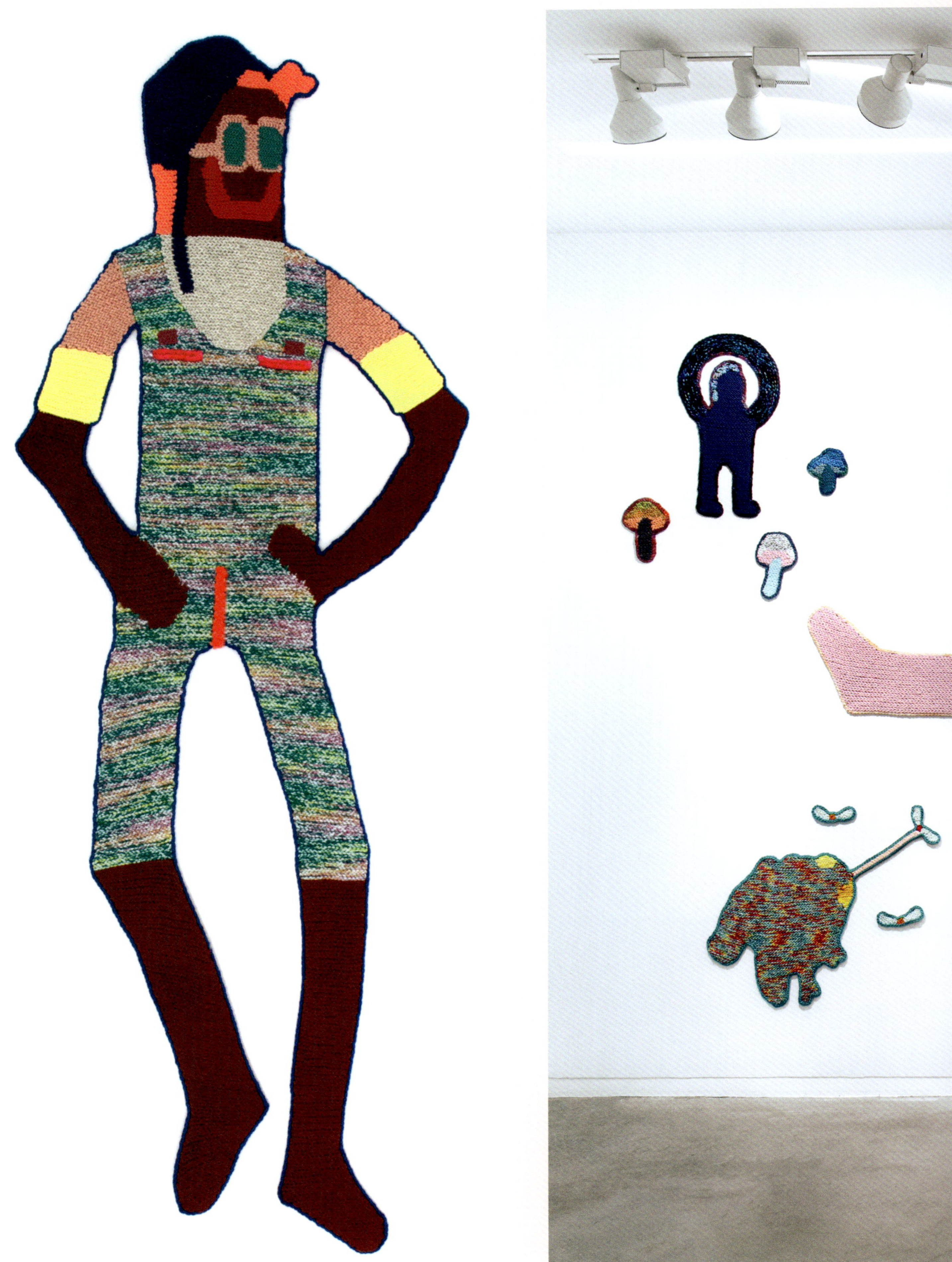

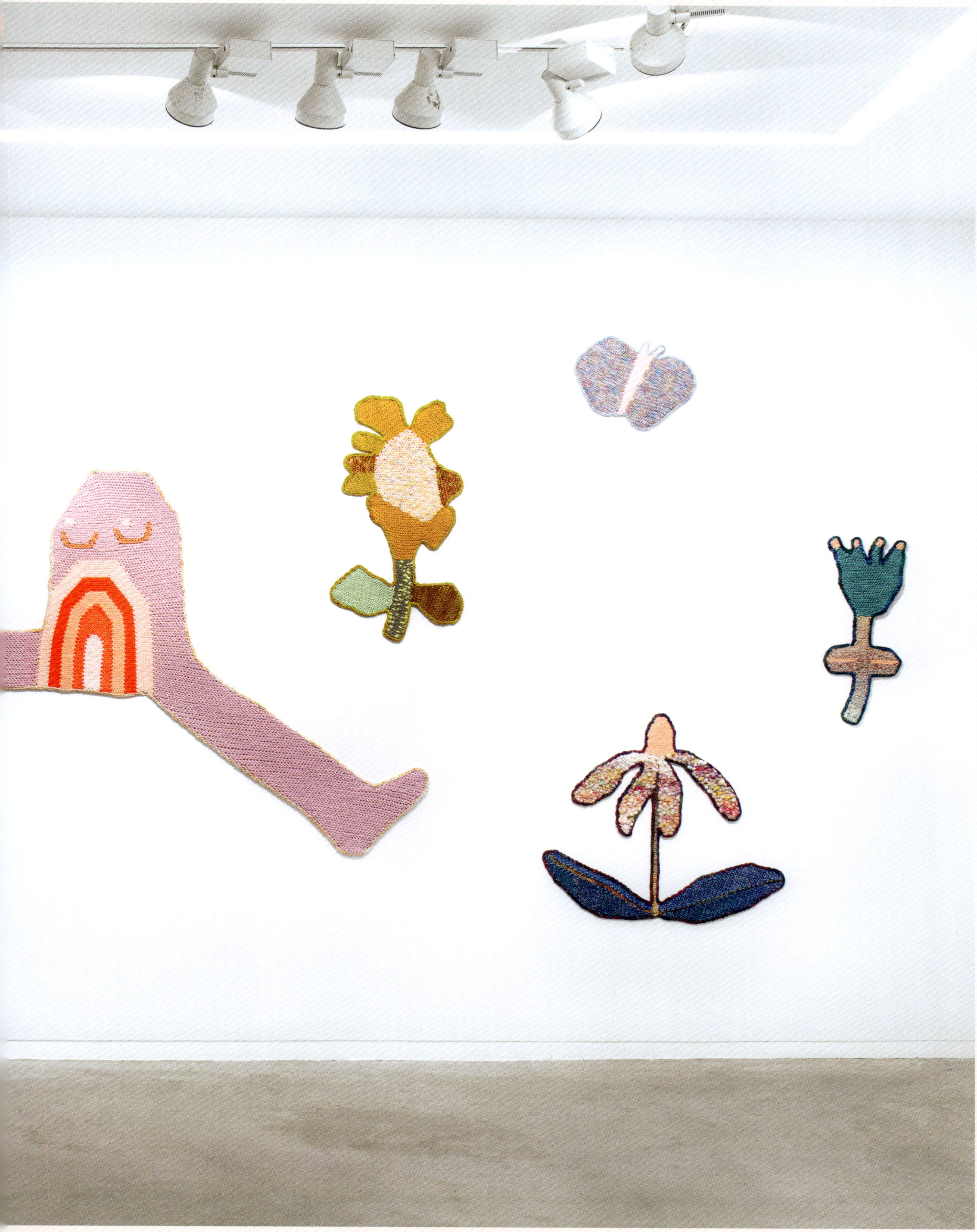

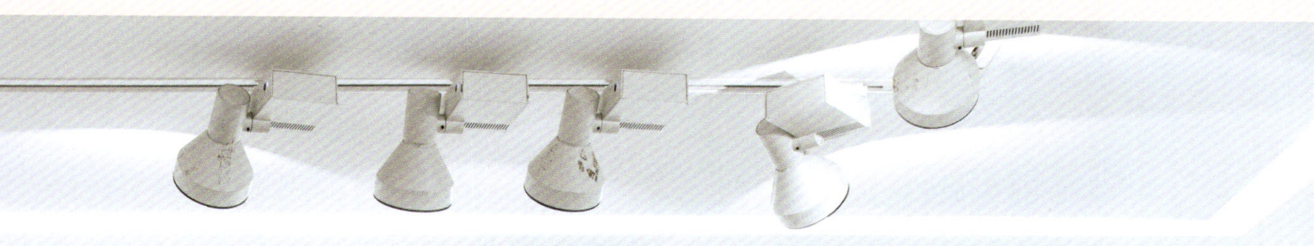

Loom

Of the three techniques covered in this book, weaving is the oldest. Textile impressions on clay fragments indicate the craft has existed since about 25,000 BCE, while the oldest known woven textile remnant has been dated to Peru, around 10,000 BCE. Today, weaving is practised across all corners of the globe, encompassing a diverse range of techniques, materials and uses.

In contrast to knitting and crochet, which are created through a continuous thread looped or hooked on itself, weaving is performed by interlacing two sets of threads. These interlocking threads are known as the warp thread (vertical) and the weft thread (horizontal). Weaving is typically performed on a loom, though the type varies widely, from backstrap and rigid heddle looms to floor and tapestry looms, which all produce different results. But this is only for making cloth. No loom is required, for example, to create baskets.

In the 19th century, the Jacquard loom introduced punch cards to weaving, creating the ability to quickly produce textiles while playing a role in the invention of early computing. This connection to computers is a central theme for Moon Bori and Kayla Mattes, who each engage with digital technology in different ways. For Moon, this includes weaving light-emitting optical fibres with hemp to centre ancient traditions in their present. Mattes, on the other hand, uses tapestry weaving to create works that pastiche a myriad of visual references and influences from internet culture.

For artists Cheong See Min, Daniela Contreras Flores and Linda Sok, weaving offers a connection to ancestry. Cheong's weavings explore the histories of Malaysian textiles, with a particular focus on the pineapple fibre. Contreras Flores, meanwhile, approaches weaving from the perspective of Andean ancestral culture through her contemporary use of local techniques and imagery. Sok, on the other hand, works collaboratively with her family to weave as an act of remembrance, referencing the lost knowledge and skills of Khmer people in Cambodia.

Historically, weavings have often been used as a canvas for storytelling. Ema Shin and Molly Kent carry on this tradition, weaving to share their personal stories. Shin's are centred in women's lives and work, shaped by growing up within a Korean family living in Japan. Kent's relationship with tapestry weaving is closely connected to her mental health and life as a neurodivergent and disabled artist. Her works give expression to her inner dreams and nightmares, as well as her recollections from her teenage diary.

A number of artists in this chapter approach weaving from a text-based perspective. Tais Rose Wae's weavings, which she creates to connect to her Indigenous lineage, are complementary to her poetry practice. Yeh Fuyu and Lin Qiqing came to weaving after respective careers in copywriting and journalism. This connection to the written word is evident in Yeh's weavings, which take an observational focus based on the places where they are made. Lin's tapestries, on the other hand, feature paper, alongside other fibres, as a weaving material to tell stories about others.

The artists in these pages demonstrate that weaving doesn't always need to create fabric or be made on a loom. Akeylah Wellington's tapestries are made from pony beads, which are also used to adorn Black children's hair. Through this material, Wellington connects her work to Black American history and life. Sophie Honess, on the other hand, is not confined by the loom, working across an expansive practice that includes basket weaving. Across her many techniques of choice, Honess brings a contemporary approach to longstanding cultural practices connected to Country.

Together, the 12 artists in this chapter offer a snapshot into a diversity of weaving practices, working across different looms and materials. Their works highlight the ongoing endurance of a millennia-old creative practice, and demonstrate its capacity for new expression.

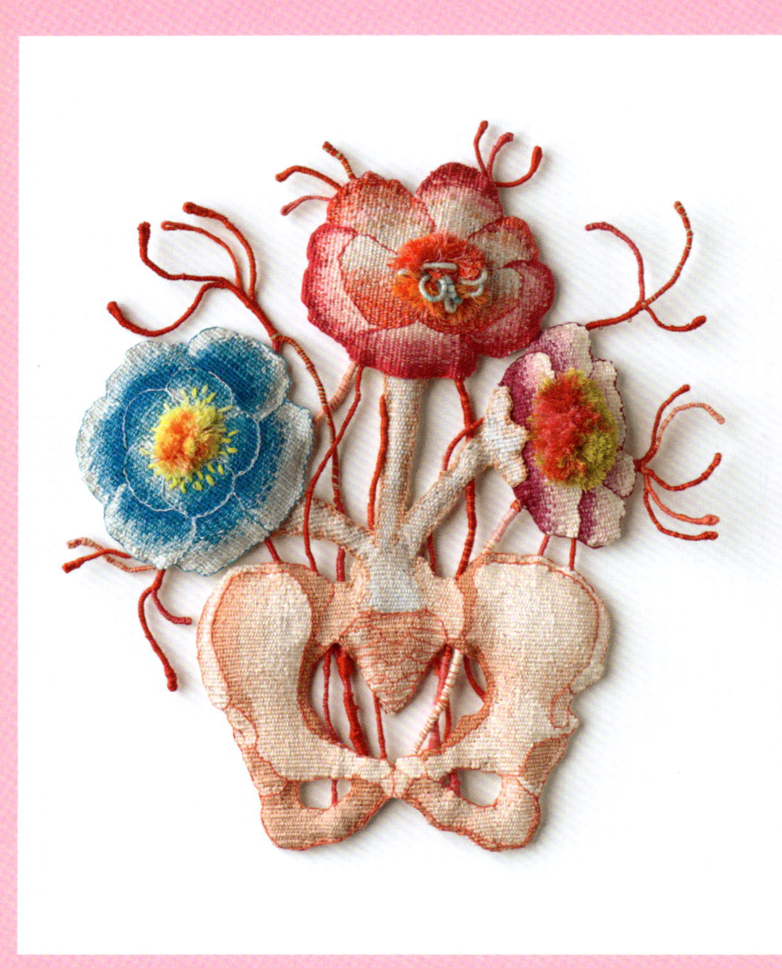

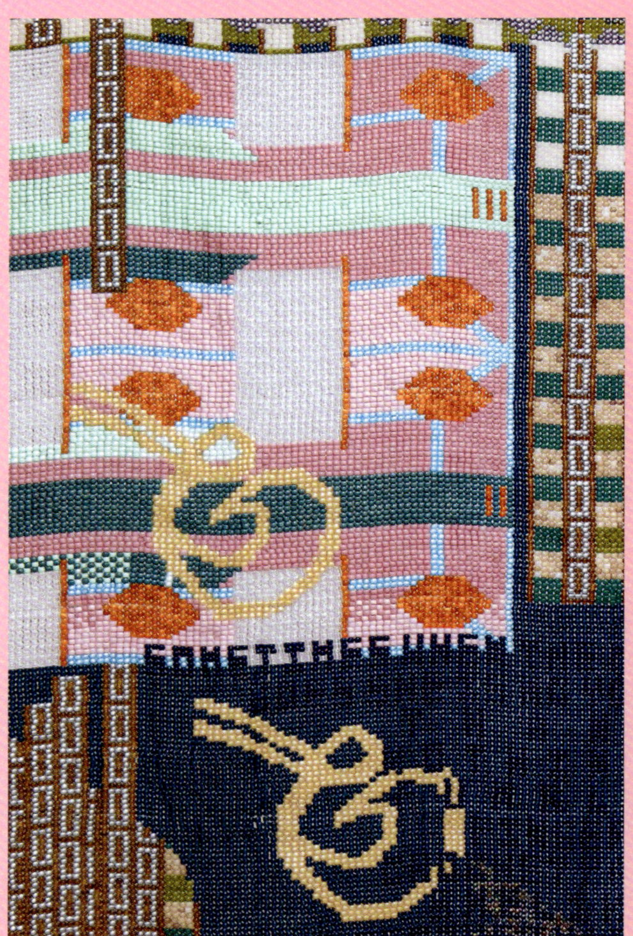

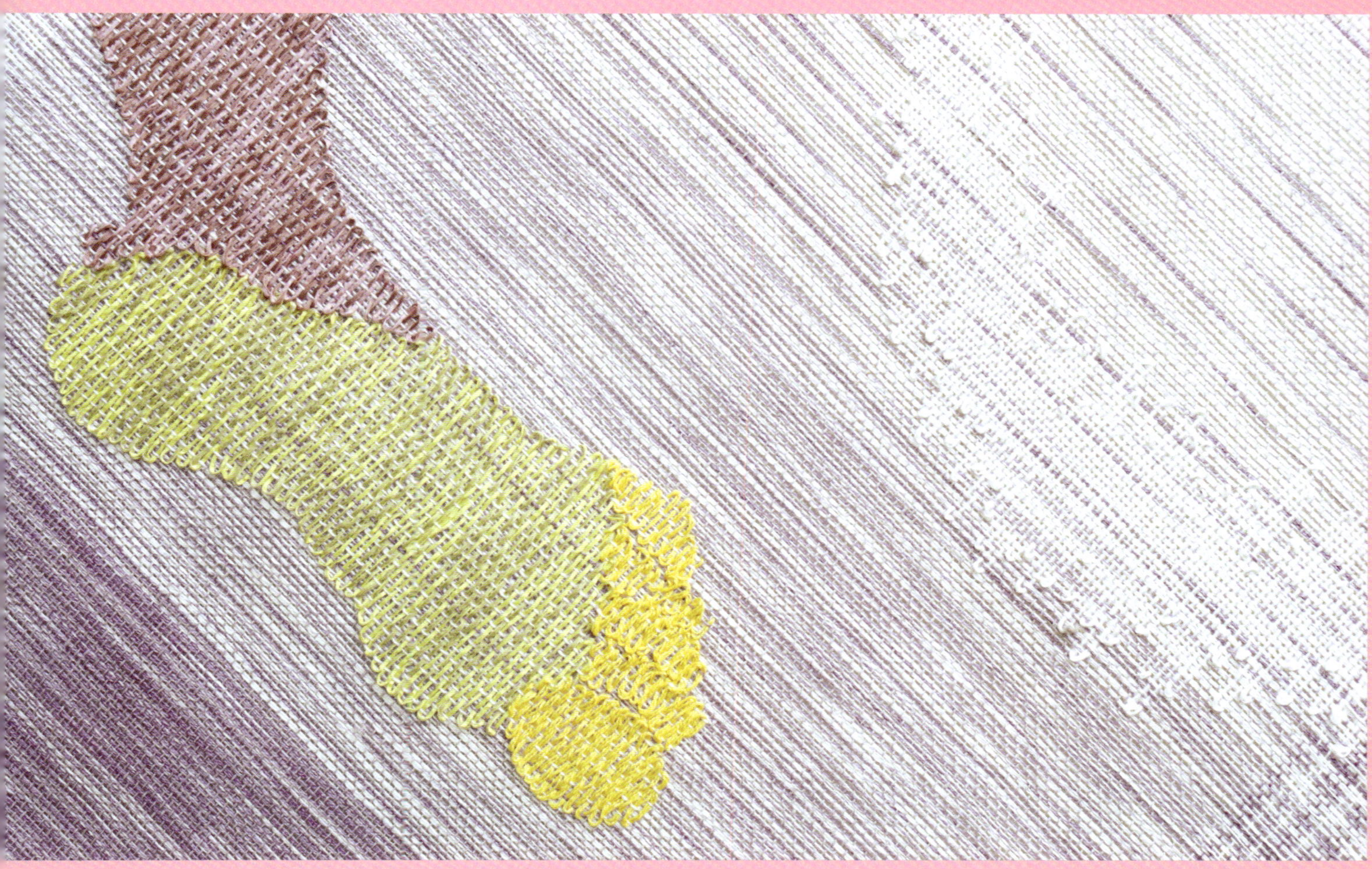

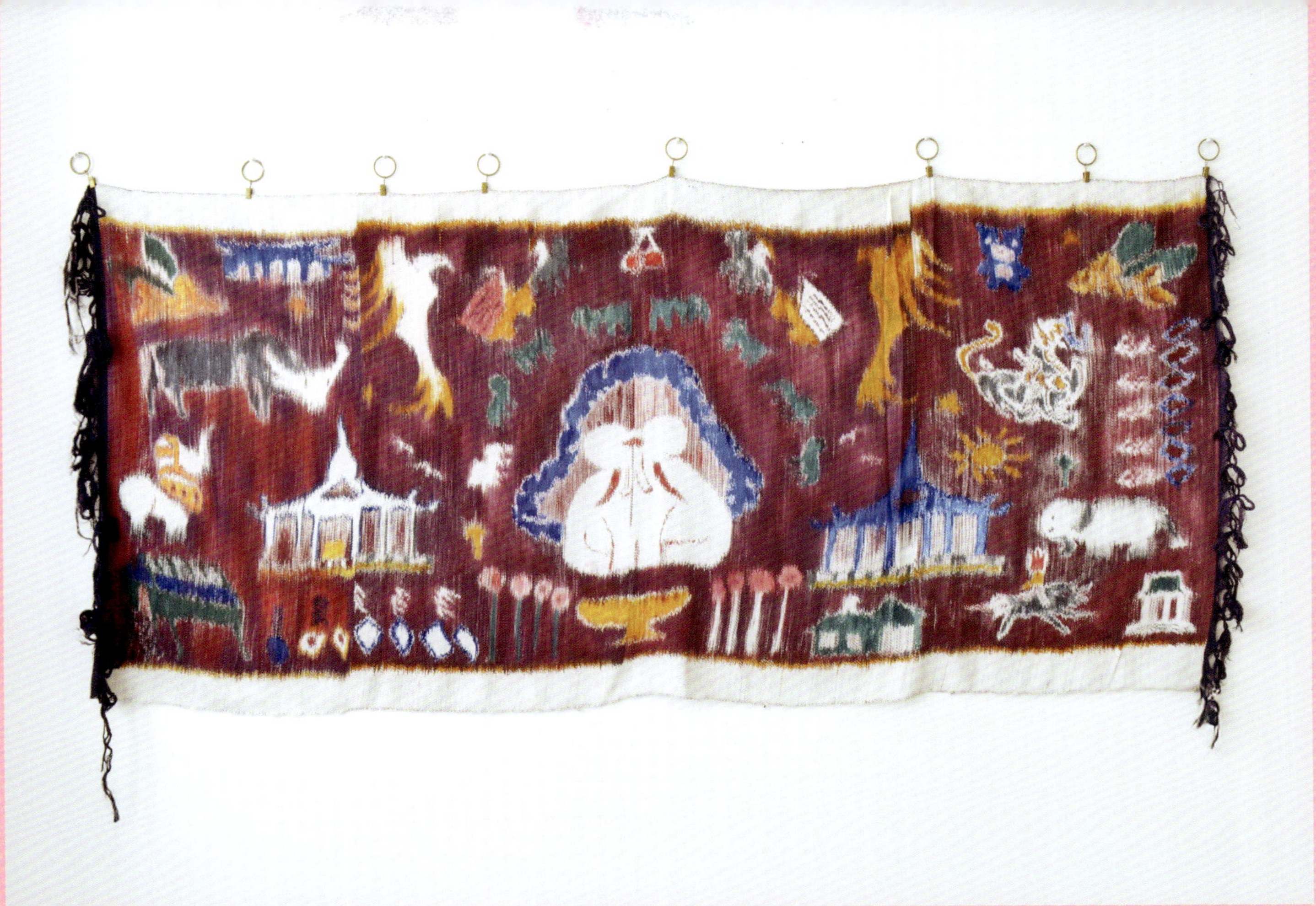

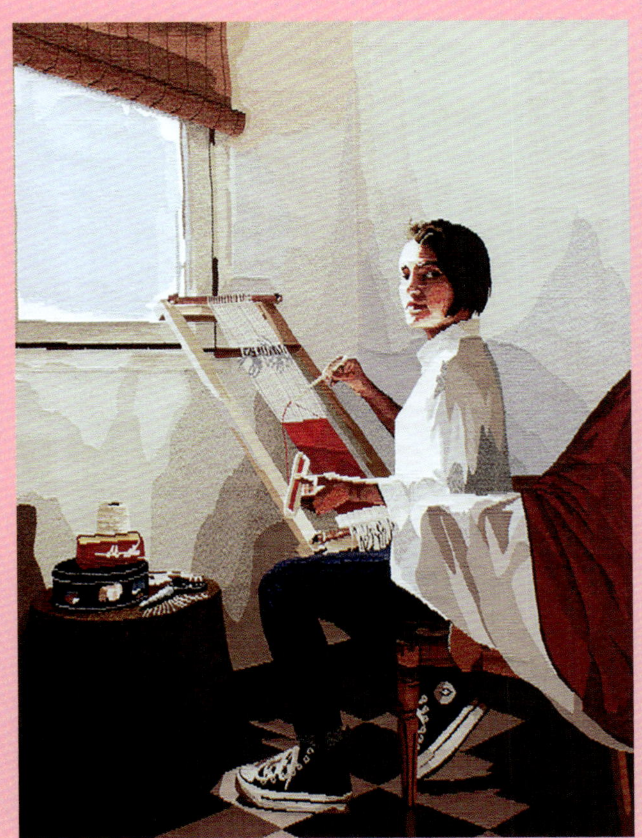

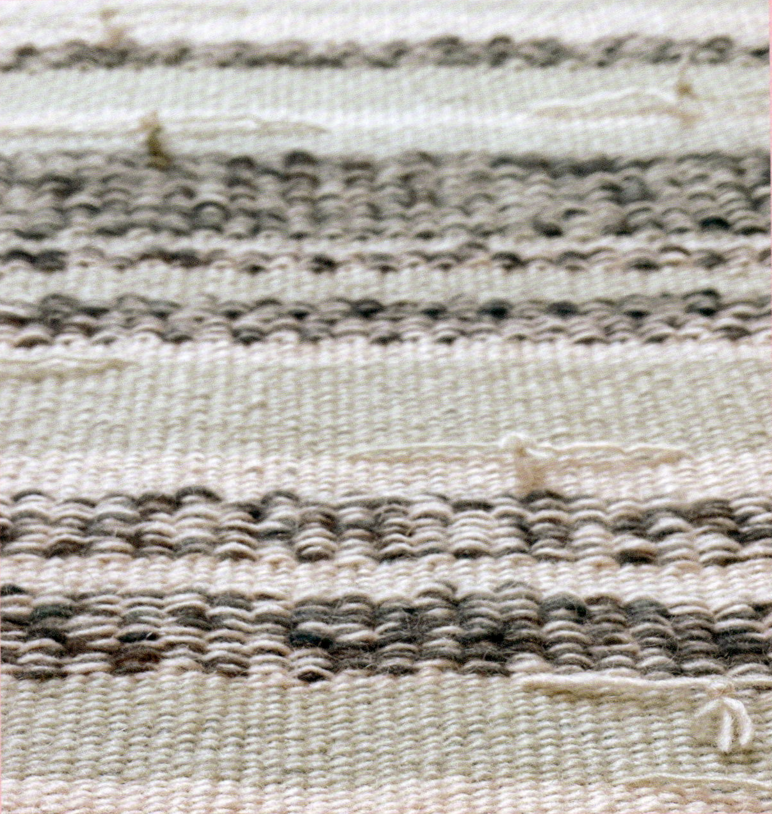

Artists clockwise from top left: Ema Shin, Akeylah Wellington, Linda Sok, Yeh Fuyu, Daniela Contreras Flores, Lin Qiqing

Akeylah Wellington

COLUMBUS

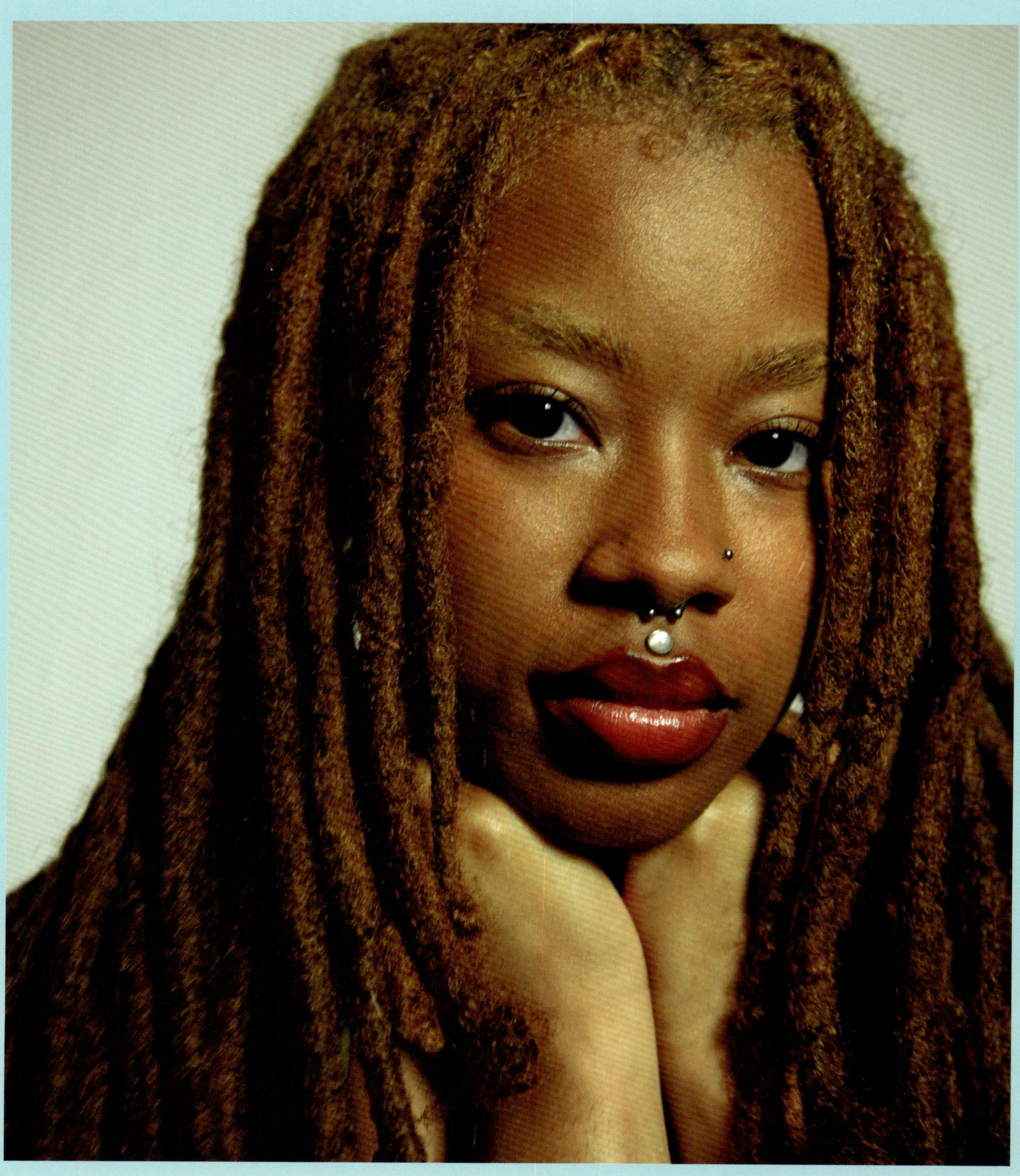

Akeylah Wellington makes woven tapestries on a loom with pony beads – the same beads that are used to adorn the hair of Black children. Wellington's fascination with beading as a creative practice started in her childhood with the discovery of a beadwork manual that she obsessively read from cover to cover. However, it wasn't until her final year of graduate studies in sculpture that Wellington decided to pursue the artform: faced with the imminent loss of a large studio space, she needed a sustainable way to work from home. Beadwork offered that option, and she purchased her first loom in 2023.

Wellington's distinctive beaded tapestries, which comprise both textual and visual forms, reflect the artist's ongoing interests in the "aughts as a historical period". For the artist, this decade in the early 2000s is an "odd soup" encompassing Web 2.0, Obama's inauguration, rhinestone jeans, Nickelodeon shows, chunky consoles, capris and CD cases (not necessarily in that order). These defining cultural references are rife in the artist's works. *Okay you'll be Jade you'll be Yasmin and I'll be Sasha* (2024), for example, is a nod to the line of Bratz fashion dolls that first entered the toy market in 2001 and still enjoy popularity today.

Many of Wellington's artworks feature poems or texts. The artist recognises that tapestries have often been used to "archive histories" and seeks to do the same in a way that "feels most authentic to me given the time I was born and what I have experienced". Wellington begins her tapestries by writing "long-form, image-heavy poem[s]", which are then "abridged and arranged acrostically". For imagery, she scours "internet archives and government databases" for archival news footage of milestone events. These records of society and culture are then translated and collaged with her poems "about domesticity, care, rest, and familial love" through a juxtaposition of text and image.

In this way, Wellington personally interprets the generational issues and themes of growing up in the Digital Age: an interpretation deepened through the visual symbol of the bead as a "pixel", which forms an image when combined with thousands of others.

Wellington's choice to work with pony beads imbues her art with both a personal and cultural connection to Black American history and life. The beads are directly connected to the artist's own experience of wearing braided hair styles, and in her view are "a cultural signifier of care: a way to declare someone loves this one and someone desires for me to enjoy myself... To adorn, in this case, is to love." Wellington highlighting these beads through artmaking can be regarded as an ode to the joys and happiness found in Black childhood, as well as a "mundane exaltation of belonging".

This process of love is translated through the laborious process of making the tapestries, which take up to 100 hours and typically between 50,000 and 100,000 individual beads to create. She works on an adapted upright tapestry loom to accommodate the size of the pony beads, and uses heavy weight monofilament thread for both warp and weft. For larger designs, Wellington breaks the tapestry into smaller panels, which are then sewn together. At times, weaving in the thread ends takes half the time that the weaving itself does. To Wellington, the repetitive and meditative nature of weaving feels "natural", given the "cyclical nature of work my family has done": rituals that include the time taken "every other Sunday for hair washing, styling and braiding". Through her own ritual of elevating the pony bead with large-scale tapestries, Wellington wants audiences to "appreciate the gorgeousness of the material", and for "people who look like me to feel seen". ■

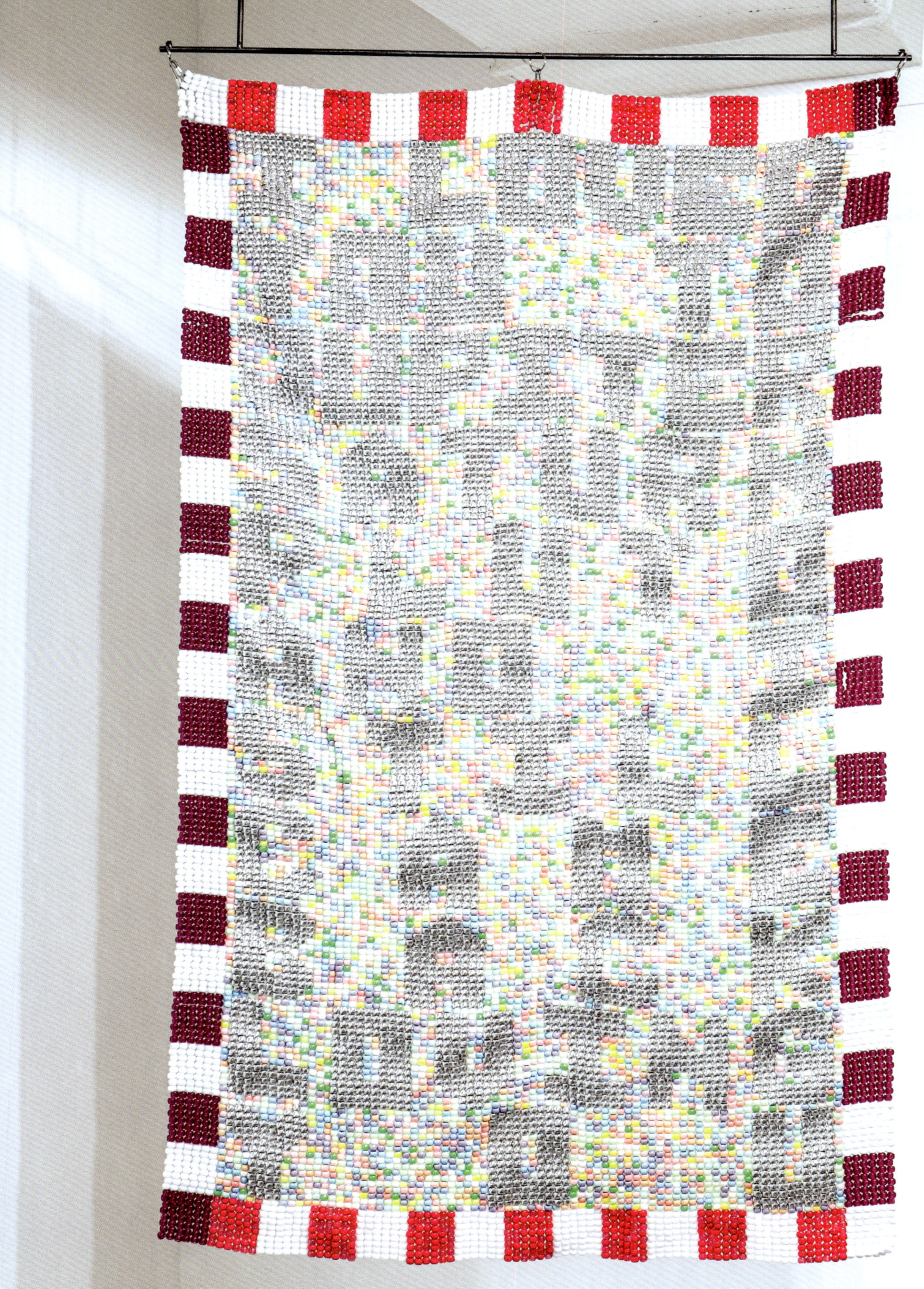

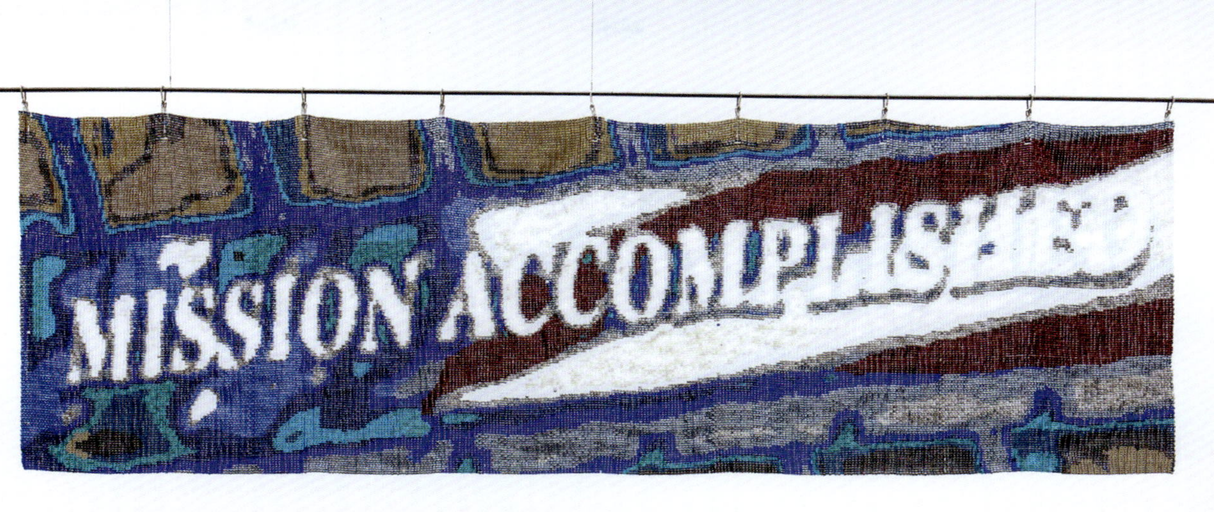

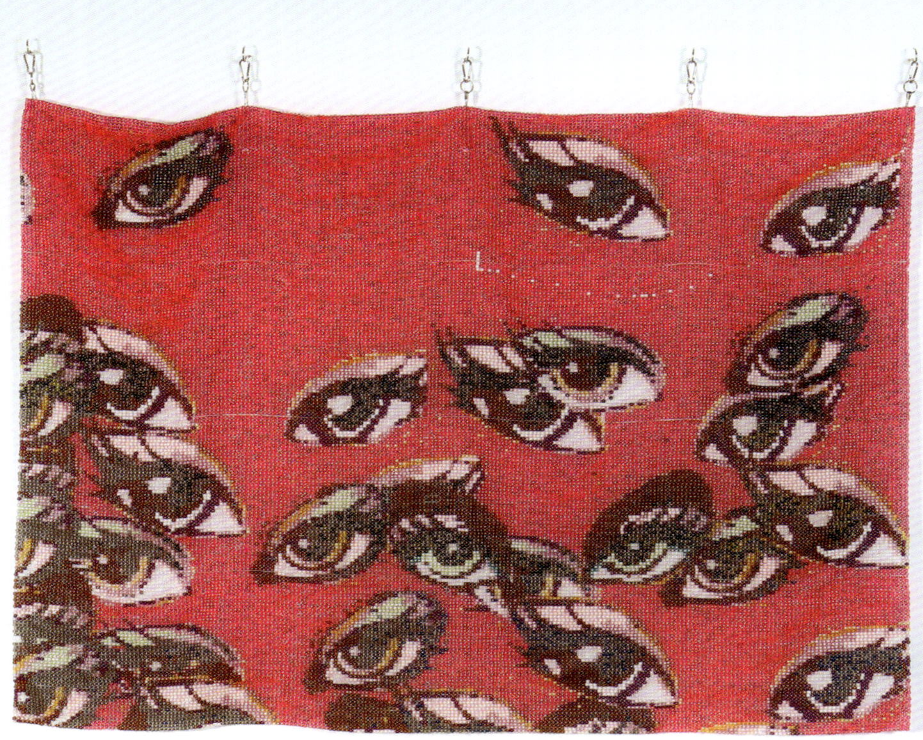

Opposite *I loved you to Jupiter Saturn Pluto and I still came back loving you*, 2023, Weaving and beadwork
This page Top: *Baby bush, you made my eyes go wide and stay there,* 2024, Weaving and beadwork; Bottom: *Okay you'll be Jade you'll be Yasmin and I'll be Sasha*, 2024, Weaving and beadwork

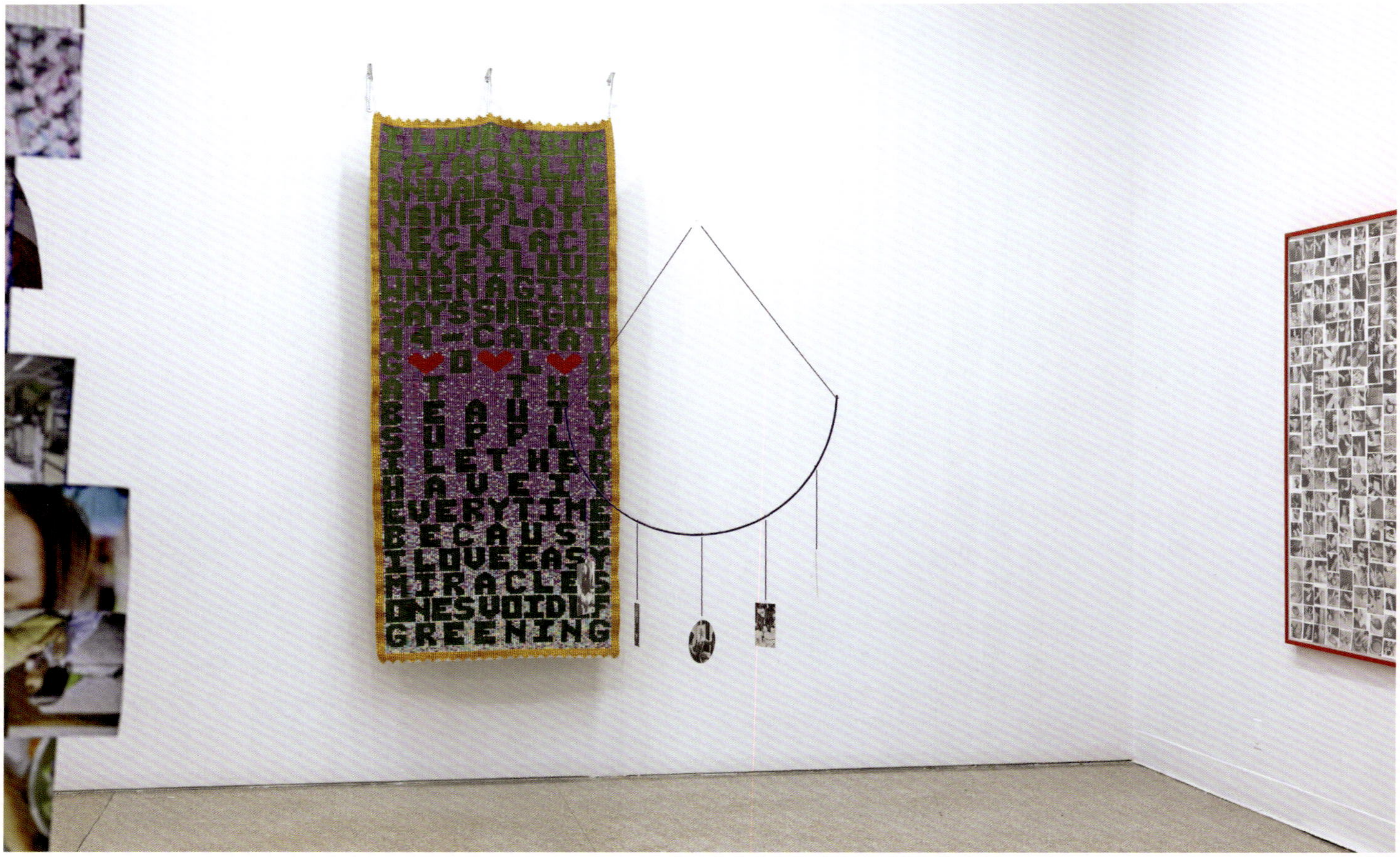

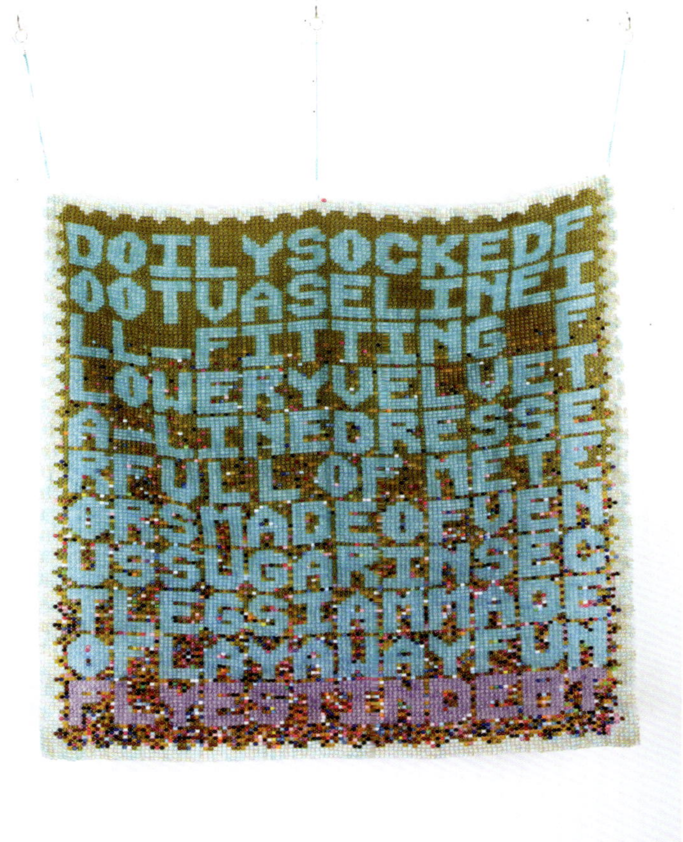

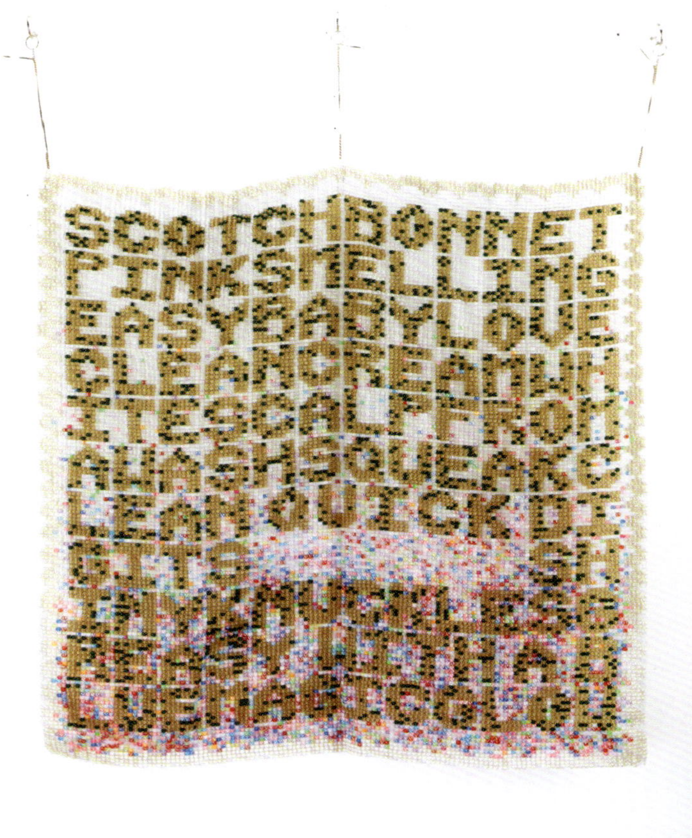

This page Clockwise from top: *I love a big fat acrylic and a little nameplate necklace …,* 2023, Weaving and beadwork; *Scotchbonnet special girl,* 2024,Weaving and beadwork; *Doily socked dollar out of fifteen cent,* 2024, Weaving and beadwork
Opposite *She was a fly bride in her denims,* 2024, Weaving and beadwork

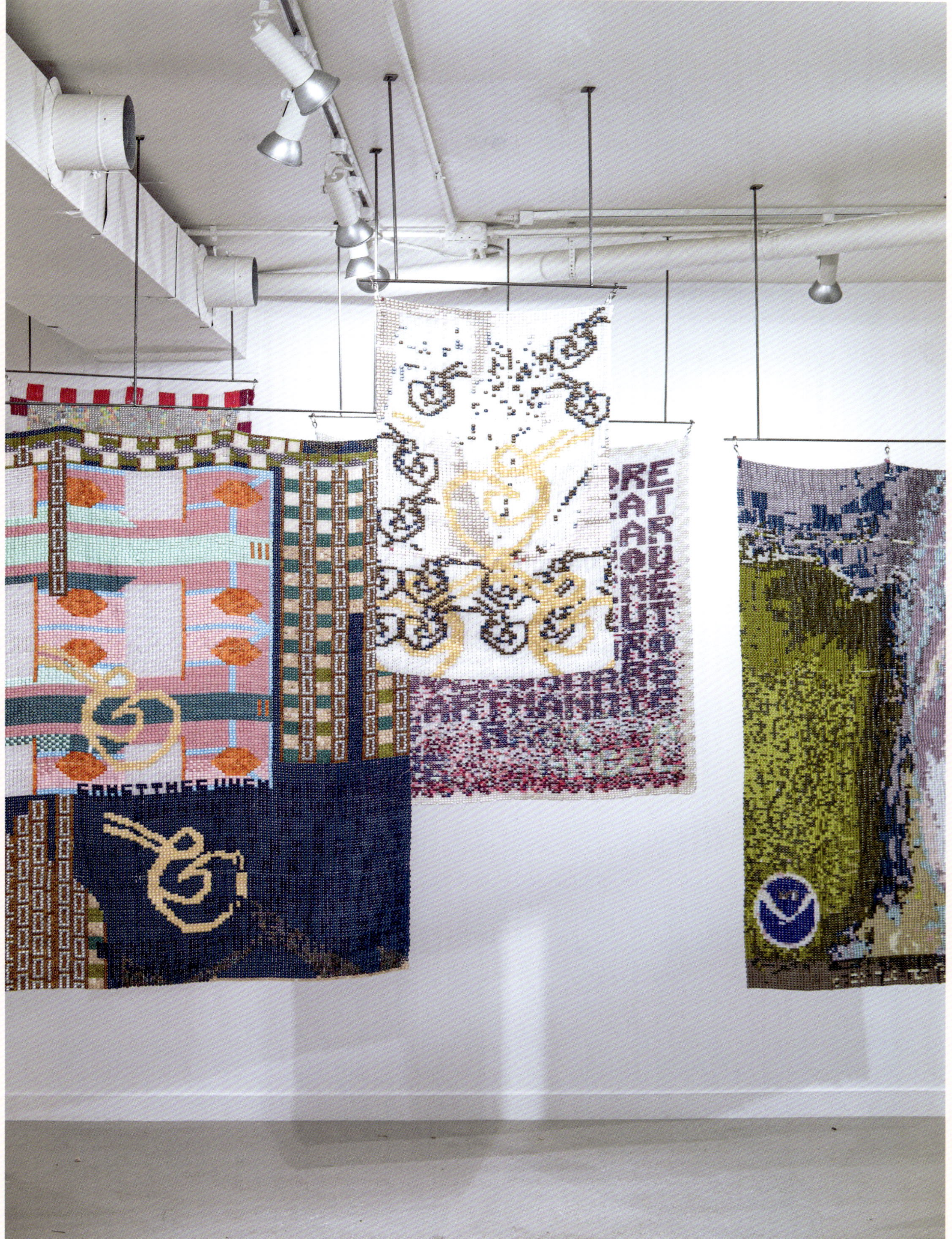

Cheong See Min 張思敏 JOHOR AND TAICHUNG

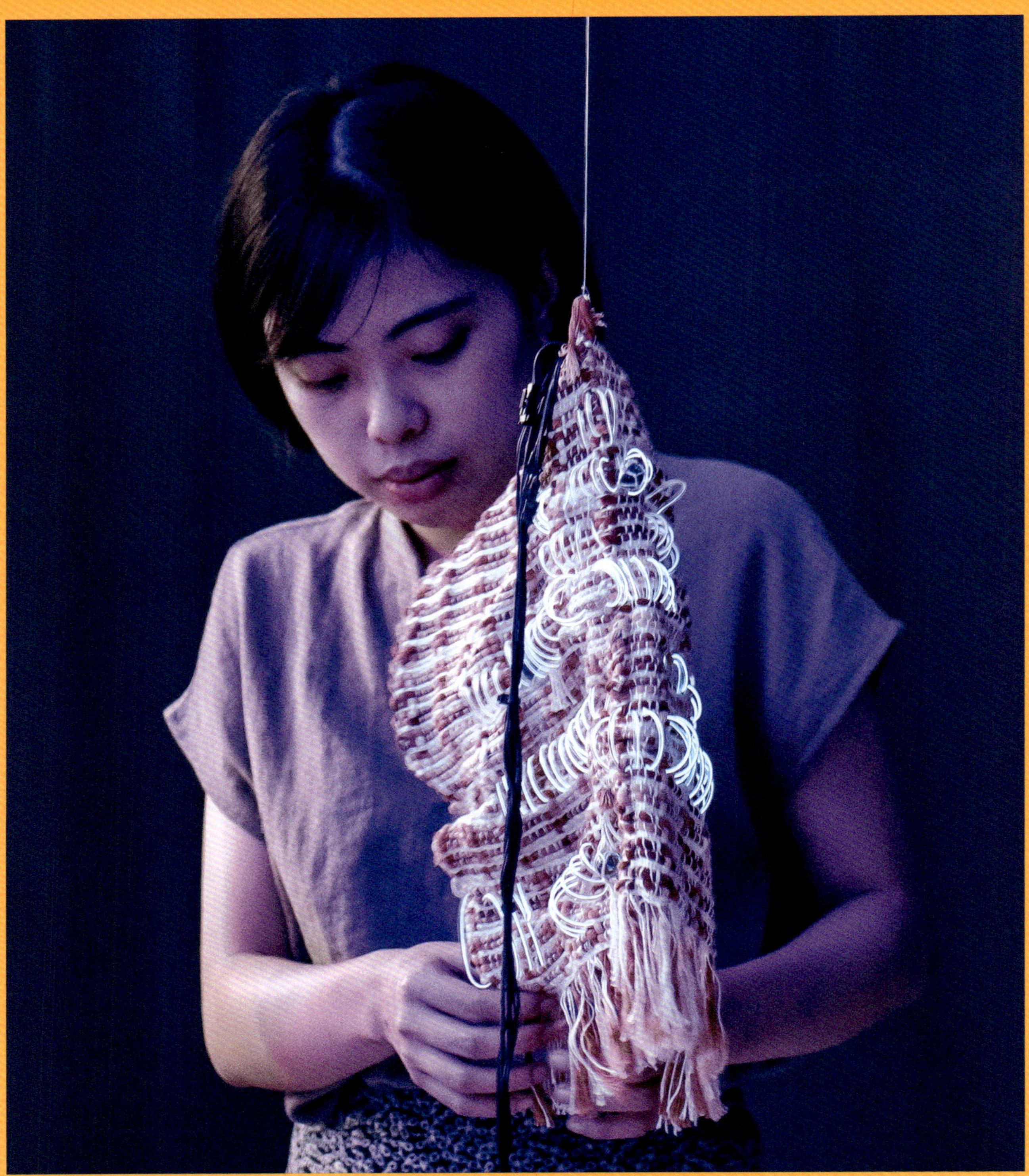

Cheong See Min's art explores the "intricate relationship between nature and human". She captures this by working with fibres and techniques deeply connected to her upbringing in Malaysia, and by examining cultural and historical contexts of textiles in the region. This includes her use of local fibres and adoption of songket, a traditional brocade technique that inserts gold and silver threads into woven fabrics. By highlighting these connections and the endurance of Malaysia's textile traditions, Cheong uses weaving as an "act of communication, a way to bridge the past and the present".

Among her material choices that connect the personal and cultural is pineapple fibre. Cheong's mother and grandmother were both pineapple farmers, and the artist grew up in a country where "natural fibres such as cotton, silk and linen were materials of fabrics I frequently encountered". She honours her lineage by harvesting and laboriously preparing the pineapple fibre for weaving, hand-scraping it from leaves and letting it soak for days.

Beyond personal links, the pineapple is a historically significant crop and trade commodity in Malaysia, as it was "introduced by colonisers and tied to the nation's economic and social history". Its presence in the country is closely connected to ongoing impacts on land, economic prosperity and, significantly, human labourers. The pineapple fibre in Cheong's works is not just a material, but a thematic focus and object of study. This is captured in *The Lost Pineapple Cannery I* (2025), which references the period in the 1960s and '70s during which Malaysian pineapple export was at its peak. This connection to industry is also revealed in works such as *A Cart of Lost Pineapple* (2023), which makes visible the labour required to maintain this crop – in this case, a bull-drawn cart. Across her art, Cheong considers the often invisible labour needed to sustain profitable export markets.

What is evident in both these works is an "absence". Where pineapples would usually appear, Cheong has left a visual gap. For the artist, this erasure "speaks to the untold or forgotten narratives in history, particularly those silenced by power structures or overlooked by mainstream accounts". This absence is utilised to critical effect in *We Walk Barefoot, They Sit in the Car* (2025), a tapestry based on archival documentation that highlights the power imbalance between two figures in a car and a labourer whose silhouette is left unfilled. This absence invites audiences to "reflect on the gaps in their own understanding of history and their personal experience".

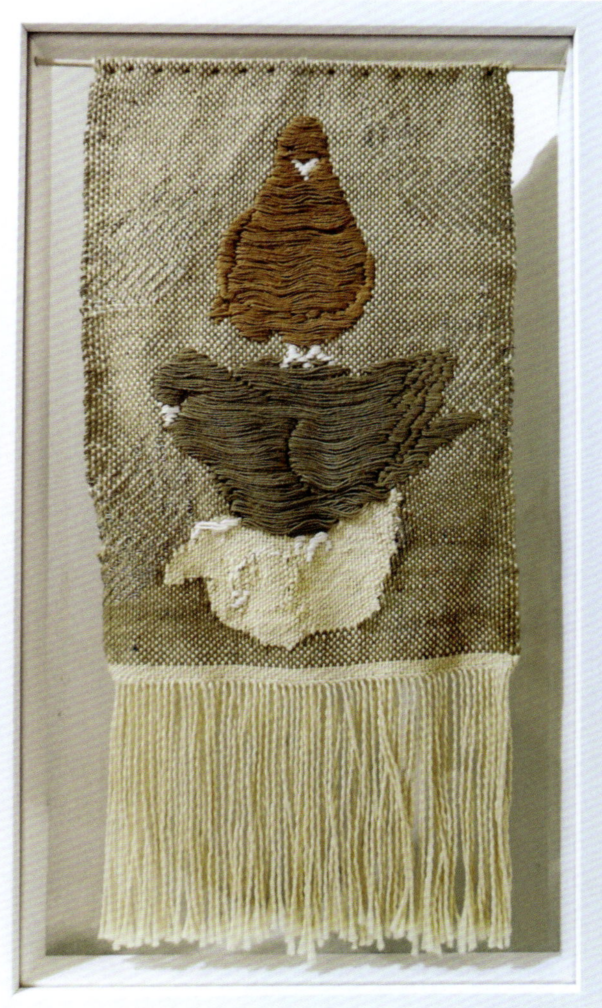

Birds on Bird, 2024, Supplementary weft and twill weaving

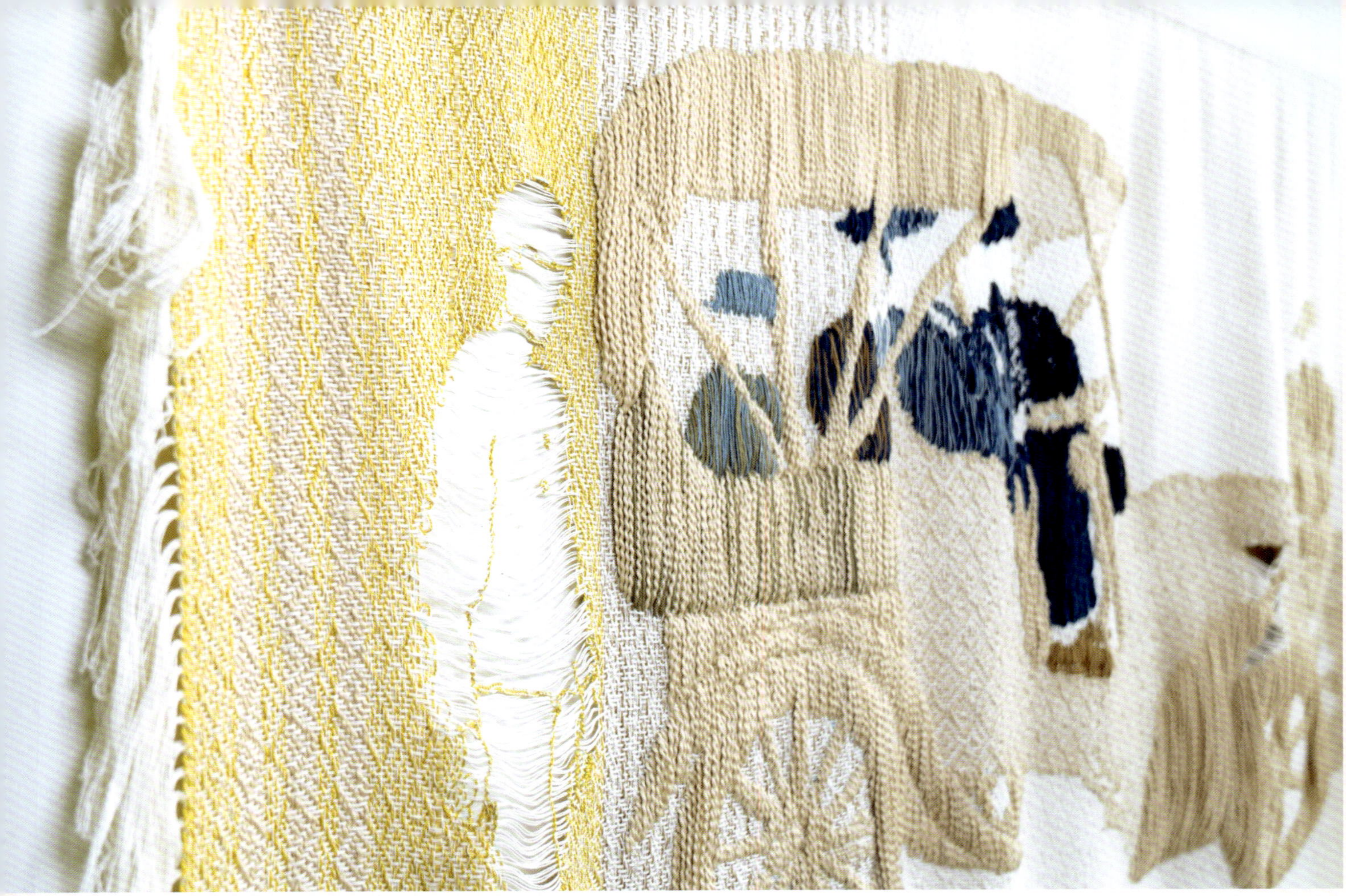

Themes of memory, loss and absence are also evident in Cheong's *Remember* series (2021–ongoing). These works, made during a residency in Taichung, are based on her "wandering experience and observation". Every day, Cheong noticed elderly men chatting in front of their stores. But during the pandemic, they vanished, leaving only empty chairs behind – a silent trace of their presence. In Cheong's weavings capturing these scenes, the chair becomes a metaphor for each life; instead of a human figure, Cheong adds a flower motif to the chairs as a symbol of mourning to highlight the transience of life and to give "more meaning" to its presence.

For this series of works, Cheong removes select weft threads from polypropylene (PP) bags to create images – the same bags widely used in Southeast Asia for a variety of uses. This material imbues each tapestry with additional pathos. As a common, everyday object, the bag's use as a weaving material brings significance and value to the plastic anew. This deliberate choice continues Cheong's goals in her art to uncover the "forgotten or untold narratives from history". ■

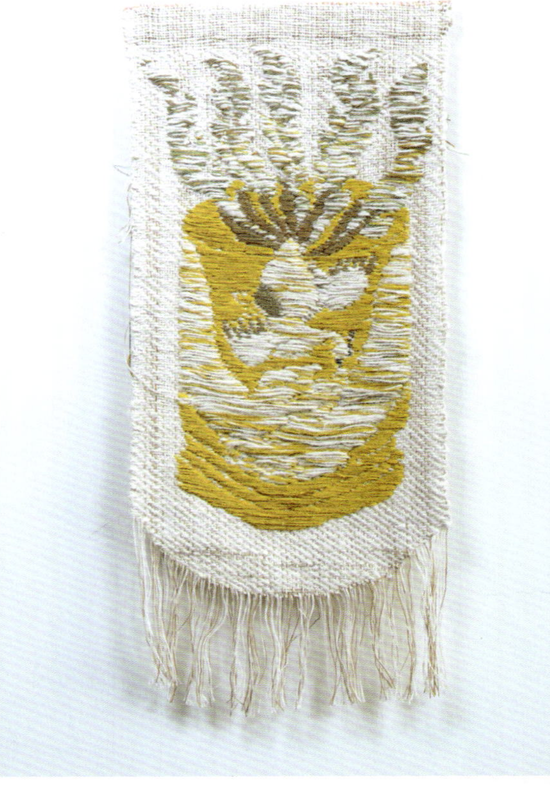

This page Top: *We Walk Barefoot, They Sit in the Car*, 2024, Supplementary weft and twill weaving; Bottom: *Pineapple I*, 2024, Supplementary weft and twill weaving **Opposite** *A Cart of Lost Pineapples*, 2023, Supplementary weft and tapestry weaving

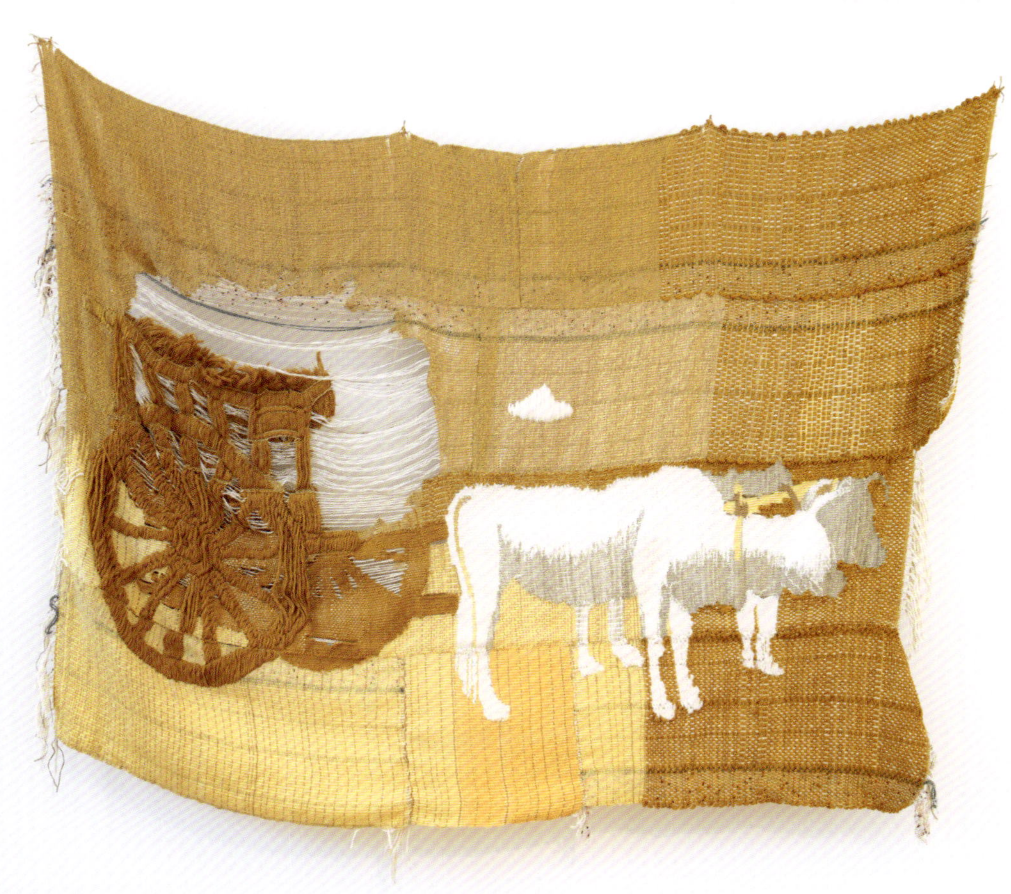

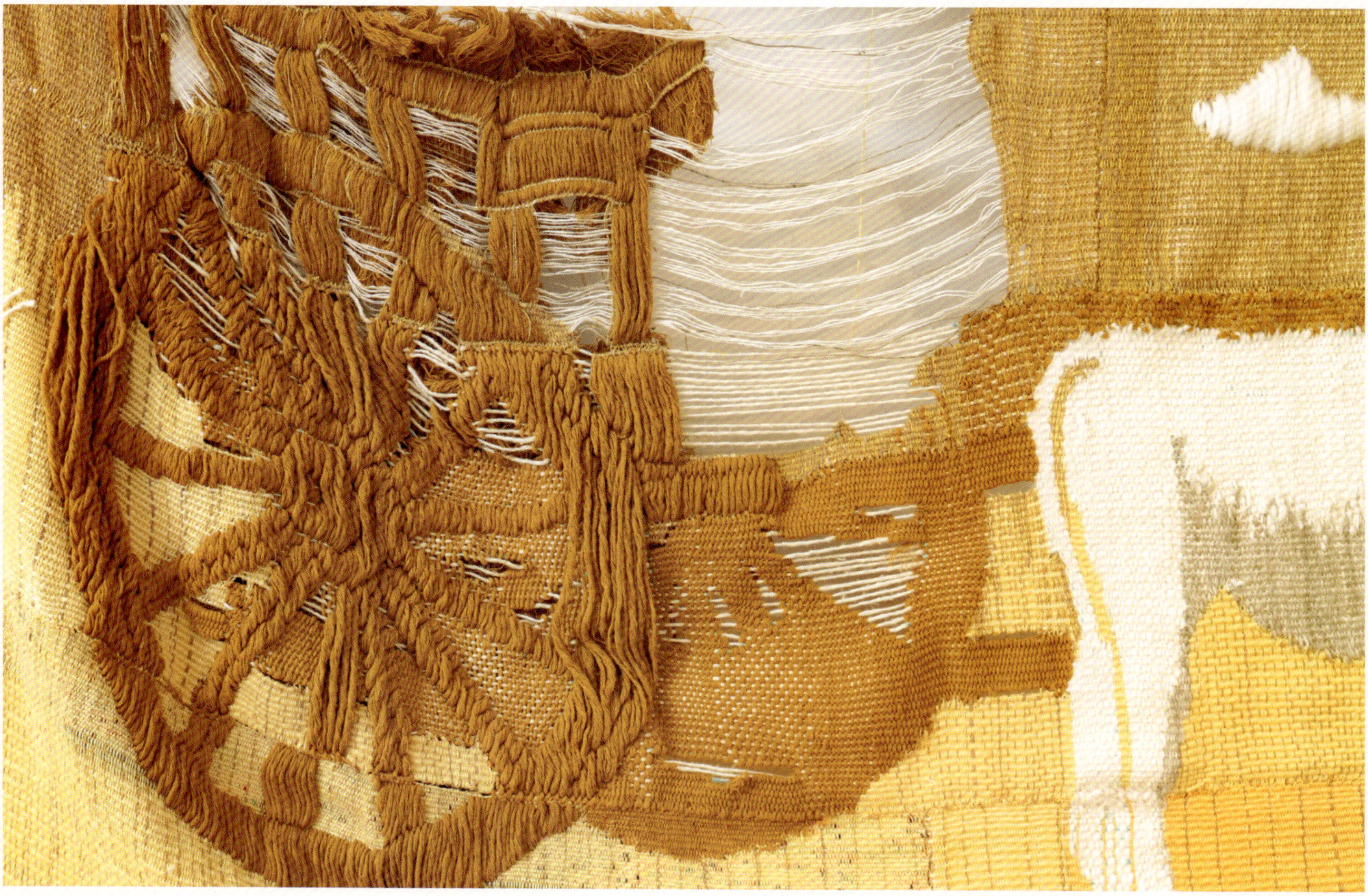

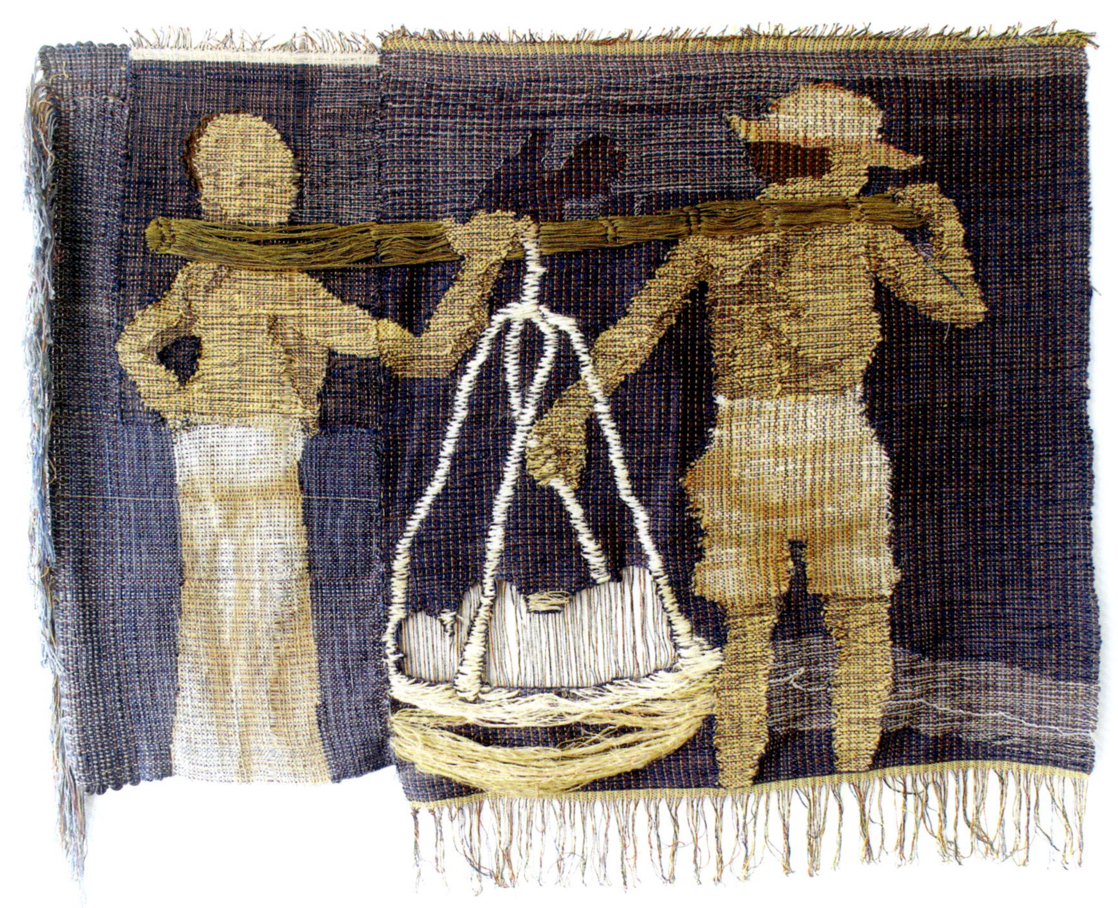

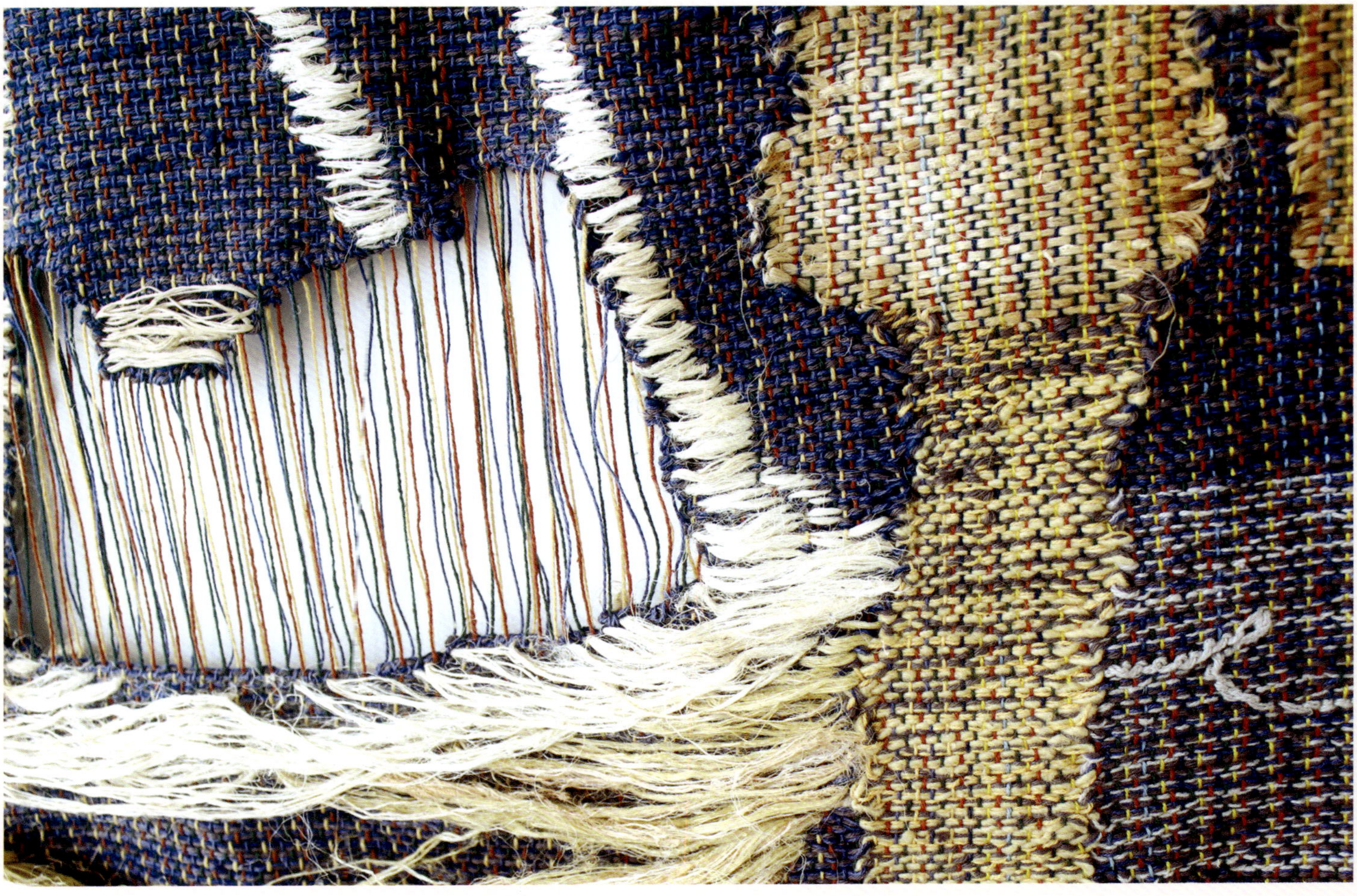

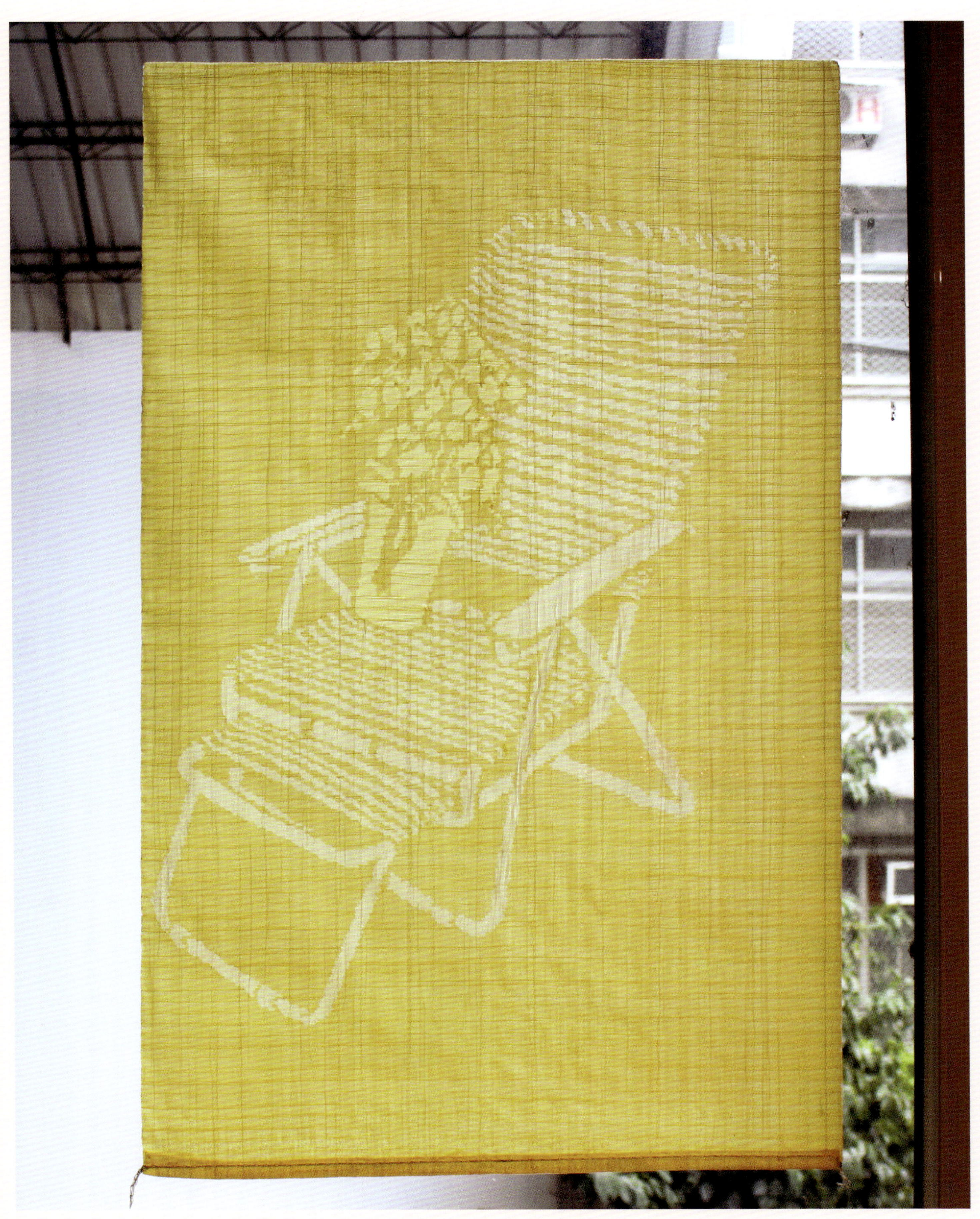

Opposite *The Lost Pineapple Cannery I*, 2025, Supplementary weft and plain weaving
This page *Remember - Don't worry me*, 2021, Drawn thread work

Daniela Contreras Flores MEXICO CITY

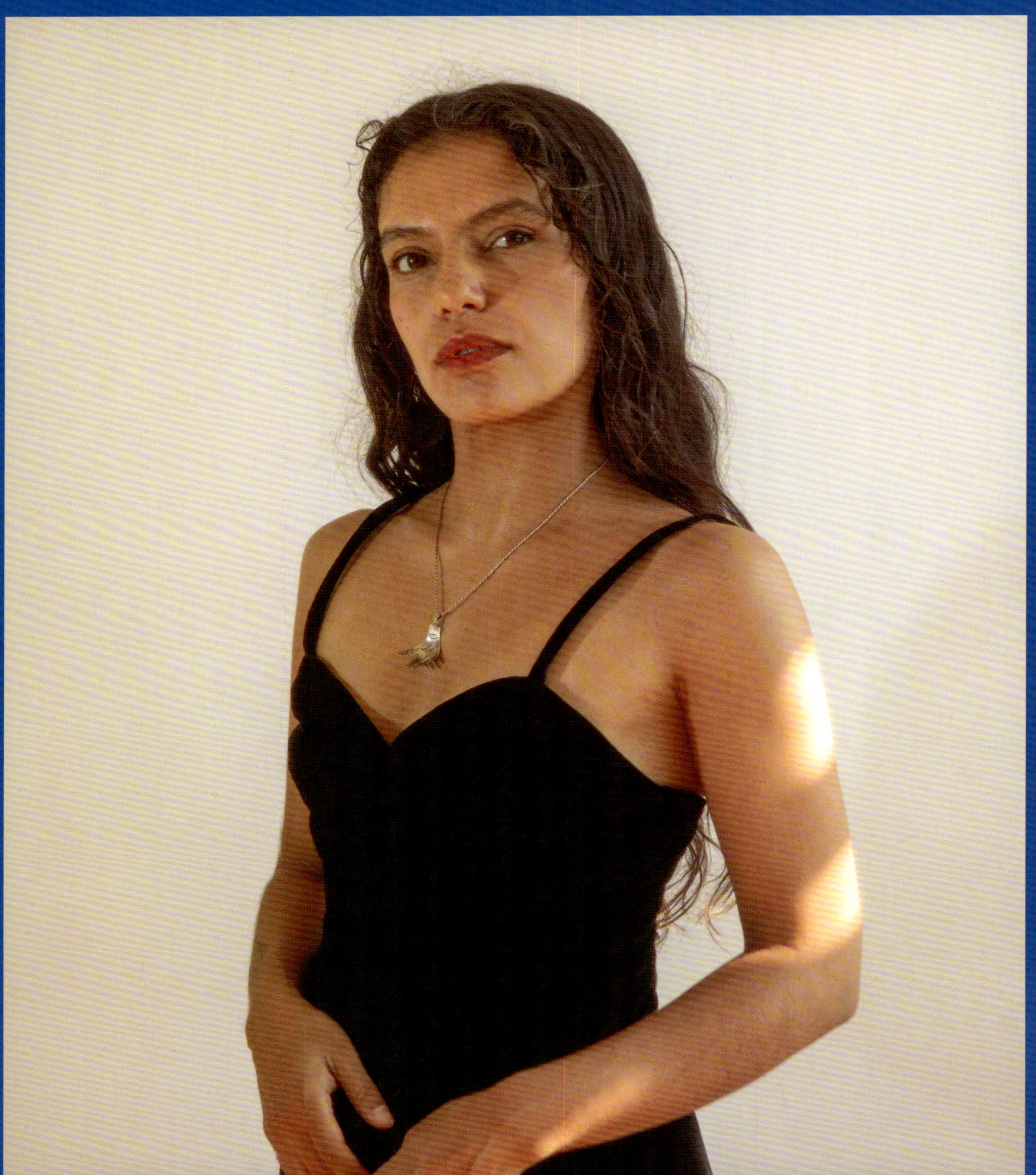

Daniela Contreras Flores grew up in Chile in a family where "craftsmanship was always part of our daily lives". As a child, she would help her mother unravel yarn from second-hand sweaters to knit anew, while her father worked as a furniture maker. Long before she went to university to study visual arts, Contreras Flores' path had been "paved with textiles and crafts". It wasn't until her time at school, though, that she learnt tapestry weaving, which she now describes as a "long-term and rather monogamous relationship that continues to this day".

During her studies, a transformative realisation occurred when Contreras Flores noted the "absence of self-portraits in the history of tapestry". For the artist, this "significant void" reflected wider issues about the "visibility of the marginalised" and what artforms are given recognition. Research driven by this focus led to *Self Portrait with Shuttle* (2015–16), which evokes 17th-century European oil self-portraits. In Contreras Flores' interpretation, the style's usual grandeur is marked by inclusions from daily life such as a pair of Converse and a biscuit tin (ostensibly containing sewing supplies). The result is a powerful portrait of self-determination, "vindicating the weaver and honoring their ancestral craft".

Since university, Contreras Flores has continued exploring weaving as a space where "politics and culture converge". For her, textiles are a "living, resilient organism" that can serve "as an accessible and powerful medium to communicate complex ideas about political violence and collective resilience through an exercise of memory and archiving". Contreras Flores locates her practice within present-day Chile's cultural context and in wider Latin American traditions and ancestral cultural frameworks, in which textiles are central. Geographically, she has a particular focus on the Andean cordillera – specifically on Chile, Peru, Bolivia and Argentina. Finding a connection with the "textile roots of this territory, where weaving was historically understood as a narrative genre...a way to narrate the world and cosmogony" has been transformative for the artist: "tapestry gave me back an identity I didn't know was mine, and with it, also restored my dignity".

A number of Contreras Flores' tapestries incorporate traditional Andean techniques. This includes the use of a circular weaving technique, originating from the Chimú culture, which Contreras Flores describes as "largely unrecognised in Latin America" and which she researched extensively for *Circular Heritage* (2019). Symbolically, Andean culture is also present in *Record of a Journey* (2018), which comprises five interrelated, suspended weavings. In each piece, Contreras Flores explores "the Andean worldview" through elements that reflect her own experience: architecture, earth and water, and three women who she describes as "guardians of textile knowledge".

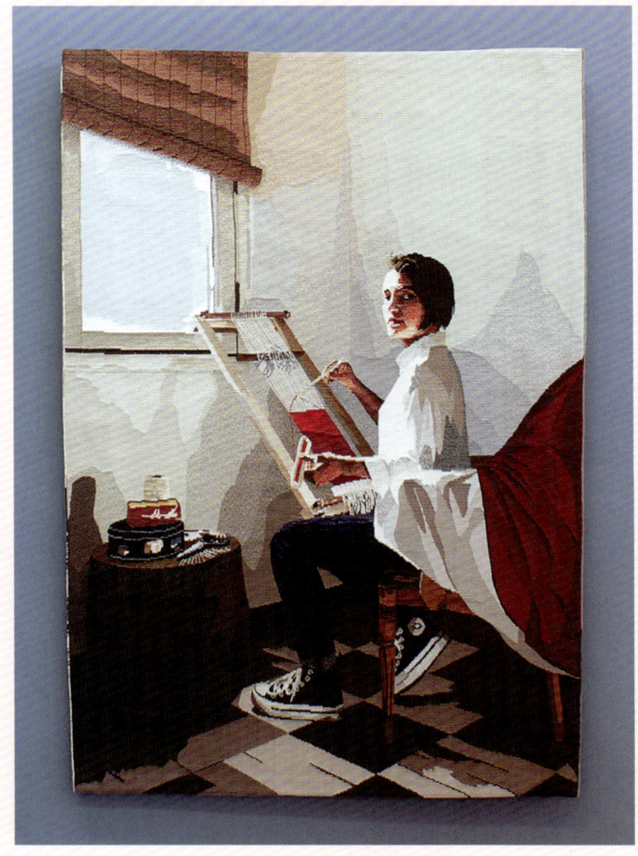

Self-Portrait with Shuttle, 2015–16, Weaving

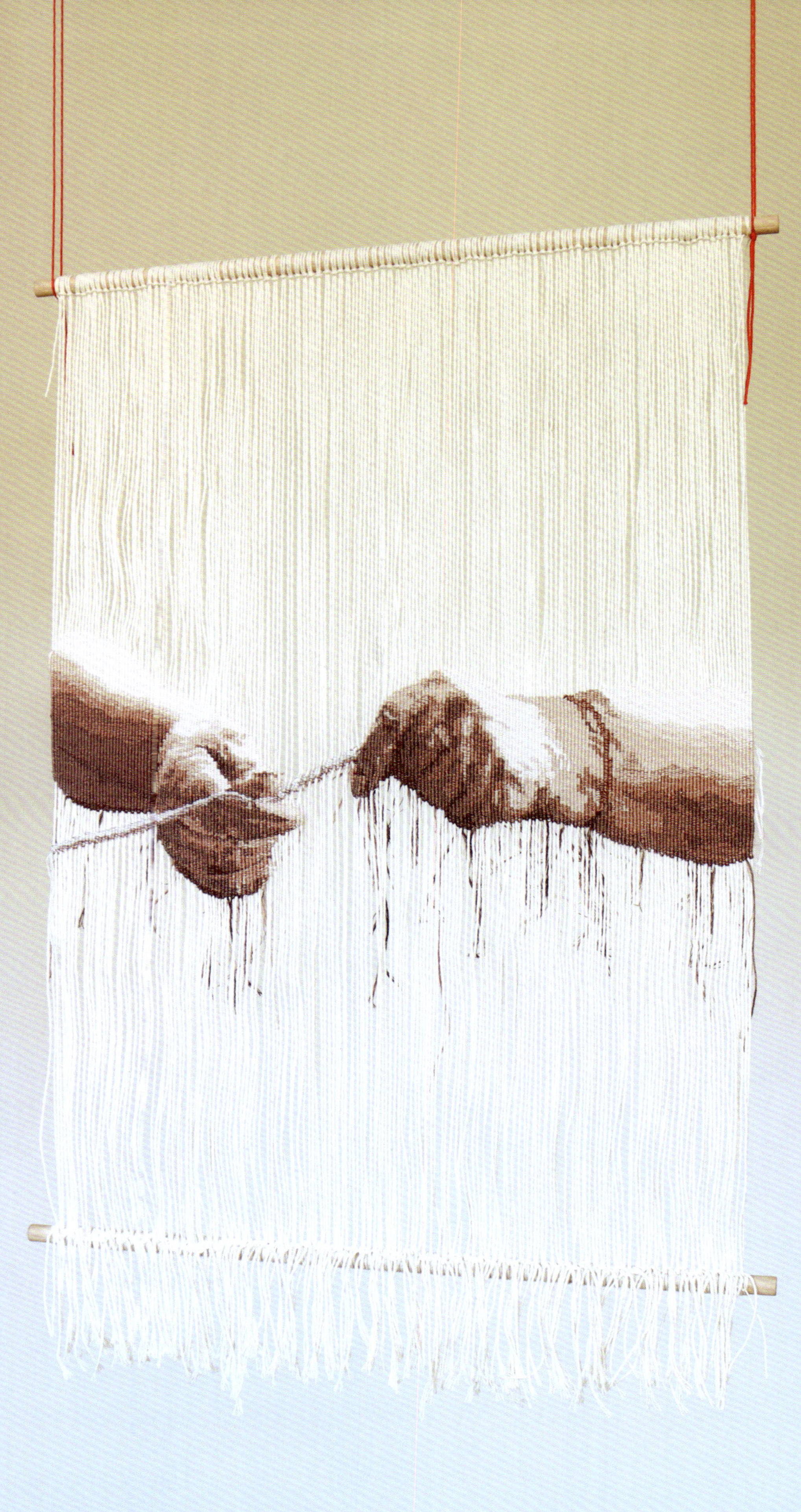

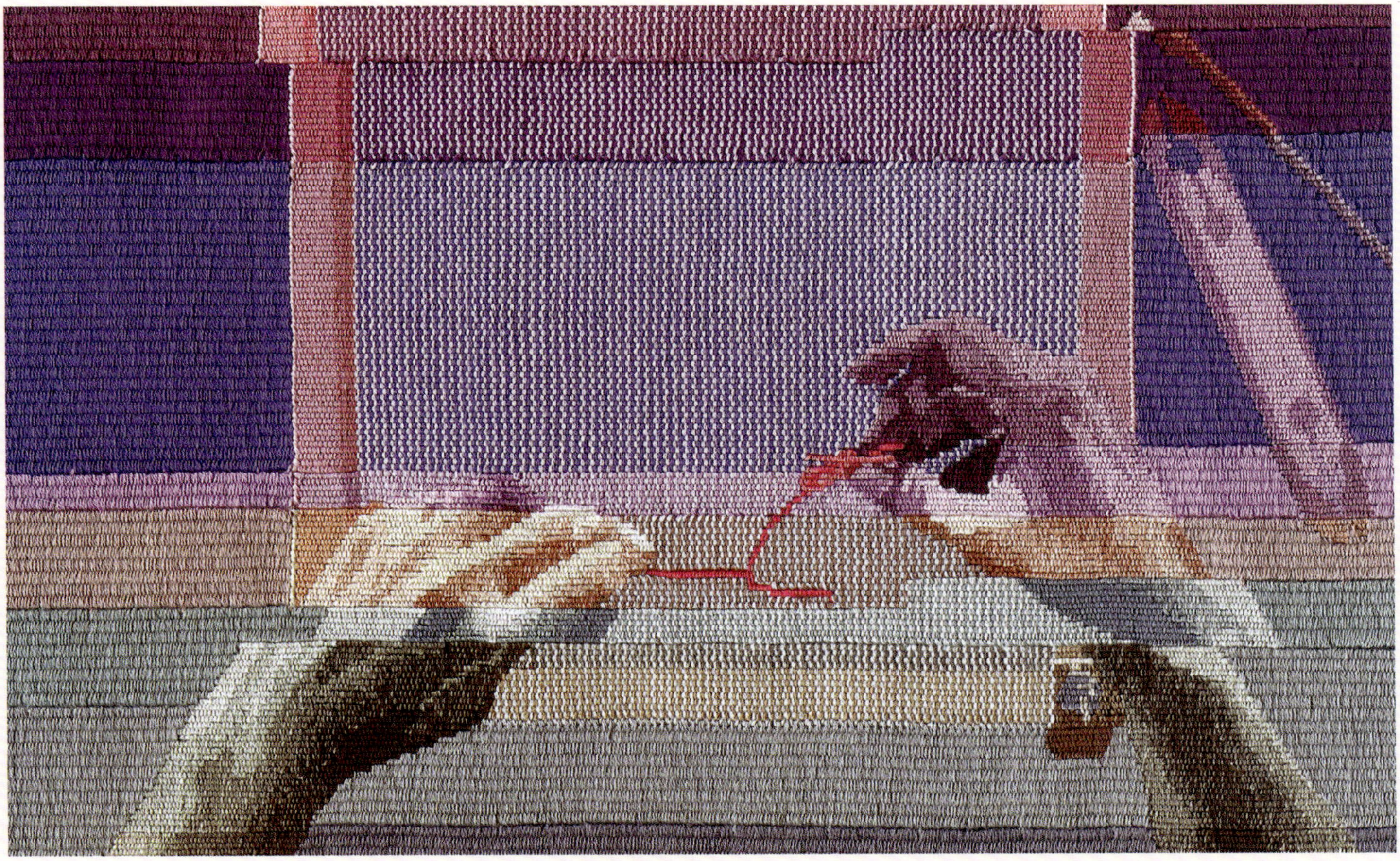

Her tapestry *Spinning Memory* (2023) depicts hands spinning yarn. They belong to Sonia, a woman in her 70s who has "devoted her life to weaving blankets". Foregrounding hands, often "invisible in this labour", elevates weaving as significant: worthy of recognition. As with *Record of a Journey*, this piece centres women's significance to the region's textiles, echoing the questions that first piqued Contreras Flores' interest: "Who and what deserve representation, who and what deserve to be woven?"

Contreras Flores' approach to tapestry is expansive; she regards it not just as a technique, but also as a "language that weaves the past, present, and identity into every one of my works". This capacity for storytelling is something she wants to share by creating works that she hopes are "universally accessible". Through her tapestries, Contreras Flores builds a bridge between the traditional and the contemporary, and her own identities as "creator, artisan, and above all, a weaver". ■

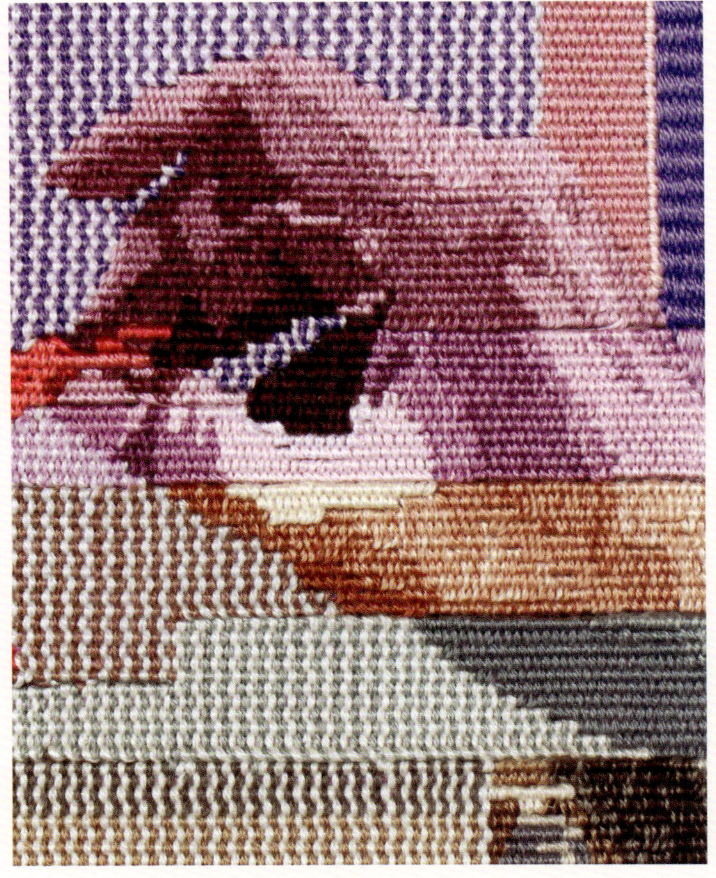

Opposite *Spinning Memory*, 2023, Weaving
This page *I Am a Weaver*, 2019, Weaving

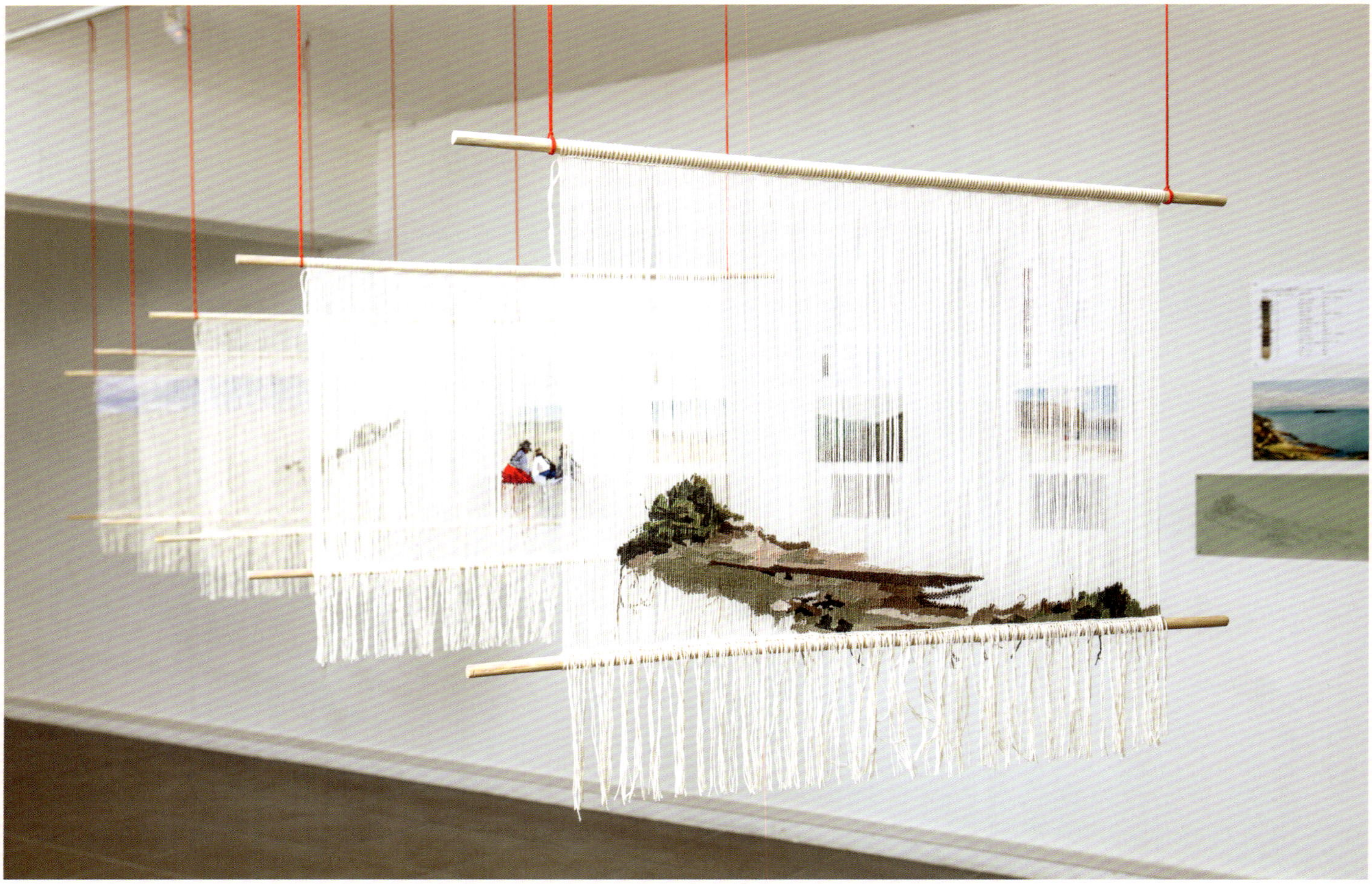

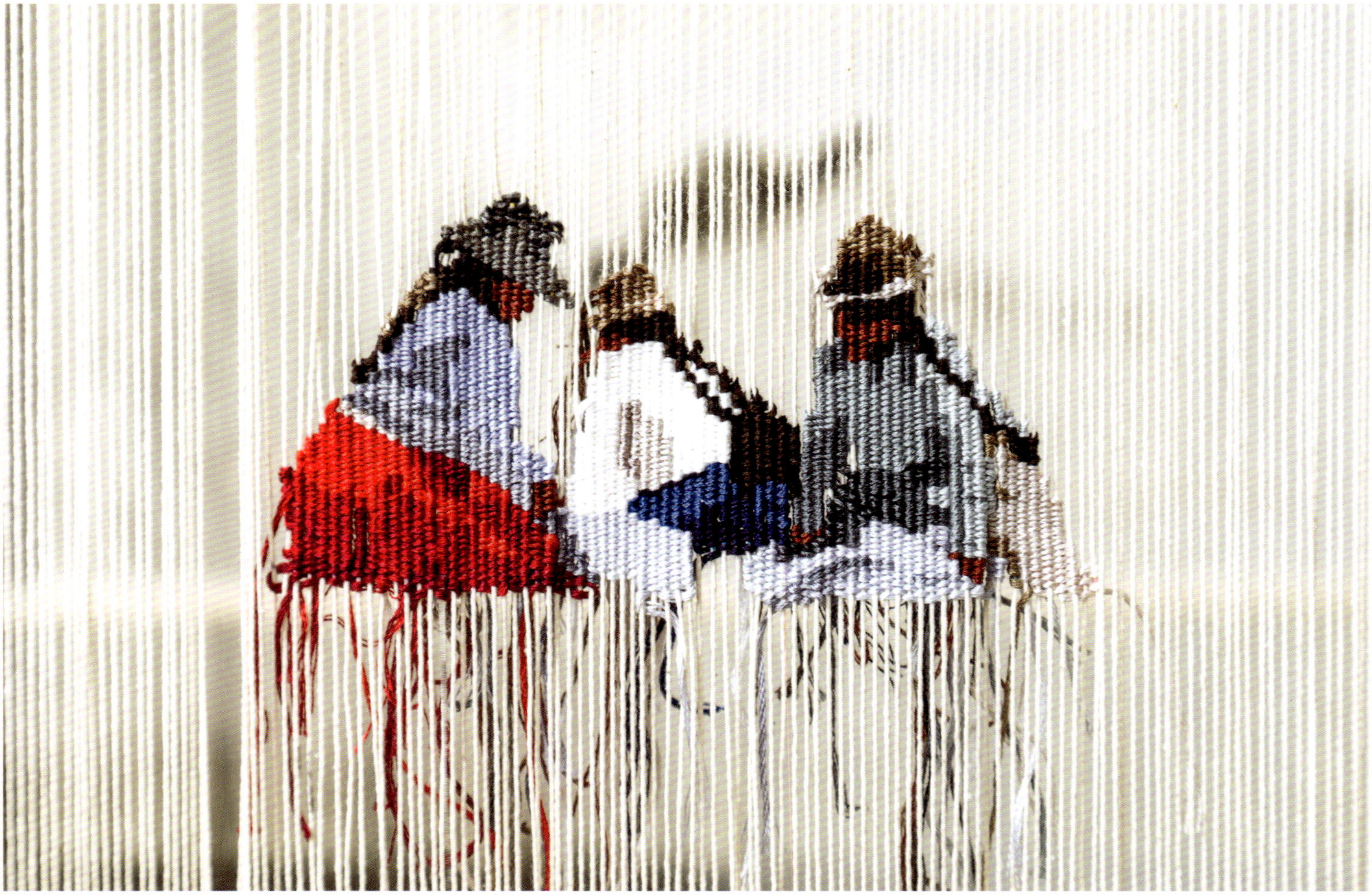

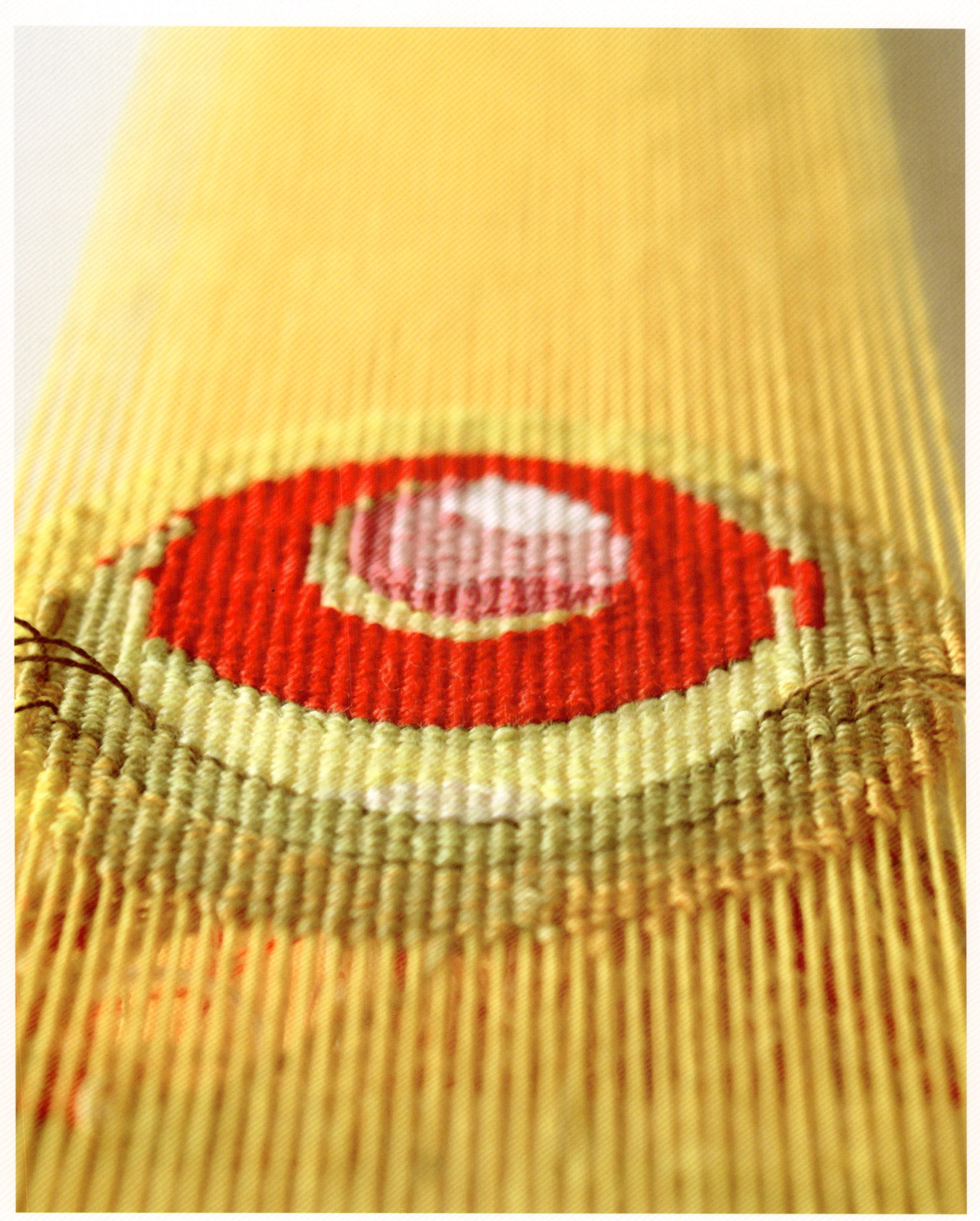

Opposite *Record of a Journey*, 2018, Weaving
This page *Amulets for Transformation* (detail), 2020, Weaving

Ema Shin 辛愛麻

NAARM/MELBOURNE

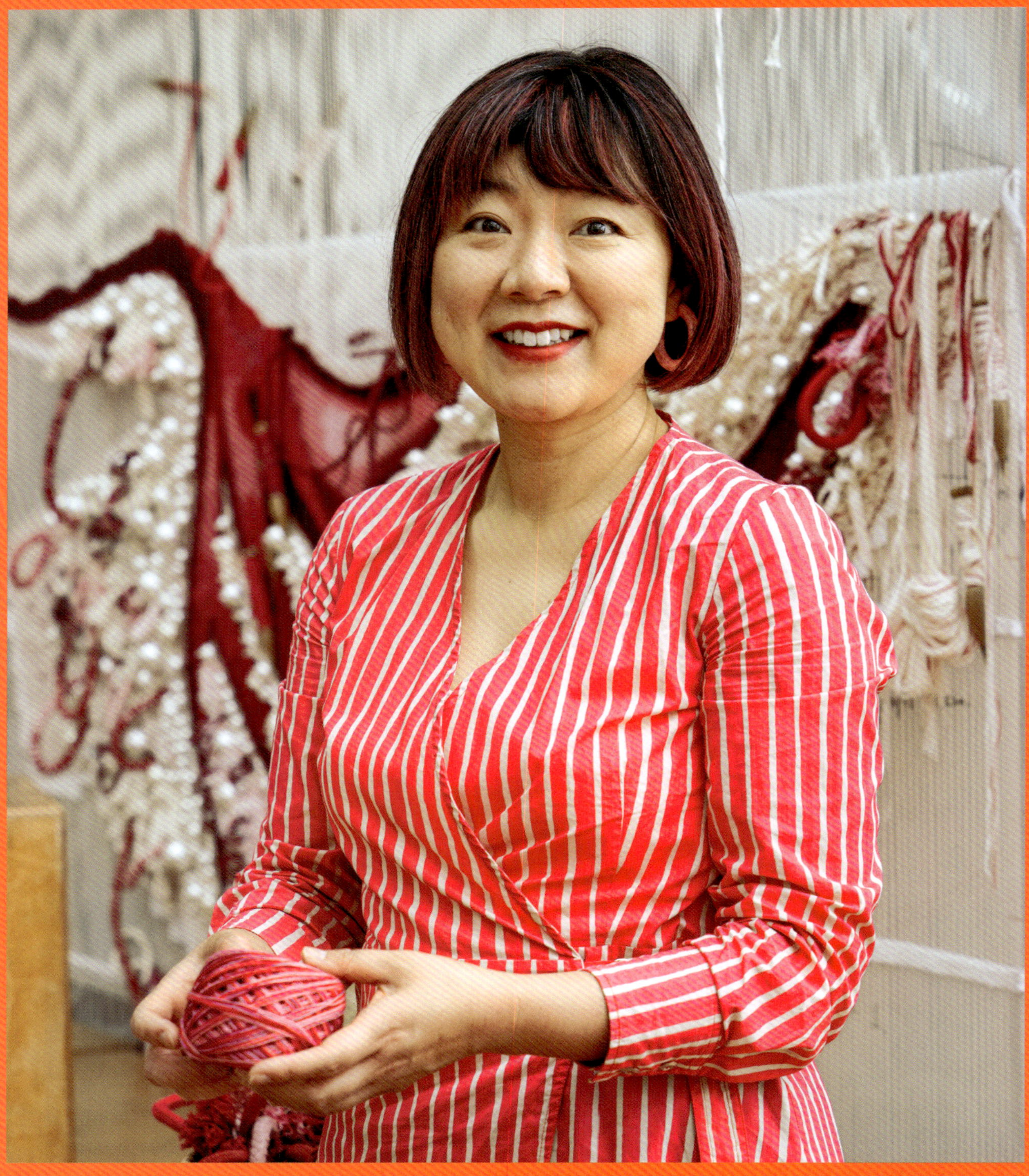

Ema Shin studied traditional and contemporary Japanese printmaking at university, but started weaving after completing an artist residency at the Australian Tapestry Workshop in Melbourne. It was there, under the guidance of the workshop's master weavers, that Shin learnt to weave tapestries on a loom. This experience would significantly shape the direction of Shin's artistic output after childbirth; working with tapestries, and later hand embroidery, afforded Shin the flexibility to set up a home studio that suited her "new lifestyle as a parent". Reflecting on this shift in her artistic output, Shin shares that "working [with] textiles made it possible to continue my creativity in short bursts of time, and I ended up creating bold, colourful works that deeply connect with women's lives and emotions".

This connection to women's work and experiences is a central theme in Shin's art. She traces this focus to her upbringing within a Korean family in Japan, where she saw "prejudice between men and women, with their family and social roles predetermined". Shin uses her art to challenge this cultural and social inequity by foregrounding women's experiences through tender depictions of the female body in tapestries and embroideries. Given textiles' close historical association with "women's crafts and lifestyles", Shin's chosen mediums add another layer of interpretation to her art. Shin shares that she believes this point of connection is "an inseparable part of my work and concept".

In the series *Soft Alchemy* (2016–ongoing), Shin employs a warm palette of pink, red and orange threads to create a striking connection between human anatomy and the shapes and forms found in plant biology. These metaphorical associations include a depiction of lung arteries as "branches" of leaves, as seen in *Soft Alchemy (Fertile Heart)* (2019), and flowers that appear to "grow" out of the pelvic bone in *Soft Alchemy (My Pelvic Bone)* (2018). The choice of colours in these works reminds the viewer of flesh and the inner body, but it also lends a warmth and sensitivity to each piece. Shin maintains traditional weaving techniques, while "adding contemporary methods" such as wrapped cord, sumac, beading and tufting, to allow for greater creative control and expression.

In addition to tapestry weaving, Shin employs embroidery to further explore women's experiences and presence in her recent body of work *Hearts of Absent Women* (2022–ongoing). These pieces, which take the form of individually embroidered hearts, are "dedicated to the lives of women who remain unrecognised". Shin started the series in response to her family tree book spanning 32 generations, which only records the names of male descendants. Daughters are "absent": as per customary Korean views, women would marry and thereafter "belong" to another family. This normalised erasure prompted Shin to consider what experiences and stories might be foregrounded by focusing on these "anonymous women" in her work. Embellished with embroidery floss in the same vivid colours that her tapestries are known for, Shin's sculptures each convey a sense of individuality and pay homage to the "physical and emotional qualities" that hearts represent.

Reflecting on her choice of mediums, Shin shares that "textiles and crafts have always been an important part of my life". This personal connection was fostered by her mother, who taught her how to sew and crochet from a young age, and by a next-door neighbour, who taught her embroidery. Beyond personal links, though, textiles are also a way for Shin to connect with her Korean ancestry and culture, which includes rich textile traditions encompassing chima jeogori dresses and souvenir cloths. The reds that are so central to Shin's creative output can also be regarded as a visual connection to Korea, as the colour is often used to represent good fortune in the country's folk art. For Shin, textiles offer a practice through which she is able to "think about my family and [revisit] my ancestors". ■

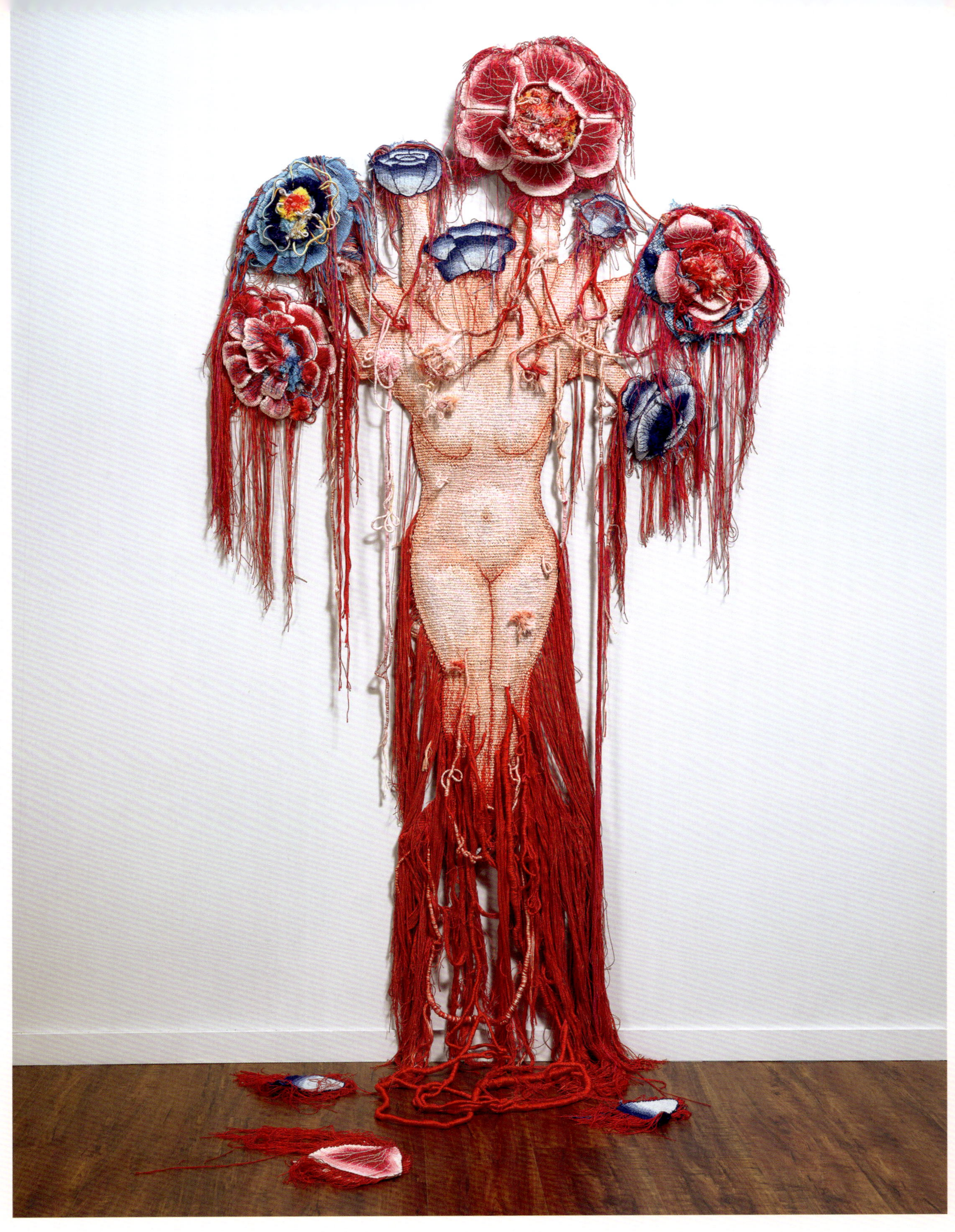

This page *Resettled Body*, 2021, Weaving **Opposite** Clockwise from top left: *Soft Alchemy (Fertile Heart)* (detail), 2022, Weaving; *Resettled Body* (detail), 2021, Weaving; *Soft Alchemy (My Pelvic Bone)*, 2018, Weaving; Studio shot, 2024

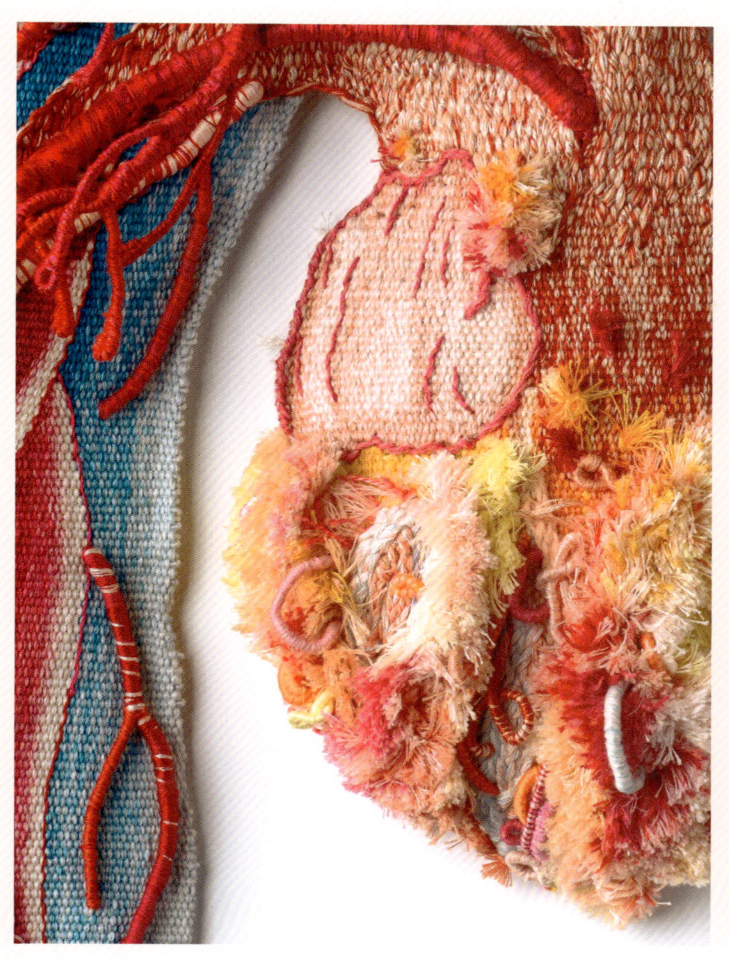
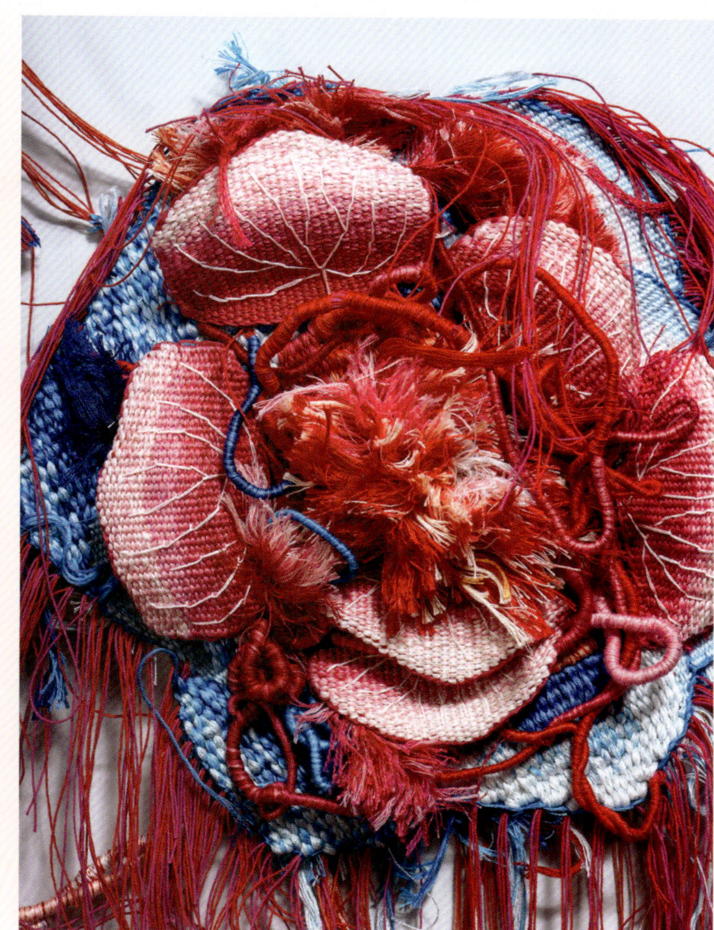
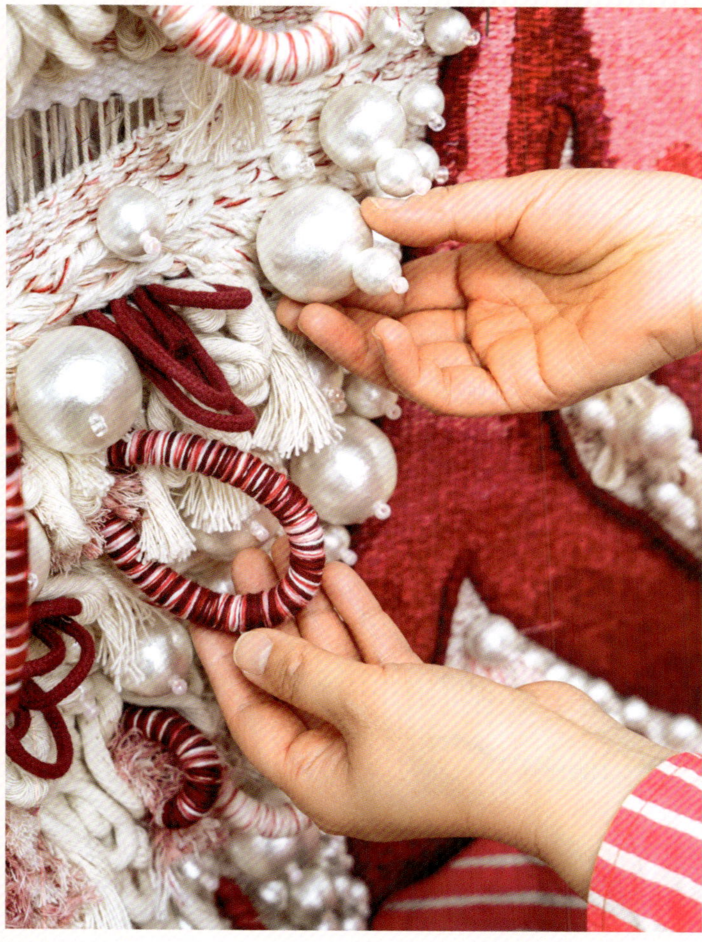
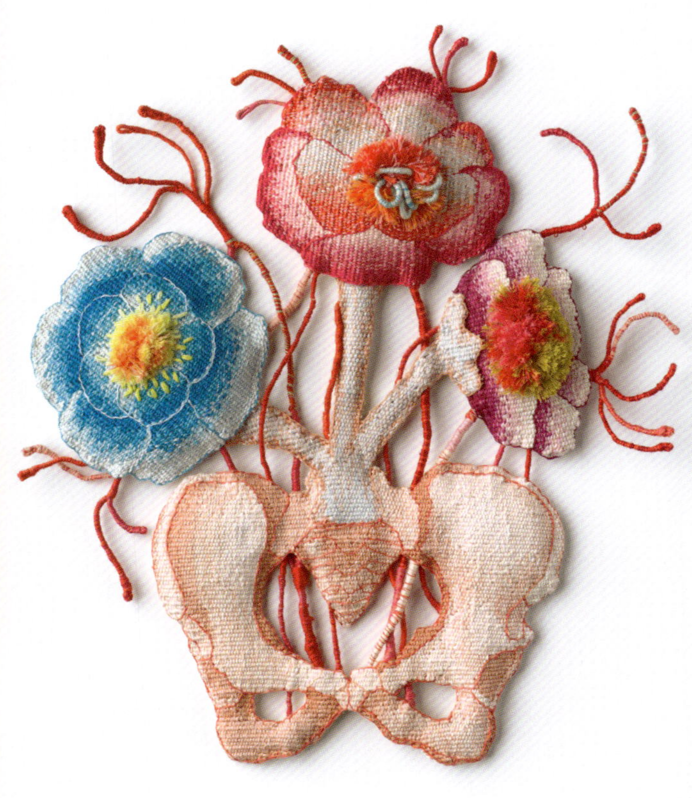

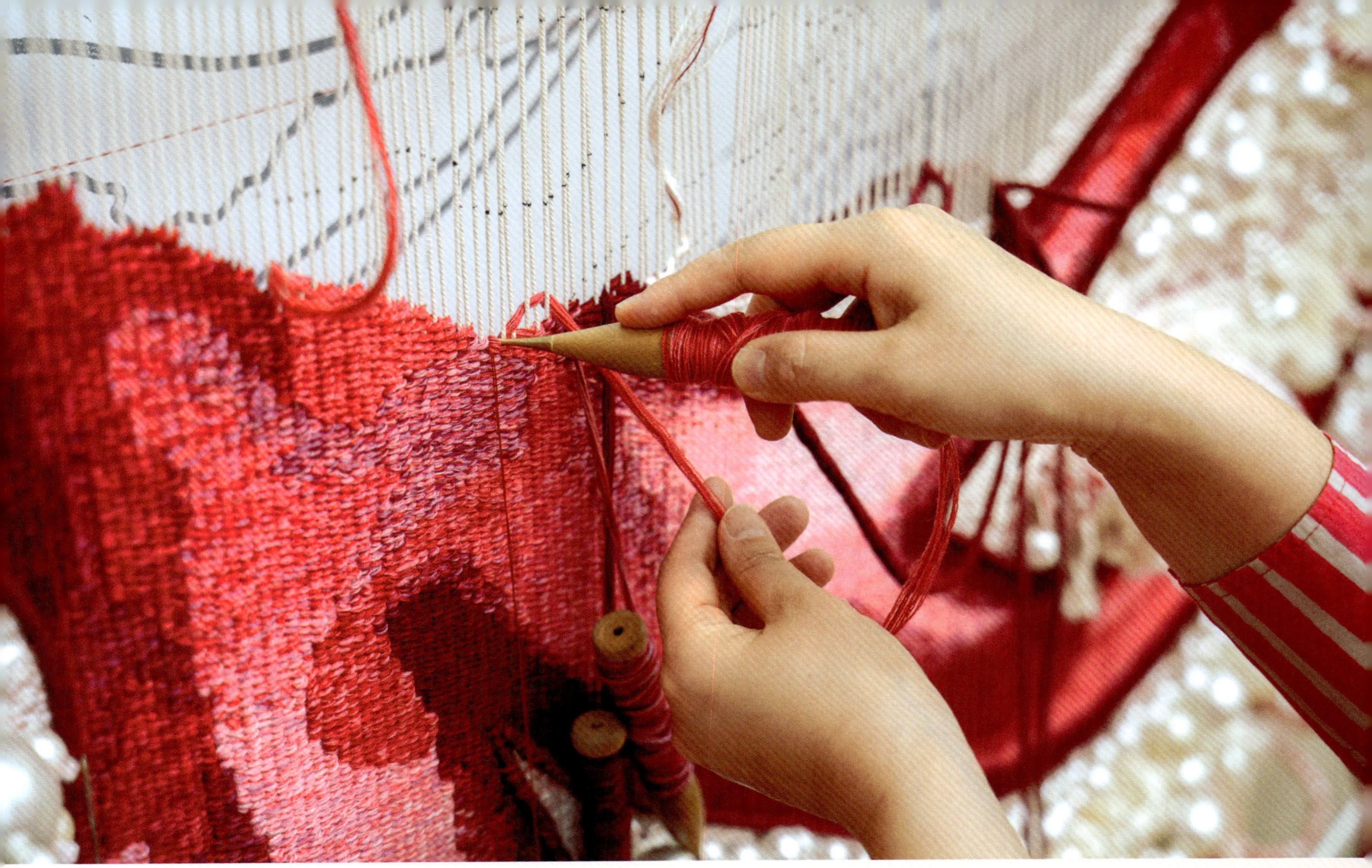

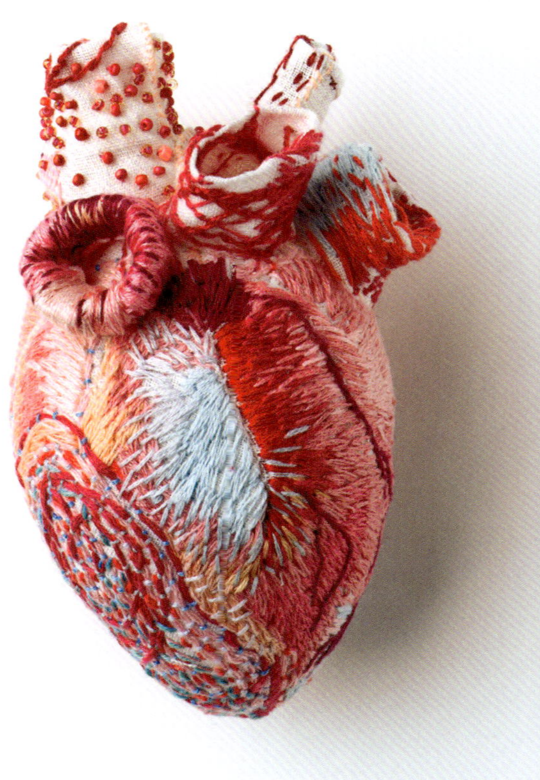

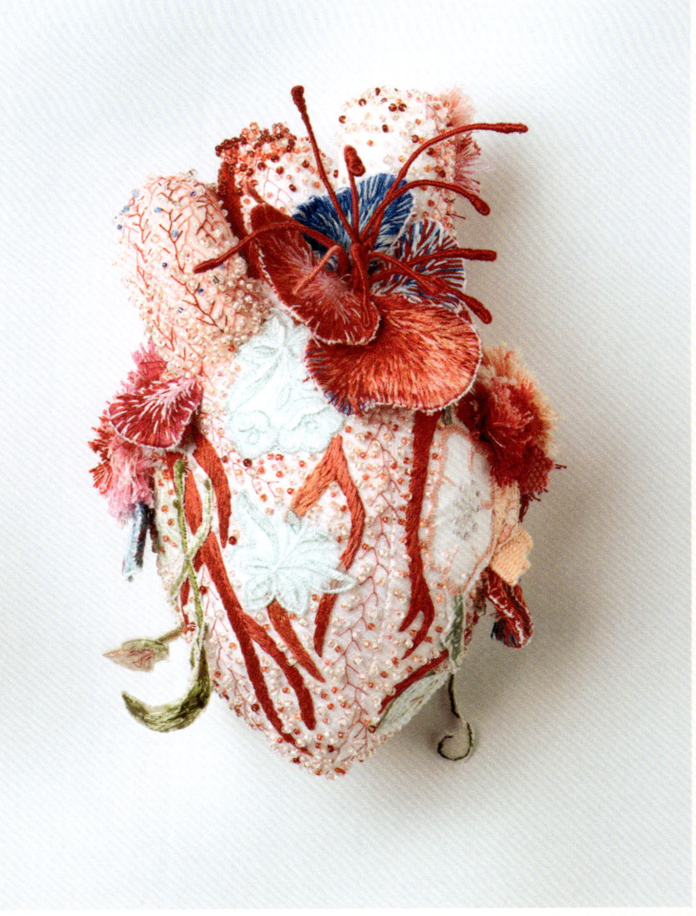

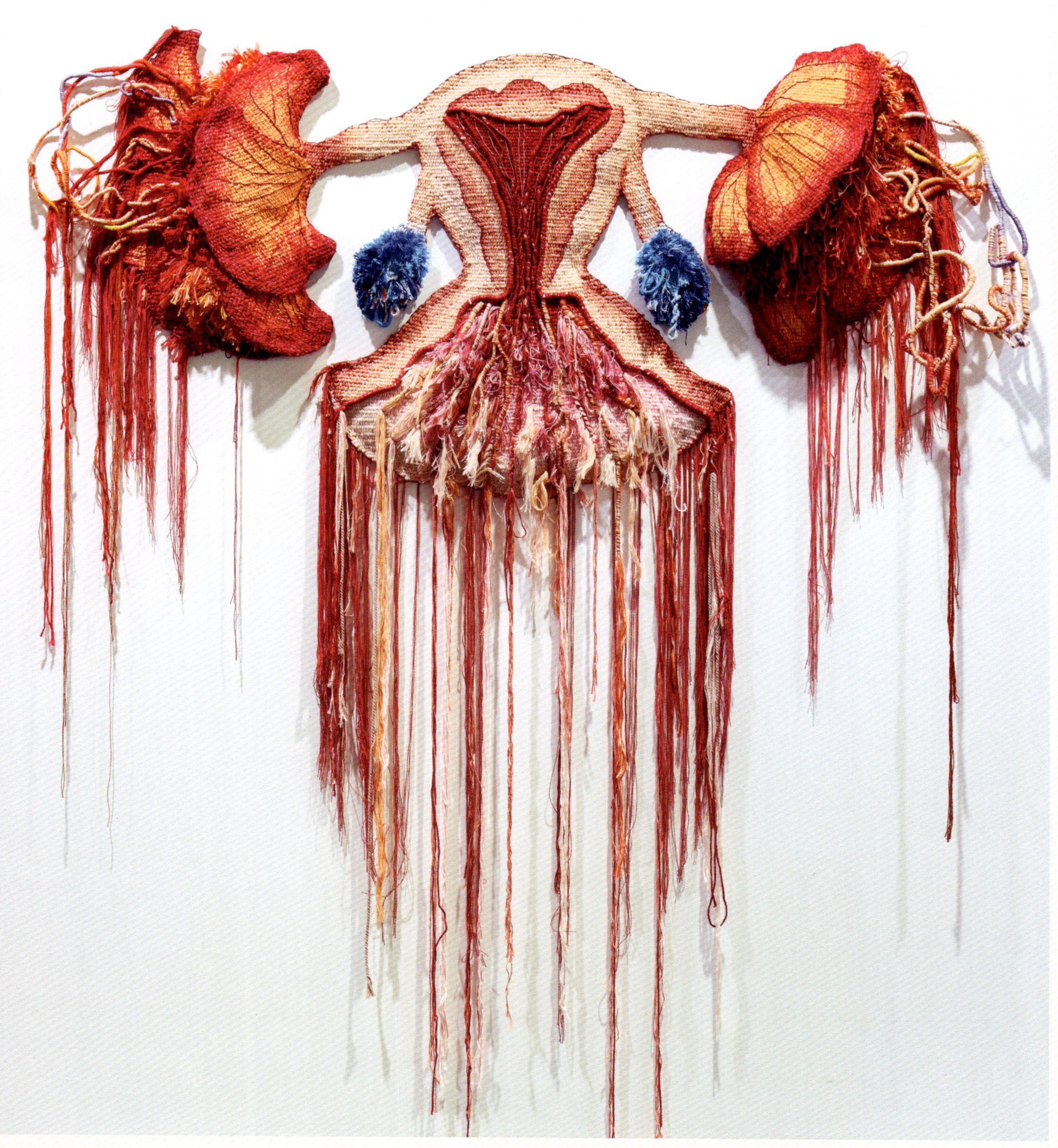

Opposite Clockwise from top: Studio shot, 2024; *Hearts of Absent Women #5*, 2022, Embroidery; *Hearts of Absent Women #16*, 2024, Embroidery **This page** *Soft Alchemy (Womb for Everyone)*, 2022, Weaving

Kayla Mattes

LOS ANGELES

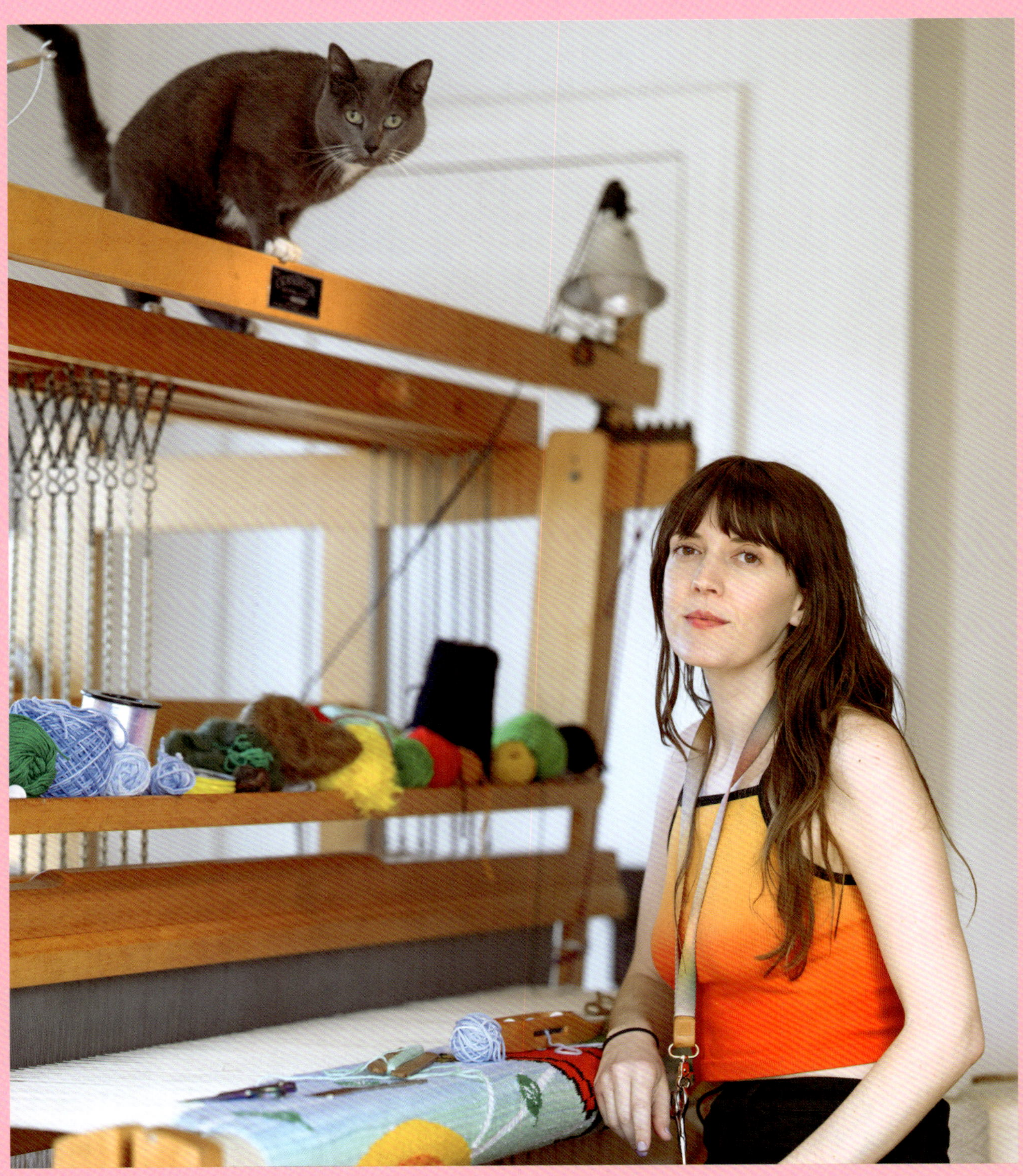

Kayla Mattes is a tapestry weaver who approaches her technique of choice as "drawing on the loom". She started weaving in 2008, but she cites a childhood spent creating on a cardboard loom. Since then, Mattes has become recognised for her distinctive tapestries that blend digital culture with an "ancient tactile art form" to create a "conversation between old and new, digitality and materiality". While her works encompass a range of sociopolitical and cultural themes, they share a visual language based on screen and internet culture.

At the heart of Mattes' tapestries are an interest in semiotics, her works exploring how we "communicate and express ourselves" through symbols in the digital age. Visually, her tapestries create a dialogue with viewers based on a shared understanding of motifs and digital references, which include "dating apps, astrology apps, meditation apps, social media formats", and "the virality of internet cats, texting, and emojis".

Many of Mattes' tapestries are presented like a collage, combining sourced images from the "screen and physical world" to capture "our collective screen anxiety fuelled by doomscrolling". *Premonitions of Smudge Lord* (2019), for instance, incorporates operating system symbols alongside internet memes and GIFs. This overlay of icons and imagery continues in Mattes' later works such as *FUN FACT* (2023), which centre a critical response to late-stage capitalism through the inclusion of incisive text.

Alongside digital imagery, fire appears across Mattes' tapestries. The motif connects her work to place – California, where she lives "alongside climate-fuelled wildfires" – while also serving as political critique. Fire appeared in Mattes' work in 2017, during the first Trump administration: a period that spurred a series of politically inspired artworks that is still evolving.

Mattes considers internet memes as "contemporary political cartoons – existing in many iterations". On screen, they are often quick to rise to virality and always shifting, but the weaving process is slow, allowing Mattes to "archive these fast and fleeting images". Recording them also injects humour into her art, which Mattes recognises as a "strategy that allows us to confront dark realities in a way that's relatable", from global warming to COVID-19. As memes reflect "cultural trends, and the state of the world", they can function as powerful tools of critique, even if they are images of an angry chihuahua.

...Baby One More Time (2024–25) reflects this duality. The weaving is centred on an image of pop star Britney Spears, which is overlaid with the edited lyrics "my government is killing me": a criticism of government politics and (in)action, framed through a shot from a music video. Mattes' marriage of "high" and "low" culture challenges the "exclusivity and

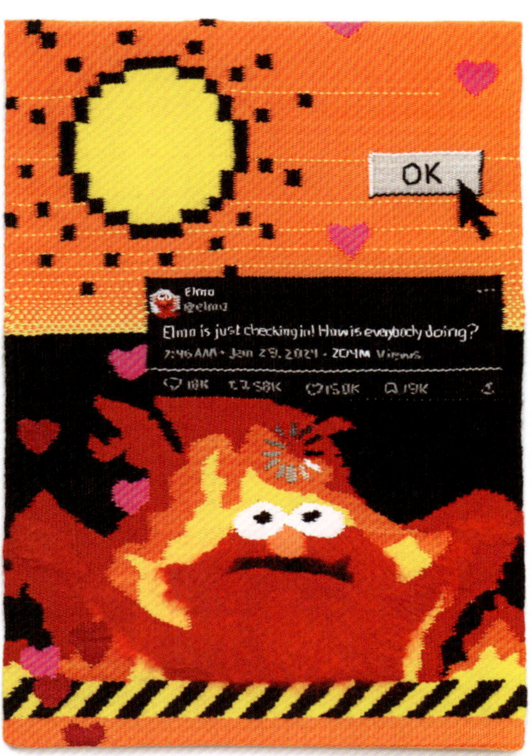

how is everybody doing?, 2024, Weaving

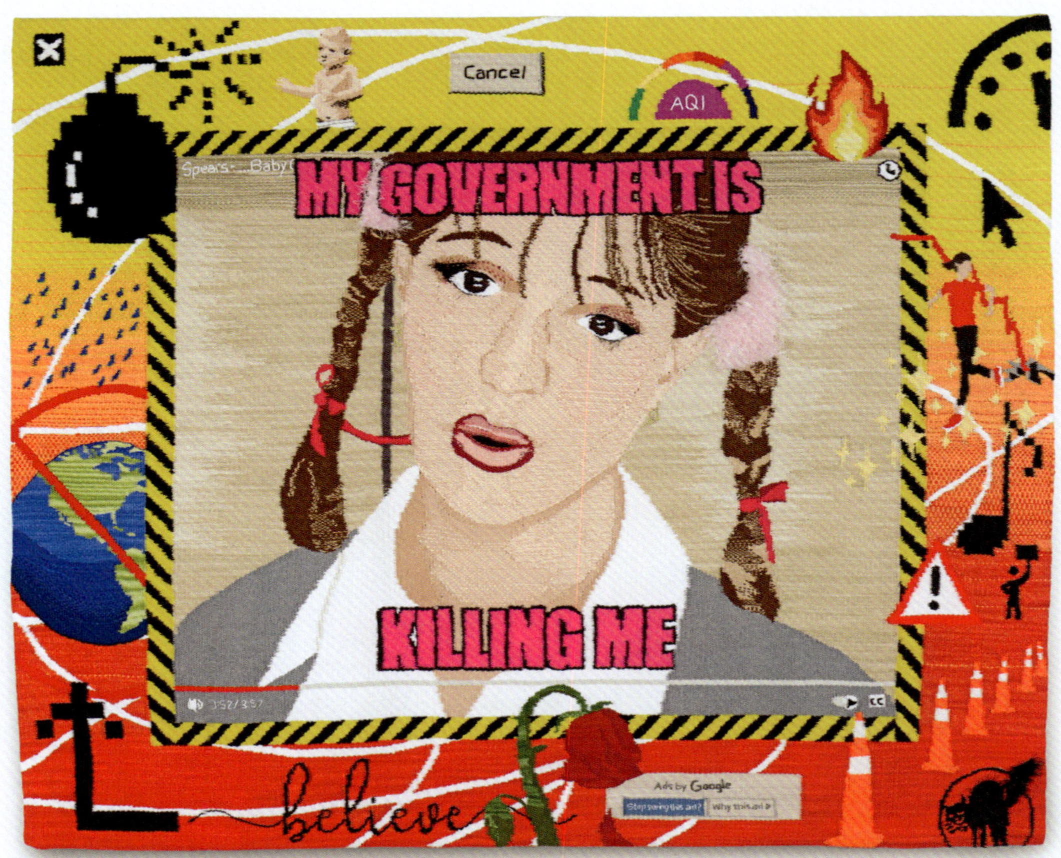

elitism of the art world" while recognising how pop culture creates powerful connections, allowing people to laugh together "when things are so bad that['s] the only thing you can do".

Both conceptually and thematically, Mattes' art reveals a deep connection between "weaving and computing", which she cites as her work's "backbone": "The way that looms operate is essentially an algorithm. It's a grid-based system". On the loom, Mattes most often works with wool and cotton yarns while weaving, often hand-dying them herself, embroidering text once the tapestries are woven. Her works build on a lineage of political weavers; she cites formative influences, such as Hannah Ryggen (1894–1970), but she is also "influenced by the creativity of people on the internet, such as meme-makers". Mattes combines these influences to carry on the possibilities of weaving as a storytelling tool, connecting her works to the "narrative history of tapestry weaving" to document our ever changing visual and cultural landscapes.

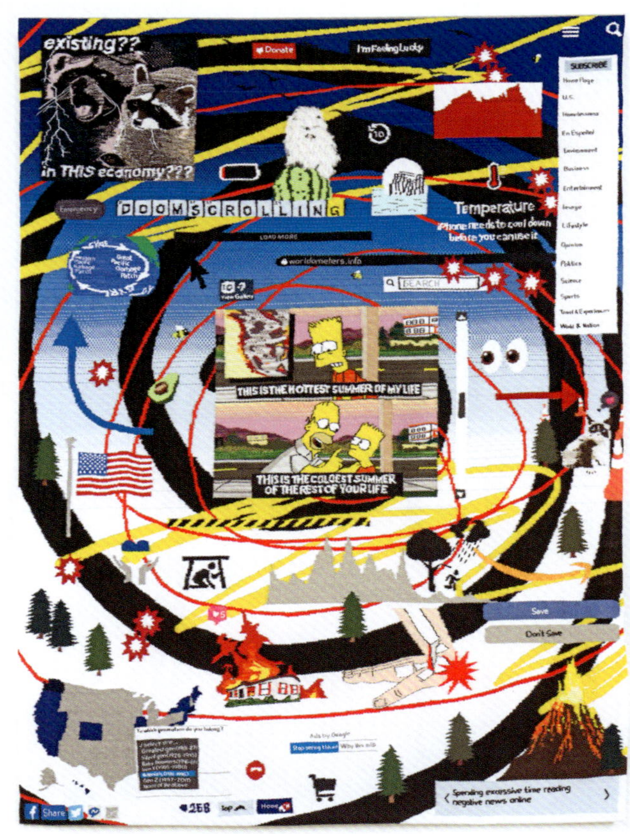

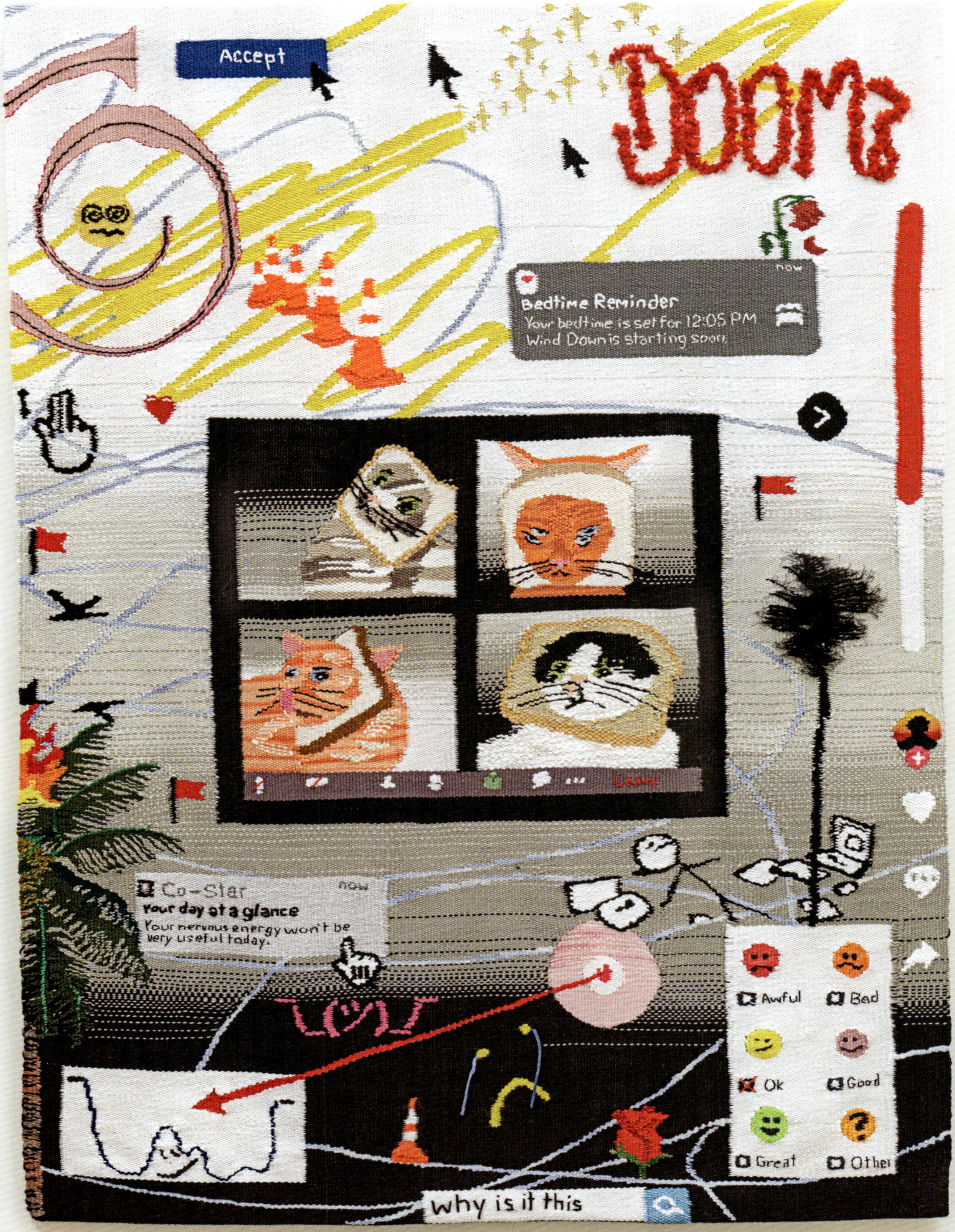
Accept
DOOM?
now
Bedtime Reminder
Your bedtime is set for 12:05 PM
Wind Down is starting soon.
Leave
Co–Star
now
Your day at a glance
Your nervous energy won't be very useful today.
Awful
Bad
Ok
Good
Great
Other
why is it this

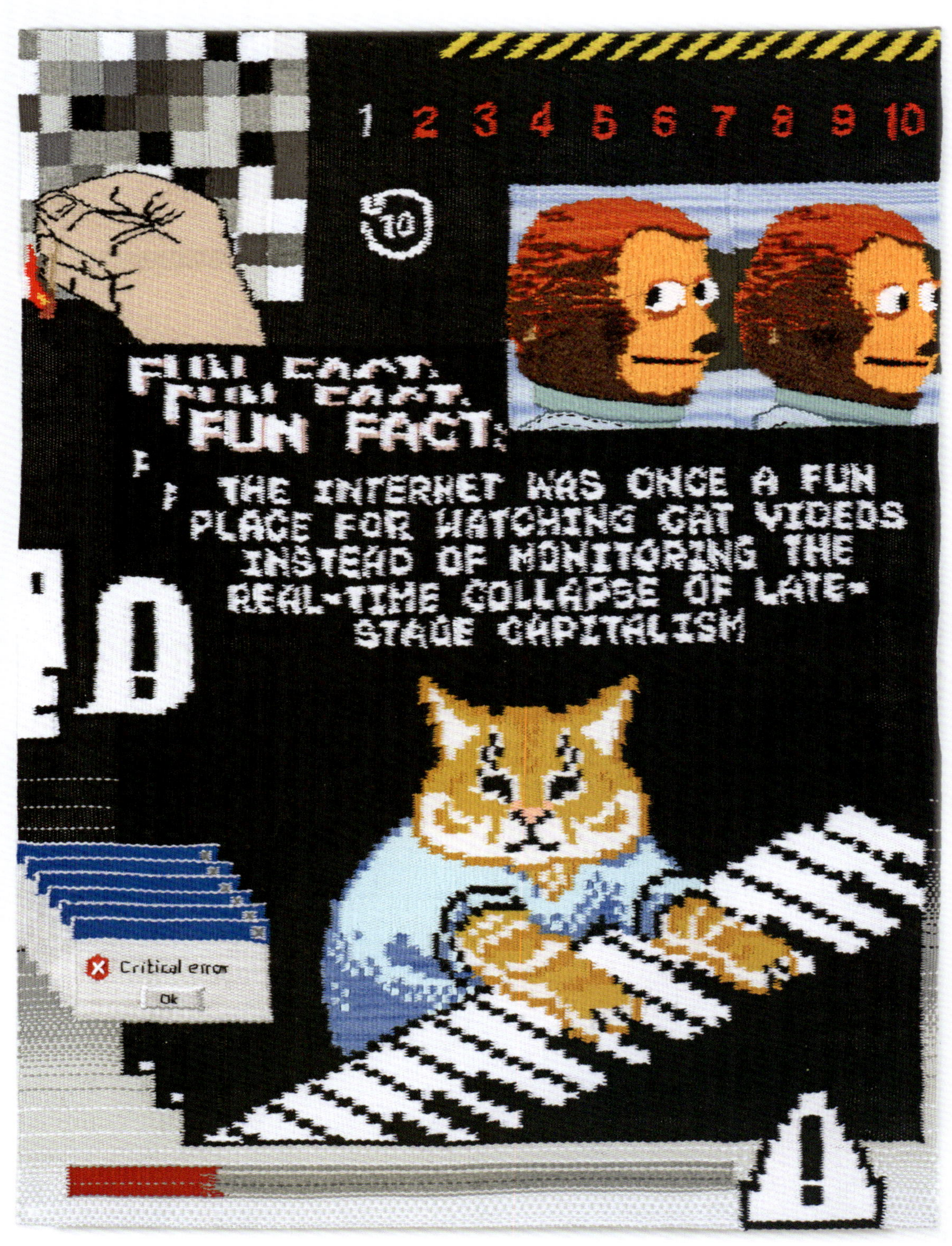

Page 198 Top: ... *Baby One More Time*, 2024–25, Weaving; Bottom: *Existing??*, 2023, Weaving **Page 199** *DOOMSCROLL*, 2022, Weaving **This page** *FUN FACT*, 2023, Weaving **Opposite** *Premonitions of Smudge Lord*, 2019, Weaving

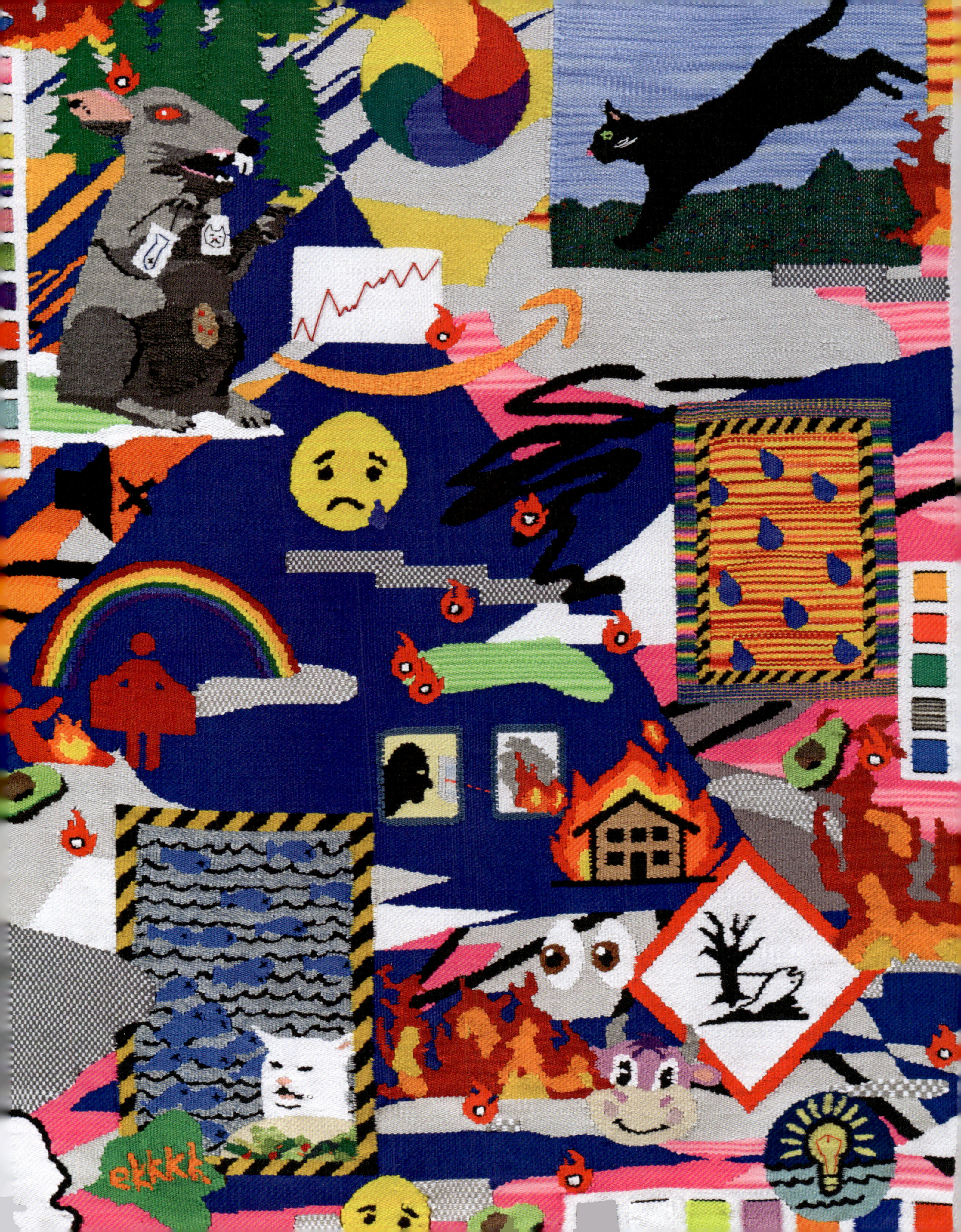
ekkk

Linda Sok លីនដា សុខ

PROVIDENCE

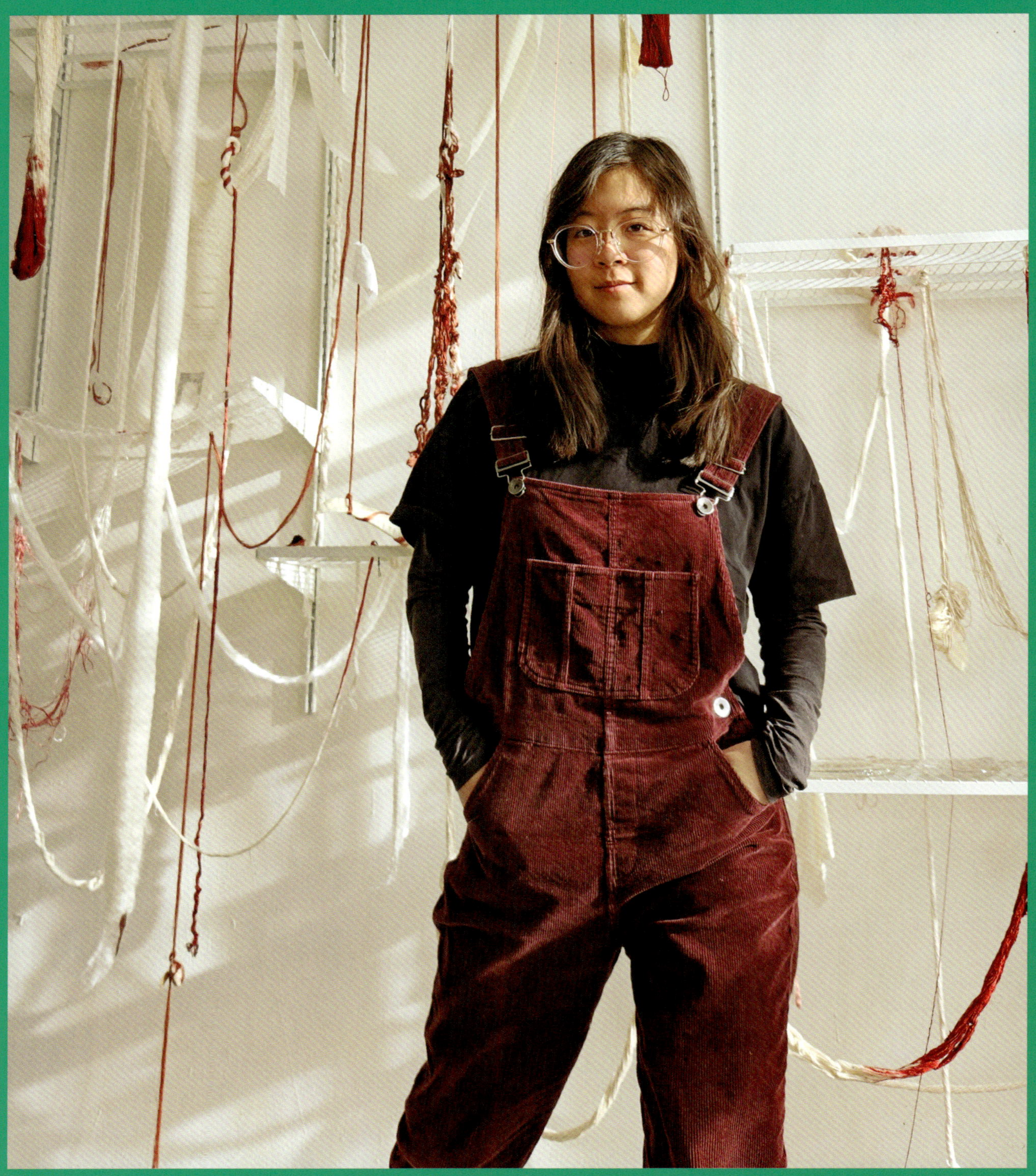

Born in Australia to Cambodian parents, Linda Sok grew up feeling a "sense of distance from my cultural roots". Today, her art embodies a practice centred on "reconstruction, healing, and remembrance", using printmaking and weaving to reconnect with historical and personal stories.

Sok's interest in textiles as a material started in childhood, when she was drawn to the "krama and silk scarves my mother would bring back from Cambodia". Over time, Sok's initial fascination with these scarves as a cultural symbol and source of national pride led her to wonder about "who made them" and the stories behind their imagery. This curiosity led Sok to research the history and techniques of pidan, a polychromatic sacred weaving tradition used for altar cloths and other ceremonial purposes by Khmer people in Cambodia. This history is one marked by loss and erasure as a direct result of the "targeted persecution of weavers during the Cambodian Khmer Rouge Regime" from 1975 to 1979, leading to a generational loss of ancestral weaving knowledge.

This cultural and historical connection to pidan is central to the series of weavings Sok made in collaboration with her family titled *Deities in Temples* (2023–25). The inspiration for this body of work is a suite of lost weavings that exist today only in the form of a single descriptive museum registration card in the National Museum of Cambodia's collection, written by French archivists as part of colonial museum projects. Sok invited her family to draw, sketch and paint visual interpretations based on these archival descriptions, blending "both the imagination and memory". The pieces by her father, mother, aunts, uncle and sisters were then silkscreened by Sok onto threads, which were used to make weavings on a loom.

This process of printing onto threads is an homage to the ikat weaving traditions of Cambodia. Ikat, called *hol* in Khmer, is a resist dyeing process in which sections of thread are bound with twine or rubber bands prior to dyeing and weaving. This allows for colour patterns to be created. While hol often "involves a whole family or community of people", Sok employs silkscreen printing as a similar process that "allows for certain parts of the imagery to be occluded in the way that ikat creates a resist". For Sok, this "approximation" is a way for her to reference the past, while also creating "my own language".

Through a process of "construction, deconstruction and reconstruction", *Deities in Temples* blends a family's personal expressions with collective knowledge. The process of translation (from drawing, to screenprint, to weaving) creates abstracted animal, plant and temple motifs that invite multiple interpretations. In a number of works from this series, Sok further highlights the lost weavings through particular techniques, including deliberate disruptions in the weaving process and highlighting signs of fabric deterioration. Through these choices, Sok's weavings reveal the ways that the connection

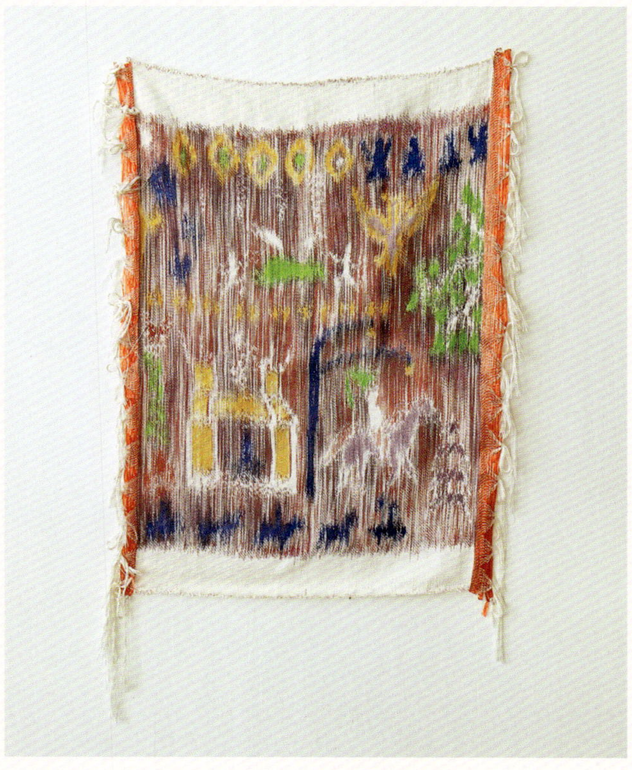

Deities in Temples X, 2024, Silk screening and weaving

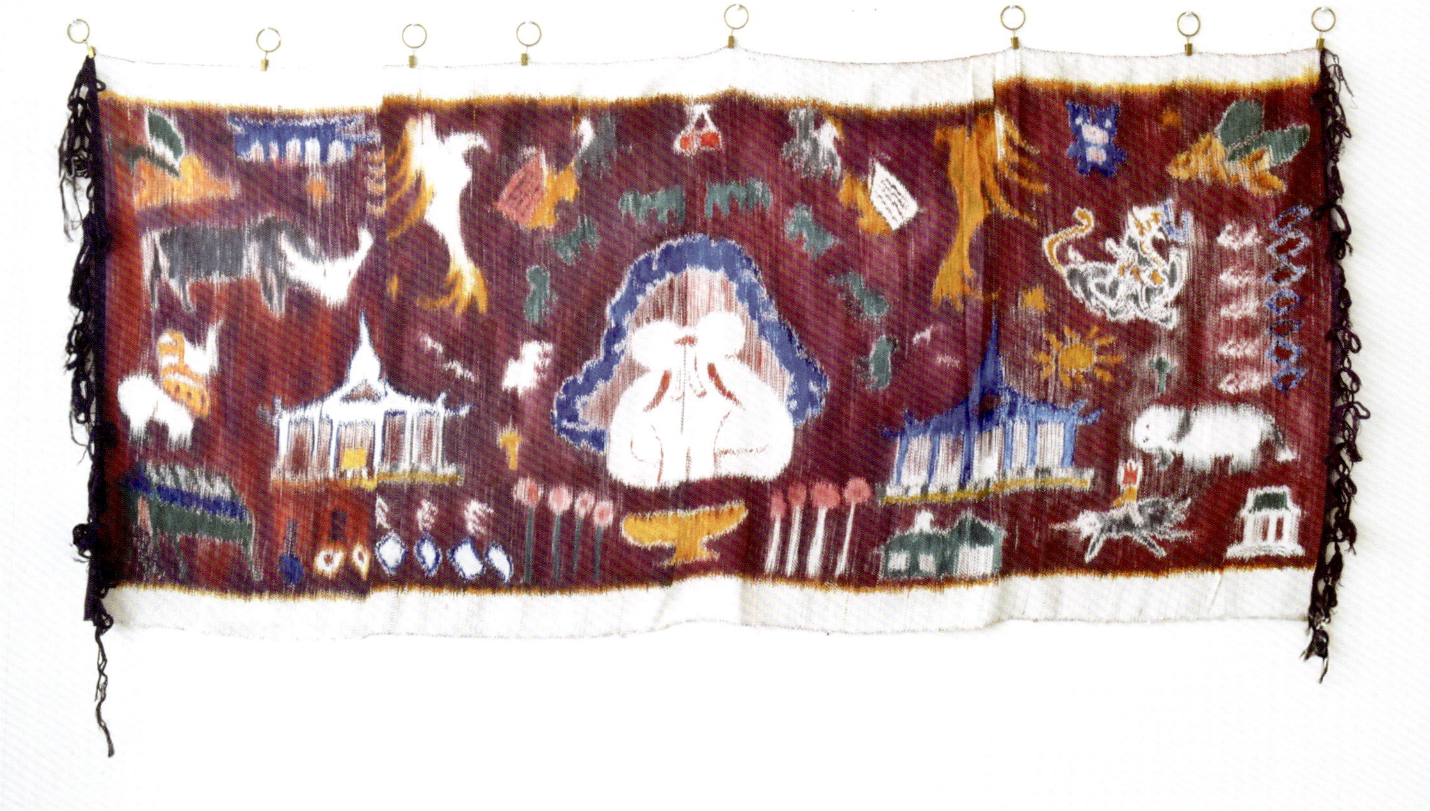

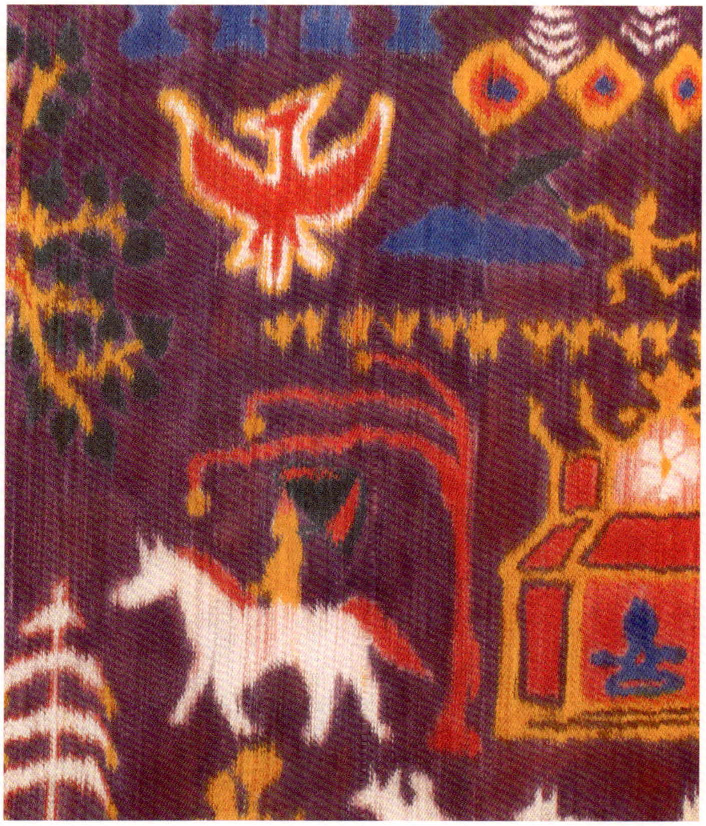

between the present and the past is not always linear or straightforward. *Deities in Temples* can also be viewed through a decolonial lens as a work that engages with inherited colonial knowledge, but as told through the lens of living culture.

Other recent artworks by Sok also use similar deconstructed and reconstructed weaving processes. *We are going to temple tomorrow, who wanna come? (Pidan)* (2022), with its focus on imagery of her family, approaches textiles as a "vessel for both personal and ancestral memory". This is because these materials "not only provide a direct connection to history but also to the body, becoming tangle carriers of memory that resonate across time". She identifies that in the English language, "the word weaving and its associated acts serve as a metaphor for rebuilding, reconstructing, and interweaving stories". For Sok, her practice gives her a means through which to connect not only with the stories and material culture of her heritage, but also with her family. ■

This page Top: *White elephants, gajasimhas and buildings*, 2025, Silk screening and weaving; Bottom: *Deities in Temples III* (detail), 2023, Silk screening and weaving **Opposite** Clockwise from top left: *We are going to temple tomorrow, who wanna come? (Pidan)* (detail), 2022, Silk screening and weaving; *Deities in Temples II* (detail), 2023, Silk screening and weaving; *We are going to temple…*

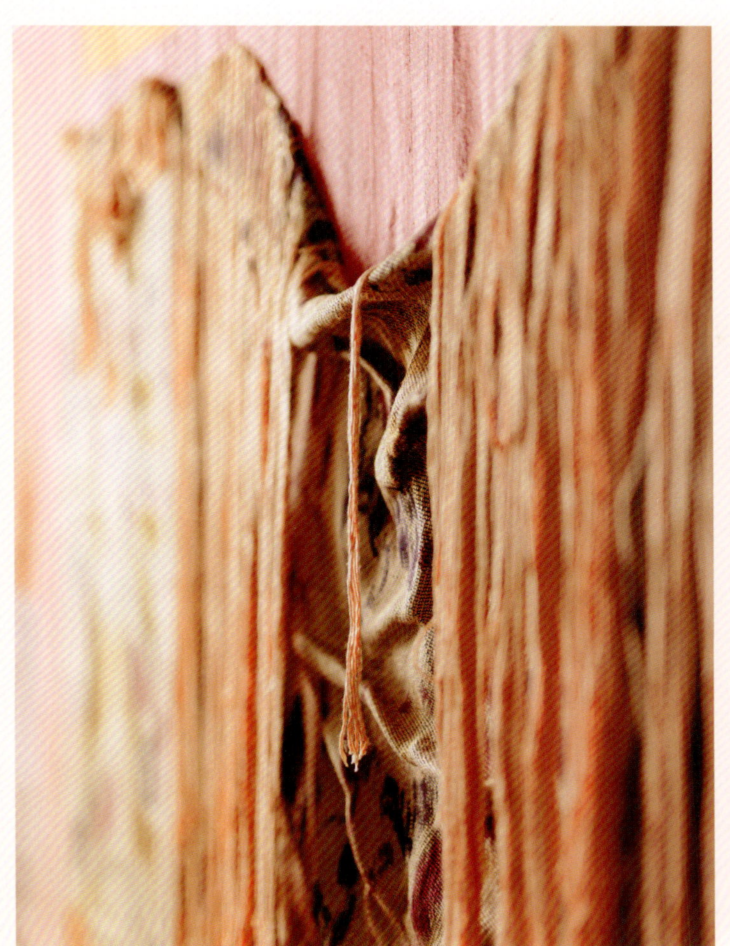

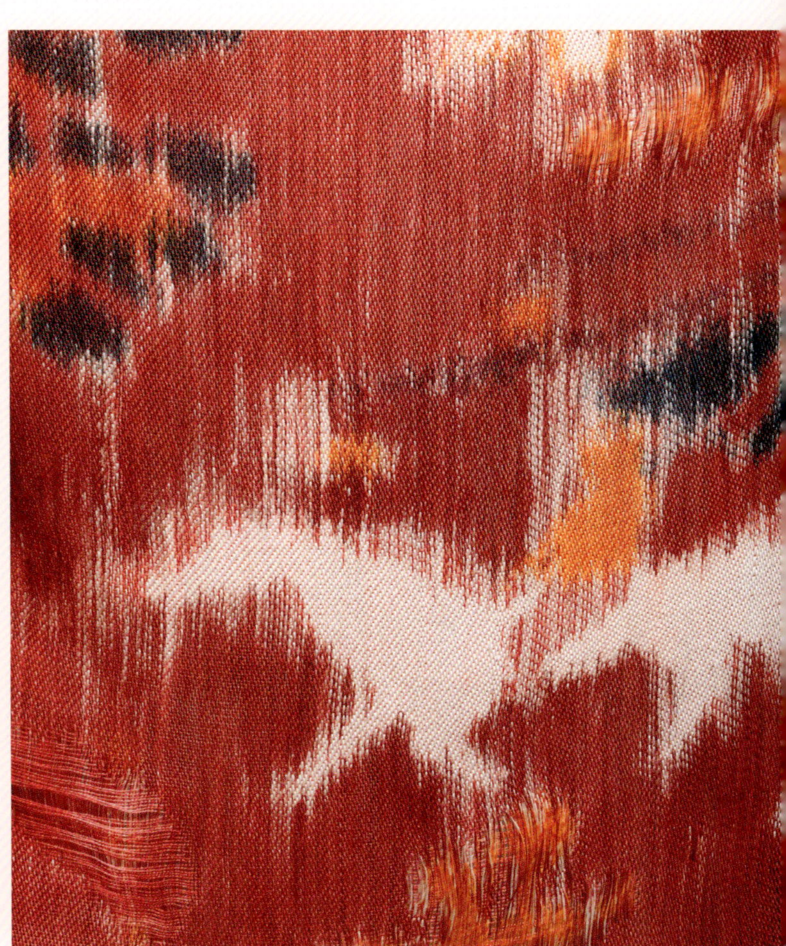

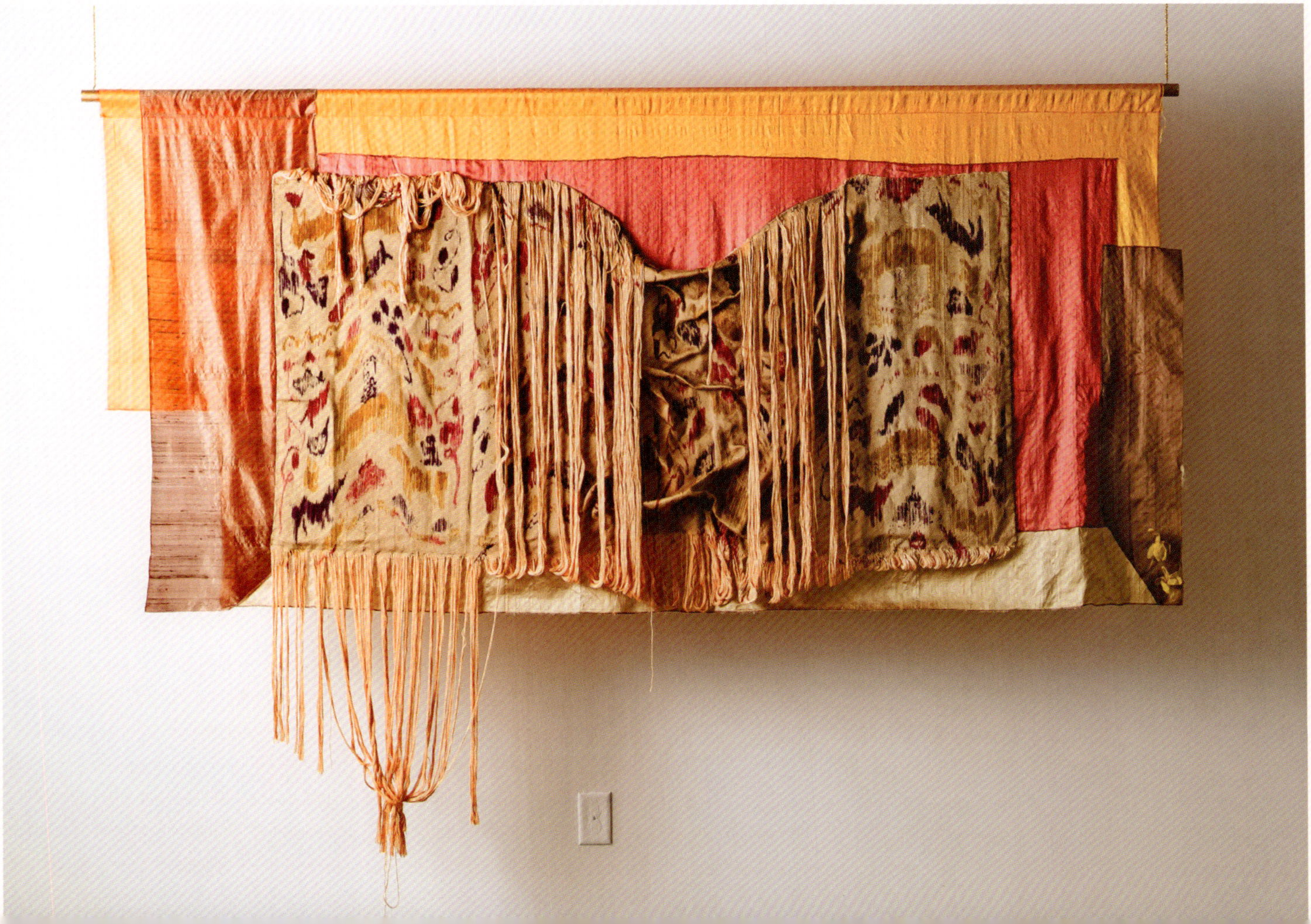

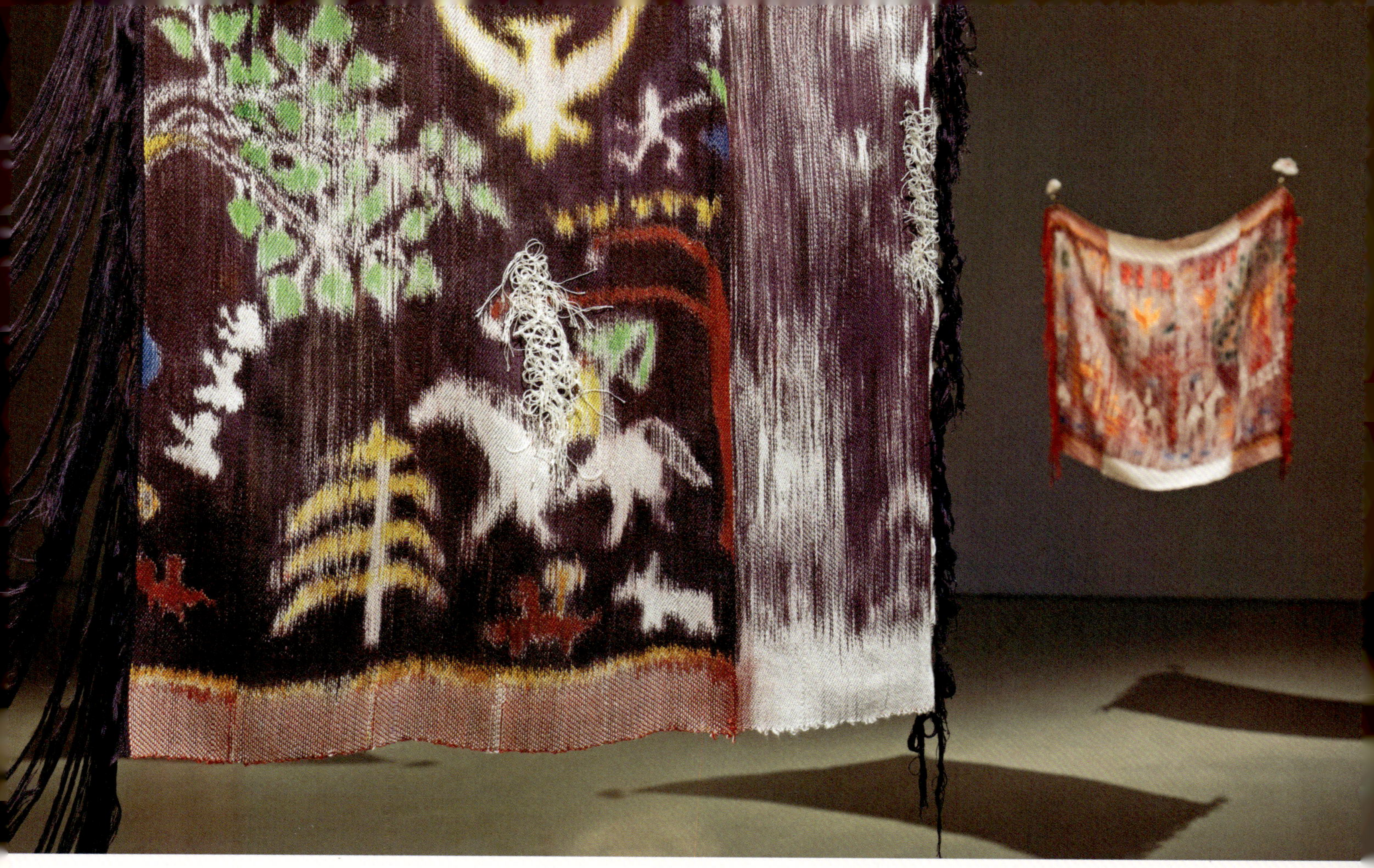

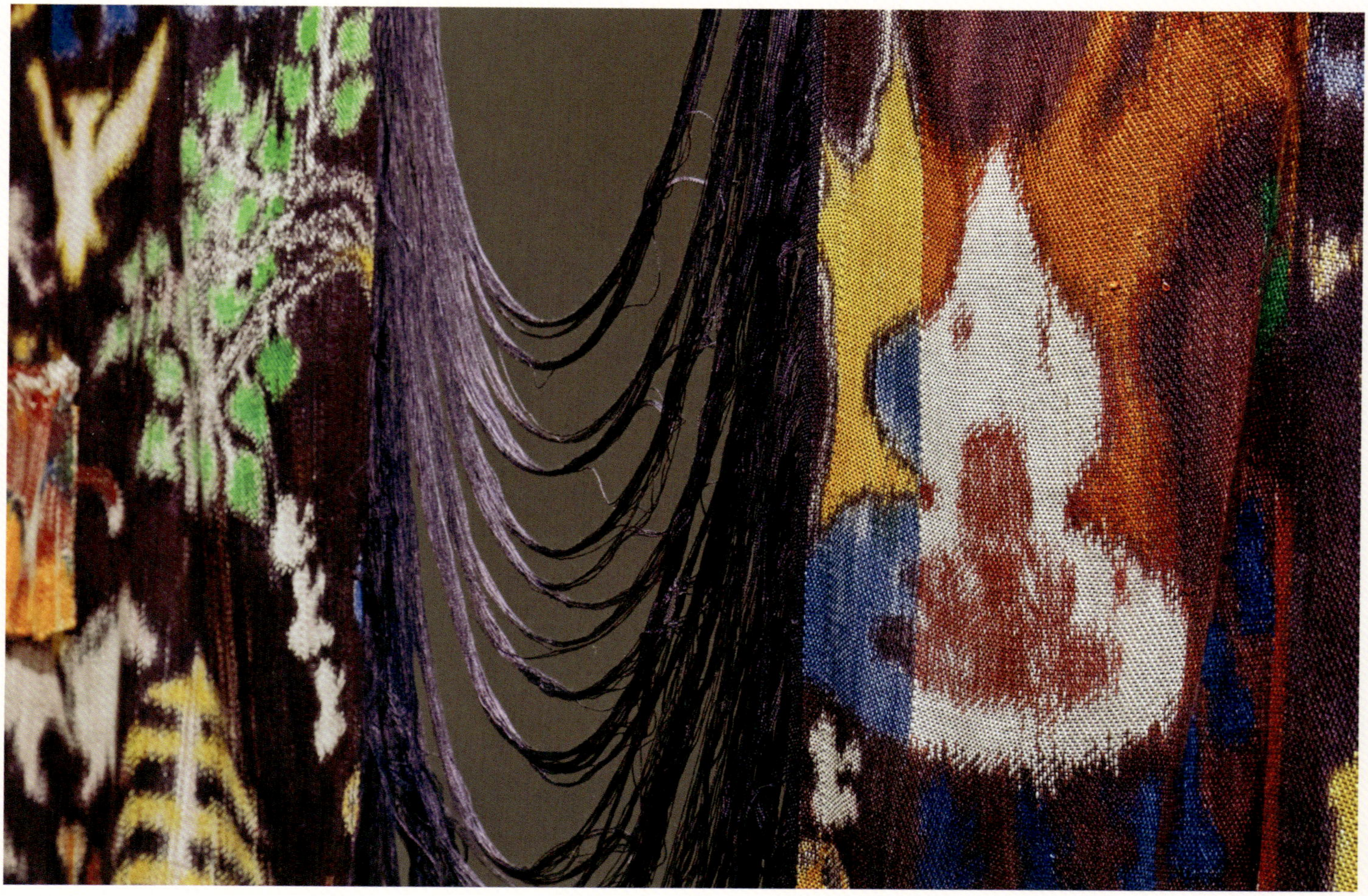

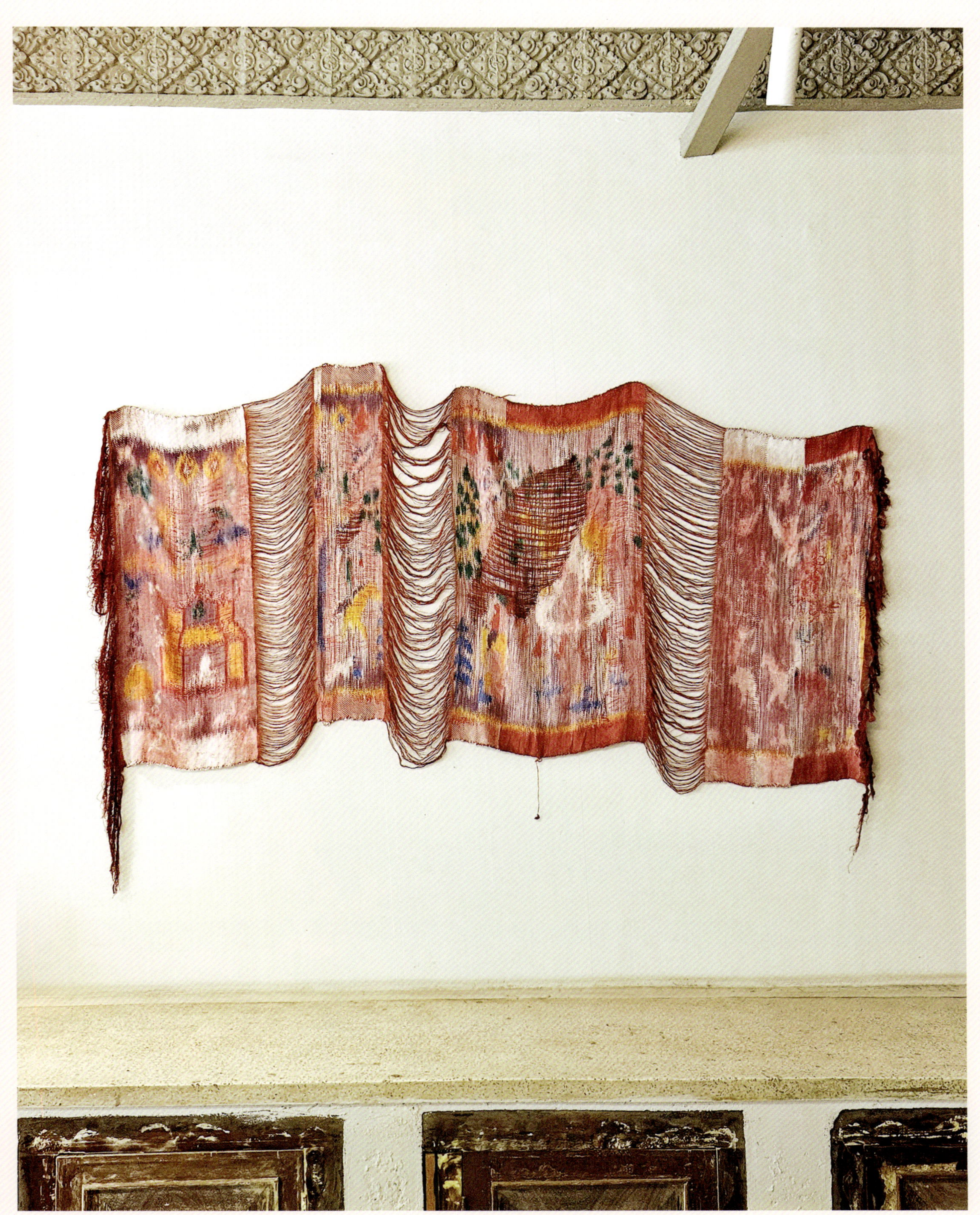

Opposite *Deities in Temples XIV*, 2025, Silk screening and weaving
This page *Deities in Temples IX*, 2024, Silk screening and weaving

Lin Qiqing 林绮晴

NEW YORK CITY

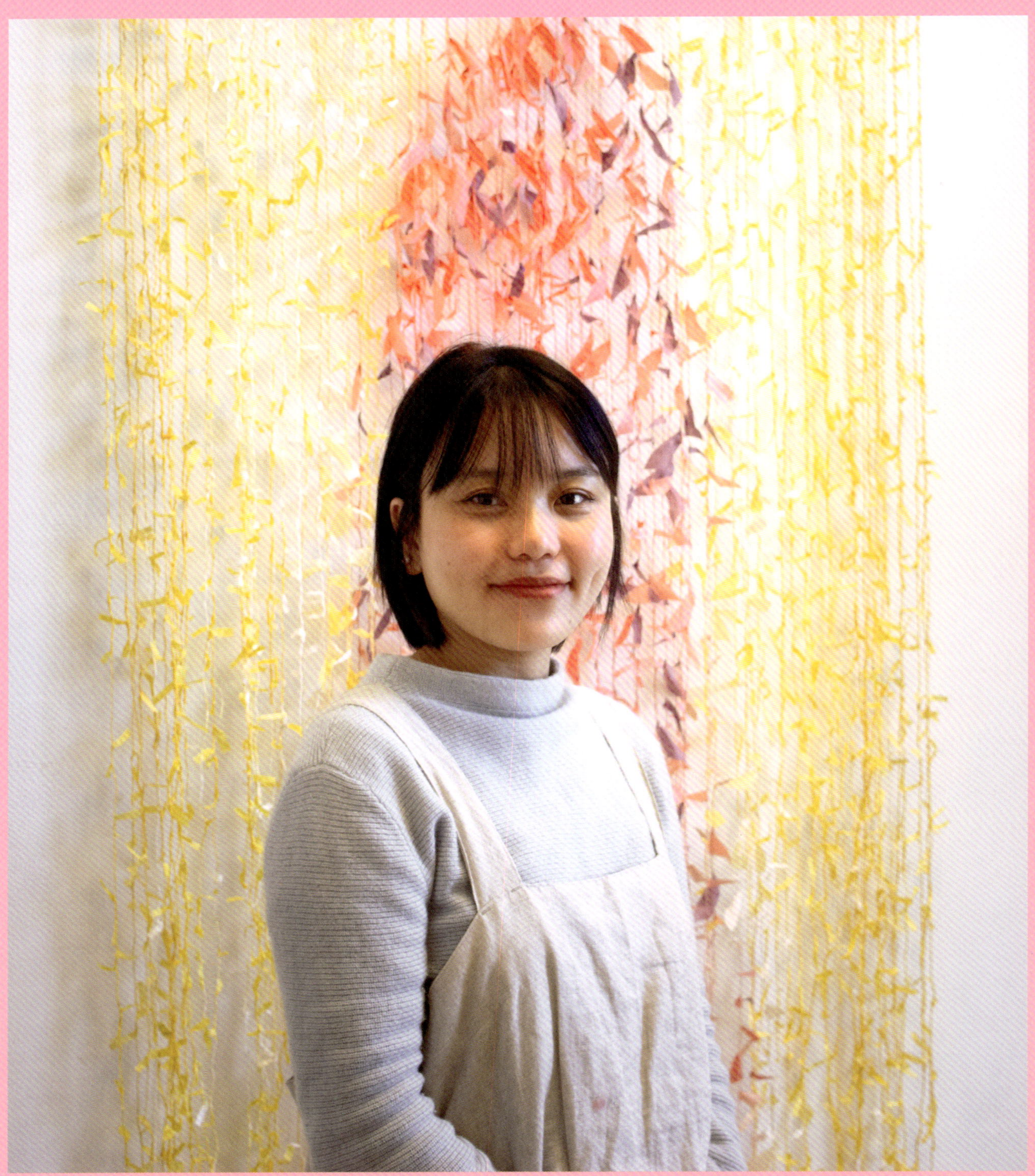

As a former award-winning journalist from China, Lin Qiqing's pathway to becoming a contemporary artist occurred later in her professional life. Lin had always enjoyed drawing and making things as a child, but she grew up in an environment where "art wasn't present much", and she "didn't know anyone who was an artist or had a creative job". It was during a two-month journalism assignment in New York City that Lin decided to sign up for a weaving class as something to do during her free weekends. She was immediately "captivated by the floor looms", and upon her return to China, decided to take any "textile workshop I could find". Her time at these classes prompted Lin to pursue textile art seriously.

Transiting from using text as a journalist, to textiles as an artist, Lin sees weaving as a "new language for telling stories". In her former career, Lin wrote about other people, and this interest in human relations is maintained in Lin's narrative weavings, which reveal "hidden emotions, struggles, and how people survive and endure life" through a figurative style. Among the themes she explores as an artist, expressions of gender, language and immigration are often present – drawn from both the artist's own experiences and her observations of others.

At the centre of many of Lin's weavings are depictions of abstracted human figures. Whether solitary, or placed in relation to others, Lin's distinct figurative style eschews identifying features or details, allowing each form to express a range of possible interpretations. In *Adrift* (2024), Lin weaves a bird's-eye perspective of two figures. Set against a white and purple background, the forms are depicted in movement, as if swimming towards (or away) from each other. This sense of "adriftness" is also captured in the diptych *The Walls* (2024), which captures two figures in motion, against a tiled background. While *Adrift* only depicts part of each body through extended limbs, *The Walls* presents two figures fully contained within the grid of the tapestry. As to whether the "walls" are a physical or emotional barrier for the depicted subjects, it is open to interpretation.

One of the distinctive features of Lin's works is her choice to use paper as a weaving material, which brings a quality of depth and structure to the surface of the works. For Lin, the use of handmade paper, which is repeatedly crumpled and smoothed out through the natural dyeing process, creates "fine wrinkles" that are "reminiscent of human skin" and its imperfect surface. Paper is also a medium that holds the potential for cultural meaning and narrative, as it can be sourced from a range of places and contexts. In Lin's works, her thread is made from calligraphy and book pages, and hints of these original texts peek through the woven fabric.

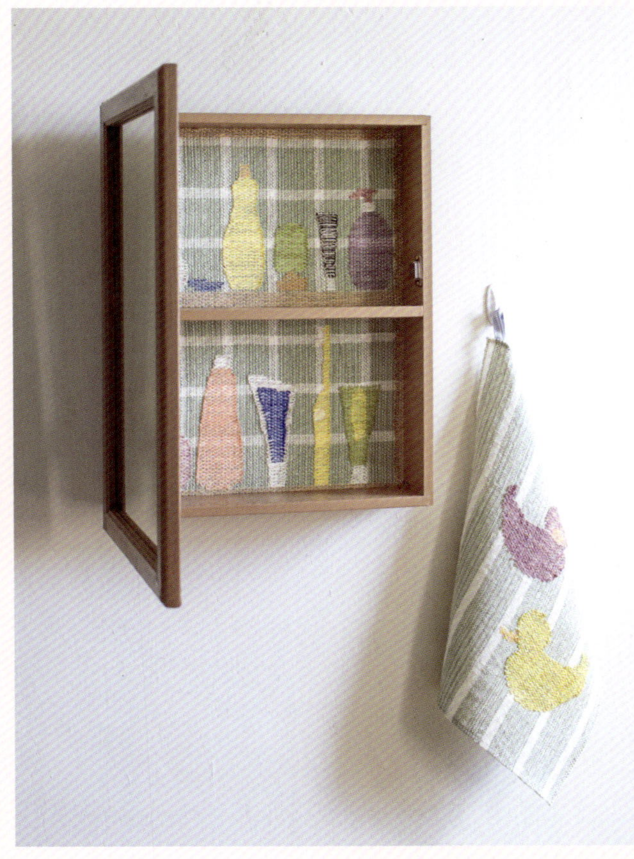

Bathroom Cabinet and Towel, 2025, Weaving

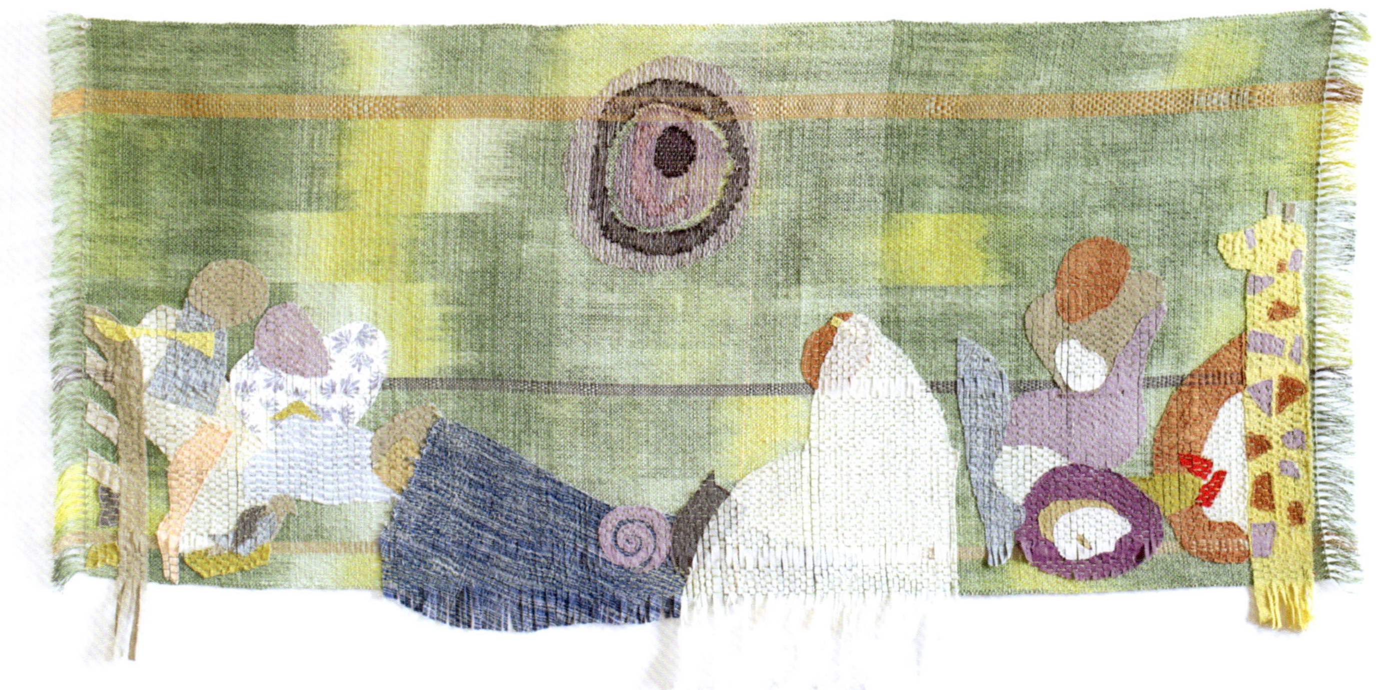

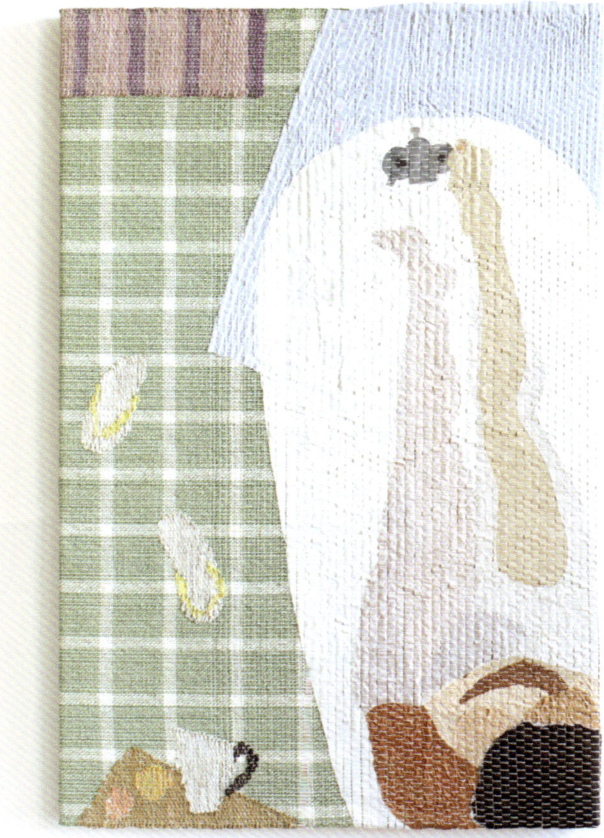

Lin is very deliberate about the range of techniques and materials applied to her artworks. She weaves on a large Leclerc floor loom, and spins paper yarn using a spinning wheel. To create her colour palettes, Lin uses natural dyes sourced from a range of materials including purple gromwell , marigold and persimmon juice, among others. After hand-dyeing the paper, yarn and fabric, she makes collages, cuts them into narrow strips and weaves them onto a linen warp.

This process, from planning, sketching, dyeing and preparing the loom to finally weaving, can take Lin several weeks to complete. Because of the time required, she approaches each project with deliberation to "choose carefully what truly matters to me to make". Among all these steps, it is the weaving process that Lin enjoys the most: "When everything is ready, shuttle in hand, and the image starts to appear row by row, it is a moment filled with pure joy and excitement."

This page Top: *The City Bathers*, 2025, Weaving and quilting; Bottom: *Bathroom II*, 2025, Weaving, quilting and collage **Opposite** *She Was Always There*, 2023, Weaving

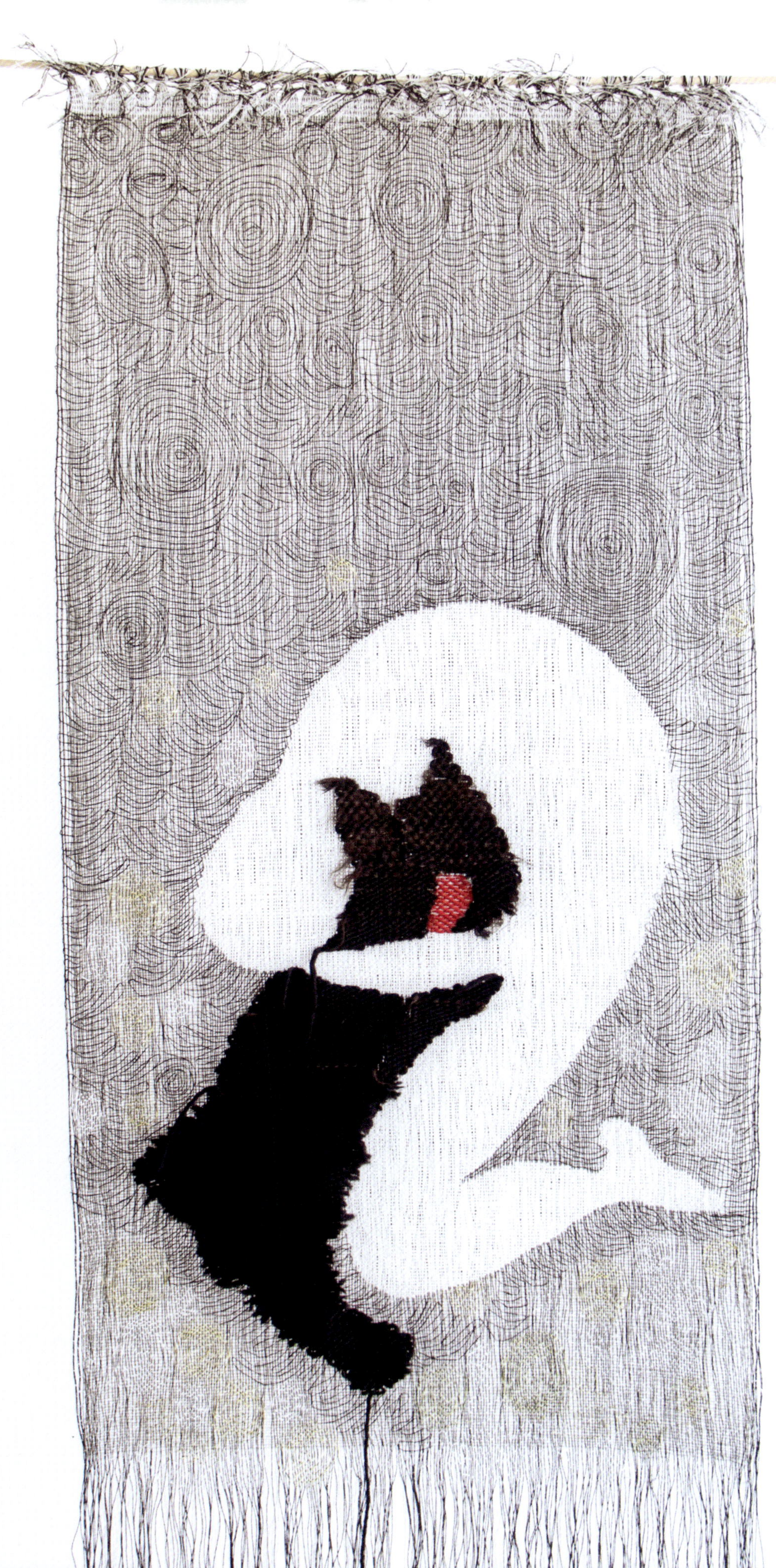

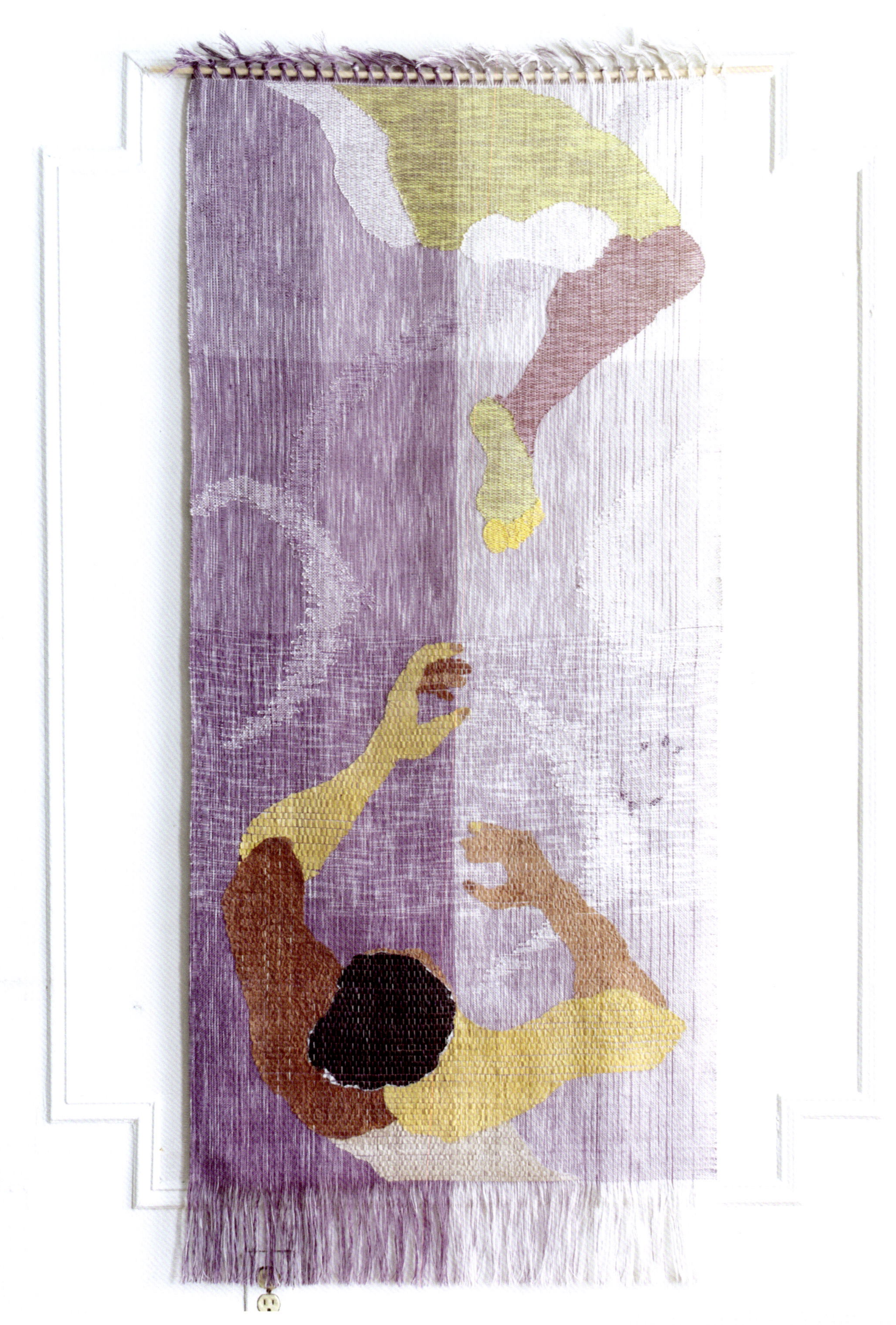

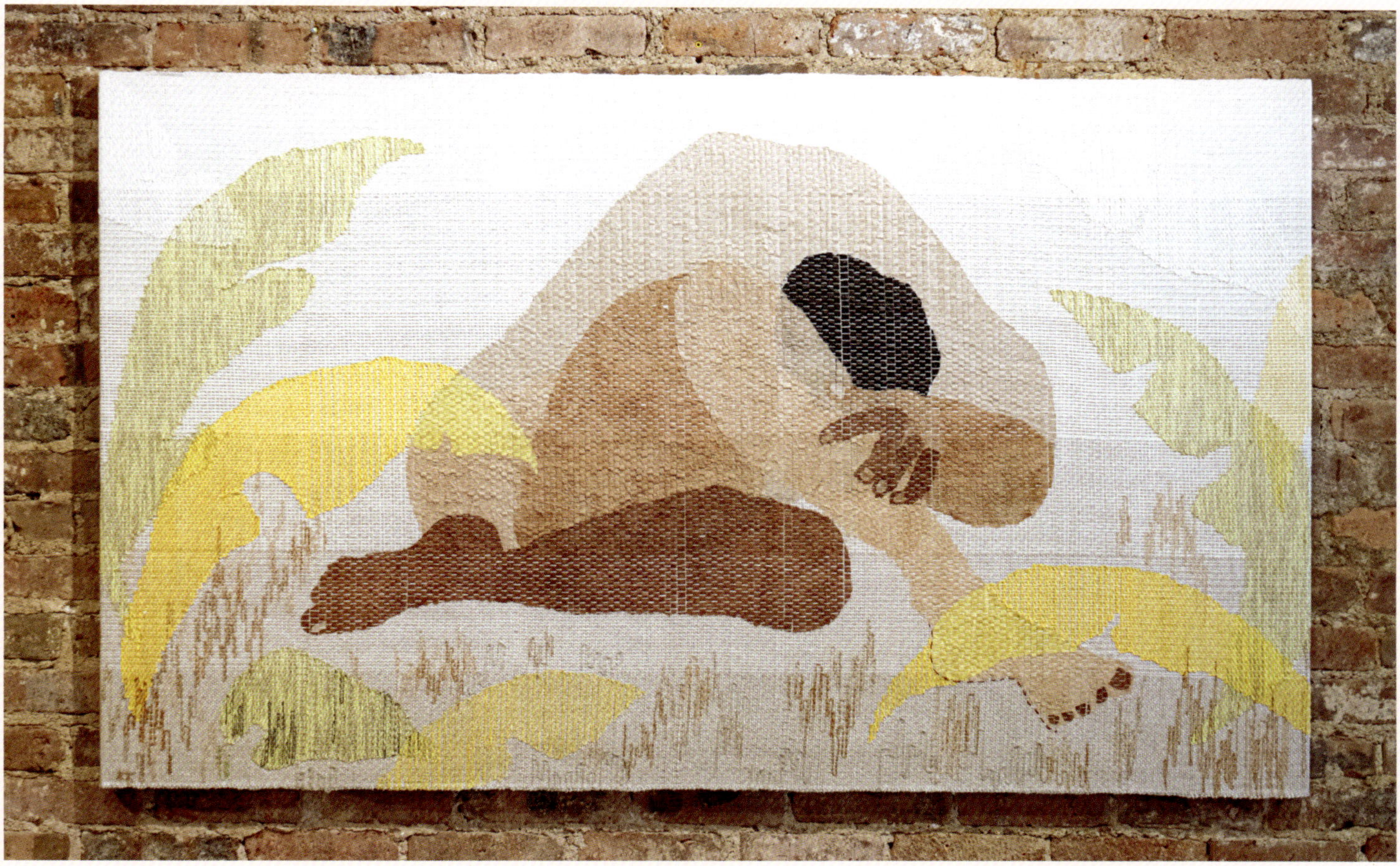

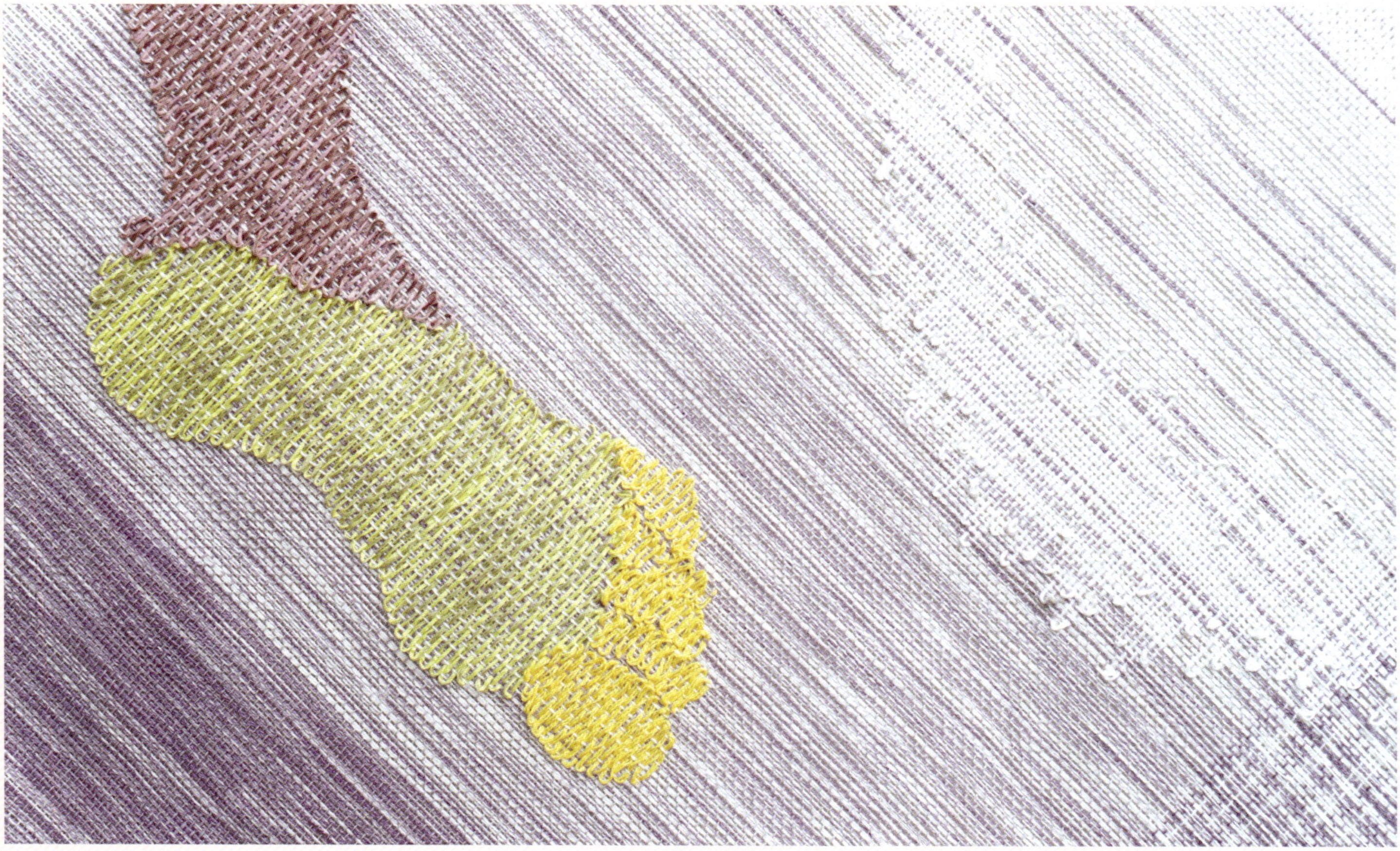

Opposite *Adrift*, 2024, Weaving and collage
This page Top: *To Yuliang*, 2024, Weaving and collage; Bottom: *Adrift* (detail)

Molly Kent

EDINBURGH

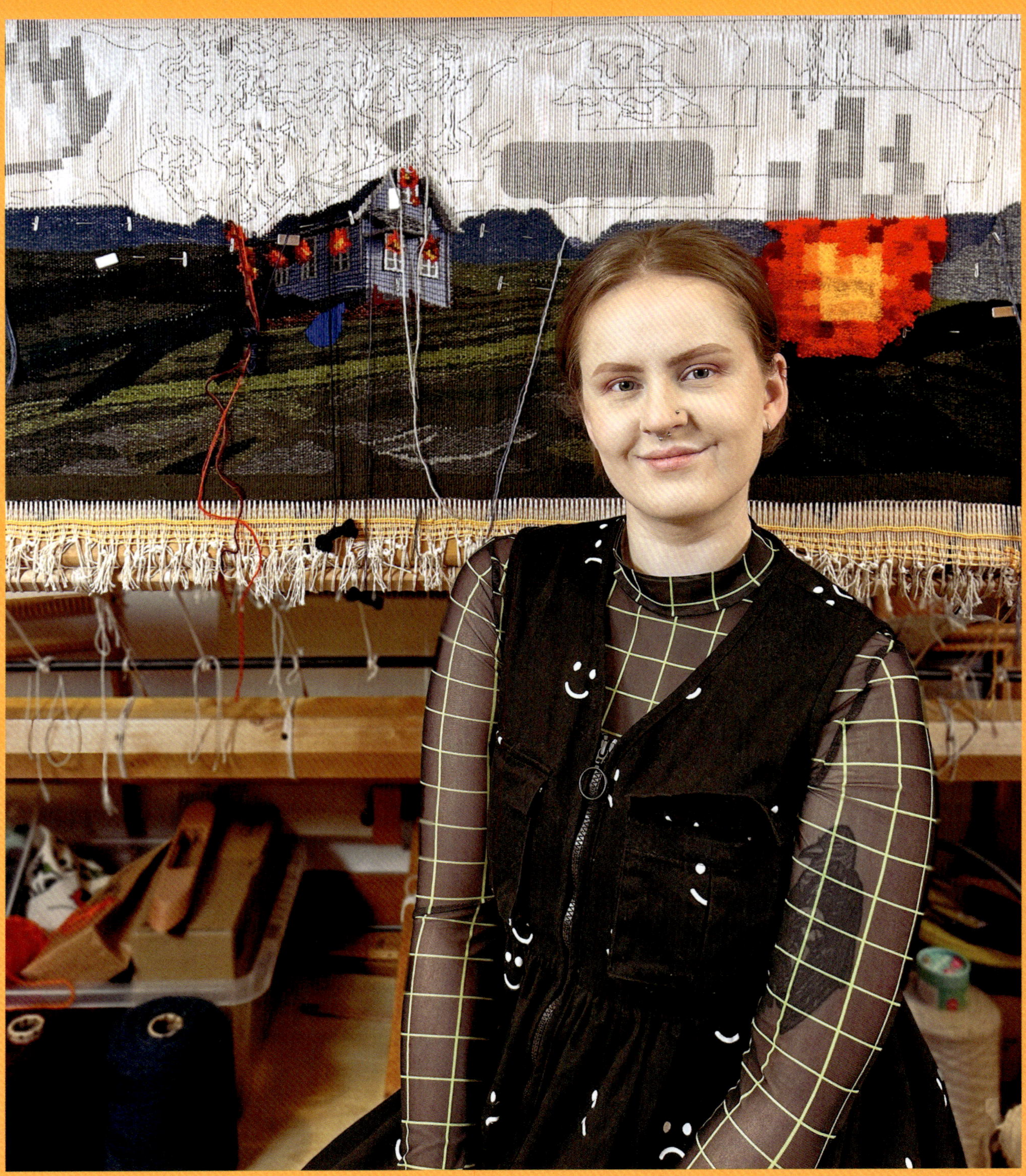

Molly Kent makes tapestries and ceramics that are shaped by mental health and her personal experiences of living with Complex Post-Traumatic Stress Disorder (CPTSD) as a neurodivergent and disabled artist. Working from this perspective, Kent seeks to use artmaking to "focus on the things that I find confusing to grasp", allowing her to "vocalise my gripes with the world in a visual way". Following the collective experiences of pandemic lockdown, Kent's works have increasingly taken on a social commentary angle, addressing broader contemporary issues including the climate crisis, health anxieties and the ways that social media and digital lives continue to shape perceptions of self.

In many of Kent's works, these markers of a "digital life" are expressed through her inclusion of recognisable digital references, including "emojis, computer windows, mouse pointers" and more. These symbols are evident across her ongoing tapestry series *Dream Weaving* (2021–now), which is a visual record of the artist's vivid dreams and nightmares. The title of the series is a pun, referring to both weaving itself and *Dreamweaver*, the Adobe software used to create webpages. In one of the larger tapestries from this series, *Everything That Could Go Wrong, Did Go Wrong (But Maybe It's Not My Fault)* (2024), Kent places computer windows and messaging texts against a ferocious stormy scene that includes a burning house. The overlay of desperate messaging ("TIME IS UP", "You only have yourself to blame", "Sometimes I feel trapped") only heightens the feelings of anxiety and claustrophobia contained in the work, providing little escape for the viewer from these calamities.

The apocalyptic visuals in *Everything That Could Go Wrong* are maintained throughout the *Dream Weaving* series, which is rich in symbolism and includes recurrent themes of falling figures, stormy skies, tornadoes and fires. These images stem from the artist's recurring dreams and nightmares, and reveal how the "study of dream psychology" can provide insight into a person's mental state. These visual representations reflect an ongoing interest by Kent in "eco-anxiety", and the daily "new images of destruction around the world and doomsday-like headlines" that are part of the 24/7 news cycle. In works such as *Ignorance is Bliss* (2023) and *Humanity Not Found* (2023), Kent draws attention to the apathy demonstrated by "so many higher powers" towards the climate crisis, and gives a visual representation to personal feelings of fear and despair in the face of this injustice.

These personal reflections are further explored in Kent's newest series of tapestries, *Dear Diary* (2022–ongoing). This collection is based on notes and pages from the artist's teenage diary, and reveal the emotions that are "often hidden amongst scribbles and desperate notes". Whereas *Dream Weaving* looks outwards, *Dear Diary* is Kent's most personal body of work yet, tracing the artist's journey with her mental health conditions and her life before and after her CPTSD and autism diagnoses. The inner turmoil and confusion caused by these experiences is encapsulated in woven texts ("I don't know who I am", "I feel lost"), which reveal the artist's struggles with making sense of her experiences, which were often disregarded as teenage angst. By translating these intimate reflections into tapestry, a medium often historically associated with narrative storytelling, Kent is healing her younger self.

For Kent, she weaves for her "well-being more than anything" as the act helps keep her "grounded". She describes how the concentration required "to build up an image" means her brain doesn't find external stimuli or input "as overwhelming". Her favourite part of weaving is that the process is "relaxing and calming", and she enjoys the "repetitiveness of the task". Since her diagnoses, Kent has also changed her approach to artmaking, preferring to work intuitively rather than "over-structure my days in the studio". In this way, both her work and her process reveal Kent's shifting relationship with her art. ■

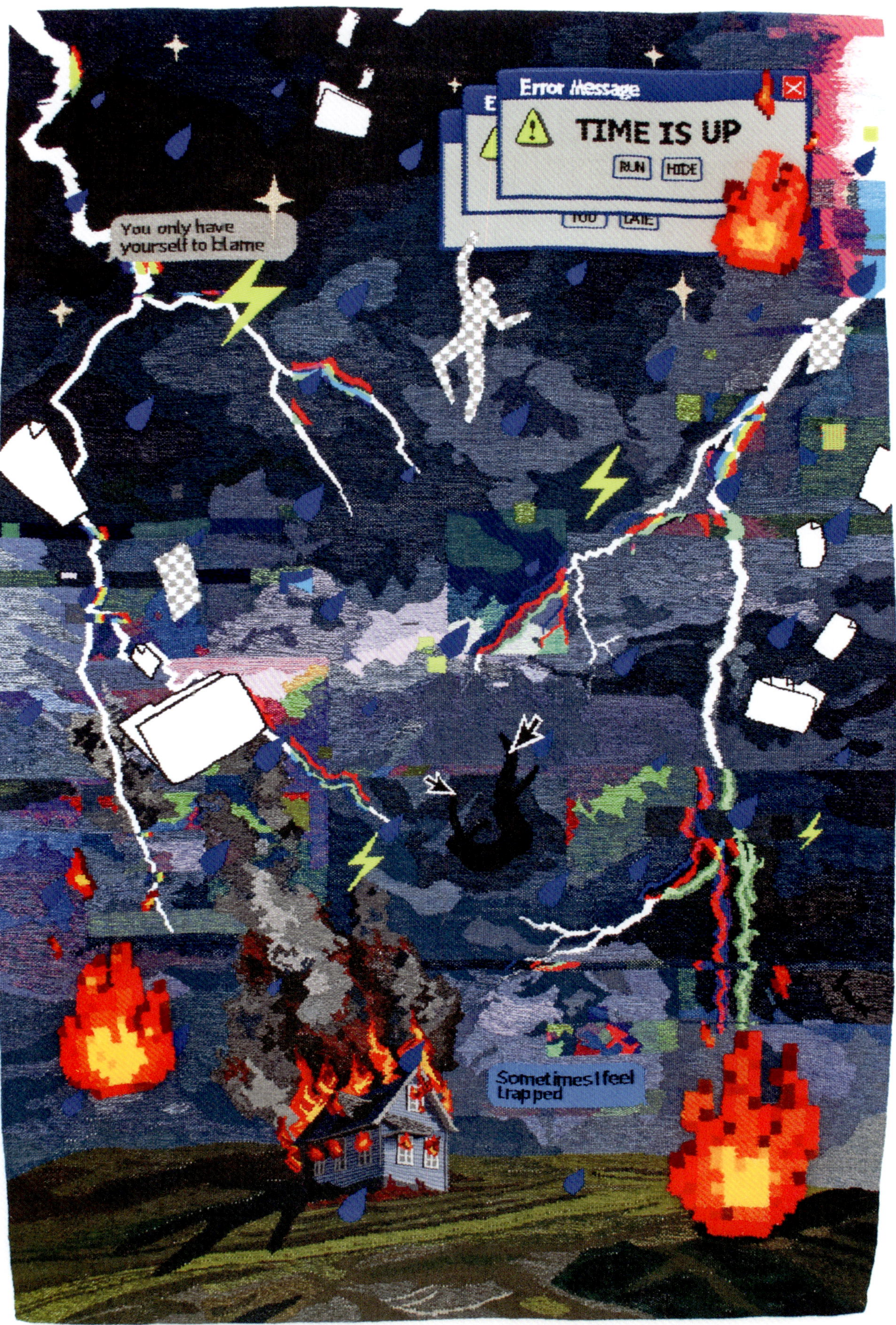

Error Message
TIME IS UP
RUN
HIDE
You only have yourself to blame
Sometimes I feel trapped

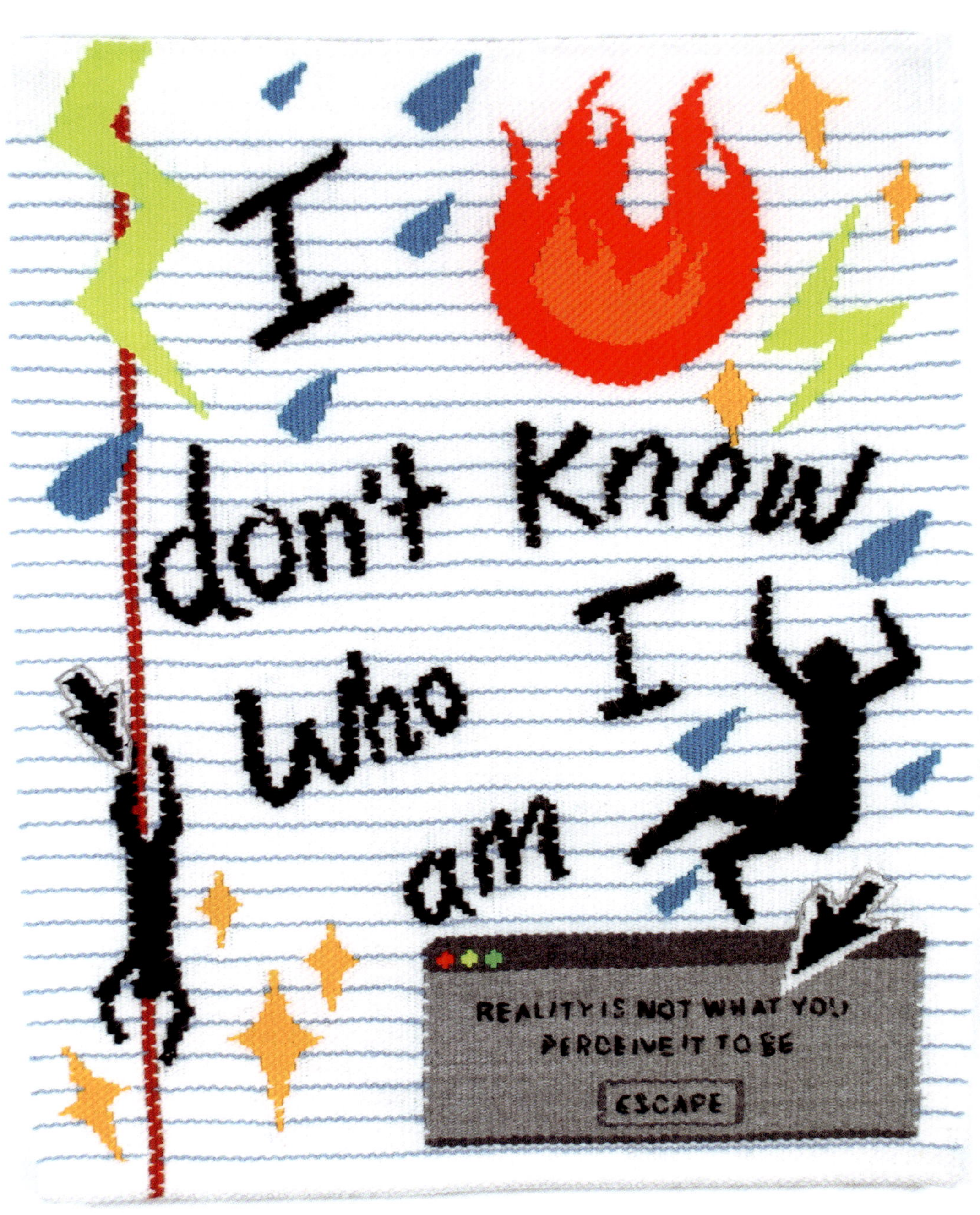

Opposite *Everything That Could Go Wrong, Did Go Wrong (But Maybe It's Not My Fault)*, 2024, Weaving
This page *Notebook Confessions*, 2022, Weaving

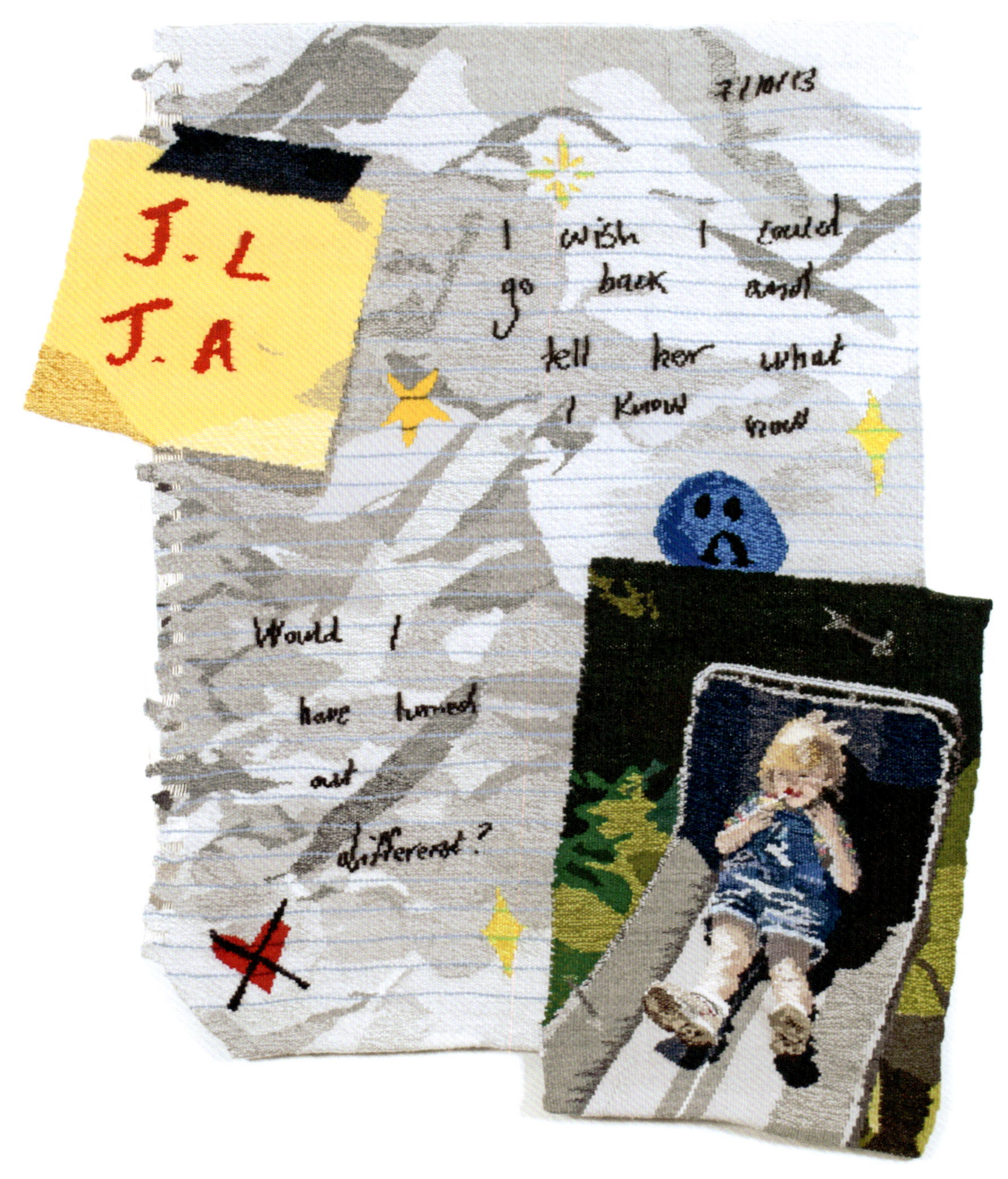

This page *I'm Sorry I Couldn't Protect You*, 2022, Weaving **Opposite** Top: *Ignorance is Bliss*, 2023, Weaving and ceramics; Bottom: *Humanity Not Found*, 2023, Weaving and ceramics

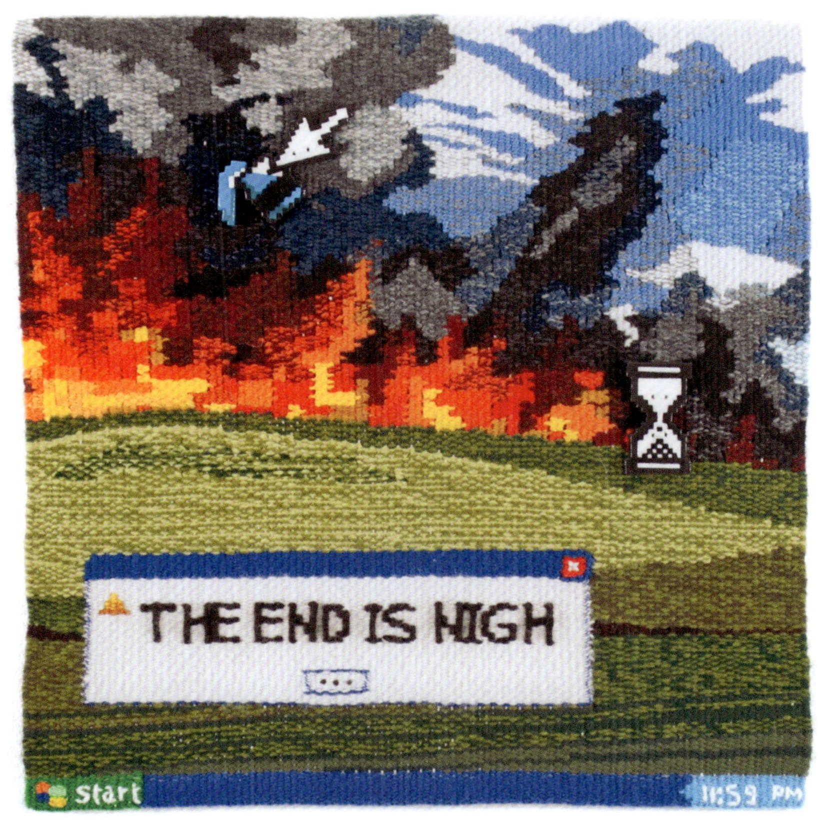
THE END IS HIGH
start
11:59 PM

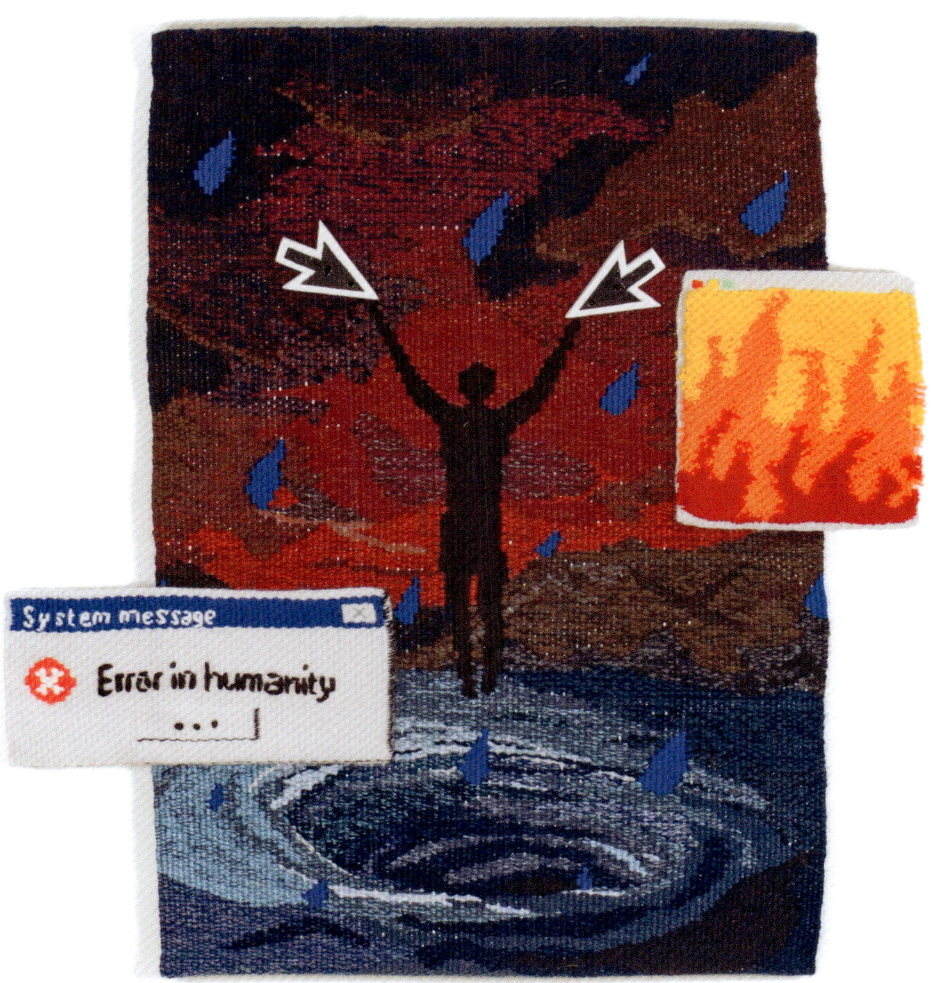
System message
Error in humanity

Moon Bori 문보리

SEOUL

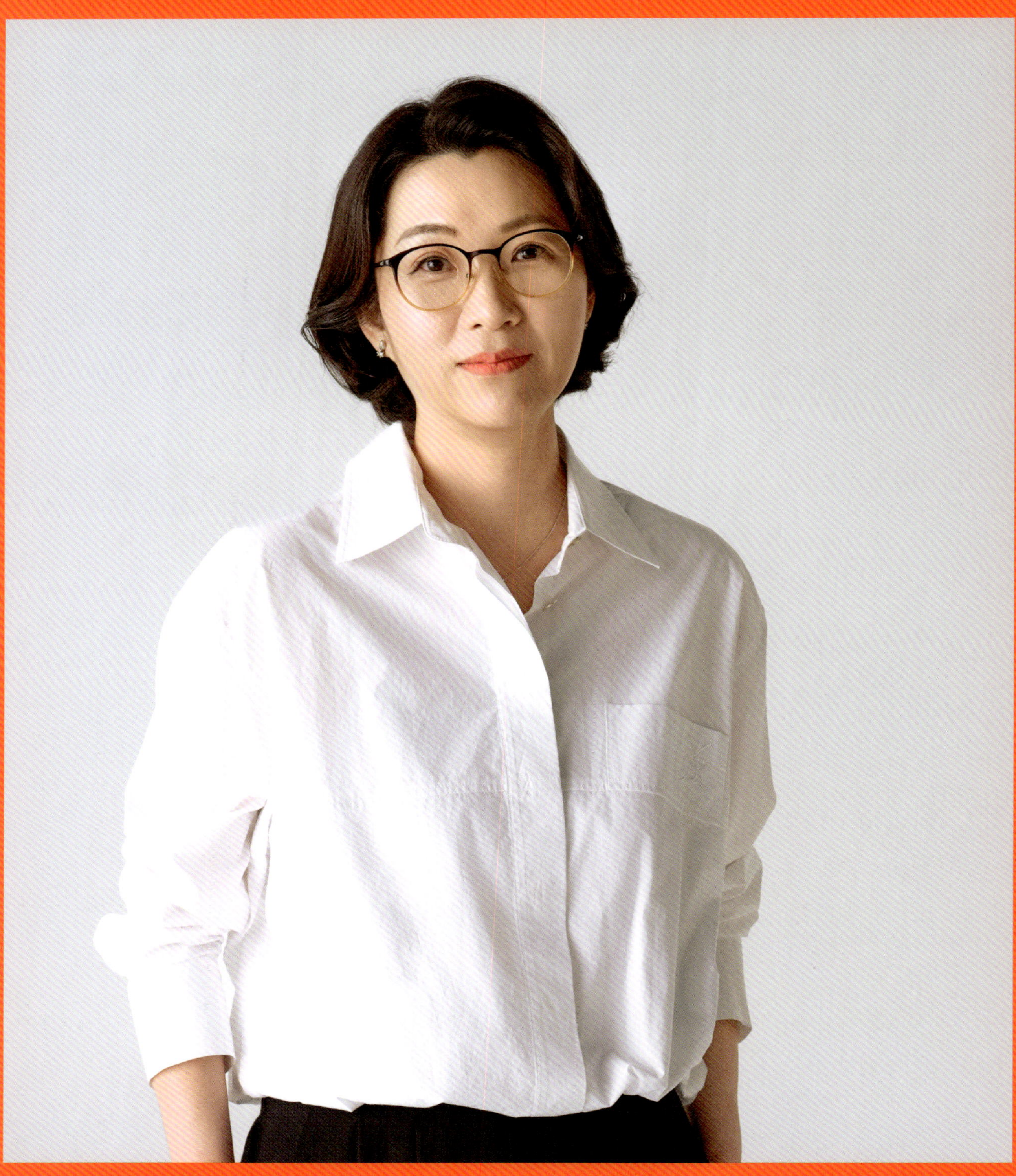

Moon Bori is an artist who uses weaving to explore the "relationship between materials" across time and cultures. She does this by combining traditional Korean materials, such as hemp, with digital elements, including optical fibre threads. This approach, which collapses binary distinctions between East and West, analogue and digital, past and present, is harnessed by Moon to "expand the field of fibre crafts" and demonstrates how weavings can take the form of contemporary sculpture to examine themes of human connection and shared experiences.

Moon's art often explores the well-established relationship between weaving and the "origins of computers and digital signals". This history can be traced to the invention of interchangeable punch cards, as used on Jacquard looms to weave patterned fabrics, which helped to inspire the adoption of binary code in early computing. For Moon, though, connections between the two extend beyond the Jacquard loom. Both computer-based programming and fabric "share an intriguing commonality" in their ability to "embody the continuity of humanity's history", visible in how codes and textiles are created and in what they capture.

In Moon's series *Memory, Algorithm, Signal* (2023–ongoing), she articulates the connection between computing and weaving processes through her choice of materials. In these works, Moon weaves light-emitting fibres into the works' other main material: hemp. Against the organic fabric, the optical fibres' luminosity stands out in stark contrast. The works in the series also incorporate heart rate and sound sensors, which allow the resulting installation to emit "light and sound in response to the viewer's heartbeat". This interactive element creates an intimate experience of Moon's work, while also introducing audiences to "synesthetic experiences based on tactility", in which the heart stimulates sight and sound.

By inviting this audience participation, Moon challenges the "depersonalised" associations of technology by instead demonstrating the way that machine output is shaped by human input.

Moon's weavings are heavily influenced by her initial education in fibre art in Korea followed by further studies on weaving design in the United States. Studying textile art in these two different contexts, using different materials and techniques, Moon became interested in the "coexistence of the past and the present in one space". This convergence is highlighted through Moon's deliberate choice to use hemp from Andong, a region in South Korea known for its traditional fibre production. For Moon, the use of Andong yarns, "which are grown in the soil", serve as not just a material choice, but also a "significant source of inspiration for my work's themes". This can be seen in *Andong-gil* (2024), which interprets the sound waves of the region, digitally recorded by the artist, through elongated lines in the woven fabric. In this work, Andong is not just the producer of the thread, but is also a central character and its own subject matter.

For Moon, working with Andong's artisans is an expression of continuing cultural practice, and the ways that the "connection between the past and present is maintained through these materials". Moon wants to anchor traditions not just in their history, but in their present, which, in the case of her hemp, is carried on by the artisans' labour. This continuity demonstrates that tradition "isn't just from the past – it exists in the present". This point of recognition is central to Moon's intentional approach to weaving as an artform: she identifies the possibilities of weaving in "connecting something to something" through the integration of warp and weft threads to create a cohesive whole. Considered in this way, we might also see the lights used in Moon's work as a symbolic gesture towards the "signals that connect us in contemporary society". ■

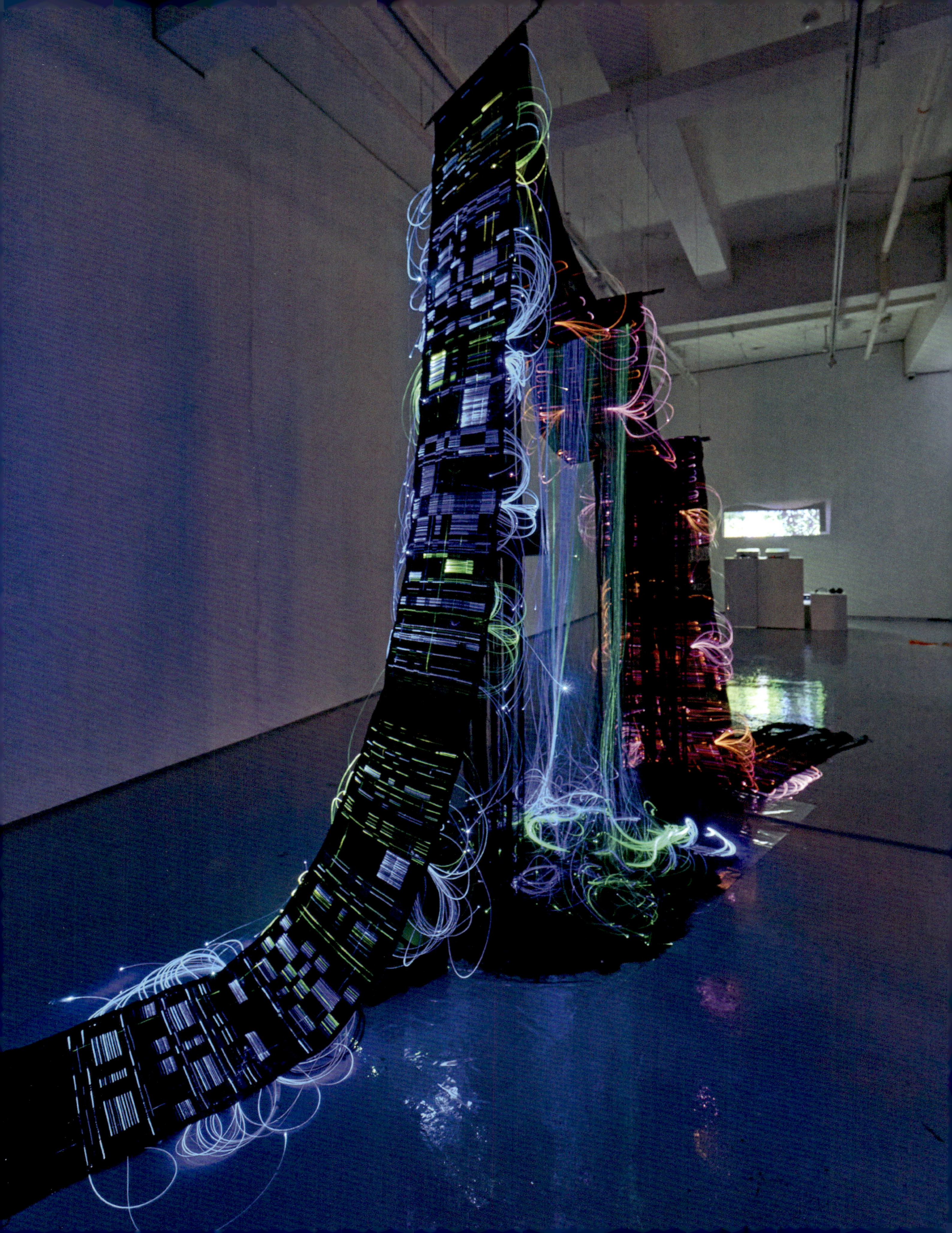

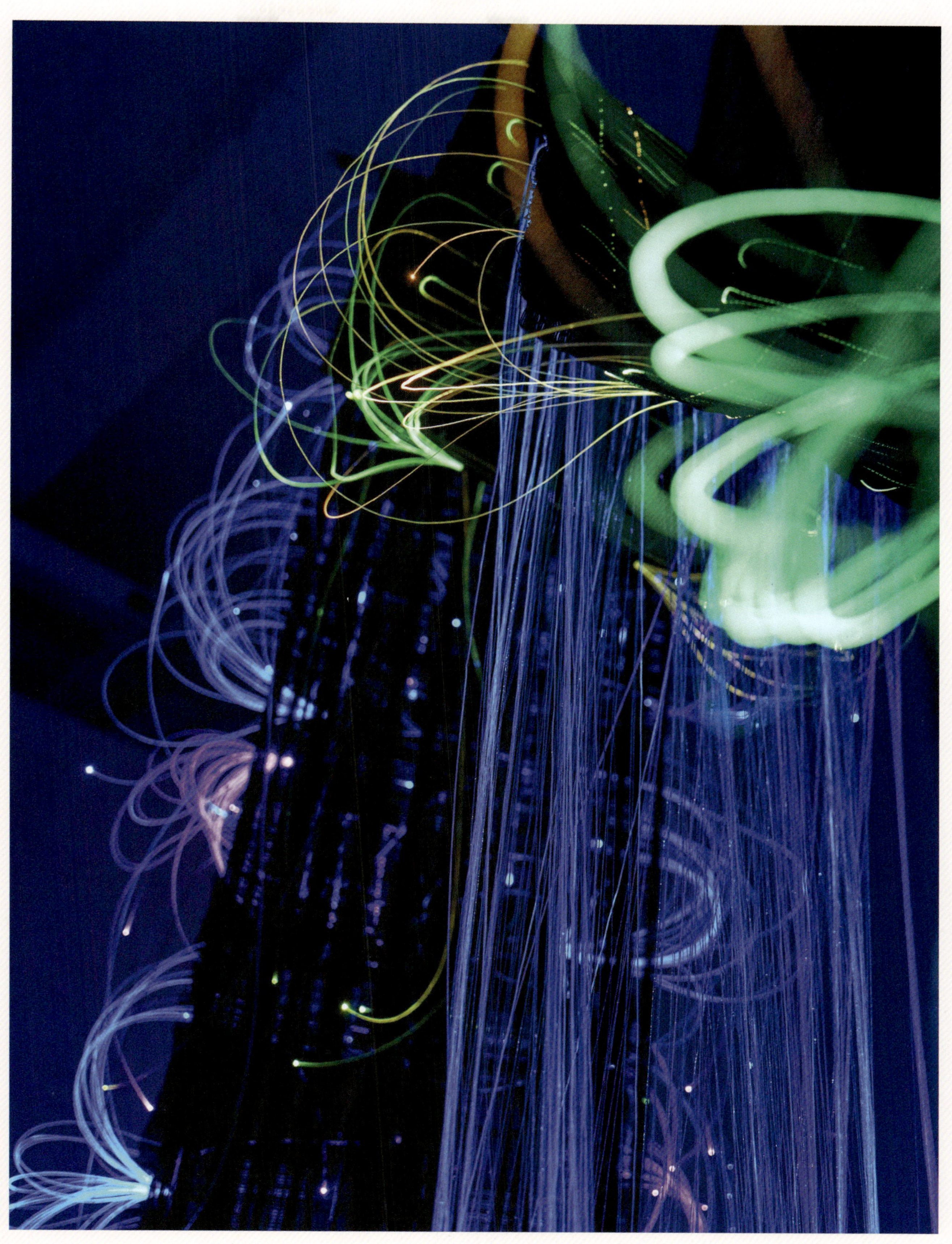

This page and opposite *Memory, Algorithm, Signal: From the Earth*, 2024–25, Weaving

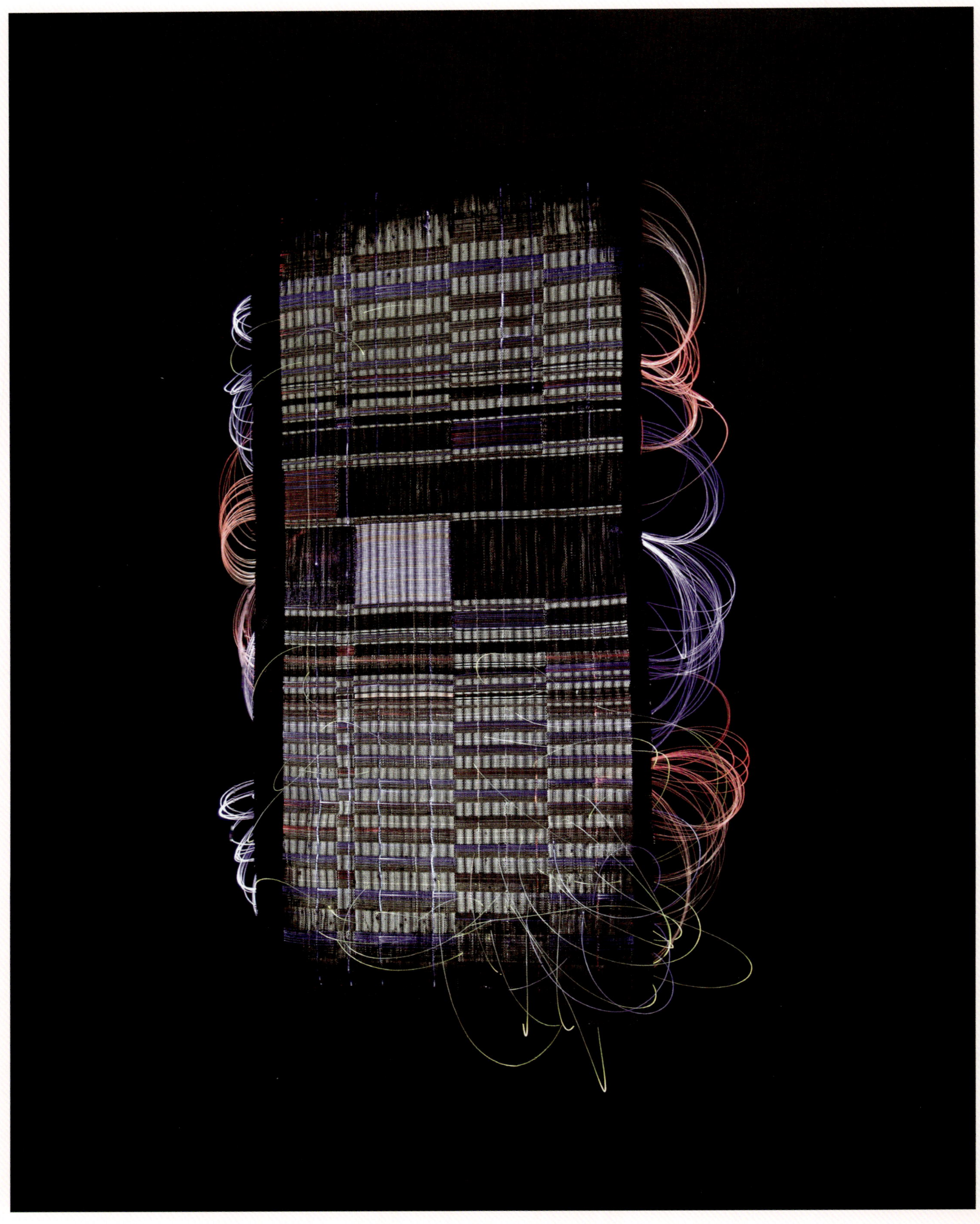

This page *Memory, Signal #1*, Weaving
Opposite Top: *Synesthetic Handloom H*, 2022, Weaving; Bottom: *Memory, Signal* (detail)

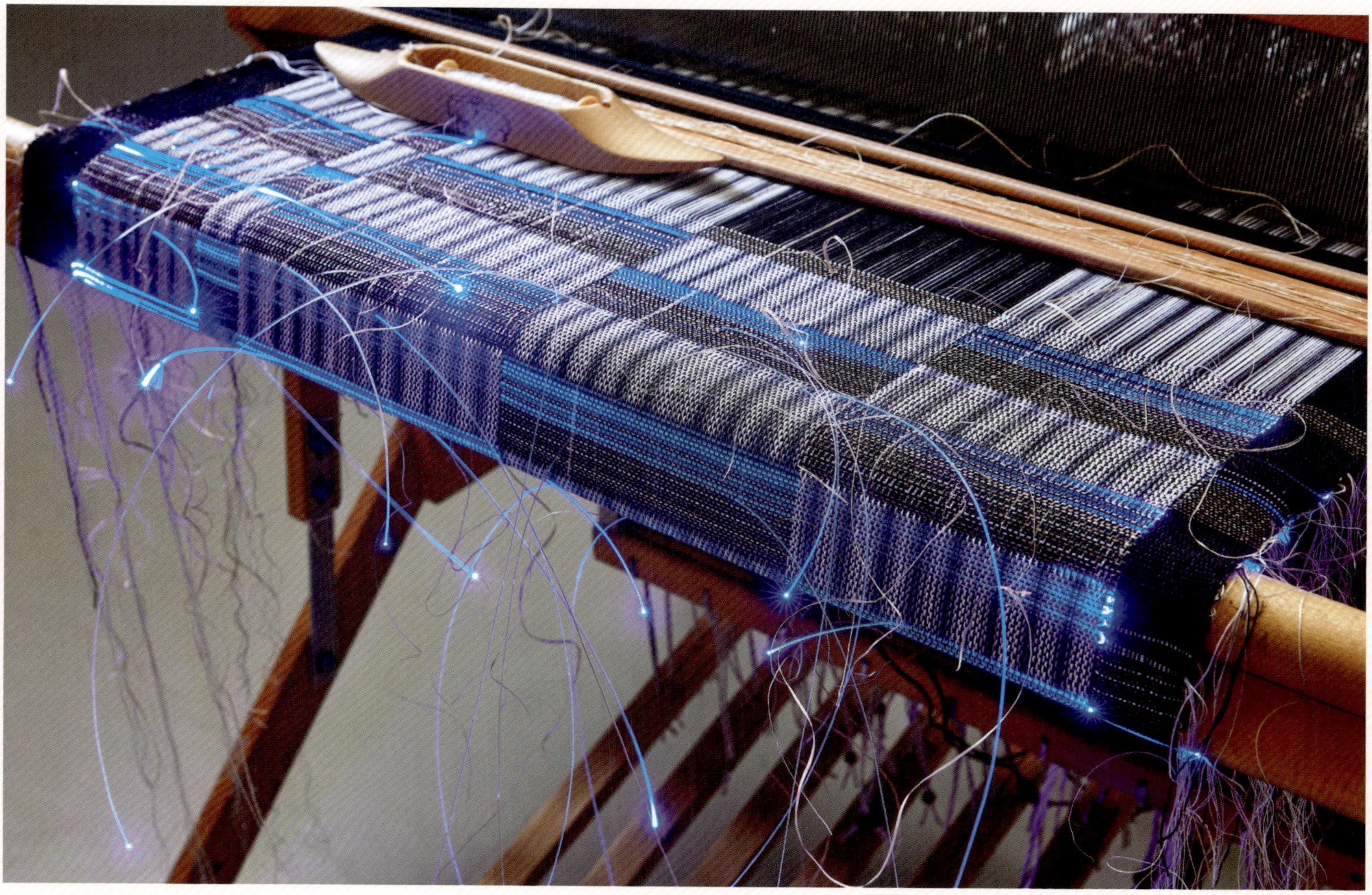

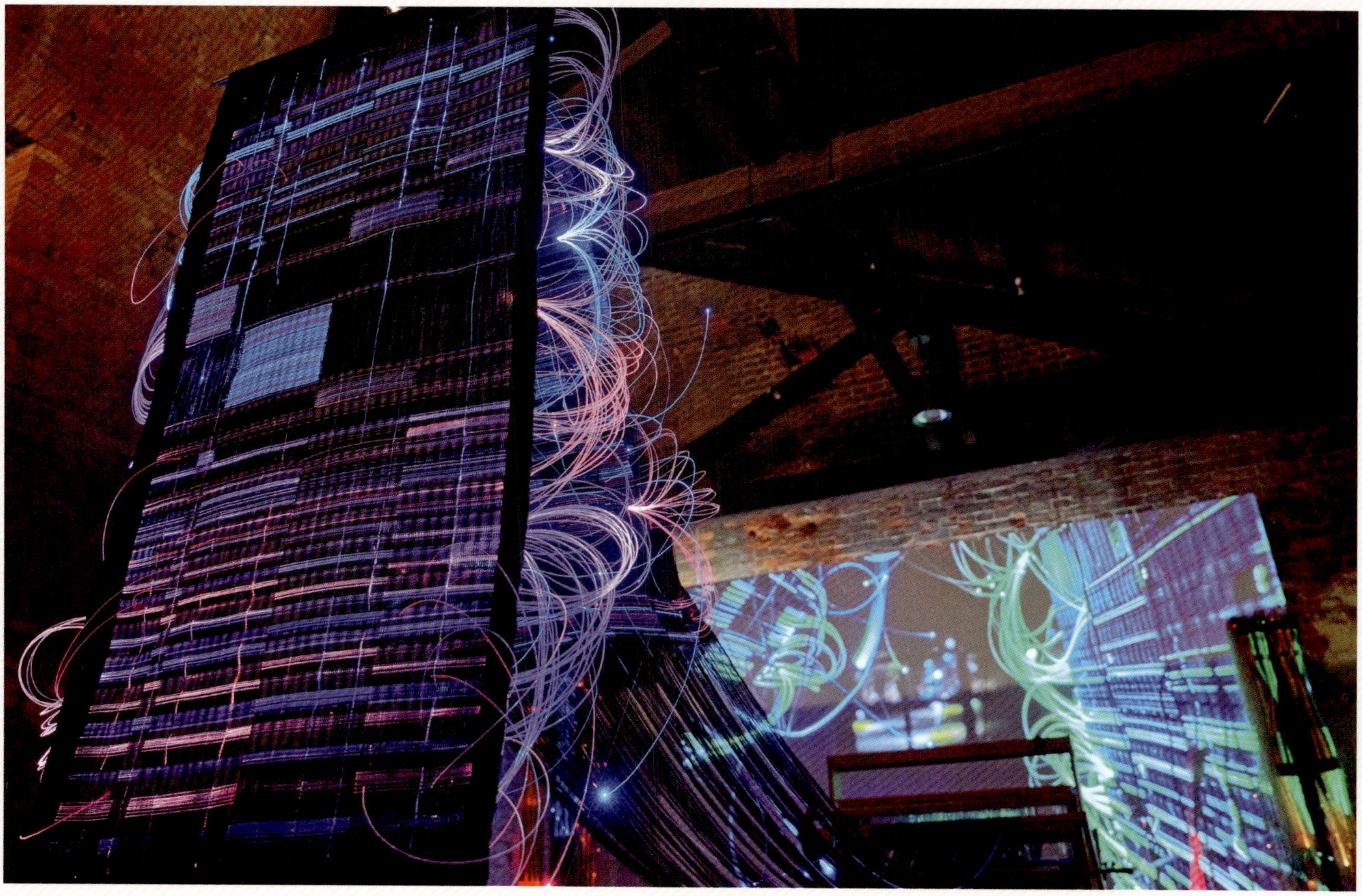

Sophie Honess

GAMILAROI COUNTRY

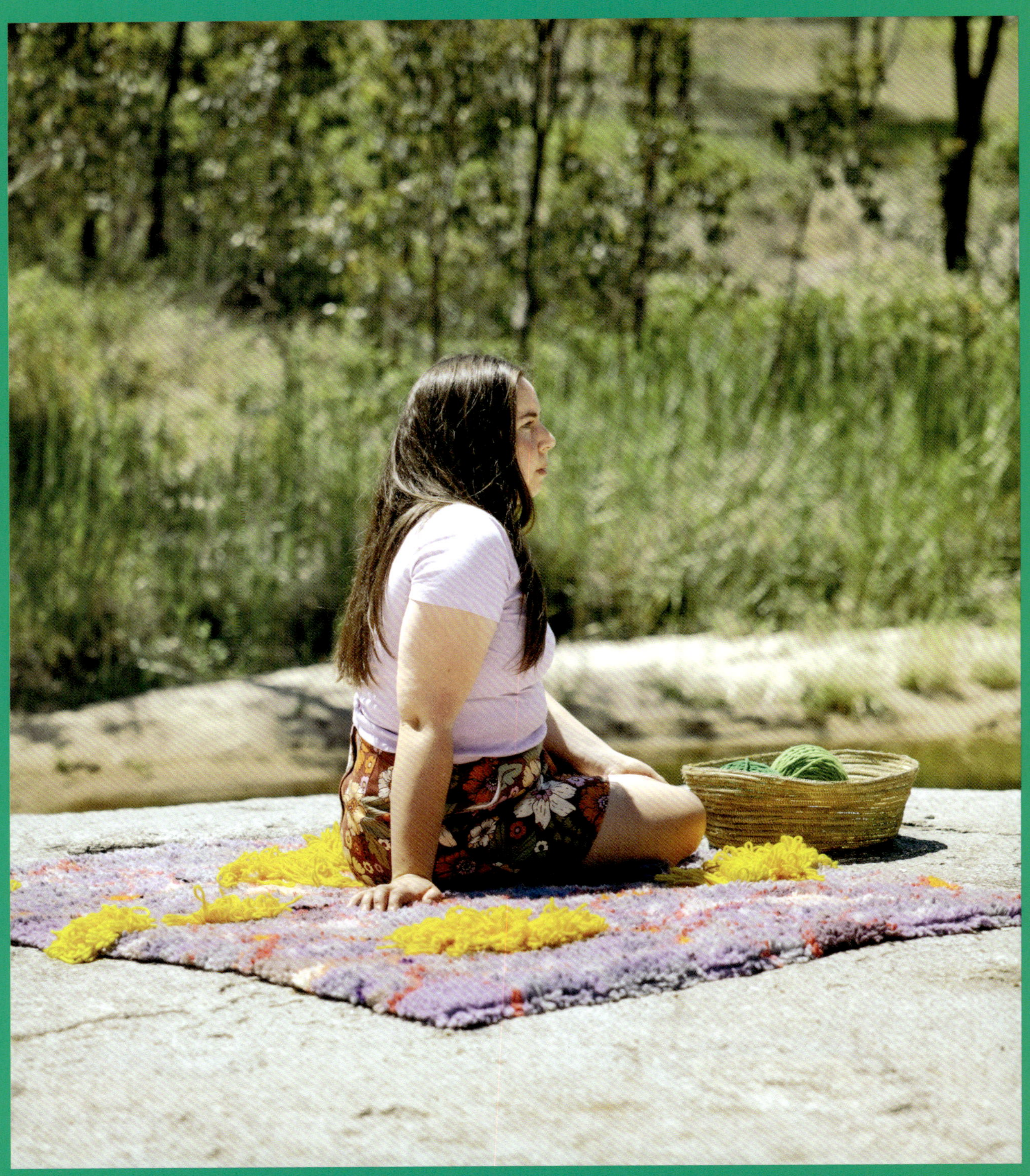

Sophie Honess is a Gamilaroi Yinarr artist whose love of textiles is embedded across her expressive practice encompassing basket weaving, embroidery, punch needle, latch hooking and rug tufting. Growing up in a regional city in Gamilaroi Country, Australia, Honess had a creative childhood, encouraged by her family from a young age to enrol in "every available art class there was" with her sister. These early forays into art were formative, but it was Honess's return to her hometown as an adult that kindled her current practice. After attending her first weaving class, she was immediately "obsessed" with the expansive possibilities for form after recognising "just how many things are made from weaving". Soon after, Honess taught herself how to weave on a loom, and also started using punch needle and rug tufting separately to create even larger, "more expressive [pieces] with line work and colour".

Honess approaches each piece afresh, allowing ideas and concepts to arise through the process of making with her hands. Her art is connected, however, by recurring themes: it "speak[s] about me, and how I fit in with my environment. Whether that be, on Country, my family and friends, how I live, how I've grown, or stayed the same, and my thoughts and ideas…" In the artist's earlier tapestries, including *Gipps Street* (2021), this connection to her environment is clearly articulated through the combination of found natural forms (gumnuts) with wool and fabric to create an impression of a native eucalyptus tree.

Today, Honess's connection to Country remains an important theme in her works; for Indigenous Australians, Country refers not just to physical space, but also the ancestral and spiritual connections to land. The connection's significance is further explored in the artist's most ambitious work to date. *Daruka – grass, water, granite* (2024) is a series of three hand-latched rugs inspired by Honess's relationship to the suburb of Daruka, a place where "my friends and I would play in… creeks, walk through fields of grass, and stand on big granite boulders". Unlike her woven tapestries made on a loom, this set of large-scale works was created through a latch-hooking technique on a gridded mat, with Honess individually knotting more than 86,000 wool strands and trimming the surface.

Daruka – grass, water, granite is striking in its vivid combination of tones, textures and colours, which work together to capture the hidden beauty and magnificence of place. Beneath this stunning relief, the rugs also present a stark reminder of the toll of colonialist expansion on both land and connection to culture. In the artist's own statement, addressed to Daruka, she writes "I've learned your story, how important you are, and see and feel your destruction." The resulting piece is a love letter to Country and demonstrates the artist's ongoing sense of awe, care and appreciation for the subject.

While Honess's tapestry weavings and latch-hooked rugs are made using wool, her basket weaving uses a native Australian grass, Lomandra. This grass is overlaid with raffia, ropes and threads in an almost neon-pink palette that includes oranges and yellows to create visually striking baskets, as well as bags. This joyous embrace of colour, which is carried across all of Honess's creative output, imbues dynamism into longstanding weaving traditions. Speaking to the inspiration behind her artistic practice, Honess shares that her art is "mainly informed by women who have always made and created works": who have woven "baskets to carry things in, [and] big woven mats to sleep on". While the materials that Honess uses may be different from those of her ancestors, Honess recognises this continuity of creative practice and locates her work within a "living culture". ■

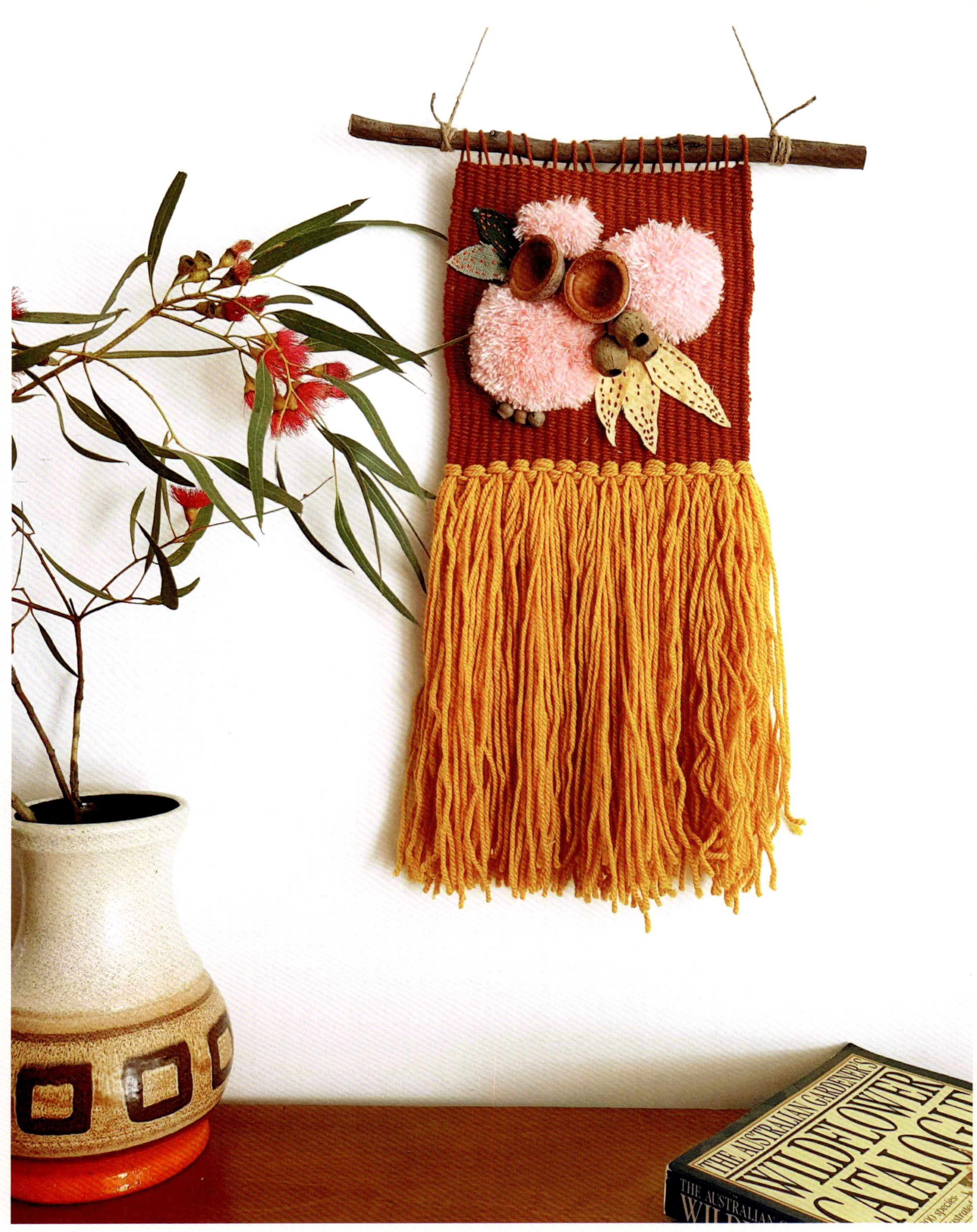

This page *Gipps Street*, 2021, Weaving
Opposite Top: *Vessels on Country*, 2024, Basket weaving; Bottom: *Lomandra Basket*, 2024, Basket weaving

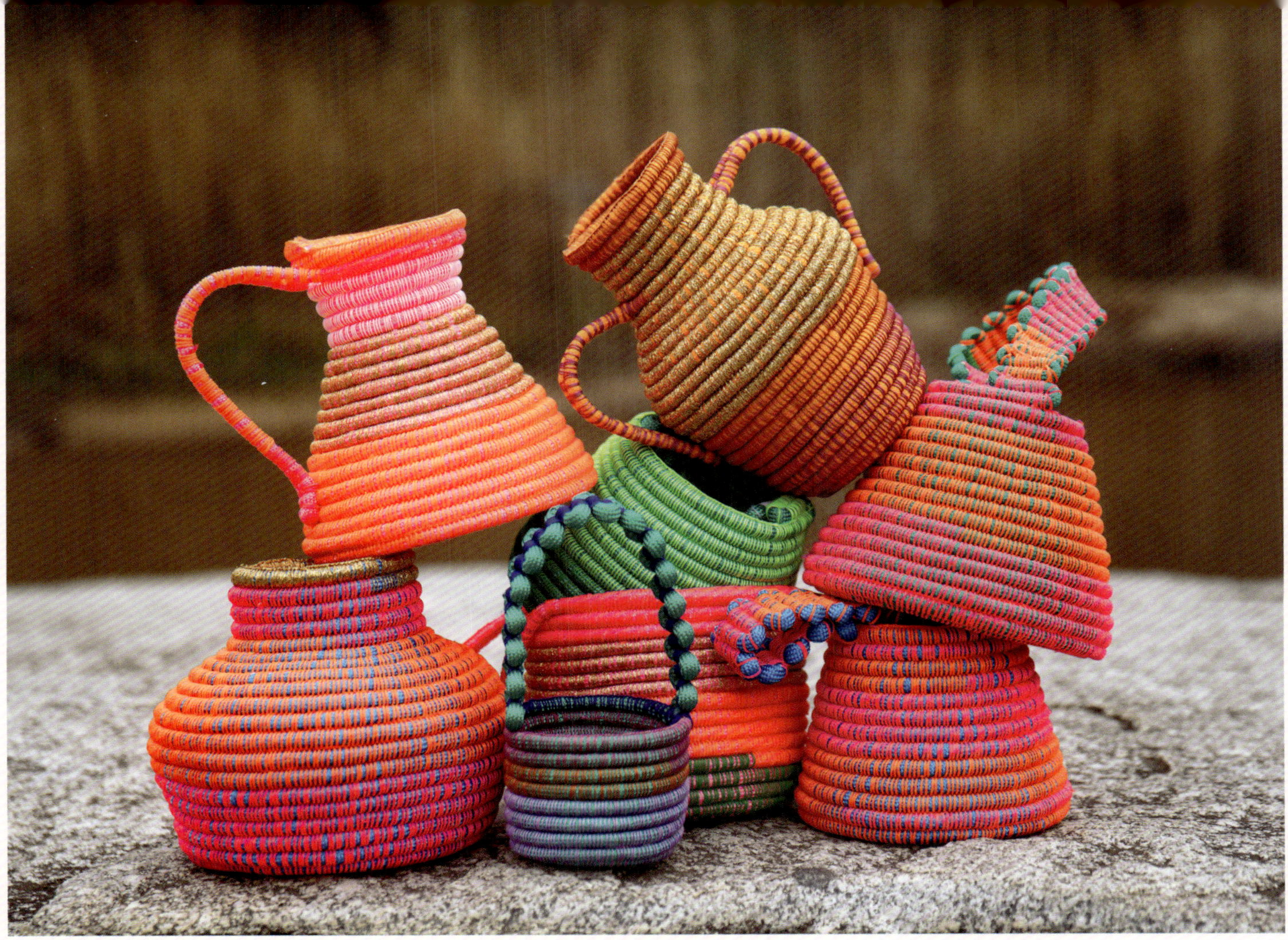

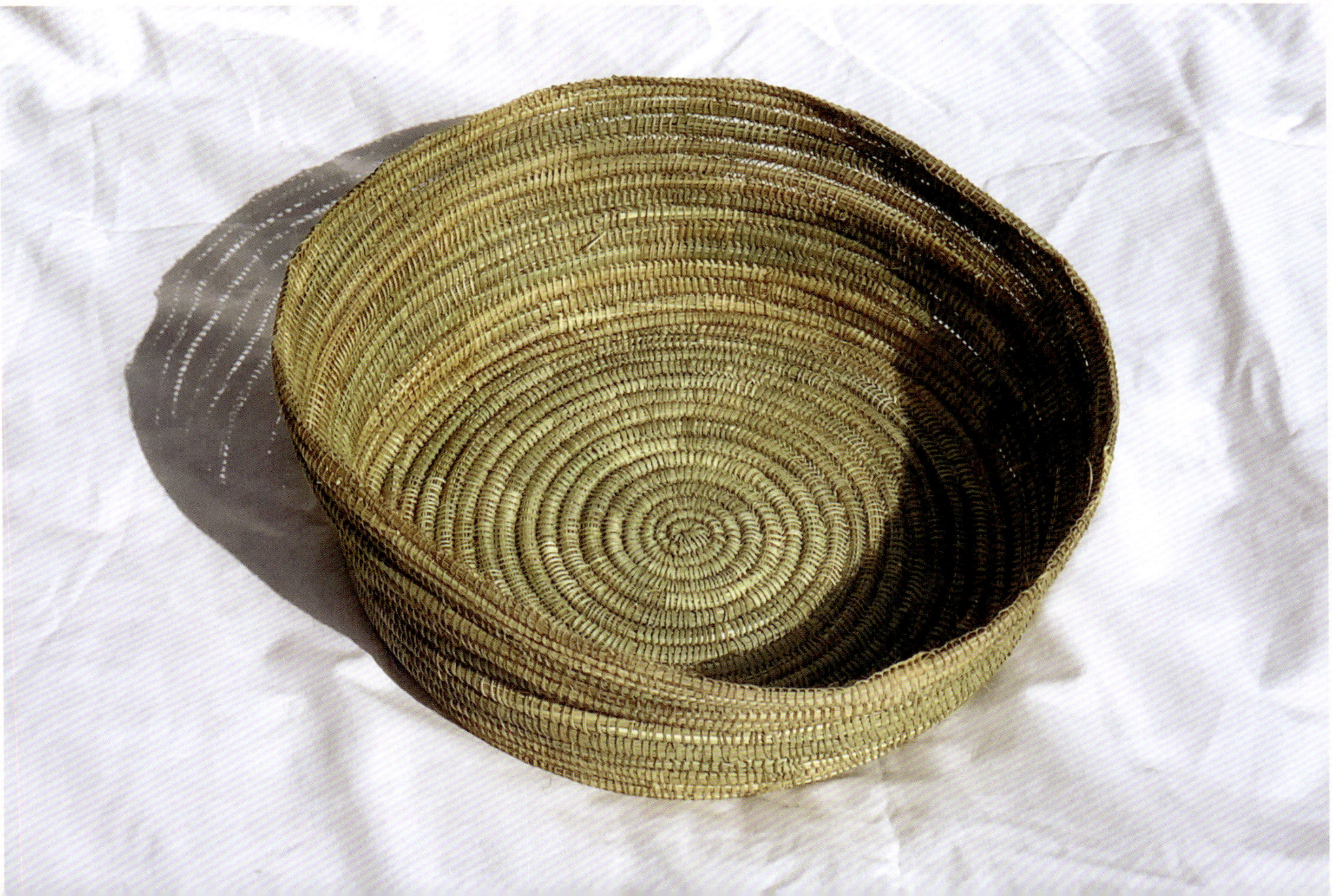

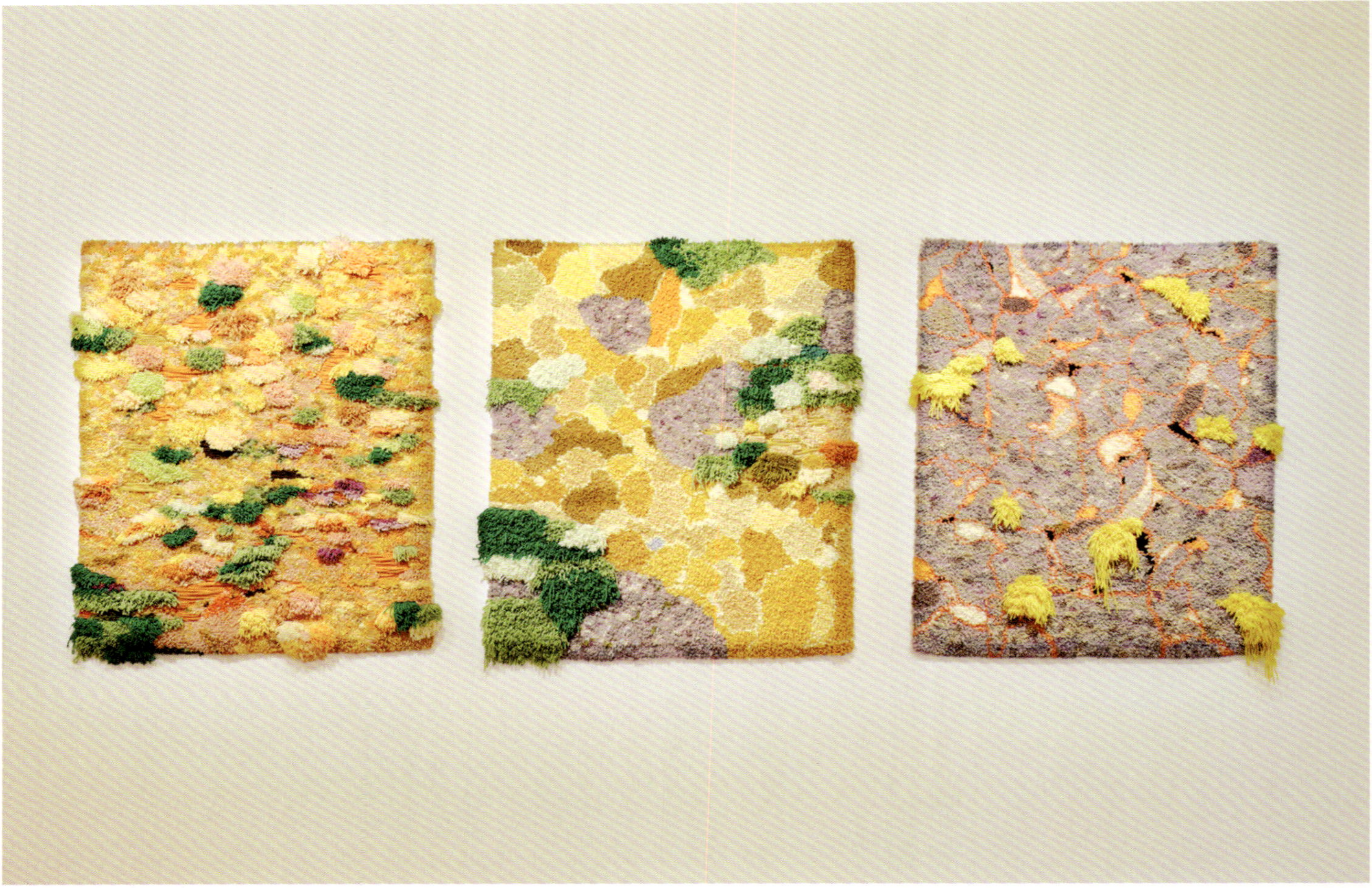

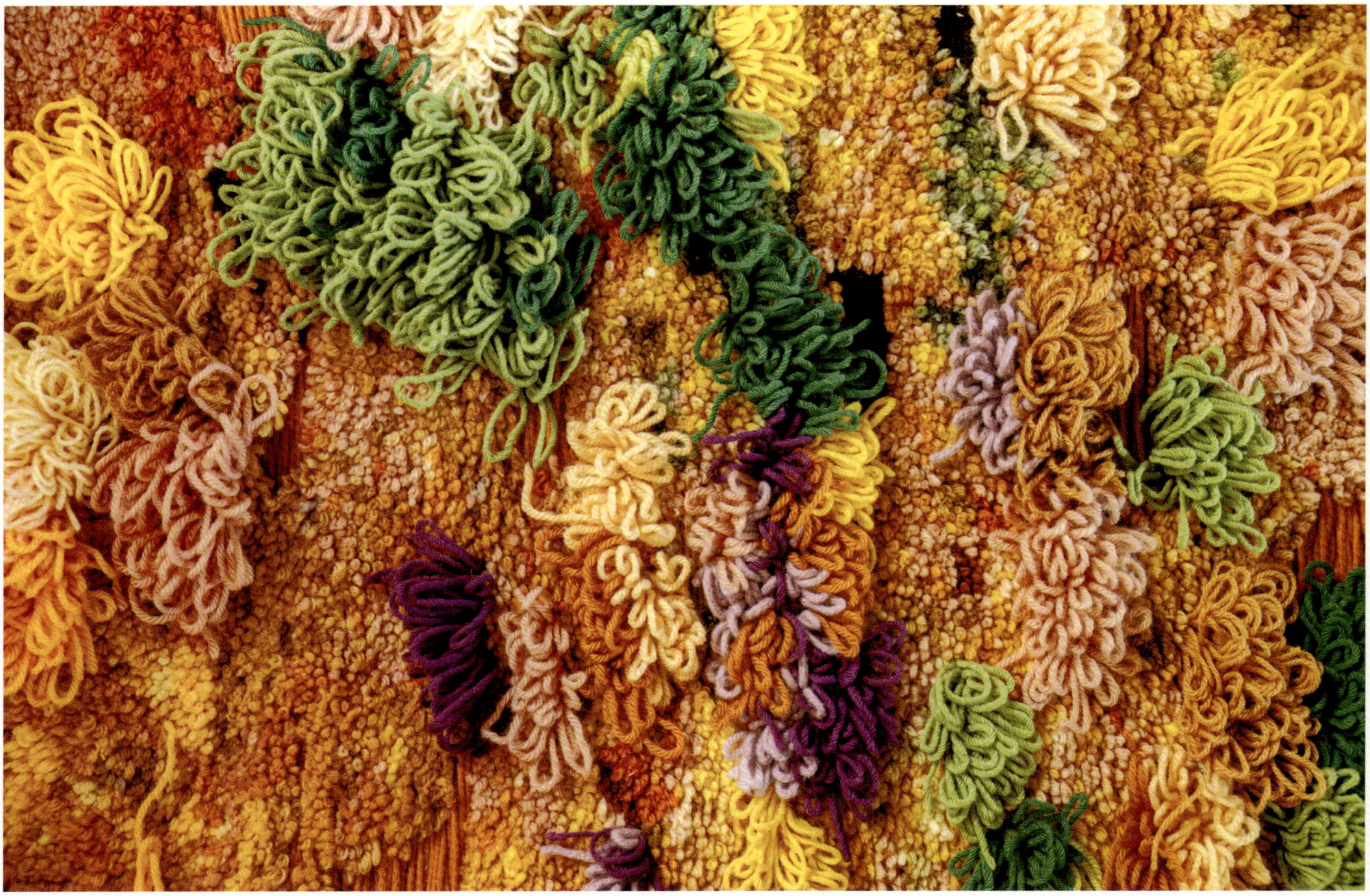

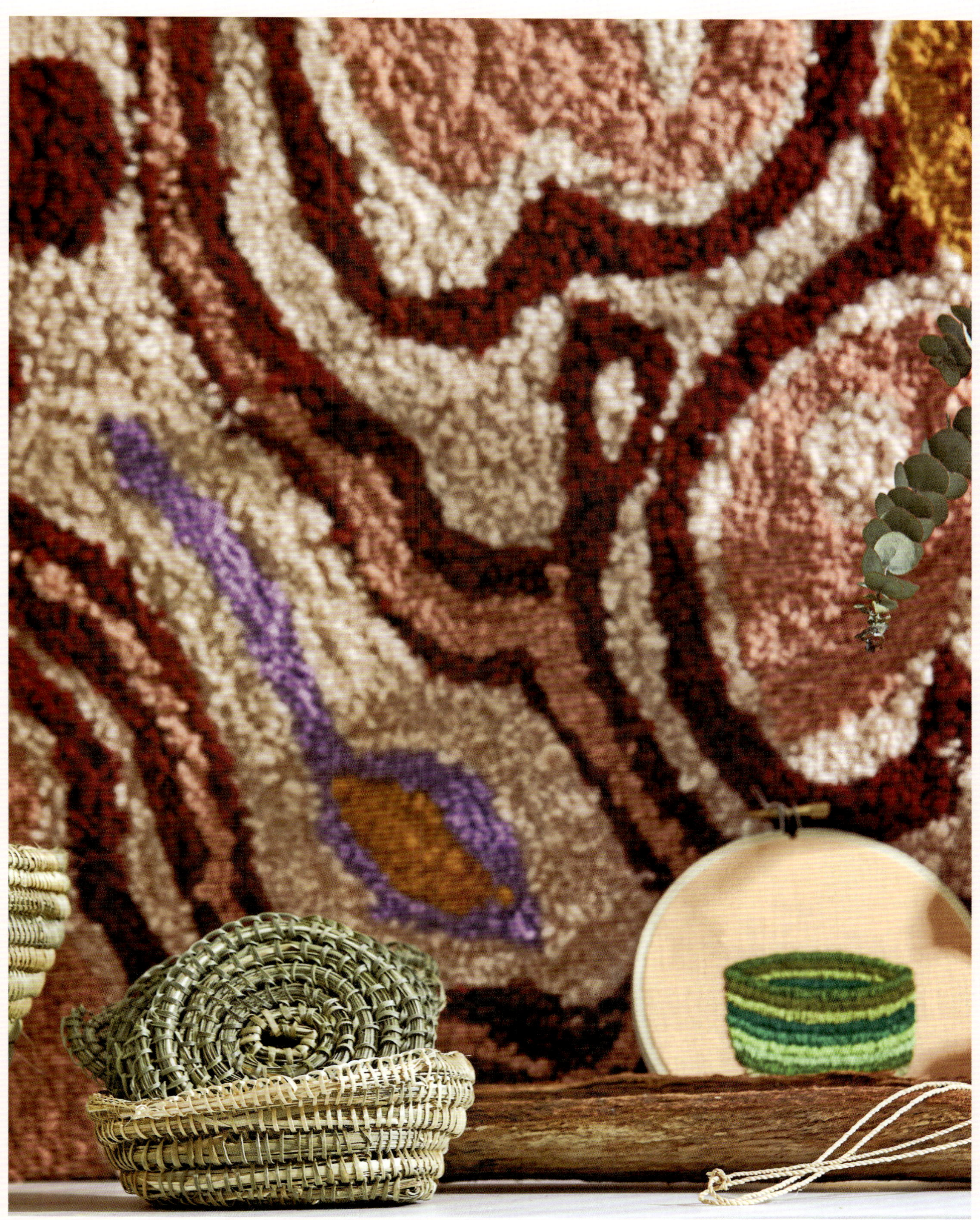

Opposite Top: *Daruka - grass, water, granite*, 2024, Latch-hooking; Bottom: *Daruka - grass*, Latch-hooking, 2024
This page Studio shot, 2022

Tais Rose Wae

BUNDJALUNG COUNTRY

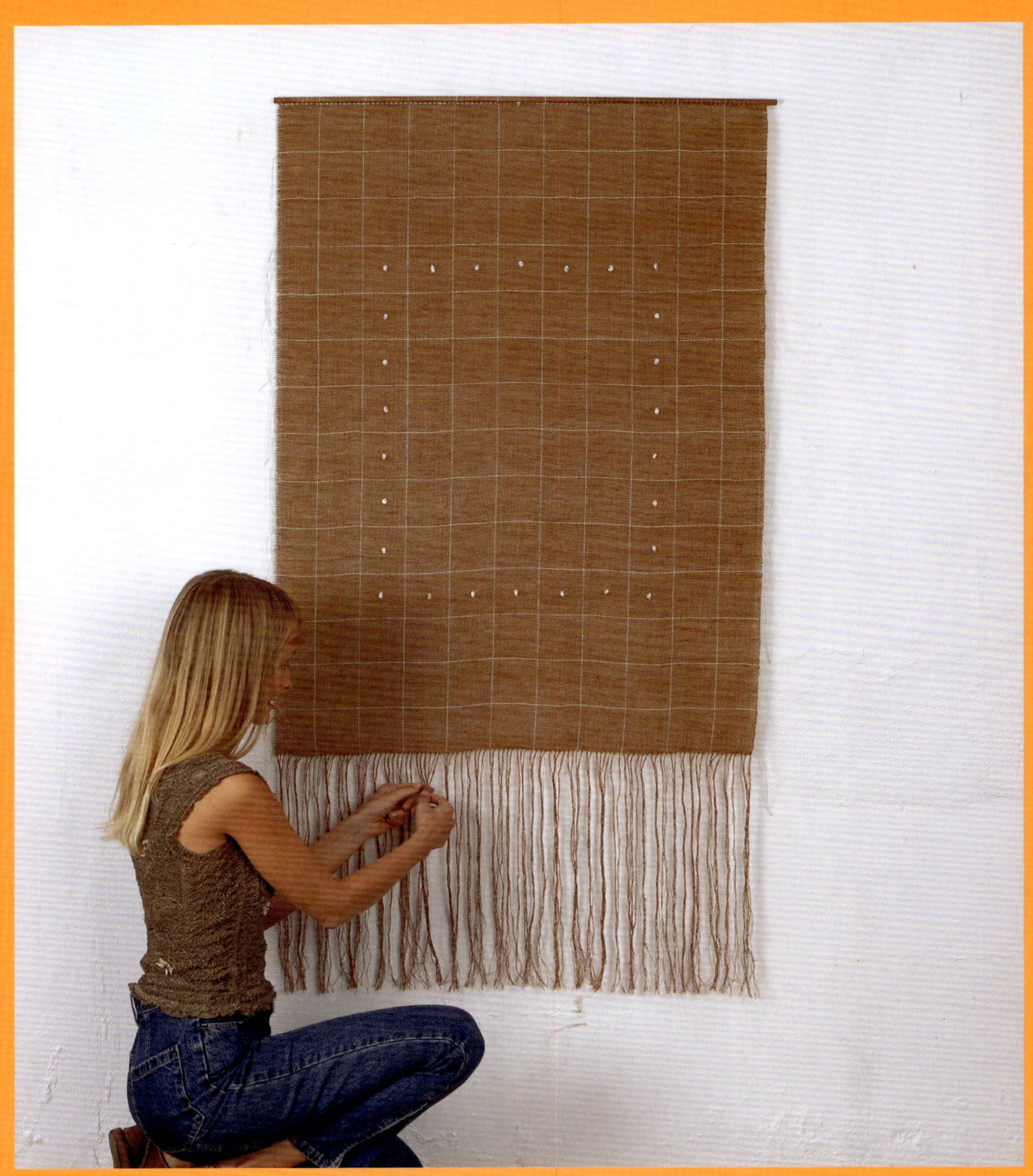

Tais Rose Wae makes weavings and writes poems that are influenced by themes including "myth, archetype, motherhood, water, spirals, dreams, memory, language, storytelling and my Aboriginal ancestry". For the artist, weaving and poetry are two complementary creative practices that are "inevitably intertwined", her weavings acting as a "tangible visual manifestation" of her writing.

Wae began weaving eight years ago after learning to make baskets, transitioning to working on a loom five years ago. In her current work, she is drawn to both natural colours and materials, which is reflected in her choice of textiles, including linen, silk and cotton, as well as "additions like seashells, pearls, seaweed, found snake bones, tree bark and gold", which are sewn in by hand at the end of the weaving process. These inclusions from the natural world are an "obvious" choice for the artist: both to incorporate the ecosystems that surround her and to exhibit a reverence for "the earth and its living beings". In addition to these embellishments, Wae uses paint, applying it on the warp threads, as well as onto the surface of the finished woven fabrics. These painterly layers serve to draw attention to particular motifs and designs as a point of detail.

Visually, Wae's weavings strike a harmonious balance between geometry and simplicity; she often employs grid-like patterns to break up the flat plane, and frequently uses spiral forms and circular motifs. These shapes, which reflect a deep connection with nature, can be interpreted as the "spiralling of rapids at the river, [or] the path of a mollusc on the water-smoothed stone at the centre of a rockpool". Structurally, Wae prefers "very simple" weaving techniques, which leave "more space for stories to emerge, for the paint and pearls and shells to tell their story on the loom". In this way, Wae does not aim to be prescriptive in meaning for audiences, preferring instead to think of her "practice as being quite watery and river-like. It expands and grows with me as a way to express that change."

Wae cites the "possibilities and limitations of weaving" as a key driver behind her artistic thinking and development. As a mother of two young children, she embraces the "ebbs and flows" that come with balancing care responsibilities and a creative practice, and admits that her approach to artmaking can be "very unstructured". Rather than see this as a hindrance, however, she explains that by the time she gets to the next weaving, "the vision... has brewed with such clarity that it almost reinvents itself on the loom". Some months, she might make multiple small weavings working on her living room floor; other times, she may not touch her loom for months.

This connection to motherhood and family is conveyed through Wae's approach to weaving as a "sentient expression", and a recognition that the physical process of passing a shuttle through the loom "with its back-and-forth motion, feels like

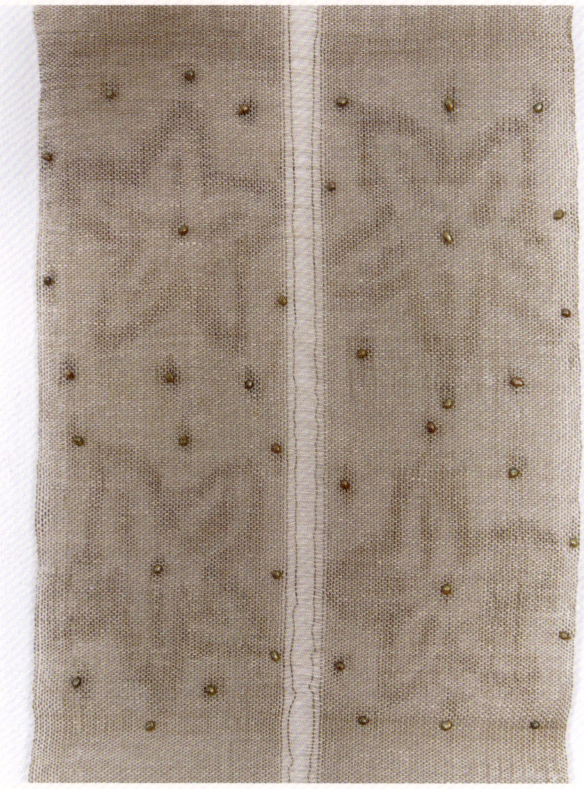

Opposite *'A Story of Lineage (in Twenty-Six Pearls)'*, 2023, Weaving **This page** *'From Upon the Riverbank, a Pearl Flowers Endlessly'*, 2023, Weaving and painting

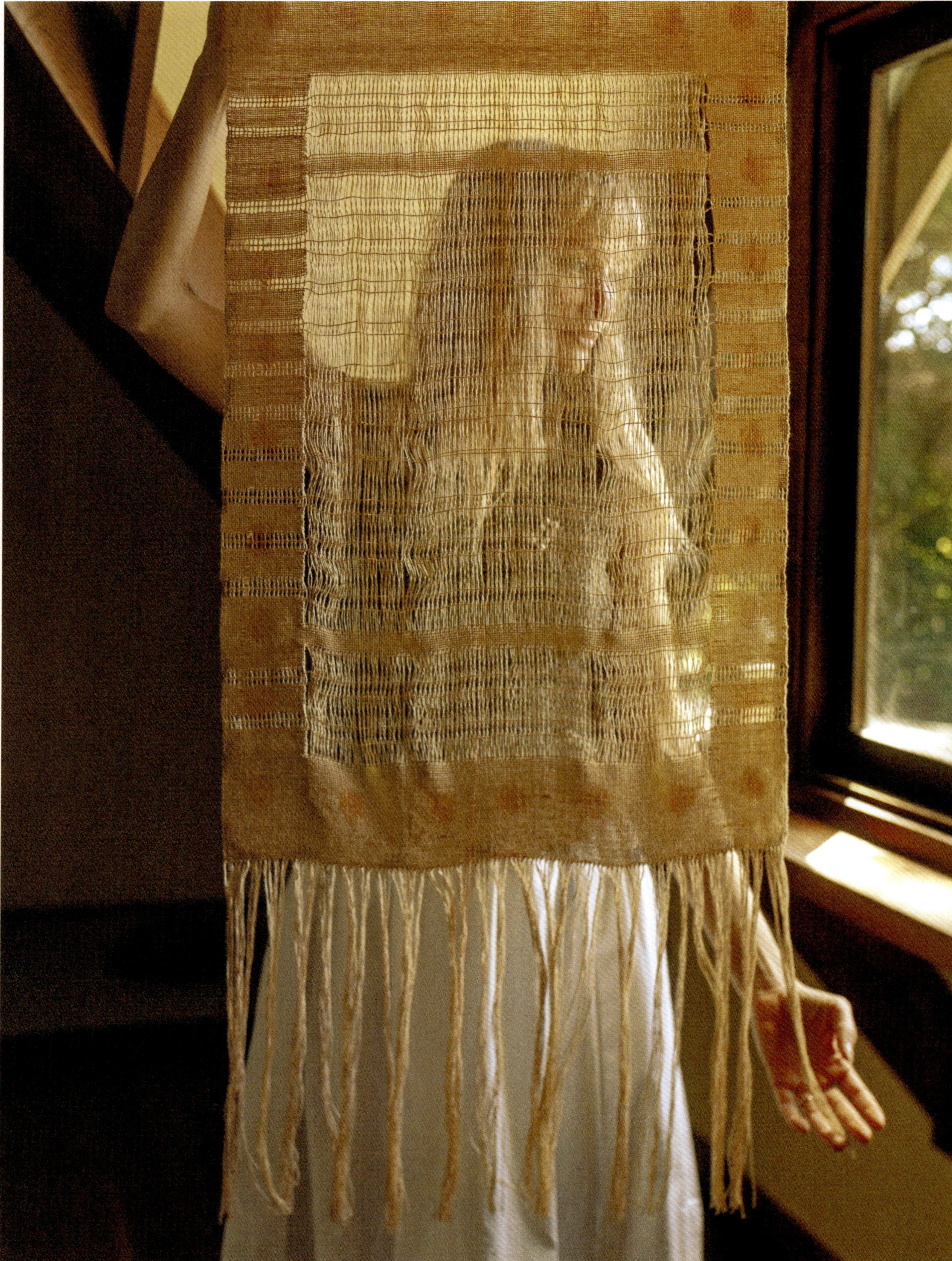

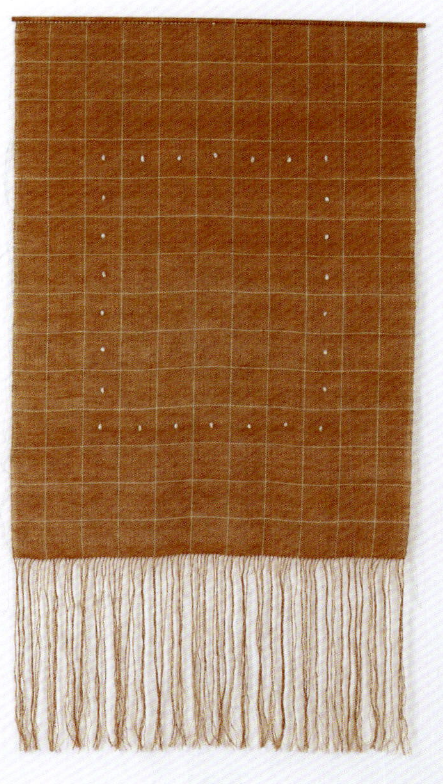

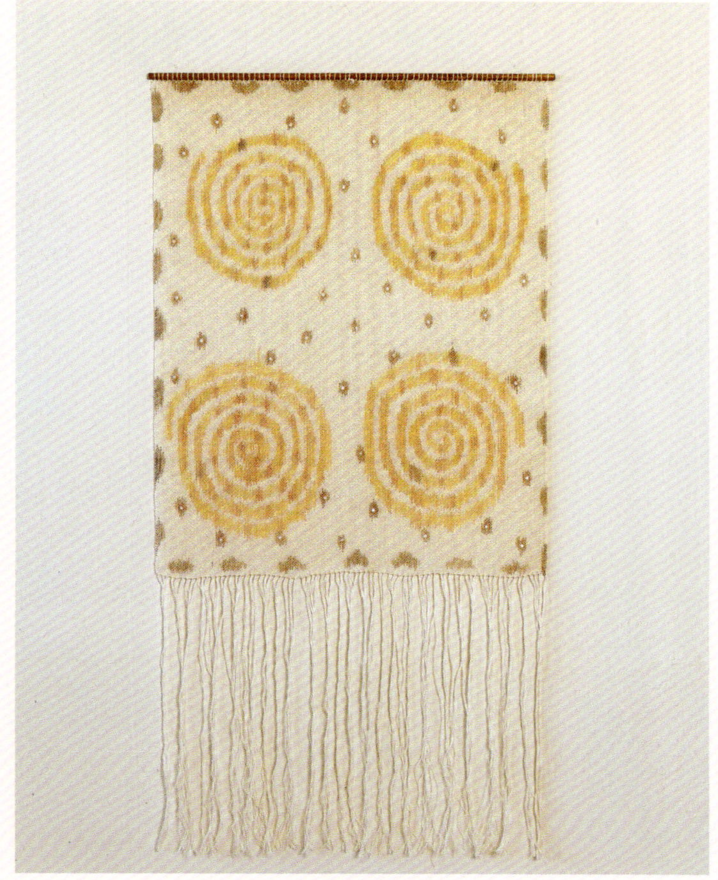

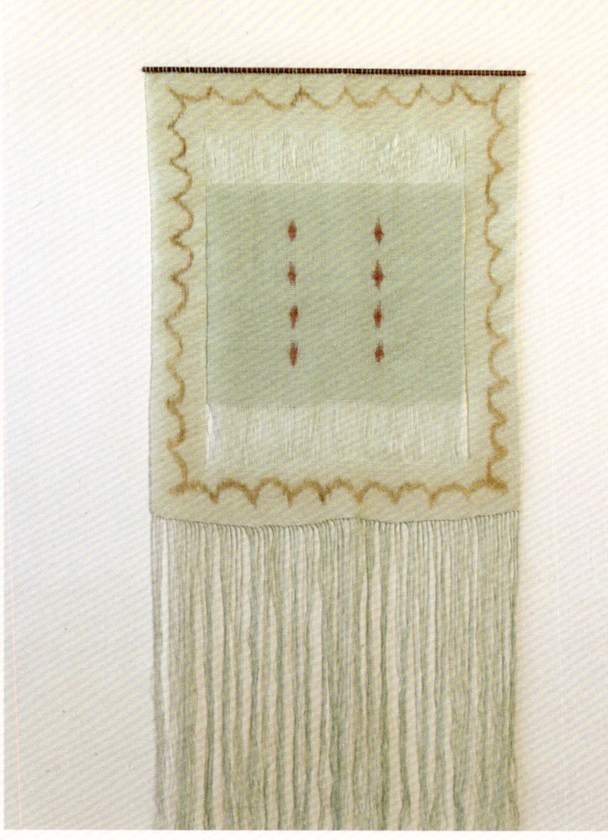

a gestation in itself". Here Wae is referring to the idea that weaving is often used as a narrative tool to tell stories, but also that "stories are woven" culturally through storytelling and oral traditions. This connection between storytelling and weaving is summarised by the artist: "Through my work and the creation of cloth from yarn, I am unravelling and making meaning of my lineage."

This connection to Aboriginal lineage remains a central focus to Wae's weaving practice. The ongoing impacts of colonisation and forced removal over generations continues to impact Wae's connection to family and ancestry. For the artist, "The questions, pain, beauty, curiosity and connection that exists in my relationship to our ancestry is really at the heart of my work." Weaving on the loom provides Wae with a material language and private dialogue through which she can explore "dreams, histories, and inner landscapes". ■

Opposite *'To Hold the Branch in its Own Dappled Light'*, 2023, Weaving **This page** Clockwise from top left: *'A Story of Lineage (in Twenty-Six Pearls)'*; *'Stone Spirit, from Upon the Silver Bank'*, 2024, Weaving and painting; *'Siren Sound from Past and Present'*, 2024, Weaving and painting

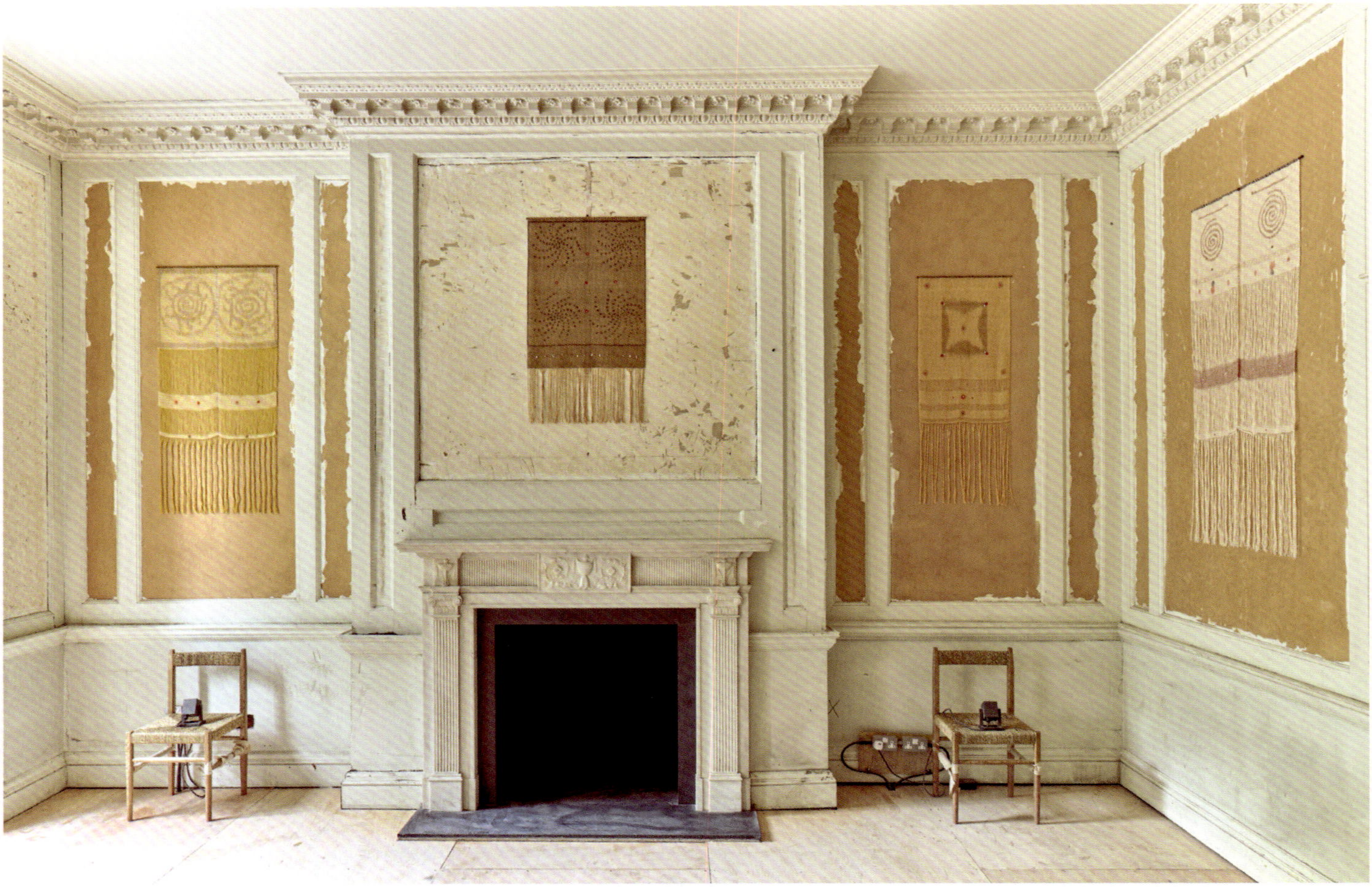

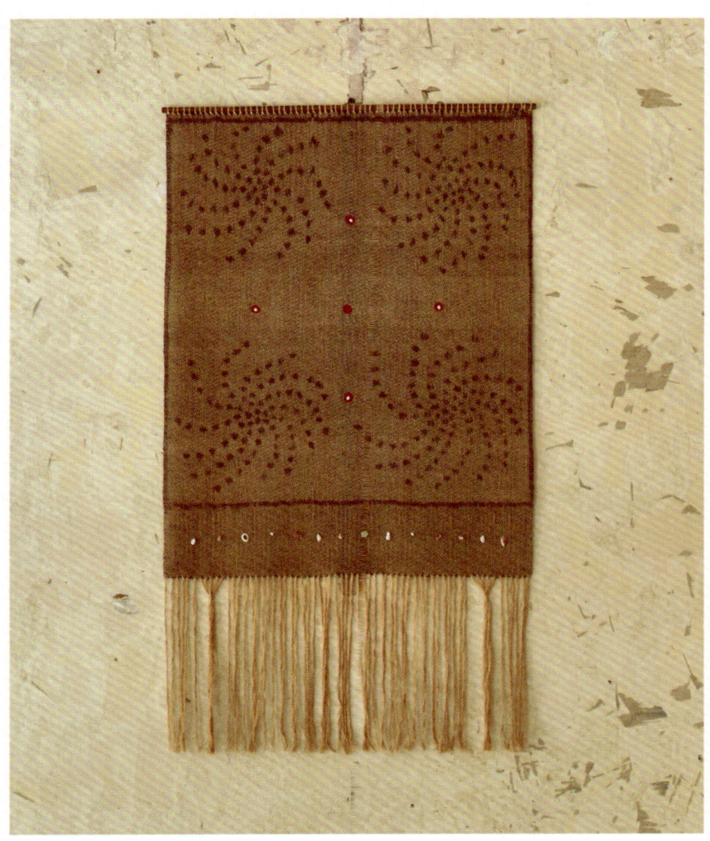

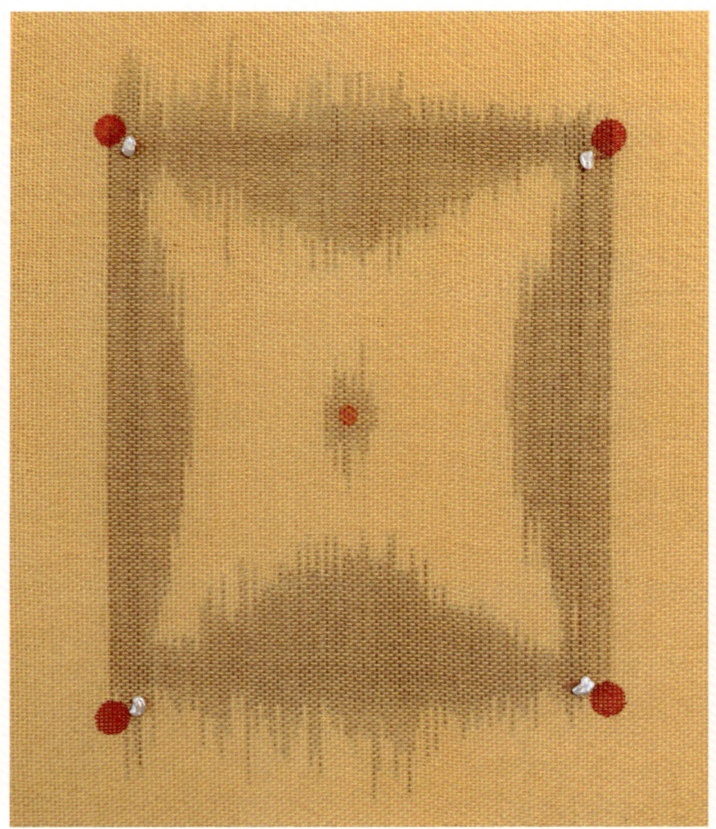

This page Clockwise from top: *'The Memory Undresses the Myth'*, 2023, Weaving and painting; *'Ephemeral Altar of Sea and Story'*, 2023, Weaving; *'On Quiet Country, a Gust Carries Gifts'*, 2024, Weaving and painting; *'Stone Spirit, from Upon the Silver Bank'*, 2024, Weaving and painting; *'On Quiet Country …'* (detail); *'Ephemeral Altar …'* **Opposite** *'Stone Spirit …'*

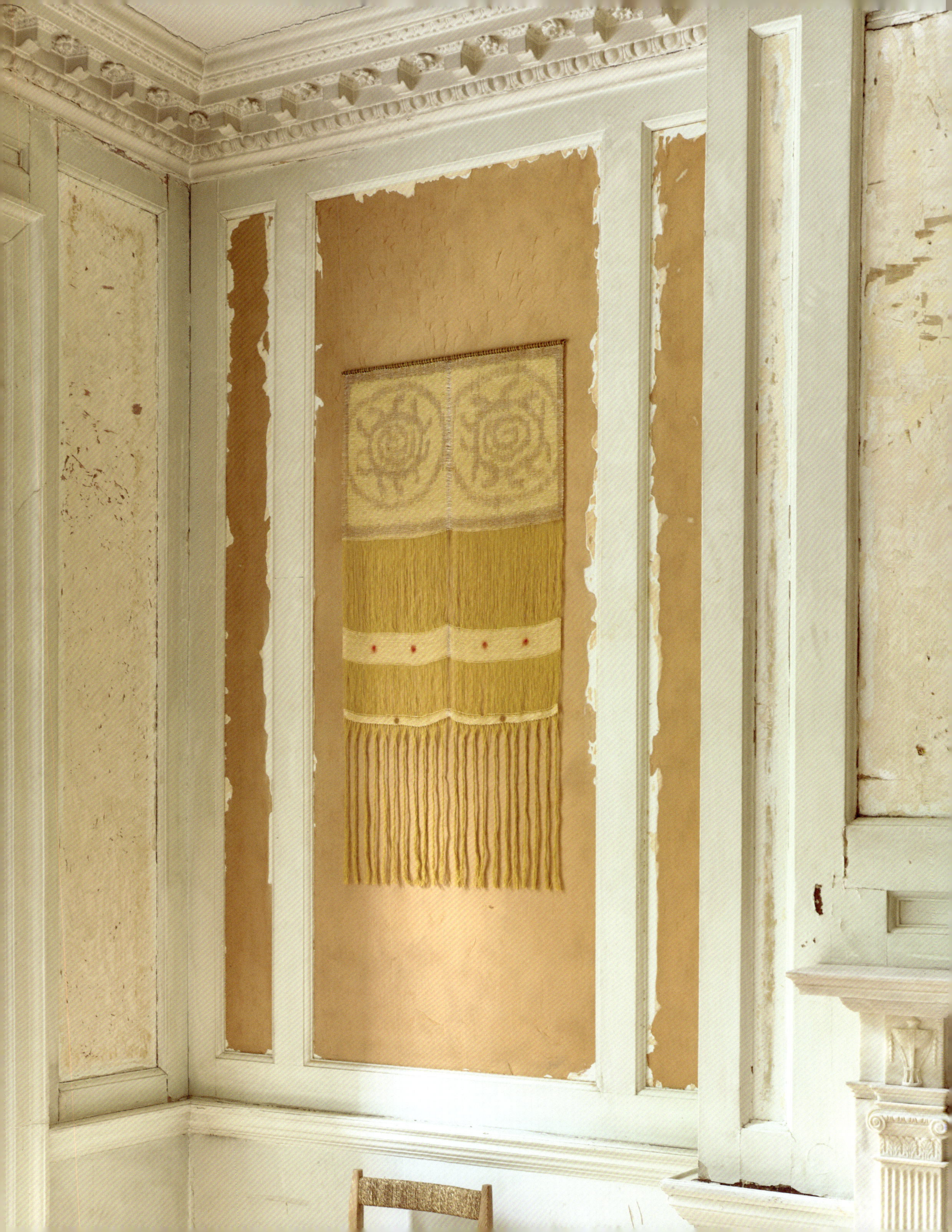

Yeh Fuyu 葉馥瑜

PINGTUNG AND PRAGUE

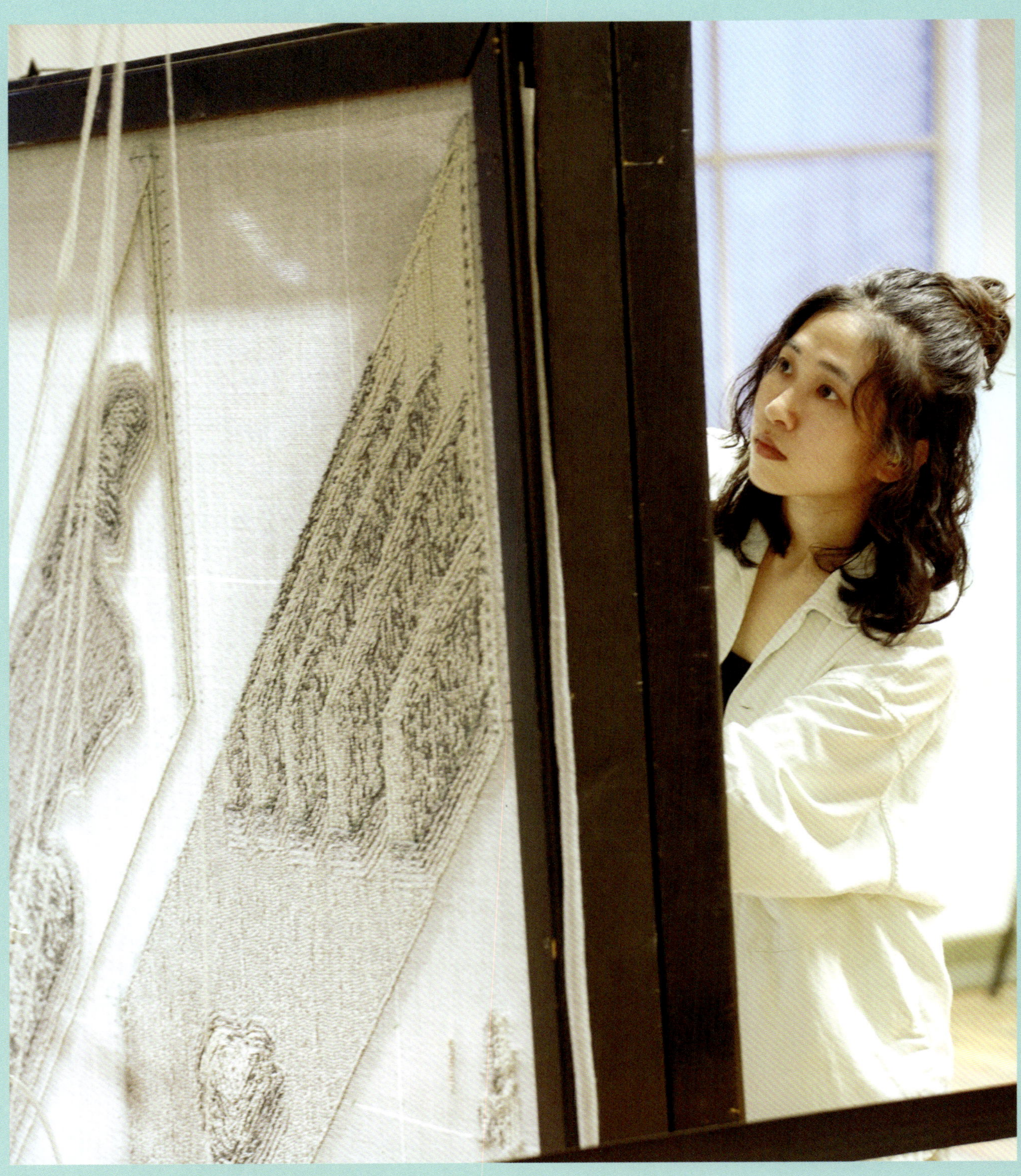

Yeh Fuyu first learnt tapestry weaving from the Indigenous Atayal and Paiwan tribes in 2018, and quickly became "enamored with the artform". After a career as an advertising copywriter, weaving offered Yeh a new creative way to process thoughts and emotions. While the similarities between textiles and words aren't immediately obvious, she regards weaving as "akin to writing" in the way tapestries are formed "line after line", with "each thread a word, the loom a page". For Yeh, weaving is her "language – a way to observe, reflect and express" her place in the world. Through the labour-intensive and often repetitive process, she seeks to "weave fragments of thought and emotion into tangible narratives".

Many of Yeh's tapestries are directly connected to the places where they are made, embedding them with local contexts and stories. This is the case for *Sketch by Weaving: a Windy Sunny Day on the Bridge* (2023) and *a bowl of the Danube* (2023), which were both completed by the artist during an extended five-month residency in Slovakia. *Sketch by Weaving* is an observational work, described as both an "artistic action and tapestry weaving". To make it, Yeh stretched 500 metres of yarn across the entire length of the Mária Valéria Bridge; as she walked back across, she cut the yarn each time she met someone new and joined a new colour using a knot. The resulting string of yarn was then woven into a unique tapestry that visibly records each of these encounters.

a bowl of the Danube was inspired by Yeh's daily views of the river during her time in Slovakia. The work is a "sketch" – an impression of her daily observations woven by the artist to "collect a piece of memory from nature". The tapestry uses wool threads that were individually hand-dyed by the artist and then woven together to encapsulate the river's "reflections and ripples". One unique feature of this work is its final presentation; instead of being hung on a wall, the tapestry was placed in a round water basin to give the visual impression of the "surface tension of a liquid". Gazing at the work from above, one gets the sense that they are gazing into a reflection pool.

Themes of waterways and rivers are also present in Yeh's other works, such as *Weavers with the River* (2018) and *Weavers with the Rivers II* (2019–20). This continued return to the natural world reveals Yeh's longstanding interest in drawing "people's attention to the small, often overlooked details in our surroundings, particularly those related to nature". These two tapestries were shaped by the artist's visits to Plum Tree Creek along the Danshui River in Taipei, as well as the nearby Sinackse River, which are all located alongside urban development sites. Yeh's tapestries invite audiences to reacquaint themselves with the waterways' colours, textures

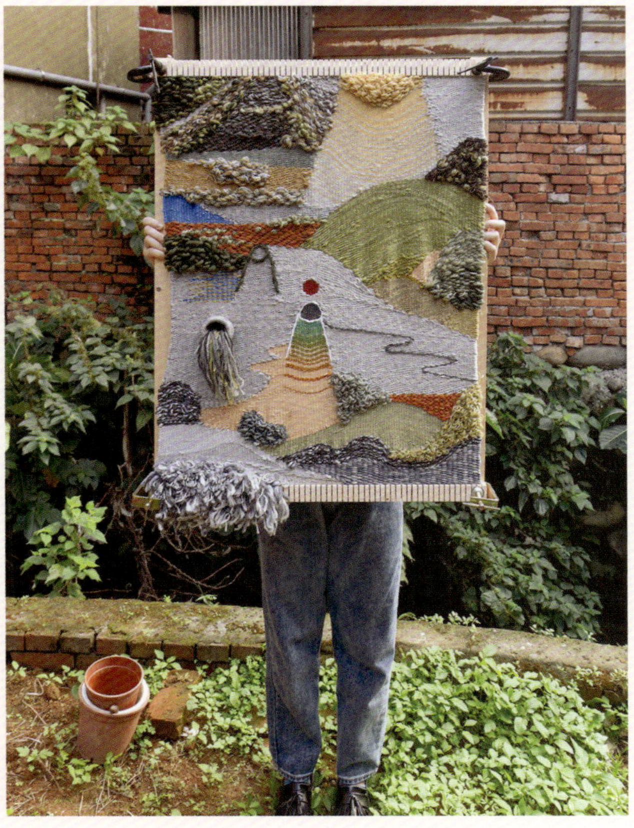

Weavers with the River, 2018, Weaving

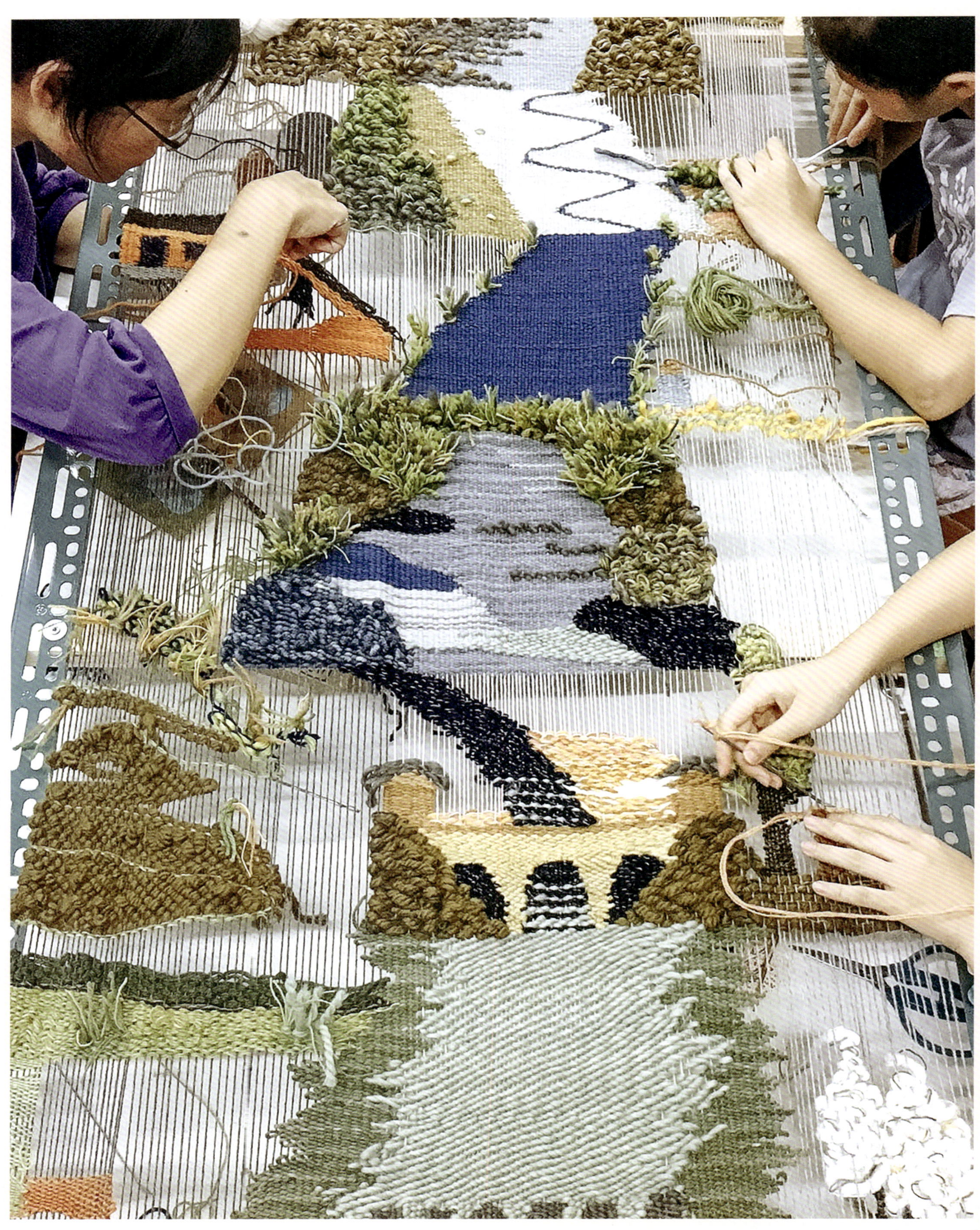

This page and opposite *Weavers with the River II*, 2019–20, Weaving **Page 242** *Sketch by Weaving: a Windy Sunny Day on the Bridge*, 2023, Artistic action and weaving **Page 243** *a bowl of the Danube*, 2023, Weaving

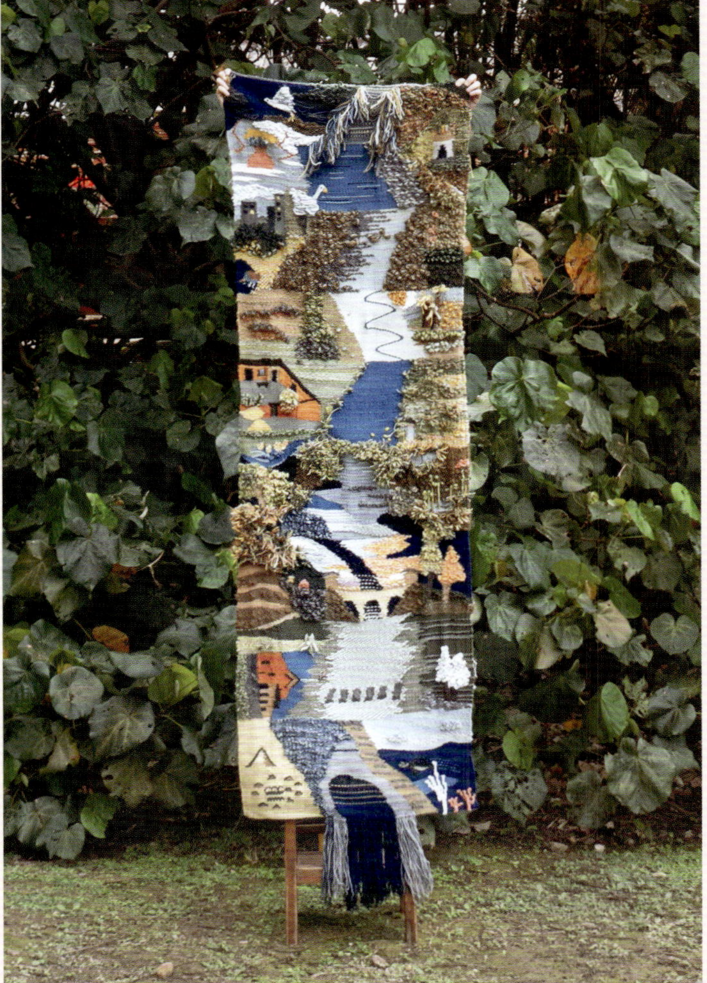

and forms. This invitation is generously extended in *Weavers with the Rivers II*, which saw Yeh ask locals living alongside the Sinackse River to complete the tapestry with simple weaving techniques, thereby "infus[ing] the piece with their vision of the river shores". This process of co-creation gives material form to the otherwise "invisible tangling relationship between people and nature", and highlights the inseparability of humans from their surroundings.

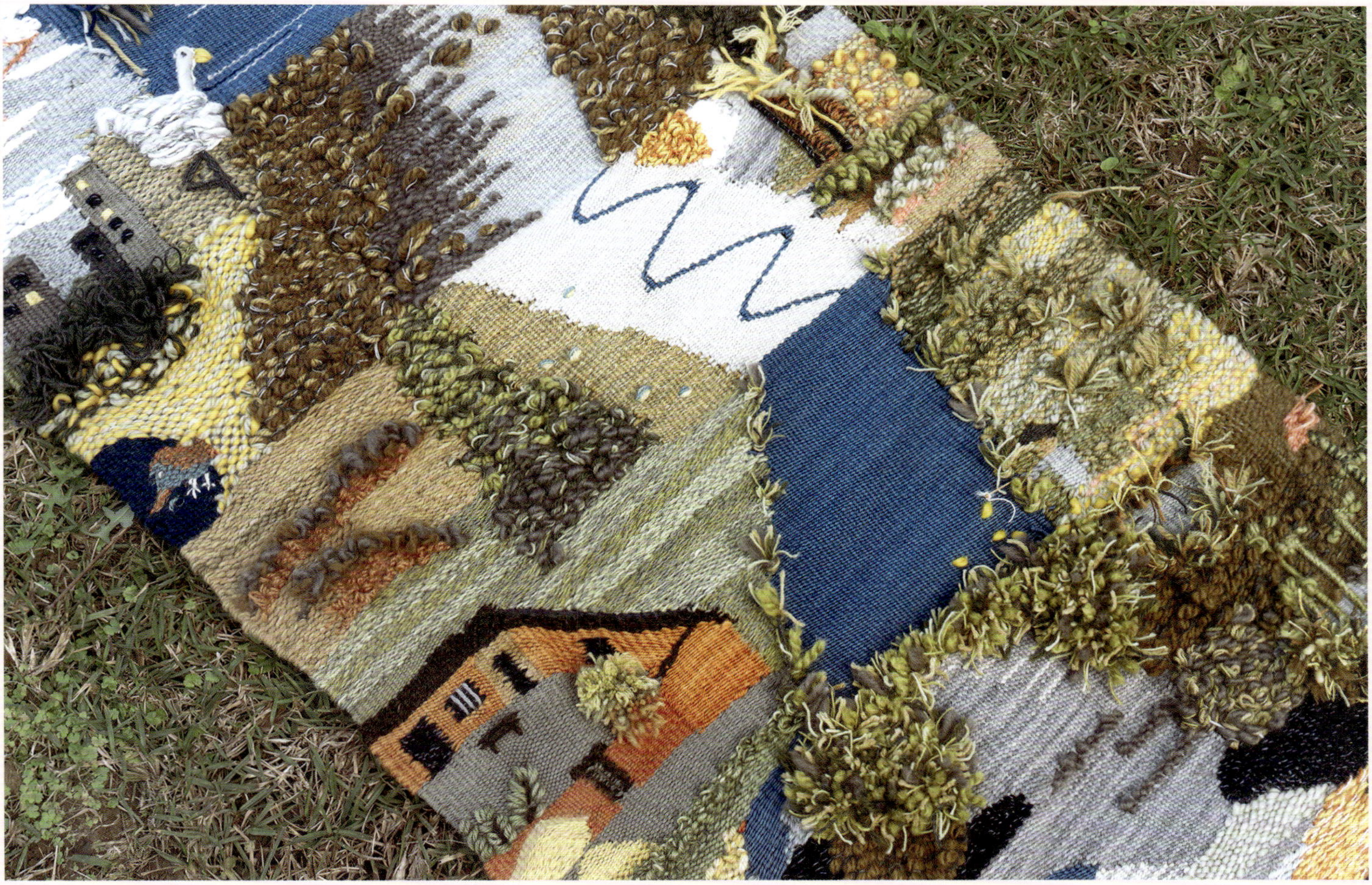

Having spent many years exploring different textile mediums and techniques, Yeh says that she still finds herself "deeply captivated by [their] diversity and versatility". For Yeh, weaving, like the other textile mediums she works with, is not just a material practice, but a methodology grounded in a meditative process – where the time invested in making contributes to a finished piece's meaning and value. She regards the weaving process "as part of the work itself" and shares that "this is what I find unique about textile art – it is, in some ways, an extension of the artist's life". ■

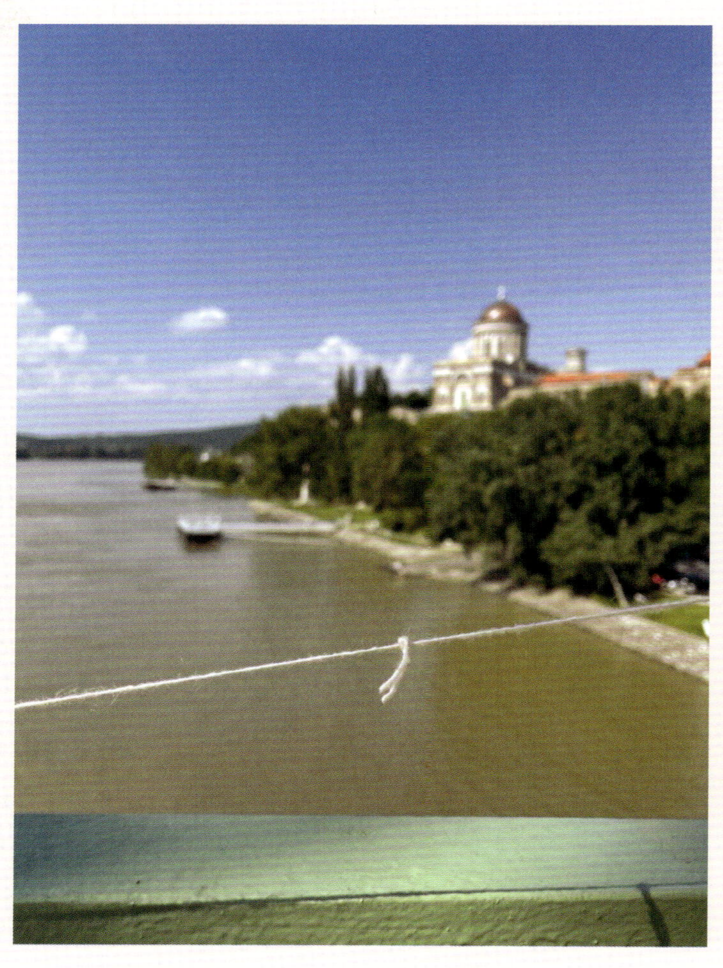
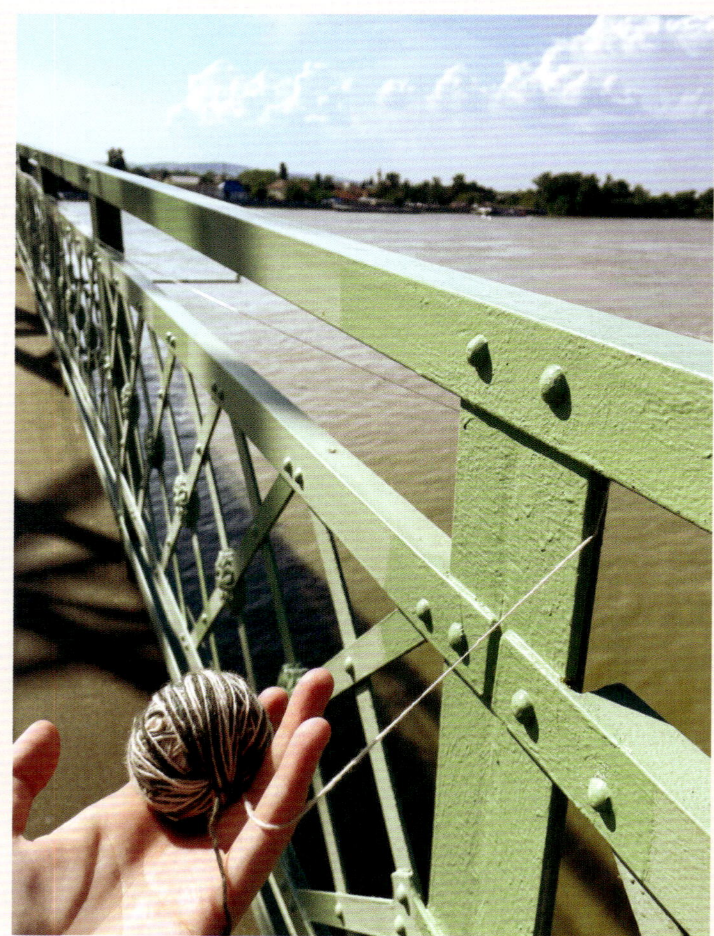
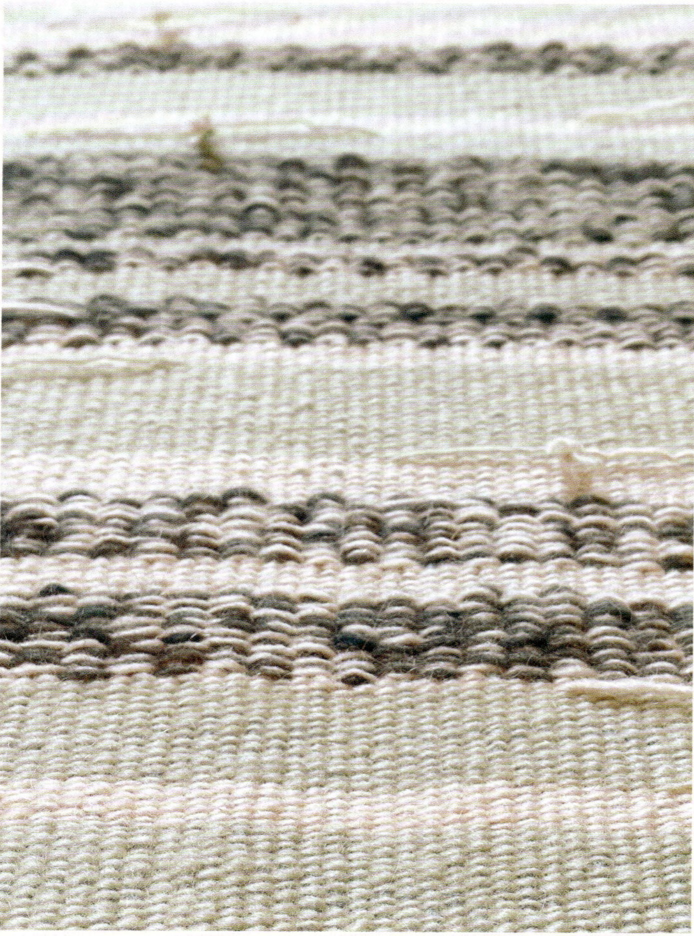
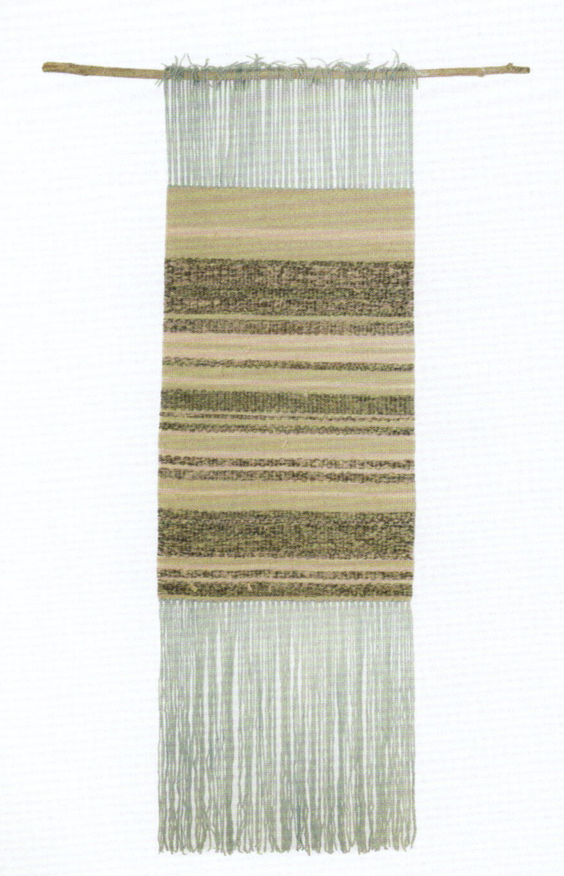

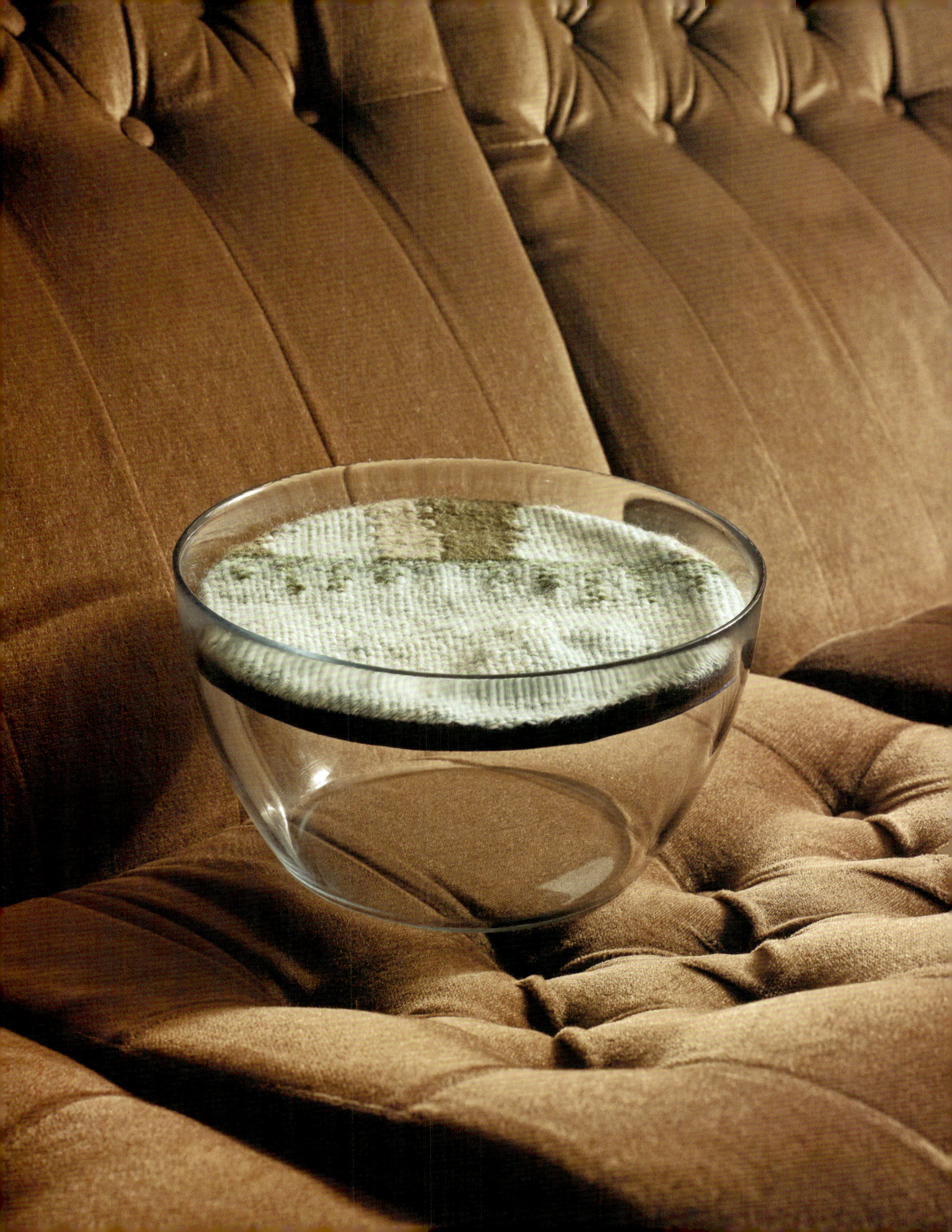

Sophia Cai 蔡晨昕

NGUNNAWAL AND NGAMBRI COUNTRY

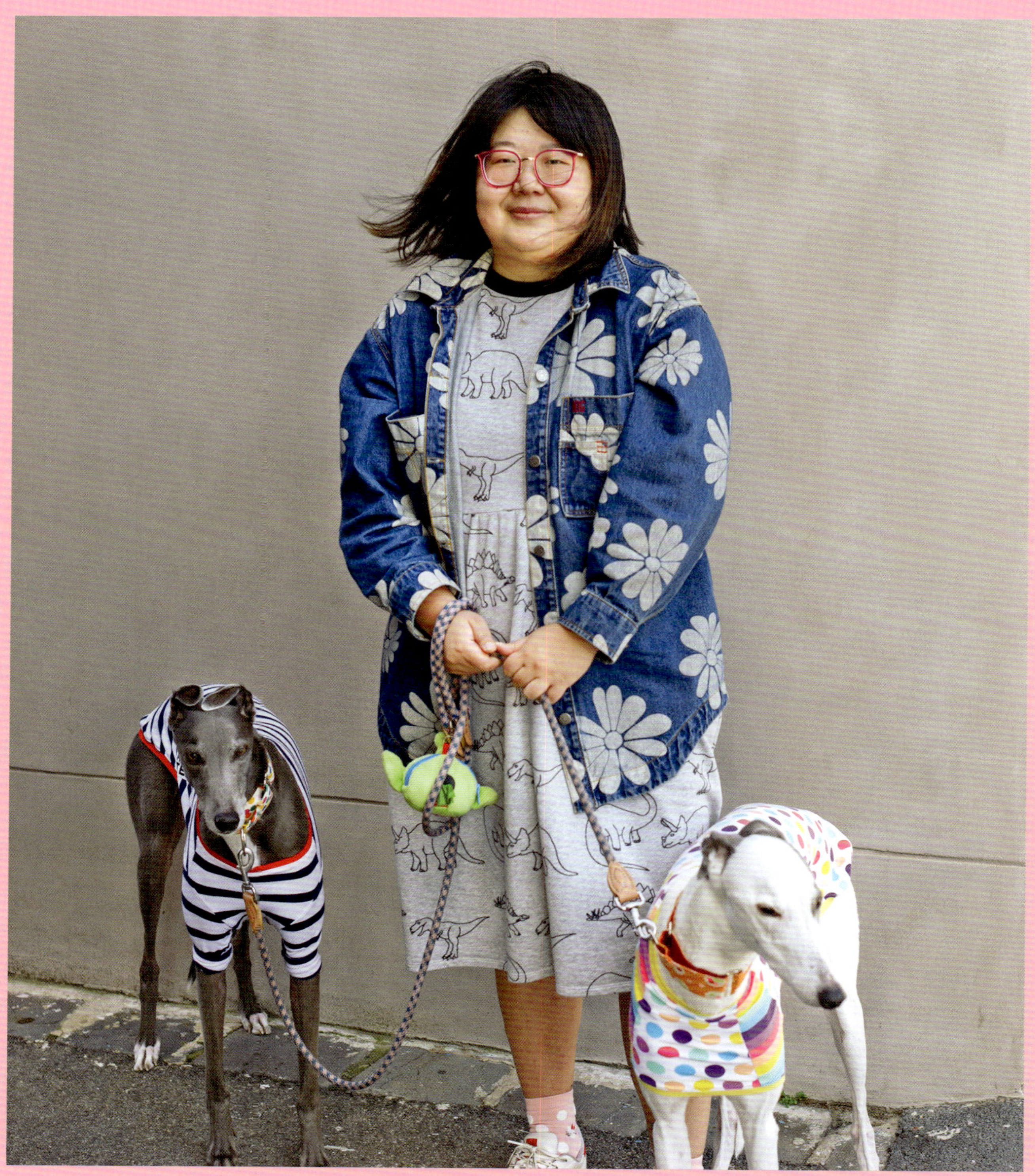

Sophia Cai is a curator, writer and knitter based in Canberra, Australia. She is the current Artistic Director and CEO of Canberra Contemporary, one of Australia's leading contemporary art organisations, and maintains an independent writing and curatorial practice. When not visiting galleries or museums, Sophia enjoys knitting and taking walks with her greyhounds, Rosie and Rocket.

This book was written on the unceded lands of the Wurundjeri people, as well as the Ngunnawal and Ngambri peoples, on whose land I presently live and work. I pay my respects to Elders past and present.

Within the context of this book and its themes, I would also like to acknowledge Aboriginal and Torres Strait Islander people as this continent's first artists and storytellers. I want like to extend this respect to all First Nations Peoples around the globe.

As with any creative project of this scale, this book was a labour of love guided and shaped by many.

First and foremost, I'd like to thank my incredible, patient and encouraging editor Avery Hayes and the whole team at Smith Street Books for supporting my writing dreams, and helping make this (second!) book a reality. I'm grateful that you continue to see the value in my words. I'd like to thank Casey Schuurman for her outstanding work in designing the book.

The cover was handknitted by me with yarns generously supplied from La Bien Aimee, and I'd like to thank them for their support.

This book wouldn't exist without the artists whose works, ideas and words fill these pages. I'd like to extend my sincere thanks to the 38 artists who spent time talking to me, answering my questions and sharing your artworks. Your works inspire me, and I'm so excited to share this book with audiences all around the world.

I'd also like to thank the dozens more artists I spoke with as part of my initial research. Seeking to connect with new voices and artistic practices previously unknown to me, I conducted part of my research through an open call on Instagram. This post gained more responses than I could have anticipated, and I'd like to thank every artist who took the time to introduce themselves to me, as well as those who kindly championed their peers and friends. While this book did not have the space to include you all, I have shared these responses on my website. Thank you to Kate Golding for your work as a research assistant to bring this digital archive to fruition.

This book was shaped by many conversations with friends and peers, who graciously shared resources, guides and books with me. I'd also like to thank my chosen art fam and dear friends, including George, Siying, Chloe, Julia, Janelle and Karima, as well as countless others – too many to name here – for their friendship and support when I needed it most. Thank you also to Shivanjani, whose contributions of artist suggestions are evident in these pages. Your generosity and support of artists is inspiring to see.

I would like to thank my family who have supported my creative and professional work over my entire life. Thank you to my mum and dad who always recognised the value of culture, and took me to museums and galleries from a young age as part of our family trips. Thank you, Dad, for driving me to galleries three hours away from home so I could see exhibitions. Thank you, Mum, for bringing back museum guides every time you went to a place without me, and making the effort to understand. As a child of migrants, I won't ever take for granted what this creative freedom you've granted me means.

Lastly, I want to acknowledge that my work is only possible because of the support of my partner, best friend and housemate, Malcolm, who helped keep me hydrated and fed while I worked on this book. I want to thank Malcolm for his patience, kindness and giving me the space to thrive. I love you.

I share my home with Rosie and Rocket, my two greyhound children, and I am thankful that their presence continued to provide a source of calm and love. As I get older, I realise more and more that I can never take these small moments for granted. Thank you to Rosie and Rocket for watching over me while I wrote this book from the sofa next to my writing desk.

Image Credits

All images in the book are courtesy of the artists and the following:

Page 2

photo by Laura Mendelin

Page 9

4A Centre for Contemporary Asian Art, photos by Kai Wasikowski

Page 12

(top left) Kouri + Corrao Gallery, Santa Fe, NM, photos by (top right) Pierfrancesco Celada, (bottom) Jack Ball

Page 13

photos by (top) Giulia Cairone, (bottom left) Simon Strong

Andrew Chan

p. 15 photo by Simon Aubor

Ben Cuevas

pp. 20–23 photos by Stacey Meinek

Emma Buswell

p. 26 photo by Ezra Alcantra, p. 28 photos by (top) Guy Louden, (bottom) Brenton McGeachie, p. 28 photos by Dan McCabe, p. 30 photos by (top) Jack Ball, (bottom) Aaron Claringbold, p. 31 photo by Sharon Baker

Emma Hasselblad

pp. 32–34 photos by Lisa Hallgren, p. 35 photos by (top left and bottom) Lisa Hallgren, (top right) Björn Strömfeldt, p. 36 photos by Giulia Cairone

Emma Roche

Emma Roche is represented by Brigitte Mulholland in Paris and supported by the Arts Council of Ireland p. 40 National Museums Liverpool

Kate Just

pp. 44–45 photos by Simon Strong, p. 46 photos by Zan Wimberley, p. 47 photo by Sam Roberts, p. 48 photo by Simon Strong, p. 49 photos by (top) Simon Strong, (bottom) Sam Roberts

Kendall Ross

p. 50 photo by Chris Rettman, p. 52 Kouri + Corrao Gallery, Santa Fe, NM, p. 53 (top left) Factory Obscura, Oklahoma City, OK, pp. 54–55 Kouri + Corrao Gallery, Santa Fe, NM

Lucas Morneau

p. 56 photo by Annie France Noël

Movana Chen

p. 63 photo by Pierfrancesco Celada, p. 64. Gyeonggi Museum of Modern Art, p. 65 Burger Collection and the TOY family p. 66 photos by (top) Scott Goldburg, (bottom) Wilson Lam, M+ Hong Kong, p. 67 photo by Tyler Weinberger

Romina Chuls

p. 68 photo by David Williams, p. 69 photo by Shawn Inglima, p. 70 photos by (top) Juan Pablo Murrugarra, (bottom) Shawn Inglima, pp. 71–72 photos by Juan Pablo Murrugarra, p. 73 photos by Shawn Inglima

Sancia Ridgeway

p. 74 photo by Tyler Patten, p. 76 photos by UTS photography studio, p. 77 photo by Tyler Patten

Shradha Kochhar

p. 80 photo by Bea Frank, p. 82 photo by Sambit Biswas, p. 83 photos by (top right) Sambit Biswas, (bottom) Bea Frank, p. 84 photos by (top) Lovebirds, (bottom left) Paul Salveson, p. 85 photo by Sambit Biswas

Page 86

(bottom left) photo by Marjaana Malkamäki

Page 87

photos by (top right) Sam Hartnett, (bottom) Paolo Jay Agbay

Baylee Schmitt

p. 90 photo by Jessica Rinaldi, p. 92 (top right and bottom) Contemporary Art Center in Cincinnati, OH

Beth Williams

p. 98 (top) photo by Mattia Trupp

Kelly Jin Mei

p. 114 photo by Art Ripple Taitung, pp. 116–119 photos by Clarence Aw

Liisa Hietanen

p. 120–121 photos by Marjaana Malkamäki, p. 122 photos by (top) Arto Liiti, (bottom) Marjaana Malkamäki, p. 123 photo by Laura Mendelin, p. 124 photo by Marjaana Malkamäki, p. 125 photos by (top left) Jari Kuusenaho, (top right and bottom) Marjaana Malkamäki

Lissy & Rudi Robinson-Cole

pp. 126–128 photos by Hōhua Kurene, pp. 129–131 photos by Sam Hartnett

Mulyana

p. 134 (top) Esplanade Singapore, p. 135 photo by Dewi Bukit, p. 137 (bottom) photo by Tarynhays Photo

Nicole Nikolich

p. 138 photo by Paolo Jay Agbay, p. 139 photo by Jason Chen, p. 140 photos by (top) Jason Chen, (bottom) Paolo Jay Agbay, p. 141 photo by Paolo Jay Agbay, p. 142 (bottom) photos by Jason Chen, p. 143 (top) photos by Jason Chen

Paula do Prado

p. 150 photo by Document Photography, p. 152 photos by (top) Document Photography, (bottom) Garry Trinh, p. 153 photo by Document Photography, p. 154 Tiwani Contemporary, photo by Deniz Guzel, p. 155 photos by (top) Garry Trinh, (bottom) Jamie James Photography

Wells Chandler

p. 162 photo by Manal Abu-Shaheen

Pages 170

photos by (top left) Matthew Stanton, (top right) Chris Schultz of Pond Gallery

Akeylah Wellington

p. 172 photo by Marcus Morris p. 174 photo by Chris Schultz of Pond Gallery, p. 175 (top) Beeler Gallery, p. 176 (top) The Anderson , (bottom left and right) photos by Joshua Simpson on behalf of Wassaic Project, p. 177 photo by Chris Schultz of Pond Gallery

Cheong See Min

p. 178 photo by Eugene Kong and Arnakhi, p. 180 (top) photo by Vivo, p. 182 photos by Jules Lister

Daniela Contreras Flores

p. 184 photo by Doye Kim

Ema Shin

p. 190 photo by Selina Ou, p. 193 photos by (top left and bottom right) Matthew Stanton, (bottom left) Selina Ou, p. 194 photos by (top) Selina Ou, (bottom right) Narelle Wilson, (bottom left) Matthew Stanton, p. 195 photo by Tania Bahr-Vollrath

Kayla Mattes

p. 196 photo by ofstudio, p. 198–200 photos by ofstudio

Linda Sok

p. 205 (top left and bottom) Center for Craft, photos by Benjamin Roberts, (top right) Campbelltown Arts Centre, photo by Silversalt Photography, p. 206 Campbelltown Arts Centre, photos by Silversalt Photography

Lin Qiqing

p. 208 photo by Terumi Saito, p. 211 photo by Kevin Schoenmakers, p. 213 (top) photo by Kevin Schoenmakers

Moon Bori

p. 220 photo by Jandee Ki

Sophie Honess

p. 226 photo by Jacquie Manning, p. 229 photo by (bottom) Danny Stanley, p. 230 photos by (top) Tom Ross, (bottom) Jacquie Manning, p. 231 photo by Phillip Castleton

Tais Rose Wae

pp. 232–233 photos by Natalie McComas, p. 234 photo by Lisa Sorgini, p. 235 photos by (top left) Natalie McComas, (top right and bottom) Tale Studio, p. 236 photos by (top and bottom left) Milo Jack Paris Hutchings, (bottom right) Tale Studio, p. 237 photo by Milo Jack Paris Hutchings

Yeh Fuyu

pp. 238–239 photos by Lu Chieh, p. 241 photos by Lu Chieh, p. 242 (bottom right) photo by Lu Chieh, p. 243 photo by Lu Chieh

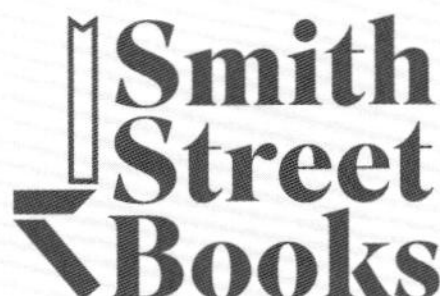

Published in 2026 by Smith Street Books
Naarm (Melbourne) | Australia
smithstreetbooks.com

Distributed outside of ANZ, North & Latin America by
Thames & Hudson Ltd., 6–24 Britannia Street,
London, WC1X 9JD
thamesandhudson.com

EU Authorised Representative: Interart S.A.R.L.
19 rue Charles Auray, 93500 Pantin, Paris, France
productsafety@thameshudson.co.uk; www.interart.fr

ISBN: 978-1-923239-84-5

Smith Street Books respectfully acknowledges the Wurundjeri People of the Kulin Nation, who are the Traditional Owners of the land on which we work, and we pay our respects to their Elders past and present.

Publisher: Paul McNally
Comissioning editor: Avery Hayes
Design concept and layout: Casey Schuurman
Cover knitting: Sophia Cai
Proofreader: Pam Dunne
Production manager: Aisling Coughlan
Prepress: Megan Ellis

Printed & bound in China by C&C Offset Printing Co., Ltd.

Book 444
10 9 8 7 6 5 4 3 2 1

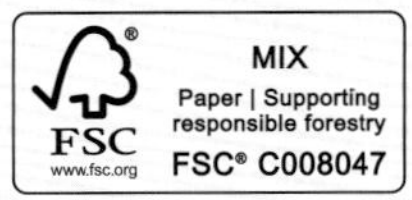

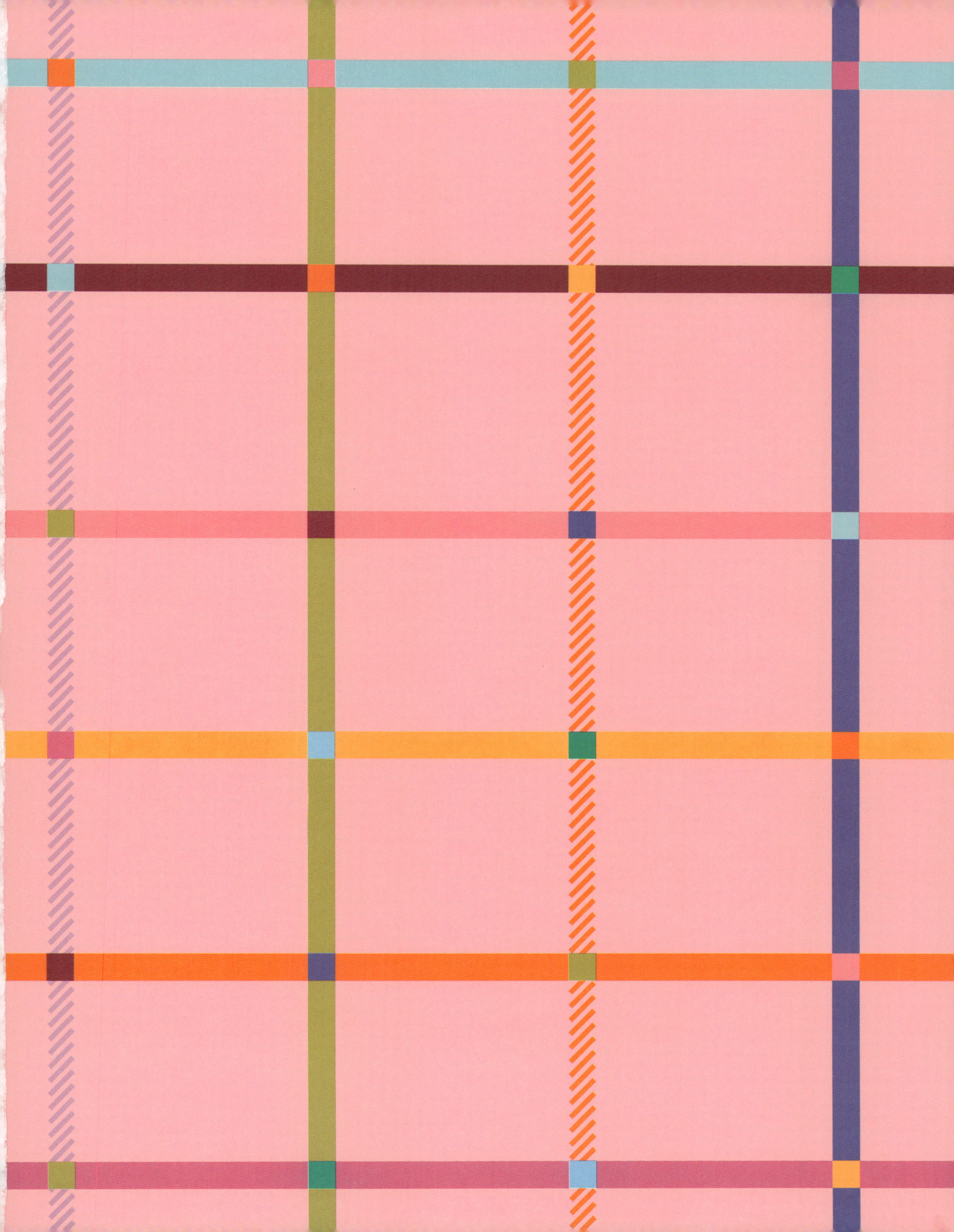

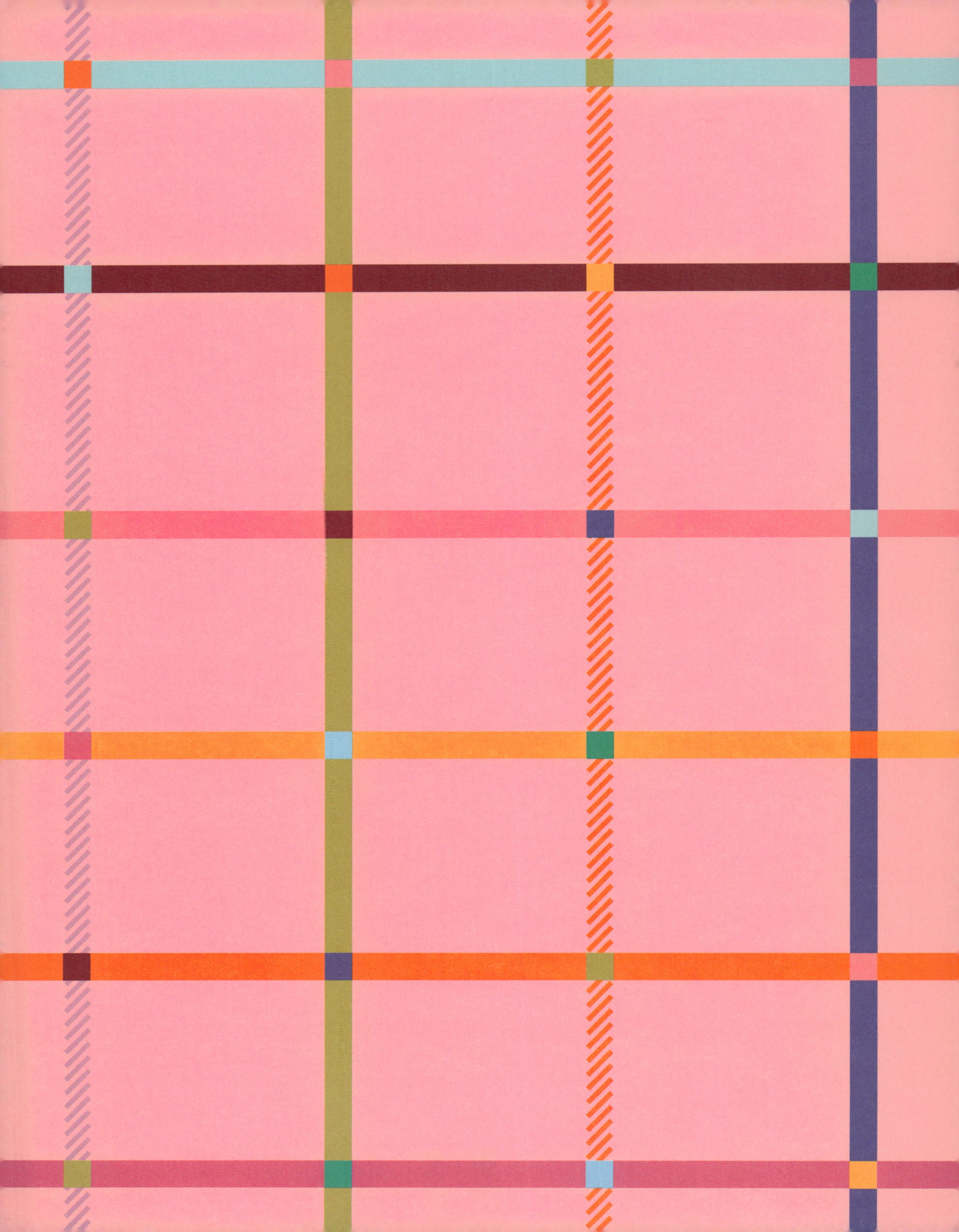